200 Best Jobs® for College Graduates

Fourth Edition

Part of JIST's Best Jobs® Series

Michael Farr and Laurence Shatkin, Ph.D.

Also in JIST's Best Jobs Series

* *300 Best Jobs Without a Four-Year Degree*
* *200 Best Jobs Through Apprenticeships*
* *Best Jobs for the 21st Century*
* *50 Best Jobs for Your Personality*
* *10 Best College Majors for Your Personality*
* *40 Best Fields for Your Career*
* *225 Best Jobs for Baby Boomers*
* *250 Best-Paying Jobs*

* *150 Best Jobs for Your Skills*
* *175 Best Jobs Not Behind a Desk*
* *150 Best Jobs Through Military Training*
* *150 Best Jobs for a Better World*
* *200 Best Jobs for Introverts*
* *150 Best Low-Stress Jobs*
* *150 Best Recession-Proof Jobs*

JIST Works
America's Career Publisher®

200 Best Jobs for College Graduates, Fourth Edition

© 2009 by JIST Publishing

Published by JIST Works, an imprint of JIST Publishing
7321 Shadeland Station, Suite 200
Indianapolis, IN 46256-3923

Phone: 800-648-JIST   Fax: 877-454-7839
E-mail: info@jist.com   Web site: www.jist.com

Some Other Books by the Authors

Michael Farr

The Quick Resume & Cover Letter Book

Same-Day Resume

Overnight Career Choice

Top 100 Careers Without a Four-Year Degree

100 Fastest-Growing Careers

Laurence Shatkin

Quick Guide to College Majors and Careers

90-Minute College Major Matcher

Your $100,000 Career Plan

New Guide for Occupational Exploration

150 Best Recession-Proof Jobs

Quantity discounts are available for JIST products. Have future editions of JIST books automatically delivered to you on publication through our convenient standing order program. Please call 800-648-JIST or visit www.jist.com for a free catalog and more information.

Visit www.jist.com for information on JIST, free job search information, tables of contents and sample pages, and ordering information on our many products.

Acquisitions Editor: Susan Pines
Development Editors: Aaron Black, Stephanie Koutek
Cover and Interior Designer: Aleata Halbig
Cover Image: Big Cheese Photo, Fotosearch

Interior Layout: Aleata Halbig
Proofreaders: Paula Lowell, Jeanne Clark
Indexer: Cheryl Lenser

Printed in the United States of America

11 10 09 08   9 8 7 6 5 4 3 2 1

Library of Congress Cataloging-in-Publication Data

Farr, J. Michael.
    200 best jobs for college graduates / Michael Farr and Laurence Shatkin. -- 4th ed.
        p. cm. -- (JIST's best jobs series)
    Includes index.
    ISBN 978-1-59357-603-5 (alk. paper)
    1. Vocational guidance. 2. College graduates--Employment. 3. Occupations--Forecasting. I. Shatkin, Laurence. II. Title. III. Title: Two hundred best jobs for college graduates.
    HF5381.F4563 2009
    331.702'35--dc22

                                    2008046426

We have been careful to provide accurate information throughout this book, but it is possible that errors and omissions have been introduced. Please consider this in making any career plans or other important decisions. Trust your own judgment above all else and in all things.

Trademarks: All brand names and product names used in this book are trade names, service marks, trademarks, or registered trademarks of their respective owners.

ISBN 978-1-59357-603-5

This Is a Big Book, But It Is Very Easy to Use

This book is for the many people who have or are considering getting a two- or four-year college degree or more and want to change or move ahead in their careers. It covers all the jobs in the U.S. Department of Labor's O*NET (Occupational Information Network) database that require a two-year associate degree, a four-year bachelor's degree, or higher.

We decided to create this book after the success of another book we did called *Best Jobs for the 21st Century*. That book covers all major jobs at all levels of education and training that met our criteria for earnings, projected growth rate, and number of job openings. It has information on about 500 jobs. But covering that many jobs required 700 pages, and the book includes many jobs that would not be of interest to people having or considering a college education.

So this book, *200 Best Jobs for College Graduates*, covers only those jobs that require a college degree. This approach allowed us to create a book that is less expensive, includes more-targeted lists, and has more useful information in the descriptions.

The nice thing about this book is that you don't have to read it all. Instead, we designed it to allow you to browse and find information that most interests you. The Table of Contents will give you a good idea of what's inside and how to use the book, so we suggest you start there. Part I of the book is made up of interesting lists that will help you explore jobs based on pay, interests, education level, personality type, and many other criteria. Part II provides descriptions for all major jobs that require a two-year associate degree, a bachelor's degree, or higher. Just find a job that interests you in one of the lists in Part I and look up its description in Part II. Simple.

Some Things You Can Do with This Book

* Identify more-interesting or better-paying jobs that don't require additional training or education.
* Develop long-term plans that may require additional training, education, or experience.
* Explore and select a college major or a training or educational program that relates to a career objective.
* Find reliable earnings information to negotiate pay.
* Prepare for interviews and the job search.

These are a few of the many ways you can use this book. We hope you find it as interesting to browse as we did to put together. We have tried to make it easy to use and as interesting as occupational information can be.

When you are done with this book, pass it along or tell someone else about it. We wish you well in your career and in your life.

Credits and Acknowledgments: While the authors created this book, it is based on the work of many others. The occupational information is based on data obtained from the U.S. Department of Labor and the U.S. Census Bureau. These sources provide the most authoritative occupational information available. The noneconomic job-related information is from the O*NET database, which was developed by researchers and developers under the direction of the U.S. Department of Labor. They, in turn, were assisted by thousands of employers who provided details on the nature of work in the many thousands of job samplings used in the database's development. We used the most recent version of the O*NET database, release 13. We appreciate and thank the staff of the U.S. Department of Labor for their efforts and expertise in providing such a rich source of data. The taxonomy of college majors (the Classification of Instructional Programs) is from the U.S. Department of Education.

Table of Contents

Summary of Major Sections

Introduction. A short overview to help you better understand and use the book. *Starts on page 1.*

Part I—The Best Jobs Lists: Jobs That Require a Two- or Four-Year College Degree or More. Very useful for exploring career options! Lists are arranged into easy-to-use groups. The first group of lists presents the best overall jobs that require a college degree as well as jobs with the highest earnings, projected growth, and number of openings. More-specialized lists follow, presenting the best jobs at various levels of education, for graduates age 20–24, for graduates 55 and older, for graduates who want to work part time, for graduates who want to be self-employed, for women graduates, and for men graduates. Other lists present the best jobs by interest and by personality type. The column starting at right presents all the list titles within the groups. *Starts on page 15.*

Part II—The Job Descriptions. Provides complete descriptions of the 200 college-grad jobs that met our criteria for high pay, fast growth, and large number of openings. Each description contains information on earnings, projected growth, job duties, skills, related job titles, education and training required, related knowledge and courses, and many other details. *Starts on page 101.*

Detailed Table of Contents

Introduction

We kept this introduction short to encourage you to scan it. For this reason, we won't provide many details on the technical issues involved in creating the job lists or descriptions. Instead, we give you short explanations to help you understand and use the information the book provides for career exploration or planning.

Where the Information Comes From

The information we used in creating this book comes from three major government sources:

❋ **The U.S. Department of Labor:** We used several data sources to construct the information we put into this book. We started with the jobs included in the U.S. Department of Labor's O*NET database. The O*NET includes information on about 950 occupations and is now the primary source of detailed information on occupations. The Labor Department updates the O*NET on a regular basis, and we used the most recent one available, version 13. Because we wanted to include earnings, growth, number of openings—information not part of the O*NET—we used sources at the U.S. Department of Labor's Bureau of Labor Statistics (BLS). The Occupational Employment Statistics survey provided the most reliable figures on earnings we could obtain, and the Employment Projections program provided the nation's best figures on job growth and openings. These two BLS programs use a slightly different system of job titles than the O*NET does, but we were able to link the BLS data to all of the O*NET job titles we used to develop this book.

❋ **The U.S. Census Bureau:** Data on the demographic characteristics of workers came from the Current Population Survey (CPS), conducted by the U.S. Census Bureau. This includes our information about the proportion of workers in each job who are men and women, in various age brackets, are self-employed, or work part time. As with the BLS data, we had to match slightly different sets of job titles, but we were able to identify CPS data for almost all the O*NET jobs.

❋ **The U.S. Department of Education:** We used the Classification of Instructional Programs, a system developed by the U.S. Department of Education, to cross-reference the education or training programs related to each job.

Of course, information in a database format can be boring and even confusing, so we did many things to help make the data useful and present it to you in a form that is easy to understand.

How We Selected the 200 Best Jobs for College Graduates

Deciding on the "best" job is a choice that only you can make, but objective criteria can help you identify jobs that are, for example, better paying than other jobs with similar duties. We have sorted through the data for *all* major jobs and selected only those jobs that meet the following criteria:

1. We began by creating our own database of information from the O*NET, Census Bureau, and other sources to include the information we wanted. This database covered about 950 job titles at all levels of education and training.

2. The U.S. Department of Labor assigns a minimum level of training or education for entry into each job they track. We cut our initial list to include only those jobs requiring an associate degree (which typically requires two years of college) or higher. A total of 346 jobs met this criterion. We removed 48 jobs for which very little information is available.

3. After we obtained the core economic information about the remaining 298 jobs, we removed one more job (Legislators) because it has annual earnings of less than $20,920, which means that 75 percent of workers earn more than the workers in this job.

4. We ranked the remaining 297 jobs three times, based on these major criteria: median annual earnings, projected growth through 2016, and number of job openings projected per year.

5. We then added the three numerical rankings for each job to calculate its overall score.

6. To emphasize jobs that tend to pay more, are likely to grow more rapidly, and have more job openings, we selected the 200 job titles with the best total overall scores.

For example, the job with the best combined score for earnings, growth, and number of job openings is Computer Software Engineers, Applications, so this job is listed first even though it is not the best-paying college-level job (which is a tie between Chief Executives, several physician jobs, and Airline Pilots, Copilots, and Flight Engineers), the fastest-growing job (which is Network Systems and Data Communications Analysts), or the job with the most openings (which is Registered Nurses).

We are not suggesting that the 200 jobs with the best overall scores for earnings, growth, and number of openings are all good ones for you to consider—some will not be. But the 200 jobs that met our criteria encompass such a wide range that you are likely to find one or more that will interest you. The jobs that met our "best jobs" criteria are also more likely than average to have higher pay, faster projected growth, and a larger number of openings than other jobs at similar levels of education and training.

Understand the Limits of the Data in This Book

In this book we use the most reliable and up-to-date information available on earnings, projected growth, number of openings, and other topics. The earnings data came from the U.S. Department of Labor's Bureau of Labor Statistics. As you look at the figures, keep in mind that they are estimates. They give you a general idea about the number of workers employed, annual earnings, rate of job growth, and annual job openings.

Understand that a problem with such data is that it describes an average. Just as there is no precisely average person, there is no such thing as a statistically average example of a particular job. We say this because data, while helpful, can also be misleading.

Take, for example, the yearly earnings information in this book. This is highly reliable data obtained from a very large U.S. working population sample by the Bureau of Labor Statistics. It tells us the average annual pay received as of May 2007 by people in various job titles (actually, it is the median annual pay, which means that half earned more and half less).

This sounds great, except that half of all people in that occupation earned less than that amount. For example, people who are new to the occupation or with only a few years of work experience often earn much less than the median amount. People who live in rural areas or who work for smaller employers typically earn less than those who do similar work in cities (where the cost of living is higher) or for bigger employers. People in certain areas of the country earn less than those in others. Other factors also influence how much you are likely to earn in a given job in your area. For example, the approximately 20,000 Computer Software Engineers, Applications, in the San Jose–Sunnyvale–Santa Clara, California, metropolitan area have median earnings of $104,550 (compared to a national average of $83,130), probably because they work where the red-hot high-tech industry is concentrated and they can collaborate productively with other workers. By comparison, petroleum is the main industry in the Casper, Wyoming, metropolitan area; the 40 workers in the same occupation there earn a median of only $53,410—a good salary, but about half of what their Silicon Valley colleagues earn.

Also keep in mind that the figures for job growth and number of openings are projections by labor economists—their best guesses about what we can expect between now and 2016. They are not guarantees. A major economic downturn, war, or technological breakthrough could change the actual outcome.

Finally, don't forget that the job market consists of both job openings and job *seekers*. The figures on job growth and openings don't tell you how many people will be competing with you to be hired. The Department of Labor does not publish figures on the supply of job candidates, so we are unable to tell you about the level of competition you can expect. Competition is an important issue that you should research for any tentative career goal. The *Occupational Outlook Handbook* provides informative statements for many occupations. You should speak to people who educate or train tomorrow's workers; they probably have a good idea of how many graduates find rewarding employment and how quickly. People in the workforce also can provide insights into this issue. Use your critical thinking skills to evaluate what people tell you. For example, educators or trainers may be trying to recruit you, whereas people in the workforce may be trying to discourage you from competing. Get a variety of opinions to balance out possible biases.

So, in reviewing the information in this book, please understand the limitations of the data. You need to use common sense in career decision making as in most other things in life. We hope that, using that approach, you find the information helpful and interesting.

Data Complexities

For those of you who like details, we present some of the complexities inherent in our sources of information and what we did to make sense of them here. You don't need to know this to use the book, so jump to the next section of the introduction if you are bored with details.

We include information on earnings, projected growth, and number of job openings for each job throughout this book. We think this information is important to most people, but getting it for each job is not a simple task.

Education or Training Required

The 200 jobs selected for this book were chosen partly on the basis of the amount of education or training that they typically require for entry: for all 200 jobs, the minimum requirement is a college degree, either two-year, four-year, or higher. We base the educational requirement on ratings supplied by the Bureau of Labor Statistics.

You should keep in mind that some people working in these jobs may have credentials that differ considerably from the level listed here. For example, although a bachelor's degree is considered the appropriate preparation for Cost Estimators, more than one-quarter of these workers have no college background at all. Conversely, although Registered Nurses can begin working after earning an associate degree, more than half have a bachelor's, and in fact career opportunities without the bachelor's are considerably more limited. The occupation Air Traffic Controllers is not even included in this book because the minimum requirement for entry is long-term on-the-job training, but more than half of the workers have some college background, and almost one-third have a bachelor's degree.

Some workers who have more than the minimum required education for their job have earned a higher degree *after* being hired, but others entered the job with this educational credential, and the more advanced degree may have given them an advantage over other job seekers with less education. Some workers with *less* than the normal minimum requirement may have been hired on the basis of their work experience in a similar job. So don't assume that the one-line statement of "Education/Training Required" in the Part II job descriptions gives a complete picture of how best to prepare for the job. If you're considering the job seriously, you need to investigate this topic in greater detail. Informative sources are listed in the last section of this introduction.

Earnings

The employment security agency of each state gathers information on earnings for various jobs and forwards it to the U.S. Bureau of Labor Statistics. This information is organized in standardized ways by a BLS program called Occupational Employment Statistics, or OES. To keep the earnings for the various jobs and regions comparable, the OES screens out certain types of earnings and includes others, so the OES earnings we use in this book represent straight-time gross pay exclusive of premium pay. More specifically, the OES earnings include the job's base rate; cost-of-living allowances; guaranteed pay; hazardous-duty pay; incentive pay, including commissions and production bonuses; on-call pay; and tips. They do not include back pay, jury duty pay, overtime pay, severance pay, shift differentials, nonproduction bonuses, or tuition reimbursements. Also, self-employed workers are not included in the estimates, and they can be a significant segment in certain occupations. When data on annual earnings for an occupation is highly unreliable, OES does not report a figure, which meant that we reluctantly had to exclude from this book a few occupations such as Actors.

For each job, we report three figures related to earnings:

* The Annual Earnings figure shows the median earnings (half earn more, half earn less).
* The Beginning Wage figure shows the 10th percentile earnings (the figure that exceeds the earnings of the lowest 10 percent of the workers). This is a rough approximation of what a beginning worker may be offered.
* The Earnings Growth Potential statement represents the gap between the 10th percentile and the median. This information answers the question, "If I started at the beginning wage and then got a raise that took me up to the median, how much of a pay boost (in percentage terms) would that be?" If this would be a big boost, the job has great potential for increasing your earnings as you gain experience and skills. If the boost would be small, you probably will need to move on to another occupation to improve your earnings substantially. Rather than use a percentage figure, which might be hard to interpret, we use a verbal tag to express the earnings growth potential: "very low" when the percentage is less than 25%, "low" for 25–35%, "medium" for 35%–40%, "high" for 40%–50%, and "very high" for any figure higher than 50%. For the highest-paying jobs, those for which the BLS reports the median earnings as "more than $145,600," we are unable to calculate a figure for earnings growth potential.

The median earnings for all workers in all occupations were $31,410 in May 2007. For occupations that require a college degree or higher, the average figure is a respectable $64,447. The 200 college-level jobs in this book were chosen partly on the basis of good earnings, so their average is even a little higher: $65,971. (These are weighted averages, which means that jobs with larger workforces are given greater weight in the computations. They also are based on the assumption that a job with income reported as "more than $145,600" pays exactly $145,600, so the actual averages are somewhat higher.)

The beginning (that is, 10th percentile) wage for all occupations in May 2007 was $16,060. For the 200 jobs in this book, the weighted average for the beginning wage is an impressive $39,423. The earnings growth potential for these jobs is rated very high for 21 jobs, high for 77 jobs, medium for 57 jobs, and low for 32 jobs. No jobs are rated very low. (Earnings growth potential cannot be calculated for 11 jobs.)

The earnings data from the OES survey is reported under a system of job titles called the Standard Occupational Classification system, or SOC. Most of these jobs have an exact counterpart in the O*NET system of job titles that we use in this book, so it is easy for us to attach earnings information to most of our job titles. But a small number of the O*NET jobs simply do not have earnings data available for them from the sources we used and therefore were not included. In some other cases, an SOC title cross-references to more than one O*NET job title. For example, the O*NET has separate information for Accountants and for Auditors, but the BLS reports earnings for a single SOC occupation called Accountants and Auditors. Therefore you may notice that the salary we report for Accountants ($57,060) is identical to the salary we report for Auditors. In reality there probably is a difference, but this is the best information that is available.

Projected Growth and Number of Job Openings

This information comes from the Office of Occupational Statistics and Employment Projections, a program within the Bureau of Labor Statistics that develops information about projected trends in the nation's labor market for the next ten years. The most recent projections available cover the years from 2006 to 2016. The projections are based on information about people moving into and out of occupations. The BLS uses data from various sources in projecting the growth and number of openings for each job title—some data comes from the Census Bureau's Current Population Survey and some comes from an OES survey. The projections assume that there will be no major war, depression, or other economic upheaval.

Like the earnings figures, the figures on projected growth and job openings are reported according to the SOC classification, so again we had to exclude a few jobs from this book because this information is not available for them. As with earnings, some of the SOC jobs crosswalk to more than one O*NET job. To continue the example we used earlier, SOC reports growth (17.7%) and openings (134,463) for one occupation called Accountants and Auditors, but in this book we report these figures separately for the occupation Accountants and for the occupation Auditors. When you see that Accountants has a 17.7% projected growth rate and 134,463 projected job openings and Auditors has the same two numbers, you should realize that the 17.7% rate of projected growth represents the *average* of these two occupations—one may actually experience higher growth than the other—and that these two occupations will *share* the 134,463 projected openings.

The Department of Labor provides a single figure (22.9%) for the projected growth of 38 postsecondary teaching jobs and also provides a single figure (237,478) for the projected annual job openings for these 38 jobs. Because these college-teaching jobs are related to very different interests—from engineering to art to forestry to social work—and because separate *earnings* figures are available for each of the 38 jobs, we thought you'd appreciate having these jobs appear separately in the lists in this book. If the trends of the last several years continue, none of these jobs can be expected to grow or take on workers at a significantly faster rate than the other 37. Therefore, in preparing the lists and in the Part II descriptions, we assumed that all of these college-teaching jobs share the same rate of job growth, 22.9%, and we computed a figure for their projected job openings by dividing the total (237,478) into 38 parts, each of which is proportional in size to the current workforce of the job.

While salary figures are fairly straightforward, you may not know what to make of job-growth figures. For example, is projected growth of 15 percent good or bad? You should keep in mind that the average (mean) growth projected for all occupations in the OES survey is 10.4 percent. For college-level jobs the growth projection is better: 15.8 percent. One-quarter of these occupations have a growth projection of 8.6 percent or lower. Growth of 14.2 percent is the median, meaning that half of the occupations are projected to have more, half less. Only one-quarter of the occupations have growth projected at more than 22.9 percent.

Remember, however, that the jobs in this book are a distinguished set—they were selected as "best" partly on the basis of high growth, so their mean growth is a lofty 16.4 percent. Among these 200 high-powered jobs, the job ranked 50th by projected growth has a figure of 22.9 percent, the job ranked 100th (the median) has a projected growth of 18.4 percent, and the job ranked 150th has a projected growth of 14.2 percent.

Some of the occupations in this book are projected to provide a larger number of annual job openings than others, so you may wonder what an average number of openings might be. Of the 751 occupations for which the BLS projects job openings, the average number is 35,805 per year. The 200 best college-level occupations tend to have smaller-than-average workforces and therefore are projected to offer an average of only 20,839 job openings. (Fortunately, competition for these openings also is limited because a college degree is usually required.) One-quarter of these occupations are projected to provide 3,572 openings or fewer. The median is 9,719. Only one-quarter of the college-level occupations are projected to offer more than 27,603 openings.

However, keep in mind that figures for job openings depend on how the BLS defines an occupation. For example, consider the college teaching jobs. The Office of Occupational Statistics and Employment Projections recognizes one occupation called Teachers, Postsecondary, and projects 237,478 annual job openings for this occupation. As explained earlier in this introduction, we divided this huge occupation into 38 separate occupations, following the practice of O*NET and of the Occupational Employment Statistics program. The "average" number of openings for all the occupations in this book would change substantially, depending on whether we treated college teachers as one occupation or as 38. So it follows that because the way BLS defines occupations is somewhat arbitrary, any "average" figure for job openings is also somewhat arbitrary.

You may wonder why we include figures about job growth *and* number of job openings in this book. Aren't they two ways of saying the same thing? Actually, they aren't. As an example, consider the occupation Athletic Trainers, which is projected to grow at the very impressive rate of 24.3 percent. There should be lots of opportunities in such a fast-growing job, right? Not exactly. This is a small occupation, with only about 17,000 people currently employed, so even though it is growing rapidly, it is expected to create only 1,669 job openings per year. Now contrast this with General and Operations Managers. This occupation is growing at the glacial rate of 1.5 percent—but it is a much larger occupation with a workforce of 1.7 million and is projected to provide 112,072 job openings per year. We base our selection of the best jobs on both of these economic indicators—growth and openings—and you should pay attention to both when you scan our lists of best jobs.

Other Job Characteristics

Like the figures for earnings, some of the other figures used to create the lists of jobs in this book—for example, figures for the percentage of female workers in a job—are shared by more than one job title. Usually this is the case for occupations that are so small that the BLS does not release separate statistics for them. For example, the occupation Cardiovascular Technologists and Technicians has a total workforce of only about 45,000 workers, so the BLS does not report a specific figure for the percentage of female workers. In this case, we had to use the figure that the BLS reports for a family of occupations it calls Diagnostic Related Technologists and Technicians. We relied on this same figure for three other jobs: Diagnostic Medical Sonographers, Nuclear Medicine Technologists, and Radiologic Technologists and Technicians. You may notice similar figure-sharing among related jobs where we list the percentages of workers in specific age brackets.

Information in the Job Descriptions

We used a variety of government and other sources to compile the job descriptions we provide in Part II. Details on these various sources are mentioned later in this introduction in the section "Part II—The Job Descriptions."

Part I—The Best Jobs Lists: Jobs That Require a Two- or Four-Year College Degree or More

There are 63 separate lists in Part I of this book—look in the Table of Contents for a complete list of them. The lists are not difficult to understand because they have clear titles and are organized into groupings of related lists.

Depending on your situation, some of the job lists in Part I will interest you more than others. For example, if you are young, you may be interested to learn the highest-paying jobs that employ high percentages of college graduates age 20–24. Other lists show jobs within interest groupings, personality types, levels of education, or other ways that you might find helpful in exploring your career options.

Whatever your situation, we suggest you use the lists that make sense for you to help explore career options. Following are the names of each group of lists along with short comments on each group. You will find additional information in a brief introduction provided at the beginning of each group of lists in Part I.

Best Jobs Overall: Lists of Jobs for College Graduates with the Highest Pay, Fastest Growth, and Most Openings

Four lists are in this group, and they are the ones that most people want to see first. The first list presents the top 200 college-grad job titles in order of their combined scores for earnings, growth, and number of job openings. Three more lists in this group are extracted from the 200 best and present the 100 jobs with the highest earnings, the 100 jobs projected to grow most rapidly, and the 100 jobs with the most openings.

Best Jobs Lists by Demographic

This group of lists presents interesting information for a variety of types of people based on data from the Current Population Survey, conducted by the U.S. Census Bureau. The lists are arranged into groups for workers age 20–24, workers 55 and older, part-time workers, self-employed workers, women, and men. We created five lists for each group, basing the last four on the information in the first list:

- ❀ The jobs having the highest percentage of people of each type
- ❀ The 25 jobs with the highest combined scores for earnings, growth, and number of openings
- ❀ The 25 jobs with the highest earnings
- ❀ The 25 jobs with the highest growth rates
- ❀ The 25 jobs with the largest number of openings

Best Jobs Lists Based on Levels of Education and Experience

We put each of the top 200 job titles into a list with the other jobs that require the same amount of education and experience for entry, according to the U.S. Department of Labor. Jobs within these lists are presented in order of their total combined scores for earnings, growth, and number of openings. The lists include jobs in these groupings:

- ❀ Associate degree
- ❀ Bachelor's degree

⊛ Work experience plus degree

⊛ Master's degree

⊛ Doctoral degree

⊛ First professional degree

Best Jobs Lists for College Graduates Based on Interests

These lists organize the 200 best jobs into groups based on interests. Within each list, jobs are presented in order of their total scores for earnings, growth, and number of openings. Here are the 15 interest areas/clusters used in these lists: Agriculture and Natural Resources; Architecture and Construction; Arts and Communication; Business and Administration; Education and Training; Finance and Insurance; Government and Public Administration; Health Science; Hospitality, Tourism, and Recreation; Human Service; Information Technology; Law and Public Safety; Retail and Wholesale Sales and Service; Scientific Research, Engineering, and Mathematics; Transportation, Distribution, and Logistics.

Best Jobs Lists for College Graduates Based on Personality Types

These lists organize the 200 best jobs into six personality types described in the introduction to the lists: Realistic, Investigative, Artistic, Social, Enterprising, and Conventional. The jobs within each list are presented in order of their total scores for earnings, growth, and number of openings.

Bonus Lists

Two bonus lists show jobs with the biggest increases and biggest decreases in growth projections over the last few years.

Part II—The Job Descriptions

This part of the book provides a brief but information-packed description for each of the 200 jobs that met our criteria for this book. The descriptions are presented in alphabetical order, which makes it easy to look up a job you've identified in a list from Part I that you want to learn more about.

We used the most current information from a variety of government sources to create the descriptions. We designed the descriptions to be easy to understand, but the sample that follows, with an explanation of each of its component parts, may help you better understand and use the descriptions.

Job Title →

Landscape Architects

Data Elements →

- ❈ Education/Training Required: Bachelor's degree
- ❈ Annual Earnings: $57,580
- ❈ Beginning Wage: $36,250
- ❈ Earnings Growth Potential: Medium
- ❈ Growth: 16.4%
- ❈ Annual Job Openings: 2,342
- ❈ Self-Employed: 18.5%
- ❈ Part-Time: 6.1%

Summary Description and Tasks →

Plan and design land areas for such projects as parks and other recreational facilities; airports; highways; hospitals; schools; land subdivisions; and commercial, industrial, and residential sites. Prepare site plans, specifications, and cost estimates for land development, coordinating arrangement of existing and proposed land features and structures. Confer with clients, engineering personnel, and architects on overall program. Compile and analyze data on conditions such as location, drainage, and location of structures for environmental reports and landscaping plans. Inspect landscape work to ensure compliance with specifications, approve quality of materials and work, and advise client and construction personnel.

Personality Type →

Personality Type: Artistic. These occupations frequently involve working with forms, designs, and patterns. They often require self-expression, and the work can be done without following a clear set of rules.

GOE Interest Areas/Clusters →

GOE—Interest Area/Cluster: 02. Architecture and Construction. **Work Group:** 02.02. Architectural Design. **Other Jobs in This Work Group:** Architects, Except Landscape and Naval.

Skills →

Skills—Operations Analysis: Analyzing needs and product requirements to create a design.

Management of Financial Resources: Determining how money will be spent to get the work done and accounting for these expenditures. **Coordination:** Adjusting actions in relation to others' actions. **Mathematics:** Using mathematics to solve problems. **Complex Problem Solving:** Identifying complex problems, reviewing the options, and implementing solutions. **Social Perceptiveness:** Being aware of others' reactions and understanding why they react the way they do. **Persuasion:** Persuading others to approach things differently. **Writing:** Communicating effectively with others in writing as indicated by the needs of the audience.

Education/Training Program(s) ←

Education and Training Programs: Environmental Design/Architecture; Landscape Architecture (BS, BSLA, BLA, MSLA, MLA, PhD). **Related Knowledge/Courses—Design:** Design techniques, principles, tools, and instruments involved in the production and use of precision technical plans, blueprints, drawings, and models. **Building and Construction:** Materials, methods, and the appropriate tools to construct objects, structures, and buildings. **Geography:** Various methods for describing the location and distribution of land, sea, and air masses, including their physical locations, relationships, and characteristics. **Biology:** Plant and animal living tissue, cells, organisms, and entities, including their functions, interdependencies, and interactions with each other and the environment. **Engineering and Technology:** Equipment, tools, and mechanical devices and their uses to produce motion, light, power, technology, and other applications. **Fine Arts:** Theory and techniques required to produce, compose, and perform works of music, dance, visual arts, drama, and sculpture.

Work Environment ←

Work Environment: More often indoors than outdoors; very hot or cold; hazardous equipment; minor burns, cuts, bites, or stings; sitting.

Here are details for each of the major parts of the job descriptions in Part II:

* **Job Title:** This is the job title for the job as defined by the U.S. Department of Labor and used in its O*NET database.

* **Data Elements:** The information on earnings, growth, and annual openings comes from the same Department of Labor databases used to create the lists, as we explain earlier in this introduction. The data on percentages of self-employed and part-time workers comes from the U.S. Census Bureau's Current Population Survey (as reported in the BLS publication *Occupational Projections and Training Data*).

* **Summary Description and Tasks:** The sentences in bold provide a summary description of the occupation. It is followed by a listing of tasks that are generally performed by people who work in the job. This information comes from the O*NET database, except that where necessary we edited the tasks to keep them from exceeding 2,200 characters.

* **Personality Type:** This part gives the name of the personality type that most closely matches each job, according to O*NET, as well as a brief definition of this personality type. You can find more information on the personality types in the introduction to the lists of jobs based on personality types in Part I.

* **GOE Interest Areas/Clusters:** This information cross-references the Guide for Occupational Exploration (or the GOE), a system developed by the U.S. Department of Labor that organizes jobs based on interests. We use the groups from the *New Guide for Occupational Exploration*, Fourth Edition, as published by JIST. That book uses a set of interest areas based on the 16 career clusters developed by the U.S. Department of Education and used in a variety of career information systems. Here we include the major Interest Area/Cluster the job fits into, its more-specific Work Group, and a list of college-level O*NET job titles that are in this same GOE Work Group. This information will help you identify other job titles that have similar interests or require similar skills. You can find more information on the GOE and its Interest Areas/Clusters in the introduction to the lists of jobs based on interests in Part I.

* **Skills:** The O*NET database provides data on 35 skills, so we decided to list only those that were most important for each job rather than list pages of unhelpful details. For each job, we identified any skill with a rating for level of mastery that was higher than the average rating for this skill for all jobs and a rating for importance that was higher than very low. We order the skills by the amount by which their ratings exceed the average rating for all occupations, from highest to lowest. If there are more than eight such skills, we include only those eight with the highest ratings. If no skill has a rating higher than the average for all jobs, we say "None met the criteria." Each listed skill is followed by a brief description of that skill.

* **Education/Training Programs:** This part of the job description provides the name of the educational or training program or programs for the job. It will help you identify sources of formal or informal training for a job that interests you. To get this information, we used a crosswalk created by the National Crosswalk Service Center to connect information in the Classification of Instructional Programs (CIP) to the O*NET job

titles we use in this book. We made various changes to connect the O*NET job titles to the education or training programs related to them and also modified the names of some education and training programs so they would be more easily understood. In 26 cases, we abbreviated the listing of related programs for the sake of space; such entries end with "others."

❋ **Related Knowledge/Courses:** This entry can help you understand the most important knowledge areas that are required for a job and the types of courses or programs you will likely need to take to prepare for it. For each job, we identified the highest-rated knowledge area in the O*NET database, so every job has at least one listed. We identified any additional knowledge area with a rating that was higher than the average rating for that knowledge area for all jobs. We listed as many as six knowledge areas in descending order.

❋ **Work Environment:** We included any work condition with a rating that exceeds the midpoint of the rating scale. The order does not indicate their frequency on the job. Consider whether you like these conditions and whether any of these conditions would make you uncomfortable. Keep in mind that when hazards are present (for example, contaminants), protective equipment and procedures are provided to keep you safe.

Getting all the information we used in the job descriptions was not a simple process, and it is not always perfect. Even so, we used the best and most recent sources of data we could find, and we think that our efforts will be helpful to many people.

Sources of Additional Information

Hundreds of sources of career information exist, so here are a few we consider most helpful in getting additional information on the jobs listed in this book.

Print References

❋ *O*NET Dictionary of Occupational Titles:* Revised on a regular basis, this book provides good descriptions for all jobs listed in the U.S. Department of Labor's O*NET database. There are about 950 job descriptions at all levels of education and training, plus lists of hundreds of related job titles in other major career information sources, educational programs, and other information. Published by JIST.

❋ *New Guide for Occupational Exploration:* The new edition of the *GOE* is cross-referenced in the descriptions in Part II. The *GOE* provides helpful information to consider on each of the interest areas/clusters and work groups, descriptions of all O*NET jobs within each GOE group, and many other features useful for exploring career options. Published by JIST.

❋ *Enhanced Occupational Outlook Handbook:* Updated regularly, this book provides thorough descriptions of the 270 major jobs in the *Occupational Outlook Handbook,* brief descriptions of the O*NET jobs that are related to each, brief descriptions of thousands of more-specialized jobs from the *Dictionary of Occupational Titles,* and other information. Published by JIST.

Internet Resources

✳ **The U.S. Department of Labor Web site:** The Department of Labor Bureau of Labor Statistics Web site (www.bls.gov) provides a lot of career information, including links to other pages that provide information on the jobs covered in this book. Their Web site is a bit formal and, well, confusing, but it will take you to the major sources of government career information if you explore its options.

✳ **Career OneStop:** Go to www.acinet.org/acinet/ for information about jobs, industries, education, and training. It includes state-specific information and links to career videos.

✳ **O*NET site:** Go to www.onetcenter.org for a wealth of information from the O*NET database, including links to sites that provide detailed information on the O*NET job titles presented in Part II of this book.

Thanks

Thanks for reading this introduction. You are surely a more thorough person than those who jumped into the book without reading it, and you will probably get more out of the book as a result.

We wish you a satisfying career and, more importantly, a good life.

PART I

The Best Jobs Lists: Jobs That Require a Two- or Four-Year College Degree or More

We've tried to make the best jobs lists in this section both fun to use and informative. You can use the Table of Contents to find a complete listing of all the list titles in this section. You can then review the lists that most interest you or simply browse the lists in this section. Most, such as the list of jobs with the highest pay, are easy to understand and require little explanation. We provide comments on each group of related lists to inform you of the selection criteria or other details we think you may want to know. As you review the lists, mark job titles that appeal to you (or, if someone else will be using this book, write them on a separate sheet of paper) so that you can look up their descriptions later in Part II.

Understand the Limitations of the Information

Most of the lists emphasize jobs with high pay, high growth, or large numbers of openings. Many people consider these factors important in selecting a desirable job, and they are also easily quantifiable. While these measures are important, we think you should also think about other factors in considering your career options. For example, location, liking the people you work with, having an opportunity to serve others, and enjoying your work are just a few of the many factors that may define the ideal job for you. These measures are difficult or impossible to objectively quantify based on the data we have available and are not, therefore, presented in this book. For this reason, we suggest that you consider the importance of these issues yourself and that you thoroughly research any job before making a firm decision.

For example, of the 200 jobs that require a college degree or more in our Best Jobs Overall list, the job ranked 200th by its combined score for earnings, growth, and number of openings is Graphic Designers. Its annual earnings—$41,280—are better than the average for all jobs, but its growth rate of 9.8% is a bit slower than average and the figure for its projected annual job openings, 26,968, is also below average. Is this a bad job, one you should avoid? No, of course not. It all depends on what you like or want to do. Another example is the job that had the very best overall score for earnings, growth, and number of openings: Computer Software Engineers, Applications. Is this job a great job to consider? Many people (the authors included) would not want to work in this job or may not have the skills or interest needed to do it well. It would be a great job for someone who was good at it and who would enjoy doing it, but it would simply not be right for someone else. On the other hand, the perfect job for some people would be Computer Software Engineers, Applications, because they enjoy it and are good at it.

So, as you look at the lists that follow, keep in mind that earnings, growth, and number of openings are just some things to consider. Also consider that half of all people in a given job earn more than the earnings you will see in this book—and half earn less. If a job really appeals to you, you should consider it even if it is not among the highest paying. And you should also consider jobs not among the fastest growing and jobs with few openings for similar reasons, because openings are always available, even for jobs with slow or negative growth projections or with small numbers of openings.

Some Details on the Lists

The sources of the information we used in constructing these lists are presented in this book's introduction. Here are some additional details on how we created the lists:

❋ **All data used to create these lists comes from the U.S. Department of Labor and the Census Bureau.** The earnings figures are based on the average annual pay received by full-time workers. Because the earnings represent the national averages, actual pay rates can vary greatly by location, amount of previous work experience, and other factors.

❋ **Many jobs have tied scores.** Many jobs have the same scores for one or more data elements. For example, in the listing of the best 200 jobs, six medical specializations— Anesthesiologists; Family and General Practitioners; Internists, General; Obstetricians and Gynecologists; Psychiatrists; and Surgeons—are listed in a row. You might think that Anesthesiologists is listed first because it has a higher rating, but that is not the case. The only data available applied to all six jobs, so they all have tied scores and are listed in alphabetical order. There was no way to avoid these issues, so simply understand that the difference of several positions on a list may not mean as much as it seems.

❋ **Likewise, it is unwise to place too much emphasis on small differences in outlook information (projections for job growth and job openings).** For example, Instructional Coordinators are projected to have 21,294 job openings per year, whereas 21,209 openings are projected for Chief Executives. This is a difference of only 85 jobs spread over the entire United States, and of course it is only a projection. Before 2007, the Bureau of Labor Statistics rounded these projections to the nearest 1,000 and would have assigned these two occupations the *same* figure (21,000), which would have given

Chief Executives the higher rank on the basis of alphabetical ordering. So, again, keep in mind that small differences of position on a list aren't very significant.

Best Jobs Overall: Lists of Jobs for College Graduates with the Highest Pay, Fastest Growth, and Most Openings

We consider the four lists that follow to be our premier lists. They are the lists that are most often mentioned in the media and the ones that most readers want to see. To create these lists, we first identified 297 jobs that typically require a two- or four-year college degree or more for entry, that offer more than minimal economic rewards, and for which we had a reasonably full set of information. We then ordered these jobs according to their individual combined rankings for pay, growth, and number of openings and extracted the top 200 jobs to create the first list that appears on the next page. This is a very popular list because it represents jobs according to quantifiable measures. We also ranked the top 200 jobs on three separate measures—annual earnings, projected percentage growth through 2016, and number of annual openings—and produced a list of the top 100 jobs for each of these measures. Descriptions for all the jobs in these lists are included in Part II.

The 200 Best Jobs Overall for College Graduates— Jobs with the Best Combination of Pay, Growth, and Openings

This list is the basis for all the lists in this book. It presents the top 200 jobs in order of their individual total scores. The job with the best overall score was Computer Software Engineers, Applications. Other jobs follow in order of their individual total scores for pay, growth, and openings. (When scores are tied, alphabetical ordering is used.) You can find descriptions for all of these jobs in Part II of this book.

The 200 Best Jobs for College Graduates			
Job	Annual Earnings	Percent Growth	Annual Openings
1. Computer Software Engineers, Applications	$83,130	44.6%	58,690
2. Computer Software Engineers, Systems Software	$89,070	28.2%	33,139
3. Computer Systems Analysts	$73,090	29.0%	63,166
4. Network Systems and Data Communications Analysts	$68,220	53.4%	35,086
5. Financial Analysts	$70,400	33.8%	29,317
6. Sales Agents, Financial Services	$68,430	24.8%	47,750

(continued)

(continued)

The 200 Best Jobs for College Graduates

Job	Annual Earnings	Percent Growth	Annual Openings
7. Sales Agents, Securities and Commodities	$68,430	24.8%	47,750
8. Health Specialties Teachers, Postsecondary	$80,700	22.9%	19,617
9. Computer Security Specialists	$64,690	27.0%	37,010
10. Network and Computer Systems Administrators	$64,690	27.0%	37,010
11. Management Analysts	$71,150	21.9%	125,669
12. Anesthesiologists	$145,600+	14.2%	38,027
13. Family and General Practitioners	$145,600+	14.2%	38,027
14. Internists, General	$145,600+	14.2%	38,027
15. Obstetricians and Gynecologists	$145,600+	14.2%	38,027
16. Psychiatrists	$145,600+	14.2%	38,027
17. Surgeons	$145,600+	14.2%	38,027
18. Computer and Information Systems Managers	$108,070	16.4%	30,887
19. Personal Financial Advisors	$67,660	41.0%	17,114
20. Pharmacists	$100,480	21.7%	16,358
21. Registered Nurses	$60,010	23.5%	233,499
22. Pediatricians, General	$140,690	14.2%	38,027
23. Physical Therapists	$69,760	27.1%	12,072
24. Financial Managers, Branch or Department	$95,310	12.6%	57,589
25. Treasurers and Controllers	$95,310	12.6%	57,589
26. Construction Managers	$76,230	15.7%	44,158
27. Physician Assistants	$78,450	27.0%	7,147
28. Medical and Health Services Managers	$76,990	16.4%	31,877
29. Lawyers	$106,120	11.0%	49,445
30. Marketing Managers	$104,400	14.4%	20,189
31. Biological Science Teachers, Postsecondary	$71,780	22.9%	9,039
32. Dental Hygienists	$64,740	30.1%	10,433
33. Veterinarians	$75,230	35.0%	5,301
34. Database Administrators	$67,250	28.6%	8,258
35. Engineering Teachers, Postsecondary	$79,510	22.9%	5,565
36. Market Research Analysts	$60,300	20.1%	45,015
37. Business Teachers, Postsecondary	$64,900	22.9%	11,643
38. Civil Engineers	$71,710	18.0%	15,979
39. Environmental Engineers	$72,350	25.4%	5,003
40. Sales Managers	$94,910	10.2%	36,392
41. Social and Community Service Managers	$54,530	24.7%	23,788
42. Actuaries	$85,690	23.7%	3,245

The 200 Best Jobs for College Graduates

Job	Annual Earnings	Percent Growth	Annual Openings
43. Accountants	$57,060	17.7%	134,463
44. Auditors	$57,060	17.7%	134,463
45. Industrial Engineers	$71,430	20.3%	11,272
46. Human Resources Managers	$87,180	12.5%	17,081
47. Education Administrators, Postsecondary	$75,780	14.2%	17,121
48. Multi-Media Artists and Animators	$54,550	25.8%	13,182
49. Occupational Therapists	$63,790	23.1%	8,338
50. Computer Systems Engineers/Architects	$71,510	15.1%	14,374
51. Network Designers	$71,510	15.1%	14,374
52. Software Quality Assurance Engineers and Testers	$71,510	15.1%	14,374
53. Web Administrators	$71,510	15.1%	14,374
54. Web Developers	$71,510	15.1%	14,374
55. Law Teachers, Postsecondary	$87,730	22.9%	2,169
56. Cost Estimators	$54,920	18.5%	38,379
57. Art, Drama, and Music Teachers, Postsecondary	$55,190	22.9%	12,707
58. Instructional Coordinators	$55,270	22.5%	21,294
59. Computer and Information Scientists, Research	$97,970	21.5%	2,901
60. Public Relations Managers	$86,470	16.9%	5,781
61. Architects, Except Landscape and Naval	$67,620	17.7%	11,324
62. Surveyors	$51,630	23.7%	14,305
63. Agricultural Sciences Teachers, Postsecondary	$78,460	22.9%	1,840
64. General and Operations Managers	$88,700	1.5%	112,072
65. Medical Scientists, Except Epidemiologists	$64,200	20.2%	10,596
66. Economics Teachers, Postsecondary	$75,300	22.9%	2,208
67. Environmental Scientists and Specialists, Including Health	$58,380	25.1%	6,961
68. Mathematical Science Teachers, Postsecondary	$58,560	22.9%	7,663
69. Administrative Services Managers	$70,990	11.7%	19,513
70. Computer Science Teachers, Postsecondary	$62,020	22.9%	5,820
71. Airline Pilots, Copilots, and Flight Engineers	$145,600+	12.9%	4,073
72. Education Administrators, Elementary and Secondary School	$80,580	7.6%	27,143
73. English Language and Literature Teachers, Postsecondary	$54,000	22.9%	10,475
74. Chief Executives	$145,600+	2.0%	21,209
75. Public Relations Specialists	$49,800	17.6%	51,216
76. Education Teachers, Postsecondary	$54,220	22.9%	9,359
77. Nursing Instructors and Teachers, Postsecondary	$57,500	22.9%	7,337

(continued)

(continued)

The 200 Best Jobs for College Graduates

Job	Annual Earnings	Percent Growth	Annual Openings
78. Mental Health Counselors	$36,000	30.0%	24,103
79. Atmospheric, Earth, Marine, and Space Sciences Teachers, Postsecondary	$73,280	22.9%	1,553
80. Physics Teachers, Postsecondary	$70,090	22.9%	2,155
81. Logisticians	$64,250	17.3%	9,671
82. Psychology Teachers, Postsecondary	$60,610	22.9%	5,261
83. Substance Abuse and Behavioral Disorder Counselors	$35,580	34.3%	20,821
84. Radiation Therapists	$70,010	24.8%	1,461
85. Medical and Public Health Social Workers	$44,670	24.2%	16,429
86. Training and Development Managers	$84,340	15.6%	3,759
87. Training and Development Specialists	$49,630	18.3%	35,862
88. Geoscientists, Except Hydrologists and Geographers	$75,800	21.9%	2,471
89. Chemistry Teachers, Postsecondary	$63,870	22.9%	3,405
90. Compensation, Benefits, and Job Analysis Specialists	$52,180	18.4%	18,761
91. Health Educators	$42,920	26.2%	13,707
92. Mental Health and Substance Abuse Social Workers	$36,640	29.9%	17,289
93. Dentists, General	$137,630	9.2%	7,106
94. Paralegals and Legal Assistants	$44,990	22.2%	22,756
95. Technical Writers	$60,390	19.5%	7,498
96. Compensation and Benefits Managers	$81,410	12.0%	6,121
97. Special Education Teachers, Preschool, Kindergarten, and Elementary School	$48,350	19.6%	20,049
98. Biomedical Engineers	$75,440	21.1%	1,804
99. History Teachers, Postsecondary	$59,160	22.9%	3,570
100. Political Science Teachers, Postsecondary	$63,100	22.9%	2,435
101. Aerospace Engineers	$90,930	10.2%	6,498
102. Rehabilitation Counselors	$29,630	23.0%	32,081
103. Veterinary Technologists and Technicians	$27,970	41.0%	14,674
104. Clinical Psychologists	$62,210	15.8%	8,309
105. Counseling Psychologists	$62,210	15.8%	8,309
106. School Psychologists	$62,210	15.8%	8,309
107. Elementary School Teachers, Except Special Education	$47,330	13.6%	181,612
108. Employment Interviewers	$44,380	18.4%	33,588
109. Loan Officers	$53,000	11.5%	54,237
110. Natural Sciences Managers	$104,040	11.4%	3,661
111. Personnel Recruiters	$44,380	18.4%	33,588
112. Engineering Managers	$111,020	7.3%	7,404

The 200 Best Jobs for College Graduates

Job	Annual Earnings	Percent Growth	Annual Openings
113. Communications Teachers, Postsecondary	$54,720	22.9%	4,074
114. Architecture Teachers, Postsecondary	$68,540	22.9%	1,044
115. Educational, Vocational, and School Counselors	$49,450	12.6%	54,025
116. Property, Real Estate, and Community Association Managers	$43,670	15.1%	49,916
117. Clergy	$40,460	18.9%	35,092
118. Foreign Language and Literature Teachers, Postsecondary	$53,610	22.9%	4,317
119. Graduate Teaching Assistants	$28,060	22.9%	20,601
120. Sociology Teachers, Postsecondary	$58,160	22.9%	2,774
121. Biochemists and Biophysicists	$79,270	15.9%	1,637
122. Child, Family, and School Social Workers	$38,620	19.1%	35,402
123. Kindergarten Teachers, Except Special Education	$45,120	16.3%	27,603
124. Philosophy and Religion Teachers, Postsecondary	$56,380	22.9%	3,120
125. Hydrologists	$68,140	24.3%	687
126. Physical Therapist Assistants	$44,130	32.4%	5,957
127. Environmental Science and Protection Technicians, Including Health	$39,370	28.0%	8,404
128. Art Directors	$72,320	9.0%	9,719
129. Insurance Sales Agents	$44,110	12.9%	64,162
130. Middle School Teachers, Except Special and Vocational Education	$47,900	11.2%	75,270
131. Marriage and Family Therapists	$43,600	29.8%	5,953
132. Sales Engineers	$80,270	8.5%	7,371
133. Copy Writers	$50,660	12.8%	24,023
134. Poets, Lyricists and Creative Writers	$50,660	12.8%	24,023
135. Computer Support Specialists	$42,400	12.9%	97,334
136. Anthropology and Archeology Teachers, Postsecondary	$64,530	22.9%	910
137. Environmental Science Teachers, Postsecondary	$64,850	22.9%	769
138. Radiologic Technicians	$50,260	15.1%	12,836
139. Radiologic Technologists	$50,260	15.1%	12,836
140. Medical Records and Health Information Technicians	$29,290	17.8%	39,048
141. Industrial-Organizational Psychologists	$80,820	21.3%	118
142. Forensic Science Technicians	$47,680	30.7%	3,074
143. Recreation and Fitness Studies Teachers, Postsecondary	$52,170	22.9%	3,010
144. Area, Ethnic, and Cultural Studies Teachers, Postsecondary	$59,150	22.9%	1,252
145. Diagnostic Medical Sonographers	$59,860	19.1%	3,211
146. Mechanical Engineers	$72,300	4.2%	12,394

(continued)

(continued)

The 200 Best Jobs for College Graduates

Job	Annual Earnings	Percent Growth	Annual Openings
147. Education Administrators, Preschool and Child Care Center/Program	$38,580	23.5%	8,113
148. Optometrists	$93,800	11.3%	1,789
149. Directors—Stage, Motion Pictures, Television, and Radio	$61,090	11.1%	8,992
150. Producers	$61,090	11.1%	8,992
151. Program Directors	$61,090	11.1%	8,992
152. Speech-Language Pathologists	$60,690	10.6%	11,160
153. Computer Programmers	$68,080	–4.1%	27,937
154. Electrical Engineers	$79,240	6.3%	6,806
155. Geography Teachers, Postsecondary	$61,310	22.9%	697
156. Respiratory Therapists	$50,070	22.6%	5,563
157. Cardiovascular Technologists and Technicians	$44,940	25.5%	3,550
158. Chiropractors	$65,890	14.4%	3,179
159. Forestry and Conservation Science Teachers, Postsecondary	$63,790	22.9%	454
160. Social Work Teachers, Postsecondary	$56,240	22.9%	1,292
161. Purchasing Managers	$85,440	3.4%	7,243
162. Adult Literacy, Remedial Education, and GED Teachers and Instructors	$44,710	14.2%	17,340
163. Criminal Justice and Law Enforcement Teachers, Postsecondary	$51,060	22.9%	1,911
164. Operations Research Analysts	$66,950	10.6%	5,727
165. Home Economics Teachers, Postsecondary	$58,170	22.9%	820
166. Chemists	$63,490	9.1%	9,024
167. Special Education Teachers, Middle School	$48,940	15.8%	8,846
168. Interior Designers	$43,970	19.5%	8,434
169. Occupational Therapist Assistants	$45,050	25.4%	2,634
170. Meeting and Convention Planners	$43,530	19.9%	8,318
171. Legal Secretaries	$38,810	11.7%	38,682
172. Medical and Clinical Laboratory Technologists	$51,720	12.4%	11,457
173. Electronics Engineers, Except Computer	$83,340	3.7%	5,699
174. Secondary School Teachers, Except Special and Vocational Education	$49,420	5.6%	93,166
175. Recreation Workers	$21,220	12.7%	61,454
176. Biological Technicians	$37,810	16.0%	15,374
177. Library Science Teachers, Postsecondary	$56,810	22.9%	702
178. Biologists	$64,920	9.2%	6,288

The 200 Best Jobs for College Graduates

Job	Annual Earnings	Percent Growth	Annual Openings
179. Computer Hardware Engineers	$91,860	4.6%	3,572
180. Directors, Religious Activities and Education	$35,370	19.7%	11,463
181. Landscape Architects	$57,580	16.4%	2,342
182. Prosthodontists	$145,600+	10.7%	54
183. Appraisers, Real Estate	$46,130	16.9%	6,493
184. Assessors	$46,130	16.9%	6,493
185. Chemical Engineers	$81,500	7.9%	2,111
186. Agents and Business Managers of Artists, Performers, and Athletes	$66,440	9.6%	3,940
187. Orthodontists	$145,600+	9.2%	479
188. Cartographers and Photogrammetrists	$49,970	20.3%	2,823
189. Probation Officers and Correctional Treatment Specialists	$44,510	10.9%	18,335
190. Environmental Engineering Technicians	$40,690	24.8%	2,162
191. Nuclear Medicine Technologists	$64,670	14.8%	1,290
192. Podiatrists	$110,510	9.5%	648
193. Advertising and Promotions Managers	$78,250	6.2%	2,955
194. Financial Examiners	$66,670	10.7%	2,449
195. Judges, Magistrate Judges, and Magistrates	$107,230	5.1%	1,567
196. Oral and Maxillofacial Surgeons	$145,600+	9.1%	400
197. Physicists	$96,850	6.8%	1,302
198. Statisticians	$69,900	8.5%	3,433
199. Curators	$46,000	23.3%	1,416
200. Graphic Designers	$41,280	9.8%	26,968

Jobs 6 and 7 share 47,750 openings. Jobs 9 and 10 share 37,010 openings. Jobs 12, 13, 14, 15, 16, 17, and 22 share 38,027 openings. Jobs 24 and 25 share 57,589 openings. Jobs 43 and 44 share 134,463 openings. Jobs 50, 51, 52, 53, and 54 share 14,374 openings. Jobs 104, 105, and 106 share 8,309 openings. Jobs 108 and 111 share 33,588 openings. Jobs 133 and 134 share 24,023 openings. Jobs 138 and 139 share 12,836 openings. Jobs 149, 150, and 151 share 8,992 openings with each other and with three other jobs not included in this list. Jobs 183 and 184 share 6,493 openings.

The 100 Best-Paying Jobs for College Graduates

We sorted the 200 best jobs that require a college degree or more based on their annual median earnings from highest to lowest. *Median earnings* means that half of all workers in these jobs earn more than that amount and half earn less. We then selected the 100 jobs with the highest earnings to create the list that follows.

It shouldn't be a big surprise to learn that most of the highest-paying jobs require advanced levels of education, training, and experience. For example, most of the 20 jobs with the highest earnings require a doctoral or professional degree, and others—such as Chief Executives and Airline Pilots, Copilots, and Flight Engineers—require extensive training and experience. Although the top 20 jobs may not appeal to you for a variety of reasons, you are likely to find others that will among the top 100 jobs with the highest earnings. Keep in mind that the earnings reflect the national average for all workers in the occupation. This is an important consideration because starting pay in the job is usually a lot less than the pay that workers can earn with several years of experience. (You can see estimates of starting pay in the Part II job descriptions.) Earnings also vary significantly by region of the country, so actual pay in your area could be substantially different.

The 100 Best-Paying Jobs for College Graduates

Job	Annual Earnings
1. Airline Pilots, Copilots, and Flight Engineers	$145,600+
2. Anesthesiologists	$145,600+
3. Chief Executives	$145,600+
4. Family and General Practitioners	$145,600+
5. Internists, General	$145,600+
6. Obstetricians and Gynecologists	$145,600+
7. Oral and Maxillofacial Surgeons	$145,600+
8. Orthodontists	$145,600+
9. Prosthodontists	$145,600+
10. Psychiatrists	$145,600+
11. Surgeons	$145,600+
12. Pediatricians, General	$140,690
13. Dentists, General	$137,630
14. Engineering Managers	$111,020
15. Podiatrists	$110,510
16. Computer and Information Systems Managers	$108,070
17. Judges, Magistrate Judges, and Magistrates	$107,230
18. Lawyers	$106,120
19. Marketing Managers	$104,400
20. Natural Sciences Managers	$104,040
21. Pharmacists	$100,480
22. Computer and Information Scientists, Research	$97,970
23. Physicists	$96,850
24. Financial Managers, Branch or Department	$95,310
25. Treasurers and Controllers	$95,310
26. Sales Managers	$94,910
27. Optometrists	$93,800
28. Computer Hardware Engineers	$91,860

The 100 Best-Paying Jobs for College Graduates

Job	Annual Earnings
29. Aerospace Engineers	$90,930
30. Computer Software Engineers, Systems Software	$89,070
31. General and Operations Managers	$88,700
32. Law Teachers, Postsecondary	$87,730
33. Human Resources Managers	$87,180
34. Public Relations Managers	$86,470
35. Actuaries	$85,690
36. Purchasing Managers	$85,440
37. Training and Development Managers	$84,340
38. Electronics Engineers, Except Computer	$83,340
39. Computer Software Engineers, Applications	$83,130
40. Chemical Engineers	$81,500
41. Compensation and Benefits Managers	$81,410
42. Industrial-Organizational Psychologists	$80,820
43. Health Specialties Teachers, Postsecondary	$80,700
44. Education Administrators, Elementary and Secondary School	$80,580
45. Sales Engineers	$80,270
46. Engineering Teachers, Postsecondary	$79,510
47. Biochemists and Biophysicists	$79,270
48. Electrical Engineers	$79,240
49. Agricultural Sciences Teachers, Postsecondary	$78,460
50. Physician Assistants	$78,450
51. Advertising and Promotions Managers	$78,250
52. Medical and Health Services Managers	$76,990
53. Construction Managers	$76,230
54. Geoscientists, Except Hydrologists and Geographers	$75,800
55. Education Administrators, Postsecondary	$75,780
56. Biomedical Engineers	$75,440
57. Economics Teachers, Postsecondary	$75,300
58. Veterinarians	$75,230
59. Atmospheric, Earth, Marine, and Space Sciences Teachers, Postsecondary	$73,280
60. Computer Systems Analysts	$73,090
61. Environmental Engineers	$72,350
62. Art Directors	$72,320
63. Mechanical Engineers	$72,300
64. Biological Science Teachers, Postsecondary	$71,780
65. Civil Engineers	$71,710

(continued)

(continued)

The 100 Best-Paying Jobs for College Graduates

Job	Annual Earnings
66. Computer Systems Engineers/Architects	$71,510
67. Network Designers	$71,510
68. Software Quality Assurance Engineers and Testers	$71,510
69. Web Administrators	$71,510
70. Web Developers	$71,510
71. Industrial Engineers	$71,430
72. Management Analysts	$71,150
73. Administrative Services Managers	$70,990
74. Financial Analysts	$70,400
75. Physics Teachers, Postsecondary	$70,090
76. Radiation Therapists	$70,010
77. Statisticians	$69,900
78. Physical Therapists	$69,760
79. Architecture Teachers, Postsecondary	$68,540
80. Sales Agents, Financial Services	$68,430
81. Sales Agents, Securities and Commodities	$68,430
82. Network Systems and Data Communications Analysts	$68,220
83. Hydrologists	$68,140
84. Computer Programmers	$68,080
85. Personal Financial Advisors	$67,660
86. Architects, Except Landscape and Naval	$67,620
87. Database Administrators	$67,250
88. Operations Research Analysts	$66,950
89. Financial Examiners	$66,670
90. Agents and Business Managers of Artists, Performers, and Athletes	$66,440
91. Chiropractors	$65,890
92. Biologists	$64,920
93. Business Teachers, Postsecondary	$64,900
94. Environmental Science Teachers, Postsecondary	$64,850
95. Dental Hygienists	$64,740
96. Computer Security Specialists	$64,690
97. Network and Computer Systems Administrators	$64,690
98. Nuclear Medicine Technologists	$64,670
99. Anthropology and Archeology Teachers, Postsecondary	$64,530
100. Logisticians	$64,250

The 100 Fastest-Growing Jobs for College Graduates

We created this list by sorting the 200 best jobs that require a college degree or more by their projected growth over a ten-year period. Growth rates are one measure to consider in exploring career options, as jobs with higher growth rates tend to provide more job opportunities.

Jobs in the computer and medical fields dominate the 20 fastest-growing jobs. Network Systems and Data Communications Analysts is the job with the highest growth rate—the number employed is projected to grow by a bit more than half during this time. You can find a wide range of rapidly growing jobs in a variety of fields and at different levels of training and education among the jobs on this list.

Job	Percent Growth
The 100 Fastest-Growing Jobs for College Graduates	
1. Network Systems and Data Communications Analysts	53.4%
2. Computer Software Engineers, Applications	44.6%
3. Personal Financial Advisors	41.0%
4. Veterinary Technologists and Technicians	41.0%
5. Veterinarians	35.0%
6. Substance Abuse and Behavioral Disorder Counselors	34.3%
7. Financial Analysts	33.8%
8. Physical Therapist Assistants	32.4%
9. Forensic Science Technicians	30.7%
10. Dental Hygienists	30.1%
11. Mental Health Counselors	30.0%
12. Mental Health and Substance Abuse Social Workers	29.9%
13. Marriage and Family Therapists	29.8%
14. Computer Systems Analysts	29.0%
15. Database Administrators	28.6%
16. Computer Software Engineers, Systems Software	28.2%
17. Environmental Science and Protection Technicians, Including Health	28.0%
18. Physical Therapists	27.1%
19. Computer Security Specialists	27.0%
20. Network and Computer Systems Administrators	27.0%
21. Physician Assistants	27.0%
22. Health Educators	26.2%
23. Multi-Media Artists and Animators	25.8%
24. Cardiovascular Technologists and Technicians	25.5%

(continued)

(continued)

The 100 Fastest-Growing Jobs for College Graduates

Job	Percent Growth
25. Environmental Engineers	25.4%
26. Occupational Therapist Assistants	25.4%
27. Environmental Scientists and Specialists, Including Health	25.1%
28. Environmental Engineering Technicians	24.8%
29. Radiation Therapists	24.8%
30. Sales Agents, Financial Services	24.8%
31. Sales Agents, Securities and Commodities	24.8%
32. Social and Community Service Managers	24.7%
33. Hydrologists	24.3%
34. Medical and Public Health Social Workers	24.2%
35. Actuaries	23.7%
36. Surveyors	23.7%
37. Education Administrators, Preschool and Child Care Center/Program	23.5%
38. Registered Nurses	23.5%
39. Curators	23.3%
40. Occupational Therapists	23.1%
41. Rehabilitation Counselors	23.0%
42. Agricultural Sciences Teachers, Postsecondary	22.9%
43. Anthropology and Archeology Teachers, Postsecondary	22.9%
44. Architecture Teachers, Postsecondary	22.9%
45. Area, Ethnic, and Cultural Studies Teachers, Postsecondary	22.9%
46. Art, Drama, and Music Teachers, Postsecondary	22.9%
47. Atmospheric, Earth, Marine, and Space Sciences Teachers, Postsecondary	22.9%
48. Biological Science Teachers, Postsecondary	22.9%
49. Business Teachers, Postsecondary	22.9%
50. Chemistry Teachers, Postsecondary	22.9%
51. Communications Teachers, Postsecondary	22.9%
52. Computer Science Teachers, Postsecondary	22.9%
53. Criminal Justice and Law Enforcement Teachers, Postsecondary	22.9%
54. Economics Teachers, Postsecondary	22.9%
55. Education Teachers, Postsecondary	22.9%
56. Engineering Teachers, Postsecondary	22.9%
57. English Language and Literature Teachers, Postsecondary	22.9%
58. Environmental Science Teachers, Postsecondary	22.9%
59. Foreign Language and Literature Teachers, Postsecondary	22.9%
60. Forestry and Conservation Science Teachers, Postsecondary	22.9%

The 100 Fastest-Growing Jobs for College Graduates

Job	Percent Growth
61. Geography Teachers, Postsecondary	22.9%
62. Graduate Teaching Assistants	22.9%
63. Health Specialties Teachers, Postsecondary	22.9%
64. History Teachers, Postsecondary	22.9%
65. Home Economics Teachers, Postsecondary	22.9%
66. Law Teachers, Postsecondary	22.9%
67. Library Science Teachers, Postsecondary	22.9%
68. Mathematical Science Teachers, Postsecondary	22.9%
69. Nursing Instructors and Teachers, Postsecondary	22.9%
70. Philosophy and Religion Teachers, Postsecondary	22.9%
71. Physics Teachers, Postsecondary	22.9%
72. Political Science Teachers, Postsecondary	22.9%
73. Psychology Teachers, Postsecondary	22.9%
74. Recreation and Fitness Studies Teachers, Postsecondary	22.9%
75. Social Work Teachers, Postsecondary	22.9%
76. Sociology Teachers, Postsecondary	22.9%
77. Respiratory Therapists	22.6%
78. Instructional Coordinators	22.5%
79. Paralegals and Legal Assistants	22.2%
80. Geoscientists, Except Hydrologists and Geographers	21.9%
81. Management Analysts	21.9%
82. Pharmacists	21.7%
83. Computer and Information Scientists, Research	21.5%
84. Industrial-Organizational Psychologists	21.3%
85. Biomedical Engineers	21.1%
86. Cartographers and Photogrammetrists	20.3%
87. Industrial Engineers	20.3%
88. Medical Scientists, Except Epidemiologists	20.2%
89. Market Research Analysts	20.1%
90. Meeting and Convention Planners	19.9%
91. Directors, Religious Activities and Education	19.7%
92. Special Education Teachers, Preschool, Kindergarten, and Elementary School	19.6%
93. Interior Designers	19.5%
94. Technical Writers	19.5%
95. Child, Family, and School Social Workers	19.1%
96. Diagnostic Medical Sonographers	19.1%
97. Clergy	18.9%

(continued)

(continued)

The 100 Fastest-Growing Jobs for College Graduates

Job	Percent Growth
98. Cost Estimators	18.5%
99. Compensation, Benefits, and Job Analysis Specialists	18.4%
100. Employment Interviewers	18.4%

The 100 Jobs with the Most Openings for College Graduates

We created this list by sorting the 200 best jobs that require a college degree or more by the number of job openings that each is expected to have per year. Jobs with the most annual openings often provide easier entry for new workers or make it easier to move from one position to another. Some of these jobs may also be attractive to people reentering the labor market, part-time workers, and workers who want to move from one employer to another.

The 100 Jobs with the Most Openings for College Graduates

Job	Annual Openings
1. Registered Nurses	233,499
2. Elementary School Teachers, Except Special Education	181,612
3. Accountants	134,463
4. Auditors	134,463
5. Management Analysts	125,669
6. General and Operations Managers	112,072
7. Computer Support Specialists	97,334
8. Secondary School Teachers, Except Special and Vocational Education	93,166
9. Middle School Teachers, Except Special and Vocational Education	75,270
10. Insurance Sales Agents	64,162
11. Computer Systems Analysts	63,166
12. Recreation Workers	61,454
13. Computer Software Engineers, Applications	58,690
14. Financial Managers, Branch or Department	57,589
15. Treasurers and Controllers	57,589
16. Loan Officers	54,237
17. Educational, Vocational, and School Counselors	54,025
18. Public Relations Specialists	51,216
19. Property, Real Estate, and Community Association Managers	49,916

The 100 Jobs with the Most Openings for College Graduates

Job	Annual Openings
20. Lawyers	49,445
21. Sales Agents, Financial Services	47,750
22. Sales Agents, Securities and Commodities	47,750
23. Market Research Analysts	45,015
24. Construction Managers	44,158
25. Medical Records and Health Information Technicians	39,048
26. Legal Secretaries	38,682
27. Cost Estimators	38,379
28. Anesthesiologists	38,027
29. Family and General Practitioners	38,027
30. Internists, General	38,027
31. Obstetricians and Gynecologists	38,027
32. Pediatricians, General	38,027
33. Psychiatrists	38,027
34. Surgeons	38,027
35. Computer Security Specialists	37,010
36. Network and Computer Systems Administrators	37,010
37. Sales Managers	36,392
38. Training and Development Specialists	35,862
39. Child, Family, and School Social Workers	35,402
40. Clergy	35,092
41. Network Systems and Data Communications Analysts	35,086
42. Employment Interviewers	33,588
43. Personnel Recruiters	33,588
44. Computer Software Engineers, Systems Software	33,139
45. Rehabilitation Counselors	32,081
46. Medical and Health Services Managers	31,877
47. Computer and Information Systems Managers	30,887
48. Financial Analysts	29,317
49. Computer Programmers	27,937
50. Kindergarten Teachers, Except Special Education	27,603
51. Education Administrators, Elementary and Secondary School	27,143
52. Graphic Designers	26,968
53. Mental Health Counselors	24,103
54. Copy Writers	24,023
55. Poets, Lyricists and Creative Writers	24,023
56. Social and Community Service Managers	23,788

(continued)

(continued)

The 100 Jobs with the Most Openings for College Graduates

Job	Annual Openings
57. Paralegals and Legal Assistants	22,756
58. Instructional Coordinators	21,294
59. Chief Executives	21,209
60. Substance Abuse and Behavioral Disorder Counselors	20,821
61. Graduate Teaching Assistants	20,601
62. Marketing Managers	20,189
63. Special Education Teachers, Preschool, Kindergarten, and Elementary School	20,049
64. Health Specialties Teachers, Postsecondary	19,617
65. Administrative Services Managers	19,513
66. Compensation, Benefits, and Job Analysis Specialists	18,761
67. Probation Officers and Correctional Treatment Specialists	18,335
68. Adult Literacy, Remedial Education, and GED Teachers and Instructors	17,340
69. Mental Health and Substance Abuse Social Workers	17,289
70. Education Administrators, Postsecondary	17,121
71. Personal Financial Advisors	17,114
72. Human Resources Managers	17,081
73. Medical and Public Health Social Workers	16,429
74. Pharmacists	16,358
75. Civil Engineers	15,979
76. Biological Technicians	15,374
77. Veterinary Technologists and Technicians	14,674
78. Computer Systems Engineers/Architects	14,374
79. Network Designers	14,374
80. Software Quality Assurance Engineers and Testers	14,374
81. Web Administrators	14,374
82. Web Developers	14,374
83. Surveyors	14,305
84. Health Educators	13,707
85. Multi-Media Artists and Animators	13,182
86. Radiologic Technicians	12,836
87. Radiologic Technologists	12,836
88. Art, Drama, and Music Teachers, Postsecondary	12,707
89. Mechanical Engineers	12,394
90. Physical Therapists	12,072
91. Business Teachers, Postsecondary	11,643
92. Directors, Religious Activities and Education	11,463

The 100 Jobs with the Most Openings for College Graduates

Job	Annual Openings
93. Medical and Clinical Laboratory Technologists	11,457
94. Architects, Except Landscape and Naval	11,324
95. Industrial Engineers	11,272
96. Speech-Language Pathologists	11,160
97. Medical Scientists, Except Epidemiologists	10,596
98. English Language and Literature Teachers, Postsecondary	10,475
99. Dental Hygienists	10,433
100. Art Directors	9,719

Jobs 3 and 4 share 134,463 openings. Jobs 14 and 15 share 57,589 openings. Jobs 21 and 22 share 47,750 openings. Jobs 28, 29, 30, 31, 32, 33, and 34 share 38,027 openings. Jobs 35 and 36 share 37,010 openings. Jobs 42 and 43 share 33,588 openings. Jobs 54 and 55 share 24,023 openings. Jobs 78, 79, 80, 81, and 82 share 14,374 openings. Jobs 86 and 87 share 12,836 openings.

Best Jobs Lists by Demographic

We decided it would be interesting to include lists in this section that show what sorts of jobs different types of people are most likely to have. For example, what jobs have the highest percentages of male college graduates or young college graduates? We're not saying that men or young grads should consider these jobs over others, but it is interesting information to know.

In some cases, the lists can give you ideas for jobs to consider that you might otherwise overlook. For example, perhaps women should consider some jobs that traditionally have high percentages of men in them. Or older workers might consider some jobs typically held by young graduates. Although these aren't obvious ways of using these lists, the lists may give you some good ideas of jobs to consider. The lists may also help you identify jobs that work well for others in your situation—for example, jobs with plentiful opportunities for part-time work, if that is something you want to do.

All lists in this section were created through a similar process. We began with the 200 best jobs that require a two- or four-year college degree or more. Next, we sorted those jobs in order of the primary criterion for each set of lists. For example, we sorted the 200 jobs based on the percentage of workers age 20 to 24 from highest to lowest percentage, and then selected the jobs with high percentages (36 jobs with a percentage greater than 7.5). From this list of jobs with a high percentage of each type of worker, we created four more-specialized lists:

❋ 25 Best Jobs Overall (the subset of jobs that have the highest combined scores for earnings, growth rate, and number of openings)

❋ 25 Best-Paying Jobs

❀ 25 Fastest-Growing Jobs

❀ 25 Jobs with the Most Openings

Again, each of these four lists includes only jobs that have high percentages of each type of worker. The same basic process was used to create all the lists in this section. The lists are very interesting, and we hope you find them helpful.

Best Jobs with a High Percentage of College Graduates Age 20–24

These jobs have higher percentages (more than 7.5%) of recent college graduates and may present more opportunities for initial entry or upward mobility. If you're wondering how 7.5% can be considered a high percentage, consider that most bachelor's degrees are awarded to people age 21 or older, and many of the jobs among our best 200 require a graduate or professional degree that is rarely attained by people in their early 20s. Many other jobs have few young workers because they usually require several years of related work experience. Therefore, many of the jobs on the following set of lists are those that require specialized training lasting two years.

Best Jobs with the Highest Percentage of College Graduates Age 20–24

Job	Percent Age 20–24
1. Recreation Workers	30.2%
2. Environmental Science and Protection Technicians, Including Health	28.0%
3. Forensic Science Technicians	28.0%
4. Veterinary Technologists and Technicians	24.7%
5. Agents and Business Managers of Artists, Performers, and Athletes	17.6%
6. Adult Literacy, Remedial Education, and GED Teachers and Instructors	17.4%
7. Physical Therapist Assistants	14.8%
8. Kindergarten Teachers, Except Special Education	13.2%
9. Computer Support Specialists	12.6%
10. Actuaries	10.5%
11. Biological Technicians	10.5%
12. Health Educators	10.5%
13. Probation Officers and Correctional Treatment Specialists	10.5%
14. Graphic Designers	10.3%
15. Interior Designers	10.3%
16. Public Relations Specialists	10.1%
17. Chemical Engineers	9.8%
18. Market Research Analysts	9.7%
19. Paralegals and Legal Assistants	9.4%

Best Jobs with the Highest Percentage of College Graduates Age 20–24

Job	Percent Age 20–24
20. Medical Records and Health Information Technicians	9.1%
21. Network Systems and Data Communications Analysts	9.1%
22. Cost Estimators	9.0%
23. Environmental Engineering Technicians	8.9%
24. Sales Agents, Financial Services	8.4%
25. Sales Agents, Securities and Commodities	8.4%
26. Computer Hardware Engineers	8.0%
27. Educational, Vocational, and School Counselors	8.0%
28. Marriage and Family Therapists	8.0%
29. Mental Health Counselors	8.0%
30. Rehabilitation Counselors	8.0%
31. Substance Abuse and Behavioral Disorder Counselors	8.0%
32. Directors—Stage, Motion Pictures, Television, and Radio	7.9%
33. Legal Secretaries	7.9%
34. Producers	7.9%
35. Program Directors	7.9%
36. Logisticians	7.7%

The jobs in the following four lists are derived from the preceding list of the jobs with the highest percentages of workers age 20–24.

25 Best Jobs Overall with a High Percentage of College Graduates Age 20–24

Job	Percent Age 20–24	Annual Earnings	Percent Growth	Annual Openings
1. Network Systems and Data Communications Analysts	9.1%	$68,220	53.4%	35,086
2. Sales Agents, Financial Services	8.4%	$68,430	24.8%	47,750
3. Sales Agents, Securities and Commodities	8.4%	$68,430	24.8%	47,750
4. Market Research Analysts	9.7%	$60,300	20.1%	45,015
5. Public Relations Specialists	10.1%	$49,800	17.6%	51,216
6. Cost Estimators	9.0%	$54,920	18.5%	38,379
7. Educational, Vocational, and School Counselors	8.0%	$49,450	12.6%	54,025
8. Actuaries	10.5%	$85,690	23.7%	3,245
9. Paralegals and Legal Assistants	9.4%	$44,990	22.2%	22,756

(continued)

(continued)

25 Best Jobs Overall with a High Percentage of College Graduates Age 20–24

Job	Percent Age 20–24	Annual Earnings	Percent Growth	Annual Openings
10. Computer Support Specialists	12.6%	$42,400	12.9%	97,334
11. Logisticians	7.7%	$64,250	17.3%	9,671
12. Kindergarten Teachers, Except Special Education	13.2%	$45,120	16.3%	27,603
13. Mental Health Counselors	8.0%	$36,000	30.0%	24,103
14. Substance Abuse and Behavioral Disorder Counselors	8.0%	$35,580	34.3%	20,821
15. Health Educators	10.5%	$42,920	26.2%	13,707
16. Physical Therapist Assistants	14.8%	$44,130	32.4%	5,957
17. Forensic Science Technicians	28.0%	$47,680	30.7%	3,074
18. Veterinary Technologists and Technicians	24.7%	$27,970	41.0%	14,674
19. Rehabilitation Counselors	8.0%	$29,630	23.0%	32,081
20. Marriage and Family Therapists	8.0%	$43,600	29.8%	5,953
21. Medical Records and Health Information Technicians	9.1%	$29,290	17.8%	39,048
22. Adult Literacy, Remedial Education, and GED Teachers and Instructors	17.4%	$44,710	14.2%	17,340
23. Directors—Stage, Motion Pictures, Television, and Radio	7.9%	$61,090	11.1%	8,992
24. Producers	7.9%	$61,090	11.1%	8,992
25. Program Directors	7.9%	$61,090	11.1%	8,992

Jobs 2 and 3 share 47,750 openings. Jobs 23, 24, and 25 share 8,992 openings with each other and with two other jobs not included in this list.

25 Best-Paying Jobs with a High Percentage of College Graduates Age 20–24

Job	Percent Age 20–24	Annual Earnings
1. Computer Hardware Engineers	8.0%	$91,860
2. Actuaries	10.5%	$85,690
3. Chemical Engineers	9.8%	$81,500
4. Sales Agents, Financial Services	8.4%	$68,430
5. Sales Agents, Securities and Commodities	8.4%	$68,430
6. Network Systems and Data Communications Analysts	9.1%	$68,220
7. Agents and Business Managers of Artists, Performers, and Athletes	17.6%	$66,440
8. Logisticians	7.7%	$64,250

200 Best Jobs for College Graduates © JIST Works

25 Best-Paying Jobs with a High Percentage of College Graduates Age 20–24

Job	Percent Age 20–24	Annual Earnings
9. Chemists	7.5%	$63,490
10. Directors—Stage, Motion Pictures, Television, and Radio	7.9%	$61,090
11. Producers	7.9%	$61,090
12. Program Directors	7.9%	$61,090
13. Market Research Analysts	9.7%	$60,300
14. Cost Estimators	9.0%	$54,920
15. Public Relations Specialists	10.1%	$49,800
16. Educational, Vocational, and School Counselors	8.0%	$49,450
17. Forensic Science Technicians	28.0%	$47,680
18. Kindergarten Teachers, Except Special Education	13.2%	$45,120
19. Paralegals and Legal Assistants	9.4%	$44,990
20. Adult Literacy, Remedial Education, and GED Teachers and Instructors	17.4%	$44,710
21. Probation Officers and Correctional Treatment Specialists	10.5%	$44,510
22. Physical Therapist Assistants	14.8%	$44,130
23. Interior Designers	10.3%	$43,970
24. Marriage and Family Therapists	8.0%	$43,600
25. Health Educators	10.5%	$42,920

25 Fastest-Growing Jobs with a High Percentage of College Graduates Age 20–24

Job	Percent Age 20–24	Percent Growth
1. Network Systems and Data Communications Analysts	9.1%	53.4%
2. Veterinary Technologists and Technicians	24.7%	41.0%
3. Substance Abuse and Behavioral Disorder Counselors	8.0%	34.3%
4. Physical Therapist Assistants	14.8%	32.4%
5. Forensic Science Technicians	28.0%	30.7%
6. Mental Health Counselors	8.0%	30.0%
7. Marriage and Family Therapists	8.0%	29.8%
8. Environmental Science and Protection Technicians, Including Health	28.0%	28.0%
9. Health Educators	10.5%	26.2%
10. Environmental Engineering Technicians	8.9%	24.8%
11. Sales Agents, Financial Services	8.4%	24.8%

(continued)

(continued)

25 Fastest-Growing Jobs with a High Percentage of College Graduates Age 20–24

Job	Percent Age 20–24	Percent Growth
12. Sales Agents, Securities and Commodities	8.4%	24.8%
13. Actuaries	10.5%	23.7%
14. Rehabilitation Counselors	8.0%	23.0%
15. Paralegals and Legal Assistants	9.4%	22.2%
16. Market Research Analysts	9.7%	20.1%
17. Interior Designers	10.3%	19.5%
18. Cost Estimators	9.0%	18.5%
19. Medical Records and Health Information Technicians	9.1%	17.8%
20. Public Relations Specialists	10.1%	17.6%
21. Logisticians	7.7%	17.3%
22. Kindergarten Teachers, Except Special Education	13.2%	16.3%
23. Biological Technicians	10.5%	16.0%
24. Adult Literacy, Remedial Education, and GED Teachers and Instructors	17.4%	14.2%
25. Computer Support Specialists	12.6%	12.9%

25 Jobs with the Most Openings with a High Percentage of College Graduates Age 20–24

Job	Percent Age 20–24	Annual Openings
1. Computer Support Specialists	12.6%	97,334
2. Recreation Workers	30.2%	61,454
3. Educational, Vocational, and School Counselors	8.0%	54,025
4. Public Relations Specialists	10.1%	51,216
5. Sales Agents, Financial Services	8.4%	47,750
6. Sales Agents, Securities and Commodities	8.4%	47,750
7. Market Research Analysts	9.7%	45,015
8. Medical Records and Health Information Technicians	9.1%	39,048
9. Legal Secretaries	7.9%	38,682
10. Cost Estimators	9.0%	38,379
11. Network Systems and Data Communications Analysts	9.1%	35,086
12. Rehabilitation Counselors	8.0%	32,081
13. Kindergarten Teachers, Except Special Education	13.2%	27,603
14. Graphic Designers	10.3%	26,968

25 Jobs with the Most Openings with a High Percentage of College Graduates Age 20–24

Job	Percent Age 20–24	Annual Openings
15. Mental Health Counselors	8.0%	24,103
16. Paralegals and Legal Assistants	9.4%	22,756
17. Substance Abuse and Behavioral Disorder Counselors	8.0%	20,821
18. Probation Officers and Correctional Treatment Specialists	10.5%	18,335
19. Adult Literacy, Remedial Education, and GED Teachers and Instructors	17.4%	17,340
20. Biological Technicians	10.5%	15,374
21. Veterinary Technologists and Technicians	24.7%	14,674
22. Health Educators	10.5%	13,707
23. Logisticians	7.7%	9,671
24. Chemists	7.5%	9,024
25. Directors—Stage, Motion Pictures, Television, and Radio	7.9%	8,992

Jobs 5 and 6 share 47,750 openings. Job 25 shares 8,992 openings with four other jobs not included in this list.

Best Jobs with a High Percentage of College Graduates Age 55 and Over

Older workers don't change careers as often as younger ones do and, on the average, they tend to have been in their jobs for quite some time. Many of the jobs with the highest percentages of college graduates age 55 and over—and those with the highest earnings—require considerable preparation, either through experience or through education and training. These are not the sort of jobs most young graduates could easily get just out of college. That should not come as a big surprise, as many of these folks would have been in the workforce for a long time and would therefore have lots of experience.

But go down the list of the jobs with the highest percentage (more than 25 percent) of older workers and you will find a variety of jobs that many older workers could more easily enter if they were changing careers. Some would make good "retirement" or "encore" jobs, particularly if they allowed for part-time work or self-employment.

Best Jobs with the Highest Percentage of College Graduates Age 55 and Over

Job	Percent Age 55 and Over
1. Clergy	42.0%
2. Property, Real Estate, and Community Association Managers	35.2%
3. Clinical Psychologists	35.0%
4. Counseling Psychologists	35.0%
5. Industrial-Organizational Psychologists	35.0%
6. School Psychologists	35.0%
7. Art Directors	33.9%
8. Multi-Media Artists and Animators	33.9%
9. Copy Writers	33.3%
10. Physicists	33.3%
11. Poets, Lyricists and Creative Writers	33.3%
12. Curators	32.5%
13. Chief Executives	31.5%
14. Natural Sciences Managers	30.9%
15. Instructional Coordinators	30.4%
16. Management Analysts	30.1%
17. Cost Estimators	29.9%
18. Education Administrators, Elementary and Secondary School	28.7%
19. Education Administrators, Postsecondary	28.7%
20. Education Administrators, Preschool and Child Care Center/Program	28.7%
21. Appraisers, Real Estate	28.6%
22. Assessors	28.6%
23. Veterinarians	28.4%
24. Judges, Magistrate Judges, and Magistrates	27.8%
25. Lawyers	27.8%
26. Directors, Religious Activities and Education	27.7%
27. Dentists, General	27.4%
28. Oral and Maxillofacial Surgeons	27.4%
29. Orthodontists	27.4%
30. Prosthodontists	27.4%
31. Anesthesiologists	27.2%
32. Family and General Practitioners	27.2%
33. Internists, General	27.2%
34. Obstetricians and Gynecologists	27.2%
35. Pediatricians, General	27.2%
36. Psychiatrists	27.2%

Best Jobs with the Highest Percentage of College Graduates Age 55 and Over

Job	Percent Age 55 and Over
37. Surgeons	27.2%
38. Administrative Services Managers	27.1%
39. Insurance Sales Agents	27.1%
40. Medical Records and Health Information Technicians	26.1%
41. Engineering Managers	25.5%
42. Legal Secretaries	25.5%
43. Educational, Vocational, and School Counselors	25.3%
44. Marriage and Family Therapists	25.3%
45. Mental Health Counselors	25.3%
46. Rehabilitation Counselors	25.3%
47. Social and Community Service Managers	25.3%
48. Substance Abuse and Behavioral Disorder Counselors	25.3%

The jobs in the following four lists are derived from the preceding list of the jobs with the highest percentages of workers age 55 and over.

25 Best Jobs Overall with a High Percentage of College Graduates Age 55 and Over

Job	Percent Age 55 and Over	Annual Earnings	Percent Growth	Annual Openings
1. Anesthesiologists	27.2%	$145,600+	14.2%	38,027
2. Family and General Practitioners	27.2%	$145,600+	14.2%	38,027
3. Internists, General	27.2%	$145,600+	14.2%	38,027
4. Obstetricians and Gynecologists	27.2%	$145,600+	14.2%	38,027
5. Psychiatrists	27.2%	$145,600+	14.2%	38,027
6. Surgeons	27.2%	$145,600+	14.2%	38,027
7. Management Analysts	30.1%	$71,150	21.9%	125,669
8. Pediatricians, General	27.2%	$140,690	14.2%	38,027
9. Cost Estimators	29.9%	$54,920	18.5%	38,379
10. Lawyers	27.8%	$106,120	11.0%	49,445
11. Social and Community Service Managers	25.3%	$54,530	24.7%	23,788
12. Instructional Coordinators	30.4%	$55,270	22.5%	21,294
13. Veterinarians	28.4%	$75,230	35.0%	5,301
14. Multi-Media Artists and Animators	33.9%	$54,550	25.8%	13,182

(continued)

(continued)

25 Best Jobs Overall with a High Percentage of College Graduates Age 55 and Over

Job	Percent Age 55 and Over	Annual Earnings	Percent Growth	Annual Openings
15. Property, Real Estate, and Community Association Managers	35.2%	$43,670	15.1%	49,916
16. Mental Health Counselors	25.3%	$36,000	30.0%	24,103
17. Education Administrators, Postsecondary	28.7%	$75,780	14.2%	17,121
18. Medical Records and Health Information Technicians	26.1%	$29,290	17.8%	39,048
19. Clergy	42.0%	$40,460	18.9%	35,092
20. Educational, Vocational, and School Counselors	25.3%	$49,450	12.6%	54,025
21. Insurance Sales Agents	27.1%	$44,110	12.9%	64,162
22. Substance Abuse and Behavioral Disorder Counselors	25.3%	$35,580	34.3%	20,821
23. Chief Executives	31.5%	$145,600+	2.0%	21,209
24. Rehabilitation Counselors	25.3%	$29,630	23.0%	32,081
25. Clinical Psychologists	35.0%	$62,210	15.8%	8,309

Jobs 1, 2, 3, 4, 5, 6, and 8 share 38,027 openings. Job 25 shares 8,309 openings with two other jobs not included in this list.

25 Best-Paying Jobs with a High Percentage of College Graduates Age 55 and Over

Job	Percent Age 55 and Over	Annual Earnings
1. Anesthesiologists	27.2%	$145,600+
2. Chief Executives	31.5%	$145,600+
3. Family and General Practitioners	27.2%	$145,600+
4. Internists, General	27.2%	$145,600+
5. Obstetricians and Gynecologists	27.2%	$145,600+
6. Oral and Maxillofacial Surgeons	27.4%	$145,600+
7. Orthodontists	27.4%	$145,600+
8. Prosthodontists	27.4%	$145,600+
9. Psychiatrists	27.2%	$145,600+
10. Surgeons	27.2%	$145,600+
11. Pediatricians, General	27.2%	$140,690
12. Dentists, General	27.4%	$137,630
13. Engineering Managers	25.5%	$111,020

25 Best-Paying Jobs with a High Percentage of College Graduates Age 55 and Over

Job	Percent Age 55 and Over	Annual Earnings
14. Judges, Magistrate Judges, and Magistrates	27.8%	$107,230
15. Lawyers	27.8%	$106,120
16. Natural Sciences Managers	30.9%	$104,040
17. Physicists	33.3%	$96,850
18. Industrial-Organizational Psychologists	35.0%	$80,820
19. Education Administrators, Elementary and Secondary School	28.7%	$80,580
20. Education Administrators, Postsecondary	28.7%	$75,780
21. Veterinarians	28.4%	$75,230
22. Art Directors	33.9%	$72,320
23. Management Analysts	30.1%	$71,150
24. Administrative Services Managers	27.1%	$70,990
25. Clinical Psychologists	35.0%	$62,210

25 Fastest-Growing Jobs with a High Percentage of College Graduates Age 55 and Over

Job	Percent Age 55 and Over	Percent Growth
1. Veterinarians	28.4%	35.0%
2. Substance Abuse and Behavioral Disorder Counselors	25.3%	34.3%
3. Mental Health Counselors	25.3%	30.0%
4. Marriage and Family Therapists	25.3%	29.8%
5. Multi-Media Artists and Animators	33.9%	25.8%
6. Social and Community Service Managers	25.3%	24.7%
7. Education Administrators, Preschool and Child Care Center/Program	28.7%	23.5%
8. Curators	32.5%	23.3%
9. Rehabilitation Counselors	25.3%	23.0%
10. Instructional Coordinators	30.4%	22.5%
11. Management Analysts	30.1%	21.9%
12. Industrial-Organizational Psychologists	35.0%	21.3%
13. Directors, Religious Activities and Education	27.7%	19.7%
14. Clergy	42.0%	18.9%
15. Cost Estimators	29.9%	18.5%
16. Medical Records and Health Information Technicians	26.1%	17.8%

(continued)

(continued)

25 Fastest-Growing Jobs with a High Percentage of College Graduates Age 55 and Over

Job	Percent Age 55 and Over	Percent Growth
17. Appraisers, Real Estate	28.6%	16.9%
18. Assessors	28.6%	16.9%
19. Clinical Psychologists	35.0%	15.8%
20. Counseling Psychologists	35.0%	15.8%
21. School Psychologists	35.0%	15.8%
22. Property, Real Estate, and Community Association Managers	35.2%	15.1%
23. Anesthesiologists	27.2%	14.2%
24. Education Administrators, Postsecondary	28.7%	14.2%
25. Family and General Practitioners	27.2%	14.2%

25 Jobs with the Most Openings with a High Percentage of College Graduates Age 55 and Over

Job	Percent Age 55 and Over	Annual Openings
1. Management Analysts	30.1%	125,669
2. Insurance Sales Agents	27.1%	64,162
3. Educational, Vocational, and School Counselors	25.3%	54,025
4. Property, Real Estate, and Community Association Managers	35.2%	49,916
5. Lawyers	27.8%	49,445
6. Medical Records and Health Information Technicians	26.1%	39,048
7. Legal Secretaries	25.5%	38,682
8. Cost Estimators	29.9%	38,379
9. Anesthesiologists	27.2%	38,027
10. Family and General Practitioners	27.2%	38,027
11. Internists, General	27.2%	38,027
12. Obstetricians and Gynecologists	27.2%	38,027
13. Pediatricians, General	27.2%	38,027
14. Psychiatrists	27.2%	38,027
15. Surgeons	27.2%	38,027
16. Clergy	42.0%	35,092
17. Rehabilitation Counselors	25.3%	32,081
18. Education Administrators, Elementary and Secondary School	28.7%	27,143
19. Mental Health Counselors	25.3%	24,103

25 Jobs with the Most Openings with a High Percentage of College Graduates Age 55 and Over

Job	Percent Age 55 and Over	Annual Openings
20. Copy Writers	33.3%	24,023
21. Poets, Lyricists and Creative Writers	33.3%	24,023
22. Social and Community Service Managers	25.3%	23,788
23. Instructional Coordinators	30.4%	21,294
24. Chief Executives	31.5%	21,209
25. Substance Abuse and Behavioral Disorder Counselors	25.3%	20,821

Jobs 9, 10, 11, 12, 13, 14, and 15 share 38,027 openings. Jobs 20 and 21 share 24,023 openings.

Best Jobs for College Graduates with a High Percentage of Part-Time Workers

These lists show jobs typically requiring a college degree or more that have a percentage of part-time workers higher than 20 percent. Look over this list and you will find some interesting things. For example, the list is dominated by postsecondary teaching jobs; many college teachers are part-timers, often referred to as adjunct faculty. You'll note that all of these jobs are estimated to have 27.8 percent part-time workers. In reality, there are probably different percentages of part-timers in these professorial jobs, but separate figures are not available. Many of the other jobs on the list involve providing services at times when most other people are not working. Some are in the field of health care.

Some part-time workers may want the freedom of time that this work arrangement can provide, but others may do so because they can't find full-time employment in these areas. These folks may work in other full- or part-time jobs to make ends meet. If you want to work part time now or in the future, these lists will help you identify jobs that are more likely to provide that opportunity. If you want full-time work, the lists may also help you identify jobs that may make such opportunities more difficult to find. In either case, it's good information to know in advance.

Note: The earnings estimates in the following lists are based on a survey of both part-time and full-time workers. On average, part-time workers earn about 40 percent less per hour than full-time workers, but some of this earnings gap can be explained by differences between the two kinds of workers in age, sex, education, experience, and employing industries.

Best Jobs for College Graduates with the Highest Percentage of Part-Time Workers

Job	Percent Part-Time
1. Dental Hygienists	58.7%
2. Adult Literacy, Remedial Education, and GED Teachers and Instructors	41.3%
3. Recreation Workers	38.2%
4. Occupational Therapists	29.8%
5. Agricultural Sciences Teachers, Postsecondary	27.8%
6. Anthropology and Archeology Teachers, Postsecondary	27.8%
7. Architecture Teachers, Postsecondary	27.8%
8. Area, Ethnic, and Cultural Studies Teachers, Postsecondary	27.8%
9. Art, Drama, and Music Teachers, Postsecondary	27.8%
10. Atmospheric, Earth, Marine, and Space Sciences Teachers, Postsecondary	27.8%
11. Biological Science Teachers, Postsecondary	27.8%
12. Business Teachers, Postsecondary	27.8%
13. Chemistry Teachers, Postsecondary	27.8%
14. Communications Teachers, Postsecondary	27.8%
15. Computer Science Teachers, Postsecondary	27.8%
16. Criminal Justice and Law Enforcement Teachers, Postsecondary	27.8%
17. Economics Teachers, Postsecondary	27.8%
18. Education Teachers, Postsecondary	27.8%
19. Engineering Teachers, Postsecondary	27.8%
20. English Language and Literature Teachers, Postsecondary	27.8%
21. Environmental Science Teachers, Postsecondary	27.8%
22. Foreign Language and Literature Teachers, Postsecondary	27.8%
23. Forestry and Conservation Science Teachers, Postsecondary	27.8%
24. Geography Teachers, Postsecondary	27.8%
25. Graduate Teaching Assistants	27.8%
26. Health Specialties Teachers, Postsecondary	27.8%
27. History Teachers, Postsecondary	27.8%
28. Home Economics Teachers, Postsecondary	27.8%
29. Law Teachers, Postsecondary	27.8%
30. Library Science Teachers, Postsecondary	27.8%
31. Mathematical Science Teachers, Postsecondary	27.8%
32. Nursing Instructors and Teachers, Postsecondary	27.8%
33. Philosophy and Religion Teachers, Postsecondary	27.8%
34. Physics Teachers, Postsecondary	27.8%
35. Political Science Teachers, Postsecondary	27.8%
36. Psychology Teachers, Postsecondary	27.8%

Best Jobs for College Graduates with the Highest Percentage of Part-Time Workers

Job	Percent Part-Time
37. Recreation and Fitness Studies Teachers, Postsecondary	27.8%
38. Social Work Teachers, Postsecondary	27.8%
39. Sociology Teachers, Postsecondary	27.8%
40. Physical Therapist Assistants	27.1%
41. Dentists, General	25.9%
42. Oral and Maxillofacial Surgeons	25.9%
43. Orthodontists	25.9%
44. Prosthodontists	25.9%
45. Directors, Religious Activities and Education	25.2%
46. Kindergarten Teachers, Except Special Education	25.1%
47. Speech-Language Pathologists	24.6%
48. Clinical Psychologists	24.0%
49. Counseling Psychologists	24.0%
50. Industrial-Organizational Psychologists	24.0%
51. School Psychologists	24.0%
52. Chiropractors	23.6%
53. Podiatrists	23.6%
54. Physical Therapists	22.7%
55. Art Directors	22.5%
56. Multi-Media Artists and Animators	22.5%
57. Copy Writers	21.8%
58. Poets, Lyricists and Creative Writers	21.8%
59. Registered Nurses	21.8%
60. Optometrists	20.8%
61. Veterinary Technologists and Technicians	20.8%

The jobs in the following four lists are derived from the preceding list of the jobs with the highest percentages of part-time workers.

25 Best Jobs Overall for College Graduates with a High Percentage of Part-Time Workers

Job	Percent Part-Time Workers	Annual Earnings	Percent Growth	Annual Openings
1. Health Specialties Teachers, Postsecondary	27.8%	$80,700	22.9%	19,617
2. Physical Therapists	22.7%	$69,760	27.1%	12,072
3. Business Teachers, Postsecondary	27.8%	$64,900	22.9%	11,643
4. Dental Hygienists	58.7%	$64,740	30.1%	10,433
5. Registered Nurses	21.8%	$60,010	23.5%	233,499
6. Biological Science Teachers, Postsecondary	27.8%	$71,780	22.9%	9,039
7. Engineering Teachers, Postsecondary	27.8%	$79,510	22.9%	5,565
8. Occupational Therapists	29.8%	$63,790	23.1%	8,338
9. Law Teachers, Postsecondary	27.8%	$87,730	22.9%	2,169
10. Economics Teachers, Postsecondary	27.8%	$75,300	22.9%	2,208
11. Multi-Media Artists and Animators	22.5%	$54,550	25.8%	13,182
12. Agricultural Sciences Teachers, Postsecondary	27.8%	$78,460	22.9%	1,840
13. Art, Drama, and Music Teachers, Postsecondary	27.8%	$55,190	22.9%	12,707
14. Chemistry Teachers, Postsecondary	27.8%	$63,870	22.9%	3,405
15. Physics Teachers, Postsecondary	27.8%	$70,090	22.9%	2,155
16. Atmospheric, Earth, Marine, and Space Sciences Teachers, Postsecondary	27.8%	$73,280	22.9%	1,553
17. Computer Science Teachers, Postsecondary	27.8%	$62,020	22.9%	5,820
18. Veterinary Technologists and Technicians	20.8%	$27,970	41.0%	14,674
19. Mathematical Science Teachers, Postsecondary	27.8%	$58,560	22.9%	7,663
20. English Language and Literature Teachers, Postsecondary	27.8%	$54,000	22.9%	10,475
21. Graduate Teaching Assistants	27.8%	$28,060	22.9%	20,601
22. Psychology Teachers, Postsecondary	27.8%	$60,610	22.9%	5,261
23. Education Teachers, Postsecondary	27.8%	$54,220	22.9%	9,359
24. Nursing Instructors and Teachers, Postsecondary	27.8%	$57,500	22.9%	7,337
25. Political Science Teachers, Postsecondary	27.8%	$63,100	22.9%	2,435

25 Best-Paying Jobs for College Graduates with a High Percentage of Part-Time Workers

Job	Percent Part-Time Workers	Annual Earnings
1. Oral and Maxillofacial Surgeons	25.9%	$145,600+
2. Orthodontists	25.9%	$145,600+
3. Prosthodontists	25.9%	$145,600+
4. Dentists, General	25.9%	$137,630
5. Podiatrists	23.6%	$110,510
6. Optometrists	20.8%	$93,800
7. Law Teachers, Postsecondary	27.8%	$87,730
8. Industrial-Organizational Psychologists	24.0%	$80,820
9. Health Specialties Teachers, Postsecondary	27.8%	$80,700
10. Engineering Teachers, Postsecondary	27.8%	$79,510
11. Agricultural Sciences Teachers, Postsecondary	27.8%	$78,460
12. Economics Teachers, Postsecondary	27.8%	$75,300
13. Atmospheric, Earth, Marine, and Space Sciences Teachers, Postsecondary	27.8%	$73,280
14. Art Directors	22.5%	$72,320
15. Biological Science Teachers, Postsecondary	27.8%	$71,780
16. Physics Teachers, Postsecondary	27.8%	$70,090
17. Physical Therapists	22.7%	$69,760
18. Architecture Teachers, Postsecondary	27.8%	$68,540
19. Chiropractors	23.6%	$65,890
20. Business Teachers, Postsecondary	27.8%	$64,900
21. Environmental Science Teachers, Postsecondary	27.8%	$64,850
22. Dental Hygienists	58.7%	$64,740
23. Anthropology and Archeology Teachers, Postsecondary	27.8%	$64,530
24. Chemistry Teachers, Postsecondary	27.8%	$63,870
25. Forestry and Conservation Science Teachers, Postsecondary	27.8%	$63,790

25 Fastest-Growing Jobs for College Graduates with a High Percentage of Part-Time Workers

Job	Percent Part-Time Workers	Percent Growth
1. Veterinary Technologists and Technicians	20.8%	41.0%
2. Physical Therapist Assistants	27.1%	32.4%

(continued)

(continued)

25 Fastest-Growing Jobs for College Graduates with a High Percentage of Part-Time Workers

Job	Percent Part-Time Workers	Percent Growth
3. Dental Hygienists	58.7%	30.1%
4. Physical Therapists	22.7%	27.1%
5. Multi-Media Artists and Animators	22.5%	25.8%
6. Registered Nurses	21.8%	23.5%
7. Occupational Therapists	29.8%	23.1%
8. Agricultural Sciences Teachers, Postsecondary	27.8%	22.9%
9. Anthropology and Archeology Teachers, Postsecondary	27.8%	22.9%
10. Architecture Teachers, Postsecondary	27.8%	22.9%
11. Area, Ethnic, and Cultural Studies Teachers, Postsecondary	27.8%	22.9%
12. Art, Drama, and Music Teachers, Postsecondary	27.8%	22.9%
13. Atmospheric, Earth, Marine, and Space Sciences Teachers, Postsecondary	27.8%	22.9%
14. Biological Science Teachers, Postsecondary	27.8%	22.9%
15. Business Teachers, Postsecondary	27.8%	22.9%
16. Chemistry Teachers, Postsecondary	27.8%	22.9%
17. Communications Teachers, Postsecondary	27.8%	22.9%
18. Computer Science Teachers, Postsecondary	27.8%	22.9%
19. Criminal Justice and Law Enforcement Teachers, Postsecondary	27.8%	22.9%
20. Economics Teachers, Postsecondary	27.8%	22.9%
21. Education Teachers, Postsecondary	27.8%	22.9%
22. Engineering Teachers, Postsecondary	27.8%	22.9%
23. English Language and Literature Teachers, Postsecondary	27.8%	22.9%
24. Environmental Science Teachers, Postsecondary	27.8%	22.9%
25. Foreign Language and Literature Teachers, Postsecondary	27.8%	22.9%

25 Jobs with the Most Openings for College Graduates with a High Percentage of Part-Time Workers

Job	Percent Part-Time Workers	Annual Openings
1. Registered Nurses	21.8%	233,499
2. Recreation Workers	38.2%	61,454
3. Kindergarten Teachers, Except Special Education	25.1%	27,603
4. Copy Writers	21.8%	24,023

25 Jobs with the Most Openings for College Graduates with a High Percentage of Part-Time Workers

Job	Percent Part-Time Workers	Annual Openings
5. Poets, Lyricists and Creative Writers	21.8%	24,023
6. Graduate Teaching Assistants	27.8%	20,601
7. Health Specialties Teachers, Postsecondary	27.8%	19,617
8. Adult Literacy, Remedial Education, and GED Teachers and Instructors	41.3%	17,340
9. Veterinary Technologists and Technicians	20.8%	14,674
10. Multi-Media Artists and Animators	22.5%	13,182
11. Art, Drama, and Music Teachers, Postsecondary	27.8%	12,707
12. Physical Therapists	22.7%	12,072
13. Business Teachers, Postsecondary	27.8%	11,643
14. Directors, Religious Activities and Education	25.2%	11,463
15. Speech-Language Pathologists	24.6%	11,160
16. English Language and Literature Teachers, Postsecondary	27.8%	10,475
17. Dental Hygienists	58.7%	10,433
18. Art Directors	22.5%	9,719
19. Education Teachers, Postsecondary	27.8%	9,359
20. Biological Science Teachers, Postsecondary	27.8%	9,039
21. Occupational Therapists	29.8%	8,338
22. Clinical Psychologists	24.0%	8,309
23. Counseling Psychologists	24.0%	8,309
24. School Psychologists	24.0%	8,309
25. Mathematical Science Teachers, Postsecondary	27.8%	7,663

Jobs 4 and 5 share 24,023 openings. Jobs 22, 23, and 24 share 8,309 openings.

Best Jobs for College Graduates with a High Percentage of Self-Employed Workers

About 8 percent of all working people are self-employed. Although you may think of the self-employed as having similar jobs, they actually work in an enormous range of situations, fields, and work environments that you may not have considered.

Among the self-employed are people who own small or large businesses, as many real estate brokers and funeral directors do; professionals who own their own practices, as many lawyers, psychologists, and medical doctors do; people working on a contract basis for one or more employers, as many editors do; people running home consulting or other businesses; and people in many other situations. They may go to the same worksite every day, as most attorneys do; visit multiple employers during the course of a week, as many models do; or do most of their work from home, as many craft artists do. Some work part time, others full time, some as a way to have fun, some so they can spend time with their kids or go to school.

The point is that there is an enormous range of situations, and one of them could make sense for you now or in the future.

The following list contains jobs in which more than 20 percent of the workers are self-employed.

Best Jobs with the Highest Percentage of Self-Employed College Graduates

Job	Percent Self-Employed Workers
1. Multi-Media Artists and Animators	69.7%
2. Copy Writers	65.9%
3. Poets, Lyricists and Creative Writers	65.9%
4. Art Directors	59.0%
5. Construction Managers	56.3%
6. Agents and Business Managers of Artists, Performers, and Athletes	55.8%
7. Chiropractors	51.7%
8. Prosthodontists	51.3%
9. Property, Real Estate, and Community Association Managers	50.9%
10. Orthodontists	43.3%
11. Industrial-Organizational Psychologists	39.3%
12. Dentists, General	36.6%
13. Clinical Psychologists	34.2%
14. Counseling Psychologists	34.2%
15. School Psychologists	34.2%
16. Appraisers, Real Estate	32.7%
17. Assessors	32.7%
18. Personal Financial Advisors	30.9%
19. Oral and Maxillofacial Surgeons	30.6%
20. Directors—Stage, Motion Pictures, Television, and Radio	29.5%
21. Producers	29.5%
22. Program Directors	29.5%
23. Management Analysts	27.0%
24. Lawyers	26.7%
25. Interior Designers	26.3%
26. Insurance Sales Agents	25.5%
27. Optometrists	25.5%
28. Graphic Designers	25.3%

Best Jobs with the Highest Percentage of Self-Employed College Graduates

Job	Percent Self-Employed Workers
29. Podiatrists	23.9%
30. Chief Executives	22.0%
31. Architects, Except Landscape and Naval	20.3%

The jobs in the following four lists are derived from the preceding list of college-level jobs with the highest percentages of self-employed workers. Where the following lists give earnings estimates, keep in mind that these figures are based on a survey that *doesn't include self-employed workers*. The median earnings for self-employed workers in these occupations may be significantly higher or lower.

25 Best Jobs Overall with a High Percentage of Self-Employed College Graduates

Job	Percent Self-Employed Workers	Annual Earnings	Percent Growth	Annual Openings
1. Management Analysts	27.0%	$71,150	21.9%	125,669
2. Personal Financial Advisors	30.9%	$67,660	41.0%	17,114
3. Construction Managers	56.3%	$76,230	15.7%	44,158
4. Architects, Except Landscape and Naval	20.3%	$67,620	17.7%	11,324
5. Lawyers	26.7%	$106,120	11.0%	49,445
6. Multi-Media Artists and Animators	69.7%	$54,550	25.8%	13,182
7. Chief Executives	22.0%	$145,600+	2.0%	21,209
8. Industrial-Organizational Psychologists	39.3%	$80,820	21.3%	118
9. Clinical Psychologists	34.2%	$62,210	15.8%	8,309
10. Counseling Psychologists	34.2%	$62,210	15.8%	8,309
11. School Psychologists	34.2%	$62,210	15.8%	8,309
12. Insurance Sales Agents	25.5%	$44,110	12.9%	64,162
13. Property, Real Estate, and Community Association Managers	50.9%	$43,670	15.1%	49,916
14. Copy Writers	65.9%	$50,660	12.8%	24,023
15. Poets, Lyricists and Creative Writers	65.9%	$50,660	12.8%	24,023
16. Interior Designers	26.3%	$43,970	19.5%	8,434
17. Optometrists	25.5%	$93,800	11.3%	1,789
18. Dentists, General	36.6%	$137,630	9.2%	7,106

(continued)

(continued)

25 Best Jobs Overall with a High Percentage of Self-Employed College Graduates

Job	Percent Self-Employed Workers	Annual Earnings	Percent Growth	Annual Openings
19. Directors—Stage, Motion Pictures, Television, and Radio	29.5%	$61,090	11.1%	8,992
20. Producers	29.5%	$61,090	11.1%	8,992
21. Program Directors	29.5%	$61,090	11.1%	8,992
22. Art Directors	59.0%	$72,320	9.0%	9,719
23. Appraisers, Real Estate	32.7%	$46,130	16.9%	6,493
24. Assessors	32.7%	$46,130	16.9%	6,493
25. Chiropractors	51.7%	$65,890	14.4%	3,179

Jobs 9, 10, and 11 share 8,309 openings. Jobs 14 and 15 share 24,023 openings. Jobs 19, 20, and 21 share 8,992 openings with each other and with two other jobs not included in this list. Jobs 23 and 24 share 6,493 openings.

25 Best-Paying Jobs with a High Percentage of Self-Employed College Graduates

Job	Percent Self-Employed Workers	Annual Earnings
1. Chief Executives	22.0%	$145,600+
2. Oral and Maxillofacial Surgeons	30.6%	$145,600+
3. Orthodontists	43.3%	$145,600+
4. Prosthodontists	51.3%	$145,600+
5. Dentists, General	36.6%	$137,630
6. Podiatrists	23.9%	$110,510
7. Lawyers	26.7%	$106,120
8. Optometrists	25.5%	$93,800
9. Industrial-Organizational Psychologists	39.3%	$80,820
10. Construction Managers	56.3%	$76,230
11. Art Directors	59.0%	$72,320
12. Management Analysts	27.0%	$71,150
13. Personal Financial Advisors	30.9%	$67,660
14. Architects, Except Landscape and Naval	20.3%	$67,620
15. Agents and Business Managers of Artists, Performers, and Athletes	55.8%	$66,440
16. Chiropractors	51.7%	$65,890
17. Clinical Psychologists	34.2%	$62,210

25 Best-Paying Jobs with a High Percentage of Self-Employed College Graduates

Job	Percent Self-Employed Workers	Annual Earnings
18. Counseling Psychologists	34.2%	$62,210
19. School Psychologists	34.2%	$62,210
20. Directors—Stage, Motion Pictures, Television, and Radio	29.5%	$61,090
21. Producers	29.5%	$61,090
22. Program Directors	29.5%	$61,090
23. Multi-Media Artists and Animators	69.7%	$54,550
24. Copy Writers	65.9%	$50,660
25. Poets, Lyricists and Creative Writers	65.9%	$50,660

25 Fastest-Growing Jobs with a High Percentage of Self-Employed College Graduates

Job	Percent Self-Employed Workers	Percent Growth
1. Personal Financial Advisors	30.9%	41.0%
2. Multi-Media Artists and Animators	69.7%	25.8%
3. Management Analysts	27.0%	21.9%
4. Industrial-Organizational Psychologists	39.3%	21.3%
5. Interior Designers	26.3%	19.5%
6. Architects, Except Landscape and Naval	20.3%	17.7%
7. Appraisers, Real Estate	32.7%	16.9%
8. Assessors	32.7%	16.9%
9. Clinical Psychologists	34.2%	15.8%
10. Counseling Psychologists	34.2%	15.8%
11. School Psychologists	34.2%	15.8%
12. Construction Managers	56.3%	15.7%
13. Property, Real Estate, and Community Association Managers	50.9%	15.1%
14. Chiropractors	51.7%	14.4%
15. Insurance Sales Agents	25.5%	12.9%
16. Copy Writers	65.9%	12.8%
17. Poets, Lyricists and Creative Writers	65.9%	12.8%
18. Optometrists	25.5%	11.3%
19. Directors—Stage, Motion Pictures, Television, and Radio	29.5%	11.1%

(continued)

(continued)

25 Fastest-Growing Jobs with a High Percentage of Self-Employed College Graduates

Job	Percent Self-Employed Workers	Percent Growth
20. Producers	29.5%	11.1%
21. Program Directors	29.5%	11.1%
22. Lawyers	26.7%	11.0%
23. Prosthodontists	51.3%	10.7%
24. Graphic Designers	25.3%	9.8%
25. Agents and Business Managers of Artists, Performers, and Athletes	55.8%	9.6%

25 Jobs with the Most Openings with a High Percentage of Self-Employed College Graduates

Job	Percent Self-Employed Workers	Annual Openings
1. Management Analysts	27.0%	125,669
2. Insurance Sales Agents	25.5%	64,162
3. Property, Real Estate, and Community Association Managers	50.9%	49,916
4. Lawyers	26.7%	49,445
5. Construction Managers	56.3%	44,158
6. Graphic Designers	25.3%	26,968
7. Copy Writers	65.9%	24,023
8. Poets, Lyricists and Creative Writers	65.9%	24,023
9. Chief Executives	22.0%	21,209
10. Personal Financial Advisors	30.9%	17,114
11. Multi-Media Artists and Animators	69.7%	13,182
12. Architects, Except Landscape and Naval	20.3%	11,324
13. Art Directors	59.0%	9,719
14. Directors—Stage, Motion Pictures, Television, and Radio	29.5%	8,992
15. Producers	29.5%	8,992
16. Program Directors	29.5%	8,992
17. Interior Designers	26.3%	8,434
18. Clinical Psychologists	34.2%	8,309
19. Counseling Psychologists	34.2%	8,309
20. School Psychologists	34.2%	8,309
21. Dentists, General	36.6%	7,106

25 Jobs with the Most Openings with a High Percentage of Self-Employed College Graduates

Job	Percent Self-Employed Workers	Annual Openings
22. Appraisers, Real Estate	32.7%	6,493
23. Assessors	32.7%	6,493
24. Agents and Business Managers of Artists, Performers, and Athletes	55.8%	3,940
25. Chiropractors	51.7%	3,179

Jobs 7 and 8 share 24,023 openings. Jobs 14, 15, and 16 share 8,992 openings with each other and with two other jobs that do not appear on this list. Jobs 18, 19, and 20 share 8,309 openings. Jobs 22 and 23 share 6,493 openings.

Best Jobs for College Graduates Employing a High Percentage of Women

To create the four lists that follow, we sorted the 200 best jobs requiring a two- or four-year college degree or more according to the percentages of women and men in the workforce. We knew we would create some controversy when we first included the best jobs lists with high percentages (more than 70 percent) of men and women in earlier editions. But these lists aren't meant to restrict women or men from considering job options; our reason for including these lists is exactly the opposite. We hope the lists help people see possibilities that they might not otherwise have considered.

The fact is that jobs with high percentages of women or high percentages of men offer good opportunities for both men and women if they want to do one of these jobs. So we suggest that women browse the lists of jobs that employ high percentages of men and that men browse the lists of jobs with high percentages of women. There are jobs among both lists that pay well, and women or men who are interested in them and who have or can obtain the necessary education and training should consider them. Some employers are seeking female recruits to correct a traditional male imbalance.

An interesting and unfortunate tidbit to bring up at your next party is that the average earnings for the 34 college-level jobs with the highest percentages of women is $50,750, compared to average earnings of $78,451 for the 46 college-level jobs with the highest percentages of men. (The calculations assumed that the five male-dominated jobs paying "$145,600+" had earnings of exactly $145,600, which means that the actual average is probably higher than $78,451.) But earnings don't tell the whole story. We computed the average growth and job openings of the female-dominated jobs and found statistics of 18.9% growth and 29,123 openings, compared to 15.2% growth and 20,422 openings for the male-dominated jobs. This discrepancy reinforces the idea that men have had more problems than women in adapting to an economy dominated by service and information-based jobs. Many women may simply be better prepared for these jobs, possessing more appropriate skills for the jobs that are now growing rapidly and have more job openings.

Best Jobs for College Graduates Employing the Highest Percentage of Women

Job	Percent Women
1. Dental Hygienists	98.6%
2. Kindergarten Teachers, Except Special Education	97.7%
3. Legal Secretaries	96.9%
4. Speech-Language Pathologists	95.3%
5. Medical Records and Health Information Technicians	92.0%
6. Registered Nurses	91.3%
7. Occupational Therapists	90.3%
8. Occupational Therapist Assistants	89.4%
9. Paralegals and Legal Assistants	89.1%
10. Special Education Teachers, Middle School	83.5%
11. Special Education Teachers, Preschool, Kindergarten, and Elementary School	83.5%
12. Child, Family, and School Social Workers	82.6%
13. Medical and Public Health Social Workers	82.6%
14. Mental Health and Substance Abuse Social Workers	82.6%
15. Elementary School Teachers, Except Special Education	82.2%
16. Middle School Teachers, Except Special and Vocational Education	82.2%
17. Veterinary Technologists and Technicians	80.1%
18. Physical Therapist Assistants	78.4%
19. Medical and Clinical Laboratory Technologists	78.1%
20. Radiation Therapists	74.1%
21. Cardiovascular Technologists and Technicians	72.9%
22. Diagnostic Medical Sonographers	72.9%
23. Nuclear Medicine Technologists	72.9%
24. Radiologic Technicians	72.9%
25. Radiologic Technologists	72.9%
26. Curators	72.4%
27. Physician Assistants	71.7%
28. Compensation, Benefits, and Job Analysis Specialists	71.5%
29. Employment Interviewers	71.5%
30. Personnel Recruiters	71.5%
31. Training and Development Specialists	71.5%
32. Directors, Religious Activities and Education	70.5%
33. Health Educators	70.5%
34. Probation Officers and Correctional Treatment Specialists	70.5%

The jobs in the following four lists are derived from the preceding list of the college-level jobs employing the highest percentages of women. Keep in mind that the earnings estimates in the following lists are based on a survey of *all* workers, not just women. On average, women earn about 75 percent of the earnings of men in the same occupation. The earnings differences for the occupations in the following lists may be significantly higher or lower.

25 Best Jobs Overall for College Graduates Employing a High Percentage of Women

Job	Percent Women	Annual Earnings	Percent Growth	Annual Openings
1. Registered Nurses	91.3%	$60,010	23.5%	233,499
2. Dental Hygienists	98.6%	$64,740	30.1%	10,433
3. Physician Assistants	71.7%	$78,450	27.0%	7,147
4. Compensation, Benefits, and Job Analysis Specialists	71.5%	$52,180	18.4%	18,761
5. Training and Development Specialists	71.5%	$49,630	18.3%	35,862
6. Radiation Therapists	74.1%	$70,010	24.8%	1,461
7. Special Education Teachers, Preschool, Kindergarten, and Elementary School	83.5%	$48,350	19.6%	20,049
8. Occupational Therapists	90.3%	$63,790	23.1%	8,338
9. Paralegals and Legal Assistants	89.1%	$44,990	22.2%	22,756
10. Elementary School Teachers, Except Special Education	82.2%	$47,330	13.6%	181,612
11. Medical and Public Health Social Workers	82.6%	$44,670	24.2%	16,429
12. Mental Health and Substance Abuse Social Workers	82.6%	$36,640	29.9%	17,289
13. Middle School Teachers, Except Special and Vocational Education	82.2%	$47,900	11.2%	75,270
14. Employment Interviewers	71.5%	$44,380	18.4%	33,588
15. Health Educators	70.5%	$42,920	26.2%	13,707
16. Personnel Recruiters	71.5%	$44,380	18.4%	33,588
17. Veterinary Technologists and Technicians	80.1%	$27,970	41.0%	14,674
18. Kindergarten Teachers, Except Special Education	97.7%	$45,120	16.3%	27,603
19. Child, Family, and School Social Workers	82.6%	$38,620	19.1%	35,402
20. Diagnostic Medical Sonographers	72.9%	$59,860	19.1%	3,211
21. Radiologic Technicians	72.9%	$50,260	15.1%	12,836
22. Radiologic Technologists	72.9%	$50,260	15.1%	12,836
23. Physical Therapist Assistants	78.4%	$44,130	32.4%	5,957
24. Cardiovascular Technologists and Technicians	72.9%	$44,940	25.5%	3,550
25. Occupational Therapist Assistants	89.4%	$45,050	25.4%	2,634

Jobs 14 and 16 share 33,588 openings. Jobs 21 and 22 share 12,836 openings.

25 Best-Paying Jobs for College Graduates Employing a High Percentage of Women

Job	Percent Women	Annual Earnings
1. Physician Assistants	71.7%	$78,450
2. Radiation Therapists	74.1%	$70,010
3. Dental Hygienists	98.6%	$64,740
4. Nuclear Medicine Technologists	72.9%	$64,670
5. Occupational Therapists	90.3%	$63,790
6. Speech-Language Pathologists	95.3%	$60,690
7. Registered Nurses	91.3%	$60,010
8. Diagnostic Medical Sonographers	72.9%	$59,860
9. Compensation, Benefits, and Job Analysis Specialists	71.5%	$52,180
10. Medical and Clinical Laboratory Technologists	78.1%	$51,720
11. Radiologic Technicians	72.9%	$50,260
12. Radiologic Technologists	72.9%	$50,260
13. Training and Development Specialists	71.5%	$49,630
14. Special Education Teachers, Middle School	83.5%	$48,940
15. Special Education Teachers, Preschool, Kindergarten, and Elementary School	83.5%	$48,350
16. Middle School Teachers, Except Special and Vocational Education	82.2%	$47,900
17. Elementary School Teachers, Except Special Education	82.2%	$47,330
18. Curators	72.4%	$46,000
19. Kindergarten Teachers, Except Special Education	97.7%	$45,120
20. Occupational Therapist Assistants	89.4%	$45,050
21. Paralegals and Legal Assistants	89.1%	$44,990
22. Cardiovascular Technologists and Technicians	72.9%	$44,940
23. Medical and Public Health Social Workers	82.6%	$44,670
24. Probation Officers and Correctional Treatment Specialists	70.5%	$44,510
25. Employment Interviewers	71.5%	$44,380

25 Fastest-Growing Jobs for College Graduates Employing a High Percentage of Women

Job	Percent Women	Percent Growth
1. Veterinary Technologists and Technicians	80.1%	41.0%
2. Physical Therapist Assistants	78.4%	32.4%
3. Dental Hygienists	98.6%	30.1%

25 Fastest-Growing Jobs for College Graduates Employing a High Percentage of Women

Job	Percent Women	Percent Growth
4. Mental Health and Substance Abuse Social Workers	82.6%	29.9%
5. Physician Assistants	71.7%	27.0%
6. Health Educators	70.5%	26.2%
7. Cardiovascular Technologists and Technicians	72.9%	25.5%
8. Occupational Therapist Assistants	89.4%	25.4%
9. Radiation Therapists	74.1%	24.8%
10. Medical and Public Health Social Workers	82.6%	24.2%
11. Registered Nurses	91.3%	23.5%
12. Curators	72.4%	23.3%
13. Occupational Therapists	90.3%	23.1%
14. Paralegals and Legal Assistants	89.1%	22.2%
15. Directors, Religious Activities and Education	70.5%	19.7%
16. Special Education Teachers, Preschool, Kindergarten, and Elementary School	83.5%	19.6%
17. Child, Family, and School Social Workers	82.6%	19.1%
18. Diagnostic Medical Sonographers	72.9%	19.1%
19. Compensation, Benefits, and Job Analysis Specialists	71.5%	18.4%
20. Employment Interviewers	71.5%	18.4%
21. Personnel Recruiters	71.5%	18.4%
22. Training and Development Specialists	71.5%	18.3%
23. Medical Records and Health Information Technicians	92.0%	17.8%
24. Kindergarten Teachers, Except Special Education	97.7%	16.3%
25. Special Education Teachers, Middle School	83.5%	15.8%

25 Jobs with the Most Openings for College Graduates Employing a High Percentage of Women

Job	Percent Women	Annual Openings
1. Registered Nurses	91.3%	233,499
2. Elementary School Teachers, Except Special Education	82.2%	181,612
3. Middle School Teachers, Except Special and Vocational Education	82.2%	75,270
4. Medical Records and Health Information Technicians	92.0%	39,048
5. Legal Secretaries	96.9%	38,682
6. Training and Development Specialists	71.5%	35,862

(continued)

(continued)

25 Jobs with the Most Openings for College Graduates Employing a High Percentage of Women		
Job	Percent Women	Annual Openings
7. Child, Family, and School Social Workers	82.6%	35,402
8. Employment Interviewers	71.5%	33,588
9. Personnel Recruiters	71.5%	33,588
10. Kindergarten Teachers, Except Special Education	97.7%	27,603
11. Paralegals and Legal Assistants	89.1%	22,756
12. Special Education Teachers, Preschool, Kindergarten, and Elementary School	83.5%	20,049
13. Compensation, Benefits, and Job Analysis Specialists	71.5%	18,761
14. Probation Officers and Correctional Treatment Specialists	70.5%	18,335
15. Mental Health and Substance Abuse Social Workers	82.6%	17,289
16. Medical and Public Health Social Workers	82.6%	16,429
17. Veterinary Technologists and Technicians	80.1%	14,674
18. Health Educators	70.5%	13,707
19. Radiologic Technicians	72.9%	12,836
20. Radiologic Technologists	72.9%	12,836
21. Directors, Religious Activities and Education	70.5%	11,463
22. Medical and Clinical Laboratory Technologists	78.1%	11,457
23. Speech-Language Pathologists	95.3%	11,160
24. Dental Hygienists	98.6%	10,433
25. Special Education Teachers, Middle School	83.5%	8,846

Jobs 8 and 9 share 33,588 openings. Jobs 19 and 20 share 12,836 openings.

Best Jobs for College Graduates Employing a High Percentage of Men

If you have not already read the intro to the previous group of lists, jobs with high percentages of women college graduates, consider doing so. Much of the content there applies to these lists as well.

We did not include these groups of lists with the assumption that men college grads should consider jobs with high percentages of men college grads or that women should consider jobs with high percentages of women. Instead, these lists are here because we think they are interesting and perhaps helpful in considering nontraditional career options. For example, some men college graduates would do very well in and enjoy some of the jobs with high percentages of women college graduates but may not have considered them seriously. In a similar way, some women college graduates would very much enjoy and do well in some jobs that have traditionally been held by high percentages of men college graduates. We hope that these lists help you consider options that you simply did not seriously consider because of gender stereotypes.

Best Jobs for College Graduates Employing the Highest Percentage of Men

Job	Percent Men
1. Mechanical Engineers	94.2%
2. Engineering Managers	92.7%
3. Electrical Engineers	92.3%
4. Electronics Engineers, Except Computer	92.3%
5. Construction Managers	92.2%
6. Cartographers and Photogrammetrists	90.1%
7. Environmental Engineering Technicians	90.1%
8. Surveyors	90.1%
9. Civil Engineers	88.1%
10. Cost Estimators	87.3%
11. Clergy	87.2%
12. Aerospace Engineers	86.9%
13. Biomedical Engineers	85.5%
14. Environmental Engineers	85.5%
15. Computer Hardware Engineers	83.8%
16. Computer Software Engineers, Applications	83.8%
17. Computer Software Engineers, Systems Software	83.8%
18. Computer Security Specialists	83.4%
19. Network and Computer Systems Administrators	83.4%
20. Network Designers	83.4%
21. Web Administrators	83.4%
22. Chemical Engineers	82.9%
23. Computer Systems Engineers/Architects	78.2%
24. Airline Pilots, Copilots, and Flight Engineers	78.0%
25. Environmental Scientists and Specialists, Including Health	78.0%
26. Architects, Except Landscape and Naval	77.8%
27. Landscape Architects	77.8%
28. Dentists, General	77.4%
29. Industrial Engineers	77.4%
30. Oral and Maxillofacial Surgeons	77.4%

(continued)

(continued)

Best Jobs for College Graduates Employing the Highest Percentage of Men

Job	Percent Men
31. Orthodontists	77.4%
32. Prosthodontists	77.4%
33. Chiropractors	76.9%
34. Chief Executives	76.6%
35. Administrative Services Managers	75.6%
36. Computer Programmers	74.7%
37. Network Systems and Data Communications Analysts	74.5%
38. Software Quality Assurance Engineers and Testers	73.3%
39. Statisticians	73.3%
40. Web Developers	73.3%
41. Computer and Information Systems Managers	72.8%
42. Sales Engineers	72.8%
43. Computer Support Specialists	71.1%
44. General and Operations Managers	70.9%
45. Sales Agents, Financial Services	70.7%
46. Sales Agents, Securities and Commodities	70.7%

The jobs in the following four lists are derived from the preceding list of the jobs employing the highest percentages of men. Keep in mind that the earnings estimates in the following lists are based on a survey of *all* workers, not just men. On average, men earn about 133 percent of the earnings of women in the same occupation. The earnings differences for the occupations in the following lists may be significantly higher or lower.

25 Best Jobs Overall for College Graduates Employing a High Percentage of Men

Job	Percent Men	Annual Earnings	Percent Growth	Annual Openings
1. Computer Software Engineers, Applications	83.8%	$83,130	44.6%	58,690
2. Computer Software Engineers, Systems Software	83.8%	$89,070	28.2%	33,139
3. Computer and Information Systems Managers	72.8%	$108,070	16.4%	30,887
4. Sales Agents, Financial Services	70.7%	$68,430	24.8%	47,750
5. Sales Agents, Securities and Commodities	70.7%	$68,430	24.8%	47,750
6. Construction Managers	92.2%	$76,230	15.7%	44,158

25 Best Jobs Overall for College Graduates Employing a High Percentage of Men

Job	Percent Men	Annual Earnings	Percent Growth	Annual Openings
7. Network Systems and Data Communications Analysts	74.5%	$68,220	53.4%	35,086
8. Computer Security Specialists	83.4%	$64,690	27.0%	37,010
9. Network and Computer Systems Administrators	83.4%	$64,690	27.0%	37,010
10. Civil Engineers	88.1%	$71,710	18.0%	15,979
11. General and Operations Managers	70.9%	$88,700	1.5%	112,072
12. Chief Executives	76.6%	$145,600+	2.0%	21,209
13. Environmental Engineers	85.5%	$72,350	25.4%	5,003
14. Computer Systems Engineers/Architects	78.2%	$71,510	15.1%	14,374
15. Network Designers	83.4%	$71,510	15.1%	14,374
16. Software Quality Assurance Engineers and Testers	73.3%	$71,510	15.1%	14,374
17. Web Administrators	83.4%	$71,510	15.1%	14,374
18. Web Developers	73.3%	$71,510	15.1%	14,374
19. Airline Pilots, Copilots, and Flight Engineers	78.0%	$145,600+	12.9%	4,073
20. Cost Estimators	87.3%	$54,920	18.5%	38,379
21. Industrial Engineers	77.4%	$71,430	20.3%	11,272
22. Dentists, General	77.4%	$137,630	9.2%	7,106
23. Clergy	87.2%	$40,460	18.9%	35,092
24. Engineering Managers	92.7%	$111,020	7.3%	7,404
25. Aerospace Engineers	86.9%	$90,930	10.2%	6,498

Jobs 4 and 5 share 47,750 openings. Jobs 8 and 9 share 37,010 openings. Jobs 14, 15, 16, 17, and 18 share 14,374 openings.

25 Best-Paying Jobs for College Graduates Employing a High Percentage of Men

Job	Percent Men	Annual Earnings
1. Airline Pilots, Copilots, and Flight Engineers	78.0%	$145,600+
2. Chief Executives	76.6%	$145,600+
3. Oral and Maxillofacial Surgeons	77.4%	$145,600+
4. Orthodontists	77.4%	$145,600+
5. Prosthodontists	77.4%	$145,600+
6. Dentists, General	77.4%	$137,630

(continued)

(continued)

25 Best-Paying Jobs for College Graduates Employing a High Percentage of Men

Job	Percent Men	Annual Earnings
7. Engineering Managers	92.7%	$111,020
8. Computer and Information Systems Managers	72.8%	$108,070
9. Computer Hardware Engineers	83.8%	$91,860
10. Aerospace Engineers	86.9%	$90,930
11. Computer Software Engineers, Systems Software	83.8%	$89,070
12. General and Operations Managers	70.9%	$88,700
13. Electronics Engineers, Except Computer	92.3%	$83,340
14. Computer Software Engineers, Applications	83.8%	$83,130
15. Chemical Engineers	82.9%	$81,500
16. Sales Engineers	72.8%	$80,270
17. Electrical Engineers	92.3%	$79,240
18. Construction Managers	92.2%	$76,230
19. Biomedical Engineers	85.5%	$75,440
20. Environmental Engineers	85.5%	$72,350
21. Mechanical Engineers	94.2%	$72,300
22. Civil Engineers	88.1%	$71,710
23. Computer Systems Engineers/Architects	78.2%	$71,510
24. Network Designers	83.4%	$71,510
25. Software Quality Assurance Engineers and Testers	73.3%	$71,510

25 Fastest-Growing Jobs for College Graduates Employing a High Percentage of Men

Job	Percent Men	Percent Growth
1. Network Systems and Data Communications Analysts	74.5%	53.4%
2. Computer Software Engineers, Applications	83.8%	44.6%
3. Computer Software Engineers, Systems Software	83.8%	28.2%
4. Computer Security Specialists	83.4%	27.0%
5. Network and Computer Systems Administrators	83.4%	27.0%
6. Environmental Engineers	85.5%	25.4%
7. Environmental Scientists and Specialists, Including Health	78.0%	25.1%
8. Environmental Engineering Technicians	90.1%	24.8%
9. Sales Agents, Financial Services	70.7%	24.8%

25 Fastest-Growing Jobs for College Graduates Employing a High Percentage of Men

Job	Percent Men	Percent Growth
10. Sales Agents, Securities and Commodities	70.7%	24.8%
11. Surveyors	90.1%	23.7%
12. Biomedical Engineers	85.5%	21.1%
13. Cartographers and Photogrammetrists	90.1%	20.3%
14. Industrial Engineers	77.4%	20.3%
15. Clergy	87.2%	18.9%
16. Cost Estimators	87.3%	18.5%
17. Civil Engineers	88.1%	18.0%
18. Architects, Except Landscape and Naval	77.8%	17.7%
19. Computer and Information Systems Managers	72.8%	16.4%
20. Landscape Architects	77.8%	16.4%
21. Construction Managers	92.2%	15.7%
22. Computer Systems Engineers/Architects	78.2%	15.1%
23. Network Designers	83.4%	15.1%
24. Software Quality Assurance Engineers and Testers	73.3%	15.1%
25. Web Administrators	83.4%	15.1%

25 Jobs with the Most Openings for College Graduates Employing a High Percentage of Men

Job	Percent Men	Annual Openings
1. General and Operations Managers	70.9%	112,072
2. Computer Support Specialists	71.1%	97,334
3. Computer Software Engineers, Applications	83.8%	58,690
4. Sales Agents, Financial Services	70.7%	47,750
5. Sales Agents, Securities and Commodities	70.7%	47,750
6. Construction Managers	92.2%	44,158
7. Cost Estimators	87.3%	38,379
8. Computer Security Specialists	83.4%	37,010
9. Network and Computer Systems Administrators	83.4%	37,010
10. Clergy	87.2%	35,092
11. Network Systems and Data Communications Analysts	74.5%	35,086
12. Computer Software Engineers, Systems Software	83.8%	33,139

(continued)

(continued)

25 Jobs with the Most Openings for College Graduates Employing a High Percentage of Men

Job	Percent Men	Annual Openings
13. Computer and Information Systems Managers	72.8%	30,887
14. Computer Programmers	74.7%	27,937
15. Chief Executives	76.6%	21,209
16. Administrative Services Managers	75.6%	19,513
17. Civil Engineers	88.1%	15,979
18. Computer Systems Engineers/Architects	78.2%	14,374
19. Network Designers	83.4%	14,374
20. Software Quality Assurance Engineers and Testers	73.3%	14,374
21. Web Administrators	83.4%	14,374
22. Web Developers	73.3%	14,374
23. Surveyors	90.1%	14,305
24. Mechanical Engineers	94.2%	12,394
25. Architects, Except Landscape and Naval	77.8%	11,324

Jobs 4 and 5 share 47,750 openings. Jobs 8 and 9 share 37,010 openings. Jobs 18, 19, 20, 21, and 22 share 14,374 openings.

Best Jobs Lists Based on Levels of Education and Experience

The lists in this section organize the 200 best jobs requiring a two- or four-year college degree or more into groups based on the education or training typically required for entry. Unlike in the previous section, here we do not include separate lists for highest pay, growth, or number of openings. Instead, for each of the education levels we provide one list for the occupations at that level, ranking them by their individual combined score for earnings, growth, and number of openings.

These lists can help you identify a job with higher earnings or upward mobility requiring a similar level of education to the job you now hold. For example, you will find jobs within the same level of education that require similar skills, yet one pays significantly better than the other, is projected to grow more rapidly, or has significantly more job openings per year. This information can help you leverage your present skills and experience into jobs that might provide better long-term career opportunities.

You can also use these lists to explore possible job options if you were to get additional training, education, or work experience. For example, students can use these lists to identify occupations that offer high potential, and graduates can use them to identify higher degrees that could improve their employment options.

The lists can also help you when you plan your education. For example, you might be thinking about a particular college major because the pay is very good, but the lists and the information in Part II may help you identify a college major that interests you more and offers even better potential for the same general educational requirements.

The Education Levels

College degrees are not based on universal standards. Each college or university determines the number of credit hours and courses that are required for a specific degree or major (within regionally agreed upon limits). For example, among three universities the total hours required to get the bachelor's degree vary from 120 to 126 hours. At one university, a Bachelor of Architecture degree requires 160 semester hours while a Bachelor of Arts in History requires 126 hours. Thus, when you consider a job that requires a bachelor's or any other degree, you should do additional research to determine how many years of college and which courses you'll need to complete for the specific degree that the occupation requires.

Nevertheless, we offer some guidelines that can help you understand what is generally required to earn each specific degree. The following definitions are used by the federal government to classify jobs based on the minimum level of education typically required for entry and are the definitions we use for constructing the lists in this section.

- ❊ **Associate degree:** This degree usually requires two years of full-time academic work beyond high school.
- ❊ **Bachelor's degree:** This degree requires approximately four to five years of full-time academic work beyond high school.
- ❊ **Work experience plus degree:** Jobs in this category are often management-related and require some experience in a related nonmanagerial position. The degree may be either a bachelor's or a master's.
- ❊ **Master's degree:** Completion of a master's degree usually requires one to two years of full-time study beyond the bachelor's degree.
- ❊ **Doctoral degree:** This degree normally requires two or more years of full-time academic work beyond the bachelor's degree.
- ❊ **First professional degree:** This type of degree normally requires a minimum of two years of education beyond the bachelor's degree and frequently requires three years.

Another Warning About the Data

We warned you in the Introduction to this book to use caution in interpreting the data we use, and we want to do it again here. The occupational data we use is the most accurate available anywhere, but it has limitations. For example, a four-year degree in accounting, finance, or a related area is typically required for entry into the accounting profession. But some people working as accountants don't have such degrees, and others have much more education than the "minimum" required for entry.

Similarly, people with graduate degrees typically earn considerably more than people with associate or bachelor's degrees. However, some people with associate degrees earn considerably more than the average for those with higher levels of education.

So as you browse the lists that follow, please use them as a way to be encouraged rather than discouraged. Education and training are very important for success in the labor market of the future, but so are ability, drive, initiative, and—yes—luck.

Having said this, we encourage you to get as much education and training as you can. You used to be able to get your schooling and then close the schoolbooks forever, but this isn't a good attitude to have now. You will probably need to continue learning new things throughout your working life. This can be done by going to school, which is a good thing for many people to do. But other workers may learn through workshops, adult education programs, certification programs, employer training, professional conferences, Internet training, or reading related books and magazines. Upgrading your computer skills—and other technical skills—is particularly important in our rapidly changing workplace, and you avoid doing so at your peril.

Best Jobs Requiring an Associate Degree

Job	Annual Earnings	Percent Growth	Annual Openings
1. Registered Nurses	$60,010	23.5%	233,499
2. Dental Hygienists	$64,740	30.1%	10,433
3. Software Quality Assurance Engineers and Testers	$71,510	15.1%	14,374
4. Paralegals and Legal Assistants	$44,990	22.2%	22,756
5. Veterinary Technologists and Technicians	$27,970	41.0%	14,674
6. Physical Therapist Assistants	$44,130	32.4%	5,957
7. Radiation Therapists	$70,010	24.8%	1,461
8. Radiologic Technicians	$50,260	15.1%	12,836
9. Radiologic Technologists	$50,260	15.1%	12,836
10. Cardiovascular Technologists and Technicians	$44,940	25.5%	3,550
11. Environmental Science and Protection Technicians, Including Health	$39,370	28.0%	8,404

Best Jobs Requiring an Associate Degree

Job	Annual Earnings	Percent Growth	Annual Openings
12. Occupational Therapist Assistants	$45,050	25.4%	2,634
13. Respiratory Therapists	$50,070	22.6%	5,563
14. Diagnostic Medical Sonographers	$59,860	19.1%	3,211
15. Computer Support Specialists	$42,400	12.9%	97,334
16. Medical Records and Health Information Technicians	$29,290	17.8%	39,048
17. Interior Designers	$43,970	19.5%	8,434
18. Environmental Engineering Technicians	$40,690	24.8%	2,162
19. Legal Secretaries	$38,810	11.7%	38,682
20. Nuclear Medicine Technologists	$64,670	14.8%	1,290

Job 3 shares 14,374 openings with four other jobs not included in this list. Jobs 8 and 9 share 12,836 openings.

Best Jobs Requiring a Bachelor's Degree

Job	Annual Earnings	Percent Growth	Annual Openings
1. Computer Software Engineers, Applications	$83,130	44.6%	58,690
2. Computer Systems Analysts	$73,090	29.0%	63,166
3. Computer Software Engineers, Systems Software	$89,070	28.2%	33,139
4. Network Systems and Data Communications Analysts	$68,220	53.4%	35,086
5. Sales Agents, Financial Services	$68,430	24.8%	47,750
6. Financial Analysts	$70,400	33.8%	29,317
7. Sales Agents, Securities and Commodities	$68,430	24.8%	47,750
8. Computer Security Specialists	$64,690	27.0%	37,010
9. Network and Computer Systems Administrators	$64,690	27.0%	37,010
10. Personal Financial Advisors	$67,660	41.0%	17,114
11. Construction Managers	$76,230	15.7%	44,158
12. Accountants	$57,060	17.7%	134,463
13. Market Research Analysts	$60,300	20.1%	45,015
14. Auditors	$57,060	17.7%	134,463
15. Cost Estimators	$54,920	18.5%	38,379
16. Civil Engineers	$71,710	18.0%	15,979
17. Social and Community Service Managers	$54,530	24.7%	23,788
18. Environmental Engineers	$72,350	25.4%	5,003
19. Database Administrators	$67,250	28.6%	8,258
20. Industrial Engineers	$71,430	20.3%	11,272

(continued)

(continued)

Best Jobs Requiring a Bachelor's Degree

Job	Annual Earnings	Percent Growth	Annual Openings
21. Public Relations Specialists	$49,800	17.6%	51,216
22. Multi-Media Artists and Animators	$54,550	25.8%	13,182
23. Computer Systems Engineers/Architects	$71,510	15.1%	14,374
24. Biomedical Engineers	$75,440	21.1%	1,804
25. Network Designers	$71,510	15.1%	14,374
26. Substance Abuse and Behavioral Disorder Counselors	$35,580	34.3%	20,821
27. Web Administrators	$71,510	15.1%	14,374
28. Web Developers	$71,510	15.1%	14,374
29. Compensation, Benefits, and Job Analysis Specialists	$52,180	18.4%	18,761
30. Elementary School Teachers, Except Special Education	$47,330	13.6%	181,612
31. Surveyors	$51,630	23.7%	14,305
32. Loan Officers	$53,000	11.5%	54,237
33. Special Education Teachers, Preschool, Kindergarten, and Elementary School	$48,350	19.6%	20,049
34. Architects, Except Landscape and Naval	$67,620	17.7%	11,324
35. Employment Interviewers	$44,380	18.4%	33,588
36. Personnel Recruiters	$44,380	18.4%	33,588
37. Medical and Public Health Social Workers	$44,670	24.2%	16,429
38. Child, Family, and School Social Workers	$38,620	19.1%	35,402
39. Middle School Teachers, Except Special and Vocational Education	$47,900	11.2%	75,270
40. Technical Writers	$60,390	19.5%	7,498
41. Airline Pilots, Copilots, and Flight Engineers	$145,600+	12.9%	4,073
42. Insurance Sales Agents	$44,110	12.9%	64,162
43. Property, Real Estate, and Community Association Managers	$43,670	15.1%	49,916
44. Secondary School Teachers, Except Special and Vocational Education	$49,420	5.6%	93,166
45. Computer Programmers	$68,080	–4.1%	27,937
46. Logisticians	$64,250	17.3%	9,671
47. Graduate Teaching Assistants	$28,060	22.9%	20,601
48. Health Educators	$42,920	26.2%	13,707
49. Kindergarten Teachers, Except Special Education	$45,120	16.3%	27,603
50. Aerospace Engineers	$90,930	10.2%	6,498
51. Forensic Science Technicians	$47,680	30.7%	3,074
52. Copy Writers	$50,660	12.8%	24,023
53. Poets, Lyricists and Creative Writers	$50,660	12.8%	24,023

Best Jobs Requiring a Bachelor's Degree

Job	Annual Earnings	Percent Growth	Annual Openings
54. Mechanical Engineers	$72,300	4.2%	12,394
55. Sales Engineers	$80,270	8.5%	7,371
56. Electrical Engineers	$79,240	6.3%	6,806
57. Cartographers and Photogrammetrists	$49,970	20.3%	2,823
58. Recreation Workers	$21,220	12.7%	61,454
59. Computer Hardware Engineers	$91,860	4.6%	3,572
60. Electronics Engineers, Except Computer	$83,340	3.7%	5,699
61. Adult Literacy, Remedial Education, and GED Teachers and Instructors	$44,710	14.2%	17,340
62. Chemical Engineers	$81,500	7.9%	2,111
63. Directors, Religious Activities and Education	$35,370	19.7%	11,463
64. Meeting and Convention Planners	$43,530	19.9%	8,318
65. Landscape Architects	$57,580	16.4%	2,342
66. Special Education Teachers, Middle School	$48,940	15.8%	8,846
67. Chemists	$63,490	9.1%	9,024
68. Medical and Clinical Laboratory Technologists	$51,720	12.4%	11,457
69. Biological Technicians	$37,810	16.0%	15,374
70. Appraisers, Real Estate	$46,130	16.9%	6,493
71. Probation Officers and Correctional Treatment Specialists	$44,510	10.9%	18,335
72. Assessors	$46,130	16.9%	6,493
73. Graphic Designers	$41,280	9.8%	26,968
74. Financial Examiners	$66,670	10.7%	2,449

Jobs 5 and 7 share 47,750 openings. Jobs 8 and 9 share 37,010 openings. Jobs 12 and 14 share 134,463 openings. Jobs 23, 25, 27, and 28 share 14,374 openings with each other and with another job not included in this list. Jobs 35 and 36 share 33,588 openings. Jobs 52 and 53 share 24,023 openings. Jobs 70 and 72 share 6,493 openings.

Best Jobs Requiring Work Experience Plus Degree

Job	Annual Earnings	Percent Growth	Annual Openings
1. Computer and Information Systems Managers	$108,070	16.4%	30,887
2. Financial Managers, Branch or Department	$95,310	12.6%	57,589
3. Treasurers and Controllers	$95,310	12.6%	57,589
4. Marketing Managers	$104,400	14.4%	20,189
5. Management Analysts	$71,150	21.9%	125,669
6. Medical and Health Services Managers	$76,990	16.4%	31,877

(continued)

(continued)

Best Jobs Requiring Work Experience Plus Degree

Job	Annual Earnings	Percent Growth	Annual Openings
7. Sales Managers	$94,910	10.2%	36,392
8. Human Resources Managers	$87,180	12.5%	17,081
9. Training and Development Specialists	$49,630	18.3%	35,862
10. Chief Executives	$145,600+	2.0%	21,209
11. Public Relations Managers	$86,470	16.9%	5,781
12. Actuaries	$85,690	23.7%	3,245
13. General and Operations Managers	$88,700	1.5%	112,072
14. Education Administrators, Postsecondary	$75,780	14.2%	17,121
15. Engineering Managers	$111,020	7.3%	7,404
16. Natural Sciences Managers	$104,040	11.4%	3,661
17. Training and Development Managers	$84,340	15.6%	3,759
18. Education Administrators, Elementary and Secondary School	$80,580	7.6%	27,143
19. Administrative Services Managers	$70,990	11.7%	19,513
20. Education Administrators, Preschool and Child Care Center/Program	$38,580	23.5%	8,113
21. Compensation and Benefits Managers	$81,410	12.0%	6,121
22. Art Directors	$72,320	9.0%	9,719
23. Directors—Stage, Motion Pictures, Television, and Radio	$61,090	11.1%	8,992
24. Judges, Magistrate Judges, and Magistrates	$107,230	5.1%	1,567
25. Producers	$61,090	11.1%	8,992
26. Program Directors	$61,090	11.1%	8,992
27. Purchasing Managers	$85,440	3.4%	7,243
28. Agents and Business Managers of Artists, Performers, and Athletes	$66,440	9.6%	3,940
29. Advertising and Promotions Managers	$78,250	6.2%	2,955

Jobs 2 and 3 share 57,589 openings. Jobs 23, 25, and 26 share 8,992 openings with each other and with two other jobs not included in this list.

Best Jobs Requiring a Master's Degree

Job	Annual Earnings	Percent Growth	Annual Openings
1. Physical Therapists	$69,760	27.1%	12,072
2. Physician Assistants	$78,450	27.0%	7,147
3. Mental Health Counselors	$36,000	30.0%	24,103
4. Mental Health and Substance Abuse Social Workers	$36,640	29.9%	17,289

Best Jobs Requiring a Master's Degree

Job	Annual Earnings	Percent Growth	Annual Openings
5. Occupational Therapists	$63,790	23.1%	8,338
6. Environmental Scientists and Specialists, Including Health	$58,380	25.1%	6,961
7. Instructional Coordinators	$55,270	22.5%	21,294
8. Educational, Vocational, and School Counselors	$49,450	12.6%	54,025
9. Marriage and Family Therapists	$43,600	29.8%	5,953
10. Geoscientists, Except Hydrologists and Geographers	$75,800	21.9%	2,471
11. Hydrologists	$68,140	24.3%	687
12. Clergy	$40,460	18.9%	35,092
13. Rehabilitation Counselors	$29,630	23.0%	32,081
14. Industrial-Organizational Psychologists	$80,820	21.3%	118
15. Speech-Language Pathologists	$60,690	10.6%	11,160
16. Operations Research Analysts	$66,950	10.6%	5,727
17. Statisticians	$69,900	8.5%	3,433
18. Curators	$46,000	23.3%	1,416

Best Jobs Requiring a Doctoral Degree

Job	Annual Earnings	Percent Growth	Annual Openings
1. Health Specialties Teachers, Postsecondary	$80,700	22.9%	19,617
2. Biological Science Teachers, Postsecondary	$71,780	22.9%	9,039
3. Business Teachers, Postsecondary	$64,900	22.9%	11,643
4. Engineering Teachers, Postsecondary	$79,510	22.9%	5,565
5. Economics Teachers, Postsecondary	$75,300	22.9%	2,208
6. Agricultural Sciences Teachers, Postsecondary	$78,460	22.9%	1,840
7. Art, Drama, and Music Teachers, Postsecondary	$55,190	22.9%	12,707
8. Chemistry Teachers, Postsecondary	$63,870	22.9%	3,405
9. Computer Science Teachers, Postsecondary	$62,020	22.9%	5,820
10. Physics Teachers, Postsecondary	$70,090	22.9%	2,155
11. Atmospheric, Earth, Marine, and Space Sciences Teachers, Postsecondary	$73,280	22.9%	1,553
12. Mathematical Science Teachers, Postsecondary	$58,560	22.9%	7,663
13. Psychology Teachers, Postsecondary	$60,610	22.9%	5,261
14. Education Teachers, Postsecondary	$54,220	22.9%	9,359
15. English Language and Literature Teachers, Postsecondary	$54,000	22.9%	10,475
16. Nursing Instructors and Teachers, Postsecondary	$57,500	22.9%	7,337

(continued)

(continued)

Best Jobs Requiring a Doctoral Degree

Job	Annual Earnings	Percent Growth	Annual Openings
17. Political Science Teachers, Postsecondary	$63,100	22.9%	2,435
18. History Teachers, Postsecondary	$59,160	22.9%	3,570
19. Architecture Teachers, Postsecondary	$68,540	22.9%	1,044
20. Anthropology and Archeology Teachers, Postsecondary	$64,530	22.9%	910
21. Environmental Science Teachers, Postsecondary	$64,850	22.9%	769
22. Communications Teachers, Postsecondary	$54,720	22.9%	4,074
23. Medical Scientists, Except Epidemiologists	$64,200	20.2%	10,596
24. Philosophy and Religion Teachers, Postsecondary	$56,380	22.9%	3,120
25. Sociology Teachers, Postsecondary	$58,160	22.9%	2,774
26. Foreign Language and Literature Teachers, Postsecondary	$53,610	22.9%	4,317
27. Computer and Information Scientists, Research	$97,970	21.5%	2,901
28. Forestry and Conservation Science Teachers, Postsecondary	$63,790	22.9%	454
29. Area, Ethnic, and Cultural Studies Teachers, Postsecondary	$59,150	22.9%	1,252
30. Recreation and Fitness Studies Teachers, Postsecondary	$52,170	22.9%	3,010
31. Biologists	$64,920	9.2%	6,288
32. Clinical Psychologists	$62,210	15.8%	8,309
33. Geography Teachers, Postsecondary	$61,310	22.9%	697
34. Counseling Psychologists	$62,210	15.8%	8,309
35. Home Economics Teachers, Postsecondary	$58,170	22.9%	820
36. School Psychologists	$62,210	15.8%	8,309
37. Social Work Teachers, Postsecondary	$56,240	22.9%	1,292
38. Criminal Justice and Law Enforcement Teachers, Postsecondary	$51,060	22.9%	1,911
39. Biochemists and Biophysicists	$79,270	15.9%	1,637
40. Library Science Teachers, Postsecondary	$56,810	22.9%	702
41. Physicists	$96,850	6.8%	1,302

Jobs 32, 34, and 36 share 8,309 openings.

Best Jobs Requiring a First Professional Degree

Job	Annual Earnings	Percent Growth	Annual Openings
1. Anesthesiologists	$145,600+	14.2%	38,027
2. Family and General Practitioners	$145,600+	14.2%	38,027

Best Jobs Requiring a First Professional Degree

Job	Annual Earnings	Percent Growth	Annual Openings
3. Internists, General	$145,600+	14.2%	38,027
4. Obstetricians and Gynecologists	$145,600+	14.2%	38,027
5. Psychiatrists	$145,600+	14.2%	38,027
6. Surgeons	$145,600+	14.2%	38,027
7. Pediatricians, General	$140,690	14.2%	38,027
8. Pharmacists	$100,480	21.7%	16,358
9. Lawyers	$106,120	11.0%	49,445
10. Veterinarians	$75,230	35.0%	5,301
11. Law Teachers, Postsecondary	$87,730	22.9%	2,169
12. Chiropractors	$65,890	14.4%	3,179
13. Dentists, General	$137,630	9.2%	7,106
14. Orthodontists	$145,600+	9.2%	479
15. Prosthodontists	$145,600+	10.7%	54
16. Oral and Maxillofacial Surgeons	$145,600+	9.1%	400
17. Optometrists	$93,800	11.3%	1,789
18. Podiatrists	$110,510	9.5%	648

Jobs 1, 2, 3, 4, 5, 6, and 7 share 38,027 openings.

Best Jobs Lists for College Graduates Based on Interests

This group of lists organizes the 200 best jobs that typically require a college degree or more into 16 interest areas. (There actually are only 15 lists, because one interest area, Manufacturing, is not linked to any of the 200 best jobs.) These interest areas are used in a variety of career exploration systems and can help you to quickly identify jobs based on your interests. They are often referred to as "career clusters," so for each job described in Part II we identify what we call the "Career Cluster/Interest Area."

Simply find the one or more areas that interest you most. Then review the jobs in those areas to identify jobs you want to explore in more detail and look up their descriptions in Part II. You can also review interest areas where you have had past experience, education, or training to see whether other jobs in those areas would meet your current requirements.

Within each interest area, jobs are listed in order of their total combined scores based on earnings, growth, and number of openings.

Some of the interest areas have just a few jobs listed in them. (In fact, Manufacturing has *no* jobs listed.) This is because few or no jobs in those interest areas typically require a college degree. Even so, if one of those areas interests you most, you can often come up with a creative way to use your education and training in that interest area. For example, you might start or manage a business in an area that interests you or work in an industry that involves your interest area.

Note: The 16 interest areas used in these lists are those used in the *New Guide for Occupational Exploration,* Fourth Edition, published by JIST. The original GOE was developed by the U.S. Department of Labor as an intuitive way to assist in career exploration. The 16 interest areas used in the *New GOE* are based on the 16 career clusters that the U.S. Department of Education's Office of Vocational and Adult Education developed around 1999 and that many states now use to organize their career-oriented programs and career information.

Descriptions for the 16 Interest Areas

Brief descriptions follow for the 16 interest areas we use in the lists. The descriptions are from the *New Guide for Occupational Exploration,* Fourth Edition. Some of them refer to job titles (as examples) that aren't included in this book.

Also note that we put each job into only one interest area list, the one it fit into best. However, many jobs could be included in more than one list, so consider reviewing several interest areas to find jobs that you might otherwise overlook. You may notice that some interest areas include very few jobs—perhaps just one. In most cases this occurs because the jobs associated with these interest areas do not typically require a college degree to enter, although people with college degrees often do work in these jobs.

* **Agriculture and Natural Resources:** *An interest in working with plants, animals, forests, or mineral resources for agriculture, horticulture, conservation, extraction, and other purposes.* You can satisfy this interest by working in farming, landscaping, forestry, fishing, mining, and related fields. You may like doing physical work outdoors, such as on a farm or ranch, in a forest, or on a drilling rig. If you have a scientific curiosity, you could study plants and animals or analyze biological or rock samples in a lab. If you have management ability, you could own, operate, or manage a fish hatchery, a landscaping business, or a greenhouse.

* **Architecture and Construction:** *An interest in designing, assembling, and maintaining components of buildings and other structures.* You may want to be part of the team of architects, drafters, and others who design buildings and render the plans. If construction interests you, you might find fulfillment in the many building projects that are being undertaken at all times. If you like to organize and plan, you can find careers in managing these projects. Or you can play a more direct role in putting up and finishing buildings by doing jobs such as plumbing, carpentry, masonry, painting, or roofing, either as a skilled craftsworker or as a helper. You can prepare the building site by operating heavy equipment or installing, maintaining, and repairing vital building equipment and systems such as electricity and heating.

❋ **Arts and Communication:** *An interest in creatively expressing feelings or ideas, in communicating news or information, or in performing.* You can satisfy this interest in creative, verbal, or performing activities. For example, if you enjoy literature, perhaps writing or editing would appeal to you. Journalism and public relations are other fields for people who like to use their writing or speaking skills. Do you prefer to work in the performing arts? If so, you could direct or perform in drama, music, or dance. If you especially enjoy the visual arts, you could create paintings, sculpture, or ceramics or design products or visual displays. A flair for technology might lead you to specialize in photography, broadcast production, or dispatching.

❋ **Business and Administration:** *An interest in making a business organization or function run smoothly.* You can satisfy this interest by working in a position of leadership or by specializing in a function that contributes to the overall effort in a business, a nonprofit organization, or a government agency. If you especially enjoy working with people, you may find fulfillment from working in human resources. An interest in numbers may lead you to consider accounting, finance, budgeting, billing, or financial record-keeping. A job as an administrative assistant may interest you if you like a variety of tasks in a busy environment. If you are good with details and word processing, you may enjoy a job as a secretary or data-entry clerk. Or perhaps you would do well as the manager of a business.

❋ **Education and Training:** *An interest in helping people learn.* You can satisfy this interest by teaching students, who may be preschoolers, retirees, or any age in between. You may specialize in a particular academic field or work with learners of a particular age, with a particular interest, or with a particular learning problem. Working in a library or museum may give you an opportunity to expand people's understanding of the world.

❋ **Finance and Insurance:** *An interest in helping businesses and people be assured of a financially secure future.* You can satisfy this interest by working in a financial or insurance business in a leadership or support role. If you like gathering and analyzing information, you may find fulfillment as an insurance adjuster or financial analyst. Or you may deal with information at the clerical level as a banking or insurance clerk or in person-to-person situations providing customer service. Another way to interact with people is to sell financial or insurance services that will meet their needs.

❋ **Government and Public Administration:** *An interest in helping a government agency serve the needs of the public.* You can satisfy this interest by working in a position of leadership or by specializing in a function that contributes to the role of government. You may help protect the public by working as an inspector or examiner to enforce standards. If you enjoy using clerical skills, you could work as a clerk in a law court or government office. Or perhaps you prefer the top-down perspective of a government executive or urban planner.

❋ **Health Science:** *An interest in helping people and animals be healthy.* You can satisfy this interest by working on a health-care team as a doctor, therapist, or nurse. You might specialize in one of the many different parts of the body (such as the teeth or eyes) or in one of the many different types of care. Or you may want to be a generalist who deals with the whole patient. If you like technology, you might find satisfaction working with

X rays or new diagnostic methods. You might work with healthy people, helping them eat right. If you enjoy working with animals, you might care for them and keep them healthy.

✳ **Hospitality, Tourism, and Recreation:** *An interest in catering to the personal wishes and needs of others so that they can enjoy a clean environment, good food and drink, comfortable lodging away from home, and recreation.* You can satisfy this interest by providing services for the convenience, care, and pampering of others in hotels, restaurants, airplanes, beauty parlors, and so on. You may want to use your love of cooking as a chef. If you like working with people, you may want to provide personal services by being a travel guide, a flight attendant, a concierge, a hairdresser, or a waiter. You may want to work in cleaning and building services if you like a clean environment. If you enjoy sports or games, you could work for an athletic team or casino.

✳ **Human Service:** *An interest in improving people's social, mental, emotional, or spiritual well-being.* You can satisfy this interest as a counselor, social worker, or religious worker who helps people sort out their complicated lives or solve personal problems. You may work as a caretaker for very young people or the elderly. Or you may interview people to help identify the social services they need.

✳ **Information Technology:** *An interest in designing, developing, managing, and supporting information systems.* You can satisfy this interest by working with hardware, software, multimedia, or integrated systems. If you like to use your organizational skills, you might work as a systems or database administrator. Or you can solve complex problems as a software engineer or systems analyst. If you enjoy getting your hands on hardware, you might find work servicing computers, peripherals, and information-intense machines such as cash registers and ATMs.

✳ **Law and Public Safety:** *An interest in upholding people's rights or in protecting people and property by using authority, inspecting, or investigating.* You can satisfy this interest by working in law, law enforcement, fire fighting, the military, and related fields. For example, if you enjoy mental challenge and intrigue, you could investigate crimes or fires for a living. If you enjoy working with verbal skills and research skills, you may want to defend citizens in court or research deeds, wills, and other legal documents. If you want to help people in critical situations, you may want to fight fires, work as a police officer, or become a paramedic. Or, if you want more routine work in public safety, perhaps a job in guarding, patrolling, or inspecting would appeal to you. If you have management ability, you could seek a leadership position in law enforcement and the protective services. Work in the military gives you a chance to use technical and leadership skills while serving your country.

✳ **Manufacturing:** *An interest in processing materials into intermediate or final products or maintaining and repairing products by using machines or hand tools.* **None of the 200 best jobs for college graduates is linked to this interest area.**

❋ **Retail and Wholesale Sales and Service:** *An interest in bringing others to a particular point of view by personal persuasion and by sales and promotional techniques.* You can satisfy this interest in various jobs that involve persuasion and selling. If you like using knowledge of science, you may enjoy selling pharmaceutical, medical, or electronic products or services. Real estate offers several kinds of sales jobs as well. If you like speaking on the phone, you could work as a telemarketer. Or you may enjoy selling apparel and other merchandise in a retail setting. If you prefer to help people, you may want a job in customer service.

❋ **Scientific Research, Engineering, and Mathematics:** *An interest in discovering, collecting, and analyzing information about the natural world; in applying scientific research findings to problems in medicine, the life sciences, human behavior, and the natural sciences; in imagining and manipulating quantitative data; and in applying technology to manufacturing, transportation, and other economic activities.* You can satisfy this interest by working with the knowledge and processes of the sciences. You may enjoy researching and developing new knowledge in mathematics, or perhaps solving problems in the physical, life, or social sciences would appeal to you. You may want to study engineering and help create new machines, processes, and structures. If you want to work with scientific equipment and procedures, you could seek a job in a research or testing laboratory.

❋ **Transportation, Distribution, and Logistics:** *An interest in operations that move people or materials.* You can satisfy this interest by managing a transportation service, by helping vehicles keep on their assigned schedules and routes, or by driving or piloting a vehicle. If you enjoy taking responsibility, perhaps managing a rail line would appeal to you. If you work well with details and can take pressure on the job, you might consider being an air traffic controller. Or would you rather get out on the highway, on the water, or up in the air? If so, you could drive a truck from state to state, be employed on a ship, or fly a crop duster over a cornfield. If you prefer to stay closer to home, you could drive a delivery van, taxi, or school bus. You can use your physical strength to load freight and arrange it so that it gets to its destination in one piece.

Best Jobs for College Graduates Interested in Agriculture and Natural Resources

Job	Annual Earnings	Percent Growth	Annual Openings
1. Environmental Science and Protection Technicians, Including Health	$39,370	28.0%	8,404
2. Environmental Engineers	$72,350	25.4%	5,003

Best Jobs for College Graduates
Interested in Architecture and Construction

Job	Annual Earnings	Percent Growth	Annual Openings
1. Construction Managers	$76,230	15.7%	44,158
2. Architects, Except Landscape and Naval	$67,620	17.7%	11,324
3. Surveyors	$51,630	23.7%	14,305
4. Landscape Architects	$57,580	16.4%	2,342

Best Jobs for College Graduates Interested in Arts and Communication

Job	Annual Earnings	Percent Growth	Annual Openings
1. Multi-Media Artists and Animators	$54,550	25.8%	13,182
2. Public Relations Specialists	$49,800	17.6%	51,216
3. Copy Writers	$50,660	12.8%	24,023
4. Poets, Lyricists and Creative Writers	$50,660	12.8%	24,023
5. Public Relations Managers	$86,470	16.9%	5,781
6. Directors—Stage, Motion Pictures, Television, and Radio	$61,090	11.1%	8,992
7. Producers	$61,090	11.1%	8,992
8. Program Directors	$61,090	11.1%	8,992
9. Technical Writers	$60,390	19.5%	7,498
10. Art Directors	$72,320	9.0%	9,719
11. Interior Designers	$43,970	19.5%	8,434
12. Graphic Designers	$41,280	9.8%	26,968
13. Agents and Business Managers of Artists, Performers, and Athletes	$66,440	9.6%	3,940

Jobs 3 and 4 share 24,023 openings. Jobs 6, 7, and 8 share 8,992 openings with each other and with two jobs not included in this list.

Best Jobs for College Graduates Interested
in Business and Administration

Job	Annual Earnings	Percent Growth	Annual Openings
1. Management Analysts	$71,150	21.9%	125,669
2. Accountants	$57,060	17.7%	134,463
3. Auditors	$57,060	17.7%	134,463
4. General and Operations Managers	$88,700	1.5%	112,072

Best Jobs for College Graduates Interested in Business and Administration

Job	Annual Earnings	Percent Growth	Annual Openings
5. Employment Interviewers	$44,380	18.4%	33,588
6. Personnel Recruiters	$44,380	18.4%	33,588
7. Training and Development Specialists	$49,630	18.3%	35,862
8. Chief Executives	$145,600+	2.0%	21,209
9. Compensation, Benefits, and Job Analysis Specialists	$52,180	18.4%	18,761
10. Human Resources Managers	$87,180	12.5%	17,081
11. Administrative Services Managers	$70,990	11.7%	19,513
12. Logisticians	$64,250	17.3%	9,671
13. Training and Development Managers	$84,340	15.6%	3,759
14. Compensation and Benefits Managers	$81,410	12.0%	6,121
15. Meeting and Convention Planners	$43,530	19.9%	8,318
16. Legal Secretaries	$38,810	11.7%	38,682
17. Operations Research Analysts	$66,950	10.6%	5,727

Jobs 2 and 3 share 134,463 openings. Jobs 5 and 6 share 33,588 openings.

Best Jobs for College Graduates Interested in Education and Training

Job	Annual Earnings	Percent Growth	Annual Openings
1. Health Specialties Teachers, Postsecondary	$80,700	22.9%	19,617
2. Biological Science Teachers, Postsecondary	$71,780	22.9%	9,039
3. Business Teachers, Postsecondary	$64,900	22.9%	11,643
4. Engineering Teachers, Postsecondary	$79,510	22.9%	5,565
5. Law Teachers, Postsecondary	$87,730	22.9%	2,169
6. Computer Science Teachers, Postsecondary	$62,020	22.9%	5,820
7. Economics Teachers, Postsecondary	$75,300	22.9%	2,208
8. Agricultural Sciences Teachers, Postsecondary	$78,460	22.9%	1,840
9. Chemistry Teachers, Postsecondary	$63,870	22.9%	3,405
10. Mathematical Science Teachers, Postsecondary	$58,560	22.9%	7,663
11. Art, Drama, and Music Teachers, Postsecondary	$55,190	22.9%	12,707
12. Psychology Teachers, Postsecondary	$60,610	22.9%	5,261
13. Physics Teachers, Postsecondary	$70,090	22.9%	2,155
14. Atmospheric, Earth, Marine, and Space Sciences Teachers, Postsecondary	$73,280	22.9%	1,553

(continued)

(continued)

Best Jobs for College Graduates Interested in Education and Training

Job	Annual Earnings	Percent Growth	Annual Openings
15. Nursing Instructors and Teachers, Postsecondary	$57,500	22.9%	7,337
16. History Teachers, Postsecondary	$59,160	22.9%	3,570
17. Education Teachers, Postsecondary	$54,220	22.9%	9,359
18. English Language and Literature Teachers, Postsecondary	$54,000	22.9%	10,475
19. Political Science Teachers, Postsecondary	$63,100	22.9%	2,435
20. Education Administrators, Elementary and Secondary School	$80,580	7.6%	27,143
21. Architecture Teachers, Postsecondary	$68,540	22.9%	1,044
22. Education Administrators, Postsecondary	$75,780	14.2%	17,121
23. Graduate Teaching Assistants	$28,060	22.9%	20,601
24. Health Educators	$42,920	26.2%	13,707
25. Sociology Teachers, Postsecondary	$58,160	22.9%	2,774
26. Anthropology and Archeology Teachers, Postsecondary	$64,530	22.9%	910
27. Philosophy and Religion Teachers, Postsecondary	$56,380	22.9%	3,120
28. Communications Teachers, Postsecondary	$54,720	22.9%	4,074
29. Environmental Science Teachers, Postsecondary	$64,850	22.9%	769
30. Foreign Language and Literature Teachers, Postsecondary	$53,610	22.9%	4,317
31. Area, Ethnic, and Cultural Studies Teachers, Postsecondary	$59,150	22.9%	1,252
32. Forestry and Conservation Science Teachers, Postsecondary	$63,790	22.9%	454
33. Education Administrators, Preschool and Child Care Center/Program	$38,580	23.5%	8,113
34. Geography Teachers, Postsecondary	$61,310	22.9%	697
35. Recreation and Fitness Studies Teachers, Postsecondary	$52,170	22.9%	3,010
36. Home Economics Teachers, Postsecondary	$58,170	22.9%	820
37. Social Work Teachers, Postsecondary	$56,240	22.9%	1,292
38. Instructional Coordinators	$55,270	22.5%	21,294
39. Criminal Justice and Law Enforcement Teachers, Postsecondary	$51,060	22.9%	1,911
40. Library Science Teachers, Postsecondary	$56,810	22.9%	702
41. Curators	$46,000	23.3%	1,416
42. Educational, Vocational, and School Counselors	$49,450	12.6%	54,025
43. Elementary School Teachers, Except Special Education	$47,330	13.6%	181,612
44. Secondary School Teachers, Except Special and Vocational Education	$49,420	5.6%	93,166
45. Special Education Teachers, Preschool, Kindergarten, and Elementary School	$48,350	19.6%	20,049
46. Kindergarten Teachers, Except Special Education	$45,120	16.3%	27,603

Best Jobs for College Graduates Interested in Education and Training

Job	Annual Earnings	Percent Growth	Annual Openings
47. Middle School Teachers, Except Special and Vocational Education	$47,900	11.2%	75,270
48. Adult Literacy, Remedial Education, and GED Teachers and Instructors	$44,710	14.2%	17,340
49. Special Education Teachers, Middle School	$48,940	15.8%	8,846

Best Jobs for College Graduates Interested in Finance and Insurance

Job	Annual Earnings	Percent Growth	Annual Openings
1. Sales Agents, Financial Services	$68,430	24.8%	47,750
2. Sales Agents, Securities and Commodities	$68,430	24.8%	47,750
3. Financial Managers, Branch or Department	$95,310	12.6%	57,589
4. Treasurers and Controllers	$95,310	12.6%	57,589
5. Financial Analysts	$70,400	33.8%	29,317
6. Personal Financial Advisors	$67,660	41.0%	17,114
7. Market Research Analysts	$60,300	20.1%	45,015
8. Cost Estimators	$54,920	18.5%	38,379
9. Insurance Sales Agents	$44,110	12.9%	64,162
10. Loan Officers	$53,000	11.5%	54,237
11. Appraisers, Real Estate	$46,130	16.9%	6,493
12. Assessors	$46,130	16.9%	6,493

Jobs 1 and 2 share 47,750 openings. Jobs 3 and 4 share 57,589 openings. Jobs 11 and 12 share 6,493 openings.

Best Jobs for College Graduates Interested in Government and Public Administration

Job	Annual Earnings	Percent Growth	Annual Openings
1. Social and Community Service Managers	$54,530	24.7%	23,788
2. Financial Examiners	$66,670	10.7%	2,449

Best Jobs for College Graduates Interested in Health Science

Job	Annual Earnings	Percent Growth	Annual Openings
1. Anesthesiologists	$145,600+	14.2%	38,027
2. Family and General Practitioners	$145,600+	14.2%	38,027
3. Internists, General	$145,600+	14.2%	38,027
4. Obstetricians and Gynecologists	$145,600+	14.2%	38,027
5. Psychiatrists	$145,600+	14.2%	38,027
6. Surgeons	$145,600+	14.2%	38,027
7. Pediatricians, General	$140,690	14.2%	38,027
8. Registered Nurses	$60,010	23.5%	233,499
9. Pharmacists	$100,480	21.7%	16,358
10. Physical Therapists	$69,760	27.1%	12,072
11. Medical and Health Services Managers	$76,990	16.4%	31,877
12. Physician Assistants	$78,450	27.0%	7,147
13. Dental Hygienists	$64,740	30.1%	10,433
14. Veterinarians	$75,230	35.0%	5,301
15. Veterinary Technologists and Technicians	$27,970	41.0%	14,674
16. Medical Records and Health Information Technicians	$29,290	17.8%	39,048
17. Occupational Therapists	$63,790	23.1%	8,338
18. Radiation Therapists	$70,010	24.8%	1,461
19. Physical Therapist Assistants	$44,130	32.4%	5,957
20. Radiologic Technicians	$50,260	15.1%	12,836
21. Radiologic Technologists	$50,260	15.1%	12,836
22. Biological Technicians	$37,810	16.0%	15,374
23. Cardiovascular Technologists and Technicians	$44,940	25.5%	3,550
24. Respiratory Therapists	$50,070	22.6%	5,563
25. Dentists, General	$137,630	9.2%	7,106
26. Diagnostic Medical Sonographers	$59,860	19.1%	3,211
27. Occupational Therapist Assistants	$45,050	25.4%	2,634
28. Prosthodontists	$145,600+	10.7%	54
29. Chiropractors	$65,890	14.4%	3,179
30. Orthodontists	$145,600+	9.2%	479
31. Oral and Maxillofacial Surgeons	$145,600+	9.1%	400
32. Medical and Clinical Laboratory Technologists	$51,720	12.4%	11,457
33. Nuclear Medicine Technologists	$64,670	14.8%	1,290
34. Optometrists	$93,800	11.3%	1,789
35. Speech-Language Pathologists	$60,690	10.6%	11,160
36. Podiatrists	$110,510	9.5%	648

Jobs 1, 2, 3, 4, 5, 6, and 7 share 38,027 openings. Jobs 20 and 21 share 12,836 openings.

Best Jobs for College Graduates Interested in Hospitality, Tourism, and Recreation

Job	Annual Earnings	Percent Growth	Annual Openings
1. Recreation Workers	$21,220	12.7%	61,454

Best Jobs for College Graduates Interested in Human Service

Job	Annual Earnings	Percent Growth	Annual Openings
1. Mental Health Counselors	$36,000	30.0%	24,103
2. Child, Family, and School Social Workers	$38,620	19.1%	35,402
3. Medical and Public Health Social Workers	$44,670	24.2%	16,429
4. Substance Abuse and Behavioral Disorder Counselors	$35,580	34.3%	20,821
5. Clergy	$40,460	18.9%	35,092
6. Mental Health and Substance Abuse Social Workers	$36,640	29.9%	17,289
7. Clinical Psychologists	$62,210	15.8%	8,309
8. Counseling Psychologists	$62,210	15.8%	8,309
9. Marriage and Family Therapists	$43,600	29.8%	5,953
10. Rehabilitation Counselors	$29,630	23.0%	32,081
11. Probation Officers and Correctional Treatment Specialists	$44,510	10.9%	18,335
12. Directors, Religious Activities and Education	$35,370	19.7%	11,463

Jobs 7 and 8 share 8,309 openings.

Best Jobs for College Graduates Interested in Information Technology

Job	Annual Earnings	Percent Growth	Annual Openings
1. Computer Software Engineers, Applications	$83,130	44.6%	58,690
2. Computer Systems Analysts	$73,090	29.0%	63,166
3. Computer Software Engineers, Systems Software	$89,070	28.2%	33,139
4. Computer and Information Systems Managers	$108,070	16.4%	30,887
5. Network Systems and Data Communications Analysts	$68,220	53.4%	35,086
6. Computer Security Specialists	$64,690	27.0%	37,010
7. Network and Computer Systems Administrators	$64,690	27.0%	37,010
8. Computer and Information Scientists, Research	$97,970	21.5%	2,901
9. Computer Systems Engineers/Architects	$71,510	15.1%	14,374

(continued)

(continued)

Best Jobs for College Graduates Interested in Information Technology

Job	Annual Earnings	Percent Growth	Annual Openings
10. Network Designers	$71,510	15.1%	14,374
11. Software Quality Assurance Engineers and Testers	$71,510	15.1%	14,374
12. Web Administrators	$71,510	15.1%	14,374
13. Web Developers	$71,510	15.1%	14,374
14. Computer Support Specialists	$42,400	12.9%	97,334
15. Database Administrators	$67,250	28.6%	8,258
16. Computer Programmers	$68,080	−4.1%	27,937

Jobs 6 and 7 share 37,010 openings. Jobs 9, 10, 11, 12, and 13 share 14,374 openings.

Best Jobs for College Graduates Interested in Law and Public Safety

Job	Annual Earnings	Percent Growth	Annual Openings
1. Lawyers	$106,120	11.0%	49,445
2. Forensic Science Technicians	$47,680	30.7%	3,074
3. Paralegals and Legal Assistants	$44,990	22.2%	22,756
4. Judges, Magistrate Judges, and Magistrates	$107,230	5.1%	1,567

Best Jobs for College Graduates Interested in Retail and Wholesale Sales and Service

Job	Annual Earnings	Percent Growth	Annual Openings
1. Marketing Managers	$104,400	14.4%	20,189
2. Sales Managers	$94,910	10.2%	36,392
3. Property, Real Estate, and Community Association Managers	$43,670	15.1%	49,916
4. Sales Engineers	$80,270	8.5%	7,371
5. Purchasing Managers	$85,440	3.4%	7,243
6. Advertising and Promotions Managers	$78,250	6.2%	2,955

Best Jobs for College Graduates Interested in Scientific Research, Engineering, and Mathematics

Job	Annual Earnings	Percent Growth	Annual Openings
1. Actuaries	$85,690	23.7%	3,245
2. Civil Engineers	$71,710	18.0%	15,979
3. Industrial Engineers	$71,430	20.3%	11,272
4. Engineering Managers	$111,020	7.3%	7,404
5. Natural Sciences Managers	$104,040	11.4%	3,661
6. Aerospace Engineers	$90,930	10.2%	6,498
7. Environmental Scientists and Specialists, Including Health	$58,380	25.1%	6,961
8. Medical Scientists, Except Epidemiologists	$64,200	20.2%	10,596
9. Geoscientists, Except Hydrologists and Geographers	$75,800	21.9%	2,471
10. Industrial-Organizational Psychologists	$80,820	21.3%	118
11. Mechanical Engineers	$72,300	4.2%	12,394
12. Biomedical Engineers	$75,440	21.1%	1,804
13. Computer Hardware Engineers	$91,860	4.6%	3,572
14. School Psychologists	$62,210	15.8%	8,309
15. Electrical Engineers	$79,240	6.3%	6,806
16. Chemists	$63,490	9.1%	9,024
17. Biochemists and Biophysicists	$79,270	15.9%	1,637
18. Electronics Engineers, Except Computer	$83,340	3.7%	5,699
19. Hydrologists	$68,140	24.3%	687
20. Biologists	$64,920	9.2%	6,288
21. Environmental Engineering Technicians	$40,690	24.8%	2,162
22. Chemical Engineers	$81,500	7.9%	2,111
23. Physicists	$96,850	6.8%	1,302
24. Cartographers and Photogrammetrists	$49,970	20.3%	2,823
25. Statisticians	$69,900	8.5%	3,433

Job 14 shares 8,309 openings with another job not included in this list.

Best Jobs for College Graduates Interested in Transportation, Distribution, and Logistics

Job	Annual Earnings	Percent Growth	Annual Openings
1. Airline Pilots, Copilots, and Flight Engineers	$145,600+	12.9%	4,073

Best Jobs Lists for College Graduates Based on Personality Types

These lists organize the 200 best jobs requiring a college degree into groups matching six personality types. The personality types are Realistic, Investigative, Artistic, Social, Enterprising, and Conventional. This system was developed by John Holland and is used in the *Self-Directed Search* (SDS) and other career assessment inventories and information systems.

If you have used one of these career inventories or systems, the lists will help you identify jobs that most closely match these personality types. Even if you have not used one of these systems, the concept of personality types and the jobs that are related to them can help you identify jobs that most closely match the type of person you are.

As we did for the education levels, we have created only one list for each personality type. We've ranked the jobs within each personality type based on their total combined scores for earnings, growth, and annual job openings. Each job is listed in the one personality type it most closely matches, even though it might also fit into others. Consider reviewing the jobs for more than one personality type so you don't overlook possible jobs that would interest you.

Descriptions of the Six Personality Types

Following are brief descriptions of the kinds of work that appeal to each of the six personality types used in the lists. Select the two or three descriptions that most closely characterize the kinds of work you prefer, then use the lists to identify jobs that best fit these personality types.

- ✻ **Realistic:** These occupations frequently involve work activities that include practical, hands-on problems and solutions. They often deal with plants; animals; and real-world materials such as wood, tools, and machinery. Many of the occupations require working outside and don't involve a lot of paperwork or working closely with others.

- ✻ **Investigative:** These occupations frequently involve working with ideas and require an extensive amount of thinking. These occupations can involve searching for facts and figuring out problems mentally.

- ✻ **Artistic:** These occupations frequently involve working with forms, designs, and patterns. They often require self-expression, and the work can be done without following a clear set of rules.

- ✻ **Social:** These occupations frequently involve working with, communicating with, and teaching people. These occupations often involve helping or providing service to others.

- ✻ **Enterprising:** These occupations frequently involve starting up and carrying out projects. These occupations can involve leading people and making many decisions. They sometimes require risk taking and often deal with business.

❋ **Conventional:** These occupations frequently involve following set procedures and routines. These occupations can include working with data and details more than with ideas. Usually there is a clear line of authority to follow.

Best Jobs for College Graduates with a Realistic Personality Type

Job	Annual Earnings	Percent Growth	Annual Openings
1. Civil Engineers	$71,710	18.0%	15,979
2. Surveyors	$51,630	23.7%	14,305
3. Veterinary Technologists and Technicians	$27,970	41.0%	14,674
4. Airline Pilots, Copilots, and Flight Engineers	$145,600+	12.9%	4,073
5. Cardiovascular Technologists and Technicians	$44,940	25.5%	3,550
6. Radiologic Technicians	$50,260	15.1%	12,836
7. Radiologic Technologists	$50,260	15.1%	12,836
8. Computer Support Specialists	$42,400	12.9%	97,334
9. Biological Technicians	$37,810	16.0%	15,374
10. Cartographers and Photogrammetrists	$49,970	20.3%	2,823
11. Environmental Engineering Technicians	$40,690	24.8%	2,162
12. Oral and Maxillofacial Surgeons	$145,600+	9.1%	400

Jobs 6 and 7 share 12,836 openings.

Best Jobs for College Graduates with an Investigative Personality Type

Job	Annual Earnings	Percent Growth	Annual Openings
1. Computer Software Engineers, Applications	$83,130	44.6%	58,690
2. Anesthesiologists	$145,600+	14.2%	38,027
3. Family and General Practitioners	$145,600+	14.2%	38,027
4. Internists, General	$145,600+	14.2%	38,027
5. Obstetricians and Gynecologists	$145,600+	14.2%	38,027
6. Psychiatrists	$145,600+	14.2%	38,027
7. Surgeons	$145,600+	14.2%	38,027
8. Computer Systems Analysts	$73,090	29.0%	63,166
9. Computer Software Engineers, Systems Software	$89,070	28.2%	33,139
10. Pediatricians, General	$140,690	14.2%	38,027
11. Pharmacists	$100,480	21.7%	16,358
12. Management Analysts	$71,150	21.9%	125,669
13. Network Systems and Data Communications Analysts	$68,220	53.4%	35,086

(continued)

(continued)

Best Jobs for College Graduates with an Investigative Personality Type

Job	Annual Earnings	Percent Growth	Annual Openings
14. Network and Computer Systems Administrators	$64,690	27.0%	37,010
15. Veterinarians	$75,230	35.0%	5,301
16. Computer and Information Scientists, Research	$97,970	21.5%	2,901
17. Engineering Teachers, Postsecondary	$79,510	22.9%	5,565
18. Market Research Analysts	$60,300	20.1%	45,015
19. Industrial Engineers	$71,430	20.3%	11,272
20. Computer Systems Engineers/Architects	$71,510	15.1%	14,374
21. Environmental Engineers	$72,350	25.4%	5,003
22. Software Quality Assurance Engineers and Testers	$71,510	15.1%	14,374
23. Dentists, General	$137,630	9.2%	7,106
24. Geoscientists, Except Hydrologists and Geographers	$75,800	21.9%	2,471
25. Environmental Science and Protection Technicians, Including Health	$39,370	28.0%	8,404
26. Medical Scientists, Except Epidemiologists	$64,200	20.2%	10,596
27. Aerospace Engineers	$90,930	10.2%	6,498
28. Environmental Scientists and Specialists, Including Health	$58,380	25.1%	6,961
29. Biomedical Engineers	$75,440	21.1%	1,804
30. Industrial-Organizational Psychologists	$80,820	21.3%	118
31. Prosthodontists	$145,600+	10.7%	54
32. Biochemists and Biophysicists	$79,270	15.9%	1,637
33. Orthodontists	$145,600+	9.2%	479
34. Clinical Psychologists	$62,210	15.8%	8,309
35. Forensic Science Technicians	$47,680	30.7%	3,074
36. School Psychologists	$62,210	15.8%	8,309
37. Hydrologists	$68,140	24.3%	687
38. Optometrists	$93,800	11.3%	1,789
39. Mechanical Engineers	$72,300	4.2%	12,394
40. Podiatrists	$110,510	9.5%	648
41. Computer Hardware Engineers	$91,860	4.6%	3,572
42. Electrical Engineers	$79,240	6.3%	6,806
43. Electronics Engineers, Except Computer	$83,340	3.7%	5,699
44. Computer Programmers	$68,080	–4.1%	27,937
45. Medical and Clinical Laboratory Technologists	$51,720	12.4%	11,457
46. Physicists	$96,850	6.8%	1,302
47. Diagnostic Medical Sonographers	$59,860	19.1%	3,211
48. Chemical Engineers	$81,500	7.9%	2,111
49. Operations Research Analysts	$66,950	10.6%	5,727

Best Jobs for College Graduates with an Investigative Personality Type

Job	Annual Earnings	Percent Growth	Annual Openings
50. Chemists	$63,490	9.1%	9,024
51. Biologists	$64,920	9.2%	6,288
52. Nuclear Medicine Technologists	$64,670	14.8%	1,290

Jobs 2, 3, 4, 5, 6, and 7 share 38,027 openings. Job 14 shares 37,010 openings with another job not included in this list. Jobs 20 and 22 share 14,374 openings with each other and with three other jobs not included in this list. Jobs 34 and 36 share 8,309 openings with each other and with another job not included in this list.

Best Jobs for College Graduates with an Artistic Personality Type

Job	Annual Earnings	Percent Growth	Annual Openings
1. Multi-Media Artists and Animators	$54,550	25.8%	13,182
2. Architects, Except Landscape and Naval	$67,620	17.7%	11,324
3. Technical Writers	$60,390	19.5%	7,498
4. Art Directors	$72,320	9.0%	9,719
5. Poets, Lyricists and Creative Writers	$50,660	12.8%	24,023
6. Interior Designers	$43,970	19.5%	8,434
7. Graphic Designers	$41,280	9.8%	26,968
8. Landscape Architects	$57,580	16.4%	2,342

Job 5 shares 24,023 openings with another job not included in this list.

Best Jobs for College Graduates with a Social Personality Type

Job	Annual Earnings	Percent Growth	Annual Openings
1. Health Specialties Teachers, Postsecondary	$80,700	22.9%	19,617
2. Registered Nurses	$60,010	23.5%	233,499
3. Physical Therapists	$69,760	27.1%	12,072
4. Dental Hygienists	$64,740	30.1%	10,433
5. Physician Assistants	$78,450	27.0%	7,147
6. Biological Science Teachers, Postsecondary	$71,780	22.9%	9,039
7. Business Teachers, Postsecondary	$64,900	22.9%	11,643
8. Occupational Therapists	$63,790	23.1%	8,338
9. Law Teachers, Postsecondary	$87,730	22.9%	2,169

(continued)

(continued)

Best Jobs for College Graduates with a Social Personality Type

Job	Annual Earnings	Percent Growth	Annual Openings
10. Economics Teachers, Postsecondary	$75,300	22.9%	2,208
11. Agricultural Sciences Teachers, Postsecondary	$78,460	22.9%	1,840
12. Art, Drama, and Music Teachers, Postsecondary	$55,190	22.9%	12,707
13. Computer Science Teachers, Postsecondary	$62,020	22.9%	5,820
14. Radiation Therapists	$70,010	24.8%	1,461
15. Chemistry Teachers, Postsecondary	$63,870	22.9%	3,405
16. Mental Health Counselors	$36,000	30.0%	24,103
17. Physics Teachers, Postsecondary	$70,090	22.9%	2,155
18. Substance Abuse and Behavioral Disorder Counselors	$35,580	34.3%	20,821
19. Atmospheric, Earth, Marine, and Space Sciences Teachers, Postsecondary	$73,280	22.9%	1,553
20. Mathematical Science Teachers, Postsecondary	$58,560	22.9%	7,663
21. English Language and Literature Teachers, Postsecondary	$54,000	22.9%	10,475
22. Psychology Teachers, Postsecondary	$60,610	22.9%	5,261
23. Education Teachers, Postsecondary	$54,220	22.9%	9,359
24. Nursing Instructors and Teachers, Postsecondary	$57,500	22.9%	7,337
25. Medical and Public Health Social Workers	$44,670	24.2%	16,429
26. Mental Health and Substance Abuse Social Workers	$36,640	29.9%	17,289
27. History Teachers, Postsecondary	$59,160	22.9%	3,570
28. Political Science Teachers, Postsecondary	$63,100	22.9%	2,435
29. Architecture Teachers, Postsecondary	$68,540	22.9%	1,044
30. Health Educators	$42,920	26.2%	13,707
31. Rehabilitation Counselors	$29,630	23.0%	32,081
32. Anthropology and Archeology Teachers, Postsecondary	$64,530	22.9%	910
33. Environmental Science Teachers, Postsecondary	$64,850	22.9%	769
34. Physical Therapist Assistants	$44,130	32.4%	5,957
35. Sociology Teachers, Postsecondary	$58,160	22.9%	2,774
36. Communications Teachers, Postsecondary	$54,720	22.9%	4,074
37. Graduate Teaching Assistants	$28,060	22.9%	20,601
38. Philosophy and Religion Teachers, Postsecondary	$56,380	22.9%	3,120
39. Foreign Language and Literature Teachers, Postsecondary	$53,610	22.9%	4,317
40. Instructional Coordinators	$55,270	22.5%	21,294
41. Forestry and Conservation Science Teachers, Postsecondary	$63,790	22.9%	454
42. Marriage and Family Therapists	$43,600	29.8%	5,953

Best Jobs for College Graduates with a Social Personality Type

Job	Annual Earnings	Percent Growth	Annual Openings
43. Area, Ethnic, and Cultural Studies Teachers, Postsecondary	$59,150	22.9%	1,252
44. Geography Teachers, Postsecondary	$61,310	22.9%	697
45. Recreation and Fitness Studies Teachers, Postsecondary	$52,170	22.9%	3,010
46. Training and Development Specialists	$49,630	18.3%	35,862
47. Education Administrators, Preschool and Child Care Center/Program	$38,580	23.5%	8,113
48. Home Economics Teachers, Postsecondary	$58,170	22.9%	820
49. Counseling Psychologists	$62,210	15.8%	8,309
50. Social Work Teachers, Postsecondary	$56,240	22.9%	1,292
51. Occupational Therapist Assistants	$45,050	25.4%	2,634
52. Elementary School Teachers, Except Special Education	$47,330	13.6%	181,612
53. Criminal Justice and Law Enforcement Teachers, Postsecondary	$51,060	22.9%	1,911
54. Educational, Vocational, and School Counselors	$49,450	12.6%	54,025
55. Library Science Teachers, Postsecondary	$56,810	22.9%	702
56. Speech-Language Pathologists	$60,690	10.6%	11,160
57. Secondary School Teachers, Except Special and Vocational Education	$49,420	5.6%	93,166
58. Special Education Teachers, Preschool, Kindergarten, and Elementary School	$48,350	19.6%	20,049
59. Chiropractors	$65,890	14.4%	3,179
60. Middle School Teachers, Except Special and Vocational Education	$47,900	11.2%	75,270
61. Kindergarten Teachers, Except Special Education	$45,120	16.3%	27,603
62. Child, Family, and School Social Workers	$38,620	19.1%	35,402
63. Clergy	$40,460	18.9%	35,092
64. Adult Literacy, Remedial Education, and GED Teachers and Instructors	$44,710	14.2%	17,340
65. Recreation Workers	$21,220	12.7%	61,454
66. Respiratory Therapists	$50,070	22.6%	5,563
67. Special Education Teachers, Middle School	$48,940	15.8%	8,846
68. Probation Officers and Correctional Treatment Specialists	$44,510	10.9%	18,335

Job 49 shares 8,309 openings with two other jobs not included in this list.

Best Jobs for College Graduates with an Enterprising Personality Type

Job	Annual Earnings	Percent Growth	Annual Openings
1. Computer and Information Systems Managers	$108,070	16.4%	30,887
2. Sales Agents, Financial Services	$68,430	24.8%	47,750
3. Sales Agents, Securities and Commodities	$68,430	24.8%	47,750
4. Financial Managers, Branch or Department	$95,310	12.6%	57,589
5. Lawyers	$106,120	11.0%	49,445
6. Marketing Managers	$104,400	14.4%	20,189
7. Construction Managers	$76,230	15.7%	44,158
8. Medical and Health Services Managers	$76,990	16.4%	31,877
9. Personal Financial Advisors	$67,660	41.0%	17,114
10. Public Relations Specialists	$49,800	17.6%	51,216
11. Sales Managers	$94,910	10.2%	36,392
12. General and Operations Managers	$88,700	1.5%	112,072
13. Social and Community Service Managers	$54,530	24.7%	23,788
14. Employment Interviewers	$44,380	18.4%	33,588
15. Personnel Recruiters	$44,380	18.4%	33,588
16. Human Resources Managers	$87,180	12.5%	17,081
17. Public Relations Managers	$86,470	16.9%	5,781
18. Chief Executives	$145,600+	2.0%	21,209
19. Education Administrators, Postsecondary	$75,780	14.2%	17,121
20. Insurance Sales Agents	$44,110	12.9%	64,162
21. Property, Real Estate, and Community Association Managers	$43,670	15.1%	49,916
22. Logisticians	$64,250	17.3%	9,671
23. Education Administrators, Elementary and Secondary School	$80,580	7.6%	27,143
24. Administrative Services Managers	$70,990	11.7%	19,513
25. Training and Development Managers	$84,340	15.6%	3,759
26. Engineering Managers	$111,020	7.3%	7,404
27. Copy Writers	$50,660	12.8%	24,023
28. Natural Sciences Managers	$104,040	11.4%	3,661
29. Directors, Religious Activities and Education	$35,370	19.7%	11,463
30. Compensation and Benefits Managers	$81,410	12.0%	6,121
31. Meeting and Convention Planners	$43,530	19.9%	8,318
32. Appraisers, Real Estate	$46,130	16.9%	6,493
33. Curators	$46,000	23.3%	1,416
34. Directors—Stage, Motion Pictures, Television, and Radio	$61,090	11.1%	8,992
35. Producers	$61,090	11.1%	8,992

Best Jobs for College Graduates with an Enterprising Personality Type

Job	Annual Earnings	Percent Growth	Annual Openings
36. Program Directors	$61,090	11.1%	8,992
37. Sales Engineers	$80,270	8.5%	7,371
38. Judges, Magistrate Judges, and Magistrates	$107,230	5.1%	1,567
39. Purchasing Managers	$85,440	3.4%	7,243
40. Advertising and Promotions Managers	$78,250	6.2%	2,955
41. Agents and Business Managers of Artists, Performers, and Athletes	$66,440	9.6%	3,940
42. Financial Examiners	$66,670	10.7%	2,449

Jobs 2 and 3 share 47,750 openings. Job 4 shares 57,589 openings with another job not included in this list. Jobs 14 and 15 share 33,588 openings. Job 27 shares 24,023 openings with another job not included in this list. Job 32 shares 6,493 openings with another job not included in this list. Job 34, 35, and 36 share 8,992 openings with each other and with two other jobs not included in this list.

Best Jobs for College Graduates with a Conventional Personality Type

Job	Annual Earnings	Percent Growth	Annual Openings
1. Financial Analysts	$70,400	33.8%	29,317
2. Treasurers and Controllers	$95,310	12.6%	57,589
3. Accountants	$57,060	17.7%	134,463
4. Auditors	$57,060	17.7%	134,463
5. Computer Security Specialists	$64,690	27.0%	37,010
6. Actuaries	$85,690	23.7%	3,245
7. Cost Estimators	$54,920	18.5%	38,379
8. Database Administrators	$67,250	28.6%	8,258
9. Network Designers	$71,510	15.1%	14,374
10. Web Administrators	$71,510	15.1%	14,374
11. Web Developers	$71,510	15.1%	14,374
12. Medical Records and Health Information Technicians	$29,290	17.8%	39,048
13. Paralegals and Legal Assistants	$44,990	22.2%	22,756
14. Compensation, Benefits, and Job Analysis Specialists	$52,180	18.4%	18,761
15. Loan Officers	$53,000	11.5%	54,237
16. Legal Secretaries	$38,810	11.7%	38,682
17. Assessors	$46,130	16.9%	6,493
18. Statisticians	$69,900	8.5%	3,433

Job 2 shares 57,589 openings with another job not included in this list. Jobs 3 and 4 share 134,463 openings. Job 5 shares 37,010 openings with another job not included in this list. Jobs 9, 10, and 11 share 14,374 openings with each other and with two other jobs not included in this list. Job 17 shares 6,493 openings with another job not included in this list.

Bonus Lists: Jobs with the Greatest Changes in Outlook Since the Previous Edition

The previous edition of this book, which came out in 2006, used job-growth figures from the Bureau of Labor Statistics that were projected for the period from 2002 to 2012. Since that edition was prepared, the BLS has updated its projections twice, based on the latest economic data and improvements to their forecasting models.

Some jobs now are expected to have much better job growth than was previously projected, but on balance the new BLS projections are less optimistic. For all the jobs with BLS projections, the average anticipated growth has changed from 14.8 percent to 10.4 percent. For the 194 jobs that were included in both editions of this book, projected growth has changed from an average of 22.2 percent to 16.6 percent.

We thought you might be interested in seeing which 25 jobs had the greatest *increases* and greatest *decreases* in job-growth projection between the two editions, so we compiled the following two lists.

25 Jobs with the Greatest Increase in Job-Growth Projection

Job	Projected Job Growth 2002–2012	Projected Job Growth 2006–2016	Change in Forecast
1. Surveyors	4.2%	23.7%	19.5%
2. Aerospace Engineers	−5.2%	10.2%	15.4%
3. Financial Analysts	18.7%	33.8%	15.1%
4. Forensic Science Technicians	18.9%	30.7%	11.8%
5. Sales Agents, Financial Services	13.0%	24.8%	11.8%
6. Sales Agents, Securities and Commodities	13.0%	24.8%	11.8%
7. Substance Abuse and Behavioral Disorder Counselors	23.3%	34.3%	11.0%
8. Geoscientists, Except Hydrologists and Geographers	11.5%	21.9%	10.4%
9. Civil Engineers	8.0%	18.0%	10.0%
10. Multi-Media Artists and Animators	15.8%	25.8%	10.0%
11. Veterinarians	25.1%	35.0%	9.9%
12. Industrial Engineers	10.6%	20.3%	9.7%
13. Actuaries	14.9%	23.7%	8.8%
14. Chemical Engineers	0.4%	7.9%	7.5%
15. Marriage and Family Therapists	22.4%	29.8%	7.4%
16. Prosthodontists	4.1%	10.7%	6.6%
17. Personal Financial Advisors	34.6%	41.0%	6.4%
18. Curators	17.0%	23.3%	6.3%

25 Jobs with the Greatest Increase in Job-Growth Projection

Job	Projected Job Growth 2002–2012	Projected Job Growth 2006–2016	Change in Forecast
19. Industrial-Organizational Psychologists	16.0%	21.3%	5.3%
20. Cartographers and Photogrammetrists	15.1%	20.3%	5.2%
21. Dentists, General	4.1%	9.2%	5.1%
22. Orthodontists	4.1%	9.2%	5.1%
23. Oral and Maxillofacial Surgeons	4.1%	9.1%	5.0%
24. Insurance Sales Agents	8.4%	12.9%	4.5%
25. Operations Research Analysts	6.2%	10.6%	4.4%

25 Jobs with the Greatest Decrease in Job-Growth Projections

Job	Projected Job Growth 2002–2012	Projected Job Growth 2006–2016	Change in Forecast
1. Medical Records and Health Information Technicians	46.8%	17.8%	−29.0%
2. Physician Assistants	48.9%	27.0%	−21.9%
3. Sales Managers	30.5%	10.2%	−20.3%
4. Computer and Information Systems Managers	36.1%	16.4%	−19.7%
5. Advertising and Promotions Managers	25.0%	6.2%	−18.8%
6. Computer Programmers	14.6%	−4.1%	−18.7%
7. Agents and Business Managers of Artists, Performers, and Athletes	27.8%	9.6%	−18.2%
8. Computer Support Specialists	30.3%	12.9%	−17.4%
9. Computer Software Engineers, Systems Software	45.5%	28.2%	−17.3%
10. General and Operations Managers	18.4%	1.5%	−16.9%
11. Speech-Language Pathologists	27.2%	10.6%	−16.6%
12. Database Administrators	44.2%	28.6%	−15.6%
13. Public Relations Specialists	32.9%	17.6%	−15.3%
14. Agricultural Sciences Teachers, Postsecondary	38.1%	22.9%	−15.2%
15. Anthropology and Archeology Teachers, Postsecondary	38.1%	22.9%	−15.2%
16. Architecture Teachers, Postsecondary	38.1%	22.9%	−15.2%
17. Area, Ethnic, and Cultural Studies Teachers, Postsecondary	38.1%	22.9%	−15.2%
18. Art, Drama, and Music Teachers, Postsecondary	38.1%	22.9%	−15.2%
19. Atmospheric, Earth, Marine, and Space Sciences Teachers, Postsecondary	38.1%	22.9%	−15.2%
20. Biological Science Teachers, Postsecondary	38.1%	22.9%	−15.2%

(continued)

(continued)

25 Jobs with the Greatest Decrease in Job-Growth Projections

Job	Projected Job Growth 2002–2012	Projected Job Growth 2006–2016	Change in Forecast
21. Business Teachers, Postsecondary	38.1%	22.9%	–15.2%
22. Chemistry Teachers, Postsecondary	38.1%	22.9%	–15.2%
23. Communications Teachers, Postsecondary	38.1%	22.9%	–15.2%
24. Computer Science Teachers, Postsecondary	38.1%	22.9%	–15.2%
25. Criminal Justice and Law Enforcement Teachers, Postsecondary	38.1%	22.9%	–15.2%

PART II

The Job Descriptions

This part provides descriptions for all the jobs included in one or more of the lists in Part I. The Introduction gives more details on how to use and interpret the job descriptions, but here is some additional information:

❋ Job descriptions are arranged in alphabetical order by job title. This approach allows you to quickly find a description if you know its correct title from one of the lists in Part I.

❋ If you are using this section to browse for interesting options, we suggest you begin with the Table of Contents. Part I features many interesting lists that will help you identify job titles to explore in more detail. If you have not browsed the lists in Part I, consider spending some time there. The lists are interesting and will help you identify job titles you can find described in the material that follows. The job titles in Part II are also listed in the table of contents.

Accountants

❋ Education/Training Required:
Bachelor's degree

❋ Annual Earnings: $57,060

❋ Beginning Wage: $35,570

❋ Earnings Growth Potential: Medium

❋ Growth: 17.7%

❋ Annual Job Openings: 134,463

❋ Self-Employed: 9.5%

❋ Part-Time: 9.3%

The job openings listed here are shared with Auditors.

Analyze financial information and prepare financial reports to determine or maintain record of assets, liabilities, profit and loss, tax liability, or other financial activities within an organization. Prepare, examine, or analyze accounting records, financial statements, or other financial reports to assess accuracy, completeness, and conformance to reporting and procedural standards. Compute taxes owed and prepare tax returns, ensuring compliance with payment, reporting, or other tax requirements. Analyze business operations, trends, costs, revenues, financial commitments, and obligations to project future revenues and expenses or to provide advice. Report to management regarding the finances of establishment. Establish tables of accounts and assign entries to proper accounts. Develop, maintain, and analyze budgets, preparing periodic reports that compare budgeted costs to actual costs. Develop, implement, modify, and document recordkeeping and accounting systems, making use of current computer technology. Prepare forms and manuals for accounting and bookkeeping personnel and direct their work activities. Survey operations to ascertain accounting needs and to recommend, develop, or maintain solutions to business and financial problems. Work as Internal Revenue Service (IRS) agents. Advise management about issues such as resource utilization, tax strategies, and the assumptions underlying budget forecasts. Provide internal and external auditing services for businesses or individuals. Advise clients in areas such as compensation, employee health-care benefits, the design of accounting or data processing systems, or long-range tax or estate plans. Investigate bankruptcies and other complex financial transactions and prepare reports summarizing the findings. Represent clients before taxing authorities and provide support during litigation involving financial issues. Appraise, evaluate, and inventory real property and equipment, recording information such as the description, value, and location of property. Maintain or examine the records of government agencies. Serve as bankruptcy trustees or business valuators.

Personality Type: Conventional. These occupations frequently involve following set procedures and routines and can include working with data and details more than with ideas. Usually there is a clear line of authority to follow.

GOE—Interest Area/Cluster: 04. Business and Administration. **Work Group:** 04.05. Accounting, Auditing, and Analytical Support. **Other Jobs in This Work Group:** Accountants and Auditors; Auditors; Budget Analysts; Industrial Engineering Technicians; Logisticians; Management Analysts; Operations Research Analysts.

Skills—Management of Financial Resources: Determining how money will be spent to get the work done and accounting for these expenditures. **Systems Analysis:** Determining how a system should work and how changes will affect outcomes. **Systems Evaluation:** Looking at many indicators of system performance and taking into account their accuracy. **Operations Analysis:** Analyzing needs and product requirements to create a design. **Judgment and Decision Making:** Weighing the relative costs and benefits of a potential action.

Programming: Writing computer programs for various purposes. **Mathematics:** Using mathematics to solve problems. **Time Management:** Managing one's own time and the time of others.

Education and Training Programs: Accounting and Computer Science; Accounting; Accounting and Finance; Accounting and Business/Management. **Related Knowledge/Courses—Economics and Accounting:** Economic and accounting principles and practices, the financial markets, banking, and the analysis and reporting of financial data. **Clerical Practices:** Administrative and clerical procedures and systems such as word-processing systems, filing and records management systems, stenography and transcription, forms, design principles, and other office procedures and terminology. **Mathematics:** Numbers and their operations and interrelationships, including arithmetic, algebra, geometry, calculus, and statistics and their applications. **Law and Government:** Laws, legal codes, court procedures, precedents, government regulations, executive orders, agency rules, and the democratic political process. **Computers and Electronics:** Electric circuit boards, processors, chips, and computer hardware and software, including applications and programming. **Personnel and Human Resources:** Principles and procedures for personnel recruitment; selection; training; compensation and benefits; labor relations and negotiation; and personnel information systems.

Work Environment: Indoors; sitting.

Actuaries

- ❀ Education/Training Required: Work experience plus degree
- ❀ Annual Earnings: $85,690
- ❀ Beginning Wage: $48,750
- ❀ Earnings Growth Potential: High
- ❀ Growth: 23.7%
- ❀ Annual Job Openings: 3,245
- ❀ Self-Employed: 0.0%
- ❀ Part-Time: 5.9%

Analyze statistical data, such as mortality, accident, sickness, disability, and retirement rates, and construct probability tables to forecast risk and liability for payment of future benefits. May ascertain premium rates required and cash reserves necessary to ensure payment of future benefits. Ascertain premium rates required and cash reserves and liabilities necessary to ensure payment of future benefits. Analyze statistical information to estimate mortality, accident, sickness, disability, and retirement rates. Design, review, and help administer insurance, annuity, and pension plans, determining financial soundness and calculating premiums. Collaborate with programmers, underwriters, accountants, claims experts, and senior management to help companies develop plans for new lines of business or for improving existing business. Determine or help determine company policy and explain complex technical matters to company executives, government officials, shareholders, policyholders, or the public. Testify before public agencies on proposed legislation affecting businesses. Provide advice to clients on a contract basis, working as a consultant. Testify in court as expert witness or to provide legal evidence on matters such as the value of potential lifetime earnings of a person who is disabled or killed in an accident. Construct probability tables for events such as fires, natural disasters, and unemployment, based on analysis of statistical data and other pertinent information. Determine policy contract provisions for each type of insurance. Manage credit and help price corporate security offerings. Provide expertise to help financial institutions manage risks and maximize returns associated with investment products or credit offerings. Determine equitable basis for distributing surplus earnings under participating insurance and annuity contracts in mutual companies. Explain changes in contract provisions to customers.

Personality Type: Conventional. These occupations frequently involve following set procedures and routines and can include working with data and details more than with ideas. Usually there is a clear line of authority to follow.

GOE—Interest Area/Cluster: 15. Scientific Research, Engineering, and Mathematics. **Work Group:** 15.06. Mathematics and Data Analysis. **Other Jobs in This Work Group:** Mathematical Technicians; Mathematicians; Social Science Research Assistants; Statisticians.

Skills—Programming: Writing computer programs for various purposes. **Mathematics:** Using mathematics to solve problems. **Operations Analysis:** Analyzing needs and product requirements to create a design. **Complex Problem Solving:** Identifying complex problems, reviewing the options, and implementing solutions. **Active Learning:** Working with new material or information to grasp its implications. **Quality Control Analysis:** Evaluating the quality or performance of products, services, or processes. **Troubleshooting:** Determining what is causing an operating error and deciding what to do about it. **Critical Thinking:** Using logic and analysis to identify the strengths and weaknesses of different approaches.

Education and Training Program: Actuarial Science. **Related Knowledge/Courses—Mathematics:** Numbers and their operations and interrelationships, including arithmetic, algebra, geometry, calculus, and statistics and their applications. **Economics and Accounting:** Economic and accounting principles and practices, the financial markets, banking, and the analysis and reporting of financial data. **Sales and Marketing:** Principles and methods involved in showing, promoting, and selling products or services. This includes marketing strategies and tactics, product demonstration and sales techniques, and sales control systems. **Computers and Electronics:** Electric circuit boards, processors, chips, and computer hardware and software, including applications and programming. **Personnel and Human Resources:** Principles and procedures for personnel recruitment; selection; training; compensation and benefits; labor relations and negotiation; and personnel information systems. **Law and Government:** Laws, legal codes, court procedures, precedents, government regulations, executive orders, agency rules, and the democratic political process.

Work Environment: Indoors; sitting; using hands on objects, tools, or controls; repetitive motions.

Administrative Services Managers

- ❀ Education/Training Required: Work experience plus degree
- ❀ Annual Earnings: $70,990
- ❀ Beginning Wage: $36,000
- ❀ Earnings Growth Potential: High
- ❀ Growth: 11.7%
- ❀ Annual Job Openings: 19,513
- ❀ Self-Employed: 0.6%
- ❀ Part-Time: 4.7%

Plan, direct, or coordinate supportive services of an organization, such as recordkeeping, mail distribution, telephone operator/receptionist, and other office support services. May oversee facilities planning and maintenance and custodial operations. Monitor the facility to ensure that it remains safe, secure, and well-maintained. Direct or coordinate the supportive services department of a business, agency, or organization. Set goals and deadlines for the department. Prepare and review operational reports and schedules to ensure accuracy and efficiency. Analyze internal processes and recommend and implement procedural or policy changes to improve operations such as supply changes or the disposal of records. Acquire, distribute, and store supplies. Plan, administer, and control budgets for contracts, equipment, and supplies. Oversee construction and renovation projects to improve efficiency and to ensure that facilities meet environmental, health, and security standards and comply with government regulations. Hire and terminate clerical and administrative personnel. Oversee the maintenance and repair of machinery, equipment, and electrical and mechanical systems. Manage leasing of facility space. Participate in architectural and engineering planning and design, including space and installation management. Conduct classes to teach procedures to staff. Dispose of, or oversee the disposal of, surplus or unclaimed property.

Personality Type: Enterprising. These occupations frequently involve starting up and carrying out projects and can involve leading people and making many decisions. They sometimes require risk taking and often deal with business.

GOE—Interest Area/Cluster: 04. Business and Administration. **Work Group:** 04.02. Managerial Work in Business Detail. **Other Jobs in This Work Group:** Meeting and Convention Planners.

Skills—Management of Financial Resources: Determining how money will be spent to get the work done and accounting for these expenditures. **Management of Personnel Resources:** Motivating, developing, and directing people as they work; identifying the best people for the job. **Programming:** Writing computer programs for various purposes. **Service Orientation:** Actively looking for ways to help people. **Coordination:** Adjusting actions in relation to others' actions. **Monitoring:** Assessing how well one is doing when learning or doing something. **Writing:** Communicating effectively with others in writing as indicated by the needs of the audience. **Speaking:** Talking to others to effectively convey information.

Education and Training Programs: Public Administration; Medical/Health Management and Clinical Assistant/Specialist; Business/Commerce, General; Business Administration and Management, General; Purchasing, Procurement/Acquisitions and Contracts Management; Transportation/Transportation Management. **Related Knowledge/Courses—Personnel and Human Resources:** Principles and procedures for personnel recruitment; selection; training; compensation and benefits; labor relations and negotiation; and personnel information systems. **Clerical Practices:** Administrative and clerical procedures and systems such as word-processing systems, filing and records management systems, stenography and transcription, forms, design principles, and other office procedures and terminology. **Economics and Accounting:** Economic and accounting principles and practices, the financial markets, banking, and the analysis and reporting of financial data. **Administration and Management:** Principles and processes involved in business and organizational planning, coordination, and execution. This includes strategic planning, resource allocation, manpower modeling, leadership techniques, and production methods. **Customer and Personal Service:** Principles and processes for providing customer and personal services, including needs assessment techniques, quality service standards, alternative delivery systems, and customer satisfaction evaluation techniques. **Law and Government:** Laws, legal codes, court procedures, precedents, government regulations, executive orders, agency rules, and the democratic political process.

Work Environment: Indoors; more often standing than sitting.

Adult Literacy, Remedial Education, and GED Teachers and Instructors

* Education/Training Required: Bachelor's degree
* Annual Earnings: $44,710
* Beginning Wage: $25,310
* Earnings Growth Potential: High
* Growth: 14.2%
* Annual Job Openings: 17,340
* Self-Employed: 0.0%
* Part-Time: 41.3%

Teach or instruct out-of-school youths and adults in remedial education classes, preparatory classes for the General Educational Development test, literacy, or English as a Second Language. Teaching may or may not take place in a traditional educational institution. Adapt teaching methods and instructional materials to meet students' varying needs, abilities, and interests. Observe and evaluate students' work to determine progress and make suggestions for improvement. Instruct students individually and in groups, using various teaching methods such as lectures, discussions, and demonstrations. Plan and conduct activities for a balanced program of instruction, demonstration, and work time that provides students with opportunities to observe, question, and investigate. Maintain accurate and complete student records as required by laws or administrative policies. Prepare materials and classrooms for class activities. Establish clear objectives for all lessons, units, and projects and communicate those objectives to students. Conduct classes, workshops, and demonstrations to teach principles, techniques, or methods in subjects such as basic English language skills, life skills, and workforce entry skills. Prepare students for further education by encouraging them to explore learning opportunities and to persevere with challenging tasks. Establish and enforce rules for behavior and procedures for maintaining order among the students for whom they are responsible. Provide information, guidance, and preparation for the General Equivalency Diploma (GED) examination. Assign and grade classwork and homework. Observe students to determine qualifications, limitations, abilities, interests, and other individual characteristics. Register, orient, and assess new students according to standards and procedures. Prepare and implement remedial programs for students requiring extra help. Prepare and administer written, oral, and performance tests and issue grades in accordance with performance. Use computers, audio-visual aids, and other equipment and materials to supplement presentations. Prepare objectives and outlines for courses of study, following curriculum guidelines or requirements of states and schools. Guide and counsel students with adjustment or academic problems or special academic interests. Enforce administration policies and rules governing students.

Personality Type: Social. These occupations frequently involve working with, communicating with, and teaching people and often involve helping or providing service to others.

GOE—Interest Area/Cluster: 05. Education and Training. **Work Group:** 05.03. Postsecondary and

Adult Teaching and Instructing. **Other Jobs in This Work Group:** Agricultural Sciences Teachers, Postsecondary; Anthropology and Archeology Teachers, Postsecondary; Architecture Teachers, Postsecondary; Area, Ethnic, and Cultural Studies Teachers, Postsecondary; Art, Drama, and Music Teachers, Postsecondary; Atmospheric, Earth, Marine, and Space Sciences Teachers, Postsecondary; Biological Science Teachers, Postsecondary; Business Teachers, Postsecondary; Chemistry Teachers, Postsecondary; Communications Teachers, Postsecondary; Computer Science Teachers, Postsecondary; Criminal Justice and Law Enforcement Teachers, Postsecondary; Economics Teachers, Postsecondary; Education Teachers, Postsecondary; Engineering Teachers, Postsecondary; English Language and Literature Teachers, Postsecondary; Environmental Science Teachers, Postsecondary; Farm and Home Management Advisors; Foreign Language and Literature Teachers, Postsecondary; Forestry and Conservation Science Teachers, Postsecondary; Geography Teachers, Postsecondary; Graduate Teaching Assistants; Health Specialties Teachers, Postsecondary; History Teachers, Postsecondary; Home Economics Teachers, Postsecondary; Law Teachers, Postsecondary; Library Science Teachers, Postsecondary; Mathematical Science Teachers, Postsecondary; Nursing Instructors and Teachers, Postsecondary; Philosophy and Religion Teachers, Postsecondary; Physics Teachers, Postsecondary; Political Science Teachers, Postsecondary; Psychology Teachers, Postsecondary; Recreation and Fitness Studies Teachers, Postsecondary; Social Work Teachers, Postsecondary; Sociology Teachers, Postsecondary.

Skills—Instructing: Teaching others how to do something. **Learning Strategies:** Using multiple approaches when learning or teaching new things. **Social Perceptiveness:** Being aware of others' reactions and understanding why they react the way they do. **Service Orientation:** Actively looking for ways to help people. **Monitoring:** Assessing how well one is doing when learning or doing something. **Speaking:** Talking to others to effectively convey information. **Persuasion:** Persuading others to approach things differently. **Writing:** Communicating effectively with others in writing as indicated by the needs of the audience.

Education and Training Programs: Bilingual and Multilingual Education; Multicultural Education; Adult and Continuing Education and Teaching; Teaching English as a Second or Foreign Language/ESL Language Instructor; Teaching French as a Second or Foreign Language; Adult Literacy Tutor/Instructor; Linguistics of ASL and Other Sign Languages. **Related Knowledge/ Courses—History and Archeology:** Historical events and their causes, indicators, and impact on particular civilizations and cultures. **Sociology and Anthropology:** Group behavior and dynamics; societal trends and influences; and cultures and their history, migrations, ethnicity, and origins. **Therapy and Counseling:** Information and techniques needed to rehabilitate physical and mental ailments and to provide career guidance, including alternative treatments, rehabilitation equipment and its proper use, and methods to evaluate treatment effects. **Geography:** Various methods for describing the location and distribution of land, sea, and air masses, including their physical locations, relationships, and characteristics. **Education and Training:** Instructional methods and training techniques, including curriculum design principles, learning theory, group and individual teaching techniques, design of individual development plans, and test design principles. **English Language:** The structure and content of the English language, including the meaning and spelling of words, rules of composition, and grammar.

Work Environment: Indoors; more often standing than sitting.

Advertising and Promotions Managers

* Education/Training Required: Work experience plus degree
* Annual Earnings: $78,250
* Beginning Wage: $38,400
* Earnings Growth Potential: Very high
* Growth: 6.2%
* Annual Job Openings: 2,955
* Self-Employed: 13.4%
* Part-Time: 4.8%

Plan and direct advertising policies and programs or produce collateral materials, such as posters, contests, coupons, or giveaways, to create extra interest in the purchase of a product or service for a department, for an entire organization, or on an account basis. Prepare budgets and submit estimates for program costs as part of campaign plan development. Plan and prepare advertising and promotional material to increase sales of products or services, working with customers, company officials, sales departments, and advertising agencies. Assist with annual budget development. Inspect layouts and advertising copy and edit scripts, audiotapes and videotapes, and other promotional material for adherence to specifications. Coordinate activities of departments, such as sales, graphic arts, media, finance, and research. Prepare and negotiate advertising and sales contracts. Identify and develop contacts for promotional campaigns and industry programs that meet identified buyer targets, such as dealers, distributors, or consumers. Gather and organize information to plan advertising campaigns. Confer with department heads or staff to discuss topics such as contracts, selection of advertising media, or product to be advertised. Confer with clients to provide marketing or technical advice. Monitor and analyze sales promotion results to determine cost-effectiveness of promotion campaigns. Read trade journals and professional literature to stay informed on trends, innovations, and changes that affect media planning. Formulate plans to extend business with established accounts and to transact business as agent for advertising accounts. Provide presentation and product demonstration support during the introduction of new products and services to field staff and customers. Direct, motivate, and monitor the mobilization of a campaign team to advance campaign goals. Plan and execute advertising policies and strategies for organizations. Track program budgets and expenses and campaign response rates to evaluate each campaign based on program objectives and industry norms. Assemble and communicate with a strong, diverse coalition of organizations or public figures, securing their cooperation, support, and action to further campaign goals. Train and direct workers engaged in developing and producing advertisements. Coordinate with the media to disseminate advertising.

Personality Type: Enterprising. These occupations frequently involve starting up and carrying out projects and can involve leading people and making many decisions. They sometimes require risk taking and often deal with business.

GOE—Interest Area/Cluster: 14. Retail and Wholesale Sales and Service. **Work Group:** 14.01. Managerial Work in Retail/Wholesale Sales and Service. **Other Jobs in This Work Group:** Funeral Directors; Marketing Managers; Property, Real Estate, and Community Association Managers; Purchasing Managers; Sales Managers.

Skills—Management of Financial Resources: Determining how money will be spent to get the work done and accounting for these expenditures. **Service Orientation:** Actively looking for ways to help people. **Persuasion:** Persuading others to approach things differently. **Negotiation:** Bringing others together and trying to reconcile differences. **Time Management:** Managing one's own time and the time of others. **Coordination:** Adjusting actions in relation to others' actions. **Management of Personnel Resources:** Motivating, developing, and directing people as they work; identifying the best people for the job. **Judgment and Decision Making:** Weighing the relative costs and benefits of a potential action.

Education and Training Programs: Public Relations/Image Management; Advertising; Marketing/Marketing Management, General. **Related Knowledge/Courses—Sales and Marketing:** Principles and methods involved in showing, promoting, and selling products or services. This includes marketing strategies and tactics, product demonstration and sales techniques, and sales control systems. **Fine Arts:** Theory and techniques required to produce, compose, and perform works of music, dance, visual arts, drama, and sculpture. **Design:** Design techniques, principles, tools, and instruments involved in the production and use of precision technical plans, blueprints, drawings, and models. **Production and Processing:** Inputs, outputs, raw materials, waste, quality control, costs, and techniques for maximizing the manufacture and distribution of goods. **Communications and Media:** Media production, communication, and dissemination techniques and methods, including alternative ways to inform and entertain via written, oral, and visual media. **Clerical Practices:** Administrative and clerical procedures and systems such as word-processing systems, filing and records management systems, stenography and transcription, forms, design principles, and other office procedures and terminology.

Work Environment: Sitting; repetitive motions.

Aerospace Engineers

- ❋ Education/Training Required: Bachelor's degree
- ❋ Annual Earnings: $90,930
- ❋ Beginning Wage: $60,760
- ❋ Earnings Growth Potential: Low
- ❋ Growth: 10.2%
- ❋ Annual Job Openings: 6,498
- ❋ Self-Employed: 1.4%
- ❋ Part-Time: 2.6%

Perform a variety of engineering work in designing, constructing, and testing aircraft, missiles, and spacecraft. May conduct basic and applied research to evaluate adaptability of materials and equipment to aircraft design and manufacture. May recommend improvements in testing equipment and techniques. Formulate conceptual design of aeronautical or aerospace products or systems to meet customer requirements. Direct and coordinate activities of engineering or technical personnel designing, fabricating, modifying, or testing aircraft or aerospace products. Develop design criteria for aeronautical or aerospace products or systems, including testing methods, production costs, quality standards, and completion dates. Plan and conduct experimental, environmental, operational, and stress tests on models and prototypes of aircraft and aerospace systems and equipment. Evaluate product data and design from inspections and reports for conformance to engineering principles, customer requirements, and quality standards. Formulate mathematical models or other methods of computer analysis to develop, evaluate, or modify design according to customer engineering requirements. Write technical reports and other documentation, such as handbooks and bulletins, for use by engineering staff, management, and customers. Analyze project requests and proposals and engineering data to determine feasibility, productibility, cost, and production time of aerospace or aeronautical product. Review performance reports and documentation from customers and field engineers and inspect malfunctioning or damaged products to determine problem. Direct research and development programs. Evaluate and approve selection of vendors by study of past performance and new advertisements. Plan and coordinate activities concerned with investigating and resolving customers' reports of technical problems with aircraft or aerospace vehicles. Maintain records of performance reports for future reference.

Personality Type: Investigative. These occupations frequently involve working with ideas and require an extensive amount of thinking. They can involve searching for facts and figuring out problems mentally.

GOE—Interest Area/Cluster: 15. Scientific Research, Engineering, and Mathematics. **Work Group:** 15.07. Research and Design Engineering. **Other Jobs in This Work Group:** Biomedical Engineers; Chemical Engineers; Civil Engineers; Computer Hardware Engineers; Electrical Engineers; Electronics Engineers, Except Computer; Marine Architects; Marine Engineers; Marine Engineers and Naval Architects; Materials Engineers; Mechanical Engineers; Nuclear Engineers.

Skills—Science: Using scientific methods to solve problems. **Systems Evaluation:** Looking at many indicators of system performance and taking into account their accuracy. **Systems Analysis:** Determining how a system should work and how changes will affect outcomes. **Judgment and Decision Making:** Weighing the relative costs and benefits of a potential action. **Technology Design:** Generating or adapting equipment and technology to serve user needs. **Persuasion:** Persuading others to approach things differently. **Operations Analysis:** Analyzing needs and product requirements to create a design. **Management of Personnel Resources:** Motivating, developing, and directing people as they work; identifying the best people for the job.

Education and Training Program: Aerospace, Aeronautical and Astronautical Engineering. **Related Knowledge/Courses—Engineering and Technology:** Equipment, tools, and mechanical devices and their uses to produce motion, light, power, technology, and other applications. **Physics:** Physical principles, laws, and applications, including air, water, material dynamics, light, atomic principles, heat, electric theory, earth formations, and meteorological and related natural phenomena. **Design:** Design techniques, principles, tools, and instruments involved in the production and use of precision technical plans, blueprints, drawings, and models. **Mechanical Devices:** Machines and tools, including their designs, uses, benefits, repair, and maintenance. **Production and Processing:** Inputs, outputs, raw materials, waste, quality control, costs, and techniques for maximizing the manufacture and distribution of goods. **Mathematics:** Numbers and their operations and interrelationships, including arithmetic, algebra, geometry, calculus, and statistics and their applications.

Work Environment: Indoors; sitting; repetitive motions.

Agents and Business Managers of Artists, Performers, and Athletes

* Education/Training Required: Work experience plus degree
* Annual Earnings: $66,440
* Beginning Wage: $30,780
* Earnings Growth Potential: Very high
* Growth: 9.6%
* Annual Job Openings: 3,940
* Self-Employed: 55.8%
* Part-Time: 18.6%

Represent and promote artists, performers, and athletes to prospective employers. May handle contract negotiation and other business matters for clients. Manage business and financial affairs for clients, such as arranging travel and lodging, selling tickets, and directing marketing and advertising activities. Obtain information about and/or inspect performance facilities, equipment, and accommodations to ensure that they meet specifications. Negotiate with managers, promoters, union officials, and other persons regarding clients' contractual rights and obligations. Advise clients on financial and legal matters such as investments and taxes. Hire trainers or coaches to advise clients on performance matters such as training techniques or performance presentations. Prepare periodic accounting statements for clients. Keep informed of industry trends and deals. Develop contacts with individuals and organizations and apply effective strategies and techniques to ensure their clients' success. Confer with clients to develop strategies for their careers and to explain actions taken on their behalf. Conduct auditions or interviews in order to evaluate potential clients. Schedule promotional or performance engagements for clients. Arrange meetings concerning issues involving their clients. Collect fees, commissions, or other payments according to contract terms.

Personality Type: Enterprising. These occupations frequently involve starting up and carrying out projects and can involve leading people and making many decisions. They sometimes require risk taking and often deal with business.

GOE—Interest Area/Cluster: 03. Arts and Communication. **Work Group:** 03.01. Managerial Work in Arts and Communication. **Other Jobs in This Work Group:** Art Directors; Producers; Producers and Directors; Program Directors; Public Relations Managers.

Skills—Management of Financial Resources: Determining how money will be spent to get the work done and accounting for these expenditures. **Negotiation:** Bringing others together and trying to reconcile differences. **Persuasion:** Persuading others to approach things differently. **Social Perceptiveness:** Being aware of others' reactions and understanding why they react the way they do. **Speaking:** Talking to others to effectively convey information. **Coordination:** Adjusting actions in relation to others' actions. **Judgment and Decision Making:** Weighing the relative costs and benefits of a potential action. **Management of Personnel Resources:** Motivating, developing, and directing people as they work; identifying the best people for the job.

Education and Training Programs: Arts Management; Purchasing, Procurement/Acquisitions and Contracts Management. **Related Knowledge/Courses—Fine Arts:** Theory and techniques required to produce, compose, and perform works of music, dance, visual arts, drama, and sculpture. **Sales and Marketing:** Principles and methods involved in showing, promoting, and selling products or services. This includes marketing strategies and tactics, product demonstration and sales techniques, and sales control systems. **Communications and Media:** Media production, communication, and dissemination techniques and methods, including alternative ways to inform and entertain via written, oral, and visual media. **Clerical Practices:** Administrative and clerical procedures and systems such as word-processing systems, filing and records management systems, stenography and transcription, forms, design principles, and other office procedures and terminology. **Customer and Personal Service:** Principles and processes for providing customer and personal services, including needs assessment techniques, quality service standards, alternative delivery systems, and customer satisfaction evaluation techniques. **Economics and Accounting:** Economic and accounting principles and practices, the financial markets, banking, and the analysis and reporting of financial data.

Work Environment: Indoors; sitting.

Agricultural Sciences Teachers, Postsecondary

- ❋ Education/Training Required: Doctoral degree
- ❋ Annual Earnings: $78,460
- ❋ Beginning Wage: $43,050
- ❋ Earnings Growth Potential: High
- ❋ Growth: 22.9%
- ❋ Annual Job Openings: 1,840
- ❋ Self-Employed: 0.4%
- ❋ Part-Time: 27.8%

Teach courses in the agricultural sciences, including agronomy, dairy sciences, fisheries management, horticultural sciences, poultry sciences, range management, and agricultural soil conservation. Prepare course materials such as syllabi, homework assignments, and handouts. Evaluate and grade students' classwork, laboratory work, assignments, and papers. Keep abreast of developments in agriculture by reading current literature, talking with colleagues, and participating in professional conferences. Prepare and deliver lectures to undergraduate and/or graduate students on topics such as crop production, plant genetics, and soil chemistry. Initiate, facilitate, and moderate classroom discussions. Conduct research in a particular field of knowledge and publish findings in professional journals, books, and/or electronic media. Supervise laboratory sessions and fieldwork and coordinate laboratory operations. Supervise undergraduate and/or graduate teaching, internship, and research work. Compile, administer, and grade examinations or assign this work to others. Advise students on academic and vocational curricula and on career issues. Plan, evaluate, and revise curricula, course content, and course materials and methods of instruction. Maintain student attendance records, grades, and other required records. Write grant proposals to procure external research funding. Collaborate with colleagues to address teaching and research issues. Maintain regularly scheduled office hours in order to advise and assist students. Participate in student recruitment, registration, and placement activities. Select and obtain materials and supplies such as textbooks and laboratory equipment. Act as advisers to student organizations. Participate in campus and community events. Serve on academic or administrative committees that deal with institutional policies, departmental matters, and academic issues. Provide professional consulting services to government and/or industry. Perform administrative duties such as serving as department head. Compile bibliographies of specialized materials for outside reading assignments.

Personality Type: Social. These occupations frequently involve working with, communicating with, and teaching people and often involve helping or providing service to others.

GOE—Interest Area/Cluster: 05. Education and Training. **Work Group:** 05.03. Postsecondary and Adult Teaching and Instructing. **Other Jobs in This Work Group:** Adult Literacy, Remedial Education, and GED Teachers and Instructors; Anthropology and Archeology Teachers, Postsecondary; Architecture Teachers, Postsecondary; Area, Ethnic, and Cultural Studies Teachers, Postsecondary; Art, Drama, and Music Teachers, Postsecondary; Atmospheric, Earth, Marine, and Space Sciences Teachers, Postsecondary; Biological Science Teachers, Postsecondary; Business Teachers, Postsecondary; Chemistry Teachers, Postsecondary; Communications Teachers, Postsecondary; Computer Science Teachers, Postsecondary; Criminal Justice and Law Enforcement Teachers, Postsecondary; Economics Teachers, Postsecondary; Education Teachers, Postsecondary; Engineering Teachers, Postsecondary; English Language and Literature Teachers, Postsecondary; Environmental Science Teachers, Postsecondary; Farm and Home Management Advisors; Foreign Language and Literature Teachers, Postsecondary; Forestry and Conservation Science Teachers, Postsecondary; Geography Teachers, Postsecondary; Graduate Teaching Assistants; Health Specialties Teachers, Postsecondary; History Teachers, Postsecondary; Home Economics Teachers, Postsecondary; Law Teachers, Postsecondary; Library Science Teachers, Postsecondary; Mathematical Science Teachers, Postsecondary; Nursing Instructors and Teachers, Postsecondary; Philosophy and Religion Teachers, Postsecondary; Physics Teachers, Postsecondary; Political Science Teachers, Postsecondary; Psychology Teachers, Postsecondary; Recreation and Fitness Studies Teachers, Postsecondary; Social Work Teachers, Postsecondary; Sociology Teachers, Postsecondary.

Skills—Science: Using scientific methods to solve problems. **Management of Financial Resources:** Determining how money will be spent to get the work done and accounting for these expenditures. **Writing:** Communicating effectively with others in writing as indicated by the needs of the audience. **Reading Comprehension:** Understanding written sentences and paragraphs in work-related documents. **Instructing:** Teaching others how to do something. **Complex Problem Solving:** Identifying complex problems, reviewing the options, and implementing solutions. **Active Learning:** Working with new material or information to grasp its implications. **Mathematics:** Using mathematics to solve problems.

Education and Training Programs: Agriculture, General; Agricultural Business and Management, General; Agribusiness/Agricultural Business Operations; Agricultural Economics; Farm/Farm and Ranch Management; Agricultural/Farm Supplies Retailing and Wholesaling; Agricultural Business and Management, Other; Agricultural Mechanization, General; Agricultural Power Machinery Operation; Agricultural Mechanization, Other; others. **Related Knowledge/Courses—Biology:** Plant and animal living tissue, cells, organisms, and entities, including their functions, interdependencies, and interactions with each other and the environment. **Food Production:** Techniques and equipment for planting, growing, and harvesting of food for consumption, including crop-rotation methods, animal husbandry, and food storage/handling techniques. **Education and Training:** Instructional methods and training techniques, including curriculum design principles, learning theory, group and individual teaching techniques, design of individual development plans, and test design principles. **Geography:** Various methods for describing the location and distribution of land, sea, and air masses, including their physical locations, relationships, and characteristics. **Chemistry:** The composition, structure, and properties of substances and of the chemical processes and transformations that they undergo. This includes uses of chemicals and their interactions, danger signs, production techniques, and disposal methods. **Communications and Media:** Media production, communication, and dissemination techniques and methods, including alternative ways to inform and entertain via written, oral, and visual media.

Work Environment: Indoors; sitting.

Airline Pilots, Copilots, and Flight Engineers

* Education/Training Required: Bachelor's degree
* Annual Earnings: More than $145,600
* Beginning Wage: $56,540
* Earnings Growth Potential: Cannot be calculated
* Growth: 12.9%
* Annual Job Openings: 4,073
* Self-Employed: 2.5%
* Part-Time: 14.2%

Pilot and navigate the flight of multi-engine aircraft in regularly scheduled service for the transport of passengers and cargo. Requires Federal Air Transport rating and certification in specific aircraft type used. Use instrumentation to guide flights when visibility is poor. Respond to and report in-flight emergencies and malfunctions. Work as part of a flight team with other crew members, especially during takeoffs and landings. Contact control towers for takeoff clearances, arrival instructions, and other information, using radio equipment. Steer aircraft along planned routes with the assistance of autopilot and flight management computers. Monitor gauges, warning devices, and control panels to verify aircraft performance and to regulate engine speed. Start engines, operate controls, and pilot airplanes to transport passengers, mail, or freight while adhering to flight plans, regulations, and procedures. Inspect aircraft for defects and malfunctions according to pre-flight checklists. Check passenger and cargo distributions and fuel amounts to ensure that weight and balance specifications are met. Monitor engine operation, fuel consumption, and functioning of aircraft systems during flights. Confer with flight dispatchers and weather forecasters to keep abreast of flight conditions. Coordinate flight activities with ground crews and air-traffic control and inform crew members of flight and test procedures. Order changes in fuel supplies, loads, routes, or schedules to ensure safety of flights. Choose routes, altitudes, and speeds that will provide the fastest, safest, and smoothest flights. Direct activities of aircraft crews during flights. Brief crews about flight details such as destinations, duties, and responsibilities. Record in logbooks information such as flight times, distances flown, and fuel consumption. Make announcements regarding flights, using public address systems. File instrument flight plans with air traffic control to ensure that flights are coordinated with other air traffic. Perform minor maintenance work or arrange for major maintenance. Instruct other pilots and student pilots in aircraft operations and the principles of flight. Conduct in-flight tests and evaluations at specified altitudes and in all types of weather to determine the receptivity and other characteristics of equipment and systems.

Personality Type: Realistic. These occupations frequently involve work activities that include practical, hands-on problems and solutions. They often deal with plants; animals; and real-world materials such as wood, tools, and machinery. Many of the occupations require working outside and don't involve a lot of paperwork or working closely with others.

GOE—Interest Area/Cluster: 16. Transportation, Distribution, and Logistics. **Work Group:**

16.02. Air Vehicle Operation. **Other Jobs in This Work Group:** No others in group.

Skills—Operation Monitoring: Watching gauges, dials, or other indicators to make sure a machine is working properly. **Operation and Control:** Controlling operations of equipment or systems. **Systems Analysis:** Determining how a system should work and how changes will affect outcomes. **Judgment and Decision Making:** Weighing the relative costs and benefits of a potential action. **Troubleshooting:** Determining what is causing an operating error and deciding what to do about it. **Science:** Using scientific methods to solve problems. **Systems Evaluation:** Looking at many indicators of system performance and taking into account their accuracy. **Monitoring:** Assessing how well one is doing when learning or doing something.

Education and Training Programs: Airline/ Commercial/Professional Pilot and Flight Crew Training; Flight Instruction. **Related Knowledge/Courses—Transportation:** Principles and methods for moving people or goods by air, rail, sea, or road, including their relative costs, advantages, and limitations. **Geography:** Various methods for describing the location and distribution of land, sea, and air masses, including their physical locations, relationships, and characteristics. **Physics:** Physical principles, laws, and applications, including air, water, material dynamics, light, atomic principles, heat, electric theory, earth formations, and meteorological and related natural phenomena. **Public Safety and Security:** Weaponry; public safety; security operations, rules, regulations, precautions, and prevention; and the protection of people, data, and property. **Psychology:** Human behavior and performance, mental processes, psychological research methods, and the assessment and treatment of behavioral and affective disorders. **Law and Government:** Laws, legal codes, court procedures, precedents, government

regulations, executive orders, agency rules, and the democratic political process.

Work Environment: Indoors; noisy; contaminants; radiation; sitting; using hands on objects, tools, or controls.

Anesthesiologists

- ✴ Education/Training Required: First professional degree
- ✴ Annual Earnings: More than $145,600
- ✴ Beginning Wage: $118,320
- ✴ Earnings Growth Potential: Cannot be calculated
- ✴ Growth: 14.2%
- ✴ Annual Job Openings: 38,027
- ✴ Self-Employed: 14.7%
- ✴ Part-Time: 8.1%

The job openings listed here are shared with Family and General Practitioners; Internists, General; Obstetricians and Gynecologists; Pediatricians, General; Psychiatrists; and Surgeons.

Administer anesthetics during surgery or other medical procedures. Administer anesthetic or sedation during medical procedures, using local, intravenous, spinal, or caudal methods. Monitor patient before, during, and after anesthesia and counteract adverse reactions or complications. Provide and maintain life support and airway management and help prepare patients for emergency surgery. Record type and amount of anesthesia and patient condition throughout procedure. Examine patient; obtain medical history; and use diagnostic tests to determine risk during surgical, obstetrical, and other medical procedures. Position patient on operating table to maximize patient comfort and surgical accessibility. Decide when patients have recovered or stabilized enough to be sent to another room or ward or to be sent home following outpatient surgery. Coordinate administration of anesthetics with surgeons during operation. Confer with other medical professionals to determine type and method of anesthetic or sedation to render patient insensible to pain. Coordinate and direct work of nurses, medical technicians, and other health-care providers. Order laboratory tests, X rays, and other diagnostic procedures. Diagnose illnesses, using examinations, tests, and reports. Manage anesthesiological services, coordinating them with other medical activities and formulating plans and procedures. Provide medical care and consultation in many settings, prescribing medication and treatment and referring patients for surgery. Inform students and staff of types and methods of anesthesia administration, signs of complications, and emergency methods to counteract reactions. Schedule and maintain use of surgical suite, including operating, wash-up, and waiting rooms and anesthetic and sterilizing equipment. Instruct individuals and groups on ways to preserve health and prevent disease. Conduct medical research to aid in controlling and curing disease, to investigate new medications, and to develop and test new medical techniques.

Personality Type: Investigative. These occupations frequently involve working with ideas and require an extensive amount of thinking. They can involve searching for facts and figuring out problems mentally.

GOE—Interest Area/Cluster: 08. Health Science. **Work Group:** 08.02. Medicine and Surgery. **Other Jobs in This Work Group:** Family and General Practitioners; Internists, General; Obstetricians and Gynecologists; Pediatricians, General; Pharmacists; Physician Assistants; Psychiatrists; Registered Nurses; Surgeons.

Skills—Operation Monitoring: Watching gauges, dials, or other indicators to make sure a machine is working properly. **Science:** Using scientific methods to solve problems. **Operation and Control:** Controlling operations of equipment or systems. **Judgment and Decision Making:** Weighing the relative costs and benefits of a potential action. **Equipment Selection:** Determining the kind of tools and equipment needed to do a job. **Monitoring:** Assessing how well one is doing when learning or doing something. **Equipment Maintenance:** Performing routine maintenance and determining when and what kind of maintenance is needed. **Complex Problem Solving:** Identifying complex problems, reviewing the options, and implementing solutions.

Education and Training Programs: Anesthesiology; Critical Care Anesthesiology. **Related Knowledge/Courses—Medicine and Dentistry:** The information and techniques needed to diagnose and treat injuries, diseases, and deformities. This includes symptoms, treatment alternatives, drug properties and interactions, and preventive health-care measures. **Biology:** Plant and animal living tissue, cells, organisms, and entities, including their functions, interdependencies, and interactions with each other and the environment. **Chemistry:** The composition, structure, and properties of substances and of the chemical processes and transformations that they undergo. This includes uses of chemicals and their interactions, danger signs, production techniques, and disposal methods. **Psychology:** Human behavior and performance, mental processes, psychological research methods, and the assessment and treatment of behavioral and affective disorders. **Physics:** Physical principles, laws, and applications, including air, water, material dynamics, light, atomic principles, heat, electric theory, earth formations, and meteorological and related natural phenomena. **Therapy and Counseling:** Information and techniques needed to rehabilitate physical and mental ailments and to provide career guidance, including alternative treatments, rehabilitation equipment and its proper use, and methods to evaluate treatment effects.

Work Environment: Indoors; contaminants; radiation; disease or infections; standing; using hands on objects, tools, or controls.

Anthropology and Archeology Teachers, Postsecondary

- ❋ Education/Training Required: Doctoral degree
- ❋ Annual Earnings: $64,530
- ❋ Beginning Wage: $38,840
- ❋ Earnings Growth Potential: Medium
- ❋ Growth: 22.9%
- ❋ Annual Job Openings: 910
- ❋ Self-Employed: 0.4%
- ❋ Part-Time: 27.8%

Teach courses in anthropology or archeology. Conduct research in a particular field of knowledge and publish findings in professional journals, books, and electronic media. Keep abreast of developments in their field by reading current literature, talking with colleagues, and participating in professional conferences. Prepare and deliver lectures to undergraduate and graduate students on topics such as research methods, urban anthropology, and language and culture. Evaluate and grade students' classwork, assignments, and papers. Initiate, facilitate, and moderate classroom discussions. Write grant proposals to procure external research funding. Supervise undergraduate and/or graduate teaching, internship, and research work. Prepare course materials such as syllabi, homework assignments, and handouts. Compile, administer, and grade examinations or assign this work to others. Supervise students' laboratory work or fieldwork. Plan, evaluate, and revise curricula, course content, and course materials and methods of instruction. Advise students on academic and vocational curricula, career issues, and laboratory and field research. Maintain student attendance records, grades, and other required records. Maintain regularly scheduled office hours in order to advise and assist students. Collaborate with colleagues to address teaching and research issues. Compile bibliographies of specialized materials for outside reading assignments. Perform administrative duties such as serving as department head. Select and obtain materials and supplies such as textbooks and laboratory equipment. Serve on academic or administrative committees that deal with institutional policies, departmental matters, and academic issues. Participate in student recruitment, registration, and placement activities. Participate in campus and community events. Provide professional consulting services to government and industry. Act as advisers to student organizations.

Personality Type: Social. These occupations frequently involve working with, communicating with, and teaching people and often involve helping or providing service to others.

GOE—Interest Area/Cluster: 05. Education and Training. **Work Group:** 05.03. Postsecondary and Adult Teaching and Instructing. **Other Jobs in This Work Group:** Adult Literacy, Remedial Education, and GED Teachers and Instructors; Agricultural Sciences Teachers, Postsecondary; Architecture Teachers, Postsecondary; Area, Ethnic, and Cultural Studies Teachers, Postsecondary; Art, Drama, and Music Teachers, Postsecondary; Atmospheric, Earth, Marine, and Space Sciences Teachers, Postsecondary; Biological Science Teachers, Postsecondary; Business Teachers, Postsecondary; Chemistry Teachers, Postsecondary; Communications Teachers, Postsecondary; Computer Science Teachers, Postsecondary; Criminal Justice and Law Enforcement Teachers, Postsecondary; Economics Teachers, Postsecondary; Education Teachers, Postsecondary; Engineering Teachers, Postsecondary; English

Language and Literature Teachers, Postsecondary; Environmental Science Teachers, Postsecondary; Farm and Home Management Advisors; Foreign Language and Literature Teachers, Postsecondary; Forestry and Conservation Science Teachers, Postsecondary; Geography Teachers, Postsecondary; Graduate Teaching Assistants; Health Specialties Teachers, Postsecondary; History Teachers, Postsecondary; Home Economics Teachers, Postsecondary; Law Teachers, Postsecondary; Library Science Teachers, Postsecondary; Mathematical Science Teachers, Postsecondary; Nursing Instructors and Teachers, Postsecondary; Philosophy and Religion Teachers, Postsecondary; Physics Teachers, Postsecondary; Political Science Teachers, Postsecondary; Psychology Teachers, Postsecondary; Recreation and Fitness Studies Teachers, Postsecondary; Social Work Teachers, Postsecondary; Sociology Teachers, Postsecondary.

Skills—Science: Using scientific methods to solve problems. **Writing:** Communicating effectively with others in writing as indicated by the needs of the audience. **Critical Thinking:** Using logic and analysis to identify the strengths and weaknesses of different approaches. **Reading Comprehension:** Understanding written sentences and paragraphs in work-related documents. **Active Learning:** Working with new material or information to grasp its implications. **Instructing:** Teaching others how to do something. **Management of Financial Resources:** Determining how money will be spent to get the work done and accounting for these expenditures. **Active Listening:** Listening to what other people are saying and asking questions as appropriate.

Education and Training Programs: Social Science Teacher Education; Anthropology; Physical Anthropology; Archeology. **Related Knowledge/ Courses—Sociology and Anthropology:** Group behavior and dynamics; societal trends and influences; and cultures and their history, migrations, ethnicity, and origins. **History and Archeology:** Historical events and their causes, indicators, and impact on particular civilizations and cultures. **Geography:** Various methods for describing the location and distribution of land, sea, and air masses, including their physical locations, relationships, and characteristics. **Foreign Language:** The structure and content of a foreign (non-English) language, including the meaning and spelling of words, rules of composition and grammar, and pronunciation. **Philosophy and Theology:** Different philosophical systems and religions, including their basic principles, values, ethics, ways of thinking, customs, and practices and their impact on human culture. **English Language:** The structure and content of the English language, including the meaning and spelling of words, rules of composition, and grammar.

Work Environment: Indoors; sitting.

Appraisers, Real Estate

- ❋ Education/Training Required: Bachelor's degree
- ❋ Annual Earnings: $46,130
- ❋ Beginning Wage: $25,110
- ❋ Earnings Growth Potential: High
- ❋ Growth: 16.9%
- ❋ Annual Job Openings: 6,493
- ❋ Self-Employed: 32.7%
- ❋ Part-Time: 8.4%

The job openings listed here are shared with Assessors.

Appraise real property to determine its value for purchase, sales, investment, mortgage, or loan purposes. Prepare written reports that estimate property values, outline methods by which the estimations were made, and meet appraisal standards. Compute final estimation of property values, taking into account such factors as depreciation, replacement costs, value comparisons of similar properties, and income potential. Search public records for transactions such as sales, leases, and assessments. Inspect properties to evaluate construction, condition, special features, and functional design and to take property measurements. Photograph interiors and exteriors of properties in order to assist in estimating property value, substantiate findings, and complete appraisal reports. Evaluate land and neighborhoods where properties are situated, considering locations and trends or impending changes that could influence future values. Obtain county land values and sales information about nearby properties in order to aid in establishment of property values. Verify legal descriptions of properties by comparing them to county records. Check building codes and zoning bylaws in order to determine any effects on the properties being appraised. Estimate building replacement costs, using building valuation manuals and professional cost estimators. Examine income records and operating costs of income properties. Interview persons familiar with properties and immediate surroundings, such as contractors, homeowners, and realtors, in order to obtain pertinent information. Examine the type and location of nearby services such as shopping centers, schools, parks, and other neighborhood features in order to evaluate their impact on property values. Draw land diagrams that will be used in appraisal reports to support findings. Testify in court as to the value of a piece of real estate property.

Personality Type: Enterprising. These occupations frequently involve starting up and carrying out projects and can involve leading people and making many decisions. They sometimes require risk taking and often deal with business.

GOE—Interest Area/Cluster: 06. Finance and Insurance. **Work Group:** 06.02. Finance/Insurance Investigation and Analysis. **Other Jobs in**

This Work Group: Appraisers and Assessors of Real Estate; Assessors; Cost Estimators; Credit Analysts; Financial Analysts; Insurance Underwriters; Loan Counselors; Loan Officers; Market Research Analysts; Survey Researchers.

Skills—Mathematics: Using mathematics to solve problems. **Writing:** Communicating effectively with others in writing as indicated by the needs of the audience. **Critical Thinking:** Using logic and analysis to identify the strengths and weaknesses of different approaches. **Management of Financial Resources:** Determining how money will be spent to get the work done and accounting for these expenditures. **Equipment Selection:** Determining the kind of tools and equipment needed to do a job. **Complex Problem Solving:** Identifying complex problems, reviewing the options, and implementing solutions. **Speaking:** Talking to others to effectively convey information. **Technology Design:** Generating or adapting equipment and technology to serve user needs.

Education and Training Program: Real Estate. **Related Knowledge/Courses—Building and Construction:** Materials, methods, and the appropriate tools to construct objects, structures, and buildings. **Economics and Accounting:** Economic and accounting principles and practices, the financial markets, banking, and the analysis and reporting of financial data. **Geography:** Various methods for describing the location and distribution of land, sea, and air masses, including their physical locations, relationships, and characteristics. **Clerical Practices:** Administrative and clerical procedures and systems such as word-processing systems, filing and records management systems, stenography and transcription, forms, design principles, and other office procedures and terminology. **Law and Government:** Laws, legal codes, court procedures, precedents, government regulations, executive orders, agency rules, and the democratic political process. **Sales and Marketing:** Principles and methods involved in showing, promoting, and selling products or services. This includes marketing strategies and tactics, product demonstration and sales techniques, and sales control systems.

Work Environment: More often outdoors than indoors; sitting.

Architects, Except Landscape and Naval

- ❀ Education/Training Required: Bachelor's degree
- ❀ Annual Earnings: $67,620
- ❀ Beginning Wage: $40,250
- ❀ Earnings Growth Potential: High
- ❀ Growth: 17.7%
- ❀ Annual Job Openings: 11,324
- ❀ Self-Employed: 20.3%
- ❀ Part-Time: 6.1%

Plan and design structures, such as private residences, office buildings, theaters, factories, and other structural property. Prepare information regarding design, structure specifications, materials, color, equipment, estimated costs, or construction time. Consult with client to determine functional and spatial requirements of structure. Direct activities of workers engaged in preparing drawings and specification documents. Plan layout of project. Prepare contract documents for building contractors. Prepare scale drawings. Integrate engineering element into unified design. Conduct periodic on-site observation of work during construction to monitor compliance with plans. Administer construction contracts. Represent client in obtaining bids and awarding construction contracts. Prepare operating and maintenance manuals, studies, and reports.

Personality Type: Artistic. These occupations frequently involve working with forms, designs, and patterns. They often require self-expression, and the work can be done without following a clear set of rules.

GOE—Interest Area/Cluster: 02. Architecture and Construction. **Work Group:** 02.02. Architectural Design. **Other Jobs in This Work Group:** Landscape Architects.

Skills—Operations Analysis: Analyzing needs and product requirements to create a design. **Management of Financial Resources:** Determining how money will be spent to get the work done and accounting for these expenditures. **Complex Problem Solving:** Identifying complex problems, reviewing the options, and implementing solutions. **Management of Personnel Resources:** Motivating, developing, and directing people as they work; identifying the best people for the job. **Coordination:** Adjusting actions in relation to others' actions. **Negotiation:** Bringing others together and trying to reconcile differences. **Persuasion:** Persuading others to approach things differently. **Science:** Using scientific methods to solve problems.

Education and Training Programs: Architecture (BArch, BA/BS, MArch, MA/MS, PhD); Environmental Design/Architecture; Architectural History and Criticism, General; Architecture and Related Services, Other. **Related Knowledge/Courses—Building and Construction:** Materials, methods, and the appropriate tools to construct objects, structures, and buildings. **Design:** Design techniques, principles, tools, and instruments involved in the production and use of precision technical plans, blueprints, drawings, and models. **Engineering and Technology:** Equipment, tools, and mechanical devices and their uses to produce motion, light, power, technology, and other applications. **Fine Arts:** Theory and techniques required to produce, compose, and perform works of music, dance, visual arts, drama, and sculpture. **Law and Government:** Laws, legal codes, court procedures, precedents, government regulations, executive orders, agency rules, and the democratic political process. **Physics:** Physical principles, laws, and applications, including air, water, material dynamics, light, atomic principles, heat, electric theory, earth formations, and meteorological and related natural phenomena.

Work Environment: Indoors; sitting.

Architecture Teachers, Postsecondary

- ❀ Education/Training Required: Doctoral degree
- ❀ Annual Earnings: $68,540
- ❀ Beginning Wage: $41,080
- ❀ Earnings Growth Potential: High
- ❀ Growth: 22.9%
- ❀ Annual Job Openings: 1,044
- ❀ Self-Employed: 0.4%
- ❀ Part-Time: 27.8%

Teach courses in architecture and architectural design, such as architectural environmental design, interior architecture/design, and landscape architecture. Evaluate and grade students' work, including work performed in design studios. Prepare and deliver lectures to undergraduate and/ or graduate students on topics such as architectural design methods, aesthetics and design, and structures and materials. Prepare course materials such as syllabi, homework assignments, and handouts. Initiate, facilitate, and moderate classroom discussions. Plan, evaluate, and revise curricula, course content, and course materials and methods of instruction. Keep abreast of developments in their field by reading current literature, talking with colleagues, and participating in professional conferences. Maintain student attendance records, grades, and other required records. Maintain regularly scheduled office hours to advise and assist students. Compile, administer, and grade examinations or assign this work to others. Conduct research in a particular field of knowledge and publish findings in professional journals, books, and/or electronic media. Supervise undergraduate and/or graduate teaching, internship, and research work. Advise students on academic and vocational curricula and on career issues. Collaborate with colleagues to address teaching and research issues. Compile bibliographies of specialized materials for outside reading assignments. Serve on academic or administrative committees that deal with institutional policies, departmental matters, and academic issues. Participate in student recruitment, registration, and placement activities. Select and obtain materials and supplies such as textbooks and laboratory equipment. Write grant proposals to procure external research funding. Provide professional consulting services to government and/ or industry. Perform administrative duties such as serving as department head. Act as advisers to student organizations. Participate in campus and community events.

Personality Type: Social. These occupations frequently involve working with, communicating with, and teaching people and often involve helping or providing service to others.

GOE—Interest Area/Cluster: 05. Education and Training. **Work Group:** 05.03. Postsecondary and Adult Teaching and Instructing. **Other Jobs in This Work Group:** Adult Literacy, Remedial Education, and GED Teachers and Instructors; Agricultural Sciences Teachers, Postsecondary; Anthropology and Archeology Teachers, Postsecondary; Area, Ethnic, and Cultural Studies Teachers, Postsecondary; Art, Drama, and Music Teachers, Postsecondary; Atmospheric, Earth, Marine, and Space Sciences Teachers, Postsecondary;

Biological Science Teachers, Postsecondary; Business Teachers, Postsecondary; Chemistry Teachers, Postsecondary; Communications Teachers, Postsecondary; Computer Science Teachers, Postsecondary; Criminal Justice and Law Enforcement Teachers, Postsecondary; Economics Teachers, Postsecondary; Education Teachers, Postsecondary; Engineering Teachers, Postsecondary; English Language and Literature Teachers, Postsecondary; Environmental Science Teachers, Postsecondary; Farm and Home Management Advisors; Foreign Language and Literature Teachers, Postsecondary; Forestry and Conservation Science Teachers, Postsecondary; Geography Teachers, Postsecondary; Graduate Teaching Assistants; Health Specialties Teachers, Postsecondary; History Teachers, Postsecondary; Home Economics Teachers, Postsecondary; Law Teachers, Postsecondary; Library Science Teachers, Postsecondary; Mathematical Science Teachers, Postsecondary; Nursing Instructors and Teachers, Postsecondary; Philosophy and Religion Teachers, Postsecondary; Physics Teachers, Postsecondary; Political Science Teachers, Postsecondary; Psychology Teachers, Postsecondary; Recreation and Fitness Studies Teachers, Postsecondary; Social Work Teachers, Postsecondary; Sociology Teachers, Postsecondary.

Skills—Technology Design: Generating or adapting equipment and technology to serve user needs. **Operations Analysis:** Analyzing needs and product requirements to create a design. **Instructing:** Teaching others how to do something. **Writing:** Communicating effectively with others in writing as indicated by the needs of the audience. **Science:** Using scientific methods to solve problems. **Complex Problem Solving:** Identifying complex problems, reviewing the options, and implementing solutions. **Speaking:** Talking to others to effectively convey information. **Critical Thinking:** Using logic and analysis to identify the strengths and weaknesses of different approaches.

Education and Training Programs: Architecture (BArch, BA/BS, MArch, MA/MS, PhD); City/Urban, Community and Regional Planning; Environmental Design/Architecture; Interior Architecture; Landscape Architecture (BS, BSLA, BLA, MSLA, MLA, PhD); Teacher Education and Professional Development, Specific Subject Areas, Other; Architectural Engineering. **Related Knowledge/Courses—Fine Arts:** Theory and techniques required to produce, compose, and perform works of music, dance, visual arts, drama, and sculpture. **Design:** Design techniques, principles, tools, and instruments involved in the production and use of precision technical plans, blueprints, drawings, and models. **Building and Construction:** Materials, methods, and the appropriate tools to construct objects, structures, and buildings. **History and Archeology:** Historical events and their causes, indicators, and impact on particular civilizations and cultures. **Philosophy and Theology:** Different philosophical systems and religions, including their basic principles, values, ethics, ways of thinking, customs, and practices and their impact on human culture. **Geography:** Various methods for describing the location and distribution of land, sea, and air masses, including their physical locations, relationships, and characteristics.

Work Environment: Indoors; sitting.

Area, Ethnic, and Cultural Studies Teachers, Postsecondary

- ❋ Education/Training Required: Doctoral degree
- ❋ Annual Earnings: $59,150
- ❋ Beginning Wage: $32,940
- ❋ Earnings Growth Potential: High
- ❋ Growth: 22.9%
- ❋ Annual Job Openings: 1,252
- ❋ Self-Employed: 0.4%
- ❋ Part-Time: 27.8%

Teach courses pertaining to the culture and development of an area (e.g., Latin America), an ethnic group, or any other group (e.g., women's studies, urban affairs). Keep abreast of developments in their field by reading current literature, talking with colleagues, and participating in professional conferences. Conduct research in a particular field of knowledge and publish findings in professional journals, books, and/or electronic media. Evaluate and grade students' classwork, assignments, and papers. Prepare course materials such as syllabi, homework assignments, and handouts. Prepare and deliver lectures to undergraduate and/or graduate students on topics such as race and ethnic relations, gender studies, and cross-cultural perspectives. Initiate, facilitate, and moderate classroom discussions. Compile, administer, and grade examinations or assign this work to others. Maintain regularly scheduled office hours in order to advise and assist students. Plan, evaluate, and revise curricula, course content, and course materials and methods of instruction. Maintain student attendance records, grades, and other required records. Advise students on academic and vocational curricula and on career issues. Supervise undergraduate and/or graduate teaching, internship, and research work. Select and obtain materials and supplies such as textbooks. Collaborate with colleagues to address teaching and research issues. Serve on academic or administrative committees that deal with institutional policies, departmental matters, and academic issues. Compile bibliographies of specialized materials for outside reading assignments. Write grant proposals to procure external research funding. Participate in campus and community events. Participate in student recruitment, registration, and placement activities. Act as advisers to student organizations. Incorporate experiential/site visit components into courses. Perform administrative duties such as serving as department head. Provide professional consulting services to government and/or industry.

Personality Type: Social. These occupations frequently involve working with, communicating with, and teaching people and often involve helping or providing service to others.

GOE—Interest Area/Cluster: 05. Education and Training. **Work Group:** 05.03. Postsecondary and Adult Teaching and Instructing. **Other Jobs in This Work Group:** Adult Literacy, Remedial Education, and GED Teachers and Instructors; Agricultural Sciences Teachers, Postsecondary; Anthropology and Archeology Teachers, Postsecondary; Architecture Teachers, Postsecondary; Art, Drama, and Music Teachers, Postsecondary; Atmospheric, Earth, Marine, and Space Sciences Teachers, Postsecondary; Biological Science Teachers, Postsecondary; Business Teachers, Postsecondary; Chemistry Teachers, Postsecondary; Communications Teachers, Postsecondary; Computer Science Teachers, Postsecondary; Criminal Justice and Law Enforcement Teachers, Postsecondary; Economics Teachers, Postsecondary; Education Teachers, Postsecondary; Engineering Teachers, Postsecondary; English Language and Literature Teachers, Postsecondary; Environmental Science Teachers, Postsecondary; Farm and

Home Management Advisors; Foreign Language and Literature Teachers, Postsecondary; Forestry and Conservation Science Teachers, Postsecondary; Geography Teachers, Postsecondary; Graduate Teaching Assistants; Health Specialties Teachers, Postsecondary; History Teachers, Postsecondary; Home Economics Teachers, Postsecondary; Law Teachers, Postsecondary; Library Science Teachers, Postsecondary; Mathematical Science Teachers, Postsecondary; Nursing Instructors and Teachers, Postsecondary; Philosophy and Religion Teachers, Postsecondary; Physics Teachers, Postsecondary; Political Science Teachers, Postsecondary; Psychology Teachers, Postsecondary; Recreation and Fitness Studies Teachers, Postsecondary; Social Work Teachers, Postsecondary; Sociology Teachers, Postsecondary.

Skills—Writing: Communicating effectively with others in writing as indicated by the needs of the audience. **Critical Thinking:** Using logic and analysis to identify the strengths and weaknesses of different approaches. **Instructing:** Teaching others how to do something. **Persuasion:** Persuading others to approach things differently. **Active Learning:** Working with new material or information to grasp its implications. **Learning Strategies:** Using multiple approaches when learning or teaching new things. **Speaking:** Talking to others to effectively convey information. **Management of Financial Resources:** Determining how money will be spent to get the work done and accounting for these expenditures.

Education and Training Programs: African Studies; American/United States Studies/Civilization; Asian Studies/Civilization; East Asian Studies; Central/Middle and Eastern European Studies; European Studies/Civilization; Latin American Studies; Near and Middle Eastern Studies; Pacific Area/Pacific Rim Studies; Russian Studies; Scandinavian Studies; South Asian Studies; Southeast Asian Studies; Western European Studies; others.

Related Knowledge/Courses—History and Archeology: Historical events and their causes, indicators, and impact on particular civilizations and cultures. **Sociology and Anthropology:** Group behavior and dynamics; societal trends and influences; and cultures and their history, migrations, ethnicity, and origins. **Foreign Language:** The structure and content of a foreign (non-English) language, including the meaning and spelling of words, rules of composition and grammar, and pronunciation. **Philosophy and Theology:** Different philosophical systems and religions, including their basic principles, values, ethics, ways of thinking, customs, and practices and their impact on human culture. **Geography:** Various methods for describing the location and distribution of land, sea, and air masses, including their physical locations, relationships, and characteristics. **Education and Training:** Instructional methods and training techniques, including curriculum design principles, learning theory, group and individual teaching techniques, design of individual development plans, and test design principles.

Work Environment: Indoors; sitting.

Art Directors

- ❋ Education/Training Required: Work experience plus degree
- ❋ Annual Earnings: $72,320
- ❋ Beginning Wage: $39,600
- ❋ Earnings Growth Potential: High
- ❋ Growth: 9.0%
- ❋ Annual Job Openings: 9,719
- ❋ Self-Employed: 59.0%
- ❋ Part-Time: 22.5%

Formulate design concepts and presentation approaches and direct workers engaged in art work, layout design, and copy writing for visual

communications media, such as magazines, books, newspapers, and packaging. Formulate basic layout design or presentation approach and specify material details, such as style and size of type, photographs, graphics, animation, video, and sound. Review and approve proofs of printed copy and art and copy materials developed by staff members. Manage own accounts and projects, working within budget and scheduling requirements. Confer with creative, art, copy-writing, or production department heads to discuss client requirements and presentation concepts and to coordinate creative activities. Present final layouts to clients for approval. Confer with clients to determine objectives; budget; background information; and presentation approaches, styles, and techniques. Hire, train, and direct staff members who develop design concepts into art layouts or who prepare layouts for printing. Work with creative directors to develop design solutions. Review illustrative material to determine if it conforms to standards and specifications. Attend photo shoots and printing sessions to ensure that the products needed are obtained. Create custom illustrations or other graphic elements. Mark up, paste, and complete layouts and write typography instructions to prepare materials for typesetting or printing. Negotiate with printers and estimators to determine what services will be performed. Conceptualize and help design interfaces for multimedia games, products, and devices. Prepare detailed storyboards showing sequence and timing of story development for television production.

Personality Type: Artistic. These occupations frequently involve working with forms, designs, and patterns. They often require self-expression, and the work can be done without following a clear set of rules.

GOE—Interest Area/Cluster: 03. Arts and Communication. **Work Group:** 03.01. Managerial Work in Arts and Communication. **Other Jobs in**

This Work Group: Agents and Business Managers of Artists, Performers, and Athletes; Producers; Producers and Directors; Program Directors; Public Relations Managers.

Skills—Operations Analysis: Analyzing needs and product requirements to create a design. **Management of Financial Resources:** Determining how money will be spent to get the work done and accounting for these expenditures. **Coordination:** Adjusting actions in relation to others' actions. **Negotiation:** Bringing others together and trying to reconcile differences. **Persuasion:** Persuading others to approach things differently. **Service Orientation:** Actively looking for ways to help people. **Systems Evaluation:** Looking at many indicators of system performance and taking into account their accuracy. **Management of Personnel Resources:** Motivating, developing, and directing people as they work; identifying the best people for the job.

Education and Training Programs: Graphic Design; Intermedia/Multimedia. **Related Knowledge/Courses—Fine Arts:** Theory and techniques required to produce, compose, and perform works of music, dance, visual arts, drama, and sculpture. **Design:** Design techniques, principles, tools, and instruments involved in the production and use of precision technical plans, blueprints, drawings, and models. **Communications and Media:** Media production, communication, and dissemination techniques and methods, including alternative ways to inform and entertain via written, oral, and visual media. **Production and Processing:** Inputs, outputs, raw materials, waste, quality control, costs, and techniques for maximizing the manufacture and distribution of goods. **Computers and Electronics:** Electric circuit boards, processors, chips, and computer hardware and software, including applications and programming. **Administration and Management:** Principles and processes involved in business and organizational planning, coordination, and execution. This includes strategic planning, resource allocation, manpower modeling, leadership techniques, and production methods.

Work Environment: Indoors; sitting; using hands on objects, tools, or controls; repetitive motions.

Art, Drama, and Music Teachers, Postsecondary

- ❈ Education/Training Required: Doctoral degree
- ❈ Annual Earnings: $55,190
- ❈ Beginning Wage: $30,340
- ❈ Earnings Growth Potential: High
- ❈ Growth: 22.9%
- ❈ Annual Job Openings: 12,707
- ❈ Self-Employed: 0.4%
- ❈ Part-Time: 27.8%

Teach courses in drama; music; and the arts, including fine and applied art, such as painting and sculpture, or design and crafts. Evaluate and grade students' classwork, performances, projects, assignments, and papers. Explain and demonstrate artistic techniques. Prepare students for performances, exams, or assessments. Prepare and deliver lectures to undergraduate or graduate students on topics such as acting techniques, fundamentals of music, and art history. Organize performance groups and direct their rehearsals. Prepare course materials such as syllabi, homework assignments, and handouts. Initiate, facilitate, and moderate classroom discussions. Keep abreast of developments in their field by reading current literature, talking with colleagues, and participating in professional conferences. Advise students on academic and vocational curricula and on career issues. Maintain student attendance records, grades, and other required records. Conduct research in a particular field of knowledge and publish findings in professional journals, books, or electronic media. Supervise undergraduate and/or graduate teaching, internship, and research work. Plan, evaluate, and revise curricula, course content, and course materials and methods of instruction. Maintain regularly scheduled office hours to advise and assist students. Compile, administer, and grade examinations or assign this work to others. Participate in student recruitment, registration, and placement activities. Select and obtain materials and supplies such as textbooks and performance pieces. Collaborate with colleagues to address teaching and research issues. Serve on academic or administrative committees that deal with institutional policies, departmental matters, and academic issues. Participate in campus and community events. Keep students informed of community events such as plays and concerts. Compile bibliographies of specialized materials for outside reading assignments. Display students' work in schools, galleries, and exhibitions. Perform administrative duties such as serving as department head. Act as advisers to student organizations. Write grant proposals to procure external research funding. Provide professional consulting services to government or industry.

Personality Type: Social. These occupations frequently involve working with, communicating with, and teaching people and often involve helping or providing service to others.

GOE—Interest Area/Cluster: 05. Education and Training. **Work Group:** 05.03. Postsecondary and Adult Teaching and Instructing. **Other Jobs in This Work Group:** Adult Literacy, Remedial Education, and GED Teachers and Instructors; Agricultural Sciences Teachers, Postsecondary; Anthropology and Archeology Teachers, Postsecondary; Architecture Teachers, Postsecondary; Area, Ethnic, and Cultural Studies Teachers, Postsecondary; Atmospheric, Earth, Marine, and

Space Sciences Teachers, Postsecondary; Biological Science Teachers, Postsecondary; Business Teachers, Postsecondary; Chemistry Teachers, Postsecondary; Communications Teachers, Postsecondary; Computer Science Teachers, Postsecondary; Criminal Justice and Law Enforcement Teachers, Postsecondary; Economics Teachers, Postsecondary; Education Teachers, Postsecondary; Engineering Teachers, Postsecondary; English Language and Literature Teachers, Postsecondary; Environmental Science Teachers, Postsecondary; Farm and Home Management Advisors; Foreign Language and Literature Teachers, Postsecondary; Forestry and Conservation Science Teachers, Postsecondary; Geography Teachers, Postsecondary; Graduate Teaching Assistants; Health Specialties Teachers, Postsecondary; History Teachers, Postsecondary; Home Economics Teachers, Postsecondary; Law Teachers, Postsecondary; Library Science Teachers, Postsecondary; Mathematical Science Teachers, Postsecondary; Nursing Instructors and Teachers, Postsecondary; Philosophy and Religion Teachers, Postsecondary; Physics Teachers, Postsecondary; Political Science Teachers, Postsecondary; Psychology Teachers, Postsecondary; Recreation and Fitness Studies Teachers, Postsecondary; Social Work Teachers, Postsecondary; Sociology Teachers, Postsecondary.

Skills—Instructing: Teaching others how to do something. **Social Perceptiveness:** Being aware of others' reactions and understanding why they react the way they do. **Speaking:** Talking to others to effectively convey information. **Active Listening:** Listening to what other people are saying and asking questions as appropriate. **Persuasion:** Persuading others to approach things differently. **Learning Strategies:** Using multiple approaches when learning or teaching new things. **Critical Thinking:** Using logic and analysis to identify the strengths and weaknesses of different approaches. **Monitoring:** Assessing how well one is doing when learning or doing something.

Education and Training Programs: Visual and Performing Arts, General; Crafts/Craft Design, Folk Art and Artisanry; Dance, General; Design and Visual Communications, General; Industrial Design; Commercial Photography; Fashion/Apparel Design; Interior Design; Graphic Design; Design and Applied Arts, Other; Drama and Dramatics/Theatre Arts, General; Technical Theatre/Theatre Design and Technology; Playwriting and Screenwriting; others. **Related Knowledge/Courses—Fine Arts:** Theory and techniques required to produce, compose, and perform works of music, dance, visual arts, drama, and sculpture. **History and Archeology:** Historical events and their causes, indicators, and impact on particular civilizations and cultures. **Philosophy and Theology:** Different philosophical systems and religions, including their basic principles, values, ethics, ways of thinking, customs, and practices and their impact on human culture. **Education and Training:** Instructional methods and training techniques, including curriculum design principles, learning theory, group and individual teaching techniques, design of individual development plans, and test design principles. **Communications and Media:** Media production, communication, and dissemination techniques and methods, including alternative ways to inform and entertain via written, oral, and visual media. **Sociology and Anthropology:** Group behavior and dynamics; societal trends and influences; and cultures and their history, migrations, ethnicity, and origins.

Work Environment: Indoors; noisy; sitting.

Assessors

- ❀ Education/Training Required:
  Bachelor's degree
- ❀ Annual Earnings: $46,130
- ❀ Beginning Wage: $25,110
- ❀ Earnings Growth Potential: High
- ❀ Growth: 16.9%
- ❀ Annual Job Openings: 6,493
- ❀ Self-Employed: 32.7%
- ❀ Part-Time: 8.4%

The job openings listed here are shared with Appraisers, Real Estate.

Appraise real and personal property to determine its fair value. May assess taxes in accordance with prescribed schedules. Determine taxability and value of properties, using methods such as field inspection, structural measurement, calculation, sales analysis, market trend studies, and income and expense analysis. Inspect new construction and major improvements to existing structures to determine values. Explain assessed values to property owners and defend appealed assessments at public hearings. Inspect properties, considering factors such as market value, location, and building or replacement costs to determine appraisal value. Prepare and maintain current data on each parcel assessed, including maps of boundaries, inventories of land and structures, property characteristics, and any applicable exemptions. Identify the ownership of each piece of taxable property. Conduct regular reviews of property within jurisdictions to determine changes in property due to construction or demolition. Complete and maintain assessment rolls that show the assessed values and status of all property in a municipality. Issue notices of assessments and taxes. Review information about transfers of property to ensure its accuracy, checking basic information on buyers, sellers, and sales prices and making corrections as necessary. Maintain familiarity with aspects of local real estate markets. Analyze trends in sales prices, construction costs, and rents to assess property values or determine the accuracy of assessments. Approve applications for property tax exemptions or deductions. Establish uniform and equitable systems for assessing all classes and kinds of property. Write and submit appraisal and tax reports for public record. Serve on assessment review boards. Hire staff members. Provide sales analyses to be used for equalization of school aid. Calculate tax bills for properties by multiplying assessed values by jurisdiction tax rates.

Personality Type: Conventional. These occupations frequently involve following set procedures and routines and can include working with data and details more than with ideas. Usually there is a clear line of authority to follow.

GOE—Interest Area/Cluster: 06. Finance and Insurance. **Work Group:** 06.02. Finance/Insurance Investigation and Analysis. **Other Jobs in This Work Group:** Appraisers and Assessors of Real Estate; Appraisers, Real Estate; Cost Estimators; Credit Analysts; Financial Analysts; Insurance Underwriters; Loan Counselors; Loan Officers; Market Research Analysts; Survey Researchers.

Skills—Mathematics: Using mathematics to solve problems. **Systems Analysis:** Determining how a system should work and how changes will affect outcomes. **Speaking:** Talking to others to effectively convey information. **Negotiation:** Bringing others together and trying to reconcile differences. **Systems Evaluation:** Looking at many indicators of system performance and taking into account their accuracy. **Active Listening:** Listening to what other people are saying and asking questions as appropriate. **Management of Financial Resources:** Determining how money will be spent to get the work done and accounting for these expenditures. **Persuasion:** Persuading others to approach things differently.

Education and Training Program: Real Estate. **Related Knowledge/Courses—Building and Construction:** Materials, methods, and the appropriate tools to construct objects, structures, and buildings. **Clerical Practices:** Administrative and clerical procedures and systems such as word-processing systems, filing and records management systems, stenography and transcription, forms, design principles, and other office procedures and terminology. **Law and Government:** Laws, legal codes, court procedures, precedents, government regulations, executive orders, agency rules, and the democratic political process. **Mathematics:** Numbers and their operations and interrelationships, including arithmetic, algebra, geometry, calculus, and statistics and their applications. **Geography:** Various methods for describing the location and distribution of land, sea, and air masses, including their physical locations, relationships, and characteristics. **Economics and Accounting:** Economic and accounting principles and practices, the financial markets, banking, and the analysis and reporting of financial data.

Work Environment: More often indoors than outdoors; sitting; using hands on objects, tools, or controls; repetitive motions.

Atmospheric, Earth, Marine, and Space Sciences Teachers, Postsecondary

❋ Education/Training Required: Doctoral degree
❋ Annual Earnings: $73,280
❋ Beginning Wage: $39,840
❋ Earnings Growth Potential: High
❋ Growth: 22.9%
❋ Annual Job Openings: 1,553
❋ Self-Employed: 0.4%
❋ Part-Time: 27.8%

Teach courses in the physical sciences, except chemistry and physics. Conduct research in a particular field of knowledge and publish findings in professional journals, books, and/or electronic media. Write grant proposals to procure external research funding. Keep abreast of developments in their field by reading current literature, talking with colleagues, and participating in professional conferences. Supervise undergraduate and/or graduate teaching, internships, and research work. Prepare and deliver lectures to undergraduate and/or graduate students on topics such as structural geology, micrometeorology, and atmospheric thermodynamics. Supervise laboratory work and field-work. Evaluate and grade students' classwork, assignments, and papers. Prepare course materials such as syllabi, homework assignments, and handouts. Collaborate with colleagues to address teaching and research issues. Compile, administer, and grade examinations or assign this work to others. Plan, evaluate, and revise curricula, course content, course materials, and methods of instruction. Initiate, facilitate, and moderate classroom discussions. Maintain regularly scheduled office hours to advise and assist students. Advise students on academic and vocational curricula and on career issues. Maintain student attendance records, grades, and other required records. Participate in student recruitment, registration, and placement activities. Perform administrative duties such as serving as department head. Select and obtain materials and supplies such as textbooks and laboratory equipment. Serve on academic or administrative committees that deal with institutional policies, departmental matters, and academic issues. Compile bibliographies of specialized materials for outside reading assignments. Provide professional consulting services to government and/or industry. Act as adviser to student organizations. Participate in campus and community events.

Personality Type: Social. These occupations frequently involve working with, communicating with, and teaching people and often involve helping or providing service to others.

GOE—Interest Area/Cluster: 05. Education and Training. **Work Group:** 05.03. Postsecondary and Adult Teaching and Instructing. **Other Jobs in This Work Group:** Adult Literacy, Remedial Education, and GED Teachers and Instructors; Agricultural Sciences Teachers, Postsecondary; Anthropology and Archeology Teachers, Postsecondary; Architecture Teachers, Postsecondary; Area, Ethnic, and Cultural Studies Teachers, Postsecondary; Art, Drama, and Music Teachers, Postsecondary; Biological Science Teachers, Postsecondary; Business Teachers, Postsecondary; Chemistry Teachers, Postsecondary; Communications Teachers, Postsecondary; Computer Science Teachers, Postsecondary; Criminal Justice and Law Enforcement Teachers, Postsecondary; Economics Teachers, Postsecondary; Education Teachers, Postsecondary; Engineering Teachers, Postsecondary; English Language and Literature Teachers, Postsecondary; Environmental Science Teachers, Postsecondary; Farm and Home Management Advisors; Foreign Language and Literature Teachers, Postsecondary; Forestry and Conservation Science Teachers,

Postsecondary; Geography Teachers, Postsecondary; Graduate Teaching Assistants; Health Specialties Teachers, Postsecondary; History Teachers, Postsecondary; Home Economics Teachers, Postsecondary; Law Teachers, Postsecondary; Library Science Teachers, Postsecondary; Mathematical Science Teachers, Postsecondary; Nursing Instructors and Teachers, Postsecondary; Philosophy and Religion Teachers, Postsecondary; Physics Teachers, Postsecondary; Political Science Teachers, Postsecondary; Psychology Teachers, Postsecondary; Recreation and Fitness Studies Teachers, Postsecondary; Social Work Teachers, Postsecondary; Sociology Teachers, Postsecondary.

Skills—Science: Using scientific methods to solve problems. **Programming:** Writing computer programs for various purposes. **Mathematics:** Using mathematics to solve problems. **Management of Financial Resources:** Determining how money will be spent to get the work done and accounting for these expenditures. **Complex Problem Solving:** Identifying complex problems, reviewing the options, and implementing solutions. **Writing:** Communicating effectively with others in writing as indicated by the needs of the audience. **Active Learning:** Working with new material or information to grasp its implications. **Reading Comprehension:** Understanding written sentences and paragraphs in work-related documents.

Education and Training Programs: Science Teacher Education/General Science Teacher Education; Physics Teacher Education; Astronomy; Astrophysics; Planetary Astronomy and Science; Atmospheric Sciences and Meteorology, General; Atmospheric Chemistry and Climatology; Atmospheric Physics and Dynamics; Meteorology; Atmospheric Sciences and Meteorology, Other; Geology/Earth Science, General; Geochemistry; Geophysics and Seismology; others. **Related Knowledge/Courses—Physics:** Physical principles, laws, and applications, including air, water, material dynamics, light, atomic principles, heat, electric theory, earth formations, and meteorological and related natural phenomena. **Geography:** Various methods for describing the location and distribution of land, sea, and air masses, including their physical locations, relationships, and characteristics. **Chemistry:** The composition, structure, and properties of substances and of the chemical processes and transformations that they undergo. This includes uses of chemicals and their interactions, danger signs, production techniques, and disposal methods. **Biology:** Plant and animal living tissue, cells, organisms, and entities, including their functions, interdependencies, and interactions with each other and the environment. **Mathematics:** Numbers and their operations and interrelationships, including arithmetic, algebra, geometry, calculus, and statistics and their applications. **Education and Training:** Instructional methods and training techniques, including curriculum design principles, learning theory, group and individual teaching techniques, design of individual development plans, and test design principles.

Work Environment: Indoors; sitting.

Auditors

- ❋ Education/Training Required: Bachelor's degree
- ❋ Annual Earnings: $57,060
- ❋ Beginning Wage: $35,570
- ❋ Earnings Growth Potential: Medium
- ❋ Growth: 17.7%
- ❋ Annual Job Openings: 134,463
- ❋ Self-Employed: 9.5%
- ❋ Part-Time: 9.3%

The job openings listed here are shared with Accountants.

Examine and analyze accounting records to determine financial status of establishment and prepare financial reports concerning operating procedures. Collect and analyze data to detect deficient controls; duplicated effort; extravagance; fraud; or non-compliance with laws, regulations, and management policies. Prepare detailed reports on audit findings. Supervise auditing of establishments and determine scope of investigation required. Report to management about asset utilization and audit results and recommend changes in operations and financial activities. Inspect account books and accounting systems for efficiency, effectiveness, and use of accepted accounting procedures to record transactions. Examine records and interview workers to ensure recording of transactions and compliance with laws and regulations. Examine and evaluate financial and information systems, recommending controls to ensure system reliability and data integrity. Review data about material assets, net worth, liabilities, capital stock, surplus, income, and expenditures. Confer with company officials about financial and regulatory matters. Examine whether the organization's objectives are reflected in its management activities and whether employees understand the objectives. Prepare, analyze, and verify annual reports, financial statements, and other records, using accepted accounting and statistical procedures to assess financial condition and facilitate financial planning. Inspect cash on hand, notes receivable and payable, negotiable securities, and canceled checks to confirm records are accurate. Examine inventory to verify journal and ledger entries. Direct activities of personnel engaged in filing, recording, compiling, and transmitting financial records. Conduct pre-implementation audits to determine whether systems and programs under development will work as planned. Audit payroll and personnel records to determine unemployment insurance premiums, workers' compensation coverage, liabilities, and compliance with tax laws. Evaluate taxpayer finances to determine tax liability, using knowledge of interest and discount rates, annuities, valuation of stocks and bonds, and amortization valuation of depletable assets. Review taxpayer accounts and conduct audits on-site, by correspondence, or by summoning taxpayers to office.

Personality Type: Conventional. These occupations frequently involve following set procedures and routines and can include working with data and details more than with ideas. Usually there is a clear line of authority to follow.

GOE—Interest Area/Cluster: 04. Business and Administration. **Work Group:** 04.05. Accounting, Auditing, and Analytical Support. **Other Jobs in This Work Group:** Accountants; Accountants and Auditors; Budget Analysts; Industrial Engineering Technicians; Logisticians; Management Analysts; Operations Research Analysts.

Skills—Systems Analysis: Determining how a system should work and how changes will affect outcomes. **Systems Evaluation:** Looking at many indicators of system performance and taking into account their accuracy.

Education and Training Programs: Accounting and Computer Science; Accounting; Auditing; Accounting and Finance; Accounting and Business/Management. **Related Knowledge/Courses—Economics and Accounting:** Economic and accounting principles and practices, the financial markets, banking, and the analysis and reporting of financial data. **Administration and Management:** Principles and processes involved in business and organizational planning, coordination, and execution. This includes strategic planning, resource allocation, manpower modeling, leadership techniques, and production methods. **Personnel and Human Resources:** Principles and procedures for personnel recruitment; selection; training; compensation and benefits; labor relations and negotiation; and personnel information

systems. **Computers and Electronics:** Electric circuit boards, processors, chips, and computer hardware and software, including applications and programming. **Law and Government:** Laws, legal codes, court procedures, precedents, government regulations, executive orders, agency rules, and the democratic political process. **English Language:** The structure and content of the English language, including the meaning and spelling of words, rules of composition, and grammar.

Work Environment: Indoors; sitting.

Biochemists and Biophysicists

❋ Education/Training Required: Doctoral degree
❋ Annual Earnings: $79,270
❋ Beginning Wage: $42,670
❋ Earnings Growth Potential: High
❋ Growth: 15.9%
❋ Annual Job Openings: 1,637
❋ Self-Employed: 2.5%
❋ Part-Time: 7.3%

Study the chemical composition and physical principles of living cells and organisms and their electrical and mechanical energy and related phenomena. May conduct research in order to further understanding of the complex chemical combinations and reactions involved in metabolism, reproduction, growth, and heredity. May determine the effects of foods, drugs, serums, hormones, and other substances on tissues and vital processes of living organisms. Design and perform experiments with equipment such as lasers, accelerators, and mass spectrometers. Analyze brain functions, such as learning, thinking, and memory, and analyze the dynamics of seeing and hearing. Share research findings by writing scientific articles and by making presentations at scientific conferences. Develop and test new drugs and medications intended for commercial distribution. Develop methods to process, store, and use foods, drugs, and chemical compounds. Develop new methods to study the mechanisms of biological processes. Examine the molecular and chemical aspects of immune system functioning. Investigate the nature, composition, and expression of genes and research how genetic engineering can impact these processes. Determine the three-dimensional structure of biological macromolecules. Prepare reports and recommendations based upon research outcomes. Design and build laboratory equipment needed for special research projects. Isolate, analyze, and synthesize vitamins, hormones, allergens, minerals, and enzymes and determine their effects on body functions. Research cancer treatment, using radiation and nuclear particles. Research transformations of substances in cells, using atomic isotopes. Study how light is absorbed in processes such as photosynthesis or vision. Analyze foods to determine their nutritional values and the effects of cooking, canning, and processing on these values. Study spatial configurations of submicroscopic molecules such as proteins, using X rays and electron microscopes. Teach and advise undergraduate and graduate students and supervise their research. Investigate the transmission of electrical impulses along nerves and muscles. Research how characteristics of plants and animals are carried through successive generations. Investigate damage to cells and tissues caused by X rays and nuclear particles. Research the chemical effects of substances such as drugs, serums, hormones, and food on tissues and vital processes. Develop and execute tests to detect diseases, genetic disorders, or other abnormalities. Produce pharmaceutically and industrially useful proteins, using recombinant DNA technology.

Personality Type: Investigative. These occupations frequently involve working with ideas and

require an extensive amount of thinking. They can involve searching for facts and figuring out problems mentally.

GOE—Interest Area/Cluster: 15. Scientific Research, Engineering, and Mathematics. **Work Group:** 15.03. Life Sciences. **Other Jobs in This Work Group:** Biologists; Environmental Scientists and Specialists, Including Health; Epidemiologists; Medical Scientists, Except Epidemiologists; Microbiologists.

Skills—Science: Using scientific methods to solve problems. **Technology Design:** Generating or adapting equipment and technology to serve user needs. **Writing:** Communicating effectively with others in writing as indicated by the needs of the audience. **Equipment Selection:** Determining the kind of tools and equipment needed to do a job. **Operations Analysis:** Analyzing needs and product requirements to create a design. **Reading Comprehension:** Understanding written sentences and paragraphs in work-related documents. **Troubleshooting:** Determining what is causing an operating error and deciding what to do about it. **Quality Control Analysis:** Evaluating the quality or performance of products, services, or processes.

Education and Training Programs: Soil Chemistry and Physics; Soil Microbiology; Biophysics; Molecular Biophysics; Biochemistry/Biophysics and Molecular Biology; Cell/Cellular Biology and Anatomical Sciences, Other. **Related Knowledge/Courses—Biology:** Plant and animal living tissue, cells, organisms, and entities, including their functions, interdependencies, and interactions with each other and the environment. **Chemistry:** The composition, structure, and properties of substances and of the chemical processes and transformations that they undergo. This includes uses of chemicals and their interactions, danger signs, production techniques, and disposal methods. **Physics:** Physical principles, laws, and applications, including air, water, material dynamics, light, atomic principles, heat, electric theory, earth formations, and meteorological and related natural phenomena. **Engineering and Technology:** Equipment, tools, and mechanical devices and their uses to produce motion, light, power, technology, and other applications. **Medicine and Dentistry:** The information and techniques needed to diagnose and treat injuries, diseases, and deformities. This includes symptoms, treatment alternatives, drug properties and interactions, and preventive health-care measures. **Design:** Design techniques, principles, tools, and instruments involved in the production and use of precision technical plans, blueprints, drawings, and models.

Work Environment: Indoors; disease or infections; sitting; using hands on objects, tools, or controls.

Biological Science Teachers, Postsecondary

- ❋ Education/Training Required: Doctoral degree
- ❋ Annual Earnings: $71,780
- ❋ Beginning Wage: $39,100
- ❋ Earnings Growth Potential: High
- ❋ Growth: 22.9%
- ❋ Annual Job Openings: 9,039
- ❋ Self-Employed: 0.4%
- ❋ Part-Time: 27.8%

Teach courses in biological sciences. Prepare and deliver lectures to undergraduate and/or graduate students on topics such as molecular biology, marine biology, and botany. Evaluate and grade students' classwork, laboratory work, assignments, and papers. Prepare course materials such as syllabi, homework assignments, and handouts. Compile, administer, and grade examinations or assign this work to others. Supervise students' laboratory work. Keep abreast of developments in their field by reading current literature, talking with colleagues, and participating in professional conferences. Maintain student attendance records, grades, and other required records. Initiate, facilitate, and moderate classroom discussions. Plan, evaluate, and revise curricula, course content, course materials, and methods of instruction. Advise students on academic and vocational curricula and on career issues. Maintain regularly scheduled office hours to advise and assist students. Supervise undergraduate and/or graduate teaching, internships, and research work. Select and obtain materials and supplies such as textbooks and laboratory equipment. Collaborate with colleagues to address teaching and research issues. Conduct research in a particular field of knowledge and publish findings in professional journals, books, and/or electronic media. Serve on academic or administrative committees that deal with institutional policies, departmental matters, and academic issues. Participate in student recruitment, registration, and placement activities. Write grant proposals to procure external research funding. Perform administrative duties such as serving as department head. Act as advisers to student organizations. Compile bibliographies of specialized materials for outside reading assignments. Participate in campus and community events. Provide professional consulting services to government and/or industry.

Personality Type: Social. These occupations frequently involve working with, communicating with, and teaching people and often involve helping or providing service to others.

GOE—Interest Area/Cluster: 05. Education and Training. **Work Group:** 05.03. Postsecondary and Adult Teaching and Instructing. **Other Jobs in This Work Group:** Adult Literacy, Remedial Education, and GED Teachers and Instructors; Agricultural Sciences Teachers, Postsecondary; Anthropology and Archeology Teachers,

Postsecondary; Architecture Teachers, Postsecondary; Area, Ethnic, and Cultural Studies Teachers, Postsecondary; Art, Drama, and Music Teachers, Postsecondary; Atmospheric, Earth, Marine, and Space Sciences Teachers, Postsecondary; Business Teachers, Postsecondary; Chemistry Teachers, Postsecondary; Communications Teachers, Postsecondary; Computer Science Teachers, Postsecondary; Criminal Justice and Law Enforcement Teachers, Postsecondary; Economics Teachers, Postsecondary; Education Teachers, Postsecondary; Engineering Teachers, Postsecondary; English Language and Literature Teachers, Postsecondary; Environmental Science Teachers, Postsecondary; Farm and Home Management Advisors; Foreign Language and Literature Teachers, Postsecondary; Forestry and Conservation Science Teachers, Postsecondary; Geography Teachers, Postsecondary; Graduate Teaching Assistants; Health Specialties Teachers, Postsecondary; History Teachers, Postsecondary; Home Economics Teachers, Postsecondary; Law Teachers, Postsecondary; Library Science Teachers, Postsecondary; Mathematical Science Teachers, Postsecondary; Nursing Instructors and Teachers, Postsecondary; Philosophy and Religion Teachers, Postsecondary; Physics Teachers, Postsecondary; Political Science Teachers, Postsecondary; Psychology Teachers, Postsecondary; Recreation and Fitness Studies Teachers, Postsecondary; Social Work Teachers, Postsecondary; Sociology Teachers, Postsecondary.

Skills—Science: Using scientific methods to solve problems. **Instructing:** Teaching others how to do something. **Writing:** Communicating effectively with others in writing as indicated by the needs of the audience. **Reading Comprehension:** Understanding written sentences and paragraphs in work-related documents. **Learning Strategies:** Using multiple approaches when learning or teaching new things. **Speaking:** Talking to others to effectively convey information. **Active Learning:** Working with new material or information to grasp its implications. **Critical Thinking:** Using logic and analysis to identify the strengths and weaknesses of different approaches.

Education and Training Programs: Biology/Biological Sciences, General; Biochemistry; Biophysics; Molecular Biology; Radiation Biology/Radiobiology; Botany/Plant Biology; Plant Pathology/Phytopathology; Plant Physiology; Cell/Cellular Biology and Histology; Anatomy; Microbiology, General; Virology; Parasitology; Immunology; Zoology/Animal Biology; Entomology; Animal Physiology; others. **Related Knowledge/Courses—Biology:** Plant and animal living tissue, cells, organisms, and entities, including their functions, interdependencies, and interactions with each other and the environment. **Chemistry:** The composition, structure, and properties of substances and of the chemical processes and transformations that they undergo. This includes uses of chemicals and their interactions, danger signs, production techniques, and disposal methods. **Education and Training:** Instructional methods and training techniques, including curriculum design principles, learning theory, group and individual teaching techniques, design of individual development plans, and test design principles. **Medicine and Dentistry:** The information and techniques needed to diagnose and treat injuries, diseases, and deformities. This includes symptoms, treatment alternatives, drug properties and interactions, and preventive health-care measures. **Physics:** Physical principles, laws, and applications, including air, water, material dynamics, light, atomic principles, heat, electric theory, earth formations, and meteorological and related natural phenomena. **Geography:** Various methods for describing the location and distribution of land, sea, and air masses, including their physical locations, relationships, and characteristics.

Work Environment: Indoors; more often sitting than standing.

Biological Technicians

- ❋ Education/Training Required: Bachelor's degree
- ❋ Annual Earnings: $37,810
- ❋ Beginning Wage: $24,360
- ❋ Earnings Growth Potential: Medium
- ❋ Growth: 16.0%
- ❋ Annual Job Openings: 15,374
- ❋ Self-Employed: 0.0%
- ❋ Part-Time: 6.2%

Assist biological and medical scientists in laboratories. Set up, operate, and maintain laboratory instruments and equipment; monitor experiments; make observations; and calculate and record results. May analyze organic substances, such as blood, food, and drugs. Keep detailed logs of all work-related activities. Monitor laboratory work to ensure compliance with set standards. Isolate, identify, and prepare specimens for examination. Use computers, computer-interfaced equipment, robotics, or high-technology industrial applications to perform work duties. Conduct research or assist in the conduct of research, including the collection of information and samples such as blood, water, soil, plants, and animals. Set up, adjust, calibrate, clean, maintain, and troubleshoot laboratory and field equipment. Provide technical support and services for scientists and engineers working in fields such as agriculture, environmental science, resource management, biology, and health sciences. Clean, maintain, and prepare supplies and work areas. Participate in the research, development, or manufacturing of medicinal and pharmaceutical preparations. Conduct standardized biological, microbiological, or biochemical tests and laboratory analyses to evaluate the quantity or quality of physical or chemical substances in food or other products. Analyze experimental data and interpret results to write reports and summaries of findings. Measure or weigh compounds and solutions for use in testing or animal feed. Monitor and observe experiments, recording production and test data for evaluation by research personnel. Examine animals and specimens to detect the presence of disease or other problems. Conduct or supervise operational programs such as fish hatcheries, greenhouses, and livestock production programs. Feed livestock or laboratory animals.

Personality Type: Realistic. These occupations frequently involve work activities that include practical, hands-on problems and solutions. They often deal with plants; animals; and real-world materials such as wood, tools, and machinery. Many of the occupations require working outside and don't involve a lot of paperwork or working closely with others.

GOE—Interest Area/Cluster: 08. Health Science. **Work Group:** 08.06. Medical Technology. **Other Jobs in This Work Group:** Cardiovascular Technologists and Technicians; Diagnostic Medical Sonographers; Medical and Clinical Laboratory Technicians; Medical and Clinical Laboratory Technologists; Medical Records and Health Information Technicians; Nuclear Medicine Technologists; Orthotists and Prosthetists; Radiologic Technicians; Radiologic Technologists; Radiologic Technologists and Technicians.

Skills—Science: Using scientific methods to solve problems. **Equipment Maintenance:** Performing routine maintenance and determining when and what kind of maintenance is needed. **Quality Control Analysis:** Evaluating the quality or performance of products, services, or processes. **Troubleshooting:** Determining what is causing an operating error and deciding what to do about it. **Mathematics:** Using mathematics to solve problems. **Active Learning:** Working with new material or information to grasp its implications. **Technology Design:** Generating or adapting equipment and technology to serve user needs. **Learning Strategies:** Using multiple approaches when learning or teaching new things.

Education and Training Program: Biology Technician/Biotechnology Laboratory Technician. **Related Knowledge/Courses—Chemistry:** The composition, structure, and properties of substances and of the chemical processes and transformations that they undergo. This includes uses of chemicals and their interactions, danger signs, production techniques, and disposal methods. **Biology:** Plant and animal living tissue, cells, organisms, and entities, including their functions, interdependencies, and interactions with each other and the environment.

Work Environment: Indoors; standing; using hands on objects, tools, or controls; repetitive motions.

Biologists

* Education/Training Required: Doctoral degree
* Annual Earnings: $64,920
* Beginning Wage: $37,770
* Earnings Growth Potential: High
* Growth: 9.2%
* Annual Job Openings: 6,288
* Self-Employed: 2.8%
* Part-Time: 0.0%

Research or study basic principles of plant and animal life, such as origin, relationship, development, anatomy, and functions. Develop and maintain liaisons and effective working relations with groups and individuals, agencies, and the public to encourage cooperative management strategies or to develop information and interpret findings. Program and use computers to store, process, and analyze data. Study aquatic plants and animals and environmental conditions affecting them, such as radioactivity or pollution. Collect and analyze biological data about relationships among and between organisms and their environment. Communicate test results to state and federal representatives and general public. Identify, classify, and study structure, behavior, ecology, physiology, nutrition, culture, and distribution of plant and animal species. Prepare environmental impact reports for industry, government, or publication. Represent employer in a technical capacity at conferences. Plan and administer biological research programs for government, research firms, medical industries, or manufacturing firms. Research environmental effects of present and potential uses of land and water areas, determining methods of improving environmental conditions or such outputs as crop yields. Review reports such as those relating to land use classifications and recreational development for accuracy and adequacy. Measure salinity, acidity, light, oxygen content, and other physical conditions of water to determine their relationship to aquatic life. Teach, supervise students, and perform research at universities and colleges. Supervise biological technicians and technologists and other scientists. Study basic principles of plant and animal life such as origin, relationship, development, anatomy, and function. Study and manage wild animal populations. Prepare requests for proposals or statements of work. Cultivate, breed, and grow aquatic life such as lobsters, clams, or fish. Prepare plans for management of renewable resources. Develop methods and apparatus for securing representative plant, animal, aquatic, or soil samples. Study reactions of plants, animals, and marine species to parasites. Develop pest management and control measures and conduct risk assessments related to pest exclusion, using scientific methods.

Personality Type: Investigative. These occupations frequently involve working with ideas and require an extensive amount of thinking. They can involve searching for facts and figuring out problems mentally.

GOE—Interest Area/Cluster: 15. Scientific Research, Engineering, and Mathematics. **Work Group:** 15.03. Life Sciences. **Other Jobs in This Work Group:** Biochemists and Biophysicists; Environmental Scientists and Specialists, Including Health; Epidemiologists; Medical Scientists, Except Epidemiologists; Microbiologists.

Skills—Science: Using scientific methods to solve problems. **Management of Financial Resources:** Determining how money will be spent to get the work done and accounting for these expenditures. **Judgment and Decision Making:** Weighing the relative costs and benefits of a potential action. **Negotiation:** Bringing others together and trying to reconcile differences. **Persuasion:** Persuading others to approach things differently. **Management of Material Resources:** Obtaining and seeing to the appropriate use of equipment, facilities, and materials needed to do certain work. **Active Learning:** Working with new material or information to grasp its implications. **Reading Comprehension:** Understanding written sentences and paragraphs in work-related documents.

Education and Training Programs: Biology/Biological Sciences, General; Biomedical Sciences, General; Biochemistry; Biophysics; Molecular Biology; Molecular Biochemistry; Molecular Biophysics; Structural Biology; Photobiology; Radiation Biology/Radiobiology; Biochemistry/Biophysics and Molecular Biology; Biochemistry, Biophysics and Molecular Biology, Other; Botany/Plant Biology; Plant Pathology/Phytopathology; others. **Related Knowledge/Courses—Biology:** Plant and animal living tissue, cells, organisms, and entities, including their functions, interdependencies, and interactions with each other and the environment. **Chemistry:** The composition, structure, and properties of substances and of the chemical

processes and transformations that they undergo. This includes uses of chemicals and their interactions, danger signs, production techniques, and disposal methods. **Law and Government:** Laws, legal codes, court procedures, precedents, government regulations, executive orders, agency rules, and the democratic political process. **Geography:** Various methods for describing the location and distribution of land, sea, and air masses, including their physical locations, relationships, and characteristics. **Physics:** Physical principles, laws, and applications, including air, water, material dynamics, light, atomic principles, heat, electric theory, earth formations, and meteorological and related natural phenomena. **Computers and Electronics:** Electric circuit boards, processors, chips, and computer hardware and software, including applications and programming.

Work Environment: Indoors; noisy; sitting.

Biomedical Engineers

* Education/Training Required: Bachelor's degree
* Annual Earnings: $75,440
* Beginning Wage: $45,910
* Earnings Growth Potential: Medium
* Growth: 21.1%
* Annual Job Openings: 1,804
* Self-Employed: 0.0%
* Part-Time: 3.4%

Apply knowledge of engineering, biology, and biomechanical principles to the design, development, and evaluation of biological and health systems and products, such as artificial organs, prostheses, instrumentation, medical information systems, and health management and care delivery systems. Evaluate the safety, efficiency, and effectiveness of biomedical equipment. Install, adjust, maintain, and/or repair biomedical equipment. Advise hospital administrators on the planning, acquisition, and use of medical equipment. Advise and assist in the application of instrumentation in clinical environments. Develop models or computer simulations of human bio-behavioral systems in order to obtain data for measuring or controlling life processes. Research new materials to be used for products such as implanted artificial organs. Design and develop medical diagnostic and clinical instrumentation, equipment, and procedures, utilizing the principles of engineering and bio-behavioral sciences. Conduct research, along with life scientists, chemists, and medical scientists, on the engineering aspects of the biological systems of humans and animals. Teach biomedical engineering or disseminate knowledge about field through writing or consulting. Design and deliver technology to assist people with disabilities. Diagnose and interpret bioelectric data, using signal-processing techniques. Adapt or design computer hardware or software for medical science uses. Analyze new medical procedures in order to forecast likely outcomes. Develop new applications for energy sources, such as using nuclear power for biomedical implants.

Personality Type: Investigative. These occupations frequently involve working with ideas and require an extensive amount of thinking. They can involve searching for facts and figuring out problems mentally.

GOE—Interest Area/Cluster: 15. Scientific Research, Engineering, and Mathematics. **Work Group:** 15.07. Research and Design Engineering. **Other Jobs in This Work Group:** Aerospace Engineers; Chemical Engineers; Civil Engineers; Computer Hardware Engineers; Electrical Engineers; Electronics Engineers, Except Computer; Marine Architects; Marine Engineers; Marine Engineers and Naval Architects; Materials Engineers; Mechanical Engineers; Nuclear Engineers.

Skills—Technology Design: Generating or adapting equipment and technology to serve user needs. **Science:** Using scientific methods to solve problems. **Installation:** Installing equipment, machines, wiring, or programs to meet specifications. **Operations Analysis:** Analyzing needs and product requirements to create a design. **Quality Control Analysis:** Evaluating the quality or performance of products, services, or processes. **Systems Evaluation:** Looking at many indicators of system performance and taking into account their accuracy. **Troubleshooting:** Determining what is causing an operating error and deciding what to do about it. **Management of Material Resources:** Obtaining and seeing to the appropriate use of equipment, facilities, and materials needed to do certain work.

Education and Training Program: Biomedical/Medical Engineering. **Related Knowledge/Courses—Engineering and Technology:** Equipment, tools, and mechanical devices and their uses to produce motion, light, power, technology, and other applications. **Computers and Electronics:** Electric circuit boards, processors, chips, and computer hardware and software, including applications and programming. **Physics:** Physical principles, laws, and applications, including air, water, material dynamics, light, atomic principles, heat, electric theory, earth formations, and meteorological and related natural phenomena. **Design:** Design techniques, principles, tools, and instruments involved in the production and use of precision technical plans, blueprints, drawings, and models. **Mechanical Devices:** Machines and tools, including their designs, uses, benefits, repair, and maintenance. **Chemistry:** The composition, structure, and properties of substances and of the chemical processes and transformations that they undergo. This includes uses of chemicals and their interactions, danger signs, production techniques, and disposal methods.

Work Environment: Indoors; contaminants; disease or infections; hazardous conditions; sitting; using hands on objects, tools, or controls.

Business Teachers, Postsecondary

- ✼ Education/Training Required: Doctoral degree
- ✼ Annual Earnings: $64,900
- ✼ Beginning Wage: $32,770
- ✼ Earnings Growth Potential: High
- ✼ Growth: 22.9%
- ✼ Annual Job Openings: 11,643
- ✼ Self-Employed: 0.4%
- ✼ Part-Time: 27.8%

Teach courses in business administration and management, such as accounting, finance, human resources, labor relations, marketing, and operations research. Prepare and deliver lectures to undergraduate and/or graduate students on topics such as financial accounting, principles of marketing, and operations management. Evaluate and grade students' classwork, assignments, and papers. Compile, administer, and grade examinations or assign this work to others. Prepare course materials such as syllabi, homework assignments, and handouts. Maintain student attendance records, grades, and other required records. Initiate, facilitate, and moderate classroom discussions. Plan, evaluate, and revise curricula, course content, and course materials and methods of instruction. Keep abreast of developments in their field by reading current literature, talking with colleagues, and participating in professional organizations and conferences. Maintain regularly scheduled office hours to advise and assist students. Advise students on academic and vocational curricula and on career issues. Select and obtain materials and supplies such as textbooks. Collaborate with colleagues to address teaching and research issues. Collaborate with members of the business community to improve programs, to develop new programs, and to provide student access to learning opportunities such as internships. Participate in student recruitment, registration, and placement activities. Serve on academic or administrative committees that deal with institutional policies, departmental matters, and academic issues. Participate in campus and community events. Compile bibliographies of specialized materials for outside reading assignments. Perform administrative duties such as serving as department head. Supervise undergraduate and/or graduate teaching, internship, and research work. Conduct research in a particular field of knowledge and publish findings in professional journals, books, and/or electronic media. Act as advisers to student organizations. Provide professional consulting services to government and/or industry. Write grant proposals to procure external research funding.

Personality Type: Social. These occupations frequently involve working with, communicating with, and teaching people and often involve helping or providing service to others.

GOE—Interest Area/Cluster: 05. Education and Training. **Work Group:** 05.03. Postsecondary and Adult Teaching and Instructing. **Other Jobs in This Work Group:** Adult Literacy, Remedial Education, and GED Teachers and Instructors; Agricultural Sciences Teachers, Postsecondary; Anthropology and Archeology Teachers, Postsecondary; Architecture Teachers, Postsecondary; Area, Ethnic, and Cultural Studies Teachers, Postsecondary; Art, Drama, and Music Teachers, Postsecondary; Atmospheric, Earth, Marine, and Space Sciences Teachers, Postsecondary; Biological Science Teachers, Postsecondary; Chemistry Teachers, Postsecondary; Communications Teachers, Postsecondary; Computer Science Teachers,

Postsecondary; Criminal Justice and Law Enforcement Teachers, Postsecondary; Economics Teachers, Postsecondary; Education Teachers, Postsecondary; Engineering Teachers, Postsecondary; English Language and Literature Teachers, Postsecondary; Environmental Science Teachers, Postsecondary; Farm and Home Management Advisors; Foreign Language and Literature Teachers, Postsecondary; Forestry and Conservation Science Teachers, Postsecondary; Geography Teachers, Postsecondary; Graduate Teaching Assistants; Health Specialties Teachers, Postsecondary; History Teachers, Postsecondary; Home Economics Teachers, Postsecondary; Law Teachers, Postsecondary; Library Science Teachers, Postsecondary; Mathematical Science Teachers, Postsecondary; Nursing Instructors and Teachers, Postsecondary; Philosophy and Religion Teachers, Postsecondary; Physics Teachers, Postsecondary; Political Science Teachers, Postsecondary; Psychology Teachers, Postsecondary; Recreation and Fitness Studies Teachers, Postsecondary; Social Work Teachers, Postsecondary; Sociology Teachers, Postsecondary.

Skills—Instructing: Teaching others how to do something. **Learning Strategies:** Using multiple approaches when learning or teaching new things. **Writing:** Communicating effectively with others in writing as indicated by the needs of the audience. **Monitoring:** Assessing how well one is doing when learning or doing something. **Speaking:** Talking to others to effectively convey information. **Active Learning:** Working with new material or information to grasp its implications. **Reading Comprehension:** Understanding written sentences and paragraphs in work-related documents. **Critical Thinking:** Using logic and analysis to identify the strengths and weaknesses of different approaches.

Education and Training Programs: Business Teacher Education; Business/Commerce, General; Business Administration and Management, General; Purchasing, Procurement/Acquisitions and Contracts Management; Logistics and Materials Management; Operations Management and Supervision; Accounting; Business/Corporate Communications; Entrepreneurship/Entrepreneurial Studies; Franchising and Franchise Operations; Finance, General; others. **Related Knowledge/Courses—Economics and Accounting:** Economic and accounting principles and practices, the financial markets, banking, and the analysis and reporting of financial data. **Education and Training:** Instructional methods and training techniques, including curriculum design principles, learning theory, group and individual teaching techniques, design of individual development plans, and test design principles. **Sociology and Anthropology:** Group behavior and dynamics; societal trends and influences; and cultures and their history, migrations, ethnicity, and origins. **Sales and Marketing:** Principles and methods involved in showing, promoting, and selling products or services. This includes marketing strategies and tactics, product demonstration and sales techniques, and sales control systems. **Philosophy and Theology:** Different philosophical systems and religions, including their basic principles, values, ethics, ways of thinking, customs, and practices and their impact on human culture. **English Language:** The structure and content of the English language, including the meaning and spelling of words, rules of composition, and grammar.

Work Environment: Indoors; sitting.

Cardiovascular Technologists and Technicians

❋ Education/Training Required:
   Associate degree
❋ Annual Earnings: $44,940
❋ Beginning Wage: $24,650
❋ Earnings Growth Potential: High
❋ Growth: 25.5%
❋ Annual Job Openings: 3,550
❋ Self-Employed: 1.1%
❋ Part-Time: 17.3%

Conduct tests on pulmonary or cardiovascular systems of patients for diagnostic purposes. May conduct or assist in electrocardiograms, cardiac catheterizations, pulmonary-functions, lung capacity, and similar tests. Monitor patients' blood pressures and heart rates, using electrocardiogram (EKG) equipment during diagnostic and therapeutic procedures to notify physicians if something appears wrong. Explain testing procedures to patients to obtain cooperation and reduce anxiety. Observe gauges, recorders, and video screens of data analysis systems during imaging of cardiovascular systems. Monitor patients' comfort and safety during tests, alerting physicians to abnormalities or changes in patient responses. Obtain and record patients' identities, medical histories, or test results. Attach electrodes to patients' chests, arms, and legs; connect electrodes to leads from electrocardiogram (EKG) machines; and operate EKG machines to obtain readings. Adjust equipment and controls according to physicians' orders or established protocol. Prepare and position patients for testing. Check, test, and maintain cardiology equipment, making minor repairs when necessary, to ensure proper operation. Supervise and train other cardiology technologists and students. Perform general administrative tasks, such as scheduling appointments or ordering supplies and equipment. Maintain a proper sterile field during surgical procedures. Assist physicians in the diagnosis and treatment of cardiac and peripheral vascular treatments, such as implanting pacemakers or assisting with balloon angioplasties to treat blood vessel blockages. Inject contrast medium into patients' blood vessels. Assess cardiac physiology and calculate valve areas from blood flow velocity measurements. Operate diagnostic imaging equipment to produce contrast enhanced radiographs of hearts and cardiovascular systems. Observe ultrasound display screens and listen to signals to record vascular information such as blood pressure, limb volume changes, oxygen saturation, and cerebral circulation. Transcribe, type, and distribute reports of diagnostic procedures for interpretation by physician. Conduct electrocardiogram (EKG), phonocardiogram, echocardiogram, stress testing, or other cardiovascular tests to record patients' cardiac activities, using specialized electronic test equipment, recording devices, and laboratory instruments.

Personality Type: Realistic. These occupations frequently involve work activities that include practical, hands-on problems and solutions. They often deal with plants; animals; and real-world materials such as wood, tools, and machinery. Many of the occupations require working outside and don't involve a lot of paperwork or working closely with others.

GOE—Interest Area/Cluster: 08. Health Science. **Work Group:** 08.06. Medical Technology. **Other Jobs in This Work Group:** Biological Technicians; Diagnostic Medical Sonographers; Medical and Clinical Laboratory Technicians; Medical and Clinical Laboratory Technologists; Medical Records and Health Information Technicians; Nuclear Medicine Technologists; Orthotists and Prosthetists; Radiologic Technicians;

Radiologic Technologists; Radiologic Technologists and Technicians.

Skills—Operation Monitoring: Watching gauges, dials, or other indicators to make sure a machine is working properly. **Management of Personnel Resources:** Motivating, developing, and directing people as they work; identifying the best people for the job. **Systems Analysis:** Determining how a system should work and how changes will affect outcomes. **Quality Control Analysis:** Evaluating the quality or performance of products, services, or processes. **Management of Material Resources:** Obtaining and seeing to the appropriate use of equipment, facilities, and materials needed to do certain work.

Education and Training Programs: Cardiovascular Technology/Technologist; Electrocardiograph Technology/Technician; Perfusion Technology/Perfusionist; Cardiopulmonary Technology/Technologist. **Related Knowledge/Courses—Medicine and Dentistry:** The information and techniques needed to diagnose and treat injuries, diseases, and deformities. This includes symptoms, treatment alternatives, drug properties and interactions, and preventive health-care measures. **Biology:** Plant and animal living tissue, cells, organisms, and entities, including their functions, interdependencies, and interactions with each other and the environment. **Psychology:** Human behavior and performance, mental processes, psychological research methods, and the assessment and treatment of behavioral and affective disorders. **Customer and Personal Service:** Principles and processes for providing customer and personal services, including needs assessment techniques, quality service standards, alternative delivery systems, and customer satisfaction evaluation techniques. **Sociology and Anthropology:** Group behavior and dynamics; societal trends and influences; and cultures and their history, migrations, ethnicity, and origins. **Chemistry:** The composition, structure, and properties of substances and of the chemical processes and transformations that they undergo. This includes uses of chemicals and their interactions, danger signs, production techniques, and disposal methods.

Work Environment: Indoors; radiation; disease or infections; standing; using hands on objects, tools, or controls; repetitive motions.

Cartographers and Photogrammetrists

- ✻ Education/Training Required: Bachelor's degree
- ✻ Annual Earnings: $49,970
- ✻ Beginning Wage: $32,380
- ✻ Earnings Growth Potential: Medium
- ✻ Growth: 20.3%
- ✻ Annual Job Openings: 2,823
- ✻ Self-Employed: 3.4%
- ✻ Part-Time: 4.6%

Collect, analyze, and interpret geographic information provided by geodetic surveys, aerial photographs, and satellite data. Research, study, and prepare maps and other spatial data in digital or graphic form for legal, social, political, educational, and design purposes. May work with Geographic Information Systems (GIS). May design and evaluate algorithms, data structures, and user interfaces for GIS and mapping systems. Identify, scale, and orient geodetic points, elevations, and other planimetric or topographic features, applying standard mathematical formulas. Collect information about specific features of the Earth, using aerial photography and other digital remote sensing techniques. Revise existing maps and charts, making all necessary corrections and adjustments. Compile data required for map preparation, including aerial photographs, survey notes, records, reports, and original maps. Inspect final compositions to ensure completeness and accuracy. Determine map content and layout, as well as production specifications such as scale, size, projection, and colors, and direct production to ensure that specifications are followed. Examine and analyze data from ground surveys, reports, aerial photographs, and satellite images to prepare topographic maps, aerial-photograph mosaics, and related charts. Select aerial photographic and remote sensing techniques and plotting equipment needed to meet required standards of accuracy. Delineate aerial photographic detail such as control points, hydrography, topography, and cultural features, using precision stereo-plotting apparatus or drafting instruments. Build and update digital databases. Prepare and alter trace maps, charts, tables, detailed drawings, and three-dimensional optical models of terrain, using stereoscopic plotting and computer graphics equipment. Determine guidelines that specify which source material is acceptable for use. Study legal records to establish boundaries of local, national, and international properties. Travel over photographed areas to observe, identify, record, and verify all relevant features.

Personality Type: Realistic. These occupations frequently involve work activities that include practical, hands-on problems and solutions. They often deal with plants; animals; and real-world materials such as wood, tools, and machinery. Many of the occupations require working outside and don't involve a lot of paperwork or working closely with others.

GOE—Interest Area/Cluster: 15. Scientific Research, Engineering, and Mathematics. **Work Group:** 15.09. Engineering Technology. **Other Jobs in This Work Group:** Aerospace Engineering and Operations Technicians; Civil Engineering Technicians; Electrical and Electronic Engineering Technicians; Electrical Engineering Technicians; Electro-Mechanical Technicians; Electronics Engineering Technicians; Environmental Engineering Technicians; Mechanical Engineering Technicians.

Skills—Science: Using scientific methods to solve problems. **Technology Design:** Generating or adapting equipment and technology to serve user needs. **Mathematics:** Using mathematics to solve problems. **Active Learning:** Working with new material or information to grasp its implications. **Troubleshooting:** Determining what is causing an operating error and deciding what to do about it. **Reading Comprehension:** Understanding written sentences and paragraphs in work-related documents. **Operation and Control:** Controlling operations of equipment or systems. **Writing:** Communicating effectively with others in writing as indicated by the needs of the audience.

Education and Training Programs: Surveying Technology/Surveying; Cartography. **Related Knowledge/Courses—Geography:** Various methods for describing the location and distribution of land, sea, and air masses, including their physical locations, relationships, and characteristics. **Design:** Design techniques, principles, tools, and instruments involved in the production and use of precision technical plans, blueprints, drawings, and models. **Engineering and Technology:** Equipment, tools, and mechanical devices and their uses to produce motion, light, power, technology, and other applications. **Computers and Electronics:** Electric circuit boards, processors, chips, and computer hardware and software, including applications and programming. **Production and Processing:** Inputs, outputs, raw materials, waste, quality control, costs, and techniques for maximizing the manufacture and distribution of goods. **Mathematics:** Numbers and their operations and interrelationships, including arithmetic, algebra, geometry, calculus, and statistics and their applications.

Work Environment: Indoors; sitting; using hands on objects, tools, or controls; repetitive motions.

Chemical Engineers

* Education/Training Required: Bachelor's degree
* Annual Earnings: $81,500
* Beginning Wage: $52,060
* Earnings Growth Potential: Medium
* Growth: 7.9%
* Annual Job Openings: 2,111
* Self-Employed: 1.9%
* Part-Time: 3.4%

Design chemical plant equipment and devise processes for manufacturing chemicals and products, such as gasoline, synthetic rubber, plastics, detergents, cement, paper, and pulp, by applying principles and technology of chemistry, physics, and engineering. Perform tests throughout stages of production to determine degree of control over variables, including temperature, density, specific gravity, and pressure. Develop safety procedures to be employed by workers operating equipment or working in close proximity to ongoing chemical reactions. Determine most effective arrangement of operations such as mixing, crushing, heat transfer, distillation, and drying. Prepare estimate of production costs and production progress reports for management. Direct activities of workers who operate or who are engaged in constructing and improving absorption, evaporation, or electromagnetic equipment. Perform laboratory studies of steps in manufacture of new product and test proposed process in small-scale operation such as a pilot plant. Develop processes to separate components of liquids or gases or generate electrical currents by using controlled chemical processes. Conduct research to develop new and improved chemical manufacturing processes. Design measurement and control systems for chemical plants based on data collected in laboratory experiments and in pilot plant operations. Design and plan layout of equipment.

Personality Type: Investigative. These occupations frequently involve working with ideas and require an extensive amount of thinking. They can involve searching for facts and figuring out problems mentally.

GOE—Interest Area/Cluster: 15. Scientific Research, Engineering, and Mathematics. **Work Group:** 15.07. Research and Design Engineering. **Other Jobs in This Work Group:** Aerospace Engineers; Biomedical Engineers; Civil Engineers; Computer Hardware Engineers; Electrical Engineers; Electronics Engineers, Except Computer; Marine Architects; Marine Engineers; Marine Engineers and Naval Architects; Materials Engineers; Mechanical Engineers; Nuclear Engineers.

Skills—Science: Using scientific methods to solve problems. **Technology Design:** Generating or adapting equipment and technology to serve user needs. **Troubleshooting:** Determining what is causing an operating error and deciding what to do about it. **Programming:** Writing computer programs for various purposes. **Operations Analysis:** Analyzing needs and product requirements to create a design. **Installation:** Installing equipment, machines, wiring, or programs to meet specifications. **Mathematics:** Using mathematics to solve problems. **Systems Analysis:** Determining how a system should work and how changes will affect outcomes.

Education and Training Program: Chemical Engineering. **Related Knowledge/Courses— Engineering and Technology:** Equipment, tools, and mechanical devices and their uses to produce motion, light, power, technology, and other applications. **Chemistry:** The composition, structure, and properties of substances and of the chemical processes and transformations that they undergo. This includes uses of chemicals and their interactions, danger signs, production techniques, and disposal methods. **Physics:** Physical principles, laws, and applications, including air, water, material dynamics, light, atomic principles, heat, electric theory, earth formations, and meteorological and related natural phenomena. **Design:** Design techniques, principles, tools, and instruments involved in the production and use of precision technical plans, blueprints, drawings, and models. **Production and Processing:** Inputs, outputs, raw materials, waste, quality control, costs, and techniques for maximizing the manufacture and distribution of goods. **Mathematics:** Numbers and their operations and interrelationships, including arithmetic, algebra, geometry, calculus, and statistics and their applications.

Work Environment: Indoors; noisy; hazardous conditions; sitting.

Chemistry Teachers, Postsecondary

- ❋ Education/Training Required: Doctoral degree
- ❋ Annual Earnings: $63,870
- ❋ Beginning Wage: $37,810
- ❋ Earnings Growth Potential: High
- ❋ Growth: 22.9%
- ❋ Annual Job Openings: 3,405
- ❋ Self-Employed: 0.4%
- ❋ Part-Time: 27.8%

Teach courses pertaining to the chemical and physical properties and compositional changes of substances. Work may include instruction in the methods of qualitative and quantitative chemical analysis. Includes both teachers primarily engaged in teaching and those who do a combination of both teaching and research. Prepare and deliver lectures to undergraduate and/or graduate students on topics such as organic chemistry, analytical chemistry, and chemical separation. Supervise students' laboratory work. Evaluate and grade students' classwork, laboratory performance, assignments, and papers. Compile, administer, and grade examinations or assign this work to others. Maintain student attendance records, grades, and other required records. Prepare course materials such as syllabi, homework assignments, and handouts. Maintain regularly scheduled office hours to advise and assist students. Plan, evaluate, and revise curricula, course content, course materials, and methods of instruction. Supervise undergraduate and/or graduate teaching, internships, and research work. Keep abreast of developments in the field by reading current literature, talking with colleagues, and participating in professional conferences. Initiate, facilitate, and moderate classroom discussions. Select and obtain materials and supplies such as textbooks and laboratory equipment. Conduct research in a particular field of knowledge and publish findings in professional journals, books, and/or electronic media. Advise students on academic and vocational curricula and on career issues. Collaborate with colleagues to address teaching and research issues. Serve on academic or administrative committees that deal with institutional policies, departmental matters, and academic issues. Write grant proposals to procure external research funding. Participate in student recruitment, registration, and placement activities. Prepare and submit required reports related to instruction. Perform administrative duties such as serving as a department head. Act as advisers to student organizations. Compile bibliographies of specialized materials for outside reading assignments. Participate in campus and community events. Provide professional consulting services to government and/or industry.

Personality Type: Social. These occupations frequently involve working with, communicating with, and teaching people and often involve helping or providing service to others.

GOE—Interest Area/Cluster: 05. Education and Training. **Work Group:** 05.03. Postsecondary and Adult Teaching and Instructing. **Other Jobs in This Work Group:** Adult Literacy, Remedial Education, and GED Teachers and Instructors; Agricultural Sciences Teachers, Postsecondary; Anthropology and Archeology Teachers, Postsecondary; Architecture Teachers, Postsecondary; Area, Ethnic, and Cultural Studies Teachers, Postsecondary; Art, Drama, and Music Teachers, Postsecondary; Atmospheric, Earth, Marine, and Space Sciences Teachers, Postsecondary; Biological Science Teachers, Postsecondary; Business Teachers, Postsecondary; Communications Teachers, Postsecondary; Computer Science Teachers, Postsecondary; Criminal Justice and Law Enforcement Teachers, Postsecondary; Economics Teachers, Postsecondary; Education Teachers, Postsecondary; Engineering Teachers, Postsecondary; English Language and Literature Teachers, Postsecondary; Environmental Science Teachers, Postsecondary; Farm and Home Management Advisors; Foreign Language and Literature Teachers, Postsecondary; Forestry and Conservation Science Teachers, Postsecondary; Geography Teachers, Postsecondary; Graduate Teaching Assistants; Health Specialties Teachers, Postsecondary; History Teachers, Postsecondary; Home Economics Teachers, Postsecondary; Law Teachers, Postsecondary; Library Science Teachers, Postsecondary; Mathematical Science Teachers, Postsecondary; Nursing Instructors and Teachers, Postsecondary; Philosophy and Religion Teachers, Postsecondary; Physics Teachers, Postsecondary; Political Science Teachers, Postsecondary; Psychology Teachers, Postsecondary; Recreation and Fitness Studies Teachers, Postsecondary; Social Work Teachers, Postsecondary; Sociology Teachers, Postsecondary.

Skills—Science: Using scientific methods to solve problems. **Mathematics:** Using mathematics to solve problems. **Instructing:** Teaching others how to do something. **Writing:** Communicating effectively with others in writing as indicated by the needs of the audience. **Reading Comprehension:** Understanding written sentences and paragraphs in work-related documents. **Active Learning:** Working with new material or information to grasp its implications. **Technology Design:** Generating or adapting equipment and technology to serve user needs. **Complex Problem Solving:** Identifying complex problems, reviewing the options, and implementing solutions.

Education and Training Programs: Chemistry, General; Analytical Chemistry; Inorganic Chemistry; Organic Chemistry; Physical and Theoretical Chemistry; Polymer Chemistry; Chemical Physics; Chemistry, Other; Geochemistry. **Related Knowledge/Courses—Chemistry:** The composition, structure, and properties of substances and of the chemical processes and transformations that they undergo. This includes uses of chemicals and their interactions, danger signs, production techniques, and disposal methods. **Biology:** Plant and animal living tissue, cells, organisms, and entities, including their functions, interdependencies, and interactions with each other and the environment. **Physics:** Physical principles, laws, and applications, including air, water, material dynamics, light, atomic principles, heat, electric theory, earth formations, and meteorological and related natural phenomena. **Education and Training:** Instructional methods and training techniques, including curriculum design principles, learning theory, group and individual teaching techniques, design of individual development plans, and test design principles. **Mathematics:** Numbers and their operations and interrelationships, including arithmetic, algebra, geometry, calculus, and statistics and their applications. **English Language:** The structure and content of the English language, including the meaning and spelling of words, rules of composition, and grammar.

Work Environment: Indoors; contaminants; hazardous conditions; sitting.

Chemists

* Education/Training Required: Bachelor's degree
* Annual Earnings: $63,490
* Beginning Wage: $36,810
* Earnings Growth Potential: High
* Growth: 9.1%
* Annual Job Openings: 9,024
* Self-Employed: 1.2%
* Part-Time: 3.9%

Conduct qualitative and quantitative chemical analyses or chemical experiments in laboratories for quality or process control or to develop new products or knowledge. Analyze organic and inorganic compounds to determine chemical and physical properties, composition, structure, relationships, and reactions, utilizing chromatography, spectroscopy, and spectrophotometry techniques. Develop, improve, and customize products, equipment, formulas, processes, and analytical methods. Compile and analyze test information to determine process or equipment operating efficiency and to diagnose malfunctions. Confer with scientists and engineers to conduct analyses of research projects, interpret test results, or develop nonstandard tests. Direct, coordinate, and advise personnel in test procedures for analyzing components and physical properties of materials. Induce changes in composition of substances by introducing heat, light, energy, and chemical catalysts for quantitative and qualitative analysis. Write technical papers and reports and prepare standards and specifications for processes, facilities, products, or tests. Study effects of various methods of processing, preserving, and packaging on composition and properties of foods. Prepare test solutions, compounds, and reagents for laboratory personnel to conduct test.

Personality Type: Investigative. These occupations frequently involve working with ideas and require an extensive amount of thinking. They can involve searching for facts and figuring out problems mentally.

GOE—Interest Area/Cluster: 15. Scientific Research, Engineering, and Mathematics. **Work Group:** 15.02. Physical Sciences. **Other Jobs in This Work Group:** Astronomers; Atmospheric and Space Scientists; Geographers; Geoscientists, Except Hydrologists and Geographers; Hydrologists; Materials Scientists; Physicists.

Skills—Science: Using scientific methods to solve problems. **Quality Control Analysis:** Evaluating the quality or performance of products, services, or processes. **Technology Design:** Generating or adapting equipment and technology to serve user needs. **Operation Monitoring:** Watching gauges, dials, or other indicators to make sure a machine is working properly. **Equipment Selection:** Determining the kind of tools and equipment needed to do a job. **Management of Material Resources:** Obtaining and seeing to the appropriate use of equipment, facilities, and materials needed to do certain work. **Management of Financial Resources:** Determining how money will be spent to get the work done and accounting for these expenditures. **Operations Analysis:** Analyzing needs and product requirements to create a design.

Education and Training Programs: Chemistry, General; Analytical Chemistry; Inorganic Chemistry; Organic Chemistry; Physical and Theoretical Chemistry; Polymer Chemistry; Chemical

C

Physics; Chemistry, Other. **Related Knowledge/ Courses—Chemistry:** The composition, structure, and properties of substances and of the chemical processes and transformations that they undergo. This includes uses of chemicals and their interactions, danger signs, production techniques, and disposal methods. **Mathematics:** Numbers and their operations and interrelationships, including arithmetic, algebra, geometry, calculus, and statistics and their applications. **Engineering and Technology:** Equipment, tools, and mechanical devices and their uses to produce motion, light, power, technology, and other applications. **Production and Processing:** Inputs, outputs, raw materials, waste, quality control, costs, and techniques for maximizing the manufacture and distribution of goods. **Computers and Electronics:** Electric circuit boards, processors, chips, and computer hardware and software, including applications and programming. **Law and Government:** Laws, legal codes, court procedures, precedents, government regulations, executive orders, agency rules, and the democratic political process.

Work Environment: Indoors; contaminants; hazardous conditions; standing.

Chief Executives

- ❋ Education/Training Required: Work experience plus degree
- ❋ Annual Earnings: More than $145,600
- ❋ Beginning Wage: $64,530
- ❋ Earnings Growth Potential: Cannot be calculated
- ❋ Growth: 2.0%
- ❋ Annual Job Openings: 21,209
- ❋ Self-Employed: 22.0%
- ❋ Part-Time: 5.5%

Determine and formulate policies and provide the overall direction of companies or private and public sector organizations within the guidelines set up by a board of directors or similar governing body. Plan, direct, or coordinate operational activities at the highest level of management with the help of subordinate executives and staff managers. Direct and coordinate an organization's financial and budget activities in order to fund operations, maximize investments, and increase efficiency. Confer with board members, organization officials, and staff members to discuss issues, coordinate activities, and resolve problems. Analyze operations to evaluate performance of a company and its staff in meeting objectives and to determine areas of potential cost reduction, program improvement, or policy change. Direct, plan, and implement policies, objectives, and activities of organizations or businesses in order to ensure continuing operations, to maximize returns on investments, and to increase productivity. Prepare budgets for approval, including those for funding and implementation of programs. Direct and coordinate activities of businesses or departments concerned with production, pricing, sales, and/ or distribution of products. Negotiate or approve contracts and agreements with suppliers, distributors, federal and state agencies, and other organizational entities. Review reports submitted by staff members in order to recommend approval or to suggest changes. Appoint department heads or managers and assign or delegate responsibilities to them. Direct human resources activities, including the approval of human resource plans and activities, the selection of directors and other high-level staff, and establishment and organization of major departments. Preside over or serve on boards of directors, management committees, or other governing boards. Prepare and present reports concerning activities, expenses, budgets, government statutes and rulings, and other items affecting businesses or program services. Establish departmental responsibilities and coordinate functions among departments and sites. Implement corrective action plans to solve organizational or departmental problems. Coordinate the development and implementation of budgetary control systems, recordkeeping systems, and other administrative control processes. Direct non-merchandising departments such as advertising, purchasing, credit, and accounting. Deliver speeches, write articles, and present information at meetings or conventions in order to promote services, exchange ideas, and accomplish objectives.

Personality Type: Enterprising. These occupations frequently involve starting up and carrying out projects and can involve leading people and making many decisions. They sometimes require risk taking and often deal with business.

GOE—Interest Area/Cluster: 04. Business and Administration. **Work Group:** 04.01. Managerial Work in General Business. **Other Jobs in This Work Group:** Compensation and Benefits Managers; General and Operations Managers; Human Resources Managers; Training and Development Managers.

Skills—Management of Financial Resources: Determining how money will be spent to get the work done and accounting for these expenditures. **Management of Material Resources:** Obtaining and seeing to the appropriate use of equipment, facilities, and materials needed to do certain work. **Judgment and Decision Making:** Weighing the relative costs and benefits of a potential action. **Negotiation:** Bringing others together and trying to reconcile differences. **Management of Personnel Resources:** Motivating, developing, and directing people as they work; identifying the best people for the job. **Systems Evaluation:** Looking at many indicators of system performance and taking into account their accuracy. **Coordination:** Adjusting actions in relation to others' actions.

Operations Analysis: Analyzing needs and product requirements to create a design.

Education and Training Programs: Business Administration/Management; Business/Commerce, General; Entrepreneurship/Entrepreneurial Studies; International Business/Trade/Commerce; International Relations and Affairs; Public Administration; Public Administration and Services, Other; Public Policy Analysis; Transportation/Transportation Management. **Related Knowledge/Courses—Economics and Accounting:** Economic and accounting principles and practices, the financial markets, banking, and the analysis and reporting of financial data. **Administration and Management:** Principles and processes involved in business and organizational planning, coordination, and execution. This includes strategic planning, resource allocation, manpower modeling, leadership techniques, and production methods. **Sales and Marketing:** Principles and methods involved in showing, promoting, and selling products or services. This includes marketing strategies and tactics, product demonstration and sales techniques, and sales control systems. **Personnel and Human Resources:** Principles and procedures for personnel recruitment; selection; training; compensation and benefits; labor relations and negotiation; and personnel information systems. **Law and Government:** Laws, legal codes, court procedures, precedents, government regulations, executive orders, agency rules, and the democratic political process. **Medicine and Dentistry:** The information and techniques needed to diagnose and treat injuries, diseases, and deformities. This includes symptoms, treatment alternatives, drug properties and interactions, and preventive health-care measures.

Work Environment: Indoors; sitting.

Child, Family, and School Social Workers

* Education/Training Required: Bachelor's degree
* Annual Earnings: $38,620
* Beginning Wage: $25,160
* Earnings Growth Potential: Low
* Growth: 19.1%
* Annual Job Openings: 35,402
* Self-Employed: 2.8%
* Part-Time: 9.4%

Provide social services and assistance to improve the social and psychological functioning of children and their families and to maximize the family well-being and the academic functioning of children. May assist single parents, arrange adoptions, and find foster homes for abandoned or abused children. In schools, they address such problems as teenage pregnancy, misbehavior, and truancy. May also advise teachers on how to deal with problem children. Interview clients individually, in families, or in groups, assessing their situations, capabilities, and problems, to determine what services are required to meet their needs. Counsel individuals, groups, families, or communities regarding issues including mental health, poverty, unemployment, substance abuse, physical abuse, rehabilitation, social adjustment, child care, or medical care. Maintain case history records and prepare reports. Counsel students whose behavior, school progress, or mental or physical impairment indicate a need for assistance, diagnosing students' problems and arranging for needed services. Consult with parents, teachers, and other school personnel to determine causes of problems such as truancy and misbehavior and to implement solutions. Counsel parents with child rearing problems, interviewing the child and family to determine whether further action is required. Develop and review service plans in consultation with clients and perform follow-ups assessing the quantity and quality of services provided. Collect supplementary information needed to assist clients, such as employment records, medical records, or school reports. Address legal issues, such as child abuse and discipline, assisting with hearings and providing testimony to inform custody arrangements. Provide, find, or arrange for support services, such as child care, homemaker service, prenatal care, substance abuse treatment, job training, counseling, or parenting classes, to prevent more serious problems from developing. Refer clients to community resources for services such as job placement, debt counseling, legal aid, housing, medical treatment, or financial assistance and provide concrete information, such as where to go and how to apply. Arrange for medical, psychiatric, and other tests that may disclose causes of difficulties and indicate remedial measures. Work in child and adolescent residential institutions. Administer welfare programs. Evaluate personal characteristics and home conditions of foster home or adoption applicants. Serve as liaisons between students, homes, schools, family services, child guidance clinics, courts, protective services, doctors, and other contacts to help children who face problems such as disabilities, abuse, or poverty.

Personality Type: Social. These occupations frequently involve working with, communicating with, and teaching people and often involve helping or providing service to others.

GOE—Interest Area/Cluster: 10. Human Service. **Work Group:** 10.01. Counseling and Social Work. **Other Jobs in This Work Group:** Clinical Psychologists; Clinical, Counseling, and School Psychologists; Counseling Psychologists; Marriage and Family Therapists; Medical and Public Health Social Workers; Mental Health and Substance Abuse Social Workers; Mental Health Counselors;

Probation Officers and Correctional Treatment Specialists; Rehabilitation Counselors; Substance Abuse and Behavioral Disorder Counselors.

Skills—Social Perceptiveness: Being aware of others' reactions and understanding why they react the way they do. **Service Orientation:** Actively looking for ways to help people. **Speaking:** Talking to others to effectively convey information. **Monitoring:** Assessing how well one is doing when learning or doing something. **Writing:** Communicating effectively with others in writing as indicated by the needs of the audience. **Learning Strategies:** Using multiple approaches when learning or teaching new things. **Negotiation:** Bringing others together and trying to reconcile differences. **Active Listening:** Listening to what other people are saying and asking questions as appropriate.

Education and Training Programs: Juvenile Corrections; Social Work; Youth Services/Administration. **Related Knowledge/Courses—Therapy and Counseling:** Information and techniques needed to rehabilitate physical and mental ailments and to provide career guidance, including alternative treatments, rehabilitation equipment and its proper use, and methods to evaluate treatment effects. **Psychology:** Human behavior and performance, mental processes, psychological research methods, and the assessment and treatment of behavioral and affective disorders. **Sociology and Anthropology:** Group behavior and dynamics; societal trends and influences; and cultures and their history, migrations, ethnicity, and origins. **Philosophy and Theology:** Different philosophical systems and religions, including their basic principles, values, ethics, ways of thinking, customs, and practices and their impact on human culture. **Customer and Personal Service:** Principles and processes for providing customer and personal services, including needs assessment techniques, quality service standards, alternative

delivery systems, and customer satisfaction evaluation techniques. **Law and Government:** Laws, legal codes, court procedures, precedents, government regulations, executive orders, agency rules, and the democratic political process.

Work Environment: Indoors; sitting.

Chiropractors

- Education/Training Required: First professional degree
- Annual Earnings: $65,890
- Beginning Wage: $32,530
- Earnings Growth Potential: Very high
- Growth: 14.4%
- Annual Job Openings: 3,179
- Self-Employed: 51.7%
- Part-Time: 23.6%

Adjust spinal column and other articulations of the body to correct abnormalities of the human body believed to be caused by interference with the nervous system. Examine patients to determine nature and extent of disorders. Manipulate spines or other involved areas. May utilize supplementary measures such as exercise, rest, water, light, heat, and nutritional therapy. Diagnose health problems by reviewing patients' health and medical histories; questioning, observing, and examining patients; and interpreting X rays. Maintain accurate case histories of patients. Evaluate the functioning of the neuromuscularskeletal system and the spine, using systems of chiropractic diagnosis. Perform a series of manual adjustments to spines, or other articulations of the body, to correct musculoskeletal systems. Obtain and record patients' medical histories. Advise patients about recommended courses of treatment. Consult with and refer patients to appropriate health practitioners when necessary. Analyze X rays to locate the sources of patients' difficulties and to rule out fractures or diseases as sources of problems. Counsel patients about nutrition, exercise, sleeping habits, stress management, and other matters. Arrange for diagnostic X rays to be taken. Suggest and apply the use of supports such as straps, tapes, bandages, and braces if necessary.

Personality Type: Social. These occupations frequently involve working with, communicating with, and teaching people and often involve helping or providing service to others.

GOE—Interest Area/Cluster: 08. Health Science. **Work Group:** 08.04. Health Specialties. **Other Jobs in This Work Group:** Optometrists; Podiatrists.

Skills—Service Orientation: Actively looking for ways to help people. **Systems Analysis:** Determining how a system should work and how changes will affect outcomes. **Systems Evaluation:** Looking at many indicators of system performance and taking into account their accuracy. **Management of Personnel Resources:** Motivating, developing, and directing people as they work; identifying the best people for the job. **Writing:** Communicating effectively with others in writing as indicated by the needs of the audience.

Education and Training Program: Chiropractic (DC). **Related Knowledge/Courses— Medicine and Dentistry:** The information and techniques needed to diagnose and treat injuries, diseases, and deformities. This includes symptoms, treatment alternatives, drug properties and interactions, and preventive health-care measures. **Therapy and Counseling:** Information and techniques needed to rehabilitate physical and mental ailments and to provide career guidance, including alternative treatments, rehabilitation equipment and its proper use, and methods to evaluate treatment effects. **Biology:** Plant and animal living tissue, cells, organisms, and entities, including their

functions, interdependencies, and interactions with each other and the environment. **Psychology:** Human behavior and performance, mental processes, psychological research methods, and the assessment and treatment of behavioral and affective disorders. **Personnel and Human Resources:** Principles and procedures for personnel recruitment; selection; training; compensation and benefits; labor relations and negotiation; and personnel information systems. **Sales and Marketing:** Principles and methods involved in showing, promoting, and selling products or services. This includes marketing strategies and tactics, product demonstration and sales techniques, and sales control systems.

Work Environment: Indoors; disease or infections; standing; using hands on objects, tools, or controls; bending or twisting the body; repetitive motions.

Civil Engineers

* Education/Training Required: Bachelor's degree
* Annual Earnings: $71,710
* Beginning Wage: $46,420
* Earnings Growth Potential: Medium
* Growth: 18.0%
* Annual Job Openings: 15,979
* Self-Employed: 4.9%
* Part-Time: 3.2%

Perform engineering duties in planning, designing, and overseeing construction and maintenance of building structures and facilities such as roads, railroads, airports, bridges, harbors, channels, dams, irrigation projects, pipelines, power plants, water and sewage systems, and waste disposal units. Includes architectural, structural, traffic, ocean, and geo-technical

engineers. Manage and direct staff members and the construction, operations, or maintenance activities at project site. Provide technical advice regarding design, construction, or program modifications and structural repairs to industrial and managerial personnel. Inspect project sites to monitor progress and ensure conformance to design specifications and safety or sanitation standards. Estimate quantities and cost of materials, equipment, or labor to determine project feasibility. Test soils and materials to determine the adequacy and strength of foundations, concrete, asphalt, or steel. Compute load and grade requirements, water flow rates, and material stress factors to determine design specifications. Plan and design transportation or hydraulic systems and structures, following construction and government standards and using design software and drawing tools. Analyze survey reports, maps, drawings, blueprints, aerial photography, and other topographical or geologic data to plan projects. Prepare or present public reports on topics such as bid proposals, deeds, environmental impact statements, or property and right-of-way descriptions. Direct or participate in surveying to lay out installations and establish reference points, grades, and elevations to guide construction. Conduct studies of traffic patterns or environmental conditions to identify engineering problems and assess the potential impact of projects.

Personality Type: Realistic. These occupations frequently involve work activities that include practical, hands-on problems and solutions. They often deal with plants; animals; and real-world materials such as wood, tools, and machinery. Many of the occupations require working outside and don't involve a lot of paperwork or working closely with others.

GOE—Interest Area/Cluster: 15. Scientific Research, Engineering, and Mathematics. **Work Group:** 15.07. Research and Design Engineering. **Other Jobs in This Work Group:** Aerospace Engineers; Biomedical Engineers; Chemical Engineers; Computer Hardware Engineers; Electrical Engineers; Electronics Engineers, Except Computer; Marine Architects; Marine Engineers; Marine Engineers and Naval Architects; Materials Engineers; Mechanical Engineers; Nuclear Engineers.

Skills—Management of Personnel Resources: Motivating, developing, and directing people as they work; identifying the best people for the job. **Systems Analysis:** Determining how a system should work and how changes will affect outcomes. **Systems Evaluation:** Looking at many indicators of system performance and taking into account their accuracy. **Management of Material Resources:** Obtaining and seeing to the appropriate use of equipment, facilities, and materials needed to do certain work. **Management of Financial Resources:** Determining how money will be spent to get the work done and accounting for these expenditures. **Operation Monitoring:** Watching gauges, dials, or other indicators to make sure a machine is working properly. **Negotiation:** Bringing others together and trying to reconcile differences. **Complex Problem Solving:** Identifying complex problems, reviewing the options, and implementing solutions.

Education and Training Programs: Civil Engineering, General; Transportation and Highway Engineering; Water Resources Engineering; Civil Engineering, Other. **Related Knowledge/ Courses—Engineering and Technology:** Equipment, tools, and mechanical devices and their uses to produce motion, light, power, technology, and other applications. **Design:** Design techniques, principles, tools, and instruments involved in the production and use of precision technical plans, blueprints, drawings, and models. **Building and Construction:** Materials, methods, and the appropriate tools to construct objects, structures, and buildings. **Physics:** Physical principles, laws, and applications, including air, water, material dynamics, light, atomic principles, heat, electric theory, earth formations, and meteorological and related natural phenomena. **Transportation:** Principles and methods for moving people or goods by air, rail, sea, or road, including their relative costs, advantages, and limitations. **Geography:** Various methods for describing the location and distribution of land, sea, and air masses, including their physical locations, relationships, and characteristics.

Work Environment: Indoors; sitting.

Clergy

* Education/Training Required: Master's degree
* Annual Earnings: $40,460
* Beginning Wage: $20,240
* Earnings Growth Potential: High
* Growth: 18.9%
* Annual Job Openings: 35,092
* Self-Employed: 0.1%
* Part-Time: 10.0%

Conduct religious worship and perform other spiritual functions associated with beliefs and practices of religious faith or denomination. Provide spiritual and moral guidance and assistance to members. Pray and promote spirituality. Read from sacred texts such as the Bible, Torah, or Koran. Prepare and deliver sermons and other talks. Organize and lead regular religious services. Share information about religious issues by writing articles, giving speeches, or teaching. Instruct people who seek conversion to a particular faith. Visit people in homes, hospitals, and prisons to provide them with comfort and support. Counsel individuals and groups concerning their spiritual, emotional, and personal needs. Train leaders of church, community, and youth groups. Administer

religious rites or ordinances. Study and interpret religious laws, doctrines, or traditions. Conduct special ceremonies such as weddings, funerals, and confirmations. Plan and lead religious education programs for congregation. Respond to requests for assistance during emergencies or crises. Devise ways in which congregation membership can be expanded. Collaborate with committees and individuals to address financial and administrative issues pertaining to congregation. Prepare people for participation in religious ceremonies. Perform administrative duties such as overseeing building management, ordering supplies, contracting for services and repairs, and supervising the work of staff members and volunteers. Refer people to community support services, psychologists, and doctors as necessary. Participate in fundraising activities to support congregation activities and facilities. Organize and engage in interfaith, community, civic, educational, and recreational activities sponsored by or related to their religion.

Personality Type: Social. These occupations frequently involve working with, communicating with, and teaching people and often involve helping or providing service to others.

GOE—Interest Area/Cluster: 10. Human Service. **Work Group:** 10.02. Religious Work. **Other Jobs in This Work Group:** Directors, Religious Activities and Education.

Skills—Management of Personnel Resources: Motivating, developing, and directing people as they work; identifying the best people for the job. **Management of Financial Resources:** Determining how money will be spent to get the work done and accounting for these expenditures. **Service Orientation:** Actively looking for ways to help people. **Negotiation:** Bringing others together and trying to reconcile differences. **Judgment and Decision Making:** Weighing the relative costs and benefits of a potential action. **Persuasion:** Persuading others to approach things differently. **Social**

Perceptiveness: Being aware of others' reactions and understanding why they react the way they do. **Coordination:** Adjusting actions in relation to others' actions.

Education and Training Programs: Theology/Theological Studies; Divinity/Ministry (BD, MDiv.); Pre-Theology/Pre-Ministerial Studies; Rabbinical Studies; Theological and Ministerial Studies, Other; Pastoral Studies/Counseling; Youth Ministry; Pastoral Counseling and Specialized Ministries, Other; Theology and Religious Vocations, Other; Clinical Pastoral Counseling/Patient Counseling. **Related Knowledge/Courses—Philosophy and Theology:** Different philosophical systems and religions, including their basic principles, values, ethics, ways of thinking, customs, and practices and their impact on human culture. **Therapy and Counseling:** Information and techniques needed to rehabilitate physical and mental ailments and to provide career guidance, including alternative treatments, rehabilitation equipment and its proper use, and methods to evaluate treatment effects. **Sociology and Anthropology:** Group behavior and dynamics; societal trends and influences; and cultures and their history, migrations, ethnicity, and origins. **Psychology:** Human behavior and performance, mental processes, psychological research methods, and the assessment and treatment of behavioral and affective disorders. **Public Safety and Security:** Weaponry; public safety; security operations, rules, regulations, precautions, and prevention; and the protection of people, data, and property. **Customer and Personal Service:** Principles and processes for providing customer and personal services, including needs assessment techniques, quality service standards, alternative delivery systems, and customer satisfaction evaluation techniques.

Work Environment: Indoors; sitting.

Clinical Psychologists

- ❋ Education/Training Required: Doctoral degree
- ❋ Annual Earnings: $62,210
- ❋ Beginning Wage: $37,300
- ❋ Earnings Growth Potential: High
- ❋ Growth: 15.8%
- ❋ Annual Job Openings: 8,309
- ❋ Self-Employed: 34.2%
- ❋ Part-Time: 24.0%

The job openings listed here are shared with Counseling Psychologists and with School Psychologists.

Diagnose or evaluate mental and emotional disorders of individuals through observation, interview, and psychological tests and formulate and administer programs of treatment. Identify psychological, emotional, or behavioral issues and diagnose disorders, using information obtained from interviews, tests, records, and reference materials. Develop and implement individual treatment plans, specifying type, frequency, intensity, and duration of therapy. Interact with clients to assist them in gaining insight, defining goals, and planning action to achieve effective personal, social, educational, and vocational development and adjustment. Discuss the treatment of problems with clients. Utilize a variety of treatment methods such as psychotherapy, hypnosis, behavior modification, stress reduction therapy, psychodrama, and play therapy. Counsel individuals and groups regarding problems such as stress, substance abuse, and family situations to modify behavior or to improve personal, social, and vocational adjustment. Write reports on clients and maintain required paperwork. Evaluate the effectiveness of counseling or treatments and the accuracy and completeness of diagnoses; then modify plans and diagnoses as necessary. Obtain and study medical, psychological, social, and family histories by interviewing individuals, couples, or families and by reviewing records. Consult reference material such as textbooks, manuals, and journals to identify symptoms, make diagnoses, and develop approaches to treatment. Maintain current knowledge of relevant research. Observe individuals at play, in group interactions, or in other contexts to detect indications of mental deficiency, abnormal behavior, or maladjustment. Select, administer, score, and interpret psychological tests to obtain information on individuals' intelligence, achievements, interests, and personalities. Refer clients to other specialists, institutions, or support services as necessary. Develop, direct, and participate in training programs for staff and students. Provide psychological or administrative services and advice to private firms and community agencies regarding mental health programs or individual cases. Provide occupational, educational, and other information to individuals so that they can make educational and vocational plans.

Personality Type: Investigative. These occupations frequently involve working with ideas and require an extensive amount of thinking. They can involve searching for facts and figuring out problems mentally.

GOE—Interest Area/Cluster: 10. Human Service. **Work Group:** 10.01. Counseling and Social Work. **Other Jobs in This Work Group:** Child, Family, and School Social Workers; Clinical, Counseling, and School Psychologists; Counseling Psychologists; Marriage and Family Therapists; Medical and Public Health Social Workers; Mental Health and Substance Abuse Social Workers; Mental Health Counselors; Probation Officers and Correctional Treatment Specialists; Rehabilitation Counselors; Substance Abuse and Behavioral Disorder Counselors.

Skills—Social Perceptiveness: Being aware of others' reactions and understanding why they react the way they do. **Service Orientation:** Actively looking for ways to help people. **Complex Problem Solving:** Identifying complex problems, reviewing the options, and implementing solutions. **Learning Strategies:** Using multiple approaches when learning or teaching new things. **Active Listening:** Listening to what other people are saying and asking questions as appropriate. **Negotiation:** Bringing others together and trying to reconcile differences. **Active Learning:** Working with new material or information to grasp its implications. **Critical Thinking:** Using logic and analysis to identify the strengths and weaknesses of different approaches.

Education and Training Programs: Psychology, General; Clinical Psychology; Counseling Psychology; Developmental and Child Psychology; School Psychology; Clinical Child Psychology; Psychoanalysis and Psychotherapy. **Related Knowledge/Courses—Therapy and Counseling:** Information and techniques needed to rehabilitate physical and mental ailments and to provide career guidance, including alternative treatments, rehabilitation equipment and its proper use, and methods to evaluate treatment effects. **Psychology:** Human behavior and performance, mental processes, psychological research methods, and the assessment and treatment of behavioral and affective disorders. **Sociology and Anthropology:** Group behavior and dynamics; societal trends and influences; and cultures and their history, migrations, ethnicity, and origins. **Philosophy and Theology:** Different philosophical systems and religions, including their basic principles, values, ethics, ways of thinking, customs, and practices and their impact on human culture. **Customer and Personal Service:** Principles and processes for providing customer and personal services, including needs assessment techniques, quality service standards, alternative delivery systems, and customer satisfaction evaluation techniques. **Medicine and Dentistry:** The information and techniques needed to diagnose and treat injuries, diseases, and deformities. This includes symptoms, treatment alternatives, drug properties and interactions, and preventive health-care measures.

Work Environment: Indoors; sitting.

Communications Teachers, Postsecondary

* Education/Training Required: Doctoral degree
* Annual Earnings: $54,720
* Beginning Wage: $29,700
* Earnings Growth Potential: High
* Growth: 22.9%
* Annual Job Openings: 4,074
* Self-Employed: 0.4%
* Part-Time: 27.8%

Teach courses in communications, such as organizational communications, public relations, radio/television broadcasting, and journalism. Evaluate and grade students' classwork, assignments, and papers. Prepare course materials such as syllabi, homework assignments, and handouts. Initiate, facilitate, and moderate classroom discussions. Prepare and deliver lectures to undergraduate or graduate students on topics such as public speaking, media criticism, and oral traditions. Compile, administer, and grade examinations or assign this work to others. Maintain student attendance records, grades, and other required records. Plan, evaluate, and revise curricula, course content, and course materials and methods of instruction. Maintain regularly scheduled office hours to advise and assist students. Keep abreast of developments in their field by reading current literature, talking with colleagues, and participating in professional conferences. Advise students on academic and vocational curricula and on career issues. Supervise undergraduate or graduate teaching, internship, and research work. Select and obtain materials and supplies such as textbooks. Collaborate with colleagues to address teaching and research issues. Conduct research in a particular field of knowledge and publish findings in professional journals, books, or electronic media. Participate in student recruitment, registration, and placement activities. Serve on academic or administrative committees that deal with institutional policies, departmental matters, and academic issues. Compile bibliographies of specialized materials for outside reading assignments. Act as advisers to student organizations. Participate in campus and community events. Perform administrative duties such as serving as department head. Write grant proposals to procure external research funding. Provide professional consulting services to government or industry.

Personality Type: Social. These occupations frequently involve working with, communicating with, and teaching people and often involve helping or providing service to others.

GOE—Interest Area/Cluster: 05. Education and Training. **Work Group:** 05.03. Postsecondary and Adult Teaching and Instructing. **Other Jobs in This Work Group:** Adult Literacy, Remedial Education, and GED Teachers and Instructors; Agricultural Sciences Teachers, Postsecondary; Anthropology and Archeology Teachers, Postsecondary; Architecture Teachers, Postsecondary; Area, Ethnic, and Cultural Studies Teachers, Postsecondary; Art, Drama, and Music Teachers, Postsecondary; Atmospheric, Earth, Marine, and Space Sciences Teachers, Postsecondary; Biological Science Teachers, Postsecondary; Business Teachers, Postsecondary; Chemistry Teachers, Postsecondary; Computer Science Teachers, Postsecondary; Criminal Justice and Law Enforcement Teachers, Postsecondary; Economics Teachers,

Postsecondary; Education Teachers, Postsecondary; Engineering Teachers, Postsecondary; English Language and Literature Teachers, Postsecondary; Environmental Science Teachers, Postsecondary; Farm and Home Management Advisors; Foreign Language and Literature Teachers, Postsecondary; Forestry and Conservation Science Teachers, Postsecondary; Geography Teachers, Postsecondary; Graduate Teaching Assistants; Health Specialties Teachers, Postsecondary; History Teachers, Postsecondary; Home Economics Teachers, Postsecondary; Law Teachers, Postsecondary; Library Science Teachers, Postsecondary; Mathematical Science Teachers, Postsecondary; Nursing Instructors and Teachers, Postsecondary; Philosophy and Religion Teachers, Postsecondary; Physics Teachers, Postsecondary; Political Science Teachers, Postsecondary; Psychology Teachers, Postsecondary; Recreation and Fitness Studies Teachers, Postsecondary; Social Work Teachers, Postsecondary; Sociology Teachers, Postsecondary.

Skills—Instructing: Teaching others how to do something. **Writing:** Communicating effectively with others in writing as indicated by the needs of the audience. **Persuasion:** Persuading others to approach things differently. **Learning Strategies:** Using multiple approaches when learning or teaching new things. **Monitoring:** Assessing how well one is doing when learning or doing something. **Speaking:** Talking to others to effectively convey information. **Social Perceptiveness:** Being aware of others' reactions and understanding why they react the way they do. **Critical Thinking:** Using logic and analysis to identify the strengths and weaknesses of different approaches.

Education and Training Programs: Communication Studies/Speech Communication and Rhetoric; Mass Communication/Media Studies; Journalism; Broadcast Journalism; Journalism, Other; Radio and Television; Digital Communication and Media/Multimedia; Public Relations/

Image Management; Advertising; Political Communication; Health Communication; Communication, Journalism, and Related Programs, Other. **Related Knowledge/Courses—Communications and Media:** Media production, communication, and dissemination techniques and methods, including alternative ways to inform and entertain via written, oral, and visual media. **Education and Training:** Instructional methods and training techniques, including curriculum design principles, learning theory, group and individual teaching techniques, design of individual development plans, and test design principles. **Philosophy and Theology:** Different philosophical systems and religions, including their basic principles, values, ethics, ways of thinking, customs, and practices and their impact on human culture. **Sociology and Anthropology:** Group behavior and dynamics; societal trends and influences; and cultures and their history, migrations, ethnicity, and origins. **English Language:** The structure and content of the English language, including the meaning and spelling of words, rules of composition, and grammar. **History and Archeology:** Historical events and their causes, indicators, and impact on particular civilizations and cultures.

Work Environment: Indoors; sitting.

Compensation and Benefits Managers

- ❋ Education/Training Required: Work experience plus degree
- ❋ Annual Earnings: $81,410
- ❋ Beginning Wage: $46,050
- ❋ Earnings Growth Potential: High
- ❋ Growth: 12.0%
- ❋ Annual Job Openings: 6,121
- ❋ Self-Employed: 1.4%
- ❋ Part-Time: 2.7%

Plan, direct, or coordinate compensation and benefits activities and staff of an organization. Design, evaluate, and modify benefits policies to ensure that programs are current, competitive, and in compliance with legal requirements. Analyze compensation policies, government regulations, and prevailing wage rates to develop competitive compensation plans. Fulfill all reporting requirements of all relevant government rules and regulations, including the Employee Retirement Income Security Act (ERISA). Direct preparation and distribution of written and verbal information to inform employees of benefits, compensation, and personnel policies. Administer, direct, and review employee benefit programs, including the integration of benefit programs following mergers and acquisitions. Plan, direct, supervise, and coordinate work activities of subordinates and staff relating to employment, compensation, labor relations, and employee relations. Identify and implement benefits to increase the quality of life for employees by working with brokers and researching benefits issues. Manage the design and development of tools to assist employees in benefits selection and to guide managers through compensation decisions. Prepare detailed job descriptions and classification systems and define job levels and families in partnership with other managers. Prepare budgets for personnel operations. Formulate policies, procedures, and programs for recruitment, testing, placement, classification, orientation, benefits and compensation, and labor and industrial relations. Mediate between benefits providers and employees, such as by assisting in handling employees' benefits-related questions or taking suggestions. Develop methods to improve employment policies, processes, and practices and recommend changes to management. Study legislation, arbitration decisions, and collective bargaining contracts to assess industry trends. Maintain records and compile statistical reports concerning personnel-related data such as hires, transfers, performance appraisals, and absenteeism rates. Negotiate bargaining agreements. Conduct exit interviews to identify reasons for employee termination. Plan and conduct new employee orientations to foster positive attitude toward organizational objectives.

Personality Type: Enterprising. These occupations frequently involve starting up and carrying out projects and can involve leading people and making many decisions. They sometimes require risk taking and often deal with business.

GOE—Interest Area/Cluster: 04. Business and Administration. **Work Group:** 04.01. Managerial Work in General Business. **Other Jobs in This Work Group:** Chief Executives; General and Operations Managers; Human Resources Managers; Training and Development Managers.

Skills—Management of Financial Resources: Determining how money will be spent to get the work done and accounting for these expenditures. **Management of Personnel Resources:** Motivating, developing, and directing people as they work; identifying the best people for the job. **Systems Analysis:** Determining how a system should work and how changes will affect outcomes. **Systems Evaluation:** Looking at many indicators of system performance and taking into account their accuracy. **Negotiation:** Bringing others together and trying to reconcile differences. **Writing:** Communicating effectively with others in writing as indicated by the needs of the audience. **Persuasion:** Persuading others to approach things differently. **Judgment and Decision Making:** Weighing the relative costs and benefits of a potential action.

Education and Training Programs: Human Resources Management/Personnel Administration, General; Labor and Industrial Relations. **Related Knowledge/Courses—Personnel and Human Resources:** Principles and procedures for personnel recruitment; selection; training; compensation and benefits; labor relations and negotiation; and personnel information systems. **Economics and Accounting:** Economic and accounting principles and practices, the financial markets, banking, and the analysis and reporting of financial data. **Administration and Management:** Principles and processes involved in business and organizational planning, coordination, and execution. This includes strategic planning, resource allocation, manpower modeling, leadership techniques, and production methods. **Mathematics:** Numbers and their operations and interrelationships, including arithmetic, algebra, geometry, calculus, and statistics and their applications. **Law and Government:** Laws, legal codes, court procedures, precedents, government regulations, executive orders, agency rules, and the democratic political process. **Communications and Media:** Media production, communication, and dissemination techniques and methods, including alternative ways to inform and entertain via written, oral, and visual media.

Work Environment: Indoors; sitting.

Compensation, Benefits, and Job Analysis Specialists

- ❋ Education/Training Required: Bachelor's degree
- ❋ Annual Earnings: $52,180
- ❋ Beginning Wage: $33,450
- ❋ Earnings Growth Potential: Medium
- ❋ Growth: 18.4%
- ❋ Annual Job Openings: 18,761
- ❋ Self-Employed: 2.1%
- ❋ Part-Time: 7.6%

Conduct programs of compensation and benefits and job analysis for employer. May specialize in specific areas, such as position classification and pension programs. Evaluate job positions, determining classification, exempt or non-exempt status, and salary. Ensure company compliance with federal and state laws, including reporting requirements. Advise managers and employees on state and federal employment regulations, collective agreements, benefit and compensation policies, personnel procedures, and classification programs. Plan, develop, evaluate, improve, and communicate methods and techniques for selecting, promoting, compensating, evaluating, and training workers. Provide advice on the resolution of classification and salary complaints. Prepare occupational classifications, job descriptions, and salary scales. Assist in preparing and maintaining personnel records and handbooks. Prepare reports such as organization and flow charts and career path reports to summarize job analysis and evaluation and compensation analysis information. Administer employee insurance, pension, and savings plans, working with insurance brokers and plan carriers. Negotiate collective agreements on behalf of employers or workers and mediate labor disputes and grievances. Develop, implement, administer, and evaluate personnel and labor relations programs, including performance appraisal, affirmative action, and employment equity programs. Perform multifactor data and cost analyses that may be used in areas such as support of collective bargaining agreements. Research employee benefit and health and safety practices and recommend changes or modifications to existing policies. Analyze organizational, occupational, and industrial data to facilitate organizational functions and provide technical information to business, industry, and government. Advise staff of individuals' qualifications. Assess need for and develop job analysis instruments and materials. Review occupational data on Alien Employment Certification Applications to determine the appropriate occupational title and code; provide local offices with information about immigration and occupations. Research job and worker requirements, structural and functional relationships among jobs and occupations, and occupational trends.

Personality Type: Conventional. These occupations frequently involve following set procedures and routines and can include working with data and details more than with ideas. Usually there is a clear line of authority to follow.

GOE—Interest Area/Cluster: 04. Business and Administration. **Work Group:** 04.03. Human Resources Support. **Other Jobs in This Work Group:** Employment Interviewers; Employment, Recruitment, and Placement Specialists; Personnel Recruiters; Training and Development Specialists.

Skills—Service Orientation: Actively looking for ways to help people. **Judgment and Decision Making:** Weighing the relative costs and benefits of a potential action. **Management of Financial Resources:** Determining how money will be spent to get the work done and accounting for these expenditures. **Persuasion:** Persuading others to approach things differently. **Active Listening:** Listening to what other people are saying and asking questions as appropriate. **Negotiation:** Bringing others together and trying to reconcile differences. **Monitoring:** Assessing how well one is doing when learning or doing something. **Coordination:** Adjusting actions in relation to others' actions.

Education and Training Programs: Human Resources Management/Personnel Administration, General; Labor and Industrial Relations. **Related Knowledge/Courses—Personnel and Human Resources:** Principles and procedures for personnel recruitment; selection; training; compensation and benefits; labor relations and negotiation; and personnel information systems. **Clerical Practices:** Administrative and clerical procedures and systems such as word-processing systems, filing and records management systems, stenography and transcription, forms, design principles, and other office procedures and terminology. **Customer and Personal Service:** Principles and processes for providing customer and personal services, including needs assessment techniques, quality service standards, alternative delivery systems, and customer satisfaction evaluation techniques. **English Language:** The structure and content of the English language, including the meaning and spelling of words, rules of composition, and grammar. **Administration and Management:** Principles and processes involved in business and organizational planning, coordination, and execution. This includes strategic planning, resource allocation, manpower modeling, leadership techniques, and production methods. **Law and Government:** Laws, legal codes, court procedures, precedents, government regulations, executive orders, agency rules, and the democratic political process.

Work Environment: Indoors; noisy; sitting; using hands on objects, tools, or controls; repetitive motions.

Computer and Information Scientists, Research

* Education/Training Required: Doctoral degree
* Annual Earnings: $97,970
* Beginning Wage: $55,930
* Earnings Growth Potential: High
* Growth: 21.5%
* Annual Job Openings: 2,901
* Self-Employed: 5.3%
* Part-Time: 5.6%

Conduct research into fundamental computer and information science as theorists, designers, or inventors. Solve or develop solutions to problems in the field of computer hardware and software. Analyze problems to develop solutions involving computer hardware and software. Assign or schedule tasks in order to meet work priorities and goals. Evaluate project plans and proposals to assess feasibility issues. Apply theoretical expertise and innovation to create or apply new technology, such as adapting principles for applying computers to new uses. Consult with users, management, vendors, and technicians to determine computing needs and system requirements. Meet with managers, vendors, and others to solicit cooperation and resolve problems. Conduct logical analyses of business, scientific, engineering, and other technical problems, formulating mathematical models of problems for solution by computers. Develop and interpret organizational goals, policies, and procedures. Participate in staffing decisions and direct training of subordinates. Develop performance standards and evaluate work in light of established standards. Design computers and the software that runs them. Maintain network hardware and software, direct network security measures, and monitor networks to ensure availability to system users.

Participate in multidisciplinary projects in areas such as virtual reality, human-computer interaction, or robotics. Approve, prepare, monitor, and adjust operational budgets. Direct daily operations of departments, coordinating project activities with other departments.

Personality Type: Investigative. These occupations frequently involve working with ideas and require an extensive amount of thinking. They can involve searching for facts and figuring out problems mentally.

GOE—Interest Area/Cluster: 11. Information Technology. **Work Group:** 11.02. Information Technology Specialties. **Other Jobs in This Work Group:** Computer Programmers; Computer Security Specialists; Computer Software Engineers, Applications; Computer Software Engineers, Systems Software; Computer Support Specialists; Computer Systems Analysts; Computer Systems Engineers/Architects; Database Administrators; Network Designers; Network Systems and Data Communications Analysts; Software Quality Assurance Engineers and Testers; Web Administrators; Web Developers.

Skills—Programming: Writing computer programs for various purposes. **Science:** Using scientific methods to solve problems. **Systems Analysis:** Determining how a system should work and how changes will affect outcomes. **Operations Analysis:** Analyzing needs and product requirements to create a design. **Technology Design:** Generating or adapting equipment and technology to serve user needs. **Active Learning:** Working with new material or information to grasp its implications. **Complex Problem Solving:** Identifying complex problems, reviewing the options, and implementing solutions. **Mathematics:** Using mathematics to solve problems.

Education and Training Programs: Computer and Information Sciences, General; Artificial

Intelligence and Robotics; Information Science/ Studies; Computer Systems Analysis/Analyst; Computer Science; Computer and Information Sciences and Support Services, Other; Medical Informatics. **Related Knowledge/Courses— Computers and Electronics:** Electric circuit boards, processors, chips, and computer hardware and software, including applications and programming. **Telecommunications:** Transmission, broadcasting, switching, control, and operation of telecommunications systems. **Engineering and Technology:** Equipment, tools, and mechanical devices and their uses to produce motion, light, power, technology, and other applications. **Mathematics:** Numbers and their operations and interrelationships, including arithmetic, algebra, geometry, calculus, and statistics and their applications. **Design:** Design techniques, principles, tools, and instruments involved in the production and use of precision technical plans, blueprints, drawings, and models. **Education and Training:** Instructional methods and training techniques, including curriculum design principles, learning theory, group and individual teaching techniques, design of individual development plans, and test design principles.

Work Environment: Indoors; sitting; using hands on objects, tools, or controls; repetitive motions.

Computer and Information Systems Managers

* Education/Training Required: Work experience plus degree
* Annual Earnings: $108,070
* Beginning Wage: $65,760
* Earnings Growth Potential: Medium
* Growth: 16.4%
* Annual Job Openings: 30,887
* Self-Employed: 1.4%
* Part-Time: 2.1%

Plan, direct, or coordinate activities in such fields as electronic data processing, information systems, systems analysis, and computer programming. Review project plans to plan and coordinate project activity. Manage backup, security, and user help systems. Develop and interpret organizational goals, policies, and procedures. Develop computer information resources, providing for data security and control, strategic computing, and disaster recovery. Consult with users, management, vendors, and technicians to assess computing needs and system requirements. Stay abreast of advances in technology. Meet with department heads, managers, supervisors, vendors, and others to solicit cooperation and resolve problems. Provide users with technical support for computer problems. Recruit, hire, train, and supervise staff or participate in staffing decisions. Evaluate data processing proposals to assess project feasibility and requirements. Review and approve all systems charts and programs prior to their implementation. Control operational budget and expenditures. Direct daily operations of department, analyzing workflow, establishing priorities, developing standards, and setting deadlines. Assign and review the work of systems analysts, programmers, and other computer-related workers. Evaluate the organization's technology use and needs and recommend improvements such as hardware and software upgrades. Prepare and review operational reports or project progress reports. Purchase necessary equipment.

Personality Type: Enterprising. These occupations frequently involve starting up and carrying out projects and can involve leading people and making many decisions. They sometimes require risk taking and often deal with business.

GOE—Interest Area/Cluster: 11. Information Technology. **Work Group:** 11.01. Managerial Work in Information Technology. **Other Jobs in This Work Group:** Network and Computer Systems Administrators.

Skills—Programming: Writing computer programs for various purposes. **Systems Analysis:** Determining how a system should work and how changes will affect outcomes. **Management of Financial Resources:** Determining how money will be spent to get the work done and accounting for these expenditures. **Systems Evaluation:** Looking at many indicators of system performance and taking into account their accuracy. **Management of Material Resources:** Obtaining and seeing to the appropriate use of equipment, facilities, and materials needed to do certain work. **Management of Personnel Resources:** Motivating, developing, and directing people as they work; identifying the best people for the job. **Operation Monitoring:** Watching gauges, dials, or other indicators to make sure a machine is working properly. **Quality Control Analysis:** Evaluating the quality or performance of products, services, or processes.

Education and Training Programs: Computer and Information Sciences, General; Information Science/Studies; Computer Science; System Administration/Administrator; Operations Management and Supervision; Management Information Systems, General; Information Resources Management/CIO Training; Knowledge Management. **Related Knowledge/Courses—Telecommunications:** Transmission, broadcasting, switching, control, and operation of telecommunications systems. **Computers and Electronics:** Electric circuit boards, processors, chips, and computer hardware and software, including applications and programming. **Economics and Accounting:** Economic and accounting principles and practices, the financial markets, banking, and the analysis and reporting of financial data. **Personnel and Human Resources:** Principles and procedures for personnel recruitment; selection; training; compensation and benefits; labor relations and negotiation; and personnel information systems. **Production and Processing:** Inputs, outputs, raw materials, waste, quality control, costs, and techniques for maximizing the manufacture and distribution of goods. **Administration and Management:** Principles and processes involved in business and organizational planning, coordination, and execution. This includes strategic planning, resource allocation, manpower modeling, leadership techniques, and production methods.

Work Environment: Indoors; sitting; using hands on objects, tools, or controls.

Computer Hardware Engineers

* Education/Training Required: Bachelor's degree
* Annual Earnings: $91,860
* Beginning Wage: $55,880
* Earnings Growth Potential: Medium
* Growth: 4.6%
* Annual Job Openings: 3,572
* Self-Employed: 3.6%
* Part-Time: 2.7%

Research, design, develop, and test computer or computer-related equipment for commercial, industrial, military, or scientific use. May supervise the manufacturing and installation of computer or computer-related equipment and components. Update knowledge and skills to keep up with rapid advancements in computer technology. Provide technical support to designers, marketing and sales departments, suppliers, engineers, and other team members throughout the product development and implementation process. Test and verify hardware and support peripherals to ensure that they meet specifications and requirements, analyzing and recording test data. Monitor functioning of equipment and make necessary modifications to ensure system operates in conformance with specifications. Analyze information to determine, recommend, and plan layout, including type of computers and peripheral equipment modifications. Build, test, and modify product prototypes, using working models or theoretical models constructed using computer simulation. Analyze user needs and recommend appropriate hardware. Direct technicians, engineering designers, or other technical support personnel as needed. Confer with engineering staff and consult specifications to evaluate interface between hardware and software and operational and performance requirements of overall system. Select hardware and material, assuring compliance with specifications and product requirements. Store, retrieve, and manipulate data for analysis of system capabilities and requirements. Write detailed functional specifications that document the hardware development process and support hardware introduction. Specify power supply requirements and configuration, drawing on system performance expectations and design specifications. Provide training and support to system designers and users. Assemble and modify existing pieces of equipment to meet special needs. Evaluate factors such as reporting formats required, cost constraints, and need for security restrictions

to determine hardware configuration. Design and develop computer hardware and support peripherals, including central processing units (CPUs), support logic, microprocessors, custom integrated circuits, and printers and disk drives. Recommend purchase of equipment to control dust, temperature, and humidity in area of system installation.

Personality Type: Investigative. These occupations frequently involve working with ideas and require an extensive amount of thinking. They can involve searching for facts and figuring out problems mentally.

GOE—Interest Area/Cluster: 15. Scientific Research, Engineering, and Mathematics. **Work Group:** 15.07. Research and Design Engineering. **Other Jobs in This Work Group:** Aerospace Engineers; Biomedical Engineers; Chemical Engineers; Civil Engineers; Electrical Engineers; Electronics Engineers, Except Computer; Marine Architects; Marine Engineers; Marine Engineers and Naval Architects; Materials Engineers; Mechanical Engineers; Nuclear Engineers.

Skills—Programming: Writing computer programs for various purposes. **Operations Analysis:** Analyzing needs and product requirements to create a design. **Systems Analysis:** Determining how a system should work and how changes will affect outcomes. **Systems Evaluation:** Looking at many indicators of system performance and taking into account their accuracy. **Troubleshooting:** Determining what is causing an operating error and deciding what to do about it. **Technology Design:** Generating or adapting equipment and technology to serve user needs. **Science:** Using scientific methods to solve problems. **Quality Control Analysis:** Evaluating the quality or performance of products, services, or processes.

Education and Training Programs: Computer Engineering, General; Computer Hardware Engineering. **Related Knowledge/**

Courses—Computers and Electronics: Electric circuit boards, processors, chips, and computer hardware and software, including applications and programming. **Engineering and Technology:** Equipment, tools, and mechanical devices and their uses to produce motion, light, power, technology, and other applications. **Telecommunications:** Transmission, broadcasting, switching, control, and operation of telecommunications systems. **Design:** Design techniques, principles, tools, and instruments involved in the production and use of precision technical plans, blueprints, drawings, and models. **Physics:** Physical principles, laws, and applications, including air, water, material dynamics, light, atomic principles, heat, electric theory, earth formations, and meteorological and related natural phenomena. **Communications and Media:** Media production, communication, and dissemination techniques and methods, including alternative ways to inform and entertain via written, oral, and visual media.

Work Environment: Indoors; sitting.

Computer Programmers

- ❈ Education/Training Required: Bachelor's degree
- ❈ Annual Earnings: $68,080
- ❈ Beginning Wage: $39,500
- ❈ Earnings Growth Potential: High
- ❈ Growth: –4.1%
- ❈ Annual Job Openings: 27,937
- ❈ Self-Employed: 3.9%
- ❈ Part-Time: 4.7%

Convert project specifications and statements of problems and procedures to detailed logical flow charts for coding into computer language. Develop and write computer programs to store, locate, and retrieve specific documents, data, and information. May program Web sites. Correct errors by making appropriate changes and rechecking the program to ensure that the desired results are produced. Conduct trial runs of programs and software applications to be sure that they will produce the desired information and that the instructions are correct. Compile and write documentation of program development and subsequent revisions, inserting comments in the coded instructions so others can understand the program. Write, update, and maintain computer programs or software packages to handle specific jobs such as tracking inventory, storing or retrieving data, or controlling other equipment. Consult with managerial, engineering, and technical personnel to clarify program intent, identify problems, and suggest changes. Perform or direct revision, repair, or expansion of existing programs to increase operating efficiency or adapt to new requirements. Write, analyze, review, and rewrite programs, using workflow chart and diagram and applying knowledge of computer capabilities, subject matter, and symbolic logic. Write or contribute to instructions or manuals to guide end users. Investigate whether networks, workstations, the central processing unit of the system, or peripheral equipment are responding to a program's instructions. Prepare detailed workflow charts and diagrams that describe input, output, and logical operation and convert them into a series of instructions coded in a computer language. Perform systems analysis and programming tasks to maintain and control the use of computer systems software as a systems programmer. Consult with and assist computer operators or system analysts to define and resolve problems in running computer programs. Assign, coordinate, and review work and activities of programming personnel. Collaborate with computer manufacturers and other users to develop new programming methods. Train subordinates in programming and program coding.

Personality Type: Investigative. These occupations frequently involve working with ideas and require an extensive amount of thinking. They can involve searching for facts and figuring out problems mentally.

GOE—Interest Area/Cluster: 11. Information Technology. **Work Group:** 11.02. Information Technology Specialties. **Other Jobs in This Work Group:** Computer and Information Scientists, Research; Computer Security Specialists; Computer Software Engineers, Applications; Computer Software Engineers, Systems Software; Computer Support Specialists; Computer Systems Analysts; Computer Systems Engineers/Architects; Database Administrators; Network Designers; Network Systems and Data Communications Analysts; Software Quality Assurance Engineers and Testers; Web Administrators; Web Developers.

Skills—Programming: Writing computer programs for various purposes. **Operations Analysis:** Analyzing needs and product requirements to create a design. **Technology Design:** Generating or adapting equipment and technology to serve user needs. **Systems Analysis:** Determining how a system should work and how changes will affect outcomes. **Troubleshooting:** Determining what is causing an operating error and deciding what to do about it. **Installation:** Installing equipment, machines, wiring, or programs to meet specifications. **Complex Problem Solving:** Identifying complex problems, reviewing the options, and implementing solutions. **Systems Evaluation:** Looking at many indicators of system performance and taking into account their accuracy.

Education and Training Programs: Artificial Intelligence and Robotics; Computer Programming/Programmer, General; Computer Programming, Specific Applications; Computer Programming, Vendor/Product Certification; Web Page, Digital/Multimedia and Information Resources Design; Computer Graphics; Web/Multimedia Management and Webmaster; Bioinformatics; Medical Office Computer Specialist/Assistant; Medical Informatics; E-Commerce/Electronic Commerce; others. **Related Knowledge/Courses—Computers and Electronics:** Electric circuit boards, processors, chips, and computer hardware and software, including applications and programming. **Design:** Design techniques, principles, tools, and instruments involved in the production and use of precision technical plans, blueprints, drawings, and models. **Telecommunications:** Transmission, broadcasting, switching, control, and operation of telecommunications systems. **Mathematics:** Numbers and their operations and interrelationships, including arithmetic, algebra, geometry, calculus, and statistics and their applications. **Economics and Accounting:** Economic and accounting principles and practices, the financial markets, banking, and the analysis and reporting of financial data. **Engineering and Technology:** Equipment, tools, and mechanical devices and their uses to produce motion, light, power, technology, and other applications.

Work Environment: Indoors; sitting; using hands on objects, tools, or controls; repetitive motions.

Computer Science Teachers, Postsecondary

- ❋ Education/Training Required: Doctoral degree
- ❋ Annual Earnings: $62,020
- ❋ Beginning Wage: $33,720
- ❋ Earnings Growth Potential: High
- ❋ Growth: 22.9%
- ❋ Annual Job Openings: 5,820
- ❋ Self-Employed: 0.4%
- ❋ Part-Time: 27.8%

Teach courses in computer science. May specialize in a field of computer science, such as the design and function of computers or operations and research analysis. Evaluate and grade students' classwork, laboratory work, assignments, and papers. Maintain student attendance records, grades, and other required records. Prepare and deliver lectures to undergraduate and/or graduate students on topics such as programming, data structures, and software design. Prepare course materials such as syllabi, homework assignments, and handouts. Compile, administer, and grade examinations or assign this work to others. Keep abreast of developments in their field by reading current literature, talking with colleagues, and participating in professional conferences. Initiate, facilitate, and moderate classroom discussions. Plan, evaluate, and revise curricula, course content, and course materials and methods of instruction. Supervise students' laboratory work. Maintain regularly scheduled office hours to advise and assist students. Select and obtain materials and supplies such as textbooks and laboratory equipment. Advise students on academic and vocational curricula and on career issues. Participate in student recruitment, registration, and placement activities. Collaborate with colleagues to address teaching and research issues. Serve on academic or administrative committees that deal with institutional policies, departmental matters, and academic issues. Act as advisers to student organizations. Supervise undergraduate and/or graduate teaching, internship, and research work. Perform administrative duties such as serving as department head. Conduct research in a particular field of knowledge and publish findings in professional journals, books, and/or electronic media. Direct research of other teachers or of graduate students working for advanced academic degrees. Provide professional consulting services to government and/or industry. Participate in campus and community events. Compile bibliographies of specialized materials for outside reading assignments. Write grant proposals to procure external research funding.

Personality Type: Social. These occupations frequently involve working with, communicating with, and teaching people and often involve helping or providing service to others.

GOE—Interest Area/Cluster: 05. Education and Training. **Work Group:** 05.03. Postsecondary and Adult Teaching and Instructing. **Other Jobs in This Work Group:** Adult Literacy, Remedial Education, and GED Teachers and Instructors; Agricultural Sciences Teachers, Postsecondary; Anthropology and Archeology Teachers, Postsecondary; Architecture Teachers, Postsecondary; Area, Ethnic, and Cultural Studies Teachers, Postsecondary; Art, Drama, and Music Teachers, Postsecondary; Atmospheric, Earth, Marine, and Space Sciences Teachers, Postsecondary; Biological Science Teachers, Postsecondary; Business Teachers, Postsecondary; Chemistry Teachers, Postsecondary; Communications Teachers, Postsecondary; Criminal Justice and Law Enforcement Teachers, Postsecondary; Economics Teachers, Postsecondary; Education Teachers, Postsecondary; Engineering Teachers, Postsecondary; English Language and Literature Teachers, Postsecondary; Environmental Science Teachers, Postsecondary; Farm and Home Management Advisors; Foreign Language and Literature Teachers, Postsecondary; Forestry and Conservation Science Teachers, Postsecondary; Geography Teachers, Postsecondary; Graduate Teaching Assistants; Health Specialties Teachers, Postsecondary; History Teachers, Postsecondary; Home Economics Teachers, Postsecondary; Law Teachers, Postsecondary; Library Science Teachers, Postsecondary; Mathematical Science Teachers, Postsecondary; Nursing Instructors and Teachers, Postsecondary; Philosophy and Religion Teachers, Postsecondary; Physics Teachers, Postsecondary; Political Science Teachers, Postsecondary; Psychology Teachers, Postsecondary;

Recreation and Fitness Studies Teachers, Postsecondary; Social Work Teachers, Postsecondary; Sociology Teachers, Postsecondary.

Skills—Programming: Writing computer programs for various purposes. **Instructing:** Teaching others how to do something. **Operations Analysis:** Analyzing needs and product requirements to create a design. **Technology Design:** Generating or adapting equipment and technology to serve user needs. **Science:** Using scientific methods to solve problems. **Mathematics:** Using mathematics to solve problems. **Learning Strategies:** Using multiple approaches when learning or teaching new things. **Complex Problem Solving:** Identifying complex problems, reviewing the options, and implementing solutions.

Education and Training Programs: Computer and Information Sciences, General; Computer Programming/Programmer, General; Information Science/Studies; Computer Systems Analysis/Analyst; Computer Science. **Related Knowledge/Courses—Computers and Electronics:** Electric circuit boards, processors, chips, and computer hardware and software, including applications and programming. **Education and Training:** Instructional methods and training techniques, including curriculum design principles, learning theory, group and individual teaching techniques, design of individual development plans, and test design principles. **Telecommunications:** Transmission, broadcasting, switching, control, and operation of telecommunications systems. **Mathematics:** Numbers and their operations and interrelationships, including arithmetic, algebra, geometry, calculus, and statistics and their applications. **Engineering and Technology:** Equipment, tools, and mechanical devices and their uses to produce motion, light, power, technology, and other applications. **English Language:** The structure and content of the English language, including the meaning and spelling of words, rules of composition, and grammar.

Work Environment: Indoors; sitting.

Computer Security Specialists

* Education/Training Required: Bachelor's degree
* Annual Earnings: $64,690
* Beginning Wage: $39,970
* Earnings Growth Potential: Medium
* Growth: 27.0%
* Annual Job Openings: 37,010
* Self-Employed: 0.4%
* Part-Time: 3.1%

The job openings listed here are shared with Network and Computer Systems Administrators.

Plan, coordinate, and implement security measures for information systems to regulate access to computer data files and prevent unauthorized modification, destruction, or disclosure of information. Train users and promote security awareness to ensure system security and to improve server and network efficiency. Develop plans to safeguard computer files against accidental or unauthorized modification, destruction, or disclosure and to meet emergency data processing needs. Confer with users to discuss issues such as computer data access needs, security violations, and programming changes. Monitor current reports of computer viruses to determine when to update virus protection systems. Modify computer security files to incorporate new software, correct errors, or change individual access status. Coordinate implementation of computer system plan with establishment personnel and outside vendors. Monitor use of data files and regulate access to safeguard information in computer files. Perform risk assessments and execute tests of data-processing system to ensure functioning of data-processing activities and security measures. Encrypt data transmissions and erect firewalls to conceal confidential information as it is being transmitted and to keep out tainted digital transfers. Document computer security and emergency measures policies, procedures, and tests. Review violations of computer security procedures and discuss procedures with violators to ensure violations are not repeated. Maintain permanent fleet cryptologic and carry-on direct support systems required in special land, sea surface, and subsurface operations.

Personality Type: Conventional. These occupations frequently involve following set procedures and routines and can include working with data and details more than with ideas. Usually there is a clear line of authority to follow.

GOE—Interest Area/Cluster: 11. Information Technology. **Work Group:** 11.02. Information Technology Specialties. **Other Jobs in This Work Group:** Computer and Information Scientists, Research; Computer Programmers; Computer Software Engineers, Applications; Computer Software Engineers, Systems Software; Computer Support Specialists; Computer Systems Analysts; Computer Systems Engineers/Architects; Database Administrators; Network Designers; Network Systems and Data Communications Analysts; Software Quality Assurance Engineers and Testers; Web Administrators; Web Developers.

Skills—Systems Evaluation: Looking at many indicators of system performance and taking into account their accuracy. **Systems Analysis:** Determining how a system should work and how changes will affect outcomes. **Operations Analysis:** Analyzing needs and product requirements to create a design. **Programming:** Writing computer programs for various purposes. **Installation:** Installing equipment, machines, wiring, or programs to meet specifications. **Management of Material Resources:** Obtaining and seeing to the appropriate use of equipment, facilities, and materials needed to do certain work. **Troubleshooting:** Determining what is causing an operating error and deciding what to do about it. **Management of Financial Resources:** Determining how money will be spent to get the work done and accounting for these expenditures.

Education and Training Programs: Computer and Information Sciences, General; Information Science/Studies; Computer Systems Analysis/Analyst; Computer Systems Networking and Telecommunications; System Administration/Administrator; System, Networking, and LAN/WAN Management/Manager; Computer and Information Systems Security; Computer and Information Sciences and Support Services, Other. **Related Knowledge/Courses—Computers and Electronics:** Electric circuit boards, processors, chips, and computer hardware and software, including applications and programming. **Telecommunications:** Transmission, broadcasting, switching, control, and operation of telecommunications systems. **Engineering and Technology:** Equipment, tools, and mechanical devices and their uses to produce motion, light, power, technology, and other applications. **Design:** Design techniques, principles, tools, and instruments involved in the production and use of precision technical plans, blueprints, drawings, and models. **Education and Training:** Instructional methods and training techniques, including curriculum design principles, learning theory, group and individual teaching techniques, design of individual development plans, and test design principles. **Therapy and Counseling:** Information and techniques needed to rehabilitate physical and mental ailments and to provide career guidance, including alternative treatments, rehabilitation equipment and its proper use, and methods to evaluate treatment effects.

Work Environment: Indoors; sitting.

Computer Software Engineers, Applications

- ❋ Education/Training Required: Bachelor's degree
- ❋ Annual Earnings: $83,130
- ❋ Beginning Wage: $52,090
- ❋ Earnings Growth Potential: Medium
- ❋ Growth: 44.6%
- ❋ Annual Job Openings: 58,690
- ❋ Self-Employed: 2.0%
- ❋ Part-Time: 2.6%

Develop, create, and modify general computer applications software or specialized utility programs. Analyze user needs and develop software solutions. Design software or customize software for client use with the aim of optimizing operational efficiency. May analyze and design databases within an application area, working individually or coordinating database development as part of a team. Confer with systems analysts, engineers, programmers, and others to design system and to obtain information on project limitations and capabilities, performance requirements, and interfaces. Modify existing software to correct errors, allow it to adapt to new hardware, or improve its performance. Analyze user needs and software requirements to determine feasibility of design within time and cost constraints. Consult with customers about software system design and maintenance. Coordinate software system installation and monitor equipment functioning to ensure specifications are met. Design, develop, and modify software systems, using scientific analysis and mathematical models to predict and measure outcome and consequences of design. Develop and direct software system testing and validation procedures, programming, and documentation. Analyze information to determine, recommend, and plan computer specifications and layouts and peripheral equipment modifications. Supervise the work of programmers, technologists, and technicians and other engineering and scientific personnel. Obtain and evaluate information on factors such as reporting formats required, costs, and security needs to determine hardware configuration. Determine system performance standards. Train users to use new or modified equipment. Store, retrieve, and manipulate data for analysis of system capabilities and requirements. Specify power supply requirements and configuration. Recommend purchase of equipment to control dust, temperature, and humidity in area of system installation.

Personality Type: Investigative. These occupations frequently involve working with ideas and require an extensive amount of thinking. They can involve searching for facts and figuring out problems mentally.

GOE—Interest Area/Cluster: 11. Information Technology. **Work Group:** 11.02. Information Technology Specialties. **Other Jobs in This Work Group:** Computer and Information Scientists, Research; Computer Programmers; Computer Security Specialists; Computer Software Engineers, Systems Software; Computer Support Specialists; Computer Systems Analysts; Computer Systems Engineers/Architects; Database Administrators; Network Designers; Network Systems and Data Communications Analysts; Software Quality Assurance Engineers and Testers; Web Administrators; Web Developers.

Skills—Programming: Writing computer programs for various purposes. **Troubleshooting:** Determining what is causing an operating error and deciding what to do about it. **Technology Design:** Generating or adapting equipment and technology to serve user needs. **Systems Analysis:** Determining how a system should work and how changes will affect outcomes. **Quality Control Analysis:** Evaluating the quality or performance of products, services, or processes. **Operations Analysis:** Analyzing needs and product requirements to create a design. **Installation:** Installing equipment, machines, wiring, or programs to meet specifications. **Complex Problem Solving:** Identifying complex problems, reviewing the options, and implementing solutions.

Education and Training Programs: Artificial Intelligence and Robotics; Information Technology; Computer Science; Computer Engineering, General; Computer Software Engineering; Computer Engineering Technologies/Technicians, Other; Bioinformatics; Medical Informatics; Medical Illustration and Informatics, Other. **Related Knowledge/Courses—Computers and Electronics:** Electric circuit boards, processors, chips, and computer hardware and software, including applications and programming. **Telecommunications:** Transmission, broadcasting, switching, control, and operation of telecommunications systems. **Engineering and Technology:** Equipment, tools, and mechanical devices and their uses to produce motion, light, power, technology, and other applications. **Design:** Design techniques, principles, tools, and instruments involved in the production and use of precision technical plans, blueprints, drawings, and models. **Mathematics:** Numbers and their operations and interrelationships, including arithmetic, algebra, geometry, calculus, and statistics and their applications. **Physics:** Physical principles, laws, and applications, including air, water, material dynamics, light, atomic principles, heat, electric theory, earth formations, and meteorological and related natural phenomena.

Work Environment: Indoors; sitting; using hands on objects, tools, or controls; repetitive motions.

Computer Software Engineers, Systems Software

* Education/Training Required: Bachelor's degree
* Annual Earnings: $89,070
* Beginning Wage: $55,870
* Earnings Growth Potential: Medium
* Growth: 28.2%
* Annual Job Openings: 33,139
* Self-Employed: 2.1%
* Part-Time: 2.6%

Research, design, develop, and test operating systems-level software, compilers, and network distribution software for medical, industrial, military, communications, aerospace, business, scientific, and general computing applications. Set operational specifications and formulate and analyze software requirements. Apply principles and techniques of computer science, engineering, and mathematical analysis. Modify existing software to correct errors, to adapt it to new hardware, or to upgrade interfaces and improve performance. Design and develop software systems, using scientific analysis and mathematical models to predict and measure outcome and consequences of design. Consult with engineering staff to evaluate interface between hardware and software, develop specifications and performance requirements, and resolve customer problems. Analyze information to determine, recommend, and plan installation of a new system or modification of an existing system. Develop and direct software system testing and validation procedures. Direct software programming and development of documentation. Consult with customers or other departments on project status, proposals, and technical issues such as software system design and maintenance. Advise customer about, or perform, maintenance of software system. Coordinate installation of software system. Monitor functioning of equipment to ensure system operates in conformance with specifications. Store, retrieve, and manipulate data for analysis of system capabilities and requirements. Confer with data processing and project managers to obtain information on limitations and capabilities for data-processing projects. Prepare reports and correspondence concerning project specifications, activities, and status. Evaluate factors such as reporting formats required, cost constraints, and need for security restrictions to determine hardware configuration. Supervise and assign work to programmers, designers, technologists and technicians, and other engineering and scientific personnel. Train users to use new or modified equipment. Utilize microcontrollers to develop control signals; implement control algorithms; and measure process variables such as temperatures, pressures, and positions. Recommend purchase of equipment to control dust, temperature, and humidity in area of system installation. Specify power supply requirements and configuration.

Personality Type: Investigative. These occupations frequently involve working with ideas and require an extensive amount of thinking. They can involve searching for facts and figuring out problems mentally.

GOE—Interest Area/Cluster: 11. Information Technology. **Work Group:** 11.02. Information Technology Specialties. **Other Jobs in This Work Group:** Computer and Information Scientists, Research; Computer Programmers; Computer Security Specialists; Computer Software Engineers, Applications; Computer Support Specialists; Computer Systems Analysts; Computer Systems Engineers/Architects; Database Administrators; Network Designers; Network Systems and Data Communications Analysts; Software Quality Assurance Engineers and Testers; Web Administrators; Web Developers.

Skills—Programming: Writing computer programs for various purposes. **Technology Design:** Generating or adapting equipment and technology to serve user needs. **Systems Analysis:** Determining how a system should work and how changes will affect outcomes. **Troubleshooting:** Determining what is causing an operating error and deciding what to do about it. **Operations Analysis:** Analyzing needs and product requirements to create a design. **Complex Problem Solving:** Identifying complex problems, reviewing the options, and implementing solutions. **Science:** Using scientific methods to solve problems. **Mathematics:** Using mathematics to solve problems.

Education and Training Programs: Artificial Intelligence and Robotics; Information Technology; Information Science/Studies; Computer Science; System, Networking, and LAN/WAN Management/Manager; Computer Engineering, General; Computer Engineering Technologies/Technicians, Other. **Related Knowledge/Courses—Computers and Electronics:** Electric circuit boards, processors, chips, and computer hardware and software, including applications and programming. **Design:** Design techniques, principles, tools, and instruments involved in the production and use of precision technical plans, blueprints, drawings, and models. **Engineering and Technology:** Equipment, tools, and mechanical devices and their uses to produce motion, light, power, technology, and other applications. **Telecommunications:** Transmission, broadcasting, switching, control, and operation of telecommunications systems. **Mathematics:** Numbers and their operations and interrelationships, including arithmetic, algebra, geometry, calculus, and statistics and their applications. **Communications and**

Media: Media production, communication, and dissemination techniques and methods, including alternative ways to inform and entertain via written, oral, and visual media.

Work Environment: Indoors; sitting; using hands on objects, tools, or controls; repetitive motions.

Computer Support Specialists

- ❋ Education/Training Required: Associate degree
- ❋ Annual Earnings: $42,400
- ❋ Beginning Wage: $25,950
- ❋ Earnings Growth Potential: Medium
- ❋ Growth: 12.9%
- ❋ Annual Job Openings: 97,334
- ❋ Self-Employed: 1.3%
- ❋ Part-Time: 6.9%

Provide technical assistance to computer system users. Answer questions or resolve computer problems for clients in person, via telephone, or from remote locations. May provide assistance concerning the use of computer hardware and software, including printing, installation, word processing, e-mail, and operating systems. Oversee the daily performance of computer systems. Answer user inquiries regarding computer software or hardware operation to resolve problems. Enter commands and observe system functioning to verify correct operations and detect errors. Set up equipment for employee use, performing or ensuring proper installation of cables, operating systems, or appropriate software. Install and perform minor repairs to hardware, software, or peripheral equipment, following design or installation specifications. Maintain records of daily data communication transactions, problems and remedial actions taken, or installation activities. Read technical manuals, confer with users, or conduct computer diagnostics to investigate and resolve problems or to provide technical assistance and support. Refer major hardware or software problems or defective products to vendors or technicians for service. Develop training materials and procedures or train users in the proper use of hardware or software. Confer with staff, users, and management to establish requirements for new systems or modifications. Prepare evaluations of software or hardware and recommend improvements or upgrades. Read trade magazines and technical manuals or attend conferences and seminars to maintain knowledge of hardware and software. Hire, supervise, and direct workers engaged in special project work, problem solving, monitoring, and installing data communication equipment and software. Inspect equipment and read order sheets to prepare for delivery to users. Modify and customize commercial programs for internal needs. Conduct office automation feasibility studies, including workflow analysis, space design, or cost comparison analysis.

Personality Type: Realistic. These occupations frequently involve work activities that include practical, hands-on problems and solutions. They often deal with plants; animals; and real-world materials such as wood, tools, and machinery. Many of the occupations require working outside and don't involve a lot of paperwork or working closely with others.

GOE—Interest Area/Cluster: 11. Information Technology. **Work Group:** 11.02. Information Technology Specialties. **Other Jobs in This Work Group:** Computer and Information Scientists, Research; Computer Programmers; Computer Security Specialists; Computer Software Engineers, Applications; Computer Software Engineers, Systems Software; Computer Systems Analysts; Computer Systems Engineers/Architects; Database Administrators; Network Designers;

Network Systems and Data Communications Analysts; Software Quality Assurance Engineers and Testers; Web Administrators; Web Developers.

Skills—Programming: Writing computer programs for various purposes. **Installation:** Installing equipment, machines, wiring, or programs to meet specifications. **Systems Analysis:** Determining how a system should work and how changes will affect outcomes. **Operation Monitoring:** Watching gauges, dials, or other indicators to make sure a machine is working properly. **Repairing:** Repairing machines or systems, using the needed tools. **Systems Evaluation:** Looking at many indicators of system performance and taking into account their accuracy. **Troubleshooting:** Determining what is causing an operating error and deciding what to do about it. **Operation and Control:** Controlling operations of equipment or systems.

Education and Training Programs: Agricultural Business Technology; Data Processing and Data Processing Technology/Technician; Computer Hardware Technology/Technician; Computer Software Technology/Technician; Accounting and Computer Science; Medical Office Computer Specialist/Assistant. **Related Knowledge/Courses—Computers and Electronics:** Electric circuit boards, processors, chips, and computer hardware and software, including applications and programming. **Telecommunications:** Transmission, broadcasting, switching, control, and operation of telecommunications systems. **Engineering and Technology:** Equipment, tools, and mechanical devices and their uses to produce motion, light, power, technology, and other applications. **Clerical Practices:** Administrative and clerical procedures and systems such as word-processing systems, filing and records management systems, stenography and transcription, forms, design principles, and other office procedures and terminology. **Customer and Personal Service:** Principles and processes for providing customer and personal services, including

needs assessment techniques, quality service standards, alternative delivery systems, and customer satisfaction evaluation techniques. **Communications and Media:** Media production, communication, and dissemination techniques and methods, including alternative ways to inform and entertain via written, oral, and visual media.

Work Environment: Indoors; sitting; using hands on objects, tools, or controls.

Computer Systems Analysts

- ❊ Education/Training Required: Bachelor's degree
- ❊ Annual Earnings: $73,090
- ❊ Beginning Wage: $43,930
- ❊ Earnings Growth Potential: Medium
- ❊ Growth: 29.0%
- ❊ Annual Job Openings: 63,166
- ❊ Self-Employed: 5.8%
- ❊ Part-Time: 5.6%

Analyze science, engineering, business, and all other data-processing problems for application to electronic data processing systems. Analyze user requirements, procedures, and problems to automate or improve existing systems and review computer system capabilities, workflow, and scheduling limitations. May analyze or recommend commercially available software. May supervise computer programmers. Provide staff and users with assistance solving computer-related problems, such as malfunctions and program problems. Test, maintain, and monitor computer programs and systems, including coordinating the installation of computer programs and systems. Use object-oriented programming languages as well as client and server applications development processes and multimedia and Internet technology. Confer with clients regarding the nature of the information processing or computation needs a computer program is to address. Coordinate and link the computer systems within an organization to increase compatibility and so information can be shared. Consult with management to ensure agreement on system principles. Expand or modify system to serve new purposes or improve workflow. Interview or survey workers, observe job performance, or perform the job to determine what information is processed and how it is processed. Determine computer software or hardware needed to set up or alter system. Train staff and users to work with computer systems and programs. Analyze information processing or computation needs and plan and design computer systems, using techniques such as structured analysis, data modeling, and information engineering. Assess the usefulness of pre-developed application packages and adapt them to a user environment. Define the goals of the system and devise flow charts and diagrams describing logical operational steps of programs. Develop, document, and revise system design procedures, test procedures, and quality standards. Review and analyze computer printouts and performance indicators to locate code problems; correct errors by correcting codes. Recommend new equipment or software packages. Read manuals, periodicals, and technical reports to learn how to develop programs that meet staff and user requirements. Supervise computer programmers or other systems analysts or serve as project leaders for particular systems projects. Utilize the computer in the analysis and solution of business problems such as development of integrated production and inventory control and cost analysis systems.

Personality Type: Investigative. These occupations frequently involve working with ideas and require an extensive amount of thinking. They can involve searching for facts and figuring out problems mentally.

GOE—Interest Area/Cluster: 11. Information Technology. **Work Group:** 11.02. Information Technology Specialties. **Other Jobs in This Work Group:** Computer and Information Scientists, Research; Computer Programmers; Computer Security Specialists; Computer Software Engineers, Applications; Computer Software Engineers, Systems Software; Computer Support Specialists; Computer Systems Engineers/Architects; Database Administrators; Network Designers; Network Systems and Data Communications Analysts; Software Quality Assurance Engineers and Testers; Web Administrators; Web Developers.

Skills—Installation: Installing equipment, machines, wiring, or programs to meet specifications. **Quality Control Analysis:** Evaluating the quality or performance of products, services, or processes. **Technology Design:** Generating or adapting equipment and technology to serve user needs. **Programming:** Writing computer programs for various purposes. **Systems Analysis:** Determining how a system should work and how changes will affect outcomes. **Troubleshooting:** Determining what is causing an operating error and deciding what to do about it. **Operations Analysis:** Analyzing needs and product requirements to create a design. **Systems Evaluation:** Looking at many indicators of system performance and taking into account their accuracy.

Education and Training Programs: Computer and Information Sciences, General; Information Technology; Computer Systems Analysis/Analyst; Web/Multimedia Management and Webmaster. **Related Knowledge/Courses—Computers and Electronics:** Electric circuit boards, processors, chips, and computer hardware and software, including applications and programming. **Telecommunications:** Transmission, broadcasting, switching, control, and operation of telecommunications systems. **Design:** Design techniques, principles, tools, and instruments involved in the production and use of precision technical plans, blueprints, drawings, and models. **Customer and Personal Service:** Principles and processes for providing customer and personal services, including needs assessment techniques, quality service standards, alternative delivery systems, and customer satisfaction evaluation techniques. **Law and Government:** Laws, legal codes, court procedures, precedents, government regulations, executive orders, agency rules, and the democratic political process. **Communications and Media:** Media production, communication, and dissemination techniques and methods, including alternative ways to inform and entertain via written, oral, and visual media.

Work Environment: Indoors; sitting.

Computer Systems Engineers/Architects

- ❋ Education/Training Required: Bachelor's degree
- ❋ Annual Earnings: $71,510
- ❋ Beginning Wage: $37,600
- ❋ Earnings Growth Potential: High
- ❋ Growth: 15.1%
- ❋ Annual Job Openings: 14,374
- ❋ Self-Employed: 6.6%
- ❋ Part-Time: 5.6%

The job openings listed here are shared with Network Designers; Software Quality Assurance Engineers and Testers; Web Administrators; and Web Developers.

Design and develop solutions to complex applications problems, system administration issues, or network concerns. Perform systems management and integration functions. Communicate with staff or clients to understand specific system requirements. Provide advice on project costs, design concepts, or design changes. Document design specifications, installation instructions, and other system-related information. Verify stability, interoperability, portability, security, or scalability of system architecture. Collaborate with engineers or software developers to select appropriate design solutions or ensure the compatibility of system components. Provide technical guidance or support for the development or troubleshooting of systems. Evaluate current or emerging technologies to consider factors such as cost, portability, compatibility, or usability. Identify system data, hardware, or software components required to meet user needs. Provide guidelines for implementing secure systems to customers or installation teams. Monitor system operation to detect potential problems. Direct the analysis, development, and operation of complete computer systems. Investigate system component suitability for specified purposes and make recommendations regarding component use. Perform ongoing hardware and software maintenance operations, including installing or upgrading hardware or software. Develop or approve project plans, schedules, or budgets. Configure servers to meet functional specifications. Design and conduct hardware or software tests. Define and analyze objectives, scope, issues, or organizational impact of information systems. Develop system engineering, software engineering, system integration, or distributed system architectures. Establish functional or system standards to ensure operational requirements, quality requirements, and design constraints are addressed. Evaluate existing systems to determine effectiveness and suggest changes to meet organizational requirements. Research, test, or verify proper functioning of software patches and fixes. Communicate project information through presentations, technical reports, or white papers. Complete models and simulations, using manual or automated tools, to analyze or predict system performance under different operating conditions.

Personality Type: Investigative. These occupations frequently involve working with ideas and require an extensive amount of thinking. They can involve searching for facts and figuring out problems mentally.

GOE—Interest Area/Cluster: 11. Information Technology. **Work Group:** 11.02. Information Technology Specialties. **Other Jobs in This Work Group:** Computer and Information Scientists, Research; Computer Programmers; Computer Security Specialists; Computer Software Engineers, Applications; Computer Software Engineers, Systems Software; Computer Support Specialists; Computer Systems Analysts; Database Administrators; Network Designers; Network Systems and Data Communications Analysts; Software Quality Assurance Engineers and Testers; Web Administrators; Web Developers.

Skills—Programming: Writing computer programs for various purposes. **Systems Evaluation:** Looking at many indicators of system performance and taking into account their accuracy. **Technology Design:** Generating or adapting equipment and technology to serve user needs. **Systems Analysis:** Determining how a system should work and how changes will affect outcomes. **Troubleshooting:** Determining what is causing an operating error and deciding what to do about it. **Operations Analysis:** Analyzing needs and product requirements to create a design. **Installation:** Installing equipment, machines, wiring, or programs to meet specifications. **Science:** Using scientific methods to solve problems.

Education and Training Programs: Computer Engineering, General; Computer Software Engineering. **Related Knowledge/Courses—Computers and Electronics:** Electric circuit boards, processors, chips, and computer hardware and software, including applications and programming. **Engineering and Technology:** Equipment, tools, and mechanical devices and their uses

to produce motion, light, power, technology, and other applications. **Telecommunications:** Transmission, broadcasting, switching, control, and operation of telecommunications systems. **Design:** Design techniques, principles, tools, and instruments involved in the production and use of precision technical plans, blueprints, drawings, and models. **Mathematics:** Numbers and their operations and interrelationships, including arithmetic, algebra, geometry, calculus, and statistics and their applications. **Sales and Marketing:** Principles and methods involved in showing, promoting, and selling products or services. This includes marketing strategies and tactics, product demonstration and sales techniques, and sales control systems.

Work Environment: Indoors; sitting; repetitive motions.

Construction Managers

* Education/Training Required: Bachelor's degree
* Annual Earnings: $76,230
* Beginning Wage: $44,630
* Earnings Growth Potential: High
* Growth: 15.7%
* Annual Job Openings: 44,158
* Self-Employed: 56.3%
* Part-Time: 4.9%

Plan, direct, coordinate, or budget, usually through subordinate supervisory personnel, activities concerned with the construction and maintenance of structures, facilities, and systems. Participate in the conceptual development of a construction project and oversee its organization, scheduling, and implementation. Schedule the project in logical steps and budget time required to meet deadlines. Confer with supervisory personnel, owners, contractors, and design professionals to discuss and resolve matters such as work procedures, complaints, and construction problems. Prepare contracts and negotiate revisions, changes, and additions to contractual agreements with architects, consultants, clients, suppliers, and subcontractors. Prepare and submit budget estimates and progress and cost tracking reports. Interpret and explain plans and contract terms to administrative staff, workers, and clients, representing the owner or developer. Plan, organize, and direct activities concerned with the construction and maintenance of structures, facilities, and systems. Take actions to deal with the results of delays, bad weather, or emergencies at construction sites. Inspect and review projects to monitor compliance with building and safety codes and other regulations. Study job specifications to determine appropriate construction methods. Select, contract, and oversee workers who complete specific pieces of the project such as painting or plumbing. Obtain all necessary permits and licenses. Direct and supervise workers. Develop and implement quality control programs. Investigate damage, accidents, or delays at construction sites to ensure that proper procedures are being carried out. Determine labor requirements and dispatch workers to construction sites. Evaluate construction methods and determine cost-effectiveness of plans, using computers. Requisition supplies and materials to complete construction projects. Direct acquisition of land for construction projects.

Personality Type: Enterprising. These occupations frequently involve starting up and carrying out projects and can involve leading people and making many decisions. They sometimes require risk taking and often deal with business.

GOE—Interest Area/Cluster: 02. Architecture and Construction. **Work Group:** 02.01. Managerial Work in Architecture and Construction. **Other Jobs in This Work Group:** No others in group.

Skills—Management of Financial Resources: Determining how money will be spent to get the work done and accounting for these expenditures. **Management of Material Resources:** Obtaining and seeing to the appropriate use of equipment, facilities, and materials needed to do certain work. **Management of Personnel Resources:** Motivating, developing, and directing people as they work; identifying the best people for the job. **Systems Analysis:** Determining how a system should work and how changes will affect outcomes. **Systems Evaluation:** Looking at many indicators of system performance and taking into account their accuracy. **Negotiation:** Bringing others together and trying to reconcile differences. **Persuasion:** Persuading others to approach things differently. **Monitoring:** Assessing how well one is doing when learning or doing something.

Education and Training Programs: Construction Engineering Technology/Technician; Business/Commerce, General; Business Administration and Management, General; Operations Management and Supervision; Construction Management. **Related Knowledge/Courses—Building and Construction:** Materials, methods, and the appropriate tools to construct objects, structures, and buildings. **Design:** Design techniques, principles, tools, and instruments involved in the production and use of precision technical plans, blueprints, drawings, and models. **Engineering and Technology:** Equipment, tools, and mechanical devices and their uses to produce motion, light, power, technology, and other applications. **Mechanical Devices:** Machines and tools, including their designs, uses, benefits, repair, and maintenance. **Administration and Management:** Principles and processes involved in business and organizational planning, coordination, and execution. This includes strategic planning, resource allocation, manpower modeling, leadership techniques, and production methods. **Personnel and**

Human Resources: Principles and procedures for personnel recruitment; selection; training; compensation and benefits; labor relations and negotiation; and personnel information systems.

Work Environment: More often outdoors than indoors; noisy; contaminants; hazardous equipment; sitting.

Copy Writers

❋ Education/Training Required: Bachelor's degree
❋ Annual Earnings: $50,660
❋ Beginning Wage: $26,530
❋ Earnings Growth Potential: High
❋ Growth: 12.8%
❋ Annual Job Openings: 24,023
❋ Self-Employed: 65.9%
❋ Part-Time: 21.8%

The job openings listed here are shared with Poets, Lyricists, and Creative Writers.

Write advertising copy for use by publication or broadcast media to promote sale of goods and services. Write advertising copy for use by publication, broadcast, or Internet media to promote the sale of goods and services. Present drafts and ideas to clients. Discuss with the client the product, advertising themes and methods, and any changes that should be made in advertising copy. Consult with sales, media, and marketing representatives to obtain information on product or service and discuss style and length of advertising copy. Vary language and tone of messages based on product and medium. Edit or rewrite existing copy as necessary and submit copy for approval by supervisor. Write to customers in their terms and on their level so that the advertiser's sales message is more readily received. Write articles; bulletins; sales letters; speeches; and other related informative, marketing, and promotional material. Invent names for products and write the slogans that appear on packaging, brochures, and other promotional material. Review advertising trends, consumer surveys, and other data regarding marketing of goods and services to determine the best way to promote products. Develop advertising campaigns for a wide range of clients, working with an advertising agency's creative director and art director to determine the best way to present advertising information. Conduct research and interviews to determine which of a product's selling features should be promoted.

Personality Type: Enterprising. These occupations frequently involve starting up and carrying out projects and can involve leading people and making many decisions. They sometimes require risk taking and often deal with business.

GOE—Interest Area/Cluster: 03. Arts and Communication. **Work Group:** 03.02. Writing and Editing. **Other Jobs in This Work Group:** Editors; Poets, Lyricists and Creative Writers; Technical Writers; Writers and Authors.

Skills—Persuasion: Persuading others to approach things differently. **Technology Design:** Generating or adapting equipment and technology to serve user needs. **Equipment Selection:** Determining the kind of tools and equipment needed to do a job. **Quality Control Analysis:** Evaluating the quality or performance of products, services, or processes. **Time Management:** Managing one's own time and the time of others. **Writing:** Communicating effectively with others in writing as indicated by the needs of the audience. **Active Listening:** Listening to what other people are saying and asking questions as appropriate. **Negotiation:** Bringing others together and trying to reconcile differences.

Education and Training Programs: Communication Studies/Speech Communication and Rhetoric; Mass Communication/Media Studies; Journalism; Broadcast Journalism; Communication, Journalism, and Related Programs, Other; English Composition. **Related Knowledge/ Courses—Communications and Media:** Media production, communication, and dissemination techniques and methods, including alternative ways to inform and entertain via written, oral, and visual media. **Sales and Marketing:** Principles and methods involved in showing, promoting, and selling products or services. This includes marketing strategies and tactics, product demonstration and sales techniques, and sales control systems. **Sociology and Anthropology:** Group behavior and dynamics; societal trends and influences; and cultures and their history, migrations, ethnicity, and origins. **English Language:** The structure and content of the English language, including the meaning and spelling of words, rules of composition, and grammar. **Computers and Electronics:** Electric circuit boards, processors, chips, and computer hardware and software, including applications and programming. **Psychology:** Human behavior and performance, mental processes, psychological research methods, and the assessment and treatment of behavioral and affective disorders.

Work Environment: Indoors; sitting; using hands on objects, tools, or controls; repetitive motions.

Cost Estimators

* Education/Training Required: Bachelor's degree
* Annual Earnings: $54,920
* Beginning Wage: $32,470
* Earnings Growth Potential: High
* Growth: 18.5%
* Annual Job Openings: 38,379
* Self-Employed: 1.1%
* Part-Time: 5.8%

Prepare cost estimates for product manufacturing, construction projects, or services to aid management in bidding on or determining prices of products or services. May specialize according to particular service performed or type of product manufactured. Consult with clients, vendors, personnel in other departments, or construction foremen to discuss and formulate estimates and resolve issues. Analyze blueprints and other documentation to prepare time, cost, materials, and labor estimates. Prepare estimates for use in selecting vendors or subcontractors. Confer with engineers, architects, owners, contractors, and subcontractors on changes and adjustments to cost estimates. Prepare estimates used by management for purposes such as planning, organizing, and scheduling work. Prepare cost and expenditure statements and other necessary documentation at regular intervals for the duration of the project. Assess cost-effectiveness of products, projects, or services, tracking actual costs relative to bids as projects develop. Set up cost-monitoring and cost-reporting systems and procedures. Conduct special studies to develop and establish standard hour and related cost data or to effect cost reductions. Review material and labor requirements to decide whether it is more cost-effective to produce or purchase components. Prepare and maintain a directory of suppliers, contractors, and subcontractors. Establish and maintain tendering processes and conduct negotiations. Visit sites and record information about access, drainage and topography, and availability of services such as water and electricity.

Personality Type: Conventional. These occupations frequently involve following set procedures and routines and can include working with data and details more than with ideas. Usually there is a clear line of authority to follow.

GOE—Interest Area/Cluster: 06. Finance and Insurance. **Work Group:** 06.02. Finance/Insurance Investigation and Analysis. **Other Jobs in This Work Group:** Appraisers and Assessors of Real Estate; Appraisers, Real Estate; Assessors; Credit Analysts; Financial Analysts; Insurance Underwriters; Loan Counselors; Loan Officers; Market Research Analysts; Survey Researchers.

Skills—Systems Analysis: Determining how a system should work and how changes will affect outcomes. **Management of Financial Resources:** Determining how money will be spent to get the work done and accounting for these expenditures. **Mathematics:** Using mathematics to solve problems. **Systems Evaluation:** Looking at many indicators of system performance and taking into account their accuracy. **Writing:** Communicating effectively with others in writing as indicated by the needs of the audience. **Negotiation:** Bringing others together and trying to reconcile differences.

Education and Training Programs: Materials Engineering; Mechanical Engineering; Construction Engineering; Manufacturing Engineering; Construction Engineering Technology/Technician; Business/Commerce, General; Business Administration and Management, General. **Related Knowledge/Courses—Engineering and Technology:** Equipment, tools, and mechanical devices and their uses to produce motion, light, power, technology, and other applications.

Mathematics: Numbers and their operations and interrelationships, including arithmetic, algebra, geometry, calculus, and statistics and their applications. **Economics and Accounting:** Economic and accounting principles and practices, the financial markets, banking, and the analysis and reporting of financial data. **Building and Construction:** Materials, methods, and the appropriate tools to construct objects, structures, and buildings. **Design:** Design techniques, principles, tools, and instruments involved in the production and use of precision technical plans, blueprints, drawings, and models. **Computers and Electronics:** Electric circuit boards, processors, chips, and computer hardware and software, including applications and programming.

Work Environment: Indoors; sitting.

Counseling Psychologists

* Education/Training Required: Doctoral degree
* Annual Earnings: $62,210
* Beginning Wage: $37,300
* Earnings Growth Potential: High
* Growth: 15.8%
* Annual Job Openings: 8,309
* Self-Employed: 34.2%
* Part-Time: 24.0%

The job openings listed here are shared with Clinical Psychologists and with School Psychologists.

Assess and evaluate individuals' problems through the use of case history, interview, and observation and provide individual or group counseling services to assist individuals in achieving more effective personal, social, educational, and vocational development and adjustment. Collect information about individuals or clients, using interviews, case histories, observational techniques, and other assessment methods. Counsel individuals, groups, or families to help them understand problems, define goals, and develop realistic action plans. Develop therapeutic and treatment plans based on clients' interests, abilities, and needs. Consult with other professionals to discuss therapies, treatments, counseling resources, or techniques and to share occupational information. Analyze data such as interview notes, test results, and reference manuals in order to identify symptoms and to diagnose the nature of clients' problems. Advise clients on how they could be helped by counseling. Evaluate the results of counseling methods to determine the reliability and validity of treatments. Provide consulting services to schools, social service agencies, and businesses. Refer clients to specialists or to other institutions for non-counseling treatment of problems. Select, administer, and interpret psychological tests to assess intelligence, aptitudes, abilities, or interests. Conduct research to develop or improve diagnostic or therapeutic counseling techniques.

Personality Type: Social. These occupations frequently involve working with, communicating with, and teaching people and often involve helping or providing service to others.

GOE—Interest Area/Cluster: 10. Human Service. **Work Group:** 10.01. Counseling and Social Work. **Other Jobs in This Work Group:** Child, Family, and School Social Workers; Clinical Psychologists; Clinical, Counseling, and School Psychologists; Marriage and Family Therapists; Medical and Public Health Social Workers; Mental Health and Substance Abuse Social Workers; Mental Health Counselors; Probation Officers and Correctional Treatment Specialists; Rehabilitation Counselors; Substance Abuse and Behavioral Disorder Counselors.

Skills—Social Perceptiveness: Being aware of others' reactions and understanding why they react the way they do. **Active Listening:** Listening to what other people are saying and asking questions as appropriate. **Persuasion:** Persuading others to approach things differently. **Service Orientation:** Actively looking for ways to help people. **Coordination:** Adjusting actions in relation to others' actions. **Monitoring:** Assessing how well one is doing when learning or doing something. **Negotiation:** Bringing others together and trying to reconcile differences. **Learning Strategies:** Using multiple approaches when learning or teaching new things.

Education and Training Programs: Psychology, General; Clinical Psychology; Counseling Psychology; Developmental and Child Psychology; School Psychology; Clinical Child Psychology; Psychoanalysis and Psychotherapy. **Related Knowledge/Courses—Therapy and Counseling:** Information and techniques needed to rehabilitate physical and mental ailments and to provide career guidance, including alternative treatments, rehabilitation equipment and its proper use, and methods to evaluate treatment effects. **Philosophy and Theology:** Different philosophical systems and religions, including their basic principles, values, ethics, ways of thinking, customs, and practices and their impact on human culture. **Sociology and Anthropology:** Group behavior and dynamics; societal trends and influences; and cultures and their history, migrations, ethnicity, and origins. **Psychology:** Human behavior and performance, mental processes, psychological research methods, and the assessment and treatment of behavioral and affective disorders. **English Language:** The structure and content of the English language, including the meaning and spelling of words, rules of composition, and grammar. **Customer and Personal Service:** Principles and processes for providing customer and personal services, including needs assessment techniques, quality service standards, alternative delivery systems, and customer satisfaction evaluation techniques.

Work Environment: Indoors; sitting.

Criminal Justice and Law Enforcement Teachers, Postsecondary

✹ Education/Training Required: Doctoral degree
✹ Annual Earnings: $51,060
✹ Beginning Wage: $30,420
✹ Earnings Growth Potential: High
✹ Growth: 22.9%
✹ Annual Job Openings: 1,911
✹ Self-Employed: 0.4%
✹ Part-Time: 27.8%

Teach courses in criminal justice, corrections, and law enforcement administration. Initiate, facilitate, and moderate classroom discussions. Keep abreast of developments in their field by reading current literature, talking with colleagues, and participating in professional conferences. Evaluate and grade students' classwork, assignments, and papers. Compile, administer, and grade examinations or assign this work to others. Prepare and deliver lectures to undergraduate or graduate students on topics such as criminal law, defensive policing, and investigation techniques. Prepare course materials such as syllabi, homework assignments, and handouts. Conduct research in a particular field of knowledge and publish findings in professional journals, books, and/or electronic media. Plan, evaluate, and revise curricula, course content, and course materials and methods of instruction. Supervise undergraduate and/or graduate teaching, internship, and research work. Maintain student attendance records, grades, and other required records. Select and obtain materials and supplies such as textbooks. Advise students on academic and vocational curricula and on career issues. Maintain regularly scheduled office hours to advise and assist students. Collaborate with colleagues to address teaching and research issues. Write grant proposals to procure external research funding. Serve on academic or administrative committees that deal with institutional policies, departmental matters, and academic issues. Compile bibliographies of specialized materials for outside reading assignments. Participate in student recruitment, registration, and placement activities. Provide professional consulting services to government and/or industry. Perform administrative duties such as serving as department head. Participate in campus and community events. Act as advisers to student organizations.

Personality Type: Social. These occupations frequently involve working with, communicating with, and teaching people and often involve helping or providing service to others.

GOE—Interest Area/Cluster: 05. Education and Training. **Work Group:** 05.03. Postsecondary and Adult Teaching and Instructing. **Other Jobs in This Work Group:** Adult Literacy, Remedial Education, and GED Teachers and Instructors; Agricultural Sciences Teachers, Postsecondary; Anthropology and Archeology Teachers, Postsecondary; Architecture Teachers, Postsecondary; Area, Ethnic, and Cultural Studies Teachers, Postsecondary; Art, Drama, and Music Teachers, Postsecondary; Atmospheric, Earth, Marine, and Space Sciences Teachers, Postsecondary; Biological Science Teachers, Postsecondary; Business Teachers, Postsecondary; Chemistry Teachers, Postsecondary; Communications Teachers, Postsecondary; Computer Science Teachers, Postsecondary; Economics Teachers, Postsecondary; Education Teachers, Postsecondary; Engineering Teachers, Postsecondary; English Language and Literature Teachers, Postsecondary; Environmental Science Teachers, Postsecondary; Farm and Home Management Advisors; Foreign Language and Literature Teachers, Postsecondary; Forestry and Conservation Science Teachers, Postsecondary; Geography Teachers, Postsecondary; Graduate Teaching Assistants; Health Specialties Teachers, Postsecondary; History Teachers, Postsecondary; Home Economics Teachers, Postsecondary; Law Teachers, Postsecondary; Library Science Teachers, Postsecondary; Mathematical Science Teachers, Postsecondary; Nursing Instructors and Teachers, Postsecondary; Philosophy and Religion Teachers, Postsecondary; Physics Teachers, Postsecondary; Political Science Teachers, Postsecondary; Psychology Teachers, Postsecondary; Recreation and Fitness Studies Teachers, Postsecondary; Social Work Teachers, Postsecondary; Sociology Teachers, Postsecondary.

Skills—Writing: Communicating effectively with others in writing as indicated by the needs of the audience. **Critical Thinking:** Using logic and analysis to identify the strengths and weaknesses of different approaches. **Instructing:** Teaching others how to do something. **Active Learning:** Working with new material or information to grasp its implications. **Reading Comprehension:** Understanding written sentences and paragraphs in work-related documents. **Persuasion:** Persuading others to approach things differently. **Science:** Using scientific methods to solve problems. **Speaking:** Talking to others to effectively convey information.

Education and Training Programs: Teacher Education and Professional Development, Specific Subject Areas, Other; Corrections; Criminal Justice/Law Enforcement Administration; Criminal Justice/Safety Studies; Forensic Science and Technology; Criminal Justice/Police Science; Security and Loss Prevention Services; Juvenile Corrections; Criminalistics and Criminal Science; Corrections Administration; Corrections and Criminal Justice, Other. **Related Knowledge/Courses—Sociology and Anthropology:** Group behavior and dynamics; societal trends and influences; and cultures and their history, migrations, ethnicity, and origins. **Philosophy and Theology:** Different philosophical systems and religions, including their basic principles, values, ethics, ways of thinking, customs, and practices and their impact on human culture. **History and Archeology:** Historical events and their causes, indicators, and impact on particular civilizations and cultures. **Law and Government:** Laws, legal codes, court procedures, precedents, government regulations, executive orders, agency rules, and the democratic political process. **English Language:** The structure and content of the English language, including the meaning and spelling of words, rules of composition, and grammar. **Education and Training:** Instructional methods and training techniques, including curriculum design principles, learning theory, group and individual teaching techniques, design of individual development plans, and test design principles.

Work Environment: Indoors; sitting.

Curators

- Education/Training Required: Master's degree
- Annual Earnings: $46,000
- Beginning Wage: $26,100
- Earnings Growth Potential: High
- Growth: 23.3%
- Annual Job Openings: 1,416
- Self-Employed: 1.3%
- Part-Time: 18.4%

Administer affairs of museum and conduct research programs. Direct instructional, research, and public service activities of institution. Plan and organize the acquisition, storage, and exhibition of collections and related materials, including the selection of exhibition themes and designs. Develop and maintain an institution's registration, cataloging, and basic recordkeeping systems, using computer databases. Provide information from the institution's holdings to other curators and to the public. Inspect premises to assess the need for repairs and to ensure that climate and pest-control issues are addressed. Train and supervise curatorial, fiscal, technical, research, and clerical staff, as well as volunteers or interns. Negotiate and authorize purchase, sale, exchange, or loan of collections. Plan and conduct special research projects in area of interest or expertise. Conduct or organize tours, workshops, and instructional sessions to acquaint individuals with an institution's facilities and materials. Confer with the board of directors to formulate and interpret policies, to determine budget requirements, and to plan overall operations. Attend meetings, conventions, and civic events to promote use of institution's services, to seek financing, and to maintain community alliances. Schedule events and organize details, including refreshment, entertainment, decorations, and the collection of any fees. Write and review grant proposals, journal articles, institutional reports, and publicity materials. Study, examine, and test acquisitions to authenticate their origin, composition, and history and to assess their current value. Arrange insurance coverage for objects on loan or for special exhibits and recommend changes in coverage for the entire collection. Establish specifications for reproductions and oversee their manufacture or select items from commercially available replica sources.

Personality Type: Enterprising. These occupations frequently involve starting up and carrying out projects and can involve leading people and making many decisions. They sometimes require risk taking and often deal with business.

GOE—Interest Area/Cluster: 05. Education and Training. **Work Group:** 05.05. Archival and Museum Services. **Other Jobs in This Work Group:** Archivists; Audio-Visual Collections Specialists; Museum Technicians and Conservators.

Skills—Management of Financial Resources: Determining how money will be spent to get the work done and accounting for these expenditures. **Management of Personnel Resources:** Motivating, developing, and directing people as they work; identifying the best people for the job. **Writing:** Communicating effectively with others in writing as indicated by the needs of the audience. **Time Management:** Managing one's own time and the time of others. **Speaking:** Talking to others to effectively convey information. **Persuasion:** Persuading others to approach things differently. **Monitoring:** Assessing how well one is doing when learning or doing something. **Negotiation:** Bringing others together and trying to reconcile differences.

Education and Training Programs: Museology/Museum Studies; Art History, Criticism and Conservation; Public/Applied History and Archival Administration. **Related Knowledge/Courses—Fine Arts:** Theory and techniques required to produce, compose, and perform works of music, dance, visual arts, drama, and sculpture. **History and Archeology:** Historical events and their causes, indicators, and impact on particular civilizations and cultures. **Clerical Practices:** Administrative and clerical procedures and systems such as word-processing systems, filing and records management systems, stenography and transcription, forms, design principles, and other office procedures and terminology. **Philosophy and Theology:** Different philosophical systems and religions, including their basic principles, values, ethics, ways of thinking, customs, and practices and their impact on human culture. **Sociology and Anthropology:** Group behavior and dynamics; societal trends and influences; and cultures and their history, migrations, ethnicity, and origins. **Geography:** Various methods for describing the location and distribution of land, sea, and air masses, including their physical locations, relationships, and characteristics.

Work Environment: Indoors; sitting.

Database Administrators

- ❀ Education/Training Required: Bachelor's degree
- ❀ Annual Earnings: $67,250
- ❀ Beginning Wage: $38,890
- ❀ Earnings Growth Potential: High
- ❀ Growth: 28.6%
- ❀ Annual Job Openings: 8,258
- ❀ Self-Employed: 1.3%
- ❀ Part-Time: 5.3%

Coordinate changes to computer databases. Test and implement the databases, applying knowledge of database management systems. May plan, coordinate, and implement security measures to safeguard computer databases. Test programs or databases, correct errors, and make necessary modifications. Modify existing databases and database management systems or direct programmers and analysts to make changes. Plan, coordinate, and implement security measures to safeguard information in computer files against accidental or unauthorized damage, modification, or disclosure. Work as part of project teams to coordinate database development and determine project scope and limitations. Write and code logical and physical database descriptions and specify identifiers of database to management system or direct others in coding descriptions. Train users and answer questions. Specify users and user access levels for each segment of databases. Approve, schedule, plan, and supervise the installation and testing of new products and improvements to computer systems such as the installation of new databases.

Review project requests describing database user needs to estimate time and cost required to accomplish project. Develop standards and guidelines to guide the use and acquisition of software and to protect vulnerable information. Review procedures in database management system manuals for making changes to database. Develop methods for integrating different products so they work properly together such as customizing commercial databases to fit specific needs. Develop data models describing data elements and how they are used, following procedures and using pen, template, or computer software. Select and enter codes to monitor database performances and to create production databases. Establish and calculate optimum values for database parameters, using manuals and calculators. Revise company definition of data as defined in data dictionary. Review workflow charts developed by programmer analysts to understand tasks computer will perform, such as updating records. Identify and evaluate industry trends in database systems to serve as a source of information and advice for upper management.

Personality Type: Conventional. These occupations frequently involve following set procedures and routines and can include working with data and details more than with ideas. Usually there is a clear line of authority to follow.

GOE—Interest Area/Cluster: 11. Information Technology. **Work Group:** 11.02. Information Technology Specialties. **Other Jobs in This Work Group:** Computer and Information Scientists, Research; Computer Programmers; Computer Security Specialists; Computer Software Engineers, Applications; Computer Software Engineers, Systems Software; Computer Support Specialists; Computer Systems Analysts; Computer Systems Engineers/Architects; Network Designers; Network Systems and Data Communications Analysts; Software Quality Assurance Engineers and Testers; Web Administrators; Web Developers.

D

Skills—Programming: Writing computer programs for various purposes. **Systems Analysis:** Determining how a system should work and how changes will affect outcomes. **Systems Evaluation:** Looking at many indicators of system performance and taking into account their accuracy.

Education and Training Programs: Computer and Information Sciences, General; Computer Systems Analysis/Analyst; Data Modeling/Warehousing and Database Administration; Computer and Information Systems Security; Management Information Systems, General. **Related Knowledge/ Courses—Computers and Electronics:** Electric circuit boards, processors, chips, and computer hardware and software, including applications and programming. **Telecommunications:** Transmission, broadcasting, switching, control, and operation of telecommunications systems. **Clerical Practices:** Administrative and clerical procedures and systems such as word-processing systems, filing and records management systems, stenography and transcription, forms, design principles, and other office procedures and terminology. **Communications and Media:** Media production, communication, and dissemination techniques and methods, including alternative ways to inform and entertain via written, oral, and visual media. **Engineering and Technology:** Equipment, tools, and mechanical devices and their uses to produce motion, light, power, technology, and other applications. **Mathematics:** Numbers and their operations and interrelationships, including arithmetic, algebra, geometry, calculus, and statistics and their applications.

Work Environment: Indoors; noisy; sitting; using hands on objects, tools, or controls; repetitive motions.

Dental Hygienists

* Education/Training Required: Associate degree
* Annual Earnings: $64,740
* Beginning Wage: $42,480
* Earnings Growth Potential: Low
* Growth: 30.1%
* Annual Job Openings: 10,433
* Self-Employed: 0.1%
* Part-Time: 58.7%

Clean teeth and examine oral areas, head, and neck for signs of oral disease. May educate patients on oral hygiene, take and develop X rays, or apply fluoride or sealants. Clean calcareous deposits, accretions, and stains from teeth and beneath margins of gums, using dental instruments. Feel and visually examine gums for sores and signs of disease. Chart conditions of decay and disease for diagnosis and treatment by dentist. Feel lymph nodes under patient's chin to detect swelling or tenderness that could indicate presence of oral cancer. Apply fluorides and other cavity-preventing agents to arrest dental decay. Examine gums, using probes, to locate periodontal recessed gums and signs of gum disease. Expose and develop X-ray film. Provide clinical services and health education to improve and maintain oral health of schoolchildren. Remove excess cement from coronal surfaces of teeth. Make impressions for study casts. Place, carve, and finish amalgam restorations. Administer local anesthetic agents. Conduct dental health clinics for community groups to augment services of dentist. Remove sutures and dressings. Place and remove rubber dams, matrices, and temporary restorations.

Personality Type: Social. These occupations frequently involve working with, communicating with, and teaching people and often involve helping or providing service to others.

GOE—Interest Area/Cluster: 08. Health Science. **Work Group:** 08.03. Dentistry. **Other Jobs in This Work Group:** Dentists, General; Oral and Maxillofacial Surgeons; Orthodontists; Prosthodontists.

Skills—Science: Using scientific methods to solve problems. **Active Learning:** Working with new material or information to grasp its implications. **Reading Comprehension:** Understanding written sentences and paragraphs in work-related documents. **Time Management:** Managing one's own time and the time of others. **Equipment Selection:** Determining the kind of tools and equipment needed to do a job. **Persuasion:** Persuading others to approach things differently. **Social Perceptiveness:** Being aware of others' reactions and understanding why they react the way they do. **Writing:** Communicating effectively with others in writing as indicated by the needs of the audience.

Education and Training Program: Dental Hygiene/Hygienist. **Related Knowledge/Courses—Biology:** Plant and animal living tissue, cells, organisms, and entities, including their functions, interdependencies, and interactions with each other and the environment. **Medicine and Dentistry:** The information and techniques needed to diagnose and treat injuries, diseases, and deformities. This includes symptoms, treatment alternatives, drug properties and interactions, and preventive health-care measures. **Chemistry:** The composition, structure, and properties of substances and of the chemical processes and transformations that they undergo. This includes uses of chemicals and their interactions, danger signs, production techniques, and disposal methods. **Psychology:** Human behavior and performance, mental processes, psychological research methods, and the assessment and treatment of behavioral and affective disorders. **Therapy and Counseling:** Information and techniques needed to rehabilitate physical and mental ailments and to provide career guidance, including alternative treatments, rehabilitation equipment and its proper use, and methods to evaluate treatment effects. **Sales and Marketing:** Principles and methods involved in showing, promoting, and selling products or services. This includes marketing strategies and tactics, product demonstration and sales techniques, and sales control systems.

Work Environment: Indoors; radiation; disease or infections; sitting; using hands on objects, tools, or controls; repetitive motions.

Dentists, General

- ✳ Education/Training Required: First professional degree
- ✳ Annual Earnings: $137,630
- ✳ Beginning Wage: $71,520
- ✳ Earnings Growth Potential: High
- ✳ Growth: 9.2%
- ✳ Annual Job Openings: 7,106
- ✳ Self-Employed: 36.6%
- ✳ Part-Time: 25.9%

Diagnose and treat diseases, injuries, and malformations of teeth and gums and related oral structures. May treat diseases of nerve, pulp, and other dental tissues affecting vitality of teeth. Use masks, gloves, and safety glasses to protect themselves and their patients from infectious diseases. Administer anesthetics to limit the amount of pain experienced by patients during procedures. Examine teeth, gums, and related tissues, using dental instruments, X rays, and other diagnostic equipment, to evaluate dental health, diagnose diseases or abnormalities, and plan appropriate treatments. Formulate plan of treatment for patient's teeth and mouth tissue. Use air turbine and hand instruments, dental appliances, and surgical implements. Advise and instruct patients regarding preventive dental care, the causes and treatment of dental problems, and oral health-care services. Design, make, and fit prosthodontic appliances such as space maintainers, bridges, and dentures or write fabrication instructions or prescriptions for denturists and dental technicians. Diagnose and treat diseases, injuries, and malformations of teeth, gums, and related oral structures and provide preventive and corrective services. Fill pulp chamber and canal with endodontic materials. Write prescriptions for antibiotics and other medications. Analyze and evaluate dental needs to determine changes and trends in patterns of dental disease. Treat exposure of pulp by pulp capping, removal of pulp from pulp chamber, or root canal, using dental instruments. Eliminate irritating margins of fillings and correct occlusions, using dental instruments. Perform oral and periodontal surgery on the jaw or mouth. Remove diseased tissue, using surgical instruments. Apply fluoride and sealants to teeth. Manage business, employing and supervising staff and handling paperwork and insurance claims. Bleach, clean, or polish teeth to restore natural color. Plan, organize, and maintain dental health programs. Produce and evaluate dental health educational materials.

Personality Type: Investigative. These occupations frequently involve working with ideas and require an extensive amount of thinking. They can involve searching for facts and figuring out problems mentally.

GOE—Interest Area/Cluster: 08. Health Science. **Work Group:** 08.03. Dentistry. **Other Jobs in This Work Group:** Dental Hygienists; Oral and Maxillofacial Surgeons; Orthodontists; Prosthodontists.

Skills—Science: Using scientific methods to solve problems. **Management of Financial Resources:** Determining how money will be spent to get the work done and accounting for these expenditures. **Management of Material Resources:** Obtaining and seeing to the appropriate use of equipment, facilities, and materials needed to do certain work. **Equipment Selection:** Determining the kind of tools and equipment needed to do a job. **Complex Problem Solving:** Identifying complex problems, reviewing the options, and implementing solutions. **Reading Comprehension:** Understanding written sentences and paragraphs in work-related documents. **Service Orientation:** Actively looking for ways to help people. **Management of Personnel Resources:** Motivating, developing, and directing people as they work; identifying the best people for the job.

Education and Training Programs: Dentistry (DDS, DMD); Dental Clinical Sciences, General (MS, PhD); Advanced General Dentistry (Cert, MS, PhD); Oral Biology and Oral Pathology (MS, PhD); Dental Public Health and Education (Cert, MS/MPH, PhD/DPH); Dental Materials (MS, PhD); Pediatric Dentistry/Pedodontics (Cert, MS, PhD); Dental Public Health Specialty; Pedodontics Specialty. **Related Knowledge/Courses—Medicine and Dentistry:** The information and techniques needed to diagnose and treat injuries, diseases, and deformities. This includes symptoms, treatment alternatives, drug properties and interactions, and preventive health-care measures. **Biology:** Plant and animal living tissue, cells, organisms, and entities, including their functions, interdependencies, and interactions with each other and the environment. **Psychology:** Human behavior and performance, mental processes, psychological research methods, and the assessment and treatment of behavioral and affective disorders. **Chemistry:** The composition, structure, and properties of substances and of the chemical processes and transformations that they undergo. This includes uses of chemicals and their interactions, danger signs, production techniques, and disposal methods. **Personnel and Human Resources:** Principles and procedures for personnel recruitment; selection; training; compensation and benefits; labor relations and negotiation; and personnel information systems. **Economics and Accounting:** Economic and accounting principles and practices, the financial markets, banking, and the analysis and reporting of financial data.

Work Environment: Indoors; contaminants; radiation; disease or infections; sitting; using hands on objects, tools, or controls.

Diagnostic Medical Sonographers

- ❀ Education/Training Required: Associate degree
- ❀ Annual Earnings: $59,860
- ❀ Beginning Wage: $42,250
- ❀ Earnings Growth Potential: Low
- ❀ Growth: 19.1%
- ❀ Annual Job Openings: 3,211
- ❀ Self-Employed: 1.1%
- ❀ Part-Time: 17.3%

Produce ultrasonic recordings of internal organs for use by physicians. Provide sonograms and oral or written summaries of technical findings to physicians for use in medical diagnosis. Decide which images to include, looking for differences between healthy and pathological areas. Operate ultrasound equipment to produce and record images of the motion, shape, and composition of blood, organs, tissues, and bodily masses such as fluid accumulations. Select appropriate equipment settings and adjust patient positions to obtain the best sites and angles. Observe screens during scans to ensure that images produced are satisfactory for diagnostic purposes, making adjustments to equipment as required. Prepare patients for exams by explaining procedures, transferring them to ultrasound tables, scrubbing skin and applying gel, and positioning them properly. Observe and care for patients throughout examinations to ensure their safety and comfort. Obtain and record accurate patient histories, including prior test results and information from physical examinations. Determine whether scope of exams should be extended, based on findings. Maintain records that include patient information; sonographs and interpretations; files of correspondence; publications and regulations; or quality assurance records such as pathology, biopsy, or post-operative reports. Record and store suitable images, using camera unit connected to the ultrasound equipment. Coordinate work with physicians and other health-care team members, including providing assistance during invasive procedures. Perform clerical duties such as scheduling exams and special procedures, keeping records, and archiving computerized images. Perform legal and ethical duties, including preparing safety and accident reports, obtaining written consent from patients to perform invasive procedures, and reporting symptoms of abuse and neglect. Clean, check, and maintain sonographic equipment, submitting maintenance requests or performing minor repairs as necessary. Supervise and train students and other medical sonographers. Maintain stock and supplies, preparing supplies for special examinations and ordering supplies when necessary. Process and code film from procedures and complete appropriate documentation.

Personality Type: Investigative. These occupations frequently involve working with ideas and require an extensive amount of thinking. They can involve searching for facts and figuring out problems mentally.

D

GOE—Interest Area/Cluster: 08. Health Science. **Work Group:** 08.06. Medical Technology. **Other Jobs in This Work Group:** Biological Technicians; Cardiovascular Technologists and Technicians; Medical and Clinical Laboratory Technicians; Medical and Clinical Laboratory Technologists; Medical Records and Health Information Technicians; Nuclear Medicine Technologists; Orthotists and Prosthetists; Radiologic Technicians; Radiologic Technologists; Radiologic Technologists and Technicians.

Skills—Operation Monitoring: Watching gauges, dials, or other indicators to make sure a machine is working properly. **Service Orientation:** Actively looking for ways to help people. **Systems Analysis:** Determining how a system should work and how changes will affect outcomes. **Systems Evaluation:** Looking at many indicators of system performance and taking into account their accuracy.

Education and Training Programs: Diagnostic Medical Sonography/Sonographer and Ultrasound Technician; Allied Health Diagnostic, Intervention, and Treatment Professions, Other. **Related Knowledge/Courses—Medicine and Dentistry:** The information and techniques needed to diagnose and treat injuries, diseases, and deformities. This includes symptoms, treatment alternatives, drug properties and interactions, and preventive health-care measures. **Physics:** Physical principles, laws, and applications, including air, water, material dynamics, light, atomic principles, heat, electric theory, earth formations, and meteorological and related natural phenomena. **Biology:** Plant and animal living tissue, cells, organisms, and entities, including their functions, interdependencies, and interactions with each other and the environment. **Psychology:** Human behavior and performance, mental processes, psychological research methods, and the assessment and treatment of behavioral and affective disorders. **Customer and**

Personal Service: Principles and processes for providing customer and personal services, including needs assessment techniques, quality service standards, alternative delivery systems, and customer satisfaction evaluation techniques. **Clerical Practices:** Administrative and clerical procedures and systems such as word-processing systems, filing and records management systems, stenography and transcription, forms, design principles, and other office procedures and terminology.

Work Environment: Indoors; disease or infections; standing; using hands on objects, tools, or controls; bending or twisting the body; repetitive motions.

Directors, Religious Activities and Education

- ✳ Education/Training Required: Bachelor's degree
- ✳ Annual Earnings: $35,370
- ✳ Beginning Wage: $19,850
- ✳ Earnings Growth Potential: High
- ✳ Growth: 19.7%
- ✳ Annual Job Openings: 11,463
- ✳ Self-Employed: 0.0%
- ✳ Part-Time: 25.2%

Direct and coordinate activities of their chosen denominational groups to meet religious needs of students. Plan, direct, or coordinate church school programs designed to promote religious education among church membership. May provide counseling and guidance relative to marital, health, financial, and religious problems. Analyze member participation and changes in congregation emphasis to determine needs for religious education. Collaborate with other ministry members to establish goals and objectives for religious education programs and to develop ways to encourage program participation. Interpret religious education activities to the public through speaking, leading discussions, and writing articles for local and national publications. Implement program plans by ordering needed materials, scheduling speakers, reserving spaces, and handling other administrative details. Confer with clergy members, congregation officials, and congregation organizations to encourage support of and participation in religious education activities. Develop and direct study courses and religious education programs within congregations. Locate and distribute resources such as periodicals and curricula in order to enhance the effectiveness of educational programs. Visit congregation members' homes, or arrange for pastoral visits, in order to provide information and resources regarding religious education programs. Identify and recruit potential volunteer workers. Participate in denominational activities aimed at goals such as promoting interfaith understanding or providing aid to new or small congregations. Publicize programs through sources such as newsletters, bulletins, and mailings. Counsel individuals regarding interpersonal, health, financial, and religious problems. Attend workshops, seminars, and conferences to obtain program ideas, information, and resources. Analyze revenue and program cost data to determine budget priorities. Train and supervise religious education instructional staffs. Select appropriate curricula and class structures for educational programs. Schedule special events such as camps, conferences, meetings, seminars, and retreats. Plan and conduct conferences dealing with the interpretation of religious ideas and convictions.

Personality Type: Enterprising. These occupations frequently involve starting up and carrying out projects and can involve leading people and making many decisions. They sometimes require risk taking and often deal with business.

GOE—Interest Area/Cluster: 10. Human Service. **Work Group:** 10.02. Religious Work. **Other Jobs in This Work Group:** Clergy.

Skills—Management of Personnel Resources: Motivating, developing, and directing people as they work; identifying the best people for the job. **Social Perceptiveness:** Being aware of others' reactions and understanding why they react the way they do. **Negotiation:** Bringing others together and trying to reconcile differences. **Speaking:** Talking to others to effectively convey information. **Management of Financial Resources:** Determining how money will be spent to get the work done and accounting for these expenditures. **Service Orientation:** Actively looking for ways to help people. **Coordination:** Adjusting actions in relation to others' actions. **Management of Material Resources:** Obtaining and seeing to the appropriate use of equipment, facilities, and materials needed to do certain work.

Education and Training Programs: Bible/Biblical Studies; Missions/Missionary Studies and Missiology; Religious Education; Youth Ministry. **Related Knowledge/Courses—Philosophy and Theology:** Different philosophical systems and religions, including their basic principles, values, ethics, ways of thinking, customs, and practices and their impact on human culture. **Education and Training:** Instructional methods and training techniques, including curriculum design principles, learning theory, group and individual teaching techniques, design of individual development plans, and test design principles. **Therapy and Counseling:** Information and techniques needed to rehabilitate physical and mental ailments and to provide career guidance, including alternative treatments, rehabilitation equipment and its proper use, and methods to evaluate treatment effects. **Sales and Marketing:** Principles and methods involved in showing, promoting, and selling products or services. This includes marketing strategies and tactics, product demonstration and sales techniques, and sales control systems. **History and Archeology:** Historical events and their causes, indicators, and impact on particular civilizations and cultures. **Economics and Accounting:** Economic and accounting principles and practices, the financial markets, banking, and the analysis and reporting of financial data.

Work Environment: Indoors; standing.

Directors—Stage, Motion Pictures, Television, and Radio

* Education/Training Required: Work experience plus degree
* Annual Earnings: $61,090
* Beginning Wage: $28,980
* Earnings Growth Potential: Very high
* Growth: 11.1%
* Annual Job Openings: 8,992
* Self-Employed: 29.5%
* Part-Time: 9.0%

The job openings listed here are shared with Producers, Program Directors, Talent Directors, and Technical Directors/Managers.

Interpret script, conduct rehearsals, and direct activities of cast and technical crew for stage, motion pictures, television, or radio programs. Direct live broadcasts, films and recordings, or non-broadcast programming for public entertainment or education. Supervise and coordinate the work of camera, lighting, design, and sound crew members. Study and research scripts to determine how they should be directed. Cut and edit film or tape to integrate component parts into desired sequences. Collaborate with film and sound editors during the post-production process as films are edited and soundtracks are added. Confer with technical directors, managers, crew members, and writers to discuss details of production, such as photography, script, music, sets, and costumes. Plan details such as framing, composition, camera movement, sound, and actor movement for each shot or scene. Communicate to actors the approach, characterization, and movement needed for each scene in such a way that rehearsals and takes are minimized. Establish pace of programs and sequences of scenes according to time requirements and cast and set accessibility. Choose settings and locations for films and determine how scenes will be shot in these settings. Identify and approve equipment and elements required for productions, such as scenery, lights, props, costumes, choreography, and music. Compile scripts, program notes, and other material related to productions. Perform producers' duties such as securing financial backing, establishing and administering budgets, and recruiting cast and crew. Select plays or scripts for production and determine how material should be interpreted and performed. Compile cue words and phrases; cue announcers, cast members, and technicians during performances. Consult with writers, producers, or actors about script changes or "workshop" scripts, through rehearsal with writers and actors, to create final drafts. Collaborate with producers to hire crew members such as art directors, cinematographers, and costumer designers. Review film daily to check on work in progress and to plan for future filming. Interpret stage-set diagrams to determine stage layouts and supervise placement of equipment and scenery. Hold auditions for parts or negotiate contracts with actors determined suitable for specific roles, working in conjunction with producers.

Personality Type: Enterprising. These occupations frequently involve starting up and carrying out projects and can involve leading people and making many decisions. They sometimes require risk taking and often deal with business.

GOE—Interest Area/Cluster: 03. Arts and Communication. **Work Group:** 03.06. Drama. **Other Jobs in This Work Group:** No others in group.

Skills—Management of Personnel Resources: Motivating, developing, and directing people as they work; identifying the best people for the job. **Time Management:** Managing one's own time and the time of others. **Judgment and Decision Making:** Weighing the relative costs and benefits of a potential action. **Operations Analysis:** Analyzing needs and product requirements to create a design. **Equipment Selection:** Determining the kind of tools and equipment needed to do a job. **Active Listening:** Listening to what other people are saying and asking questions as appropriate. **Speaking:** Talking to others to effectively convey information. **Critical Thinking:** Using logic and analysis to identify the strengths and weaknesses of different approaches.

Education and Training Programs: Radio and Television; Drama and Dramatics/Theatre Arts, General; Directing and Theatrical Production; Theatre/Theatre Arts Management; Dramatic/Theatre Arts and Stagecraft, Other; Film/Cinema Studies; Cinematography and Film/Video Production. **Related Knowledge/Courses—Communications and Media:** Media production, communication, and dissemination techniques and methods, including alternative ways to inform and entertain via written, oral, and visual media. **Telecommunications:** Transmission, broadcasting, switching, control, and operation of telecommunications systems. **Fine Arts:** Theory and techniques required to produce, compose, and perform works of music, dance, visual arts, drama, and sculpture. **Geography:** Various methods for describing the location and distribution of land, sea, and air masses, including their physical locations, relationships, and characteristics. **Computers and Electronics:** Electric circuit boards, processors, chips, and computer hardware and software, including applications and programming. **Education and Training:** Instructional methods and training techniques, including curriculum design principles, learning theory, group and individual teaching techniques, design of individual development plans, and test design principles.

Work Environment: More often indoors than outdoors; noisy; sitting; using hands on objects, tools, or controls.

Economics Teachers, Postsecondary

- ❋ Education/Training Required: Doctoral degree
- ❋ Annual Earnings: $75,300
- ❋ Beginning Wage: $41,650
- ❋ Earnings Growth Potential: High
- ❋ Growth: 22.9%
- ❋ Annual Job Openings: 2,208
- ❋ Self-Employed: 0.4%
- ❋ Part-Time: 27.8%

Teach courses in economics. Prepare and deliver lectures to undergraduate and/or graduate students on topics such as econometrics, price theory, and macroeconomics. Prepare course materials such as syllabi, homework assignments, and handouts. Evaluate and grade students' classwork, assignments, and papers. Compile, administer, and grade examinations or assign this work to others. Keep abreast of developments in their field by reading current literature, talking with colleagues, and participating in professional conferences. Maintain student attendance records, grades, and other required records. Initiate, facilitate, and moderate classroom discussions. Maintain regularly scheduled office hours in order to advise and assist students. Select and obtain materials and supplies such as textbooks. Plan, evaluate, and revise curricula, course content, and course materials and methods of instruction. Conduct research in a particular field of knowledge and publish findings in professional journals, books, and/or electronic media. Supervise undergraduate and/or graduate teaching, internship, and research work. Advise students on academic and vocational curricula and on career issues. Serve on academic or administrative committees that deal with institutional policies, departmental matters, and academic issues. Collaborate with colleagues to address teaching and research issues. Compile bibliographies of specialized materials for outside reading assignments. Participate in student recruitment, registration, and placement activities. Perform administrative duties such as serving as department head. Write grant proposals to procure external research funding. Participate in campus and community events. Provide professional consulting services to government and/or industry. Act as advisers to student organizations.

Personality Type: Social. These occupations frequently involve working with, communicating with, and teaching people and often involve helping or providing service to others.

GOE—Interest Area/Cluster: 05. Education and Training. **Work Group:** 05.03. Postsecondary and Adult Teaching and Instructing. **Other Jobs in This Work Group:** Adult Literacy, Remedial Education, and GED Teachers and Instructors; Agricultural Sciences Teachers, Postsecondary; Anthropology and Archeology Teachers, Postsecondary; Architecture Teachers, Postsecondary; Area, Ethnic, and Cultural Studies Teachers, Postsecondary; Art, Drama, and Music Teachers, Postsecondary; Atmospheric, Earth, Marine, and Space Sciences Teachers, Postsecondary; Biological Science Teachers, Postsecondary; Business Teachers, Postsecondary; Chemistry Teachers, Postsecondary; Communications Teachers, Postsecondary; Computer Science Teachers, Postsecondary; Criminal Justice and Law Enforcement Teachers, Postsecondary; Education Teachers, Postsecondary; Engineering Teachers, Postsecondary; English Language and Literature Teachers, Postsecondary; Environmental Science Teachers, Postsecondary; Farm and Home Management Advisors; Foreign Language and Literature Teachers, Postsecondary; Forestry and Conservation Science Teachers, Postsecondary; Geography Teachers, Postsecondary; Graduate Teaching Assistants; Health Specialties Teachers, Postsecondary; History Teachers, Postsecondary; Home Economics Teachers, Postsecondary; Law Teachers, Postsecondary; Library Science Teachers, Postsecondary; Mathematical Science Teachers, Postsecondary; Nursing Instructors and Teachers, Postsecondary; Philosophy and Religion Teachers, Postsecondary; Physics Teachers, Postsecondary; Political Science Teachers, Postsecondary; Psychology Teachers, Postsecondary; Recreation and Fitness Studies Teachers, Postsecondary; Social Work Teachers, Postsecondary; Sociology Teachers, Postsecondary.

Skills—Mathematics: Using mathematics to solve problems. **Writing:** Communicating effectively with others in writing as indicated by the needs of the audience. **Instructing:** Teaching others how to do something. **Speaking:** Talking to others to effectively convey information. **Reading Comprehension:** Understanding written sentences and paragraphs in work-related documents. **Critical Thinking:** Using logic and analysis to identify the strengths and weaknesses of different approaches. **Learning Strategies:** Using multiple approaches when learning or teaching new things. **Active Learning:** Working with new material or information to grasp its implications.

Education and Training Programs: Social Science Teacher Education; Economics, General;

Applied Economics; Econometrics and Quantitative Economics; Development Economics and International Development; International Economics; Economics, Other; Business/Managerial Economics. **Related Knowledge/Courses—Economics and Accounting:** Economic and accounting principles and practices, the financial markets, banking, and the analysis and reporting of financial data. **History and Archeology:** Historical events and their causes, indicators, and impact on particular civilizations and cultures. **Mathematics:** Numbers and their operations and interrelationships, including arithmetic, algebra, geometry, calculus, and statistics and their applications. **Philosophy and Theology:** Different philosophical systems and religions, including their basic principles, values, ethics, ways of thinking, customs, and practices and their impact on human culture. **Education and Training:** Instructional methods and training techniques, including curriculum design principles, learning theory, group and individual teaching techniques, design of individual development plans, and test design principles. **English Language:** The structure and content of the English language, including the meaning and spelling of words, rules of composition, and grammar.

Work Environment: Indoors; sitting.

Education Administrators, Elementary and Secondary School

❋ Education/Training Required: Work experience plus degree
❋ Annual Earnings: $80,580
❋ Beginning Wage: $52,940
❋ Earnings Growth Potential: Low
❋ Growth: 7.6%
❋ Annual Job Openings: 27,143
❋ Self-Employed: 3.3%
❋ Part-Time: 8.3%

Plan, direct, or coordinate the academic, clerical, or auxiliary activities of public or private elementary or secondary-level schools. Review and approve new programs or recommend modifications to existing programs, submitting program proposals for school board approval as necessary. Prepare, maintain, or oversee the preparation and maintenance of attendance, activity, planning, or personnel reports and records. Confer with parents and staff to discuss educational activities, policies, and student behavioral or learning problems. Prepare and submit budget requests and recommendations or grant proposals to solicit program funding. Direct and coordinate school maintenance services and the use of school facilities. Counsel and provide guidance to students regarding personal, academic, vocational, or behavioral issues. Organize and direct committees of specialists, volunteers, and staff to provide technical and advisory assistance for programs. Teach classes or courses to students. Advocate for new schools to be built or for existing facilities to be repaired or remodeled. Plan and develop instructional methods and content for educational, vocational, or student activity programs. Develop partnerships with businesses, communities, and other organizations to help meet identified educational needs and to provide school-to-work programs. Direct and coordinate activities of teachers, administrators, and support staff at schools, public agencies, and institutions. Evaluate curricula, teaching methods, and programs to determine their effectiveness, efficiency, and utilization and to ensure that school activities comply with federal, state, and local regulations. Set educational standards and goals and help establish policies and procedures to carry them out. Recruit, hire, train, and evaluate primary and supplemental staff. Enforce discipline and attendance rules. Observe teaching methods and examine learning materials to evaluate and standardize curricula and teaching techniques and to determine areas where improvement is needed. Establish, coordinate, and oversee particular programs across school districts, such as programs to evaluate student academic achievement. Review and interpret government codes and develop programs to ensure adherence to codes and facility safety, security, and maintenance.

Personality Type: Enterprising. These occupations frequently involve starting up and carrying out projects and can involve leading people and making many decisions. They sometimes require risk taking and often deal with business.

GOE—Interest Area/Cluster: 05. Education and Training. **Work Group:** 05.01. Managerial Work in Education. **Other Jobs in This Work Group:** Education Administrators, Postsecondary; Education Administrators, Preschool and Child Care Center/Program; Instructional Coordinators.

Skills—Management of Personnel Resources: Motivating, developing, and directing people as they work; identifying the best people for the job. **Management of Financial Resources:** Determining how money will be spent to get the work done and accounting for these expenditures. **Negotiation:** Bringing others together and trying to reconcile differences. **Learning Strategies:** Using multiple approaches when learning or teaching new things. **Monitoring:** Assessing how well one is doing when learning or doing something. **Management of Material Resources:** Obtaining and seeing to the appropriate use of equipment, facilities, and materials needed to do certain work. **Systems Evaluation:** Looking at many indicators of system performance and taking into account their accuracy. **Social Perceptiveness:** Being aware of others' reactions and understanding why they react the way they do.

Education and Training Programs: Educational Leadership and Administration, General; Educational, Instructional, and Curriculum Supervision; Elementary and Middle School Administration/Principalship; Secondary School Administration/Principalship; Educational Administration and Supervision, Other. **Related Knowledge/Courses—Therapy and Counseling:** Information and techniques needed to rehabilitate physical and mental ailments and to provide career guidance, including alternative treatments, rehabilitation equipment and its proper use, and methods to evaluate treatment effects. **Education and Training:** Instructional methods and training techniques, including curriculum design principles, learning theory, group and individual teaching techniques, design of individual development plans, and test design principles. **Personnel and Human Resources:** Principles and procedures for personnel recruitment; selection; training; compensation and benefits; labor relations and negotiation; and personnel information systems. **Psychology:** Human behavior and performance, mental processes, psychological research methods, and the assessment and treatment of behavioral and affective disorders. **Sociology and Anthropology:** Group behavior and dynamics; societal trends and influences; and cultures and their history, migrations, ethnicity, and origins. **History**

and Archeology: Historical events and their causes, indicators, and impact on particular civilizations and cultures.

Work Environment: Indoors; standing.

Education Administrators, Postsecondary

* Education/Training Required: Work experience plus degree
* Annual Earnings: $75,780
* Beginning Wage: $41,910
* Earnings Growth Potential: High
* Growth: 14.2%
* Annual Job Openings: 17,121
* Self-Employed: 3.3%
* Part-Time: 8.3%

Plan, direct, or coordinate research, instructional, student administration and services, and other educational activities at postsecondary institutions, including universities, colleges, and junior and community colleges. Recruit, hire, train, and terminate departmental personnel. Plan, administer, and control budgets; maintain financial records; and produce financial reports. Represent institutions at community and campus events, in meetings with other institution personnel, and during accreditation processes. Participate in faculty and college committee activities. Provide assistance to faculty and staff in duties such as teaching classes, conducting orientation programs, issuing transcripts, and scheduling events. Establish operational policies and procedures and make any necessary modifications, based on analysis of operations, demographics, and other research information. Confer with other academic staff to explain and formulate admission requirements and course credit policies. Appoint individuals to faculty positions and evaluate their performance. Direct activities of administrative departments such as admissions, registration, and career services. Develop curricula and recommend curricula revisions and additions. Determine course schedules and coordinate teaching assignments and room assignments to ensure optimum use of buildings and equipment. Consult with government regulatory and licensing agencies to ensure the institution's conformance with applicable standards. Direct, coordinate, and evaluate the activities of personnel engaged in administering academic institutions, departments, and/or alumni organizations. Teach courses within their department. Participate in student recruitment, selection, and admission, making admissions recommendations when required to do so. Review student misconduct reports requiring disciplinary action and counsel students regarding such reports. Supervise coaches. Assess and collect tuition and fees. Direct scholarship, fellowship, and loan programs, performing activities such as selecting recipients and distributing aid. Coordinate the production and dissemination of university publications such as course catalogs and class schedules. Review registration statistics and consult with faculty officials to develop registration policies. Audit the financial status of student organizations and facility accounts.

Personality Type: Enterprising. These occupations frequently involve starting up and carrying out projects and can involve leading people and making many decisions. They sometimes require risk taking and often deal with business.

GOE—Interest Area/Cluster: 05. Education and Training. **Work Group:** 05.01. Managerial Work in Education. **Other Jobs in This Work Group:** Education Administrators, Elementary and Secondary School; Education Administrators, Preschool and Child Care Center/Program; Instructional Coordinators.

Skills—Management of Financial Resources: Determining how money will be spent to get the work done and accounting for these expenditures. **Management of Personnel Resources:** Motivating, developing, and directing people as they work; identifying the best people for the job. **Systems Evaluation:** Looking at many indicators of system performance and taking into account their accuracy. **Persuasion:** Persuading others to approach things differently. **Monitoring:** Assessing how well one is doing when learning or doing something. **Judgment and Decision Making:** Weighing the relative costs and benefits of a potential action. **Management of Material Resources:** Obtaining and seeing to the appropriate use of equipment, facilities, and materials needed to do certain work. **Operations Analysis:** Analyzing needs and product requirements to create a design.

Education and Training Programs: Educational Leadership and Administration, General; Educational, Instructional, and Curriculum Supervision; Higher Education/Higher Education Administration; Community College Education; Educational Administration and Supervision, Other. **Related Knowledge/Courses—Personnel and Human Resources:** Principles and procedures for personnel recruitment; selection; training; compensation and benefits; labor relations and negotiation; and personnel information systems. **Education and Training:** Instructional methods and training techniques, including curriculum design principles, learning theory, group and individual teaching techniques, design of individual development plans, and test design principles. **Sociology and Anthropology:** Group behavior and dynamics; societal trends and influences; and cultures and their history, migrations, ethnicity, and origins. **Administration and Management:** Principles and processes involved in business and organizational planning, coordination, and execution. This includes strategic planning, resource allocation, manpower modeling, leadership techniques, and production methods. **Philosophy and Theology:** Different philosophical systems and religions, including their basic principles, values, ethics, ways of thinking, customs, and practices and their impact on human culture. **English Language:** The structure and content of the English language, including the meaning and spelling of words, rules of composition, and grammar.

Work Environment: Indoors; sitting.

Education Administrators, Preschool and Child Care Center/Program

* Education/Training Required: Work experience plus degree
* Annual Earnings: $38,580
* Beginning Wage: $25,340
* Earnings Growth Potential: Low
* Growth: 23.5%
* Annual Job Openings: 8,113
* Self-Employed: 3.4%
* Part-Time: 8.3%

Plan, direct, or coordinate the academic and nonacademic activities of preschool and child care centers or programs. Confer with parents and staff to discuss educational activities and policies and students' behavioral or learning problems. Prepare and maintain attendance, activity, planning, accounting, or personnel reports and records for officials and agencies or direct preparation and maintenance activities. Set educational standards and goals and help establish policies, procedures, and programs to carry them out. Monitor students' progress and provide students and teachers with assistance in resolving any problems. Determine allocations of funds for staff, supplies, materials, and equipment and authorize purchases. Recruit, hire, train, and evaluate primary and supplemental staff and recommend personnel actions for programs and services. Direct and coordinate activities of teachers or administrators at daycare centers, schools, public agencies, or institutions. Plan, direct, and monitor instructional methods and content of educational, vocational, or student activity programs. Review and interpret government codes and develop procedures to meet codes and to ensure facility safety, security, and maintenance. Determine the scope of educational program offerings and prepare drafts of program schedules and descriptions to estimate staffing and facility requirements. Review and evaluate new and current programs to determine their efficiency; effectiveness; and compliance with state, local, and federal regulations, and recommend any necessary modifications. Teach classes or courses or provide direct care to children. Prepare and submit budget requests or grant proposals to solicit program funding. Write articles, manuals, and other publications and assist in the distribution of promotional literature about programs and facilities. Collect and analyze survey data, regulatory information, and demographic and employment trends to forecast enrollment patterns and the need for curriculum changes. Inform businesses, community groups, and governmental agencies about educational needs, available programs, and program policies. Organize and direct committees of specialists, volunteers, and staff to provide technical and advisory assistance for programs.

Personality Type: Social. These occupations frequently involve working with, communicating with, and teaching people and often involve helping or providing service to others.

GOE—Interest Area/Cluster: 05. Education and Training. **Work Group:** 05.01. Managerial Work in Education. **Other Jobs in This Work Group:** Education Administrators, Elementary

and Secondary School; Education Administrators, Postsecondary; Instructional Coordinators.

Skills—Management of Financial Resources: Determining how money will be spent to get the work done and accounting for these expenditures. **Management of Personnel Resources:** Motivating, developing, and directing people as they work; identifying the best people for the job. **Management of Material Resources:** Obtaining and seeing to the appropriate use of equipment, facilities, and materials needed to do certain work. **Learning Strategies:** Using multiple approaches when learning or teaching new things. **Monitoring:** Assessing how well one is doing when learning or doing something. **Social Perceptiveness:** Being aware of others' reactions and understanding why they react the way they do. **Negotiation:** Bringing others together and trying to reconcile differences. **Persuasion:** Persuading others to approach things differently.

Education and Training Programs: Educational Leadership and Administration, General; Educational, Instructional, and Curriculum Supervision; Elementary and Middle School Administration/Principalship; Educational Administration and Supervision, Other. **Related Knowledge/Courses—Personnel and Human Resources:** Principles and procedures for personnel recruitment; selection; training; compensation and benefits; labor relations and negotiation; and personnel information systems. **Education and Training:** Instructional methods and training techniques, including curriculum design principles, learning theory, group and individual teaching techniques, design of individual development plans, and test design principles. **Clerical Practices:** Administrative and clerical procedures and systems such as word-processing systems, filing and records management systems, stenography and transcription, forms, design principles, and other office procedures and terminology. **Philosophy and**

Theology: Different philosophical systems and religions, including their basic principles, values, ethics, ways of thinking, customs, and practices and their impact on human culture. **Therapy and Counseling:** Information and techniques needed to rehabilitate physical and mental ailments and to provide career guidance, including alternative treatments, rehabilitation equipment and its proper use, and methods to evaluate treatment effects. **Sociology and Anthropology:** Group behavior and dynamics; societal trends and influences; and cultures and their history, migrations, ethnicity, and origins.

Work Environment: Indoors; standing.

Education Teachers, Postsecondary

- ✸ Education/Training Required: Doctoral degree
- ✸ Annual Earnings: $54,220
- ✸ Beginning Wage: $29,060
- ✸ Earnings Growth Potential: High
- ✸ Growth: 22.9%
- ✸ Annual Job Openings: 9,359
- ✸ Self-Employed: 0.4%
- ✸ Part-Time: 27.8%

Teach courses pertaining to education, such as counseling, curriculum, guidance, instruction, teacher education, and teaching English as a second language. Prepare course materials such as syllabi, homework assignments, and handouts. Prepare and deliver lectures to undergraduate and/or graduate students on topics such as children's literature, learning and development, and reading instruction. Initiate, facilitate, and moderate classroom discussions. Evaluate and grade students' classwork, assignments, and papers. Plan, evaluate, and revise curricula, course content, and course

materials and methods of instruction. Supervise students' fieldwork, internship, and research work. Keep abreast of developments in their field by reading current literature, talking with colleagues, and participating in professional conferences. Advise students on academic and vocational curricula and on career issues. Maintain regularly scheduled office hours to advise and assist students. Maintain student attendance records, grades, and other required records. Collaborate with colleagues to address teaching and research issues. Compile, administer, and grade examinations or assign this work to others. Conduct research in a particular field of knowledge and publish findings in professional journals, books, or electronic media. Select and obtain materials and supplies such as textbooks. Participate in student recruitment, registration, and placement activities. Advise and instruct teachers employed in school systems by providing activities such as in-service seminars. Serve on academic or administrative committees that deal with institutional policies, departmental matters, and academic issues. Compile bibliographies of specialized materials for outside reading assignments. Write grant proposals to procure external research funding. Participate in campus and community events. Perform administrative duties such as serving as department head. Act as advisers to student organizations. Provide professional consulting services to government and/or industry.

Personality Type: Social. These occupations frequently involve working with, communicating with, and teaching people and often involve helping or providing service to others.

GOE—Interest Area/Cluster: 05. Education and Training. **Work Group:** 05.03. Postsecondary and Adult Teaching and Instructing. **Other Jobs in This Work Group:** Adult Literacy, Remedial Education, and GED Teachers and Instructors; Agricultural Sciences Teachers, Postsecondary; Anthropology and Archeology Teachers, Postsecondary;

Architecture Teachers, Postsecondary; Area, Ethnic, and Cultural Studies Teachers, Postsecondary; Art, Drama, and Music Teachers, Postsecondary; Atmospheric, Earth, Marine, and Space Sciences Teachers, Postsecondary; Biological Science Teachers, Postsecondary; Business Teachers, Postsecondary; Chemistry Teachers, Postsecondary; Communications Teachers, Postsecondary; Computer Science Teachers, Postsecondary; Criminal Justice and Law Enforcement Teachers, Postsecondary; Economics Teachers, Postsecondary; Engineering Teachers, Postsecondary; English Language and Literature Teachers, Postsecondary; Environmental Science Teachers, Postsecondary; Farm and Home Management Advisors; Foreign Language and Literature Teachers, Postsecondary; Forestry and Conservation Science Teachers, Postsecondary; Geography Teachers, Postsecondary; Graduate Teaching Assistants; Health Specialties Teachers, Postsecondary; History Teachers, Postsecondary; Home Economics Teachers, Postsecondary; Law Teachers, Postsecondary; Library Science Teachers, Postsecondary; Mathematical Science Teachers, Postsecondary; Nursing Instructors and Teachers, Postsecondary; Philosophy and Religion Teachers, Postsecondary; Physics Teachers, Postsecondary; Political Science Teachers, Postsecondary; Psychology Teachers, Postsecondary; Recreation and Fitness Studies Teachers, Postsecondary; Social Work Teachers, Postsecondary; Sociology Teachers, Postsecondary.

Skills—Learning Strategies: Using multiple approaches when learning or teaching new things. **Instructing:** Teaching others how to do something. **Writing:** Communicating effectively with others in writing as indicated by the needs of the audience. **Social Perceptiveness:** Being aware of others' reactions and understanding why they react the way they do. **Speaking:** Talking to others to effectively convey information. **Persuasion:** Persuading others to approach things differently.

Science: Using scientific methods to solve problems. **Monitoring:** Assessing how well one is doing when learning or doing something.

Education and Training Programs: Education, General; Indian/Native American Education; Social and Philosophical Foundations of Education; Agricultural Teacher Education; Art Teacher Education; Business Teacher Education; Driver and Safety Teacher Education; English/Language Arts Teacher Education; Foreign Language Teacher Education; Health Teacher Education; Family and Consumer Sciences/Home Economics Teacher Education; others. **Related Knowledge/Courses—Therapy and Counseling:** Information and techniques needed to rehabilitate physical and mental ailments and to provide career guidance, including alternative treatments, rehabilitation equipment and its proper use, and methods to evaluate treatment effects. **Education and Training:** Instructional methods and training techniques, including curriculum design principles, learning theory, group and individual teaching techniques, design of individual development plans, and test design principles. **Sociology and Anthropology:** Group behavior and dynamics; societal trends and influences; and cultures and their history, migrations, ethnicity, and origins. **Philosophy and Theology:** Different philosophical systems and religions, including their basic principles, values, ethics, ways of thinking, customs, and practices and their impact on human culture. **Psychology:** Human behavior and performance, mental processes, psychological research methods, and the assessment and treatment of behavioral and affective disorders. **English Language:** The structure and content of the English language, including the meaning and spelling of words, rules of composition, and grammar.

Work Environment: Indoors; sitting.

Educational, Vocational, and School Counselors

* Education/Training Required: Master's degree
* Annual Earnings: $49,450
* Beginning Wage: $28,430
* Earnings Growth Potential: High
* Growth: 12.6%
* Annual Job Openings: 54,025
* Self-Employed: 6.1%
* Part-Time: 15.4%

Counsel individuals and provide group educational and vocational guidance services. Counsel students regarding educational issues such as course and program selection, class scheduling, school adjustment, truancy, study habits, and career planning. Counsel individuals to help them understand and overcome personal, social, or behavioral problems affecting their educational or vocational situations. Maintain accurate and complete student records as required by laws, district policies, and administrative regulations. Confer with parents or guardians, teachers, other counselors, and administrators to resolve students' behavioral, academic, and other problems. Provide crisis intervention to students when difficult situations occur at schools. Identify cases involving domestic abuse or other family problems affecting students' development. Meet with parents and guardians to discuss their children's progress and to determine their priorities for their children and their resource needs. Prepare students for later educational experiences by encouraging them to explore learning opportunities and to persevere with challenging tasks. Encourage students and/or parents to seek additional assistance from mental health professionals when necessary. Observe and evaluate students' performance, behavior, social development, and physical health. Enforce all administration policies and rules governing students. Meet with other professionals to discuss individual students' needs and progress. Provide students with information on such topics as college degree programs and admission requirements, financial aid opportunities, trade and technical schools, and apprenticeship programs. Evaluate individuals' abilities, interests, and personality characteristics, using tests, records, interviews, and professional sources. Collaborate with teachers and administrators in the development, evaluation, and revision of school programs. Establish and enforce behavioral rules and procedures to maintain order among students. Teach classes and present self-help or information sessions on subjects related to education and career planning. Attend professional meetings, educational conferences, and teacher training workshops to maintain and improve professional competence.

Personality Type: Social. These occupations frequently involve working with, communicating with, and teaching people and often involve helping or providing service to others.

GOE—Interest Area/Cluster: 05. Education and Training. **Work Group:** 05.06. Counseling, Health, and Fitness Education. **Other Jobs in This Work Group:** Health Educators.

Skills—Social Perceptiveness: Being aware of others' reactions and understanding why they react the way they do. **Service Orientation:** Actively looking for ways to help people. **Negotiation:** Bringing others together and trying to reconcile differences. **Active Listening:** Listening to what other people are saying and asking questions as appropriate. **Persuasion:** Persuading others to approach things differently. **Learning Strategies:** Using multiple approaches when learning or teaching new things. **Writing:** Communicating effectively with others in writing as indicated by the needs of the audience. **Monitoring:** Assessing how well one is doing when learning or doing something.

Education and Training Programs: Counselor Education/School Counseling and Guidance Services; College Student Counseling and Personnel Services. **Related Knowledge/Courses—Therapy and Counseling:** Information and techniques needed to rehabilitate physical and mental ailments and to provide career guidance, including alternative treatments, rehabilitation equipment and its proper use, and methods to evaluate treatment effects. **Psychology:** Human behavior and performance, mental processes, psychological research methods, and the assessment and treatment of behavioral and affective disorders. **Sociology and Anthropology:** Group behavior and dynamics; societal trends and influences; and cultures and their history, migrations, ethnicity, and origins. **Education and Training:** Instructional methods and training techniques, including curriculum design principles, learning theory, group and individual teaching techniques, design of individual development plans, and test design principles. **Philosophy and Theology:** Different philosophical systems and religions, including their basic principles, values, ethics, ways of thinking, customs, and practices and their impact on human culture. **Clerical Practices:** Administrative and clerical procedures and systems such as word-processing systems, filing and records management systems, stenography and transcription, forms, design principles, and other office procedures and terminology.

Work Environment: Indoors; sitting.

Electrical Engineers

- ❋ Education/Training Required: Bachelor's degree
- ❋ Annual Earnings: $79,240
- ❋ Beginning Wage: $51,220
- ❋ Earnings Growth Potential: Medium
- ❋ Growth: 6.3%
- ❋ Annual Job Openings: 6,806
- ❋ Self-Employed: 2.1%
- ❋ Part-Time: 2.0%

Design, develop, test, or supervise the manufacturing and installation of electrical equipment, components, or systems for commercial, industrial, military, or scientific use. Confer with engineers, customers, and others to discuss existing or potential engineering projects and products. Design, implement, maintain, and improve electrical instruments, equipment, facilities, components, products, and systems for commercial, industrial, and domestic purposes. Operate computer-assisted engineering and design software and equipment to perform engineering tasks. Direct and coordinate manufacturing, construction, installation, maintenance, support, documentation, and testing activities to ensure compliance with specifications, codes, and customer requirements. Perform detailed calculations to compute and establish manufacturing, construction, and installation standards and specifications. Inspect completed installations and observe operations to ensure conformance to design and equipment specifications and compliance with operational and safety standards. Plan and implement research methodology and procedures to apply principles of electrical theory to engineering projects. Prepare specifications for purchase of materials and equipment. Supervise and train project team members as necessary. Investigate and test vendors' and competitors' products. Oversee project production efforts to assure projects are completed satisfactorily, on time, and within budget. Prepare and study technical drawings, specifications of electrical systems, and topographical maps to ensure that installation and operations conform to standards and customer requirements. Investigate customer or public complaints, determine nature and extent of problem, and recommend remedial measures. Plan layout of electric-power-generating plants and distribution lines and stations. Assist in developing capital project programs for new equipment and major repairs. Develop budgets, estimating labor, material, and construction costs. Compile data and write reports regarding existing and potential engineering studies and projects. Collect data relating to commercial and residential development, population, and power system interconnection to determine operating efficiency of electrical systems. Conduct field surveys and study maps, graphs, diagrams, and other data to identify and correct power system problems.

Personality Type: Investigative. These occupations frequently involve working with ideas and require an extensive amount of thinking. They can involve searching for facts and figuring out problems mentally.

GOE—Interest Area/Cluster: 15. Scientific Research, Engineering, and Mathematics. **Work Group:** 15.07. Research and Design Engineering. **Other Jobs in This Work Group:** Aerospace Engineers; Biomedical Engineers; Chemical Engineers; Civil Engineers; Computer Hardware Engineers; Electronics Engineers, Except Computer; Marine Architects; Marine Engineers; Marine Engineers and Naval Architects; Materials Engineers; Mechanical Engineers; Nuclear Engineers.

Skills—Technology Design: Generating or adapting equipment and technology to serve user needs. **Science:** Using scientific methods to solve problems. **Systems Analysis:** Determining how a system should work and how changes will affect

outcomes. **Troubleshooting:** Determining what is causing an operating error and deciding what to do about it. **Systems Evaluation:** Looking at many indicators of system performance and taking into account their accuracy. **Equipment Selection:** Determining the kind of tools and equipment needed to do a job. **Management of Material Resources:** Obtaining and seeing to the appropriate use of equipment, facilities, and materials needed to do certain work. **Programming:** Writing computer programs for various purposes.

Education and Training Program: Electrical, Electronics and Communications Engineering. **Related Knowledge/Courses—Engineering and Technology:** Equipment, tools, and mechanical devices and their uses to produce motion, light, power, technology, and other applications. **Design:** Design techniques, principles, tools, and instruments involved in the production and use of precision technical plans, blueprints, drawings, and models. **Physics:** Physical principles, laws, and applications, including air, water, material dynamics, light, atomic principles, heat, electric theory, earth formations, and meteorological and related natural phenomena. **Telecommunications:** Transmission, broadcasting, switching, control, and operation of telecommunications systems. **Computers and Electronics:** Electric circuit boards, processors, chips, and computer hardware and software, including applications and programming. **Mathematics:** Numbers and their operations and interrelationships, including arithmetic, algebra, geometry, calculus, and statistics and their applications.

Work Environment: Indoors; sitting.

Electronics Engineers, Except Computer

❋ Education/Training Required: Bachelor's degree
❋ Annual Earnings: $83,340
❋ Beginning Wage: $53,710
❋ Earnings Growth Potential: Medium
❋ Growth: 3.7%
❋ Annual Job Openings: 5,699
❋ Self-Employed: 2.2%
❋ Part-Time: 2.0%

Research, design, develop, and test electronic components and systems for commercial, industrial, military, or scientific use, utilizing knowledge of electronic theory and materials properties. Design electronic circuits and components for use in fields such as telecommunications, aerospace guidance and propulsion control, acoustics, or instruments and controls. Design electronic components, software, products, or systems for commercial, industrial, medical, military, or scientific applications. Provide technical support and instruction to staff or customers regarding equipment standards, assisting with specific, difficult in-service engineering. Operate computer-assisted engineering and design software and equipment to perform engineering tasks. Analyze system requirements, capacity, cost, and customer needs to determine feasibility of project and develop system plan. Confer with engineers, customers, vendors, or others to discuss existing and potential engineering projects or products. Review and evaluate work of others inside and outside the organization to ensure effectiveness, technical adequacy, and compatibility in the resolution of complex engineering problems. Determine material and equipment needs and order supplies. Inspect electronic equipment, instruments, products, and

systems to ensure conformance to specifications, safety standards, and applicable codes and regulations. Evaluate operational systems, prototypes, and proposals and recommend repair or design modifications based on factors such as environment, service, cost, and system capabilities. Prepare documentation containing information such as confidential descriptions and specifications of proprietary hardware and software, product development and introduction schedules, product costs, and information about product performance weaknesses. Direct and coordinate activities concerned with manufacture, construction, installation, maintenance, operation, and modification of electronic equipment, products, and systems. Develop and perform operational, maintenance, and testing procedures for electronic products, components, equipment, and systems. Plan and develop applications and modifications for electronic properties used in components, products, and systems to improve technical performance. Plan and implement research, methodology, and procedures to apply principles of electronic theory to engineering projects. Prepare engineering sketches and specifications for construction, relocation, and installation of equipment, facilities, products, and systems.

Personality Type: Investigative. These occupations frequently involve working with ideas and require an extensive amount of thinking. They can involve searching for facts and figuring out problems mentally.

GOE—Interest Area/Cluster: 15. Scientific Research, Engineering, and Mathematics. **Work Group:** 15.07. Research and Design Engineering. **Other Jobs in This Work Group:** Aerospace Engineers; Biomedical Engineers; Chemical Engineers; Civil Engineers; Computer Hardware Engineers; Electrical Engineers; Marine Architects; Marine Engineers; Marine Engineers and Naval Architects; Materials Engineers; Mechanical Engineers; Nuclear Engineers.

Skills—Troubleshooting: Determining what is causing an operating error and deciding what to do about it. **Installation:** Installing equipment, machines, wiring, or programs to meet specifications. **Science:** Using scientific methods to solve problems. **Operations Analysis:** Analyzing needs and product requirements to create a design. **Technology Design:** Generating or adapting equipment and technology to serve user needs. **Equipment Selection:** Determining the kind of tools and equipment needed to do a job. **Systems Evaluation:** Looking at many indicators of system performance and taking into account their accuracy. **Quality Control Analysis:** Evaluating the quality or performance of products, services, or processes.

Education and Training Program: Electrical, Electronics and Communications Engineering. **Related Knowledge/Courses—Engineering and Technology:** Equipment, tools, and mechanical devices and their uses to produce motion, light, power, technology, and other applications. **Design:** Design techniques, principles, tools, and instruments involved in the production and use of precision technical plans, blueprints, drawings, and models. **Physics:** Physical principles, laws, and applications, including air, water, material dynamics, light, atomic principles, heat, electric theory, earth formations, and meteorological and related natural phenomena. **Computers and Electronics:** Electric circuit boards, processors, chips, and computer hardware and software, including applications and programming. **Telecommunications:** Transmission, broadcasting, switching, control, and operation of telecommunications systems. **Production and Processing:** Inputs, outputs, raw materials, waste, quality control, costs, and techniques for maximizing the manufacture and distribution of goods.

Work Environment: Indoors; noisy; sitting.

Elementary School Teachers, Except Special Education

* Education/Training Required: Bachelor's degree
* Annual Earnings: $47,330
* Beginning Wage: $31,480
* Earnings Growth Potential: Low
* Growth: 13.6%
* Annual Job Openings: 181,612
* Self-Employed: 0.0%
* Part-Time: 9.5%

Teach pupils in public or private schools at the elementary level basic academic, social, and other formative skills. Establish and enforce rules for behavior and procedures for maintaining order among the students for whom they are responsible. Observe and evaluate students' performance, behavior, social development, and physical health. Prepare materials and classrooms for class activities. Adapt teaching methods and instructional materials to meet students' varying needs and interests. Plan and conduct activities for a balanced program of instruction, demonstration, and work time that provides students with opportunities to observe, question, and investigate. Instruct students individually and in groups, using various teaching methods such as lectures, discussions, and demonstrations. Establish clear objectives for all lessons, units, and projects and communicate those objectives to students. Assign and grade classwork and homework. Read books to entire classes or small groups. Prepare, administer, and grade tests and assignments in order to evaluate students' progress. Confer with parents or guardians, teachers, counselors, and administrators to resolve students' behavioral and academic problems. Meet with parents and guardians to discuss their children's progress and to determine their priorities for their children and their resource needs. Prepare students for later grades by encouraging them to explore learning opportunities and to persevere with challenging tasks. Maintain accurate and complete student records as required by laws, district policies, and administrative regulations. Guide and counsel students with adjustment or academic problems or special academic interests. Prepare and implement remedial programs for students requiring extra help. Prepare objectives and outlines for courses of study, following curriculum guidelines or requirements of states and schools. Provide a variety of materials and resources for children to explore, manipulate, and use, both in learning activities and in imaginative play. Enforce administration policies and rules governing students. Confer with other staff members to plan and schedule lessons promoting learning, following approved curricula.

Personality Type: Social. These occupations frequently involve working with, communicating with, and teaching people and often involve helping or providing service to others.

GOE—Interest Area/Cluster: 05. Education and Training. **Work Group:** 05.02. Preschool, Elementary, and Secondary Teaching and Instructing. **Other Jobs in This Work Group:** Kindergarten Teachers, Except Special Education; Middle School Teachers, Except Special and Vocational Education; Secondary School Teachers, Except Special and Vocational Education; Special Education Teachers, Middle School; Special Education Teachers, Preschool, Kindergarten, and Elementary School; Special Education Teachers, Secondary School; Vocational Education Teachers, Middle School; Vocational Education Teachers, Secondary School.

Skills—Instructing: Teaching others how to do something. **Learning Strategies:** Using multiple approaches when learning or teaching new things. **Monitoring:** Assessing how well one is doing when learning or doing something. **Social Perceptiveness:** Being aware of others' reactions and understanding why they react the way they do. **Speaking:** Talking to others to effectively convey information. **Persuasion:** Persuading others to approach things differently. **Writing:** Communicating effectively with others in writing as indicated by the needs of the audience. **Service Orientation:** Actively looking for ways to help people.

Education and Training Programs: Elementary Education and Teaching; Teacher Education, Multiple Levels; Montessori Teacher Education. **Related Knowledge/Courses—Geography:** Various methods for describing the location and distribution of land, sea, and air masses, including their physical locations, relationships, and characteristics. **History and Archeology:** Historical events and their causes, indicators, and impact on particular civilizations and cultures. **Sociology and Anthropology:** Group behavior and dynamics; societal trends and influences; and cultures and their history, migrations, ethnicity, and origins. **Therapy and Counseling:** Information and techniques needed to rehabilitate physical and mental ailments and to provide career guidance, including alternative treatments, rehabilitation equipment and its proper use, and methods to evaluate treatment effects. **Philosophy and Theology:** Different philosophical systems and religions, including their basic principles, values, ethics, ways of thinking, customs, and practices and their impact on human culture. **Education and Training:** Instructional methods and training techniques, including curriculum design principles, learning theory, group and individual teaching techniques, design of individual development plans, and test design principles.

Work Environment: Indoors; noisy; disease or infections; standing.

Employment Interviewers

* Education/Training Required: Bachelor's degree
* Annual Earnings: $44,380
* Beginning Wage: $27,340
* Earnings Growth Potential: Medium
* Growth: 18.4%
* Annual Job Openings: 33,588
* Self-Employed: 2.1%
* Part-Time: 7.6%

The job openings listed here are shared with Personnel Recruiters.

Interview job applicants in employment office and refer them to prospective employers for consideration. Search application files, notify selected applicants of job openings, and refer qualified applicants to prospective employers. Contact employers to verify referral results. Record and evaluate various pertinent data. Inform applicants of job openings and details such as duties and responsibilities, compensation, benefits, schedules, working conditions, and promotion opportunities. Interview job applicants to match their qualifications with employers' needs, recording and evaluating applicant experience, education, training, and skills. Review employment applications and job orders to match applicants with job requirements, using manual or computerized file searches. Select qualified applicants or refer them to employers according to organization policy. Perform reference and background checks on applicants. Maintain records of applicants not selected for employment. Instruct job applicants in presenting a positive image by providing help with resume writing, personal appearance, and interview techniques. Refer applicants to services such as vocational counseling, literacy or language instruction, transportation assistance, vocational training, and child care. Contact employers to solicit orders for job vacancies, determining their requirements and recording relevant data such as job descriptions. Conduct workshops and demonstrate the use of job listings to assist applicants with skill building. Search for and recruit applicants for open positions through campus job fairs and advertisements. Provide background information on organizations with which interviews are scheduled. Administer assessment tests to identify skill-building needs. Conduct or arrange for skill, intelligence, or psychological testing of applicants and current employees. Hire workers and place them with employers needing temporary help. Evaluate selection and testing techniques by conducting research or follow-up activities and conferring with management and supervisory personnel.

Personality Type: Enterprising. These occupations frequently involve starting up and carrying out projects and can involve leading people and making many decisions. They sometimes require risk taking and often deal with business.

GOE—Interest Area/Cluster: 04. Business and Administration. **Work Group:** 04.03. Human Resources Support. **Other Jobs in This Work Group:** Compensation, Benefits, and Job Analysis Specialists; Employment, Recruitment, and Placement Specialists; Personnel Recruiters; Training and Development Specialists.

Skills—Management of Personnel Resources: Motivating, developing, and directing people as they work; identifying the best people for the job. **Service Orientation:** Actively looking for ways to help people. **Social Perceptiveness:** Being aware of others' reactions and understanding why they react the way they do. **Persuasion:** Persuading others to approach things differently. **Negotiation:** Bringing others together and trying to reconcile differences. **Writing:** Communicating effectively with others in writing as indicated by the needs of the audience. **Speaking:** Talking to others to effectively convey information. **Instructing:** Teaching others how to do something.

Education and Training Programs: Human Resources Management/Personnel Administration, General; Labor and Industrial Relations. **Related Knowledge/Courses—Foreign Language:** The structure and content of a foreign (non-English) language, including the meaning and spelling of words, rules of composition and grammar, and pronunciation. **Clerical Practices:** Administrative and clerical procedures and systems such as word-processing systems, filing and records management systems, stenography and transcription, forms, design principles, and other office procedures and terminology. **Personnel and Human Resources:** Principles and procedures for personnel recruitment; selection; training; compensation and benefits; labor relations and negotiation; and personnel information systems. **Sales and Marketing:** Principles and methods involved in showing, promoting, and selling products or services. This includes marketing strategies and tactics, product demonstration and sales techniques, and sales control systems. **Customer and Personal Service:** Principles and processes for providing customer and personal services, including needs assessment techniques, quality service standards, alternative delivery systems, and customer satisfaction evaluation techniques. **English Language:** The structure and content of the English language, including the meaning and spelling of words, rules of composition, and grammar.

Work Environment: Indoors; sitting; repetitive motions.

Engineering Managers

- ❈ Education/Training Required: Work experience plus degree
- ❈ Annual Earnings: $111,020
- ❈ Beginning Wage: $70,640
- ❈ Earnings Growth Potential: Medium
- ❈ Growth: 7.3%
- ❈ Annual Job Openings: 7,404
- ❈ Self-Employed: 0.0%
- ❈ Part-Time: 2.0%

Plan, direct, or coordinate activities or research and development in such fields as architecture and engineering. Coordinate and direct projects, making detailed plans to accomplish goals and directing the integration of technical activities. Consult or negotiate with clients to prepare project specifications. Present and explain proposals, reports, and findings to clients. Direct, review, and approve product design and changes. Recruit employees, assign, direct, and evaluate their work, and oversee the development and maintenance of staff competence. Perform administrative functions such as reviewing and writing reports, approving expenditures, enforcing rules, and making decisions about the purchase of materials or services. Prepare budgets, bids, and contracts, and direct the negotiation of research contracts. Analyze technology, resource needs, and market demand, to plan and assess the feasibility of projects. Confer with management, production, and marketing staff to discuss project specifications and procedures. Review and recommend or approve contracts and cost estimates. Develop and implement policies, standards, and procedures for the engineering and technical work performed in the department, service, laboratory, or firm. Plan and direct the installation, testing, operation, maintenance, and repair of facilities and equipment. Administer highway planning, construction, and maintenance. Confer with and report to officials and the public to provide information and solicit support for projects. Set scientific and technical goals within broad outlines provided by top management. Direct the engineering of water control, treatment, and distribution projects. Plan, direct, and coordinate survey work with other staff activities, certifying survey work, and writing land legal descriptions.

Personality Type: Enterprising. These occupations frequently involve starting up and carrying out projects and can involve leading people and making many decisions. They sometimes require risk taking and often deal with business.

GOE—Interest Area/Cluster: 15. Scientific Research, Engineering, and Mathematics. **Work Group:** 15.01. Managerial Work in Scientific Research, Engineering, and Mathematics. **Other Jobs in This Work Group:** Natural Sciences Managers.

Skills—Management of Financial Resources: Determining how money will be spent to get the work done and accounting for these expenditures. **Management of Personnel Resources:** Motivating, developing, and directing people as they work; identifying the best people for the job. **Systems Analysis:** Determining how a system should work and how changes will affect outcomes. **Management of Material Resources:** Obtaining and seeing to the appropriate use of equipment, facilities, and materials needed to do certain work. **Systems Evaluation:** Looking at many indicators of system performance and taking into account their accuracy. **Negotiation:** Bringing others together and trying to reconcile differences. **Mathematics:** Using mathematics to solve problems. **Writing:** Communicating effectively with others in writing as indicated by the needs of the audience.

Education and Training Programs: Architecture (BArch, BA/BS, MArch, MA/MS, PhD); City/Urban, Community and Regional Planning;

Environmental Design/Architecture; Interior Architecture; Landscape Architecture (BS, BSLA, BLA, MSLA, MLA, PhD); Engineering, General; Aerospace, Aeronautical and Astronautical Engineering; Agricultural/Biological Engineering and Bioengineering; Architectural Engineering; Biomedical/Medical Engineering; others. **Related Knowledge/Courses—Engineering and Technology:** Equipment, tools, and mechanical devices and their uses to produce motion, light, power, technology, and other applications. **Design:** Design techniques, principles, tools, and instruments involved in the production and use of precision technical plans, blueprints, drawings, and models. **Physics:** Physical principles, laws, and applications, including air, water, material dynamics, light, atomic principles, heat, electric theory, earth formations, and meteorological and related natural phenomena. **Building and Construction:** Materials, methods, and the appropriate tools to construct objects, structures, and buildings. **Computers and Electronics:** Electric circuit boards, processors, chips, and computer hardware and software, including applications and programming. **Mathematics:** Numbers and their operations and interrelationships, including arithmetic, algebra, geometry, calculus, and statistics and their applications.

Work Environment: Indoors; noisy; sitting.

Engineering Teachers, Postsecondary

❀ Education/Training Required: Doctoral degree

❀ Annual Earnings: $79,510

❀ Beginning Wage: $43,090

❀ Earnings Growth Potential: High

❀ Growth: 22.9%

❀ Annual Job Openings: 5,565

❀ Self-Employed: 0.4%

❀ Part-Time: 27.8%

Teach courses pertaining to the application of physical laws and principles of engineering for the development of machines, materials, instruments, processes, and services. Includes teachers of subjects such as chemical, civil, electrical, industrial, mechanical, mineral, and petroleum engineering. Includes both teachers primarily engaged in teaching and those who do a combination of both teaching and research. Prepare and deliver lectures to undergraduate and/or graduate students on topics such as mechanics, hydraulics, and robotics. Keep abreast of developments in their field by reading current literature, talking with colleagues, and participating in professional conferences. Supervise undergraduate and/or graduate teaching, internship, and research work. Evaluate and grade students' classwork, laboratory work, assignments, and papers. Conduct research in a particular field of knowledge and publish findings in professional journals, books, and/or electronic media. Prepare course materials such as syllabi, homework assignments, and handouts. Compile, administer, and grade examinations or assign this work to others. Write grant proposals to procure external research funding. Supervise students' laboratory work. Initiate, facilitate, and moderate class discussions. Maintain regularly scheduled office hours to advise and assist students. Plan, evaluate, and revise curricula, course content, and course materials and methods of instruction. Advise students on academic and vocational curricula and on career issues. Maintain student attendance records, grades, and other required records. Collaborate with colleagues to address teaching and research issues. Select and obtain materials and supplies such as textbooks and laboratory equipment. Participate in student recruitment, registration, and placement activities. Serve on academic or administrative committees that deal with institutional policies, departmental matters, and academic issues. Perform administrative duties such as serving as department head. Provide professional consulting services to government and/or industry. Compile bibliographies of specialized materials for outside reading assignments. Act as advisers to student organizations. Participate in campus and community events.

Personality Type: Investigative. These occupations frequently involve working with ideas and require an extensive amount of thinking. They can involve searching for facts and figuring out problems mentally.

GOE—Interest Area/Cluster: 05. Education and Training. **Work Group:** 05.03. Postsecondary and Adult Teaching and Instructing. **Other Jobs in This Work Group:** Adult Literacy, Remedial Education, and GED Teachers and Instructors; Agricultural Sciences Teachers, Postsecondary; Anthropology and Archeology Teachers, Postsecondary; Architecture Teachers, Postsecondary; Area, Ethnic, and Cultural Studies Teachers, Postsecondary; Art, Drama, and Music Teachers, Postsecondary; Atmospheric, Earth, Marine, and Space Sciences Teachers, Postsecondary; Biological Science Teachers, Postsecondary; Business Teachers, Postsecondary; Chemistry Teachers, Postsecondary; Communications Teachers, Postsecondary; Computer Science Teachers, Postsecondary;

Criminal Justice and Law Enforcement Teachers, Postsecondary; Economics Teachers, Postsecondary; Education Teachers, Postsecondary; English Language and Literature Teachers, Postsecondary; Environmental Science Teachers, Postsecondary; Farm and Home Management Advisors; Foreign Language and Literature Teachers, Postsecondary; Forestry and Conservation Science Teachers, Postsecondary; Geography Teachers, Postsecondary; Graduate Teaching Assistants; Health Specialties Teachers, Postsecondary; History Teachers, Postsecondary; Home Economics Teachers, Postsecondary; Law Teachers, Postsecondary; Library Science Teachers, Postsecondary; Mathematical Science Teachers, Postsecondary; Nursing Instructors and Teachers, Postsecondary; Philosophy and Religion Teachers, Postsecondary; Physics Teachers, Postsecondary; Political Science Teachers, Postsecondary; Psychology Teachers, Postsecondary; Recreation and Fitness Studies Teachers, Postsecondary; Social Work Teachers, Postsecondary; Sociology Teachers, Postsecondary.

Skills—Science: Using scientific methods to solve problems. **Programming:** Writing computer programs for various purposes. **Mathematics:** Using mathematics to solve problems. **Technology Design:** Generating or adapting equipment and technology to serve user needs. **Complex Problem Solving:** Identifying complex problems, reviewing the options, and implementing solutions. **Management of Financial Resources:** Determining how money will be spent to get the work done and accounting for these expenditures. **Critical Thinking:** Using logic and analysis to identify the strengths and weaknesses of different approaches. **Operations Analysis:** Analyzing needs and product requirements to create a design.

Education and Training Programs: Teacher Education and Professional Development, Specific Subject Areas, Other; Engineering, General; Aerospace, Aeronautical and Astronautical Engineering; Agricultural/Biological Engineering and Bioengineering; Architectural Engineering; Biomedical/Medical Engineering; Ceramic Sciences and Engineering; Chemical Engineering; Civil Engineering, General; Geotechnical Engineering; Structural Engineering; others. **Related Knowledge/Courses—Engineering and Technology:** Equipment, tools, and mechanical devices and their uses to produce motion, light, power, technology, and other applications. **Physics:** Physical principles, laws, and applications, including air, water, material dynamics, light, atomic principles, heat, electric theory, earth formations, and meteorological and related natural phenomena. **Design:** Design techniques, principles, tools, and instruments involved in the production and use of precision technical plans, blueprints, drawings, and models. **Mathematics:** Numbers and their operations and interrelationships, including arithmetic, algebra, geometry, calculus, and statistics and their applications. **Education and Training:** Instructional methods and training techniques, including curriculum design principles, learning theory, group and individual teaching techniques, design of individual development plans, and test design principles. **Telecommunications:** Transmission, broadcasting, switching, control, and operation of telecommunications systems.

Work Environment: Indoors; sitting.

English Language and Literature Teachers, Postsecondary

- ❋ Education/Training Required: Doctoral degree
- ❋ Annual Earnings: $54,000
- ❋ Beginning Wage: $30,680
- ❋ Earnings Growth Potential: High
- ❋ Growth: 22.9%
- ❋ Annual Job Openings: 10,475
- ❋ Self-Employed: 0.4%
- ❋ Part-Time: 27.8%

Teach courses in English language and literature, including linguistics and comparative literature. Initiate, facilitate, and moderate classroom discussions. Evaluate and grade students' classwork, assignments, and papers. Prepare course materials such as syllabi, homework assignments, and handouts. Prepare and deliver lectures to undergraduate and graduate students on topics such as poetry, novel structure, and translation and adaptation. Maintain student attendance records, grades, and other required records. Plan, evaluate, and revise curricula, course content, and course materials and methods of instruction. Compile, administer, and grade examinations or assign this work to others. Maintain regularly scheduled office hours in order to advise and assist students. Keep abreast of developments in their field by reading current literature, talking with colleagues, and participating in professional conferences. Select and obtain materials and supplies such as textbooks. Advise students on academic and vocational curricula and on career issues. Conduct research in a particular field of knowledge and publish findings in professional journals, books, or electronic media. Collaborate with colleagues to address teaching and research issues. Serve on academic or administrative committees that deal with institutional policies, departmental matters, and academic issues. Participate in campus and community events. Participate in student recruitment, registration, and placement activities. Compile bibliographies of specialized materials for outside reading assignments. Supervise undergraduate and/or graduate teaching, internship, and research work. Provide assistance to students in college writing centers. Perform administrative duties such as serving as department head. Recruit, train, and supervise student writing instructors. Act as advisers to student organizations. Write grant proposals to procure external research funding. Provide professional consulting services to government or industry.

Personality Type: Social. These occupations frequently involve working with, communicating with, and teaching people and often involve helping or providing service to others.

GOE—Interest Area/Cluster: 05. Education and Training. **Work Group:** 05.03. Postsecondary and Adult Teaching and Instructing. **Other Jobs in This Work Group:** Adult Literacy, Remedial Education, and GED Teachers and Instructors; Agricultural Sciences Teachers, Postsecondary; Anthropology and Archeology Teachers, Postsecondary; Architecture Teachers, Postsecondary; Area, Ethnic, and Cultural Studies Teachers, Postsecondary; Art, Drama, and Music Teachers, Postsecondary; Atmospheric, Earth, Marine, and Space Sciences Teachers, Postsecondary; Biological Science Teachers, Postsecondary; Business Teachers, Postsecondary; Chemistry Teachers, Postsecondary; Communications Teachers, Postsecondary; Computer Science Teachers, Postsecondary; Criminal Justice and Law Enforcement Teachers, Postsecondary; Economics Teachers, Postsecondary; Education Teachers, Postsecondary; Engineering Teachers, Postsecondary; Environmental Science Teachers, Postsecondary; Farm and Home Management Advisors; Foreign

E

Language and Literature Teachers, Postsecondary; Forestry and Conservation Science Teachers, Postsecondary; Geography Teachers, Postsecondary; Graduate Teaching Assistants; Health Specialties Teachers, Postsecondary; History Teachers, Postsecondary; Home Economics Teachers, Postsecondary; Law Teachers, Postsecondary; Library Science Teachers, Postsecondary; Mathematical Science Teachers, Postsecondary; Nursing Instructors and Teachers, Postsecondary; Philosophy and Religion Teachers, Postsecondary; Physics Teachers, Postsecondary; Political Science Teachers, Postsecondary; Psychology Teachers, Postsecondary; Recreation and Fitness Studies Teachers, Postsecondary; Social Work Teachers, Postsecondary; Sociology Teachers, Postsecondary.

Skills—Instructing: Teaching others how to do something. **Writing:** Communicating effectively with others in writing as indicated by the needs of the audience. **Learning Strategies:** Using multiple approaches when learning or teaching new things. **Social Perceptiveness:** Being aware of others' reactions and understanding why they react the way they do. **Reading Comprehension:** Understanding written sentences and paragraphs in work-related documents. **Persuasion:** Persuading others to approach things differently. **Critical Thinking:** Using logic and analysis to identify the strengths and weaknesses of different approaches. **Active Learning:** Working with new material or information to grasp its implications.

Education and Training Programs: Comparative Literature; English Language and Literature, General; English Composition; Creative Writing; American Literature (United States); American Literature (Canadian); English Literature (British and Commonwealth); Technical and Business Writing; English Language and Literature/Letters, Other. **Related Knowledge/Courses—Philosophy and Theology:** Different philosophical systems and religions, including their basic principles, values, ethics, ways of thinking, customs, and practices and their impact on human culture. **English Language:** The structure and content of the English language, including the meaning and spelling of words, rules of composition, and grammar. **History and Archeology:** Historical events and their causes, indicators, and impact on particular civilizations and cultures. **Education and Training:** Instructional methods and training techniques, including curriculum design principles, learning theory, group and individual teaching techniques, design of individual development plans, and test design principles. **Fine Arts:** Theory and techniques required to produce, compose, and perform works of music, dance, visual arts, drama, and sculpture. **Sociology and Anthropology:** Group behavior and dynamics; societal trends and influences; and cultures and their history, migrations, ethnicity, and origins.

Work Environment: Indoors; sitting.

Environmental Engineering Technicians

- ❈ Education/Training Required: Associate degree
- ❈ Annual Earnings: $40,690
- ❈ Beginning Wage: $25,360
- ❈ Earnings Growth Potential: Medium
- ❈ Growth: 24.8%
- ❈ Annual Job Openings: 2,162
- ❈ Self-Employed: 0.8%
- ❈ Part-Time: 5.9%

Apply theory and principles of environmental engineering to modify, test, and operate equipment and devices used in the prevention, control, and remediation of environmental pollution, including waste treatment and site remediation. May assist in the development of environmental

pollution remediation devices under direction of engineer. Receive, set up, test, and decontaminate equipment. Maintain project logbook records and computer program files. Perform environmental quality work in field and office settings. Conduct pollution surveys, collecting and analyzing samples such as air and groundwater. Review technical documents to ensure completeness and conformance to requirements. Perform laboratory work such as logging numerical and visual observations, preparing and packaging samples, recording test results, and performing photo documentation. Review work plans to schedule activities. Obtain product information, identify vendors and suppliers, and order materials and equipment to maintain inventory. Arrange for the disposal of lead, asbestos, and other hazardous materials. Inspect facilities to monitor compliance with regulations governing substances such as asbestos, lead, and wastewater. Provide technical engineering support in the planning of projects such as wastewater treatment plants to ensure compliance with environmental regulations and policies. Improve chemical processes to reduce toxic emissions. Oversee support staff. Assist in the cleanup of hazardous material spills. Produce environmental assessment reports, tabulating data and preparing charts, graphs, and sketches. Maintain process parameters and evaluate process anomalies. Work with customers to assess the environmental impact of proposed construction and to develop pollution prevention programs. Perform statistical analysis and correction of air or water pollution data submitted by industry and other agencies. Develop work plans, including writing specifications and establishing material, manpower, and facilities needs.

Personality Type: Realistic. These occupations frequently involve work activities that include practical, hands-on problems and solutions. They often deal with plants; animals; and real-world materials

such as wood, tools, and machinery. Many of the occupations require working outside and don't involve a lot of paperwork or working closely with others.

GOE—Interest Area/Cluster: 15. Scientific Research, Engineering, and Mathematics. **Work Group:** 15.09. Engineering Technology. **Other Jobs in This Work Group:** Aerospace Engineering and Operations Technicians; Cartographers and Photogrammetrists; Civil Engineering Technicians; Electrical and Electronic Engineering Technicians; Electrical Engineering Technicians; Electro-Mechanical Technicians; Electronics Engineering Technicians; Mechanical Engineering Technicians.

Skills—Science: Using scientific methods to solve problems. **Repairing:** Repairing machines or systems, using the needed tools. **Troubleshooting:** Determining what is causing an operating error and deciding what to do about it. **Equipment Maintenance:** Performing routine maintenance and determining when and what kind of maintenance is needed. **Operation Monitoring:** Watching gauges, dials, or other indicators to make sure a machine is working properly. **Mathematics:** Using mathematics to solve problems. **Quality Control Analysis:** Evaluating the quality or performance of products, services, or processes. **Installation:** Installing equipment, machines, wiring, or programs to meet specifications.

Education and Training Programs: Environmental Engineering Technology/Environmental Technology; Hazardous Materials Information Systems Technology/Technician. **Related Knowledge/Courses—Engineering and Technology:** Equipment, tools, and mechanical devices and their uses to produce motion, light, power, technology, and other applications. **Building and Construction:** Materials, methods, and the appropriate tools to construct objects, structures, and buildings. **Physics:** Physical principles, laws, and applications, including air, water, material dynamics, light, atomic principles, heat, electric theory, earth formations, and meteorological and related natural phenomena. **Design:** Design techniques, principles, tools, and instruments involved in the production and use of precision technical plans, blueprints, drawings, and models. **Biology:** Plant and animal living tissue, cells, organisms, and entities, including their functions, interdependencies, and interactions with each other and the environment. **Chemistry:** The composition, structure, and properties of substances and of the chemical processes and transformations that they undergo. This includes uses of chemicals and their interactions, danger signs, production techniques, and disposal methods.

Work Environment: More often indoors than outdoors; contaminants; hazardous conditions; hazardous equipment; standing.

Environmental Engineers

- ❋ Education/Training Required: Bachelor's degree
- ❋ Annual Earnings: $72,350
- ❋ Beginning Wage: $44,090
- ❋ Earnings Growth Potential: Medium
- ❋ Growth: 25.4%
- ❋ Annual Job Openings: 5,003
- ❋ Self-Employed: 2.7%
- ❋ Part-Time: 3.0%

Design, plan, or perform engineering duties in the prevention, control, and remediation of environmental health hazards, using various engineering disciplines. Work may include waste treatment, site remediation, or pollution control technology. Collaborate with environmental scientists, planners, hazardous waste technicians, engineers, and other specialists, and experts in law and business to address environmental problems. Inspect industrial and municipal facilities and programs to evaluate operational effectiveness and ensure compliance with environmental regulations. Prepare, review, and update environmental investigation and recommendation reports. Design and supervise the development of systems processes or equipment for control, management, or remediation of water, air, or soil quality. Provide environmental engineering assistance in network analysis, regulatory analysis, and planning or reviewing database development. Obtain, update, and maintain plans, permits, and standard operating procedures. Provide technical-level support for environmental remediation and litigation projects, including remediation system design and determination of regulatory applicability. Monitor progress of environmental improvement programs. Inform company employees and other interested parties of environmental issues. Advise corporations and government agencies of procedures to follow in cleaning up contaminated sites to protect people and the environment. Develop proposed project objectives and targets, and report to management on progress in attaining them. Request bids from suppliers or consultants. Advise industries and government agencies about environmental policies and standards. Assess the existing or potential environmental impact of land use projects on air, water, and land. Assist in budget implementation, forecasts, and administration. Serve on teams conducting multimedia inspections at complex facilities, providing assistance with planning, quality assurance, safety inspection protocols, and sampling. Coordinate and manage environmental protection programs and projects, assigning and evaluating work. Maintain, write, and revise quality assurance documentation and procedures. Provide administrative support for projects by collecting data, providing project documentation, training staff, and performing other general administrative duties.

Personality Type: Investigative. These occupations frequently involve working with ideas and require an extensive amount of thinking. They can involve searching for facts and figuring out problems mentally.

GOE—Interest Area/Cluster: 01. Agriculture and Natural Resources. **Work Group:** 01.02. Resource Science/Engineering for Plants, Animals, and the Environment. **Other Jobs in This Work Group:** Agricultural Engineers; Animal Scientists; Conservation Scientists; Foresters; Mining and Geological Engineers, Including Mining Safety Engineers; Petroleum Engineers; Range Managers; Soil and Plant Scientists; Soil and Water Conservationists; Zoologists and Wildlife Biologists.

Skills—Management of Financial Resources: Determining how money will be spent to get the work done and accounting for these expenditures. **Systems Analysis:** Determining how a system should work and how changes will affect outcomes. **Mathematics:** Using mathematics to solve problems. **Systems Evaluation:** Looking at many indicators of system performance and taking into account their accuracy. **Management of Personnel Resources:** Motivating, developing, and directing people as they work; identifying the best people for the job. **Writing:** Communicating effectively with others in writing as indicated by the needs of the audience. **Operation Monitoring:** Watching gauges, dials, or other indicators to make sure a machine is working properly. **Complex Problem Solving:** Identifying complex problems, reviewing the options, and implementing solutions.

Education and Training Program: Environmental/Environmental Health Engineering. **Related Knowledge/Courses—Engineering and Technology:** Equipment, tools, and mechanical devices and their uses to produce motion, light, power, technology, and other applications. **Physics:** Physical principles, laws, and applications, including air, water, material dynamics, light, atomic

principles, heat, electric theory, earth formations, and meteorological and related natural phenomena. **Design:** Design techniques, principles, tools, and instruments involved in the production and use of precision technical plans, blueprints, drawings, and models. **Chemistry:** The composition, structure, and properties of substances and of the chemical processes and transformations that they undergo. This includes uses of chemicals and their interactions, danger signs, production techniques, and disposal methods. **Building and Construction:** Materials, methods, and the appropriate tools to construct objects, structures, and buildings. **Biology:** Plant and animal living tissue, cells, organisms, and entities, including their functions, interdependencies, and interactions with each other and the environment.

Work Environment: More often indoors than outdoors; noisy; contaminants; sitting; using hands on objects, tools, or controls.

Environmental Science and Protection Technicians, Including Health

* Education/Training Required: Associate degree
* Annual Earnings: $39,370
* Beginning Wage: $25,090
* Earnings Growth Potential: Medium
* Growth: 28.0%
* Annual Job Openings: 8,404
* Self-Employed: 1.5%
* Part-Time: 19.4%

Perform laboratory and field tests to monitor the environment and investigate sources of pollution, including those that affect health. Under direction of environmental scientists or

specialists, may collect samples of gases, soil, water, and other materials for testing and take corrective actions as assigned. Collect samples of gases, soils, water, industrial wastewater, and asbestos products to conduct tests on pollutant levels and identify sources of pollution. Record test data and prepare reports, summaries, and charts that interpret test results. Develop and implement programs for monitoring of environmental pollution and radiation. Discuss test results and analyses with customers. Set up equipment or stations to monitor and collect pollutants from sites such as smoke stacks, manufacturing plants, or mechanical equipment. Maintain files such as hazardous waste databases, chemical usage data, personnel exposure information, and diagrams showing equipment locations. Develop testing procedures or direct activities of workers in laboratory. Prepare samples or photomicrographs for testing and analysis. Calibrate microscopes and test instruments. Examine and analyze material for presence and concentration of contaminants such as asbestos, using variety of microscopes. Calculate amount of pollutant in samples or compute air pollution or gas flow in industrial processes, using chemical and mathematical formulas. Make recommendations to control or eliminate unsafe conditions at workplaces or public facilities. Weigh, analyze, and measure collected sample particles such as lead, coal dust, or rock, to determine concentration of pollutants. Provide information and technical and program assistance to government representatives, employers, and the general public on the issues of public health, environmental protection, or workplace safety. Conduct standardized tests to ensure materials and supplies used throughout power supply systems meet processing and safety specifications. Perform statistical analysis of environmental data. Respond to and investigate hazardous conditions or spills or outbreaks of disease or food poisoning, collecting samples for analysis. Determine amounts and kinds of chemicals to use

in destroying harmful organisms and removing impurities from purification systems. Inspect sanitary conditions at public facilities. Inspect workplaces to ensure the absence of health and safety hazards such as high noise levels, radiation, or potential lighting hazards.

Personality Type: Investigative. These occupations frequently involve working with ideas and require an extensive amount of thinking. They can involve searching for facts and figuring out problems mentally.

GOE—Interest Area/Cluster: 01. Agriculture and Natural Resources. **Work Group:** 01.03. Resource Technologies for Plants, Animals, and the Environment. **Other Jobs in This Work Group:** Agricultural and Food Science Technicians; Agricultural Technicians; Food Science Technicians; Food Scientists and Technologists; Geological and Petroleum Technicians; Geological Sample Test Technicians; Geophysical Data Technicians.

Skills—Quality Control Analysis: Evaluating the quality or performance of products, services, or processes. **Systems Analysis:** Determining how a system should work and how changes will affect outcomes. **Systems Evaluation:** Looking at many indicators of system performance and taking into account their accuracy. **Operation Monitoring:** Watching gauges, dials, or other indicators to make sure a machine is working properly. **Operation and Control:** Controlling operations of equipment or systems. **Science:** Using scientific methods to solve problems.

Education and Training Programs: Environmental Studies; Environmental Science; Physical Science Technologies/Technicians, Other; Science Technologies/Technicians, Other. **Related Knowledge/Courses—Biology:** Plant and animal living tissue, cells, organisms, and entities, including their functions, interdependencies, and interactions with each other and the environment.

Chemistry: The composition, structure, and properties of substances and of the chemical processes and transformations that they undergo. This includes uses of chemicals and their interactions, danger signs, production techniques, and disposal methods. **Geography:** Various methods for describing the location and distribution of land, sea, and air masses, including their physical locations, relationships, and characteristics. **Physics:** Physical principles, laws, and applications, including air, water, material dynamics, light, atomic principles, heat, electric theory, earth formations, and meteorological and related natural phenomena. **Computers and Electronics:** Electric circuit boards, processors, chips, and computer hardware and software, including applications and programming. **Building and Construction:** Materials, methods, and the appropriate tools to construct objects, structures, and buildings.

Work Environment: More often outdoors than indoors; very hot or cold; contaminants; hazardous equipment; standing.

Environmental Science Teachers, Postsecondary

- ❋ Education/Training Required: Doctoral degree
- ❋ Annual Earnings: $64,850
- ❋ Beginning Wage: $35,120
- ❋ Earnings Growth Potential: High
- ❋ Growth: 22.9%
- ❋ Annual Job Openings: 769
- ❋ Self-Employed: 0.4%
- ❋ Part-Time: 27.8%

Teach courses in environmental science. Supervise undergraduate and/or graduate teaching, internship, and research work. Conduct research in a particular field of knowledge and publish findings in professional journals, books, and/or electronic media. Keep abreast of developments in their field by reading current literature, talking with colleagues, and participating in professional conferences. Evaluate and grade students' classwork, laboratory work, assignments, and papers. Write grant proposals to procure external research funding. Supervise students' laboratory work and fieldwork. Prepare course materials such as syllabi, homework assignments, and handouts. Plan, evaluate, and revise curricula, course content, and course materials and methods of instruction. Compile, administer, and grade examinations or assign this work to others. Initiate, facilitate, and moderate classroom discussions. Advise students on academic and vocational curricula and on career issues. Prepare and deliver lectures to undergraduate and/or graduate students on topics such as hazardous waste management, industrial safety, and environmental toxicology. Maintain student attendance records, grades, and other required records. Select and obtain materials and supplies such as textbooks and laboratory equipment. Maintain regularly scheduled office hours in order to advise and assist students. Collaborate with colleagues to address teaching and research issues. Perform administrative duties such as serving as department head. Participate in student recruitment, registration, and placement activities. Provide professional consulting services to government and/or industry. Serve on academic or administrative committees that deal with institutional policies, departmental matters, and academic issues. Compile bibliographies of specialized materials for outside reading assignments. Participate in campus and community events. Act as advisers to student organizations.

Personality Type: Social. These occupations frequently involve working with, communicating with, and teaching people and often involve helping or providing service to others.

GOE—Interest Area/Cluster: 05. Education and Training. **Work Group:** 05.03. Postsecondary and Adult Teaching and Instructing. **Other Jobs in This Work Group:** Adult Literacy, Remedial Education, and GED Teachers and Instructors; Agricultural Sciences Teachers, Postsecondary; Anthropology and Archeology Teachers, Postsecondary; Architecture Teachers, Postsecondary; Area, Ethnic, and Cultural Studies Teachers, Postsecondary; Art, Drama, and Music Teachers, Postsecondary; Atmospheric, Earth, Marine, and Space Sciences Teachers, Postsecondary; Biological Science Teachers, Postsecondary; Business Teachers, Postsecondary; Chemistry Teachers, Postsecondary; Communications Teachers, Postsecondary; Computer Science Teachers, Postsecondary; Criminal Justice and Law Enforcement Teachers, Postsecondary; Economics Teachers, Postsecondary; Education Teachers, Postsecondary; Engineering Teachers, Postsecondary; English Language and Literature Teachers, Postsecondary; Farm and Home Management Advisors; Foreign Language and Literature Teachers, Postsecondary; Forestry and Conservation Science Teachers, Postsecondary; Geography Teachers, Postsecondary; Graduate Teaching Assistants; Health Specialties Teachers, Postsecondary; History Teachers, Postsecondary; Home Economics Teachers, Postsecondary; Law Teachers, Postsecondary; Library Science Teachers, Postsecondary; Mathematical Science Teachers, Postsecondary; Nursing Instructors and Teachers, Postsecondary; Philosophy and Religion Teachers, Postsecondary; Physics Teachers, Postsecondary; Political Science Teachers, Postsecondary; Psychology Teachers, Postsecondary; Recreation and Fitness Studies Teachers, Postsecondary; Social Work Teachers, Postsecondary; Sociology Teachers, Postsecondary.

Skills—Science: Using scientific methods to solve problems. **Writing:** Communicating effectively with others in writing as indicated by the needs of the audience. **Reading Comprehension:** Understanding written sentences and paragraphs in work-related documents. **Instructing:** Teaching others how to do something. **Mathematics:** Using mathematics to solve problems. **Management of Financial Resources:** Determining how money will be spent to get the work done and accounting for these expenditures. **Programming:** Writing computer programs for various purposes. **Critical Thinking:** Using logic and analysis to identify the strengths and weaknesses of different approaches.

Education and Training Programs: Environmental Studies; Environmental Science; Science Teacher Education/General Science Teacher Education. **Related Knowledge/Courses—Biology:** Plant and animal living tissue, cells, organisms, and entities, including their functions, interdependencies, and interactions with each other and the environment. **Geography:** Various methods for describing the location and distribution of land, sea, and air masses, including their physical locations, relationships, and characteristics. **Chemistry:** The composition, structure, and properties of substances and of the chemical processes and transformations that they undergo. This includes uses of chemicals and their interactions, danger signs, production techniques, and disposal methods. **Education and Training:** Instructional methods and training techniques, including curriculum design principles, learning theory, group and individual teaching techniques, design of individual development plans, and test design principles. **Physics:** Physical principles, laws, and applications, including air, water, material dynamics, light, atomic principles, heat, electric theory, earth formations, and meteorological and related natural phenomena. **History and Archeology:** Historical events and their causes, indicators, and impact on particular civilizations and cultures.

Work Environment: Indoors; sitting.

Environmental Scientists and Specialists, Including Health

⁕ Education/Training Required: Master's degree

⁕ Annual Earnings: $58,380

⁕ Beginning Wage: $35,630

⁕ Earnings Growth Potential: Medium

⁕ Growth: 25.1%

⁕ Annual Job Openings: 6,961

⁕ Self-Employed: 2.2%

⁕ Part-Time: 5.3%

Conduct research or perform investigation for the purpose of identifying, abating, or eliminating sources of pollutants or hazards that affect either the environment or the health of the population. Using knowledge of various scientific disciplines, may collect, synthesize, study, report, and take action based on data derived from measurements or observations of air, food, soil, water, and other sources. Collect, synthesize, analyze, manage, and report environmental data such as pollution emission measurements, atmospheric monitoring measurements, meteorological and mineralogical information, and soil or water samples. Analyze data to determine validity, quality, and scientific significance, and to interpret correlations between human activities and environmental effects. Communicate scientific and technical information to the public, organizations, or internal audiences through oral briefings, written documents, workshops, conferences, training sessions, or public hearings. Provide scientific and technical guidance, support, coordination, and oversight to governmental agencies, environmental programs, industry, or the public. Process and review environmental permits, licenses, and related materials. Review and implement environmental technical standards, guidelines, policies, and formal regulations that meet all appropriate requirements. Prepare charts or graphs from data samples, providing summary information on the environmental relevance of the data. Determine data collection methods to be employed in research projects and surveys. Investigate and report on accidents affecting the environment. Research sources of pollution to determine their effects on the environment and to develop theories or methods of pollution abatement or control. Provide advice on proper standards and regulations or the development of policies, strategies, and codes of practice for environmental management. Monitor effects of pollution and land degradation, and recommend means of prevention or control. Supervise or train students, environmental technologists, technicians, or other related staff. Evaluate violations or problems discovered during inspections to determine appropriate regulatory actions or to provide advice on the development and prosecution of regulatory cases. Conduct environmental audits and inspections, and investigations of violations. Plan and develop research models, using knowledge of mathematical and statistical concepts. Conduct applied research on environmental topics such as waste control and treatment and pollution abatement methods.

Personality Type: Investigative. These occupations frequently involve working with ideas and require an extensive amount of thinking. They can involve searching for facts and figuring out problems mentally.

GOE—Interest Area/Cluster: 15. Scientific Research, Engineering, and Mathematics. **Work Group:** 15.03. Life Sciences. **Other Jobs in This Work Group:** Biochemists and Biophysicists; Biologists; Epidemiologists; Medical Scientists, Except Epidemiologists; Microbiologists.

Skills—Science: Using scientific methods to solve problems. **Systems Analysis:** Determining how a

E

system should work and how changes will affect outcomes. **Systems Evaluation:** Looking at many indicators of system performance and taking into account their accuracy. **Writing:** Communicating effectively with others in writing as indicated by the needs of the audience. **Reading Comprehension:** Understanding written sentences and paragraphs in work-related documents. **Management of Personnel Resources:** Motivating, developing, and directing people as they work; identifying the best people for the job. **Management of Material Resources:** Obtaining and seeing to the appropriate use of equipment, facilities, and materials needed to do certain work. **Operation Monitoring:** Watching gauges, dials, or other indicators to make sure a machine is working properly.

Education and Training Programs: Environmental Studies; Environmental Science. **Related Knowledge/Courses—Biology:** Plant and animal living tissue, cells, organisms, and entities, including their functions, interdependencies, and interactions with each other and the environment. **Geography:** Various methods for describing the location and distribution of land, sea, and air masses, including their physical locations, relationships, and characteristics. **Chemistry:** The composition, structure, and properties of substances and of the chemical processes and transformations that they undergo. This includes uses of chemicals and their interactions, danger signs, production techniques, and disposal methods. **Physics:** Physical principles, laws, and applications, including air, water, material dynamics, light, atomic principles, heat, electric theory, earth formations, and meteorological and related natural phenomena. **Law and Government:** Laws, legal codes, court procedures, precedents, government regulations, executive orders, agency rules, and the democratic political process. **Engineering and Technology:** Equipment, tools, and mechanical devices and their uses to produce motion, light, power, technology, and other applications.

Work Environment: More often indoors than outdoors; noisy; sitting.

Family and General Practitioners

* Education/Training Required: First professional degree
* Annual Earnings: More than $145,600
* Beginning Wage: $67,400
* Earnings Growth Potential: Cannot be calculated
* Growth: 14.2%
* Annual Job Openings: 38,027
* Self-Employed: 14.7%
* Part-Time: 8.1%

The job openings listed here are shared with Anesthesiologists; Internists, General; Obstetricians and Gynecologists; Pediatricians, General; Psychiatrists; and Surgeons.

Diagnose, treat, and help prevent diseases and injuries that commonly occur in the general population. Prescribe or administer treatment, therapy, medication, vaccination, and other specialized medical care to treat or prevent illness, disease, or injury. Order, perform, and interpret tests and analyze records, reports, and examination information to diagnose patients' condition. Monitor the patients' conditions and progress and re-evaluate treatments as necessary. Explain procedures and discuss test results or prescribed treatments with patients. Collect, record, and maintain patient information, such as medical history, reports, and examination results. Advise patients and community members concerning diet, activity, hygiene, and disease prevention. Refer patients to medical specialists or other practitioners when necessary. Direct and coordinate activities of nurses, students, assistants, specialists, therapists, and other medical staff. Coordinate work with nurses, social workers, rehabilitation therapists, pharmacists, psychologists, and other health-care providers. Deliver babies. Operate on patients to remove, repair, or improve functioning of diseased or injured body parts and systems. Plan, implement, or administer health programs or standards in hospital, business, or community for information, prevention, or treatment of injury or illness. Prepare reports for government or management of birth, death, and disease statistics; workforce evaluations; or medical status of individuals. Conduct research to study anatomy and develop or test medications, treatments, or procedures to prevent or control disease or injury.

Personality Type: Investigative. These occupations frequently involve working with ideas and require an extensive amount of thinking. They can involve searching for facts and figuring out problems mentally.

GOE—Interest Area/Cluster: 08. Health Science. **Work Group:** 08.02. Medicine and Surgery. **Other Jobs in This Work Group:** Anesthesiologists; Internists, General; Obstetricians and Gynecologists; Pediatricians, General; Pharmacists; Physician Assistants; Psychiatrists; Registered Nurses; Surgeons.

Skills—Science: Using scientific methods to solve problems. **Social Perceptiveness:** Being aware of others' reactions and understanding why they react the way they do. **Reading Comprehension:** Understanding written sentences and paragraphs in work-related documents. **Complex Problem Solving:** Identifying complex problems, reviewing the options, and implementing solutions. **Persuasion:** Persuading others to approach things differently. **Service Orientation:** Actively looking for ways to help people. **Management of Financial Resources:** Determining how money will be spent to get the work done and accounting for these expenditures. **Active Learning:** Working with new material or information to grasp its implications.

Education and Training Programs: Medicine (MD); Osteopathic Medicine/Osteopathy (DO); Family Medicine. **Related Knowledge/Courses— Medicine and Dentistry:** The information and techniques needed to diagnose and treat injuries, diseases, and deformities. This includes symptoms, treatment alternatives, drug properties and interactions, and preventive health-care measures. **Biology:** Plant and animal living tissue, cells, organisms, and entities, including their functions, interdependencies, and interactions with each other and the environment. **Therapy and Counseling:** Information and techniques needed to rehabilitate physical and mental ailments and to provide career guidance, including alternative treatments, rehabilitation equipment and its proper use, and methods to evaluate treatment effects. **Psychology:** Human behavior and performance, mental processes, psychological research methods, and the assessment and treatment of behavioral and affective disorders. **Sociology and Anthropology:** Group behavior and dynamics; societal trends and influences; and cultures and their history, migrations, ethnicity, and origins. **Chemistry:** The composition, structure, and properties of substances and of the chemical processes and transformations that they undergo. This includes uses of chemicals and their interactions, danger signs, production techniques, and disposal methods.

Work Environment: Indoors; disease or infections; standing; using hands on objects, tools, or controls.

Financial Analysts

- ❋ Education/Training Required: Bachelor's degree
- ❋ Annual Earnings: $70,400
- ❋ Beginning Wage: $42,280
- ❋ Earnings Growth Potential: Medium
- ❋ Growth: 33.8%
- ❋ Annual Job Openings: 29,317
- ❋ Self-Employed: 8.3%
- ❋ Part-Time: 7.1%

Conduct quantitative analyses of information affecting investment programs of public or private institutions. Assemble spreadsheets and draw charts and graphs used to illustrate technical reports, using computer. Analyze financial information to produce forecasts of business, industry, and economic conditions for use in making investment decisions. Maintain knowledge and stay abreast of developments in the fields of industrial technology, business, finance, and economic theory. Interpret data affecting investment programs, such as price, yield, stability, future trends in investment risks, and economic influences. Monitor fundamental economic, industrial, and corporate developments through the analysis of information obtained from financial publications and services, investment banking firms, government agencies, trade publications, company sources, and personal interviews. Recommend investments and investment timing to companies, investment firm staff, or the investing public. Determine the prices at which securities should be syndicated and offered to the public. Prepare plans of action for investment based on financial analyses. Evaluate and compare the relative quality of various securities in a given industry. Present oral and written reports on general economic trends, individual corporations, and entire industries. Contact brokers and purchase investments for companies according to company policy. Collaborate with investment bankers to attract new corporate clients to securities firms.

Personality Type: Conventional. These occupations frequently involve following set procedures and routines and can include working with data and details more than with ideas. Usually there is a clear line of authority to follow.

GOE—Interest Area/Cluster: 06. Finance and Insurance. **Work Group:** 06.02. Finance/Insurance Investigation and Analysis. **Other Jobs in This Work Group:** Appraisers and Assessors of Real Estate; Appraisers, Real Estate; Assessors; Cost Estimators; Credit Analysts; Insurance Underwriters; Loan Counselors; Loan Officers; Market Research Analysts; Survey Researchers.

Skills—Management of Financial Resources: Determining how money will be spent to get the work done and accounting for these expenditures. **Judgment and Decision Making:** Weighing the relative costs and benefits of a potential action. **Mathematics:** Using mathematics to solve problems. **Systems Evaluation:** Looking at many indicators of system performance and taking into account their accuracy. **Programming:** Writing computer programs for various purposes. **Complex Problem Solving:** Identifying complex problems, reviewing the options, and implementing solutions. **Operations Analysis:** Analyzing needs and product requirements to create a design. **Systems Analysis:** Determining how a system should work and how changes will affect outcomes.

Education and Training Programs: Accounting and Finance; Accounting and Business/Management; Finance, General. **Related Knowledge/Courses—Economics and Accounting:** Economic and accounting principles and practices, the financial markets, banking, and the analysis and reporting of financial data. **Mathematics:** Numbers and their operations and interrelationships, including arithmetic, algebra, geometry, calculus, and statistics and their applications. **Law and Government:** Laws, legal codes, court procedures, precedents, government regulations, executive orders, agency rules, and the democratic political process. **Clerical Practices:** Administrative and clerical procedures and systems such as word-processing systems, filing and records management systems, stenography and transcription, forms, design principles, and other office procedures and terminology. **English Language:** The structure and content of the English language, including the meaning and spelling of words, rules of composition, and grammar. **Administration and Management:** Principles and processes involved in business and organizational planning, coordination, and execution. This includes strategic planning, resource allocation, manpower modeling, leadership techniques, and production methods.

Work Environment: Indoors; sitting.

Financial Examiners

* Education/Training Required: Bachelor's degree
* Annual Earnings: $66,670
* Beginning Wage: $36,400
* Earnings Growth Potential: High
* Growth: 10.7%
* Annual Job Openings: 2,449
* Self-Employed: 0.0%
* Part-Time: 9.3%

Enforce or ensure compliance with laws and regulations governing financial and securities institutions and financial and real estate transactions. May examine, verify correctness of, or establish authenticity of records. Investigate activities of institutions in order to enforce laws and regulations and to ensure legality of transactions and operations or financial solvency. Review and analyze new, proposed, or revised laws, regulations, policies, and procedures in order to interpret their meaning and determine their impact. Plan, supervise, and review work of assigned subordinates. Recommend actions to ensure compliance with laws and regulations or to protect solvency of institutions. Examine the minutes of meetings of directors, stockholders, and committees in order to investigate the specific authority extended at various levels of management. Prepare reports, exhibits, and other supporting schedules that detail an institution's safety and soundness, compliance with laws and regulations, and recommended solutions to questionable financial conditions. Review balance sheets, operating income and expense accounts, and loan documentation in order to confirm institution assets and liabilities. Review audit reports of internal and external auditors in order to monitor adequacy of scope of reports or to discover specific weaknesses in internal routines. Train other examiners in the financial examination process. Establish guidelines for procedures and policies that comply with new and revised regulations and direct their implementation. Direct and participate in formal and informal meetings with bank directors, trustees, senior management, counsels, outside accountants, and consultants in order to gather information and discuss findings. Verify and inspect cash reserves, assigned collateral, and bank-owned securities in order to check internal control procedures. Review applications for mergers, acquisitions, establishment of new institutions, acceptance in Federal Reserve System, or registration of securities sales in order to determine their public interest value and conformance to regulations and recommend acceptance or rejection. Resolve problems concerning the overall financial integrity of banking institutions, including loan investment portfolios, capital, earnings, and specific or large troubled accounts.

Personality Type: Enterprising. These occupations frequently involve starting up and carrying out projects and can involve leading people and making many decisions. They sometimes require risk taking and often deal with business.

GOE—Interest Area/Cluster: 07. Government and Public Administration. **Work Group:** 07.03. Regulations Enforcement. **Other Jobs in This Work Group:** Fish and Game Wardens; Nuclear Monitoring Technicians; Occupational Health and Safety Specialists; Occupational Health and Safety Technicians; Tax Examiners, Collectors, and Revenue Agents.

Skills—Quality Control Analysis: Evaluating the quality or performance of products, services, or processes. **Monitoring:** Assessing how well one is doing when learning or doing something. **Management of Financial Resources:** Determining how money will be spent to get the work done and accounting for these expenditures. **Systems Analysis:** Determining how a system should work and how changes will affect outcomes. **Systems Evaluation:** Looking at many indicators of system performance and taking into account their accuracy. **Operations Analysis:** Analyzing needs and product requirements to create a design. **Writing:** Communicating effectively with others in writing as indicated by the needs of the audience. **Reading Comprehension:** Understanding written sentences and paragraphs in work-related documents.

Education and Training Programs: Accounting; Taxation. **Related Knowledge/Courses—Economics and Accounting:** Economic and accounting principles and practices, the financial markets, banking, and the analysis and reporting of financial data. **Law and Government:** Laws, legal codes, court procedures, precedents, government regulations, executive orders, agency rules, and the democratic political process. **Clerical Practices:** Administrative and clerical procedures and systems such as word-processing systems, filing and records management systems, stenography and transcription, forms, design principles, and other office procedures and terminology. **Mathematics:** Numbers and their operations and interrelationships, including arithmetic, algebra, geometry, calculus, and statistics and their applications. **English Language:** The structure and content of the English language, including the meaning and spelling of words, rules of composition, and grammar. **Administration and Management:** Principles and processes involved in business and organizational planning, coordination, and execution. This includes strategic planning, resource allocation, manpower modeling, leadership techniques, and production methods.

Work Environment: Indoors; sitting.

Financial Managers, Branch or Department

* Education/Training Required: Work experience plus degree
* Annual Earnings: $95,310
* Beginning Wage: $51,910
* Earnings Growth Potential: High
* Growth: 12.6%
* Annual Job Openings: 57,589
* Self-Employed: 4.6%
* Part-Time: 4.2%

The job openings listed here are shared with Treasurers and Controllers.

Direct and coordinate financial activities of workers in a branch, office, or department of an establishment, such as branch bank, brokerage

firm, risk and insurance department, or credit department. Establish and maintain relationships with individual and business customers and provide assistance with problems these customers may encounter. Examine, evaluate, and process loan applications. Plan, direct, and coordinate the activities of workers in branches, offices, or departments of such establishments as branch banks, brokerage firms, risk and insurance departments, or credit departments. Oversee the flow of cash and financial instruments. Recruit staff members and oversee training programs. Network within communities to find and attract new business. Approve or reject, or coordinate the approval and rejection of, lines of credit and commercial, real estate, and personal loans. Prepare financial and regulatory reports required by laws, regulations, and boards of directors. Establish procedures for custody and control of assets, records, loan collateral, and securities in order to ensure safekeeping. Review collection reports to determine the status of collections and the amounts of outstanding balances. Prepare operational and risk reports for management analysis. Evaluate financial reporting systems, accounting and collection procedures, and investment activities and make recommendations for changes to procedures, operating systems, budgets, and other financial control functions. Plan, direct, and coordinate risk and insurance programs of establishments to control risks and losses. Submit delinquent accounts to attorneys or outside agencies for collection. Communicate with stockholders and other investors to provide information and to raise capital. Evaluate data pertaining to costs in order to plan budgets. Analyze and classify risks and investments to determine their potential impacts on companies. Review reports of securities transactions and price lists in order to analyze market conditions. Develop and analyze information to assess the current and future financial status of firms. Direct insurance negotiations, select insurance brokers and carriers, and place insurance.

Personality Type: Enterprising. These occupations frequently involve starting up and carrying out projects and can involve leading people and making many decisions. They sometimes require risk taking and often deal with business.

GOE—Interest Area/Cluster: 06. Finance and Insurance. **Work Group:** 06.01. Managerial Work in Finance and Insurance. **Other Jobs in This Work Group:** Financial Managers; Treasurers and Controllers.

Skills—Management of Personnel Resources: Motivating, developing, and directing people as they work; identifying the best people for the job. **Management of Financial Resources:** Determining how money will be spent to get the work done and accounting for these expenditures. **Service Orientation:** Actively looking for ways to help people. **Time Management:** Managing one's own time and the time of others. **Persuasion:** Persuading others to approach things differently. **Negotiation:** Bringing others together and trying to reconcile differences. **Instructing:** Teaching others how to do something. **Systems Evaluation:** Looking at many indicators of system performance and taking into account their accuracy.

Education and Training Programs: Accounting and Finance; Finance, General; International Finance; Public Finance; Credit Management; Finance and Financial Management Services, Other. **Related Knowledge/Courses—Economics and Accounting:** Economic and accounting principles and practices, the financial markets, banking, and the analysis and reporting of financial data. **Sales and Marketing:** Principles and methods involved in showing, promoting, and selling products or services. This includes marketing strategies and tactics, product demonstration and sales techniques, and sales control systems. **Personnel and Human Resources:** Principles and procedures for personnel recruitment; selection; training; compensation and benefits; labor relations and negotiation; and personnel information systems. **Clerical Practices:** Administrative and clerical procedures and systems such as word-processing systems, filing and records management systems, stenography and transcription, forms, design principles, and other office procedures and terminology. **Customer and Personal Service:** Principles and processes for providing customer and personal services, including needs assessment techniques, quality service standards, alternative delivery systems, and customer satisfaction evaluation techniques. **Mathematics:** Numbers and their operations and interrelationships, including arithmetic, algebra, geometry, calculus, and statistics and their applications.

Work Environment: Indoors; sitting.

Foreign Language and Literature Teachers, Postsecondary

- ❀ Education/Training Required: Doctoral degree
- ❀ Annual Earnings: $53,610
- ❀ Beginning Wage: $30,590
- ❀ Earnings Growth Potential: High
- ❀ Growth: 22.9%
- ❀ Annual Job Openings: 4,317
- ❀ Self-Employed: 0.4%
- ❀ Part-Time: 27.8%

Teach courses in foreign (i.e., other than English) languages and literature. Evaluate and grade students' classwork, assignments, and papers. Prepare course materials such as syllabi, homework assignments, and handouts. Initiate, facilitate, and moderate classroom discussions. Maintain student attendance records, grades, and other required records. Compile, administer, and grade examinations or assign this work to others. Plan, evaluate, and revise curricula, course content, and course materials and methods of instruction. Prepare and deliver lectures to undergraduate and graduate students on topics such as how to speak and write a foreign language and the cultural aspects of areas where a particular language is used. Maintain regularly scheduled office hours to advise and assist students. Select and obtain materials and supplies such as textbooks. Keep abreast of developments in their field by reading current literature, talking with colleagues, and participating in professional organizations and activities. Advise students on academic and vocational curricula and on career issues. Conduct research in a particular field of knowledge and publish findings in scholarly journals, books, and/or electronic media. Collaborate with colleagues to address teaching and research issues. Serve on academic or administrative committees that deal with institutional policies, departmental matters, and academic issues. Participate in student recruitment, registration, and placement activities. Compile bibliographies of specialized materials for outside reading assignments. Participate in campus and community events. Act as advisers to student organizations. Perform administrative duties such as serving as department head. Supervise undergraduate and graduate teaching, internship, and research work. Write grant proposals to procure external research funding. Provide professional consulting services to government or industry.

Personality Type: Social. These occupations frequently involve working with, communicating with, and teaching people and often involve helping or providing service to others.

GOE—Interest Area/Cluster: 05. Education and Training. **Work Group:** 05.03. Postsecondary and Adult Teaching and Instructing. **Other Jobs in This Work Group:** Adult Literacy, Remedial Education, and GED Teachers and Instructors;

Agricultural Sciences Teachers, Postsecondary; Anthropology and Archeology Teachers, Postsecondary; Architecture Teachers, Postsecondary; Area, Ethnic, and Cultural Studies Teachers, Postsecondary; Art, Drama, and Music Teachers, Postsecondary; Atmospheric, Earth, Marine, and Space Sciences Teachers, Postsecondary; Biological Science Teachers, Postsecondary; Business Teachers, Postsecondary; Chemistry Teachers, Postsecondary; Communications Teachers, Postsecondary; Computer Science Teachers, Postsecondary; Criminal Justice and Law Enforcement Teachers, Postsecondary; Economics Teachers, Postsecondary; Education Teachers, Postsecondary; Engineering Teachers, Postsecondary; English Language and Literature Teachers, Postsecondary; Environmental Science Teachers, Postsecondary; Farm and Home Management Advisors; Forestry and Conservation Science Teachers, Postsecondary; Geography Teachers, Postsecondary; Graduate Teaching Assistants; Health Specialties Teachers, Postsecondary; History Teachers, Postsecondary; Home Economics Teachers, Postsecondary; Law Teachers, Postsecondary; Library Science Teachers, Postsecondary; Mathematical Science Teachers, Postsecondary; Nursing Instructors and Teachers, Postsecondary; Philosophy and Religion Teachers, Postsecondary; Physics Teachers, Postsecondary; Political Science Teachers, Postsecondary; Psychology Teachers, Postsecondary; Recreation and Fitness Studies Teachers, Postsecondary; Social Work Teachers, Postsecondary; Sociology Teachers, Postsecondary.

Skills—Learning Strategies: Using multiple approaches when learning or teaching new things. **Instructing:** Teaching others how to do something. **Writing:** Communicating effectively with others in writing as indicated by the needs of the audience. **Reading Comprehension:** Understanding written sentences and paragraphs in work-related documents. **Speaking:** Talking to others to effectively convey information. **Persuasion:** Persuading others to approach things differently. **Social Perceptiveness:** Being aware of others' reactions and understanding why they react the way they do. **Critical Thinking:** Using logic and analysis to identify the strengths and weaknesses of different approaches.

Education and Training Programs: Latin Teacher Education; Foreign Languages and Literatures, General; Linguistics; Language Interpretation and Translation; African Languages, Literatures, and Linguistics; East Asian Languages, Literatures, and Linguistics, General; Chinese Language and Literature; Japanese Language and Literature; Korean Language and Literature; Tibetan Language and Literature; others. **Related Knowledge/Courses—Foreign Language:** The structure and content of a foreign (non-English) language, including the meaning and spelling of words, rules of composition and grammar, and pronunciation. **Philosophy and Theology:** Different philosophical systems and religions, including their basic principles, values, ethics, ways of thinking, customs, and practices and their impact on human culture. **History and Archeology:** Historical events and their causes, indicators, and impact on particular civilizations and cultures. **Sociology and Anthropology:** Group behavior and dynamics; societal trends and influences; and cultures and their history, migrations, ethnicity, and origins. **Geography:** Various methods for describing the location and distribution of land, sea, and air masses, including their physical locations, relationships, and characteristics. **English Language:** The structure and content of the English language, including the meaning and spelling of words, rules of composition, and grammar.

Work Environment: Indoors; sitting.

Forensic Science Technicians

- ❋ Education/Training Required: Bachelor's degree
- ❋ Annual Earnings: $47,680
- ❋ Beginning Wage: $29,170
- ❋ Earnings Growth Potential: Medium
- ❋ Growth: 30.7%
- ❋ Annual Job Openings: 3,074
- ❋ Self-Employed: 1.3%
- ❋ Part-Time: 19.4%

Collect, identify, classify, and analyze physical evidence related to criminal investigations. Perform tests on weapons or substances such as fiber, hair, and tissue to determine significance to investigation. May testify as expert witnesses on evidence or crime laboratory techniques. May serve as specialists in area of expertise, such as ballistics, fingerprinting, handwriting, or biochemistry. Testify in court about investigative and analytical methods and findings. Keep records and prepare reports detailing findings, investigative methods, and laboratory techniques. Interpret laboratory findings and test results to identify and classify substances, materials, and other evidence collected at crime scenes. Operate and maintain laboratory equipment and apparatus. Prepare solutions, reagents, and sample formulations needed for laboratory work. Analyze and classify biological fluids, using DNA typing or serological techniques. Collect evidence from crime scenes, storing it in conditions that preserve its integrity. Identify and quantify drugs and poisons found in biological fluids and tissues, in foods, and at crime scenes. Analyze handwritten and machine-produced textual evidence to decipher altered or obliterated text or to determine authorship, age, or source. Reconstruct crime scenes to determine relationships among pieces of evidence. Examine DNA samples to determine if they match other samples. Collect impressions of dust from surfaces to obtain and identify fingerprints. Analyze gunshot residue and bullet paths to determine how shootings occurred. Visit morgues, examine scenes of crimes, or contact other sources to obtain evidence or information to be used in investigations. Examine physical evidence such as hair, fiber, wood, or soil residues to obtain information about its source and composition. Determine types of bullets used in shooting and whether they were fired from a specific weapon. Examine firearms to determine mechanical condition and legal status, performing restoration work on damaged firearms to obtain information such as serial numbers. Confer with ballistics, fingerprinting, handwriting, document, electronics, medical, chemical, or metallurgical experts concerning evidence and its interpretation. Interpret the pharmacological effects of a drug or a combination of drugs on an individual. Compare objects such as tools with impression marks to determine whether a specific object is responsible for a specific mark.

Personality Type: Investigative. These occupations frequently involve working with ideas and require an extensive amount of thinking. They can involve searching for facts and figuring out problems mentally.

GOE—Interest Area/Cluster: 12. Law and Public Safety. **Work Group:** 12.04. Law Enforcement and Public Safety. **Other Jobs in This Work Group:** No others in group.

Skills—Science: Using scientific methods to solve problems. **Quality Control Analysis:** Evaluating the quality or performance of products, services, or processes. **Troubleshooting:** Determining what is causing an operating error and deciding what to do about it. **Speaking:** Talking to others to effectively convey information. **Equipment Selection:** Determining the kind of tools and equipment needed to do a job. **Active Learning:** Working with new material or information to grasp its implications. **Reading Comprehension:** Understanding written sentences and paragraphs in work-related documents. **Monitoring:** Assessing how well one is doing when learning or doing something.

Education and Training Program: Forensic Science and Technology. **Related Knowledge/Courses—Chemistry:** The composition, structure, and properties of substances and of the chemical processes and transformations that they undergo. This includes uses of chemicals and their interactions, danger signs, production techniques, and disposal methods. **Law and Government:** Laws, legal codes, court procedures, precedents, government regulations, executive orders, agency rules, and the democratic political process. **Biology:** Plant and animal living tissue, cells, organisms, and entities, including their functions, interdependencies, and interactions with each other and the environment. **Public Safety and Security:** Weaponry; public safety; security operations, rules, regulations, precautions, and prevention; and the protection of people, data, and property. **English Language:** The structure and content of the English language, including the meaning and spelling of words, rules of composition, and grammar. **Clerical Practices:** Administrative and clerical procedures and systems such as word-processing systems, filing and records management systems, stenography and transcription, forms, design principles, and other office procedures and terminology.

Work Environment: Indoors; contaminants; disease or infections; hazardous conditions; sitting.

Forestry and Conservation Science Teachers, Postsecondary

- ❋ Education/Training Required: Doctoral degree
- ❋ Annual Earnings: $63,790
- ❋ Beginning Wage: $36,270
- ❋ Earnings Growth Potential: High
- ❋ Growth: 22.9%
- ❋ Annual Job Openings: 454
- ❋ Self-Employed: 0.4%
- ❋ Part-Time: 27.8%

Teach courses in environmental and conservation science. Conduct research in a particular field of knowledge and publish findings in books, professional journals, and/or electronic media. Keep abreast of developments in their field by reading current literature, talking with colleagues, and participating in professional conferences. Prepare and deliver lectures to undergraduate and/or graduate students on topics such as forest resource policy, forest pathology, and mapping. Evaluate and grade students' classwork, assignments, and papers. Write grant proposals to procure external research funding. Supervise undergraduate and/or graduate teaching, internship, and research work. Plan, evaluate, and revise curricula, course content, and course materials and methods of instruction. Prepare course materials such as syllabi, homework assignments, and handouts. Compile, administer, and grade examinations or assign this work to others. Advise students on academic and vocational curricula and on career issues. Initiate, facilitate, and moderate classroom discussions. Supervise students' laboratory work and fieldwork. Maintain student attendance records, grades, and other required records. Collaborate with colleagues to address teaching and research issues. Maintain regularly scheduled office hours in order to advise and assist students. Select and obtain materials and supplies such as textbooks and laboratory equipment. Participate in student recruitment, registration, and placement activities. Serve on academic or administrative committees that deal with institutional policies, departmental matters, and academic issues. Provide professional consulting services to government and/or industry. Perform administrative duties such as serving as department head. Compile bibliographies of specialized materials for outside reading assignments. Act as advisers to student organizations. Participate in campus and community events.

Personality Type: Social. These occupations frequently involve working with, communicating with, and teaching people and often involve helping or providing service to others.

GOE—Interest Area/Cluster: 05. Education and Training. **Work Group:** 05.03. Postsecondary and Adult Teaching and Instructing. **Other Jobs in This Work Group:** Adult Literacy, Remedial Education, and GED Teachers and Instructors; Agricultural Sciences Teachers, Postsecondary; Anthropology and Archeology Teachers, Postsecondary; Architecture Teachers, Postsecondary; Area, Ethnic, and Cultural Studies Teachers, Postsecondary; Art, Drama, and Music Teachers, Postsecondary; Atmospheric, Earth, Marine, and Space Sciences Teachers, Postsecondary; Biological Science Teachers, Postsecondary; Business Teachers, Postsecondary; Chemistry Teachers, Postsecondary; Communications Teachers, Postsecondary; Computer Science Teachers, Postsecondary; Criminal Justice and Law Enforcement Teachers, Postsecondary; Economics Teachers, Postsecondary; Education Teachers, Postsecondary; Engineering Teachers, Postsecondary; English Language and Literature Teachers, Postsecondary; Environmental Science Teachers, Postsecondary; Farm and Home Management Advisors; Foreign Language and Literature Teachers, Postsecondary; Geography Teachers, Postsecondary; Graduate Teaching Assistants; Health Specialties Teachers, Postsecondary; History Teachers, Postsecondary; Home Economics Teachers, Postsecondary; Law Teachers, Postsecondary; Library Science Teachers, Postsecondary; Mathematical Science Teachers, Postsecondary; Nursing Instructors and Teachers, Postsecondary; Philosophy and Religion Teachers, Postsecondary; Physics Teachers, Postsecondary; Political Science Teachers, Postsecondary; Psychology Teachers, Postsecondary; Recreation and Fitness Studies Teachers, Postsecondary; Social Work Teachers, Postsecondary; Sociology Teachers, Postsecondary.

Skills—Science: Using scientific methods to solve problems. **Management of Financial Resources:** Determining how money will be spent to get the work done and accounting for these expenditures. **Writing:** Communicating effectively with others in writing as indicated by the needs of the audience. **Instructing:** Teaching others how to do something. **Mathematics:** Using mathematics to solve problems. **Management of Personnel Resources:** Motivating, developing, and directing people as they work; identifying the best people for the job. **Complex Problem Solving:** Identifying complex problems, reviewing the options, and implementing solutions. **Active Learning:** Working with new material or information to grasp its implications.

Education and Training Program: Science Teacher Education/General Science Teacher Education. **Related Knowledge/Courses—Biology:** Plant and animal living tissue, cells, organisms, and entities, including their functions, interdependencies, and interactions with each other and the environment. **Geography:** Various methods for describing the location and distribution of land, sea, and air masses, including their physical locations, relationships, and characteristics.

Education and Training: Instructional methods and training techniques, including curriculum design principles, learning theory, group and individual teaching techniques, design of individual development plans, and test design principles. **Mathematics:** Numbers and their operations and interrelationships, including arithmetic, algebra, geometry, calculus, and statistics and their applications. **Chemistry:** The composition, structure, and properties of substances and of the chemical processes and transformations that they undergo. This includes uses of chemicals and their interactions, danger signs, production techniques, and disposal methods. **History and Archeology:** Historical events and their causes, indicators, and impact on particular civilizations and cultures.

Work Environment: Indoors; sitting.

General and Operations Managers

- ❋ Education/Training Required: Work experience plus degree
- ❋ Annual Earnings: $88,700
- ❋ Beginning Wage: $43,990
- ❋ Earnings Growth Potential: Very high
- ❋ Growth: 1.5%
- ❋ Annual Job Openings: 112,072
- ❋ Self-Employed: 0.9%
- ❋ Part-Time: 3.2%

Plan, direct, or coordinate the operations of companies or public and private sector organizations. Duties and responsibilities include formulating policies, managing daily operations, and planning the use of materials and human resources, but are too diverse and general in nature to be classified in any one functional area of management or administration, such as personnel, purchasing, or administrative services.

Includes owners and managers who head small business establishments whose duties are primarily managerial. Oversee activities directly related to making products or providing services. Direct and coordinate activities of businesses or departments concerned with the production, pricing, sales, or distribution of products. Review financial statements, sales and activity reports, and other performance data to measure productivity and goal achievement and to determine areas needing cost reduction and program improvement. Manage staff, preparing work schedules and assigning specific duties. Direct and coordinate organization's financial and budget activities to fund operations, maximize investments, and increase efficiency. Establish and implement departmental policies, goals, objectives, and procedures, conferring with board members, organization officials, and staff members as necessary. Determine staffing requirements, and interview, hire, and train new employees, or oversee those personnel processes. Plan and direct activities such as sales promotions, coordinating with other department heads as required. Determine goods and services to be sold, and set prices and credit terms based on forecasts of customer demand. Monitor businesses and agencies to ensure that they efficiently and effectively provide needed services while staying within budgetary limits. Locate, select, and procure merchandise for resale, representing management in purchase negotiations. Perform sales floor work such as greeting and assisting customers, stocking shelves, and taking inventory. Manage the movement of goods into and out of production facilities. Develop and implement product marketing strategies including advertising campaigns and sales promotions. Recommend locations for new facilities or oversee the remodeling of current facilities. Direct non-merchandising departments of businesses such as advertising and purchasing. Plan store layouts, and design displays.

Personality Type: Enterprising. These occupations frequently involve starting up and carrying out projects and can involve leading people and making many decisions. They sometimes require risk taking and often deal with business.

GOE—Interest Area/Cluster: 04. Business and Administration. **Work Group:** 04.01. Managerial Work in General Business. **Other Jobs in This Work Group:** Chief Executives; Compensation and Benefits Managers; Human Resources Managers; Training and Development Managers.

Skills—Management of Financial Resources: Determining how money will be spent to get the work done and accounting for these expenditures. **Management of Material Resources:** Obtaining and seeing to the appropriate use of equipment, facilities, and materials needed to do certain work. **Systems Analysis:** Determining how a system should work and how changes will affect outcomes. **Management of Personnel Resources:** Motivating, developing, and directing people as they work; identifying the best people for the job. **Systems Evaluation:** Looking at many indicators of system performance and taking into account their accuracy. **Negotiation:** Bringing others together and trying to reconcile differences. **Persuasion:** Persuading others to approach things differently. **Operation Monitoring:** Watching gauges, dials, or other indicators to make sure a machine is working properly.

Education and Training Programs: Public Administration; Business/Commerce, General; Business Administration and Management, General; Entrepreneurship/Entrepreneurial Studies; International Business/Trade/Commerce. **Related Knowledge/Courses—Economics and Accounting:** Economic and accounting principles and practices, the financial markets, banking, and the analysis and reporting of financial data. **Personnel and Human Resources:** Principles and procedures for personnel recruitment; selection;

training; compensation and benefits; labor relations and negotiation; and personnel information systems. **Administration and Management:** Principles and processes involved in business and organizational planning, coordination, and execution. This includes strategic planning, resource allocation, manpower modeling, leadership techniques, and production methods. **Sales and Marketing:** Principles and methods involved in showing, promoting, and selling products or services. This includes marketing strategies and tactics, product demonstration and sales techniques, and sales control systems. **Clerical Practices:** Administrative and clerical procedures and systems such as word-processing systems, filing and records management systems, stenography and transcription, forms, design principles, and other office procedures and terminology. **Building and Construction:** Materials, methods, and the appropriate tools to construct objects, structures, and buildings.

Work Environment: Indoors; noisy; more often sitting than standing.

Geography Teachers, Postsecondary

* Education/Training Required: Doctoral degree
* Annual Earnings: $61,310
* Beginning Wage: $36,070
* Earnings Growth Potential: High
* Growth: 22.9%
* Annual Job Openings: 697
* Self-Employed: 0.4%
* Part-Time: 27.8%

Teach courses in geography. Prepare and deliver lectures to undergraduate and/or graduate students on topics such as urbanization, environmental systems, and cultural geography. Evaluate and grade students' classwork, assignments, and papers. Compile, administer, and grade examinations or assign this work to others. Initiate, facilitate, and moderate classroom discussions. Maintain student attendance records, grades, and other required records. Prepare course materials such as syllabi, homework assignments, and handouts. Keep abreast of developments in their field by reading current literature, talking with colleagues, and participating in professional conferences. Supervise undergraduate and/or graduate teaching, internship, and research work. Plan, evaluate, and revise curricula, course content, and course materials and methods of instruction. Maintain regularly scheduled office hours to advise and assist students. Supervise students' laboratory work and fieldwork. Conduct research in a particular field of knowledge and publish findings in professional journals, books, and electronic media. Collaborate with colleagues to address teaching and research issues. Select and obtain materials and supplies such as textbooks. Advise students on academic and vocational curricula and on career issues. Serve on academic or administrative committees that deal with institutional policies, departmental matters, and academic issues. Participate in student recruitment, registration, and placement activities. Participate in campus and community events. Compile bibliographies of specialized materials for outside reading assignments. Perform administrative duties such as serving as department head. Write grant proposals to procure external research funding. Maintain geographic information systems laboratories, performing duties such as updating software. Perform spatial analysis and modeling, using geographic information system techniques. Act as advisers to student organizations. Provide professional consulting services to government and industry.

Personality Type: Social. These occupations frequently involve working with, communicating with, and teaching people and often involve helping or providing service to others.

GOE—Interest Area/Cluster: 05. Education and Training. **Work Group:** 05.03. Postsecondary and Adult Teaching and Instructing. **Other Jobs in This Work Group:** Adult Literacy, Remedial Education, and GED Teachers and Instructors; Agricultural Sciences Teachers, Postsecondary; Anthropology and Archeology Teachers, Postsecondary; Architecture Teachers, Postsecondary; Area, Ethnic, and Cultural Studies Teachers, Postsecondary; Art, Drama, and Music Teachers, Postsecondary; Atmospheric, Earth, Marine, and Space Sciences Teachers, Postsecondary; Biological Science Teachers, Postsecondary; Business Teachers, Postsecondary; Chemistry Teachers, Postsecondary; Communications Teachers, Postsecondary; Computer Science Teachers, Postsecondary; Criminal Justice and Law Enforcement Teachers, Postsecondary; Economics Teachers, Postsecondary; Education Teachers, Postsecondary; Engineering Teachers, Postsecondary; English Language and Literature Teachers, Postsecondary; Environmental Science Teachers, Postsecondary; Farm and Home Management Advisors; Foreign Language and Literature Teachers, Postsecondary; Forestry and Conservation Science Teachers, Postsecondary; Graduate Teaching Assistants; Health Specialties Teachers, Postsecondary; History Teachers, Postsecondary; Home Economics Teachers, Postsecondary; Law Teachers, Postsecondary; Library Science Teachers, Postsecondary; Mathematical Science Teachers, Postsecondary; Nursing Instructors and Teachers, Postsecondary; Philosophy and Religion Teachers, Postsecondary; Physics Teachers, Postsecondary; Political Science Teachers, Postsecondary; Psychology Teachers, Postsecondary; Recreation and Fitness Studies Teachers, Postsecondary; Social Work Teachers, Postsecondary; Sociology Teachers, Postsecondary.

Skills—Science: Using scientific methods to solve problems. **Writing:** Communicating effectively with others in writing as indicated by the needs of the audience. **Instructing:** Teaching others how to do something. **Learning Strategies:** Using multiple approaches when learning or teaching new things. **Reading Comprehension:** Understanding written sentences and paragraphs in work-related documents. **Speaking:** Talking to others to effectively convey information. **Critical Thinking:** Using logic and analysis to identify the strengths and weaknesses of different approaches. **Active Learning:** Working with new material or information to grasp its implications.

Education and Training Programs: Geography Teacher Education; Geography. **Related Knowledge/Courses—Geography:** Various methods for describing the location and distribution of land, sea, and air masses, including their physical locations, relationships, and characteristics. **Sociology and Anthropology:** Group behavior and dynamics; societal trends and influences; and cultures and their history, migrations, ethnicity, and origins. **History and Archeology:** Historical events and their causes, indicators, and impact on particular civilizations and cultures. **Philosophy and Theology:** Different philosophical systems and religions, including their basic principles, values, ethics, ways of thinking, customs, and practices and their impact on human culture. **Education and Training:** Instructional methods and training techniques, including curriculum design principles, learning theory, group and individual teaching techniques, design of individual development plans, and test design principles. **Communications and Media:** Media production, communication, and dissemination techniques and methods, including alternative ways to inform and entertain via written, oral, and visual media.

Work Environment: Indoors; sitting.

Geoscientists, Except Hydrologists and Geographers

- ✷ Education/Training Required: Master's degree
- ✷ Annual Earnings: $75,800
- ✷ Beginning Wage: $41,020
- ✷ Earnings Growth Potential: High
- ✷ Growth: 21.9%
- ✷ Annual Job Openings: 2,471
- ✷ Self-Employed: 2.2%
- ✷ Part-Time: 5.3%

Study the composition, structure, and other physical aspects of the Earth. May use knowledge of geology, physics, and mathematics in exploration for oil, gas, minerals, or underground water or in waste disposal, land reclamation, or other environmental problems. May study the Earth's internal composition, atmospheres, and oceans and its magnetic, electrical, and gravitational forces. Includes mineralogists, crystallographers, paleontologists, stratigraphers, geodesists, and seismologists. Analyze and interpret geological, geochemical, and geophysical information from sources such as survey data, well logs, bore holes, and aerial photos. Locate and estimate probable natural gas, oil, and mineral ore deposits and underground water resources, using aerial photographs, charts, or research and survey results. Plan and conduct geological, geochemical, and geophysical field studies and surveys, sample collection, or drilling and testing programs used to collect data for research or application. Analyze and interpret geological data, using computer software. Search for and review research articles or environmental, historical, and technical reports. Assess ground and surface water movement to provide advice regarding issues such as waste management, route and site selection, and the restoration of contaminated sites. Prepare geological maps, cross-sectional diagrams, charts, and reports concerning mineral extraction, land use, and resource management, using results of field work and laboratory research. Investigate the composition, structure, and history of the Earth's crust through the collection, examination, measurement, and classification of soils, minerals, rocks, or fossil remains. Conduct geological and geophysical studies to provide information for use in regional development, site selection, and development of public works projects. Measure characteristics of the Earth, such as gravity and magnetic fields, using equipment such as seismographs, gravimeters, torsion balances, and magnetometers. Inspect construction projects to analyze engineering problems, applying geological knowledge and using test equipment and drilling machinery. Design geological mine maps, monitor mine structural integrity, or advise and monitor mining crews. Identify risks for natural disasters such as mud slides, earthquakes, and volcanic eruptions, providing advice on mitigation of potential damage. Advise construction firms and government agencies on dam and road construction, foundation design, or land use and resource management. Test industrial diamonds and abrasives, soil, or rocks to determine their geological characteristics, using optical, x-ray, heat, acid, and precision instruments.

Personality Type: Investigative. These occupations frequently involve working with ideas and require an extensive amount of thinking. They can involve searching for facts and figuring out problems mentally.

GOE—Interest Area/Cluster: 15. Scientific Research, Engineering, and Mathematics. **Work Group:** 15.02. Physical Sciences. **Other Jobs in This Work Group:** Astronomers; Atmospheric and Space Scientists; Chemists; Geographers; Hydrologists; Materials Scientists; Physicists.

Skills—Systems Analysis: Determining how a system should work and how changes will affect outcomes. **Science:** Using scientific methods to solve problems. **Systems Evaluation:** Looking at many indicators of system performance and taking into account their accuracy. **Mathematics:** Using mathematics to solve problems. **Writing:** Communicating effectively with others in writing as indicated by the needs of the audience. **Operation Monitoring:** Watching gauges, dials, or other indicators to make sure a machine is working properly. **Speaking:** Talking to others to effectively convey information.

Education and Training Programs: Geology/Earth Science, General; Geochemistry; Geophysics and Seismology; Paleontology; Geochemistry and Petrology; Oceanography, Chemical and Physical; Geological and Earth Sciences/Geosciences, Other. **Related Knowledge/Courses—Geography:** Various methods for describing the location and distribution of land, sea, and air masses, including their physical locations, relationships, and characteristics. **Engineering and Technology:** Equipment, tools, and mechanical devices and their uses to produce motion, light, power, technology, and other applications. **Physics:** Physical principles, laws, and applications, including air, water, material dynamics, light, atomic principles, heat, electric theory, earth formations, and meteorological and related natural phenomena. **Chemistry:** The composition, structure, and properties of substances and of the chemical processes and transformations that they undergo. This includes uses of chemicals and their interactions, danger signs, production techniques, and disposal methods. **Mathematics:** Numbers and their operations and interrelationships, including arithmetic, algebra, geometry, calculus, and statistics and their applications. **Design:** Design techniques, principles, tools, and instruments involved in the production and use of precision technical plans, blueprints, drawings, and models.

Work Environment: Indoors; sitting.

Graduate Teaching Assistants

❋ Education/Training Required: Bachelor's degree
❋ Annual Earnings: $28,060
❋ Beginning Wage: $15,660
❋ Earnings Growth Potential: High
❋ Growth: 22.9%
❋ Annual Job Openings: 20,601
❋ Self-Employed: 0.4%
❋ Part-Time: 27.8%

Assist department chairperson, faculty members, or other professional staff members in colleges or universities by performing teaching or teaching-related duties such as teaching lower-level courses, developing teaching materials, preparing and giving examinations, and grading examinations or papers. Graduate assistants must be enrolled in graduate school programs. Graduate assistants who primarily perform non-teaching duties such as laboratory research, should be reported in the occupational category related to the work performed. Lead discussion sections, tutorials, and laboratory sections. Evaluate and grade examinations, assignments, and papers, and record grades. Return assignments to students in accordance with established deadlines. Schedule and maintain regular office hours to meet with students. Inform students of the procedures for completing and submitting class work such as lab reports. Prepare and proctor examinations. Notify instructors of errors or problems with assignments. Meet with supervisors to discuss students' grades, and to complete required grade-related paperwork. Copy and distribute classroom materials. Demonstrate use of laboratory equipment, and enforce laboratory rules. Teach undergraduate level courses. Complete laboratory projects prior to assigning them to students so that any needed modifications can be made. Develop teaching materials such as syllabi, visual aids, answer keys, supplementary notes, and course websites. Provide assistance to faculty members or staff with laboratory or field research. Arrange for supervisors to conduct teaching observations; meet with supervisors to receive feedback about teaching performance. Attend lectures given by the instructors whom they are assisting. Order or obtain materials needed for classes. Provide instructors with assistance in the use of audio-visual equipment. Assist faculty members or staff with student conferences.

Personality Type: Social. These occupations frequently involve working with, communicating with, and teaching people and often involve helping or providing service to others.

GOE—Interest Area/Cluster: 05. Education and Training. **Work Group:** 05.03. Postsecondary and Adult Teaching and Instructing. **Other Jobs in This Work Group:** Adult Literacy, Remedial Education, and GED Teachers and Instructors; Agricultural Sciences Teachers, Postsecondary; Anthropology and Archeology Teachers, Postsecondary; Architecture Teachers, Postsecondary; Area, Ethnic, and Cultural Studies Teachers, Postsecondary; Art, Drama, and Music Teachers, Postsecondary; Atmospheric, Earth, Marine, and Space Sciences Teachers, Postsecondary; Biological Science Teachers, Postsecondary; Business Teachers, Postsecondary; Chemistry Teachers, Postsecondary; Communications Teachers, Postsecondary; Computer Science Teachers, Postsecondary; Criminal Justice and Law Enforcement Teachers, Postsecondary; Economics Teachers, Postsecondary; Education Teachers, Postsecondary; Engineering Teachers, Postsecondary; English Language and Literature Teachers, Postsecondary; Environmental

Science Teachers, Postsecondary; Farm and Home Management Advisors; Foreign Language and Literature Teachers, Postsecondary; Forestry and Conservation Science Teachers, Postsecondary; Geography Teachers, Postsecondary; Health Specialties Teachers, Postsecondary; History Teachers, Postsecondary; Home Economics Teachers, Postsecondary; Law Teachers, Postsecondary; Library Science Teachers, Postsecondary; Mathematical Science Teachers, Postsecondary; Nursing Instructors and Teachers, Postsecondary; Philosophy and Religion Teachers, Postsecondary; Physics Teachers, Postsecondary; Political Science Teachers, Postsecondary; Psychology Teachers, Postsecondary; Recreation and Fitness Studies Teachers, Postsecondary; Social Work Teachers, Postsecondary; Sociology Teachers, Postsecondary.

Skills—Learning Strategies: Using multiple approaches when learning or teaching new things. **Instructing:** Teaching others how to do something. **Social Perceptiveness:** Being aware of others' reactions and understanding why they react the way they do. **Reading Comprehension:** Understanding written sentences and paragraphs in work-related documents. **Writing:** Communicating effectively with others in writing as indicated by the needs of the audience. **Speaking:** Talking to others to effectively convey information. **Time Management:** Managing one's own time and the time of others. **Active Learning:** Working with new material or information to grasp its implications.

Education and Training Program: Education, General. **Related Knowledge/Courses—Sociology and Anthropology:** Group behavior and dynamics; societal trends and influences; and cultures and their history, migrations, ethnicity, and origins. **Education and Training:** Instructional methods and training techniques, including curriculum design principles, learning theory, group and individual teaching techniques, design of

individual development plans, and test design principles. **English Language:** The structure and content of the English language, including the meaning and spelling of words, rules of composition, and grammar. **Philosophy and Theology:** Different philosophical systems and religions, including their basic principles, values, ethics, ways of thinking, customs, and practices and their impact on human culture. **Communications and Media:** Media production, communication, and dissemination techniques and methods, including alternative ways to inform and entertain via written, oral, and visual media. **Psychology:** Human behavior and performance, mental processes, psychological research methods, and the assessment and treatment of behavioral and affective disorders.

Work Environment: Indoors; sitting.

Graphic Designers

- ❋ Education/Training Required: Bachelor's degree
- ❋ Annual Earnings: $41,280
- ❋ Beginning Wage: $25,090
- ❋ Earnings Growth Potential: Medium
- ❋ Growth: 9.8%
- ❋ Annual Job Openings: 26,968
- ❋ Self-Employed: 25.3%
- ❋ Part-Time: 16.7%

Design or create graphics to meet specific commercial or promotional needs such as packaging, displays, or logos. May use a variety of media to achieve artistic or decorative effects. Create designs, concepts, and sample layouts based on knowledge of layout principles and esthetic design concepts. Determine size and arrangement of illustrative material and copy, and select style and size of type. Confer with clients to discuss and determine layout designs. Develop graphics and layouts for product illustrations, company logos, and Internet Web sites. Review final layouts and suggest improvements as needed. Prepare illustrations or rough sketches of material, discussing them with clients or supervisors and making necessary changes. Use computer software to generate new images. Key information into computer equipment to create layouts for client or supervisor. Maintain archive of images, photos, or previous work products. Prepare notes and instructions for workers who assemble and prepare final layouts for printing. Draw and print charts, graphs, illustrations, and other artwork, using computer. Study illustrations and photographs to plan presentations of materials, products, or services. Research new software or design concepts. Mark up, paste, and assemble final layouts to prepare layouts for printer. Produce still and animated graphics for on-air and taped portions of television news broadcasts, using electronic video equipment. Photograph layouts, using cameras, to make layout prints for supervisors or clients. Develop negatives and prints to produce layout photographs, using negative and print developing equipment and tools.

Personality Type: Artistic. These occupations frequently involve working with forms, designs, and patterns. They often require self-expression, and the work can be done without following a clear set of rules.

GOE—Interest Area/Cluster: 03. Arts and Communication. **Work Group:** 03.05. Design. **Other Jobs in This Work Group:** Commercial and Industrial Designers; Fashion Designers; Interior Designers; Set and Exhibit Designers.

Skills—Programming: Writing computer programs for various purposes. **Systems Analysis:** Determining how a system should work and how changes will affect outcomes.

Education and Training Programs: Agricultural Communication/Journalism; Web Page, Digital/

Multimedia and Information Resources Design; Computer Graphics; Design and Visual Communications, General; Commercial and Advertising Art; Industrial Design; Graphic Design. **Related Knowledge/Courses—Fine Arts:** Theory and techniques required to produce, compose, and perform works of music, dance, visual arts, drama, and sculpture. **Design:** Design techniques, principles, tools, and instruments involved in the production and use of precision technical plans, blueprints, drawings, and models. **Communications and Media:** Media production, communication, and dissemination techniques and methods, including alternative ways to inform and entertain via written, oral, and visual media. **Sales and Marketing:** Principles and methods involved in showing, promoting, and selling products or services. This includes marketing strategies and tactics, product demonstration and sales techniques, and sales control systems. **Sociology and Anthropology:** Group behavior and dynamics; societal trends and influences; and cultures and their history, migrations, ethnicity, and origins. **Computers and Electronics:** Electric circuit boards, processors, chips, and computer hardware and software, including applications and programming.

Work Environment: Indoors; sitting; using hands on objects, tools, or controls; repetitive motions.

Health Educators

- ❋ Education/Training Required: Bachelor's degree
- ❋ Annual Earnings: $42,920
- ❋ Beginning Wage: $25,340
- ❋ Earnings Growth Potential: High
- ❋ Growth: 26.2%
- ❋ Annual Job Openings: 13,707
- ❋ Self-Employed: 0.1%
- ❋ Part-Time: 12.0%

Promote, maintain, and improve individual and community health by assisting individuals and communities to adopt healthy behaviors. Collect and analyze data to identify community needs prior to planning, implementing, monitoring, and evaluating programs designed to encourage healthy lifestyles, policies, and environments. May also serve as a resource to assist individuals, other professionals, or the community and may administer fiscal resources for health education programs. Document activities, recording information such as the numbers of applications completed, presentations conducted, and persons assisted. Develop and present health education and promotion programs such as training workshops, conferences, and school or community presentations. Develop and maintain cooperative working relationships with agencies and organizations interested in public health care. Prepare and distribute health education materials, including reports; bulletins; and visual aids such as films, videotapes, photographs, and posters. Develop operational plans and policies necessary to achieve health education objectives and services. Collaborate with health specialists and civic groups to determine community health needs and the availability of services and to develop goals for meeting needs. Maintain databases, mailing lists, telephone networks, and other information to facilitate the functioning of health education programs. Supervise professional and technical staff in implementing health programs, objectives, and goals. Design and conduct evaluations and diagnostic studies to assess the quality and performance of health education programs. Provide program information to the public by preparing and presenting press releases, conducting media campaigns, and/or maintaining program-related Web sites. Develop, prepare, and coordinate grant applications and grant-related activities to obtain funding for health education programs and related work. Provide guidance to agencies and organizations in the assessment of health education needs and in the development and delivery of health education programs. Develop and maintain health education libraries to provide resources for staff and community agencies. Develop, conduct, or coordinate health needs assessments and other public health surveys.

Personality Type: Social. These occupations frequently involve working with, communicating with, and teaching people and often involve helping or providing service to others.

GOE—Interest Area/Cluster: 05. Education and Training. **Work Group:** 05.06. Counseling, Health, and Fitness Education. **Other Jobs in This Work Group:** Educational, Vocational, and School Counselors.

Skills—Service Orientation: Actively looking for ways to help people. **Social Perceptiveness:** Being aware of others' reactions and understanding why they react the way they do. **Monitoring:** Assessing how well one is doing when learning or doing something. **Learning Strategies:** Using multiple approaches when learning or teaching new things. **Instructing:** Teaching others how to do something. **Speaking:** Talking to others to effectively convey information. **Coordination:** Adjusting actions in relation to others' actions. **Active Learning:** Working with new material or information to grasp its implications.

Education and Training Programs: Health Communication; Community Health Services/Liaison/Counseling; Public Health Education and Promotion; Maternal and Child Health; International Public Health/International Health; Bioethics/Medical Ethics. **Related Knowledge/Courses— Sociology and Anthropology:** Group behavior and dynamics; societal trends and influences; and cultures and their history, migrations, ethnicity, and origins. **Customer and Personal Service:** Principles and processes for providing customer and personal services, including needs assessment techniques, quality service standards, alternative delivery systems, and customer satisfaction evaluation techniques. **Education and Training:** Instructional methods and training techniques, including curriculum design principles, learning theory, group and individual teaching techniques, design of individual development plans, and test design principles. **Personnel and Human Resources:** Principles and procedures for personnel recruitment; selection; training; compensation and benefits; labor relations and negotiation; and personnel information systems. **Psychology:** Human behavior and performance, mental processes, psychological research methods, and the assessment and treatment of behavioral and affective disorders. **Therapy and Counseling:** Information and techniques needed to rehabilitate physical and mental ailments and to provide career guidance, including alternative treatments, rehabilitation equipment and its proper use, and methods to evaluate treatment effects.

Work Environment: Indoors; disease or infections; sitting; using hands on objects, tools, or controls.

Health Specialties Teachers, Postsecondary

- ❋ Education/Training Required: Doctoral degree
- ❋ Annual Earnings: $80,700
- ❋ Beginning Wage: $37,890
- ❋ Earnings Growth Potential: Very high
- ❋ Growth: 22.9%
- ❋ Annual Job Openings: 1,9617
- ❋ Self-Employed: 0.4%
- ❋ Part-Time: 27.8%

Teach courses in health specialties, such as veterinary medicine, dentistry, pharmacy, therapy, laboratory technology, and public health. Initiate, facilitate, and moderate classroom discussions. Keep abreast of developments in their field by reading current literature, talking with colleagues, and participating in professional conferences. Compile, administer, and grade examinations or assign this work to others. Evaluate and grade students' classwork, assignments, and papers. Prepare course materials such as syllabi, homework assignments, and handouts. Prepare and deliver lectures to undergraduate or graduate students on topics such as public health, stress management, and worksite health promotion. Plan, evaluate, and revise curricula, course content, and course materials and methods of instruction. Supervise undergraduate or graduate teaching, internship, and research work. Conduct research in a particular field of knowledge and publish findings in professional journals, books, or electronic media. Collaborate with colleagues to address teaching and research issues. Supervise laboratory sessions. Maintain student attendance records, grades, and other required records. Maintain regularly scheduled office hours in order to advise and assist students. Advise students on academic and vocational curricula and on career issues. Participate in student recruitment, registration, and placement activities. Write grant proposals to procure external research funding. Serve on academic or administrative committees that deal with institutional policies, departmental matters, and academic issues. Select and obtain materials and supplies such as textbooks and laboratory equipment. Act as advisers to student organizations. Perform administrative duties such as serving as department head. Compile bibliographies of specialized materials for outside reading assignments. Provide professional consulting services to government and industry. Participate in campus and community events.

Personality Type: Social. These occupations frequently involve working with, communicating with, and teaching people and often involve helping or providing service to others.

GOE—Interest Area/Cluster: 05. Education and Training. **Work Group:** 05.03. Postsecondary and Adult Teaching and Instructing. **Other Jobs in This Work Group:** Adult Literacy, Remedial Education, and GED Teachers and Instructors; Agricultural Sciences Teachers, Postsecondary; Anthropology and Archeology Teachers, Postsecondary; Architecture Teachers, Postsecondary; Area, Ethnic, and Cultural Studies Teachers, Postsecondary; Art, Drama, and Music Teachers, Postsecondary; Atmospheric, Earth, Marine, and Space Sciences Teachers, Postsecondary; Biological Science Teachers, Postsecondary; Business Teachers, Postsecondary; Chemistry Teachers, Postsecondary; Communications Teachers, Postsecondary; Computer Science Teachers, Postsecondary; Criminal Justice and Law Enforcement Teachers, Postsecondary; Economics Teachers, Postsecondary; Education Teachers, Postsecondary; Engineering Teachers, Postsecondary; English Language and Literature Teachers, Postsecondary; Environmental Science Teachers, Postsecondary; Farm and Home Management Advisors; Foreign Language and Literature Teachers, Postsecondary; Forestry and Conservation Science Teachers, Postsecondary; Geography Teachers, Postsecondary; Graduate Teaching Assistants; History Teachers, Postsecondary; Home Economics Teachers, Postsecondary; Law Teachers, Postsecondary; Library Science Teachers, Postsecondary; Mathematical Science Teachers, Postsecondary; Nursing Instructors and Teachers, Postsecondary; Philosophy and Religion Teachers, Postsecondary; Physics Teachers, Postsecondary; Political Science Teachers, Postsecondary; Psychology Teachers, Postsecondary; Recreation and Fitness Studies Teachers, Postsecondary; Social Work Teachers, Postsecondary; Sociology Teachers, Postsecondary.

Skills—Science: Using scientific methods to solve problems. **Instructing:** Teaching others how to do something. **Writing:** Communicating effectively with others in writing as indicated by the needs of the audience. **Reading Comprehension:** Understanding written sentences and paragraphs in work-related documents. **Learning Strategies:** Using multiple approaches when learning or teaching new things. **Complex Problem Solving:** Identifying complex problems, reviewing the options, and implementing solutions. **Critical Thinking:** Using logic and analysis to identify the strengths and weaknesses of different approaches. **Speaking:** Talking to others to effectively convey information.

Education and Training Programs: Health Occupations Teacher Education; Biostatistics; Epidemiology; Chiropractic (DC); Communication Disorders, General; Audiology/Audiologist and Hearing Sciences; Speech-Language Pathology/Pathologist; Audiology/Audiologist and Speech-Language Pathology/Pathologist; Dentistry (DDS, DMD); Dental Clinical Sciences, General (MS, PhD); Dental Assisting/Assistant; Dental Hygiene/Hygienist; others. **Related Knowledge/Courses—Biology:** Plant and animal living tissue, cells, organisms, and entities, including their functions, interdependencies, and interactions with each other and the environment. **Medicine and Dentistry:** The information and techniques needed to diagnose and treat injuries, diseases, and deformities. This includes symptoms, treatment alternatives, drug properties and interactions, and preventive health-care measures. **Education and Training:** Instructional methods and training techniques, including curriculum design principles, learning theory, group and individual teaching techniques, design of individual development plans, and test design principles. **Therapy and Counseling:** Information and techniques needed to rehabilitate physical and mental ailments and to provide career guidance, including alternative treatments, rehabilitation equipment and its proper use, and methods to evaluate treatment effects. **Sociology and Anthropology:** Group behavior and dynamics; societal trends and influences; and cultures and their history, migrations, ethnicity, and origins. **Psychology:** Human behavior and performance, mental processes, psychological research methods, and the assessment and treatment of behavioral and affective disorders.

Work Environment: Indoors; sitting.

History Teachers, Postsecondary

* Education/Training Required: Doctoral degree
* Annual Earnings: $59,160
* Beginning Wage: $33,540
* Earnings Growth Potential: High
* Growth: 22.9%
* Annual Job Openings: 3,570
* Self-Employed: 0.4%
* Part-Time: 27.8%

Teach courses in human history and historiography. Prepare and deliver lectures to undergraduate and/or graduate students on topics such as ancient history, postwar civilizations, and the history of third-world countries. Evaluate and grade students' classwork, assignments, and papers. Prepare course materials such as syllabi, homework assignments, and handouts. Compile, administer, and grade examinations or assign this work to others. Initiate, facilitate, and moderate classroom discussions. Keep abreast of developments in their field by reading current literature, talking with colleagues, and participating in professional conferences. Plan, evaluate, and revise curricula, course content, and course materials and methods of instruction. Maintain student attendance records, grades, and other required records. Maintain regularly scheduled office hours to advise and assist students. Conduct research in a particular field of knowledge and publish findings in professional journals, books, or electronic media. Select and obtain materials and supplies such as textbooks. Advise students on academic and vocational curricula and on career issues. Collaborate with colleagues to address teaching and research issues. Serve on academic or administrative committees that deal with institutional policies, departmental matters, and academic issues. Participate in campus and community events. Act as advisers to student organizations. Participate in student recruitment, registration, and placement activities. Compile bibliographies of specialized materials for outside reading assignments. Supervise undergraduate and graduate teaching, internship, and research work. Perform administrative duties such as serving as department head. Write grant proposals to procure external research funding. Provide professional consulting services to government, educational institutions, and industry.

Personality Type: Social. These occupations frequently involve working with, communicating with, and teaching people and often involve helping or providing service to others.

GOE—Interest Area/Cluster: 05. Education and Training. **Work Group:** 05.03. Postsecondary and Adult Teaching and Instructing. **Other Jobs in This Work Group:** Adult Literacy, Remedial Education, and GED Teachers and Instructors; Agricultural Sciences Teachers, Postsecondary; Anthropology and Archeology Teachers, Postsecondary; Architecture Teachers, Postsecondary; Area, Ethnic, and Cultural Studies Teachers, Postsecondary; Art, Drama, and Music Teachers, Postsecondary; Atmospheric, Earth, Marine, and Space Sciences Teachers, Postsecondary; Biological Science Teachers, Postsecondary; Business Teachers, Postsecondary; Chemistry Teachers, Postsecondary; Communications Teachers, Postsecondary; Computer Science Teachers, Postsecondary; Criminal Justice and Law Enforcement Teachers, Postsecondary; Economics Teachers, Postsecondary; Education Teachers, Postsecondary; Engineering Teachers, Postsecondary; English Language and Literature Teachers, Postsecondary; Environmental Science Teachers, Postsecondary; Farm and Home Management Advisors; Foreign Language and Literature Teachers, Postsecondary; Forestry and Conservation Science Teachers, Postsecondary; Geography Teachers, Postsecondary; Graduate Teaching Assistants; Health Specialties Teachers, Postsecondary; Home Economics Teachers, Postsecondary; Law Teachers, Postsecondary; Library Science Teachers, Postsecondary; Mathematical Science Teachers, Postsecondary; Nursing Instructors and Teachers, Postsecondary; Philosophy and Religion Teachers, Postsecondary; Physics Teachers, Postsecondary; Political Science Teachers, Postsecondary; Psychology Teachers, Postsecondary; Recreation and Fitness Studies Teachers, Postsecondary; Social Work Teachers, Postsecondary; Sociology Teachers, Postsecondary.

Skills—Writing: Communicating effectively with others in writing as indicated by the needs of the audience. **Instructing:** Teaching others how to do something. **Learning Strategies:** Using multiple approaches when learning or teaching new things. **Reading Comprehension:** Understanding written sentences and paragraphs in work-related documents. **Speaking:** Talking to others to effectively convey information. **Persuasion:** Persuading others to approach things differently. **Critical Thinking:** Using logic and analysis to identify the strengths and weaknesses of different approaches. **Active Learning:** Working with new material or information to grasp its implications.

Education and Training Programs: History, General; American History (United States); European History; History and Philosophy of Science and Technology; Public/Applied History and Archival Administration; Asian History; Canadian History; History, Other. **Related Knowledge/Courses— History and Archeology:** Historical events and their causes, indicators, and impact on particular civilizations and cultures. **Philosophy and Theology:** Different philosophical systems and religions, including their basic principles, values, ethics, ways of thinking, customs, and practices and their impact on human culture. **Geography:** Various methods for describing the location and distribution of land, sea, and air masses, including their physical locations, relationships, and characteristics. **Sociology and Anthropology:** Group behavior and dynamics; societal trends and influences; and cultures and their history, migrations, ethnicity, and origins. **Education and Training:** Instructional methods and training techniques, including curriculum design principles, learning theory, group and individual teaching techniques, design of individual development plans, and test design principles. **English Language:** The structure and content of the English language, including the meaning and spelling of words, rules of composition, and grammar.

Work Environment: Indoors; sitting.

Home Economics Teachers, Postsecondary

* ❋ Education/Training Required: Doctoral degree
* ❋ Annual Earnings: $58,170
* ❋ Beginning Wage: $29,510
* ❋ Earnings Growth Potential: High
* ❋ Growth: 22.9%
* ❋ Annual Job Openings: 820
* ❋ Self-Employed: 0.4%
* ❋ Part-Time: 27.8%

Teach courses in child care, family relations, finance, nutrition, and related subjects as pertaining to home management. Evaluate and grade students' classwork, laboratory work, projects, assignments, and papers. Initiate, facilitate, and moderate classroom discussions. Prepare and deliver lectures to undergraduate or graduate students on topics such as food science, nutrition, and child care. Prepare course materials such as syllabi, homework assignments, and handouts. Keep abreast of developments in their field by reading current literature, talking with colleagues, and participating in professional conferences. Maintain student attendance records, grades, and other required records. Plan, evaluate, and revise curricula, course content, and course materials and methods of instruction. Compile, administer, and grade examinations or assign this work to others. Advise students on academic and vocational curricula and on career issues. Maintain regularly scheduled office hours to advise and assist students. Supervise undergraduate or graduate teaching, internship, and research work. Select and obtain materials and supplies such as textbooks. Conduct research in a particular field of knowledge and publish findings in professional journals, books, and/or electronic media. Collaborate with colleagues to address teaching and research issues. Act as advisers to student organizations. Participate in student recruitment, registration, and placement activities. Serve on academic or administrative committees that deal with institutional policies, departmental matters, and academic issues. Participate in campus and community events. Compile bibliographies of specialized materials for outside reading assignments. Perform administrative duties such as serving as department head. Write grant proposals to procure external research funding. Provide professional consulting services to government and industry.

Personality Type: Social. These occupations frequently involve working with, communicating with, and teaching people and often involve helping or providing service to others.

GOE—Interest Area/Cluster: 05. Education and Training. **Work Group:** 05.03. Postsecondary and Adult Teaching and Instructing. **Other Jobs in This Work Group:** Adult Literacy, Remedial Education, and GED Teachers and Instructors; Agricultural Sciences Teachers, Postsecondary; Anthropology and Archeology Teachers, Postsecondary; Architecture Teachers, Postsecondary; Area, Ethnic, and Cultural Studies Teachers, Postsecondary; Art, Drama, and Music Teachers, Postsecondary; Atmospheric, Earth, Marine, and Space Sciences Teachers, Postsecondary; Biological Science Teachers, Postsecondary; Business Teachers, Postsecondary; Chemistry Teachers, Postsecondary; Communications Teachers, Postsecondary; Computer Science Teachers, Postsecondary; Criminal Justice and Law Enforcement Teachers, Postsecondary; Economics Teachers, Postsecondary; Education Teachers, Postsecondary; Engineering Teachers, Postsecondary; English Language and Literature Teachers, Postsecondary; Environmental Science Teachers, Postsecondary; Farm and Home Management Advisors; Foreign Language and Literature Teachers, Postsecondary;

Forestry and Conservation Science Teachers, Postsecondary; Geography Teachers, Postsecondary; Graduate Teaching Assistants; Health Specialties Teachers, Postsecondary; History Teachers, Postsecondary; Law Teachers, Postsecondary; Library Science Teachers, Postsecondary; Mathematical Science Teachers, Postsecondary; Nursing Instructors and Teachers, Postsecondary; Philosophy and Religion Teachers, Postsecondary; Physics Teachers, Postsecondary; Political Science Teachers, Postsecondary; Psychology Teachers, Postsecondary; Recreation and Fitness Studies Teachers, Postsecondary; Social Work Teachers, Postsecondary; Sociology Teachers, Postsecondary.

Skills—Writing: Communicating effectively with others in writing as indicated by the needs of the audience. **Instructing:** Teaching others how to do something. **Learning Strategies:** Using multiple approaches when learning or teaching new things. **Service Orientation:** Actively looking for ways to help people. **Active Learning:** Working with new material or information to grasp its implications. **Operations Analysis:** Analyzing needs and product requirements to create a design. **Social Perceptiveness:** Being aware of others' reactions and understanding why they react the way they do. **Speaking:** Talking to others to effectively convey information.

Education and Training Programs: Family and Consumer Sciences/Human Sciences, General; Business Family and Consumer Sciences/Human Sciences; Foodservice Systems Administration/Management; Human Development and Family Studies, General; Child Care and Support Services Management. **Related Knowledge/Courses— Sociology and Anthropology:** Group behavior and dynamics; societal trends and influences; and cultures and their history, migrations, ethnicity, and origins. **Philosophy and Theology:** Different philosophical systems and religions, including their basic principles, values, ethics, ways of

thinking, customs, and practices and their impact on human culture. **Education and Training:** Instructional methods and training techniques, including curriculum design principles, learning theory, group and individual teaching techniques, design of individual development plans, and test design principles. **Therapy and Counseling:** Information and techniques needed to rehabilitate physical and mental ailments and to provide career guidance, including alternative treatments, rehabilitation equipment and its proper use, and methods to evaluate treatment effects. **Psychology:** Human behavior and performance, mental processes, psychological research methods, and the assessment and treatment of behavioral and affective disorders. **English Language:** The structure and content of the English language, including the meaning and spelling of words, rules of composition, and grammar.

Work Environment: Indoors; sitting.

Human Resources Managers

- ❋ Education/Training Required: Work experience plus degree
- ❋ Annual Earnings: $87,180
- ❋ Beginning Wage: $49,860
- ❋ Earnings Growth Potential: High
- ❋ Growth: 12.5%
- ❋ Annual Job Openings: 17,081
- ❋ Self-Employed: 1.4%
- ❋ Part-Time: 0.0%

Plan, direct, and coordinate human resource management activities of an organization to maximize the strategic use of human resources and maintain functions such as employee compensation, recruitment, personnel policies, and

regulatory compliance. Administer compensation, benefits, and performance management systems and safety and recreation programs. Identify staff vacancies and recruit, interview, and select applicants. Allocate human resources, ensuring appropriate matches between personnel. Provide current and prospective employees with information about policies, job duties, working conditions, wages, opportunities for promotion, and employee benefits. Perform difficult staffing duties, including dealing with understaffing, refereeing disputes, firing employees, and administering disciplinary procedures. Advise managers on organizational policy matters such as equal employment opportunity and sexual harassment and recommend needed changes. Analyze and modify compensation and benefits policies to establish competitive programs and ensure compliance with legal requirements. Plan and conduct new employee orientation to foster positive attitude toward organizational objectives. Serve as a link between management and employees by handling questions, interpreting and administering contracts, and helping resolve work-related problems. Plan, direct, supervise, and coordinate work activities of subordinates and staff relating to employment, compensation, labor relations, and employee relations. Analyze training needs to design employee development, language training, and health and safety programs. Maintain records and compile statistical reports concerning personnel-related data such as hires, transfers, performance appraisals, and absenteeism rates. Analyze statistical data and reports to identify and determine causes of personnel problems and develop recommendations for improvement of organization's personnel policies and practices. Plan, organize, direct, control, or coordinate the personnel, training, or labor relations activities of an organization. Conduct exit interviews to identify reasons for employee termination. Investigate and report on industrial accidents for insurance carriers. Represent organization at personnel-related hearings and investigations. Negotiate bargaining agreements and help interpret labor contracts.

Personality Type: Enterprising. These occupations frequently involve starting up and carrying out projects and can involve leading people and making many decisions. They sometimes require risk taking and often deal with business.

GOE—Interest Area/Cluster: 04. Business and Administration. **Work Group:** 04.01. Managerial Work in General Business. **Other Jobs in This Work Group:** Chief Executives; Compensation and Benefits Managers; General and Operations Managers; Training and Development Managers.

Skills—Management of Personnel Resources: Motivating, developing, and directing people as they work; identifying the best people for the job. **Systems Analysis:** Determining how a system should work and how changes will affect outcomes. **Systems Evaluation:** Looking at many indicators of system performance and taking into account their accuracy. **Negotiation:** Bringing others together and trying to reconcile differences. **Writing:** Communicating effectively with others in writing as indicated by the needs of the audience. **Persuasion:** Persuading others to approach things differently. **Time Management:** Managing one's own time and the time of others. **Management of Financial Resources:** Determining how money will be spent to get the work done and accounting for these expenditures.

Education and Training Program: Human Resources Management/Personnel Administration, General. **Related Knowledge/Courses—Personnel and Human Resources:** Principles and procedures for personnel recruitment; selection; training; compensation and benefits; labor relations and negotiation; and personnel information systems. **Therapy and Counseling:** Information and techniques needed to rehabilitate physical and mental ailments and to provide career guidance, including alternative treatments, rehabilitation equipment and its proper use, and methods to evaluate treatment effects. **Sociology and Anthropology:** Group behavior and dynamics; societal trends and influences; and cultures and their history, migrations, ethnicity, and origins. **Psychology:** Human behavior and performance, mental processes, psychological research methods, and the assessment and treatment of behavioral and affective disorders. **Clerical Practices:** Administrative and clerical procedures and systems such as word-processing systems, filing and records management systems, stenography and transcription, forms, design principles, and other office procedures and terminology. **Administration and Management:** Principles and processes involved in business and organizational planning, coordination, and execution. This includes strategic planning, resource allocation, manpower modeling, leadership techniques, and production methods.

Work Environment: Indoors; sitting.

Hydrologists

* Education/Training Required: Master's degree
* Annual Earnings: $68,140
* Beginning Wage: $42,450
* Earnings Growth Potential: Medium
* Growth: 24.3%
* Annual Job Openings: 687
* Self-Employed: 2.4%
* Part-Time: 5.3%

Research the distribution, circulation, and physical properties of underground and surface waters; study the form and intensity of precipitation, its rate of infiltration into the soil, its movement through the earth, and its return to the ocean and atmosphere. Study and document quantities, distribution, disposition, and development of underground and surface waters. Draft final reports describing research results, including illustrations, appendices, maps, and other attachments. Coordinate and supervise the work of professional and technical staff, including research assistants, technologists, and technicians. Prepare hydrogeologic evaluations of known or suspected hazardous waste sites and land treatment and feedlot facilities. Design and conduct scientific hydrogeological investigations to ensure that accurate and appropriate information is available for use in water resource management decisions. Study public water supply issues, including flood and drought risks, water quality, wastewater, and impacts on wetland habitats. Collect and analyze water samples as part of field investigations and/or to validate data from automatic monitors. Apply research findings to help minimize the environmental impacts of pollution, water-borne diseases, erosion, and sedimentation. Measure and graph phenomena such as lake levels, stream flows, and changes in water volumes. Investigate complaints or conflicts related to the alteration of public waters, gathering information, recommending alternatives, informing participants of progress, and preparing draft orders. Develop or modify methods of conducting hydrologic studies. Answer questions and provide technical assistance and information to contractors and/or the public regarding issues such as well drilling, code requirements, hydrology, and geology. Install, maintain, and calibrate instruments such as those that monitor water levels, rainfall, and sediments. Evaluate data and provide recommendations regarding the feasibility of municipal projects such as hydroelectric power plants, irrigation systems, flood warning systems, and waste treatment facilities. Conduct short-term and long-term climate assessments and study storm occurrences. Study and analyze the physical aspects of the Earth in terms of the hydrological components, including atmosphere, hydrosphere, and interior structure. Conduct research and communicate information to promote the conservation and preservation of water resources.

Personality Type: Investigative. These occupations frequently involve working with ideas and require an extensive amount of thinking. They can involve searching for facts and figuring out problems mentally.

GOE—Interest Area/Cluster: 15. Scientific Research, Engineering, and Mathematics. **Work Group:** 15.02. Physical Sciences. **Other Jobs in This Work Group:** Astronomers; Atmospheric and Space Scientists; Chemists; Geographers; Geoscientists, Except Hydrologists and Geographers; Materials Scientists; Physicists.

Skills—Science: Using scientific methods to solve problems. **Programming:** Writing computer programs for various purposes. **Management of Financial Resources:** Determining how money will be spent to get the work done and accounting for these expenditures. **Mathematics:** Using mathematics to solve problems. **Management of Personnel Resources:** Motivating, developing, and directing people as they work; identifying the best people for the job. **Complex Problem Solving:** Identifying complex problems, reviewing the options, and implementing solutions. **Systems Analysis:** Determining how a system should work and how changes will affect outcomes. **Management of Material Resources:** Obtaining and seeing to the appropriate use of equipment, facilities, and materials needed to do certain work.

Education and Training Programs: Geology/Earth Science, General; Hydrology and Water Resources Science; Oceanography, Chemical and Physical. **Related Knowledge/Courses—Geography:** Various methods for describing the location and distribution of land, sea, and air masses, including their physical locations, relationships, and characteristics. **Physics:** Physical principles, laws, and applications, including air, water, material dynamics, light, atomic principles, heat, electric theory, earth formations, and meteorological and related natural phenomena. **Engineering and Technology:** Equipment, tools, and mechanical devices and their uses to produce motion, light, power, technology, and other applications. **Biology:** Plant and animal living tissue, cells, organisms, and entities, including their functions, interdependencies, and interactions with each other and the environment. **Chemistry:** The composition, structure, and properties of substances and of the chemical processes and transformations that they undergo. This includes uses of chemicals and their interactions, danger signs, production techniques, and disposal methods. **Mathematics:** Numbers and their operations and interrelationships, including arithmetic, algebra, geometry, calculus, and statistics and their applications.

Work Environment: More often indoors than outdoors; sitting.

Industrial Engineers

- ❋ Education/Training Required: Bachelor's degree
- ❋ Annual Earnings: $71,430
- ❋ Beginning Wage: $46,340
- ❋ Earnings Growth Potential: Medium
- ❋ Growth: 20.3%
- ❋ Annual Job Openings: 11,272
- ❋ Self-Employed: 0.9%
- ❋ Part-Time: 2.0%

Design, develop, test, and evaluate integrated systems for managing industrial production processes, including human work factors, quality control, inventory control, logistics and material flow, cost analysis, and production coordination. Analyze statistical data and product specifications to determine standards and establish quality and reliability objectives of finished product. Develop manufacturing methods, labor utilization standards, and cost analysis systems to promote efficient staff and facility utilization. Recommend methods for improving utilization of personnel, material, and utilities. Plan and establish sequence of operations to fabricate and assemble parts or products and to promote efficient utilization. Apply statistical methods and perform mathematical calculations to determine manufacturing processes, staff requirements, and production standards. Coordinate quality control objectives and activities to resolve production problems, maximize product reliability, and minimize cost. Confer with vendors, staff, and management personnel regarding purchases, procedures, product specifications, manufacturing capabilities, and project status. Draft and design layout of equipment, materials, and workspace to illustrate maximum efficiency, using drafting tools and computer. Review production schedules, engineering specifications, orders, and related information to obtain knowledge of manufacturing methods, procedures, and activities. Communicate with management and user personnel to develop production and design standards. Estimate production cost and effect of product design changes for management review, action, and control. Formulate sampling procedures and designs and develop forms and instructions for recording, evaluating, and reporting quality and reliability data. Record or oversee recording of information to ensure currency of engineering drawings and documentation of production problems. Study operations sequence, material flow, functional statements, organization charts, and project information to determine worker functions and responsibilities. Direct workers engaged in product measurement, inspection, and testing activities to ensure quality control and reliability. Implement methods and procedures for disposition of discrepant material and defective or damaged parts and assess cost and responsibility.

Personality Type: Investigative. These occupations frequently involve working with ideas and require an extensive amount of thinking. They can involve searching for facts and figuring out problems mentally.

GOE—Interest Area/Cluster: 15. Scientific Research, Engineering, and Mathematics. **Work Group:** 15.08. Industrial and Safety Engineering. **Other Jobs in This Work Group:** Fire-Prevention and Protection Engineers; Health and Safety Engineers, Except Mining Safety Engineers and Inspectors; Industrial Safety and Health Engineers; Product Safety Engineers.

Skills—Equipment Selection: Determining the kind of tools and equipment needed to do a job. **Technology Design:** Generating or adapting equipment and technology to serve user needs. **Troubleshooting:** Determining what is causing an operating error and deciding what to do about it. **Installation:** Installing equipment, machines, wiring, or programs to meet specifications. **Systems**

Analysis: Determining how a system should work and how changes will affect outcomes. **Mathematics:** Using mathematics to solve problems. **Judgment and Decision Making:** Weighing the relative costs and benefits of a potential action. **Negotiation:** Bringing others together and trying to reconcile differences.

Education and Training Program: Industrial Engineering. **Related Knowledge/Courses— Engineering and Technology:** Equipment, tools, and mechanical devices and their uses to produce motion, light, power, technology, and other applications. **Design:** Design techniques, principles, tools, and instruments involved in the production and use of precision technical plans, blueprints, drawings, and models. **Production and Processing:** Inputs, outputs, raw materials, waste, quality control, costs, and techniques for maximizing the manufacture and distribution of goods. **Mechanical Devices:** Machines and tools, including their designs, uses, benefits, repair, and maintenance. **Physics:** Physical principles, laws, and applications, including air, water, material dynamics, light, atomic principles, heat, electric theory, earth formations, and meteorological and related natural phenomena. **Mathematics:** Numbers and their operations and interrelationships, including arithmetic, algebra, geometry, calculus, and statistics and their applications.

Work Environment: Indoors; noisy; contaminants; hazardous equipment; more often sitting than standing.

Industrial-Organizational Psychologists

* Education/Training Required: Master's degree
* Annual Earnings: $80,820
* Beginning Wage: $38,910
* Earnings Growth Potential: Very high
* Growth: 21.3%
* Annual Job Openings: 118
* Self-Employed: 39.3%
* Part-Time: 24.0%

Apply principles of psychology to personnel, administration, management, sales, and marketing problems. Activities may include policy planning; employee screening, training, and development; and organizational development and analysis. May work with management to reorganize the work setting to improve worker productivity. Develop and implement employee selection and placement programs. Analyze job requirements and content to establish criteria for classification, selection, training, and other related personnel functions. Develop interview techniques, rating scales, and psychological tests used to assess skills, abilities, and interests for the purpose of employee selection, placement, and promotion. Advise management concerning personnel, managerial, and marketing policies and practices and their potential effects on organizational effectiveness and efficiency. Analyze data, using statistical methods and applications, to evaluate the outcomes and effectiveness of workplace programs. Assess employee performance. Observe and interview workers to obtain information about the physical, mental, and educational requirements of jobs as well as information about aspects such as job satisfaction. Write reports on research findings and implications to contribute to general knowledge and to suggest potential changes in organizational functioning. Facilitate organizational development and change. Identify training and development needs. Formulate and implement training programs, applying principles of learning and individual differences. Study organizational effectiveness, productivity, and efficiency, including the nature of workplace supervision and leadership. Conduct research studies of physical work environments, organizational structures, communication systems, group interactions, morale, and motivation to assess organizational functioning. Counsel workers about job and career-related issues. Study consumers' reactions to new products and package designs, and to advertising efforts, using surveys and tests. Participate in mediation and dispute resolution.

Personality Type: Investigative. These occupations frequently involve working with ideas and require an extensive amount of thinking. They can involve searching for facts and figuring out problems mentally.

GOE—Interest Area/Cluster: 15. Scientific Research, Engineering, and Mathematics. **Work Group:** 15.04. Social Sciences. **Other Jobs in This Work Group:** Anthropologists; Anthropologists and Archeologists; Archeologists; Economists; Historians; Political Scientists; School Psychologists; Sociologists.

Skills—Science: Using scientific methods to solve problems. **Systems Evaluation:** Looking at many indicators of system performance and taking into account their accuracy. **Judgment and Decision Making:** Weighing the relative costs and benefits of a potential action. **Writing:** Communicating effectively with others in writing as indicated by the needs of the audience. **Monitoring:** Assessing how well one is doing when learning or doing something. **Time Management:** Managing one's own time and the time of others. **Coordination:** Adjusting actions in relation to others' actions.

Critical Thinking: Using logic and analysis to identify the strengths and weaknesses of different approaches.

Education and Training Programs: Psychology, General; Industrial and Organizational Psychology. **Related Knowledge/Courses—Personnel and Human Resources:** Principles and procedures for personnel recruitment; selection; training; compensation and benefits; labor relations and negotiation; and personnel information systems. **Psychology:** Human behavior and performance, mental processes, psychological research methods, and the assessment and treatment of behavioral and affective disorders. **Sociology and Anthropology:** Group behavior and dynamics; societal trends and influences; and cultures and their history, migrations, ethnicity, and origins. **Education and Training:** Instructional methods and training techniques, including curriculum design principles, learning theory, group and individual teaching techniques, design of individual development plans, and test design principles. **Therapy and Counseling:** Information and techniques needed to rehabilitate physical and mental ailments and to provide career guidance, including alternative treatments, rehabilitation equipment and its proper use, and methods to evaluate treatment effects. **Mathematics:** Numbers and their operations and interrelationships, including arithmetic, algebra, geometry, calculus, and statistics and their applications.

Work Environment: Indoors; sitting.

Instructional Coordinators

- ✸ Education/Training Required: Master's degree
- ✸ Annual Earnings: $55,270
- ✸ Beginning Wage: $30,580
- ✸ Earnings Growth Potential: High
- ✸ Growth: 22.5%
- ✸ Annual Job Openings: 21,294
- ✸ Self-Employed: 3.1%
- ✸ Part-Time: 19.7%

Develop instructional material, coordinate educational content, and incorporate current technology in specialized fields that provide guidelines to educators and instructors for developing curricula and conducting courses. Conduct or participate in workshops, committees, and conferences designed to promote the intellectual, social, and physical welfare of students. Plan and conduct teacher training programs and conferences dealing with new classroom procedures, instructional materials and equipment, and teaching aids. Advise teaching and administrative staff in curriculum development, use of materials and equipment, and implementation of state and federal programs and procedures. Recommend, order, or authorize purchase of instructional materials, supplies, equipment, and visual aids designed to meet student educational needs and district standards. Interpret and enforce provisions of state education codes and rules and regulations of state education boards. Confer with members of educational committees and advisory groups to obtain knowledge of subject areas and to relate curriculum materials to specific subjects, individual student needs, and occupational areas. Organize production and design of curriculum materials. Research, evaluate, and prepare recommendations on curricula, instructional methods, and materials for school systems. Observe work of teaching staff to evaluate performance and to recommend changes that could strengthen teaching skills. Develop instructional materials to be used by educators and instructors. Prepare grant proposals, budgets, and program policies and goals or assist in their preparation. Develop tests, questionnaires, and procedures that measure the effectiveness of curricula and use these tools to determine whether program objectives are being met. Update the content of educational programs to ensure that students are being trained with equipment and processes that are technologically current. Address public audiences to explain program objectives and to elicit support. Advise and teach students. Prepare or approve manuals, guidelines, and reports on state educational policies and practices for distribution to school districts. Develop classroom-based and distance-learning training courses, using needs assessments and skill level analyses. Inspect instructional equipment to determine if repairs are needed and authorize necessary repairs.

Personality Type: Social. These occupations frequently involve working with, communicating with, and teaching people and often involve helping or providing service to others.

GOE—Interest Area/Cluster: 05. Education and Training. **Work Group:** 05.01. Managerial Work in Education. **Other Jobs in This Work Group:** Education Administrators, Elementary and Secondary School; Education Administrators, Postsecondary; Education Administrators, Preschool and Child Care Center/Program.

Skills—Management of Financial Resources: Determining how money will be spent to get the work done and accounting for these expenditures. **Learning Strategies:** Using multiple approaches when learning or teaching new things. **Monitoring:** Assessing how well one is doing when learning or doing something. **Social Perceptiveness:** Being aware of others' reactions and understanding why they react the way they do. **Coordination:**

Adjusting actions in relation to others' actions. **Time Management:** Managing one's own time and the time of others. **Management of Personnel Resources:** Motivating, developing, and directing people as they work; identifying the best people for the job. **Persuasion:** Persuading others to approach things differently.

Education and Training Programs: Curriculum and Instruction; Educational/Instructional Media Design; International and Comparative Education. **Related Knowledge/Courses—Education and Training:** Instructional methods and training techniques, including curriculum design principles, learning theory, group and individual teaching techniques, design of individual development plans, and test design principles. **Sociology and Anthropology:** Group behavior and dynamics; societal trends and influences; and cultures and their history, migrations, ethnicity, and origins. **English Language:** The structure and content of the English language, including the meaning and spelling of words, rules of composition, and grammar. **Personnel and Human Resources:** Principles and procedures for personnel recruitment; selection; training; compensation and benefits; labor relations and negotiation; and personnel information systems. **Communications and Media:** Media production, communication, and dissemination techniques and methods, including alternative ways to inform and entertain via written, oral, and visual media. **Psychology:** Human behavior and performance, mental processes, psychological research methods, and the assessment and treatment of behavioral and affective disorders.

Work Environment: Indoors; sitting.

Insurance Sales Agents

- Education/Training Required: Bachelor's degree
- Annual Earnings: $44,110
- Beginning Wage: $25,230
- Earnings Growth Potential: High
- Growth: 12.9%
- Annual Job Openings: 64,162
- Self-Employed: 25.5%
- Part-Time: 9.8%

Sell life, property, casualty, health, automotive, or other types of insurance. May refer clients to independent brokers, work as independent broker, or be employed by an insurance company. Call on policyholders to deliver and explain policy, to analyze insurance program and suggest additions or changes, or to change beneficiaries. Calculate premiums and establish payment method. Customize insurance programs to suit individual customers, often covering a variety of risks. Sell various types of insurance policies to businesses and individuals on behalf of insurance companies, including automobile, fire, life, property, medical, and dental insurance or specialized policies such as marine, farm/crop, and medical malpractice. Interview prospective clients to obtain data about their financial resources and needs and the physical condition of the person or property to be insured and to discuss any existing coverage. Seek out new clients and develop clientele by networking to find new customers and generate lists of prospective clients. Explain features, advantages, and disadvantages of various policies to promote sale of insurance plans. Contact underwriter and submit forms to obtain binder coverage. Ensure that policy requirements are fulfilled, including any necessary medical examinations and the completion of appropriate forms. Confer with clients to obtain and provide information when claims are made on a policy. Perform administrative tasks, such as maintaining records and handling policy renewals. Select company that offers type of coverage requested by client to underwrite policy. Monitor insurance claims to ensure that they are settled equitably for both the client and the insurer. Develop marketing strategies to compete with other individuals or companies who sell insurance. Attend meetings, seminars, and programs to learn about new products and services, learn new skills, and receive technical assistance in developing new accounts. Inspect property, examining its general condition, type of construction, age, and other characteristics, to decide if it is a good insurance risk. Install bookkeeping systems and resolve system problems. Plan and oversee incorporation of insurance program into bookkeeping system of company. Explain necessary bookkeeping requirements for customer to implement and provide group insurance program.

Personality Type: Enterprising. These occupations frequently involve starting up and carrying out projects and can involve leading people and making many decisions. They sometimes require risk taking and often deal with business.

GOE—Interest Area/Cluster: 06. Finance and Insurance. **Work Group:** 06.05. Finance/Insurance Sales and Support. **Other Jobs in This Work Group:** Personal Financial Advisors; Sales Agents, Financial Services; Sales Agents, Securities and Commodities; Securities, Commodities, and Financial Services Sales Agents.

Skills—Persuasion: Persuading others to approach things differently. **Judgment and Decision Making:** Weighing the relative costs and benefits of a potential action. **Time Management:** Managing one's own time and the time of others. **Negotiation:** Bringing others together and trying to reconcile differences. **Service Orientation:** Actively looking for ways to help people. **Speaking:** Talking to others to effectively convey information.

Active Listening: Listening to what other people are saying and asking questions as appropriate. **Social Perceptiveness:** Being aware of others' reactions and understanding why they react the way they do.

Education and Training Program: Insurance. **Related Knowledge/Courses—Sales and Marketing:** Principles and methods involved in showing, promoting, and selling products or services. This includes marketing strategies and tactics, product demonstration and sales techniques, and sales control systems. **Economics and Accounting:** Economic and accounting principles and practices, the financial markets, banking, and the analysis and reporting of financial data. **Customer and Personal Service:** Principles and processes for providing customer and personal services, including needs assessment techniques, quality service standards, alternative delivery systems, and customer satisfaction evaluation techniques. **Computers and Electronics:** Electric circuit boards, processors, chips, and computer hardware and software, including applications and programming. **Clerical Practices:** Administrative and clerical procedures and systems such as word-processing systems, filing and records management systems, stenography and transcription, forms, design principles, and other office procedures and terminology. **Law and Government:** Laws, legal codes, court procedures, precedents, government regulations, executive orders, agency rules, and the democratic political process.

Work Environment: Indoors; sitting.

Interior Designers

- Education/Training Required: Associate degree
- Annual Earnings: $43,970
- Beginning Wage: $25,920
- Earnings Growth Potential: High
- Growth: 19.5%
- Annual Job Openings: 8,434
- Self-Employed: 26.3%
- Part-Time: 16.7%

Plan, design, and furnish interiors of residential, commercial, or industrial buildings. Formulate design that is practical, aesthetic, and conducive to intended purposes, such as raising productivity, selling merchandise, or improving lifestyle. May specialize in a particular field, style, or phase of interior design. Estimate material requirements and costs and present design to client for approval. Confer with client to determine factors affecting planning interior environments, such as budget, architectural preferences, and purpose and function. Advise client on interior design factors such as space planning, layout, and utilization of furnishings or equipment and color coordination. Select or design and purchase furnishings, artwork, and accessories. Formulate environmental plan to be practical, esthetic, and conducive to intended purposes such as raising productivity or selling merchandise. Subcontract fabrication, installation, and arrangement of carpeting, fixtures, accessories, draperies, paint and wall coverings, artwork, furniture, and related items. Render design ideas in form of paste-ups or drawings. Plan and design interior environments for boats, planes, buses, trains, and other enclosed spaces.

Personality Type: Artistic. These occupations frequently involve working with forms, designs, and patterns. They often require self-expression, and the work can be done without following a clear set of rules.

GOE—Interest Area/Cluster: 03. Arts and Communication. **Work Group:** 03.05. Design. **Other Jobs in This Work Group:** Commercial and Industrial Designers; Fashion Designers; Graphic Designers; Set and Exhibit Designers.

Skills—Installation: Installing equipment, machines, wiring, or programs to meet specifications. **Management of Financial Resources:** Determining how money will be spent to get the work done and accounting for these expenditures. **Persuasion:** Persuading others to approach things differently. **Operations Analysis:** Analyzing needs and product requirements to create a design. **Negotiation:** Bringing others together and trying to reconcile differences. **Active Learning:** Working with new material or information to grasp its implications. **Mathematics:** Using mathematics to solve problems. **Speaking:** Talking to others to effectively convey information.

Education and Training Programs: Interior Architecture; Facilities Planning and Management; Textile Science; Interior Design. **Related Knowledge/Courses—Design:** Design techniques, principles, tools, and instruments involved in the production and use of precision technical plans, blueprints, drawings, and models. **Sales and Marketing:** Principles and methods involved in showing, promoting, and selling products or services. This includes marketing strategies and tactics, product demonstration and sales techniques, and sales control systems. **Building and Construction:** Materials, methods, and the appropriate tools to construct objects, structures, and buildings. **Clerical Practices:** Administrative and clerical procedures and systems such as word-processing systems, filing and records management systems, stenography and transcription, forms, design principles, and other office procedures and terminology. **Fine Arts:** Theory and techniques required to produce, compose, and perform works of music, dance, visual arts, drama, and sculpture. **Administration and Management:** Principles and processes involved in business and organizational planning, coordination, and execution. This includes strategic planning, resource allocation, manpower modeling, leadership techniques, and production methods.

Work Environment: Indoors; sitting.

Internists, General

- ❋ Education/Training Required: First professional degree
- ❋ Annual Earnings: More than $145,600
- ❋ Beginning Wage: $89,130
- ❋ Earnings Growth Potential: Cannot be calculated
- ❋ Growth: 14.2%
- ❋ Annual Job Openings: 38,027
- ❋ Self-Employed: 14.7%
- ❋ Part-Time: 8.1%

The job openings listed here are shared with Anesthesiologists; Family and General Practitioners; Obstetricians and Gynecologists; Pediatricians, General; Psychiatrists; and Surgeons.

Diagnose and provide non-surgical treatment of diseases and injuries of internal organ systems. Provide care mainly for adults who have a wide range of problems associated with the internal organs. Treat internal disorders, such as hypertension; heart disease; diabetes; and problems of the lung, brain, kidney, and gastrointestinal tract. Analyze records, reports, test results, or examination information to diagnose medical condition of patient. Prescribe or administer medication, therapy, and other specialized medical care to treat or prevent illness, disease, or injury. Provide and

manage long-term, comprehensive medical care, including diagnosis and non-surgical treatment of diseases, for adult patients in an office or hospital. Manage and treat common health problems, such as infections, influenza and pneumonia, as well as serious, chronic, and complex illnesses, in adolescents, adults, and the elderly. Monitor patients' conditions and progress and re-evaluate treatments as necessary. Collect, record, and maintain patient information, such as medical history, reports, and examination results. Make diagnoses when different illnesses occur together or in situations where the diagnosis may be obscure. Explain procedures and discuss test results or prescribed treatments with patients. Advise patients and community members concerning diet, activity, hygiene, and disease prevention. Refer patient to medical specialist or other practitioner when necessary. Immunize patients to protect them from preventable diseases. Advise surgeon of a patient's risk status and recommend appropriate intervention to minimize risk. Direct and coordinate activities of nurses, students, assistants, specialists, therapists, and other medical staff. Provide consulting services to other doctors caring for patients with special or difficult problems. Operate on patients to remove, repair, or improve functioning of diseased or injured body parts and systems. Plan, implement, or administer health programs in hospitals, businesses, or communities for prevention and treatment of injuries or illnesses. Conduct research to develop or test medications, treatments, or procedures to prevent or control disease or injury. Prepare government or organizational reports on birth, death, and disease statistics; workforce evaluations; or the medical status of individuals.

Personality Type: Investigative. These occupations frequently involve working with ideas and require an extensive amount of thinking. They can involve searching for facts and figuring out problems mentally.

GOE—Interest Area/Cluster: 08. Health Science. Work Group: 08.02. Medicine and Surgery. Other Jobs in This Work Group: Anesthesiologists; Family and General Practitioners; Obstetricians and Gynecologists; Pediatricians, General; Pharmacists; Physician Assistants; Psychiatrists; Registered Nurses; Surgeons.

Skills—Science: Using scientific methods to solve problems. Judgment and Decision Making: Weighing the relative costs and benefits of a potential action. Complex Problem Solving: Identifying complex problems, reviewing the options, and implementing solutions. Reading Comprehension: Understanding written sentences and paragraphs in work-related documents. Social Perceptiveness: Being aware of others' reactions and understanding why they react the way they do. Service Orientation: Actively looking for ways to help people. Management of Financial Resources: Determining how money will be spent to get the work done and accounting for these expenditures. Persuasion: Persuading others to approach things differently.

Education and Training Programs: Cardiology; Critical Care Medicine; Endocrinology and Metabolism; Gastroenterology; Geriatric Medicine; Hematology; Infectious Disease; Internal Medicine; Nephrology; Neurology; Nuclear Medicine; Oncology; Pulmonary Disease; Rheumatology. Related Knowledge/Courses—Medicine and Dentistry: The information and techniques needed to diagnose and treat injuries, diseases, and deformities. This includes symptoms, treatment alternatives, drug properties and interactions, and preventive health-care measures. Biology: Plant and animal living tissue, cells, organisms, and entities, including their functions, interdependencies, and interactions with each other and the environment. Therapy and Counseling: Information and techniques needed to rehabilitate physical and mental ailments and to provide career guidance, including alternative treatments, rehabilitation equipment and its proper use, and methods to evaluate treatment effects. Psychology: Human behavior and performance, mental processes, psychological research methods, and the assessment and treatment of behavioral and affective disorders. Chemistry: The composition, structure, and properties of substances and of the chemical processes and transformations that they undergo. This includes uses of chemicals and their interactions, danger signs, production techniques, and disposal methods. Education and Training: Instructional methods and training techniques, including curriculum design principles, learning theory, group and individual teaching techniques, design of individual development plans, and test design principles.

Work Environment: Indoors; disease or infections; standing.

Judges, Magistrate Judges, and Magistrates

* Education/Training Required: Work experience plus degree
* Annual Earnings: $107,230
* Beginning Wage: $31,100
* Earnings Growth Potential: Very high
* Growth: 5.1%
* Annual Job Openings: 1,567
* Self-Employed: 0.0%
* Part-Time: 5.9%

Arbitrate, advise, adjudicate, or administer justice in a court of law. May sentence defendant in criminal cases according to government statutes. May determine liability of defendant in civil cases. May issue marriage licenses and perform wedding ceremonies. Instruct juries on applicable laws, direct juries to deduce the facts from the evidence presented, and hear their verdicts. Sentence defendants in criminal cases on conviction by jury according to applicable government statutes. Rule on admissibility of evidence and methods of conducting testimony. Preside over hearings and listen to allegations made by plaintiffs to determine whether the evidence supports the charges. Read documents on pleadings and motions to ascertain facts and issues. Interpret and enforce rules of procedure or establish new rules in situations where there are no procedures already established by law. Monitor proceedings to ensure that all applicable rules and procedures are followed. Advise attorneys, juries, litigants, and court personnel regarding conduct, issues, and proceedings. Research legal issues and write opinions on the issues. Conduct preliminary hearings to decide issues such as whether there is reasonable and probable cause to hold defendants in felony cases. Write decisions on cases. Award compensation for damages to litigants in civil cases in relation to findings by juries or by the court. Settle disputes between opposing attorneys. Supervise other judges, court officers, and the court's administrative staff. Impose restrictions upon parties in civil cases until trials can be held. Rule on custody and access disputes and enforce court orders regarding custody and support of children. Grant divorces and divide assets between spouses. Participate in judicial tribunals to help resolve disputes. Perform wedding ceremonies.

Personality Type: Enterprising. These occupations frequently involve starting up and carrying out projects and can involve leading people and making many decisions. They sometimes require risk taking and often deal with business.

GOE—Interest Area/Cluster: 12. Law and Public Safety. **Work Group:** 12.02. Legal Practice and Justice Administration. **Other Jobs in This Work Group:** Administrative Law Judges, Adjudicators, and Hearing Officers; Arbitrators, Mediators, and Conciliators; Lawyers.

Skills—Judgment and Decision Making: Weighing the relative costs and benefits of a potential action. **Persuasion:** Persuading others to approach things differently. **Negotiation:** Bringing others together and trying to reconcile differences. **Critical Thinking:** Using logic and analysis to identify the strengths and weaknesses of different approaches. **Active Listening:** Listening to what other people are saying and asking questions as appropriate. **Reading Comprehension:** Understanding written sentences and paragraphs in work-related documents. **Social Perceptiveness:** Being aware of others' reactions and understanding why they react the way they do. **Management of Personnel Resources:** Motivating, developing, and directing people as they work; identifying the best people for the job.

Education and Training Programs: Law (LL.B., J.D.); Legal Professions and Studies, Other. **Related Knowledge/Courses—Law and Government:** Laws, legal codes, court procedures, precedents, government regulations, executive orders, agency rules, and the democratic political process. **Therapy and Counseling:** Information and techniques needed to rehabilitate physical and mental ailments and to provide career guidance, including alternative treatments, rehabilitation equipment and its proper use, and methods to evaluate treatment effects. **Philosophy and Theology:** Different philosophical systems and religions, including their basic principles, values, ethics, ways of thinking, customs, and practices and their impact on human culture. **English Language:** The structure and content of the English language, including the meaning and spelling of words, rules of composition, and grammar. **Psychology:** Human behavior and performance, mental processes, psychological research methods, and the assessment and treatment of behavioral and affective disorders. **Sociology and Anthropology:** Group behavior and dynamics; societal trends and influences; and cultures and their history, migrations, ethnicity, and origins.

Work Environment: Indoors; sitting.

Kindergarten Teachers, Except Special Education

- ❋ Education/Training Required: Bachelor's degree
- ❋ Annual Earnings: $45,120
- ❋ Beginning Wage: $29,300
- ❋ Earnings Growth Potential: Medium
- ❋ Growth: 16.3%
- ❋ Annual Job Openings: 27,603
- ❋ Self-Employed: 1.1%
- ❋ Part-Time: 25.1%

Teach elemental natural and social science, personal hygiene, music, art, and literature to children from 4 to 6 years old. Promote physical, mental, and social development. May be required to hold state certification. Teach basic skills such as color, shape, number, and letter recognition; personal hygiene; and social skills. Establish and enforce rules for behavior and policies and procedures to maintain order among students. Observe and evaluate children's performance, behavior, social development, and physical health. Instruct students individually and in groups, adapting teaching methods to meet students' varying needs and interests. Read books to entire classes or to small groups. Demonstrate activities to children. Provide a variety of materials and resources for children to explore, manipulate, and use, both in learning activities and in imaginative play. Plan and conduct activities for a balanced program of instruction, demonstration, and work time that provides students with opportunities to observe, question, and investigate. Confer with parents or guardians, other teachers, counselors, and administrators to resolve students' behavioral and academic problems. Prepare children for later grades by encouraging them to explore learning opportunities and to persevere with challenging tasks. Establish clear objectives for all lessons, units, and projects and communicate those objectives to children. Prepare and implement remedial programs for students requiring extra help. Meet with parents and guardians to discuss their children's progress and to determine their priorities for their children and their resource needs. Prepare objectives and outlines for courses of study, following curriculum guidelines or requirements of states and schools. Organize and lead activities designed to promote physical, mental, and social development such as games, arts and crafts, music, and storytelling. Guide and counsel students with adjustment or academic problems or special academic interests. Identify children showing signs of emotional, developmental, or health-related problems and discuss them with supervisors, parents or guardians, and child development specialists. Instruct and monitor students in the use and care of equipment and materials to prevent injuries and damage. Assimilate arriving children to the school environment by greeting them, helping them remove outerwear, and selecting activities of interest to them.

Personality Type: Social. These occupations frequently involve working with, communicating with, and teaching people and often involve helping or providing service to others.

GOE—Interest Area/Cluster: 05. Education and Training. **Work Group:** 05.02. Preschool, Elementary, and Secondary Teaching and Instructing. **Other Jobs in This Work Group:** Elementary School Teachers, Except Special Education; Middle School Teachers, Except Special and Vocational Education; Secondary School Teachers, Except Special and Vocational Education; Special Education Teachers, Middle School; Special

Education Teachers, Preschool, Kindergarten, and Elementary School; Special Education Teachers, Secondary School; Vocational Education Teachers, Middle School; Vocational Education Teachers, Secondary School.

Skills—Learning Strategies: Using multiple approaches when learning or teaching new things. **Instructing:** Teaching others how to do something. **Monitoring:** Assessing how well one is doing when learning or doing something. **Social Perceptiveness:** Being aware of others' reactions and understanding why they react the way they do. **Writing:** Communicating effectively with others in writing as indicated by the needs of the audience. **Time Management:** Managing one's own time and the time of others. **Coordination:** Adjusting actions in relation to others' actions. **Speaking:** Talking to others to effectively convey information.

Education and Training Programs: Montessori Teacher Education; Waldorf/Steiner Teacher Education; Kindergarten/Preschool Education and Teaching; Early Childhood Education and Teaching. **Related Knowledge/Courses—History and Archeology:** Historical events and their causes, indicators, and impact on particular civilizations and cultures. **Geography:** Various methods for describing the location and distribution of land, sea, and air masses, including their physical locations, relationships, and characteristics. **Sociology and Anthropology:** Group behavior and dynamics; societal trends and influences; and cultures and their history, migrations, ethnicity, and origins. **Philosophy and Theology:** Different philosophical systems and religions, including their basic principles, values, ethics, ways of thinking, customs, and practices and their impact on human culture. **Psychology:** Human behavior and performance, mental processes, psychological research methods, and the assessment and treatment of behavioral and affective disorders. **Education and Training:** Instructional methods and

training techniques, including curriculum design principles, learning theory, group and individual teaching techniques, design of individual development plans, and test design principles.

Work Environment: Indoors; disease or infections; standing.

Landscape Architects

- ❋ Education/Training Required: Bachelor's degree
- ❋ Annual Earnings: $57,580
- ❋ Beginning Wage: $36,250
- ❋ Earnings Growth Potential: Medium
- ❋ Growth: 16.4%
- ❋ Annual Job Openings: 2,342
- ❋ Self-Employed: 18.5%
- ❋ Part-Time: 6.1%

Plan and design land areas for such projects as parks and other recreational facilities; airports; highways; hospitals; schools; land subdivisions; and commercial, industrial, and residential sites. Prepare site plans, specifications, and cost estimates for land development, coordinating arrangement of existing and proposed land features and structures. Confer with clients, engineering personnel, and architects on overall program. Compile and analyze data on conditions such as location, drainage, and location of structures for environmental reports and landscaping plans. Inspect landscape work to ensure compliance with specifications, approve quality of materials and work, and advise client and construction personnel.

Personality Type: Artistic. These occupations frequently involve working with forms, designs, and patterns. They often require self-expression, and the work can be done without following a clear set of rules.

GOE—Interest Area/Cluster: 02. Architecture and Construction. **Work Group:** 02.02. Architectural Design. **Other Jobs in This Work Group:** Architects, Except Landscape and Naval.

Skills—Operations Analysis: Analyzing needs and product requirements to create a design. **Management of Financial Resources:** Determining how money will be spent to get the work done and accounting for these expenditures. **Coordination:** Adjusting actions in relation to others' actions. **Mathematics:** Using mathematics to solve problems. **Complex Problem Solving:** Identifying complex problems, reviewing the options, and implementing solutions. **Social Perceptiveness:** Being aware of others' reactions and understanding why they react the way they do. **Persuasion:** Persuading others to approach things differently. **Writing:** Communicating effectively with others in writing as indicated by the needs of the audience.

Education and Training Programs: Environmental Design/Architecture; Landscape Architecture (BS, BSLA, BLA, MSLA, MLA, PhD). **Related Knowledge/Courses—Design:** Design techniques, principles, tools, and instruments involved in the production and use of precision technical plans, blueprints, drawings, and models. **Building and Construction:** Materials, methods, and the appropriate tools to construct objects, structures, and buildings. **Geography:** Various methods for describing the location and distribution of land, sea, and air masses, including their physical locations, relationships, and characteristics. **Biology:** Plant and animal living tissue, cells, organisms, and entities, including their functions, interdependencies, and interactions with each other and the environment. **Engineering and Technology:** Equipment, tools, and mechanical devices and their uses to produce motion, light, power, technology, and other applications. **Fine Arts:** Theory and techniques required to produce, compose, and perform works of music, dance, visual arts, drama, and sculpture.

Work Environment: More often indoors than outdoors; very hot or cold; hazardous equipment; minor burns, cuts, bites, or stings; sitting.

Law Teachers, Postsecondary

- ❋ Education/Training Required: First professional degree
- ❋ Annual Earnings: $87,730
- ❋ Beginning Wage: $39,670
- ❋ Earnings Growth Potential: Very high
- ❋ Growth: 22.9%
- ❋ Annual Job Openings: 2,169
- ❋ Self-Employed: 0.4%
- ❋ Part-Time: 27.8%

Teach courses in law. Evaluate and grade students' classwork, assignments, papers, and oral presentations. Compile, administer, and grade examinations or assign this work to others. Prepare and deliver lectures to undergraduate or graduate students on topics such as civil procedure, contracts, and torts. Initiate, facilitate, and moderate classroom discussions. Prepare course materials such as syllabi, homework assignments, and handouts. Keep abreast of developments in their field by reading current literature, talking with colleagues, and participating in professional conferences. Plan, evaluate, and revise curricula, course content, and course materials and methods of instruction. Maintain regularly scheduled office hours to advise and assist students. Conduct research in a particular field of knowledge and publish findings in professional journals, books, or electronic media. Advise students on academic and vocational curricula and on career issues. Supervise undergraduate and/or graduate teaching, internship, and research work.

Select and obtain materials and supplies such as textbooks. Maintain student attendance records, grades, and other required records. Serve on academic or administrative committees that deal with institutional policies, departmental matters, and academic issues. Perform administrative duties such as serving as department head. Collaborate with colleagues to address teaching and research issues. Participate in student recruitment, registration, and placement activities. Compile bibliographies of specialized materials for outside reading assignments. Participate in campus and community events. Act as advisers to student organizations. Assign cases for students to hear and try. Provide professional consulting services to government or industry. Write grant proposals to procure external research funding.

Personality Type: Social. These occupations frequently involve working with, communicating with, and teaching people and often involve helping or providing service to others.

GOE—Interest Area/Cluster: 05. Education and Training. **Work Group:** 05.03. Postsecondary and Adult Teaching and Instructing. **Other Jobs in This Work Group:** Adult Literacy, Remedial Education, and GED Teachers and Instructors; Agricultural Sciences Teachers, Postsecondary; Anthropology and Archeology Teachers, Postsecondary; Architecture Teachers, Postsecondary; Area, Ethnic, and Cultural Studies Teachers, Postsecondary; Art, Drama, and Music Teachers, Postsecondary; Atmospheric, Earth, Marine, and Space Sciences Teachers, Postsecondary; Biological Science Teachers, Postsecondary; Business Teachers, Postsecondary; Chemistry Teachers, Postsecondary; Communications Teachers, Postsecondary; Computer Science Teachers, Postsecondary; Criminal Justice and Law Enforcement Teachers, Postsecondary; Economics Teachers, Postsecondary; Education Teachers, Postsecondary; Engineering Teachers, Postsecondary; English Language and

Literature Teachers, Postsecondary; Environmental Science Teachers, Postsecondary; Farm and Home Management Advisors; Foreign Language and Literature Teachers, Postsecondary; Forestry and Conservation Science Teachers, Postsecondary; Geography Teachers, Postsecondary; Graduate Teaching Assistants; Health Specialties Teachers, Postsecondary; History Teachers, Postsecondary; Home Economics Teachers, Postsecondary; Library Science Teachers, Postsecondary; Mathematical Science Teachers, Postsecondary; Nursing Instructors and Teachers, Postsecondary; Philosophy and Religion Teachers, Postsecondary; Physics Teachers, Postsecondary; Political Science Teachers, Postsecondary; Psychology Teachers, Postsecondary; Recreation and Fitness Studies Teachers, Postsecondary; Social Work Teachers, Postsecondary; Sociology Teachers, Postsecondary.

Skills—Instructing: Teaching others how to do something. **Critical Thinking:** Using logic and analysis to identify the strengths and weaknesses of different approaches. **Writing:** Communicating effectively with others in writing as indicated by the needs of the audience. **Reading Comprehension:** Understanding written sentences and paragraphs in work-related documents. **Persuasion:** Persuading others to approach things differently. **Speaking:** Talking to others to effectively convey information. **Active Listening:** Listening to what other people are saying and asking questions as appropriate. **Learning Strategies:** Using multiple approaches when learning or teaching new things.

Education and Training Programs: Legal Studies, General; Law (LL.B., J.D.). **Related Knowledge/Courses—Law and Government:** Laws, legal codes, court procedures, precedents, government regulations, executive orders, agency rules, and the democratic political process. **English Language:** The structure and content of the English language, including the meaning and spelling of words, rules of composition, and grammar.

History and Archeology: Historical events and their causes, indicators, and impact on particular civilizations and cultures. **Education and Training:** Instructional methods and training techniques, including curriculum design principles, learning theory, group and individual teaching techniques, design of individual development plans, and test design principles. **Philosophy and Theology:** Different philosophical systems and religions, including their basic principles, values, ethics, ways of thinking, customs, and practices and their impact on human culture. **Communications and Media:** Media production, communication, and dissemination techniques and methods, including alternative ways to inform and entertain via written, oral, and visual media.

Work Environment: Indoors; sitting.

Lawyers

- ❋ Education/Training Required: First professional degree
- ❋ Annual Earnings: $106,120
- ❋ Beginning Wage: $52,280
- ❋ Earnings Growth Potential: Very high
- ❋ Growth: 11.0%
- ❋ Annual Job Openings: 49,445
- ❋ Self-Employed: 26.7%
- ❋ Part-Time: 5.9%

Represent clients in criminal and civil litigation and other legal proceedings, draw up legal documents, and manage or advise clients on legal transactions. May specialize in a single area or may practice broadly in many areas of law. Advise clients concerning business transactions, claim liability, advisability of prosecuting or defending lawsuits, or legal rights and obligations. Interpret laws, rulings, and regulations for individuals and businesses. Analyze the probable outcomes of cases, using knowledge of legal precedents. Present and summarize cases to judges and juries. Gather evidence to formulate defense or to initiate legal actions by such means as interviewing clients and witnesses to ascertain the facts of a case. Evaluate findings and develop strategies and arguments in preparation for presentation of cases. Represent clients in court or before government agencies. Examine legal data to determine advisability of defending or prosecuting lawsuit. Select jurors, argue motions, meet with judges, and question witnesses during the course of a trial. Present evidence to defend clients or prosecute defendants in criminal or civil litigation. Study Constitution, statutes, decisions, regulations, and ordinances of quasi-judicial bodies to determine ramifications for cases. Prepare and draft legal documents, such as wills, deeds, patent applications, mortgages, leases, and contracts. Prepare legal briefs and opinions and file appeals in state and federal courts of appeal. Negotiate settlements of civil disputes. Confer with colleagues with specialties in appropriate areas of legal issue to establish and verify bases for legal proceedings. Search for and examine public and other legal records to write opinions or establish ownership. Supervise legal assistants. Perform administrative and management functions related to the practice of law. Act as agent, trustee, guardian, or executor for businesses or individuals. Probate wills and represent and advise executors and administrators of estates. Help develop federal and state programs, draft and interpret laws and legislation, and establish enforcement procedures. Work in environmental law, representing public interest groups, waste disposal companies, or construction firms in their dealings with state and federal agencies.

Personality Type: Enterprising. These occupations frequently involve starting up and carrying out projects and can involve leading people and making many decisions. They sometimes require risk taking and often deal with business.

GOE—Interest Area/Cluster: 12. Law and Public Safety. Work Group: 12.02. Legal Practice and Justice Administration. Other Jobs in This Work Group: Administrative Law Judges, Adjudicators, and Hearing Officers; Arbitrators, Mediators, and Conciliators; Judges, Magistrate Judges, and Magistrates.

Skills—Persuasion: Persuading others to approach things differently. Negotiation: Bringing others together and trying to reconcile differences. Writing: Communicating effectively with others in writing as indicated by the needs of the audience. Judgment and Decision Making: Weighing the relative costs and benefits of a potential action. Critical Thinking: Using logic and analysis to identify the strengths and weaknesses of different approaches. Reading Comprehension: Understanding written sentences and paragraphs in work-related documents. Speaking: Talking to others to effectively convey information. Active Listening: Listening to what other people are saying and asking questions as appropriate.

Education and Training Programs: Law (LL.B., J.D.); Advanced Legal Research/Studies, General (LL.M., M.C.L., M.L.I., M.S.L., J.S.D./S.J.D.); Programs for Foreign Lawyers (LL.M., M.C.L.); American/U.S. Law/Legal Studies/Jurisprudence (LL.M., M.C.J., J.S.D./S.J.D.); Canadian Law/ Legal Studies/Jurisprudence (LL.M., M.C.J., J.S.D./S.J.D.); Banking, Corporate, Finance, and Securities Law (LL.M., J.S.D./S.J.D.); Comparative Law (LL.M., M.C.L., J.S.D./S.J.D.); others. Related Knowledge/Courses—Law and Government: Laws, legal codes, court procedures, precedents, government regulations, executive orders, agency rules, and the democratic political process. English Language: The structure and content of the English language, including the meaning and spelling of words, rules of composition, and grammar. Personnel and Human Resources: Principles and procedures for personnel recruitment; selection; training; compensation and benefits; labor relations and negotiation; and personnel information systems. Economics and Accounting: Economic and accounting principles and practices, the financial markets, banking, and the analysis and reporting of financial data. Psychology: Human behavior and performance, mental processes, psychological research methods, and the assessment and treatment of behavioral and affective disorders. Administration and Management: Principles and processes involved in business and organizational planning, coordination, and execution. This includes strategic planning, resource allocation, manpower modeling, leadership techniques, and production methods.

Work Environment: Indoors; sitting.

Legal Secretaries

* Education/Training Required: Associate degree
* Annual Earnings: $38,810
* Beginning Wage: $24,380
* Earnings Growth Potential: Medium
* Growth: 11.7%
* Annual Job Openings: 38,682
* Self-Employed: 1.4%
* Part-Time: 18.9%

Perform secretarial duties, utilizing legal terminology, procedures, and documents. Prepare legal papers and correspondence, such as summonses, complaints, motions, and subpoenas. May also assist with legal research. Prepare and process legal documents and papers, such as summonses, subpoenas, complaints, appeals, motions, and pretrial agreements. Mail, fax, or arrange for delivery of legal correspondence to clients, witnesses, and court officials. Receive and place telephone calls. Schedule and make appointments.

Make photocopies of correspondence, documents, and other printed matter. Organize and maintain law libraries, documents, and case files. Assist attorneys in collecting information such as employment, medical, and other records. Attend legal meetings, such as client interviews, hearings, or depositions, and take notes. Draft and type office memos. Review legal publications and perform database searches to identify laws and court decisions relevant to pending cases. Submit articles and information from searches to attorneys for review and approval for use. Complete various forms such as accident reports, trial and courtroom requests, and applications for clients.

Personality Type: Conventional. These occupations frequently involve following set procedures and routines and can include working with data and details more than with ideas. Usually there is a clear line of authority to follow.

GOE—Interest Area/Cluster: 04. Business and Administration. **Work Group:** 04.04. Secretarial Support. **Other Jobs in This Work Group:** No others in group.

Skills—Writing: Communicating effectively with others in writing as indicated by the needs of the audience. **Reading Comprehension:** Understanding written sentences and paragraphs in work-related documents. **Time Management:** Managing one's own time and the time of others. **Social Perceptiveness:** Being aware of others' reactions and understanding why they react the way they do. **Judgment and Decision Making:** Weighing the relative costs and benefits of a potential action. **Operation and Control:** Controlling operations of equipment or systems. **Active Listening:** Listening to what other people are saying and asking questions as appropriate. **Speaking:** Talking to others to effectively convey information.

Education and Training Program: Legal Administrative Assistant/Secretary. **Related Knowledge/**

Courses—Clerical Practices: Administrative and clerical procedures and systems such as word-processing systems, filing and records management systems, stenography and transcription, forms, design principles, and other office procedures and terminology. **Law and Government:** Laws, legal codes, court procedures, precedents, government regulations, executive orders, agency rules, and the democratic political process. **Economics and Accounting:** Economic and accounting principles and practices, the financial markets, banking, and the analysis and reporting of financial data. **Computers and Electronics:** Electric circuit boards, processors, chips, and computer hardware and software, including applications and programming. **Customer and Personal Service:** Principles and processes for providing customer and personal services, including needs assessment techniques, quality service standards, alternative delivery systems, and customer satisfaction evaluation techniques.

Work Environment: Indoors; sitting; repetitive motions.

Library Science Teachers, Postsecondary

- ❋ Education/Training Required: Doctoral degree
- ❋ Annual Earnings: $56,810
- ❋ Beginning Wage: $34,850
- ❋ Earnings Growth Potential: Medium
- ❋ Growth: 22.9%
- ❋ Annual Job Openings: 702
- ❋ Self-Employed: 0.4%
- ❋ Part-Time: 27.8%

Teach courses in library science. Prepare course materials such as syllabi, homework assignments, and handouts. Prepare and deliver lectures to undergraduate or graduate students on topics such as collection development, archival methods, and indexing and abstracting. Evaluate and grade students' classwork, assignments, and papers. Keep abreast of developments in their field by reading current literature, talking with colleagues, and participating in professional conferences. Initiate, facilitate, and moderate classroom discussions. Plan, evaluate, and revise curricula, course content, and course materials and methods of instruction. Conduct research in a particular field of knowledge and publish findings in professional journals, books, and/or electronic media. Maintain student attendance records, grades, and other required records. Collaborate with colleagues to address teaching and research issues. Advise students on academic and vocational curricula and on career issues. Compile, administer, and grade examinations or assign this work to others. Supervise undergraduate or graduate teaching, internship, and research work. Maintain regularly scheduled office hours in order to advise and assist students. Write grant proposals to procure external research funding. Select and obtain materials and supplies such as textbooks. Serve on academic or administrative committees that deal with institutional policies, departmental matters, and academic issues. Compile bibliographies of specialized materials for outside reading assignments. Participate in student recruitment, registration, and placement activities. Perform administrative duties such as serving as department head. Participate in campus and community events. Act as advisers to student organizations. Provide professional consulting services to government and/or industry.

Personality Type: Social. These occupations frequently involve working with, communicating with, and teaching people and often involve helping or providing service to others.

GOE—Interest Area/Cluster: 05. Education and Training. **Work Group:** 05.03. Postsecondary

and Adult Teaching and Instructing. **Other Jobs in This Work Group:** Adult Literacy, Remedial Education, and GED Teachers and Instructors; Agricultural Sciences Teachers, Postsecondary; Anthropology and Archeology Teachers, Postsecondary; Architecture Teachers, Postsecondary; Area, Ethnic, and Cultural Studies Teachers, Postsecondary; Art, Drama, and Music Teachers, Postsecondary; Atmospheric, Earth, Marine, and Space Sciences Teachers, Postsecondary; Biological Science Teachers, Postsecondary; Business Teachers, Postsecondary; Chemistry Teachers, Postsecondary; Communications Teachers, Postsecondary; Computer Science Teachers, Postsecondary; Criminal Justice and Law Enforcement Teachers, Postsecondary; Economics Teachers, Postsecondary; Education Teachers, Postsecondary; Engineering Teachers, Postsecondary; English Language and Literature Teachers, Postsecondary; Environmental Science Teachers, Postsecondary; Farm and Home Management Advisors; Foreign Language and Literature Teachers, Postsecondary; Forestry and Conservation Science Teachers, Postsecondary; Geography Teachers, Postsecondary; Graduate Teaching Assistants; Health Specialties Teachers, Postsecondary; History Teachers, Postsecondary; Home Economics Teachers, Postsecondary; Law Teachers, Postsecondary; Mathematical Science Teachers, Postsecondary; Nursing Instructors and Teachers, Postsecondary; Philosophy and Religion Teachers, Postsecondary; Physics Teachers, Postsecondary; Political Science Teachers, Postsecondary; Psychology Teachers, Postsecondary; Recreation and Fitness Studies Teachers, Postsecondary; Social Work Teachers, Postsecondary; Sociology Teachers, Postsecondary.

Skills—Writing: Communicating effectively with others in writing as indicated by the needs of the audience. **Learning Strategies:** Using multiple approaches when learning or teaching new things. **Instructing:** Teaching others how to do something. **Reading Comprehension:** Understanding written sentences and paragraphs in work-related documents. **Active Learning:** Working with new material or information to grasp its implications. **Monitoring:** Assessing how well one is doing when learning or doing something. **Operations Analysis:** Analyzing needs and product requirements to create a design. **Speaking:** Talking to others to effectively convey information.

Education and Training Programs: Teacher Education and Professional Development, Specific Subject Areas, Other; Library Science/Librarianship. **Related Knowledge/Courses—Education and Training:** Instructional methods and training techniques, including curriculum design principles, learning theory, group and individual teaching techniques, design of individual development plans, and test design principles. **Sociology and Anthropology:** Group behavior and dynamics; societal trends and influences; and cultures and their history, migrations, ethnicity, and origins. **English Language:** The structure and content of the English language, including the meaning and spelling of words, rules of composition, and grammar. **Communications and Media:** Media production, communication, and dissemination techniques and methods, including alternative ways to inform and entertain via written, oral, and visual media. **History and Archeology:** Historical events and their causes, indicators, and impact on particular civilizations and cultures. **Philosophy and Theology:** Different philosophical systems and religions, including their basic principles, values, ethics, ways of thinking, customs, and practices and their impact on human culture.

Work Environment: Indoors; sitting.

Loan Officers

- ✱ Education/Training Required: Bachelor's degree
- ✱ Annual Earnings: $53,000
- ✱ Beginning Wage: $30,340
- ✱ Earnings Growth Potential: High
- ✱ Growth: 11.5%
- ✱ Annual Job Openings: 54,237
- ✱ Self-Employed: 2.9%
- ✱ Part-Time: 6.6%

Evaluate, authorize, or recommend approval of commercial, real estate, or credit loans. Advise borrowers on financial status and methods of payments. Includes mortgage loan officers and agents, collection analysts, loan servicing officers, and loan underwriters. Meet with applicants to obtain information for loan applications and to answer questions about the process. Approve loans within specified limits and refer loan applications outside those limits to management for approval. Analyze applicants' financial status, credit, and property evaluations to determine feasibility of granting loans. Explain to customers the different types of loans and credit options that are available, as well as the terms of those services. Obtain and compile copies of loan applicants' credit histories, corporate financial statements, and other financial information. Review and update credit and loan files. Review loan agreements to ensure that they are complete and accurate according to policy. Compute payment schedules. Stay abreast of new types of loans and other financial services and products to better meet customers' needs. Submit applications to credit analysts for verification and recommendation. Handle customer complaints and take appropriate action to resolve them. Work with clients to identify their financial goals and to find ways of reaching those goals. Confer with underwriters to aid in resolving mortgage application problems. Negotiate payment arrangements with customers who have delinquent loans. Market bank products to individuals and firms, promoting bank services that may meet customers' needs. Supervise loan personnel. Set credit policies, credit lines, procedures, and standards in conjunction with senior managers. Provide special services such as investment banking for clients with more specialized needs. Analyze potential loan markets and develop referral networks to locate prospects for loans. Prepare reports to send to customers whose accounts are delinquent and forward irreconcilable accounts for collector action. Arrange for maintenance and liquidation of delinquent properties. Interview, hire, and train new employees. Petition courts to transfer titles and deeds of collateral to banks.

Personality Type: Conventional. These occupations frequently involve following set procedures and routines and can include working with data and details more than with ideas. Usually there is a clear line of authority to follow.

GOE—Interest Area/Cluster: 06. Finance and Insurance. **Work Group:** 06.02. Finance/Insurance Investigation and Analysis. **Other Jobs in This Work Group:** Appraisers and Assessors of Real Estate; Appraisers, Real Estate; Assessors; Cost Estimators; Credit Analysts; Financial Analysts; Insurance Underwriters; Loan Counselors; Market Research Analysts; Survey Researchers.

Skills—Persuasion: Persuading others to approach things differently. **Social Perceptiveness:** Being aware of others' reactions and understanding why they react the way they do. **Service Orientation:** Actively looking for ways to help people. **Complex Problem Solving:** Identifying complex problems, reviewing the options, and implementing solutions. **Negotiation:** Bringing others together and trying to reconcile differences. **Instructing:** Teaching others how to do something. **Speaking:** Talking to others to effectively convey information.

Judgment and Decision Making: Weighing the relative costs and benefits of a potential action.

Education and Training Programs: Finance, General; Credit Management. **Related Knowledge/Courses—Economics and Accounting:** Economic and accounting principles and practices, the financial markets, banking, and the analysis and reporting of financial data. **Sales and Marketing:** Principles and methods involved in showing, promoting, and selling products or services. This includes marketing strategies and tactics, product demonstration and sales techniques, and sales control systems. **Law and Government:** Laws, legal codes, court procedures, precedents, government regulations, executive orders, agency rules, and the democratic political process. **English Language:** The structure and content of the English language, including the meaning and spelling of words, rules of composition, and grammar. **Mathematics:** Numbers and their operations and interrelationships, including arithmetic, algebra, geometry, calculus, and statistics and their applications. **Customer and Personal Service:** Principles and processes for providing customer and personal services, including needs assessment techniques, quality service standards, alternative delivery systems, and customer satisfaction evaluation techniques.

Work Environment: Indoors; sitting; repetitive motions.

Logisticians

- ❈ Education/Training Required: Bachelor's degree
- ❈ Annual Earnings: $64,250
- ❈ Beginning Wage: $38,280
- ❈ Earnings Growth Potential: High
- ❈ Growth: 17.3%
- ❈ Annual Job Openings: 9,671
- ❈ Self-Employed: 1.5%
- ❈ Part-Time: 3.6%

Analyze and coordinate the logistical functions of a firm or organization. Responsible for the entire life cycle of a product, including acquisition, distribution, internal allocation, delivery, and final disposal of resources. Maintain and develop positive business relationships with a customer's key personnel involved in or directly relevant to a logistics activity. Develop an understanding of customers' needs and take actions to ensure that such needs are met. Direct availability and allocation of materials, supplies, and finished products. Collaborate with other departments as necessary to meet customer requirements, to take advantage of sales opportunities, or, in the case of shortages, to minimize negative impacts on a business. Protect and control proprietary materials. Review logistics performance with customers against targets, benchmarks, and service agreements. Develop and implement technical project management tools such as plans, schedules, and responsibility and compliance matrices. Direct team activities, establishing task priorities, scheduling and tracking work assignments, providing guidance, and ensuring the availability of resources. Report project plans, progress, and results. Direct and support the compilation and analysis of technical source data necessary for product development. Explain proposed solutions to customers, management, or other interested parties through written proposals and oral presentations. Provide project management services, including the provision and analysis of technical data. Develop proposals that include documentation for estimates. Plan, organize, and execute logistics support activities such as maintenance planning, repair analysis, and test equipment recommendations. Participate in the assessment and review of design alternatives and design change proposal impacts. Support the development of training materials and technical manuals. Stay informed of logistics technology advances and apply appropriate technology in order to improve logistics processes. Redesign the movement of goods in order to maximize value and minimize costs. Manage subcontractor activities, reviewing proposals, developing performance specifications, and serving as liaisons between subcontractors and organizations. Manage the logistical aspects of product life cycles, including coordination or provisioning of samples and the minimization of obsolescence.

Personality Type: Enterprising. These occupations frequently involve starting up and carrying out projects and can involve leading people and making many decisions. They sometimes require risk taking and often deal with business.

GOE—Interest Area/Cluster: 04. Business and Administration. **Work Group:** 04.05. Accounting, Auditing, and Analytical Support. **Other Jobs in This Work Group:** Accountants; Accountants and Auditors; Auditors; Budget Analysts; Industrial Engineering Technicians; Management Analysts; Operations Research Analysts.

Skills—Management of Financial Resources: Determining how money will be spent to get the work done and accounting for these expenditures. **Management of Material Resources:** Obtaining and seeing to the appropriate use of equipment, facilities, and materials needed to do certain work. **Systems Analysis:** Determining how a system should work and how changes will affect outcomes.

Operations Analysis: Analyzing needs and product requirements to create a design. **Management of Personnel Resources:** Motivating, developing, and directing people as they work; identifying the best people for the job. **Service Orientation:** Actively looking for ways to help people. **Persuasion:** Persuading others to approach things differently. **Technology Design:** Generating or adapting equipment and technology to serve user needs.

Education and Training Programs: Logistics and Materials Management; Operations Management and Supervision; Transportation/Transportation Management. **Related Knowledge/Courses—Telecommunications:** Transmission, broadcasting, switching, control, and operation of telecommunications systems. **Geography:** Various methods for describing the location and distribution of land, sea, and air masses, including their physical locations, relationships, and characteristics. **Computers and Electronics:** Electric circuit boards, processors, chips, and computer hardware and software, including applications and programming. **Administration and Management:** Principles and processes involved in business and organizational planning, coordination, and execution. This includes strategic planning, resource allocation, manpower modeling, leadership techniques, and production methods. **Economics and Accounting:** Economic and accounting principles and practices, the financial markets, banking, and the analysis and reporting of financial data. **Public Safety and Security:** Weaponry; public safety; security operations, rules, regulations, precautions, and prevention; and the protection of people, data, and property.

Work Environment: Indoors; sitting.

Management Analysts

- ❋ Education/Training Required: Work experience plus degree
- ❋ Annual Earnings: $71,150
- ❋ Beginning Wage: $40,860
- ❋ Earnings Growth Potential: High
- ❋ Growth: 21.9%
- ❋ Annual Job Openings: 125,669
- ❋ Self-Employed: 27.0%
- ❋ Part-Time: 13.2%

Conduct organizational studies and evaluations, design systems and procedures, conduct work simplifications and measurement studies, and prepare operations and procedures manuals to assist management in operating more efficiently and effectively. Includes program analysts and management consultants. Gather and organize information on problems or procedures. Analyze data gathered and develop solutions or alternative methods of proceeding. Confer with personnel concerned to ensure successful functioning of newly implemented systems or procedures. Develop and implement records management program for filing, protection, and retrieval of records and assure compliance with program. Review forms and reports and confer with management and users about format, distribution, and purpose and to identify problems and improvements. Document findings of study and prepare recommendations for implementation of new systems, procedures, or organizational changes. Interview personnel and conduct on-site observation to ascertain unit functions; work performed; and methods, equipment, and personnel used. Prepare manuals and train workers in use of new forms, reports, procedures, or equipment according to organizational policy. Design, evaluate, recommend, and approve changes of forms and reports. Plan study of work problems and procedures, such as organizational change, communications, information flow, integrated production methods, inventory control, or cost analysis. Recommend purchase of storage equipment and design area layout to locate equipment in space available.

Personality Type: Investigative. These occupations frequently involve working with ideas and require an extensive amount of thinking. They can involve searching for facts and figuring out problems mentally.

GOE—Interest Area/Cluster: 04. Business and Administration. **Work Group:** 04.05. Accounting, Auditing, and Analytical Support. **Other Jobs in This Work Group:** Accountants; Accountants and Auditors; Auditors; Budget Analysts; Industrial Engineering Technicians; Logisticians; Operations Research Analysts.

Skills—Operations Analysis: Analyzing needs and product requirements to create a design. **Systems Evaluation:** Looking at many indicators of system performance and taking into account their accuracy. **Installation:** Installing equipment, machines, wiring, or programs to meet specifications. **Management of Financial Resources:** Determining how money will be spent to get the work done and accounting for these expenditures. **Quality Control Analysis:** Evaluating the quality or performance of products, services, or processes. **Operation and Control:** Controlling operations of equipment or systems. **Systems Analysis:** Determining how a system should work and how changes will affect outcomes. **Equipment Maintenance:** Performing routine maintenance and determining when and what kind of maintenance is needed.

Education and Training Programs: Business/Commerce, General; Business Administration and Management, General. **Related Knowledge/Courses—Personnel and Human Resources:** Principles and procedures for personnel recruitment; selection; training; compensation and benefits; labor relations and negotiation; and personnel information systems. **Clerical Practices:** Administrative and clerical procedures and systems such as word-processing systems, filing and records management systems, stenography and transcription, forms, design principles, and other office procedures and terminology. **Sales and Marketing:** Principles and methods involved in showing, promoting, and selling products or services. This includes marketing strategies and tactics, product demonstration and sales techniques, and sales control systems. **Economics and Accounting:** Economic and accounting principles and practices, the financial markets, banking, and the analysis and reporting of financial data. **Customer and Personal Service:** Principles and processes for providing customer and personal services, including needs assessment techniques, quality service standards, alternative delivery systems, and customer satisfaction evaluation techniques. **Administration and Management:** Principles and processes involved in business and organizational planning, coordination, and execution. This includes strategic planning, resource allocation, manpower modeling, leadership techniques, and production methods.

Work Environment: Indoors; sitting.

Market Research Analysts

- ❋ Education/Training Required: Bachelor's degree
- ❋ Annual Earnings: $60,300
- ❋ Beginning Wage: $33,310
- ❋ Earnings Growth Potential: High
- ❋ Growth: 20.1%
- ❋ Annual Job Openings: 45,015
- ❋ Self-Employed: 6.6%
- ❋ Part-Time: 12.5%

Research market conditions in local, regional, or national areas to determine potential sales of a product or service. May gather information on competitors, prices, sales, and methods of marketing and distribution. May use survey results to create a marketing campaign based on regional preferences and buying habits. Collect and analyze data on customer demographics, preferences, needs, and buying habits to identify potential markets and factors affecting product demand. Prepare reports of findings, illustrating data graphically and translating complex findings into written text. Measure and assess customer and employee satisfaction. Forecast and track marketing and sales trends, analyzing collected data. Seek and provide information to help companies determine their position in the marketplace. Measure the effectiveness of marketing, advertising, and communications programs and strategies. Conduct research on consumer opinions and marketing strategies, collaborating with marketing professionals, statisticians, pollsters, and other professionals. Attend staff conferences to provide management with information and proposals concerning the promotion, distribution, design, and pricing of company products or services. Gather data on competitors and analyze their prices, sales, and method of marketing and distribution. Monitor industry statistics and follow trends in trade literature. Devise and evaluate methods and procedures for collecting data, such as surveys, opinion polls, or questionnaires, or arrange to obtain existing data. Develop and implement procedures for identifying advertising needs. Direct trained survey interviewers.

Personality Type: Investigative. These occupations frequently involve working with ideas and require an extensive amount of thinking. They can involve searching for facts and figuring out problems mentally.

GOE—Interest Area/Cluster: 06. Finance and Insurance. **Work Group:** 06.02. Finance/Insurance Investigation and Analysis. **Other Jobs in This Work Group:** Appraisers and Assessors of Real Estate; Appraisers, Real Estate; Assessors; Cost Estimators; Credit Analysts; Financial Analysts; Insurance Underwriters; Loan Counselors; Loan Officers; Survey Researchers.

Skills—Writing: Communicating effectively with others in writing as indicated by the needs of the audience. **Negotiation:** Bringing others together and trying to reconcile differences. **Persuasion:** Persuading others to approach things differently. **Judgment and Decision Making:** Weighing the relative costs and benefits of a potential action. **Reading Comprehension:** Understanding written sentences and paragraphs in work-related documents. **Management of Financial Resources:** Determining how money will be spent to get the work done and accounting for these expenditures. **Coordination:** Adjusting actions in relation to others' actions. **Active Listening:** Listening to what other people are saying and asking questions as appropriate.

Education and Training Programs: Economics, General; Applied Economics; Econometrics and Quantitative Economics; International Economics; Business/Managerial Economics; Marketing Research. **Related Knowledge/Courses—Sales and Marketing:** Principles and methods involved in showing, promoting, and selling products or services. This includes marketing strategies and tactics, product demonstration and sales techniques, and sales control systems. **Communications and Media:** Media production, communication, and dissemination techniques and methods, including alternative ways to inform and entertain via written, oral, and visual media. **Administration and Management:** Principles and processes involved in business and organizational planning, coordination, and execution. This includes strategic planning, resource allocation, manpower modeling, leadership techniques, and production methods. **Economics and Accounting:** Economic and accounting principles and practices, the financial markets, banking, and the analysis and reporting of financial data. **Clerical Practices:** Administrative and clerical procedures and systems such as word-processing systems, filing and records management systems, stenography and transcription, forms, design principles, and other office procedures and terminology. **Computers and Electronics:** Electric circuit boards, processors, chips, and computer hardware and software, including applications and programming.

Work Environment: Indoors; sitting.

Marketing Managers

- ❋ Education/Training Required: Work experience plus degree
- ❋ Annual Earnings: $104,400
- ❋ Beginning Wage: $53,520
- ❋ Earnings Growth Potential: High
- ❋ Growth: 14.4%
- ❋ Annual Job Openings: 20,189
- ❋ Self-Employed: 2.3%
- ❋ Part-Time: 4.1%

Determine the demand for products and services offered by firms and their competitors, and identify potential customers. Develop pricing strategies with the goal of maximizing firms' profits or shares of the market while ensuring that firms' customers are satisfied. Oversee product development or monitor trends that indicate the need for new products and services. Formulate, direct, and coordinate marketing activities and policies to promote products and services, working with advertising and promotion managers. Identify, develop, and evaluate marketing strategies, based on knowledge of establishment objectives, market characteristics, and cost and markup factors. Direct the hiring, training, and performance evaluations of marketing and sales staff and oversee their daily activities. Evaluate the financial aspects of product development, such as budgets, expenditures, research and development appropriations, and return-on-investment and profit-loss projections. Develop pricing strategies, balancing firm objectives and customer satisfaction. Compile lists describing product or service offerings. Initiate market research studies and analyze their findings. Use sales forecasting and strategic planning to ensure the sale and profitability of products, lines, or services, analyzing business developments and monitoring market trends. Coordinate and participate in promotional activities and trade shows, working with developers, advertisers, and production managers, to market products and services. Consult with buying personnel to gain advice regarding the types of products or services expected to be in demand. Conduct economic and commercial surveys to identify potential markets for products and services. Select products and accessories to be displayed at trade or special production shows. Negotiate contracts with vendors and distributors to manage product distribution, establishing distribution networks and developing distribution strategies. Consult with product development personnel on product specifications such as design, color, and packaging. Advise businesses and other groups on local, national, and international factors affecting the buying and selling of products and services. Confer with legal staff to resolve problems such as copyright infringement and royalty sharing with outside producers and distributors.

Personality Type: Enterprising. These occupations frequently involve starting up and carrying out projects and can involve leading people and making many decisions. They sometimes require risk taking and often deal with business.

GOE—Interest Area/Cluster: 14. Retail and Wholesale Sales and Service. **Work Group:** 14.01. Managerial Work in Retail/Wholesale Sales and Service. **Other Jobs in This Work Group:** Advertising and Promotions Managers; Funeral Directors; Property, Real Estate, and Community Association Managers; Purchasing Managers; Sales Managers.

Skills—Management of Personnel Resources: Motivating, developing, and directing people as they work; identifying the best people for the job. **Systems Analysis:** Determining how a system should work and how changes will affect outcomes. **Systems Evaluation:** Looking at many indicators of system performance and taking into account their accuracy. **Persuasion:** Persuading others to approach things differently. **Negotiation:** Bringing others together and trying to reconcile differences. **Management of Financial Resources:** Determining how money will be spent to get the work done and accounting for these expenditures. **Writing:** Communicating effectively with others in writing as indicated by the needs of the audience. **Social Perceptiveness:** Being aware of others' reactions and understanding why they react the way they do.

Education and Training Programs: Consumer Merchandising/Retailing Management; Apparel and Textile Marketing Management; Marketing/Marketing Management, General; Marketing Research; International Marketing; Marketing, Other. **Related Knowledge/Courses—Sales and Marketing:** Principles and methods involved in showing, promoting, and selling products or services. This includes marketing strategies and tactics, product demonstration and sales techniques, and sales control systems. **Personnel and Human Resources:** Principles and procedures for personnel recruitment; selection; training; compensation and benefits; labor relations and negotiation; and personnel information systems. **Customer and Personal Service:** Principles and processes for providing customer and personal services, including needs assessment techniques, quality service standards, alternative delivery systems, and customer satisfaction evaluation techniques. **Communications and Media:** Media production, communication, and dissemination techniques and methods, including alternative ways to inform and entertain via written, oral, and visual media. **Sociology and Anthropology:** Group behavior and dynamics; societal trends and influences; and cultures and their history, migrations, ethnicity, and origins. **Economics and Accounting:** Economic and accounting principles and practices, the financial markets, banking, and the analysis and reporting of financial data.

Work Environment: Indoors; sitting.

Marriage and Family Therapists

- ❋ Education/Training Required: Master's degree
- ❋ Annual Earnings: $43,600
- ❋ Beginning Wage: $26,080
- ❋ Earnings Growth Potential: High
- ❋ Growth: 29.8%
- ❋ Annual Job Openings: 5,953
- ❋ Self-Employed: 6.2%
- ❋ Part-Time: 15.4%

Diagnose and treat mental and emotional disorders, whether cognitive, affective, or behavioral, within the context of marriage and family systems. Apply psychotherapeutic and family systems theories and techniques in the delivery of professional services to individuals, couples, and families for the purpose of treating such diagnosed nervous and mental disorders. Ask questions that will help clients identify their feelings and behaviors. Counsel clients on concerns such as unsatisfactory relationships, divorce and separation, child rearing, home management, and financial difficulties. Encourage individuals and family members to develop and use skills and strategies for confronting their problems in a constructive manner. Maintain case files that include activities, progress notes, evaluations, and recommendations. Collect information about clients, using techniques such as testing, interviewing, discussion, and observation. Develop and implement individualized treatment plans addressing family relationship problems. Determine whether clients should be counseled or referred to other specialists in such fields as medicine, psychiatry, and legal aid. Confer with clients in order to develop plans for post-treatment activities. Confer with other counselors to analyze individual cases and to coordinate counseling services. Follow up on results of counseling programs and clients' adjustments to determine effectiveness of programs. Provide instructions to clients on how to obtain help with legal, financial, and other personal issues. Contact doctors, schools, social workers, juvenile counselors, law enforcement personnel, and others to gather information in order to make recommendations to courts for the resolution of child custody or visitation disputes. Provide public education and consultation to other professionals or groups regarding counseling services, issues, and methods. Supervise other counselors, social service staff, and assistants. Provide family counseling and treatment services to inmates participating in substance abuse programs. Write evaluations of parents and children for use by courts deciding divorce and custody cases, testifying in court if necessary.

Personality Type: Social. These occupations frequently involve working with, communicating with, and teaching people and often involve helping or providing service to others.

GOE—Interest Area/Cluster: 10. Human Service. **Work Group:** 10.01. Counseling and Social Work. **Other Jobs in This Work Group:** Child, Family, and School Social Workers; Clinical Psychologists; Clinical, Counseling, and School Psychologists; Counseling Psychologists; Medical and Public Health Social Workers; Mental Health and Substance Abuse Social Workers; Mental Health Counselors; Probation Officers and Correctional Treatment Specialists; Rehabilitation Counselors; Substance Abuse and Behavioral Disorder Counselors.

Skills—Social Perceptiveness: Being aware of others' reactions and understanding why they react the way they do. **Negotiation:** Bringing others together and trying to reconcile differences. **Active Listening:** Listening to what other people are saying and asking questions as appropriate. **Persuasion:** Persuading others to approach things differently. **Service Orientation:** Actively looking for ways to help people. **Monitoring:** Assessing how well one is doing when learning or doing something. **Judgment and Decision Making:** Weighing the relative costs and benefits of a potential action. **Writing:** Communicating effectively with others in writing as indicated by the needs of the audience.

Education and Training Programs: Social Work; Marriage and Family Therapy/Counseling; Clinical Pastoral Counseling/Patient Counseling. **Related Knowledge/Courses—Therapy and Counseling:** Information and techniques needed to rehabilitate physical and mental ailments and to provide career guidance, including alternative treatments, rehabilitation equipment and its proper use, and methods to evaluate treatment effects. **Psychology:** Human behavior and performance, mental processes, psychological research methods, and the assessment and treatment of behavioral and affective disorders. **Philosophy and Theology:** Different philosophical systems and religions, including their basic principles, values, ethics, ways of thinking, customs, and practices and their impact on human culture. **Sociology and Anthropology:** Group behavior and dynamics; societal trends and influences; and cultures and their history, migrations, ethnicity, and origins. **Medicine and Dentistry:** The information and techniques needed to diagnose and treat injuries, diseases, and deformities. This includes symptoms, treatment alternatives, drug properties and interactions, and preventive health-care measures. **Customer and Personal Service:** Principles and processes for providing customer and personal services, including needs assessment techniques, quality service standards, alternative delivery systems, and customer satisfaction evaluation techniques.

Work Environment: Indoors; sitting.

Mathematical Science Teachers, Postsecondary

- ❋ Education/Training Required: Doctoral degree
- ❋ Annual Earnings: $58,560
- ❋ Beginning Wage: $32,690
- ❋ Earnings Growth Potential: High
- ❋ Growth: 22.9%
- ❋ Annual Job Openings: 7,663
- ❋ Self-Employed: 0.4%
- ❋ Part-Time: 27.8%

Teach courses pertaining to mathematical concepts, statistics, and actuarial science and to the application of original and standardized mathematical techniques in solving specific problems and situations. Evaluate and grade students' classwork, assignments, and papers. Compile, administer, and grade examinations or assign this work to others. Prepare and deliver lectures to undergraduate and/or graduate students on topics such as linear algebra, differential equations, and discrete mathematics. Prepare course materials such as syllabi, homework assignments, and handouts. Maintain student attendance records, grades, and other required records. Maintain regularly scheduled office hours to advise and assist students. Plan, evaluate, and revise curricula, course content, and course materials and methods of instruction. Initiate, facilitate, and moderate classroom discussions. Select and obtain materials and supplies such as textbooks. Keep abreast of developments in their field by reading current literature, talking with colleagues, and participating in professional conferences. Advise students on academic and vocational curricula and on career issues. Collaborate with colleagues to address teaching and research issues. Serve on academic or administrative committees that deal with institutional policies, departmental matters, and academic issues. Participate in student recruitment, registration, and placement activities. Perform administrative duties such as serving as department head. Conduct research in a particular field of knowledge and publish findings in books, professional journals, and/or electronic media. Supervise undergraduate and/or graduate teaching, internship, and research work. Act as advisers to student organizations. Participate in campus and community events. Write grant proposals to procure external research funding. Compile bibliographies of specialized materials for outside reading assignments. Provide professional consulting services to government and/or industry.

Personality Type: Social. These occupations frequently involve working with, communicating with, and teaching people and often involve helping or providing service to others.

GOE—Interest Area/Cluster: 05. Education and Training. **Work Group:** 05.03. Postsecondary and Adult Teaching and Instructing. **Other Jobs in This Work Group:** Adult Literacy, Remedial Education, and GED Teachers and Instructors;

Agricultural Sciences Teachers, Postsecondary; Anthropology and Archeology Teachers, Postsecondary; Architecture Teachers, Postsecondary; Area, Ethnic, and Cultural Studies Teachers, Postsecondary; Art, Drama, and Music Teachers, Postsecondary; Atmospheric, Earth, Marine, and Space Sciences Teachers, Postsecondary; Biological Science Teachers, Postsecondary; Business Teachers, Postsecondary; Chemistry Teachers, Postsecondary; Communications Teachers, Postsecondary; Computer Science Teachers, Postsecondary; Criminal Justice and Law Enforcement Teachers, Postsecondary; Economics Teachers, Postsecondary; Education Teachers, Postsecondary; Engineering Teachers, Postsecondary; English Language and Literature Teachers, Postsecondary; Environmental Science Teachers, Postsecondary; Farm and Home Management Advisors; Foreign Language and Literature Teachers, Postsecondary; Forestry and Conservation Science Teachers, Postsecondary; Geography Teachers, Postsecondary; Graduate Teaching Assistants; Health Specialties Teachers, Postsecondary; History Teachers, Postsecondary; Home Economics Teachers, Postsecondary; Law Teachers, Postsecondary; Library Science Teachers, Postsecondary; Nursing Instructors and Teachers, Postsecondary; Philosophy and Religion Teachers, Postsecondary; Physics Teachers, Postsecondary; Political Science Teachers, Postsecondary; Psychology Teachers, Postsecondary; Recreation and Fitness Studies Teachers, Postsecondary; Social Work Teachers, Postsecondary; Sociology Teachers, Postsecondary.

Skills—Mathematics: Using mathematics to solve problems. **Instructing:** Teaching others how to do something. **Science:** Using scientific methods to solve problems. **Learning Strategies:** Using multiple approaches when learning or teaching new things. **Critical Thinking:** Using logic and analysis to identify the strengths and weaknesses of different approaches. **Complex Problem Solving:** Identifying complex problems, reviewing the options, and implementing solutions. **Speaking:** Talking to others to effectively convey information. **Reading Comprehension:** Understanding written sentences and paragraphs in work-related documents.

Education and Training Programs: Mathematics, General; Algebra and Number Theory; Analysis and Functional Analysis; Geometry/Geometric Analysis; Topology and Foundations; Mathematics, Other; Applied Mathematics; Statistics, General; Mathematical Statistics and Probability; Mathematics and Statistics, Other; Logic; Business Statistics. **Related Knowledge/Courses—Mathematics:** Numbers and their operations and interrelationships, including arithmetic, algebra, geometry, calculus, and statistics and their applications. **Education and Training:** Instructional methods and training techniques, including curriculum design principles, learning theory, group and individual teaching techniques, design of individual development plans, and test design principles. **Physics:** Physical principles, laws, and applications, including air, water, material dynamics, light, atomic principles, heat, electric theory, earth formations, and meteorological and related natural phenomena. **Computers and Electronics:** Electric circuit boards, processors, chips, and computer hardware and software, including applications and programming. **English Language:** The structure and content of the English language, including the meaning and spelling of words, rules of composition, and grammar. **Communications and Media:** Media production, communication, and dissemination techniques and methods, including alternative ways to inform and entertain via written, oral, and visual media.

Work Environment: Indoors; more often standing than sitting.

M

Mechanical Engineers

- ❀ Education/Training Required: Bachelor's degree
- ❀ Annual Earnings: $72,300
- ❀ Beginning Wage: $46,560
- ❀ Earnings Growth Potential: Medium
- ❀ Growth: 4.2%
- ❀ Annual Job Openings: 12,394
- ❀ Self-Employed: 2.2%
- ❀ Part-Time: 1.9%

Perform engineering duties in planning and designing tools, engines, machines, and other mechanically functioning equipment. Oversee installation, operation, maintenance, and repair of such equipment as centralized heat, gas, water, and steam systems. Read and interpret blueprints, technical drawings, schematics, and computer-generated reports. Confer with engineers and other personnel to implement operating procedures, resolve system malfunctions, and provide technical information. Research and analyze customer design proposals, specifications, manuals, and other data to evaluate the feasibility, cost, and maintenance requirements of designs or applications. Specify system components or direct modification of products to ensure conformance with engineering design and performance specifications. Research, design, evaluate, install, operate, and maintain mechanical products, equipment, systems, and processes to meet requirements, applying knowledge of engineering principles. Investigate equipment failures and difficulties to diagnose faulty operation and to make recommendations to maintenance crew. Assist drafters in developing the structural design of products, using drafting tools or computer-assisted design (CAD) or drafting equipment and software. Provide feedback to design engineers on customer problems and needs. Oversee installation, operation, maintenance, and repair to ensure that machines and equipment are installed and functioning according to specifications. Conduct research that tests and analyzes the feasibility, design, operation, and performance of equipment, components, and systems. Recommend design modifications to eliminate machine or system malfunctions. Develop and test models of alternate designs and processing methods to assess feasibility, operating condition effects, possible new applications, and necessity of modification. Develop, coordinate, and monitor all aspects of production, including selection of manufacturing methods, fabrication, and operation of product designs. Estimate costs and submit bids for engineering, construction, or extraction projects and prepare contract documents. Perform personnel functions such as supervision of production workers, technicians, technologists, and other engineers or design of evaluation programs. Solicit new business and provide technical customer service. Establish and coordinate the maintenance and safety procedures, service schedule, and supply of materials required to maintain machines and equipment in the prescribed condition.

Personality Type: Investigative. These occupations frequently involve working with ideas and require an extensive amount of thinking. They can involve searching for facts and figuring out problems mentally.

GOE—Interest Area/Cluster: 15. Scientific Research, Engineering, and Mathematics. **Work Group:** 15.07. Research and Design Engineering. **Other Jobs in This Work Group:** Aerospace Engineers; Biomedical Engineers; Chemical Engineers; Civil Engineers; Computer Hardware Engineers; Electrical Engineers; Electronics Engineers, Except Computer; Marine Architects; Marine Engineers; Marine Engineers and Naval Architects; Materials Engineers; Nuclear Engineers.

Skills—Science: Using scientific methods to solve problems. **Operations Analysis:** Analyzing needs and product requirements to create a design. **Installation:** Installing equipment, machines, wiring, or programs to meet specifications. **Complex Problem Solving:** Identifying complex problems, reviewing the options, and implementing solutions. **Mathematics:** Using mathematics to solve problems. **Systems Analysis:** Determining how a system should work and how changes will affect outcomes. **Judgment and Decision Making:** Weighing the relative costs and benefits of a potential action. **Coordination:** Adjusting actions in relation to others' actions.

Education and Training Program: Mechanical Engineering. **Related Knowledge/Courses— Design:** Design techniques, principles, tools, and instruments involved in the production and use of precision technical plans, blueprints, drawings, and models. **Engineering and Technology:** Equipment, tools, and mechanical devices and their uses to produce motion, light, power, technology, and other applications. **Mechanical Devices:** Machines and tools, including their designs, uses, benefits, repair, and maintenance. **Production and Processing:** Inputs, outputs, raw materials, waste, quality control, costs, and techniques for maximizing the manufacture and distribution of goods. **Physics:** Physical principles, laws, and applications, including air, water, material dynamics, light, atomic principles, heat, electric theory, earth formations, and meteorological and related natural phenomena. **Administration and Management:** Principles and processes involved in business and organizational planning, coordination, and execution. This includes strategic planning, resource allocation, manpower modeling, leadership techniques, and production methods.

Work Environment: Indoors; sitting.

Medical and Clinical Laboratory Technologists

- ❋ Education/Training Required: Bachelor's degree
- ❋ Annual Earnings: $51,720
- ❋ Beginning Wage: $35,460
- ❋ Earnings Growth Potential: Low
- ❋ Growth: 12.4%
- ❋ Annual Job Openings: 11,457
- ❋ Self-Employed: 0.7%
- ❋ Part-Time: 14.3%

Perform complex medical laboratory tests for diagnosis, treatment, and prevention of disease. May train or supervise staff. Conduct chemical analysis of bodily fluids, including blood, urine, and spinal fluid, to determine presence of normal and abnormal components. Analyze laboratory findings to check the accuracy of the results. Enter data from analysis of medical tests and clinical results into computer for storage. Operate, calibrate, and maintain equipment used in quantitative and qualitative analysis, such as spectrophotometers, calorimeters, flame photometers, and computer-controlled analyzers. Establish and monitor quality assurance programs and activities to ensure the accuracy of laboratory results. Set up, clean, and maintain laboratory equipment. Provide technical information about test results to physicians, family members, and researchers. Supervise, train, and direct lab assistants, medical and clinical laboratory technicians and technologists, and other medical laboratory workers engaged in laboratory testing. Collect and study blood samples to determine the number of cells, their morphology, or their blood group, blood type, and compatibility for transfusion purposes, using microscopic techniques. Analyze samples of biological material for chemical content or reaction. Cultivate, isolate,

M

and assist in identifying microbial organisms, and perform various tests on these microorganisms. Obtain, cut, stain, and mount biological material on slides for microscopic study and diagnosis, following standard laboratory procedures. Select and prepare specimen and media for cell culture, using aseptic technique and knowledge of medium components and cell requirements. Develop, standardize, evaluate, and modify procedures, techniques, and tests used in the analysis of specimens and in medical laboratory experiments. Harvest cell cultures at optimum time based on knowledge of cell cycle differences and culture conditions. Conduct medical research under direction of microbiologist or biochemist.

Personality Type: Investigative. These occupations frequently involve working with ideas and require an extensive amount of thinking. They can involve searching for facts and figuring out problems mentally.

GOE—Interest Area/Cluster: 08. Health Science. **Work Group:** 08.06. Medical Technology. **Other Jobs in This Work Group:** Biological Technicians; Cardiovascular Technologists and Technicians; Diagnostic Medical Sonographers; Medical and Clinical Laboratory Technicians; Medical Records and Health Information Technicians; Nuclear Medicine Technologists; Orthotists and Prosthetists; Radiologic Technicians; Radiologic Technologists; Radiologic Technologists and Technicians.

Skills—Operation Monitoring: Watching gauges, dials, or other indicators to make sure a machine is working properly. **Management of Personnel Resources:** Motivating, developing, and directing people as they work; identifying the best people for the job. **Quality Control Analysis:** Evaluating the quality or performance of products, services, or processes.

Education and Training Programs: Cytotechnology/Cytotechnologist; Clinical Laboratory Science/Medical Technology/Technologist; Histologic Technology/Histotechnologist; Cytogenetics/Genetics/Clinical Genetics Technology/Technologist; Renal/Dialysis Technologist/Technician; Clinical/Medical Laboratory Science and Allied Professions, Other. **Related Knowledge/Courses—Biology:** Plant and animal living tissue, cells, organisms, and entities, including their functions, interdependencies, and interactions with each other and the environment. **Chemistry:** The composition, structure, and properties of substances and of the chemical processes and transformations that they undergo. This includes uses of chemicals and their interactions, danger signs, production techniques, and disposal methods. **Medicine and Dentistry:** The information and techniques needed to diagnose and treat injuries, diseases, and deformities. This includes symptoms, treatment alternatives, drug properties and interactions, and preventive health-care measures. **Mechanical Devices:** Machines and tools, including their designs, uses, benefits, repair, and maintenance. **Clerical Practices:** Administrative and clerical procedures and systems such as word-processing systems, filing and records management systems, stenography and transcription, forms, design principles, and other office procedures and terminology. **Mathematics:** Numbers and their operations and interrelationships, including arithmetic, algebra, geometry, calculus, and statistics and their applications.

Work Environment: Indoors; noisy; contaminants; disease or infections; standing; using hands on objects, tools, or controls.

Medical and Health Services Managers

- ❋ Education/Training Required: Work experience plus degree
- ❋ Annual Earnings: $76,990
- ❋ Beginning Wage: $46,860
- ❋ Earnings Growth Potential: Medium
- ❋ Growth: 16.4%
- ❋ Annual Job Openings: 31,877
- ❋ Self-Employed: 8.2%
- ❋ Part-Time: 5.5%

Plan, direct, or coordinate medicine and health services in hospitals, clinics, managed care organizations, public health agencies, or similar organizations. Conduct and administer fiscal operations, including accounting, planning budgets, authorizing expenditures, establishing rates for services, and coordinating financial reporting. Direct, supervise, and evaluate work activities of medical, nursing, technical, clerical, service, maintenance, and other personnel. Maintain communication between governing boards, medical staff, and department heads by attending board meetings and coordinating interdepartmental functioning. Review and analyze facility activities and data to aid planning and cash and risk management and to improve service utilization. Plan, implement, and administer programs and services in a health-care or medical facility, including personnel administration, training, and coordination of medical, nursing, and physical plant staff. Direct or conduct recruitment, hiring, and training of personnel. Establish work schedules and assignments for staff, according to workload, space, and equipment availability. Maintain awareness of advances in medicine, computerized diagnostic and treatment equipment, data processing technology, government regulations, health insurance changes, and financing options. Monitor the use of diagnostic services, inpatient beds, facilities, and staff to ensure effective use of resources and assess the need for additional staff, equipment, and services. Develop and maintain computerized record management systems to store and process data such as personnel activities and information and to produce reports. Establish and evaluative objectives and evaluative operational criteria for units they manage. Prepare activity reports to inform management of the status and implementation plans of programs, services, and quality initiatives. Inspect facilities and recommend building or equipment modifications to ensure emergency readiness and compliance to access, safety, and sanitation regulations. Develop and implement organizational policies and procedures for the facility or medical unit. Manage change in integrated health care delivery systems such as work restructuring, technological innovations, and shifts in the focus of care.

Personality Type: Enterprising. These occupations frequently involve starting up and carrying out projects and can involve leading people and making many decisions. They sometimes require risk taking and often deal with business.

GOE—Interest Area/Cluster: 08. Health Science. **Work Group:** 08.01. Managerial Work in Medical and Health Services. **Other Jobs in This Work Group:** No others in group.

Skills—Management of Financial Resources: Determining how money will be spent to get the work done and accounting for these expenditures. **Management of Personnel Resources:** Motivating, developing, and directing people as they work; identifying the best people for the job. **Systems Analysis:** Determining how a system should work and how changes will affect outcomes. **Systems Evaluation:** Looking at many indicators of system performance and taking into account their accuracy. **Management of Material Resources:** Obtaining and seeing to the appropriate use of equipment, facilities, and materials needed to do certain work. **Negotiation:** Bringing others together and trying to reconcile differences. **Persuasion:** Persuading others to approach things differently. **Monitoring:** Assessing how well one is doing when learning or doing something.

Education and Training Programs: Health/Health Care Administration/Management; Hospital and Health Care Facilities Administration/Management; Health Unit Manager/Ward Supervisor; Health Information/Medical Records Administration/Administrator; Medical Staff Services Technology/Technician; Health and Medical Administrative Services, Other; Nursing Administration (MSN, MS, PhD); Public Health, General (MPH, DPH); Community Health and Preventive Medicine; others. **Related Knowledge/Courses—Economics and Accounting:** Economic and accounting principles and practices, the financial markets, banking, and the analysis and reporting of financial data. **Personnel and Human Resources:** Principles and procedures for personnel recruitment; selection; training; compensation and benefits; labor relations and negotiation; and personnel information systems. **Administration and Management:** Principles and processes involved in business and organizational planning, coordination, and execution. This includes strategic planning, resource allocation, manpower modeling, leadership techniques, and production methods. **Sales and Marketing:** Principles and methods involved in showing, promoting, and selling products or services. This includes marketing strategies and tactics, product demonstration and sales techniques, and sales control systems. **Medicine and Dentistry:** The information and techniques needed to diagnose and treat injuries, diseases, and deformities. This includes symptoms, treatment alternatives, drug properties and interactions, and preventive health-care measures. **Law and Government:** Laws, legal codes, court

procedures, precedents, government regulations, executive orders, agency rules, and the democratic political process.

Work Environment: Indoors; disease or infections; sitting.

Medical and Public Health Social Workers

* Education/Training Required: Bachelor's degree
* Annual Earnings: $44,670
* Beginning Wage: $28,160
* Earnings Growth Potential: Medium
* Growth: 24.2%
* Annual Job Openings: 16,429
* Self-Employed: 2.6%
* Part-Time: 9.4%

Provide persons, families, or vulnerable populations with the psychosocial support needed to cope with chronic, acute, or terminal illnesses such as Alzheimer's, cancer, or AIDS. Services include advising family caregivers, providing patient education and counseling, and making necessary referrals for other social services. Advocate for clients or patients to resolve crises. Collaborate with other professionals to evaluate patients' medical or physical condition and to assess client needs. Refer patients, clients, or families to community resources to assist in recovery from mental or physical illnesses and to provide access to services such as financial assistance, legal aid, housing, job placement, or education. Counsel clients and patients in individual and group sessions to help them overcome dependencies, recover from illnesses, and adjust to life. Use consultation data and social work experience to plan and coordinate client or patient care and rehabilitation, following through to ensure service efficacy. Plan discharge from care facility to home or other care facility. Organize support groups or counsel family members to assist them in understanding, dealing with, and supporting clients or patients. Modify treatment plans to comply with changes in clients' statuses. Monitor, evaluate, and record client progress according to measurable goals described in treatment and care plans. Identify environmental impediments to client or patient progress through interviews and review of patient records. Supervise and direct other workers providing services to clients or patients. Develop or advise on social policy and assist in community development. Investigate child abuse or neglect cases and take authorized protective action when necessary. Oversee Medicaid- and Medicare-related paperwork and recordkeeping in hospitals. Plan and conduct programs to combat social problems, prevent substance abuse, or improve community health and counseling services. Conduct social research to advance knowledge in the social work field.

Personality Type: Social. These occupations frequently involve working with, communicating with, and teaching people and often involve helping or providing service to others.

GOE—Interest Area/Cluster: 10. Human Service. **Work Group:** 10.01. Counseling and Social Work. **Other Jobs in This Work Group:** Child, Family, and School Social Workers; Clinical Psychologists; Clinical, Counseling, and School Psychologists; Counseling Psychologists; Marriage and Family Therapists; Mental Health and Substance Abuse Social Workers; Mental Health Counselors; Probation Officers and Correctional Treatment Specialists; Rehabilitation Counselors; Substance Abuse and Behavioral Disorder Counselors.

Skills—Social Perceptiveness: Being aware of others' reactions and understanding why they react the way they do. **Systems Evaluation:** Looking at many indicators of system performance and taking into account their accuracy. **Service Orientation:**

Actively looking for ways to help people. **Systems Analysis:** Determining how a system should work and how changes will affect outcomes. **Negotiation:** Bringing others together and trying to reconcile differences. **Speaking:** Talking to others to effectively convey information. **Writing:** Communicating effectively with others in writing as indicated by the needs of the audience.

Education and Training Program: Clinical/ Medical Social Work. **Related Knowledge/ Courses—Therapy and Counseling:** Information and techniques needed to rehabilitate physical and mental ailments and to provide career guidance, including alternative treatments, rehabilitation equipment and its proper use, and methods to evaluate treatment effects. **Sociology and Anthropology:** Group behavior and dynamics; societal trends and influences; and cultures and their history, migrations, ethnicity, and origins. **Psychology:** Human behavior and performance, mental processes, psychological research methods, and the assessment and treatment of behavioral and affective disorders. **Philosophy and Theology:** Different philosophical systems and religions, including their basic principles, values, ethics, ways of thinking, customs, and practices and their impact on human culture. **Customer and Personal Service:** Principles and processes for providing customer and personal services, including needs assessment techniques, quality service standards, alternative delivery systems, and customer satisfaction evaluation techniques. **Medicine and Dentistry:** The information and techniques needed to diagnose and treat injuries, diseases, and deformities. This includes symptoms, treatment alternatives, drug properties and interactions, and preventive health-care measures.

Work Environment: Indoors; noisy; disease or infections; sitting.

M

Medical Records and Health Information Technicians

* Education/Training Required: Associate degree
* Annual Earnings: $29,290
* Beginning Wage: $19,690
* Earnings Growth Potential: Low
* Growth: 17.8%
* Annual Job Openings: 39,048
* Self-Employed: 0.2%
* Part-Time: 12.5%

Compile, process, and maintain medical records of hospital and clinic patients in a manner consistent with medical, administrative, ethical, legal, and regulatory requirements of the health care system. Process, maintain, compile, and report patient information for health requirements and standards. Protect the security of medical records to ensure that confidentiality is maintained. Review records for completeness, accuracy, and compliance with regulations. Retrieve patient medical records for physicians, technicians, or other medical personnel. Release information to persons and agencies according to regulations. Plan, develop, maintain, and operate a variety of health record indexes and storage and retrieval systems to collect, classify, store, and analyze information. Enter data such as demographic characteristics, history and extent of disease, diagnostic procedures, and treatment into computer. Process and prepare business and government forms. Compile and maintain patients' medical records to document condition and treatment and to provide data for research or cost control and care improvement efforts. Process patient admission and discharge documents. Assign the patient to diagnosis-related groups (DRGs), using appropriate computer software. Transcribe medical reports. Identify, compile, abstract, and code patient data, using standard classification systems. Resolve or clarify codes and diagnoses with conflicting, missing, or unclear information by consulting with doctors or others or by participating in the coding team's regular meetings. Compile medical care and census data for statistical reports on diseases treated, surgeries performed, or use of hospital beds. Post medical insurance billings. Train medical records staff. Prepare statistical reports, narrative reports, and graphic presentations of information such as tumor registry data for use by hospital staff, researchers, or other users. Manage the department and supervise clerical workers, directing and controlling activities of personnel in the medical records department. Develop in-service educational materials. Consult classification manuals to locate information about disease processes.

Personality Type: Conventional. These occupations frequently involve following set procedures and routines and can include working with data and details more than with ideas. Usually there is a clear line of authority to follow.

GOE—Interest Area/Cluster: 08. Health Science. **Work Group:** 08.06. Medical Technology. **Other Jobs in This Work Group:** Biological Technicians; Cardiovascular Technologists and Technicians; Diagnostic Medical Sonographers; Medical and Clinical Laboratory Technicians; Medical and Clinical Laboratory Technologists; Nuclear Medicine Technologists; Orthotists and Prosthetists; Radiologic Technicians; Radiologic Technologists; Radiologic Technologists and Technicians.

Skills—Systems Analysis: Determining how a system should work and how changes will affect outcomes.

Education and Training Programs: Health Information/Medical Records Technology/

Technician; Medical Insurance Coding Specialist/ Coder. **Related Knowledge/Courses—Clerical Practices:** Administrative and clerical procedures and systems such as word-processing systems, filing and records management systems, stenography and transcription, forms, design principles, and other office procedures and terminology. **Law and Government:** Laws, legal codes, court procedures, precedents, government regulations, executive orders, agency rules, and the democratic political process. **Customer and Personal Service:** Principles and processes for providing customer and personal services, including needs assessment techniques, quality service standards, alternative delivery systems, and customer satisfaction evaluation techniques.

Work Environment: Indoors; disease or infections; sitting; using hands on objects, tools, or controls; repetitive motions.

Medical Scientists, Except Epidemiologists

* Education/Training Required: Doctoral degree
* Annual Earnings: $64,200
* Beginning Wage: $36,730
* Earnings Growth Potential: High
* Growth: 20.2%
* Annual Job Openings: 10,596
* Self-Employed: 2.0%
* Part-Time: 5.9%

Conduct research dealing with the understanding of human diseases and the improvement of human health. Engage in clinical investigation or other research, production, technical writing, or related activities. Conduct research to develop methodologies, instrumentation, and procedures for medical application, analyzing data

and presenting findings. Plan and direct studies to investigate human or animal disease, preventive methods, and treatments for disease. Follow strict safety procedures when handling toxic materials to avoid contamination. Evaluate effects of drugs, gases, pesticides, parasites, and microorganisms at various levels. Teach principles of medicine and medical and laboratory procedures to physicians, residents, students, and technicians. Prepare and analyze organ, tissue, and cell samples to identify toxicity, bacteria, or microorganisms or to study cell structure. Standardize drug dosages, methods of immunization, and procedures for manufacture of drugs and medicinal compounds. Investigate cause, progress, life cycle, or mode of transmission of diseases or parasites. Confer with health department, industry personnel, physicians, and others to develop health safety standards and public health improvement programs. Study animal and human health and physiological processes. Consult with and advise physicians, educators, researchers, and others regarding medical applications of physics, biology, and chemistry. Use equipment such as atomic absorption spectrometers, electron microscopes, flow cytometers, and chromatography systems.

Personality Type: Investigative. These occupations frequently involve working with ideas and require an extensive amount of thinking. They can involve searching for facts and figuring out problems mentally.

GOE—Interest Area/Cluster: 15. Scientific Research, Engineering, and Mathematics. **Work Group:** 15.03. Life Sciences. **Other Jobs in This Work Group:** Biochemists and Biophysicists; Biologists; Environmental Scientists and Specialists, Including Health; Epidemiologists; Microbiologists.

Skills—Science: Using scientific methods to solve problems. **Management of Financial Resources:** Determining how money will be spent to get the work done and accounting for these expenditures. **Judgment and Decision Making:** Weighing the relative costs and benefits of a potential action. **Reading Comprehension:** Understanding written sentences and paragraphs in work-related documents. **Writing:** Communicating effectively with others in writing as indicated by the needs of the audience. **Time Management:** Managing one's own time and the time of others. **Complex Problem Solving:** Identifying complex problems, reviewing the options, and implementing solutions. **Active Listening:** Listening to what other people are saying and asking questions as appropriate.

Education and Training Programs: Biomedical Sciences, General; Biochemistry; Biophysics; Molecular Biology; Cell/Cellular Biology and Histology; Anatomy; Medical Microbiology and Bacteriology; Immunology; Human/Medical Genetics; Physiology, General; Molecular Physiology; Cell Physiology; Endocrinology; Reproductive Biology; Neurobiology and Neurophysiology; Cardiovascular Science; others. **Related Knowledge/Courses—Biology:** Plant and animal living tissue, cells, organisms, and entities, including their functions, interdependencies, and interactions with each other and the environment. **Medicine and Dentistry:** The information and techniques needed to diagnose and treat injuries, diseases, and deformities. This includes symptoms, treatment alternatives, drug properties and interactions, and preventive health-care measures. **Chemistry:** The composition, structure, and properties of substances and of the chemical processes and transformations that they undergo. This includes uses of chemicals and their interactions, danger signs, production techniques, and disposal methods. **Communications and Media:** Media production, communication, and dissemination techniques and methods, including alternative ways to inform and entertain via written, oral, and visual media. **Personnel and Human Resources:** Principles and procedures for personnel recruitment; selection; training; compensation and benefits; labor relations and negotiation; and personnel information systems. **Sociology and Anthropology:** Group behavior and dynamics; societal trends and influences; and cultures and their history, migrations, ethnicity, and origins.

Work Environment: Indoors; sitting; using hands on objects, tools, or controls.

Meeting and Convention Planners

- ❀ Education/Training Required: Bachelor's degree
- ❀ Annual Earnings: $43,530
- ❀ Beginning Wage: $26,880
- ❀ Earnings Growth Potential: Medium
- ❀ Growth: 19.9%
- ❀ Annual Job Openings: 8,318
- ❀ Self-Employed: 5.6%
- ❀ Part-Time: 13.8%

Coordinate activities of staff and convention personnel to make arrangements for group meetings and conventions. Monitor event activities to ensure compliance with applicable regulations and laws, satisfaction of participants, and resolution of any problems that arise. Confer with staffs at chosen event sites to coordinate details. Inspect event facilities to ensure that they conform to customer requirements. Coordinate services for events, such as accommodation and transportation for participants, facilities, catering, signage, displays, special needs requirements, printing, and event security. Consult with customers to determine objectives and requirements for events such as meetings, conferences, and conventions. Meet with sponsors and organizing committees to plan scope and format of events, to establish and monitor budgets, or to review administrative procedures and event progress. Review event bills for accuracy, and approve payments. Evaluate and select providers of services according to customer requirements. Arrange the availability of audio-visual equipment, transportation, displays, and other event needs. Plan and develop programs, agendas, budgets, and services according to customer requirements. Negotiate contracts with such service providers and suppliers as hotels, convention centers, and speakers. Maintain records of event aspects, including financial details. Conduct post-event evaluations to determine how future events could be improved. Organize registration of event participants. Hire, train, and supervise volunteers and support staff required for events. Read trade publications, attend seminars, and consult with other meeting professionals to keep abreast of meeting management standards and trends. Direct administrative details such as financial operations, dissemination of promotional materials, and responses to inquiries. Promote conference, convention, and trade show services by performing tasks such as meeting with professional and trade associations and producing brochures and other publications. Develop event topics and choose featured speakers. Obtain permits from fire and health departments to erect displays and exhibits and serve food at events. Design and implement efforts to publicize events and promote sponsorships.

Personality Type: Enterprising. These occupations frequently involve starting up and carrying out projects and can involve leading people and making many decisions. They sometimes require risk taking and often deal with business.

GOE—Interest Area/Cluster: 04. Business and Administration. **Work Group:** 04.02. Managerial Work in Business Detail. **Other Jobs in This Work Group:** Administrative Services Managers.

Skills—Management of Financial Resources: Determining how money will be spent to get the work done and accounting for these expenditures. **Systems Evaluation:** Looking at many indicators of system performance and taking into account their accuracy. **Management of Material Resources:** Obtaining and seeing to the appropriate use of equipment, facilities, and materials needed to do certain work. **Systems Analysis:** Determining how a system should work and how changes will affect outcomes. **Negotiation:** Bringing others together and trying to reconcile differences. **Management of Personnel Resources:** Motivating, developing, and directing people as they work; identifying the best people for the job. **Service Orientation:** Actively looking for ways to help people. **Coordination:** Adjusting actions in relation to others' actions.

Education and Training Program: Selling Skills and Sales Operations. **Related Knowledge/Courses—Sales and Marketing:** Principles and methods involved in showing, promoting, and selling products or services. This includes marketing strategies and tactics, product demonstration and sales techniques, and sales control systems. **Clerical Practices:** Administrative and clerical procedures and systems such as word-processing systems, filing and records management systems, stenography and transcription, forms, design principles, and other office procedures and terminology. **Customer and Personal Service:** Principles and processes for providing customer and personal services, including needs assessment techniques, quality service standards, alternative delivery systems, and customer satisfaction evaluation techniques. **English Language:** The structure and content of the English language, including the meaning and spelling of words, rules of composition, and grammar. **Economics and Accounting:** Economic and accounting principles and practices, the financial markets, banking, and the analysis and reporting of financial data. **Administration and Management:** Principles and processes involved in business and

M

organizational planning, coordination, and execution. This includes strategic planning, resource allocation, manpower modeling, leadership techniques, and production methods.

Work Environment: Indoors; noisy; sitting.

Mental Health and Substance Abuse Social Workers

- ❋ Education/Training Required: Master's degree
- ❋ Annual Earnings: $36,640
- ❋ Beginning Wage: $23,820
- ❋ Earnings Growth Potential: Medium
- ❋ Growth: 29.9%
- ❋ Annual Job Openings: 17,289
- ❋ Self-Employed: 2.8%
- ❋ Part-Time: 9.4%

Assess and treat individuals with mental, emotional, or substance abuse problems, including abuse of alcohol, tobacco, and/or other drugs. Activities may include individual and group therapy, crisis intervention, case management, client advocacy, prevention, and education. Counsel clients in individual and group sessions to assist them in dealing with substance abuse, mental and physical illness, poverty, unemployment, or physical abuse. Interview clients, review records, and confer with other professionals to evaluate mental or physical condition of client or patient. Collaborate with counselors, physicians, and nurses to plan and coordinate treatment, drawing on social work experience and patient needs. Monitor, evaluate, and record client progress with respect to treatment goals. Refer patient, client, or family to community resources for housing or treatment to assist in recovery from mental or physical illness, following through to ensure service efficacy. Counsel and aid family members to assist them in understanding, dealing with, and supporting the client or patient. Modify treatment plans according to changes in client status. Plan and conduct programs to prevent substance abuse, to combat social problems, or to improve health and counseling services in community. Supervise and direct other workers who provide services to clients or patients. Develop or advise on social policy and assist in community development. Conduct social research to advance knowledge in the social work field.

Personality Type: Social. These occupations frequently involve working with, communicating with, and teaching people and often involve helping or providing service to others.

GOE—Interest Area/Cluster: 10. Human Service. **Work Group:** 10.01. Counseling and Social Work. **Other Jobs in This Work Group:** Child, Family, and School Social Workers; Clinical Psychologists; Clinical, Counseling, and School Psychologists; Counseling Psychologists; Marriage and Family Therapists; Medical and Public Health Social Workers; Mental Health Counselors; Probation Officers and Correctional Treatment Specialists; Rehabilitation Counselors; Substance Abuse and Behavioral Disorder Counselors.

Skills—Social Perceptiveness: Being aware of others' reactions and understanding why they react the way they do. **Service Orientation:** Actively looking for ways to help people. **Negotiation:** Bringing others together and trying to reconcile differences. **Judgment and Decision Making:** Weighing the relative costs and benefits of a potential action. **Active Listening:** Listening to what other people are saying and asking questions as appropriate. **Persuasion:** Persuading others to approach things differently. **Complex Problem Solving:** Identifying complex problems, reviewing the options, and implementing solutions. **Writing:**

Communicating effectively with others in writing as indicated by the needs of the audience.

Education and Training Program: Clinical/Medical Social Work. **Related Knowledge/Courses— Psychology:** Human behavior and performance, mental processes, psychological research methods, and the assessment and treatment of behavioral and affective disorders. **Therapy and Counseling:** Information and techniques needed to rehabilitate physical and mental ailments and to provide career guidance, including alternative treatments, rehabilitation equipment and its proper use, and methods to evaluate treatment effects. **Sociology and Anthropology:** Group behavior and dynamics; societal trends and influences; and cultures and their history, migrations, ethnicity, and origins. **Customer and Personal Service:** Principles and processes for providing customer and personal services, including needs assessment techniques, quality service standards, alternative delivery systems, and customer satisfaction evaluation techniques.

Work Environment: Indoors; noisy; sitting.

Mental Health Counselors

- ❋ Education/Training Required: Master's degree
- ❋ Annual Earnings: $36,000
- ❋ Beginning Wage: $22,900
- ❋ Earnings Growth Potential: Medium
- ❋ Growth: 30.0%
- ❋ Annual Job Openings: 24,103
- ❋ Self-Employed: 6.1%
- ❋ Part-Time: 15.4%

Counsel with emphasis on prevention. Work with individuals and groups to promote optimum mental health. May help individuals deal with addictions and substance abuse; family, parenting, and marital problems; suicide; **stress management; problems with self-esteem; and issues associated with aging and mental and emotional health.** Maintain confidentiality of records relating to clients' treatment. Guide clients in the development of skills and strategies for dealing with their problems. Encourage clients to express their feelings and discuss what is happening in their lives and help them to develop insight into themselves and their relationships. Prepare and maintain all required treatment records and reports. Counsel clients and patients, individually and in group sessions, to assist in overcoming dependencies, adjusting to life, and making changes. Collect information about clients through interviews, observation, and tests. Act as client advocates to coordinate required services or to resolve emergency problems in crisis situations. Develop and implement treatment plans based on clinical experience and knowledge. Collaborate with other staff members to perform clinical assessments and develop treatment plans. Evaluate clients' physical or mental condition based on review of client information. Meet with families, probation officers, police, and other interested parties to exchange necessary information during the treatment process. Refer patients, clients, or family members to community resources or to specialists as necessary. Evaluate the effectiveness of counseling programs and clients' progress in resolving identified problems and moving towards defined objectives. Counsel family members to assist them in understanding, dealing with, and supporting clients or patients. Plan, organize, and lead structured programs of counseling, work, study, recreation, and social activities for clients. Modify treatment activities and approaches as needed to comply with changes in clients' status. Learn about new developments in their field by reading professional literature, attending courses and seminars, and establishing and maintaining contact with other social service agencies. Discuss with individual patients their plans for life after leaving therapy. Gather information about community mental health needs and resources that could be used in conjunction with therapy. Monitor clients' use of medications. Supervise other counselors, social service staff, and assistants.

Personality Type: Social. These occupations frequently involve working with, communicating with, and teaching people and often involve helping or providing service to others.

GOE—Interest Area/Cluster: 10. Human Service. **Work Group:** 10.01. Counseling and Social Work. **Other Jobs in This Work Group:** Child, Family, and School Social Workers; Clinical Psychologists; Clinical, Counseling, and School Psychologists; Counseling Psychologists; Marriage and Family Therapists; Medical and Public Health Social Workers; Mental Health and Substance Abuse Social Workers; Probation Officers and Correctional Treatment Specialists; Rehabilitation Counselors; Substance Abuse and Behavioral Disorder Counselors.

Skills—Social Perceptiveness: Being aware of others' reactions and understanding why they react the way they do. **Service Orientation:** Actively looking for ways to help people. **Negotiation:** Bringing others together and trying to reconcile differences. **Active Listening:** Listening to what other people are saying and asking questions as appropriate. **Persuasion:** Persuading others to approach things differently. **Learning Strategies:** Using multiple approaches when learning or teaching new things. **Speaking:** Talking to others to effectively convey information. **Critical Thinking:** Using logic and analysis to identify the strengths and weaknesses of different approaches.

Education and Training Programs: Substance Abuse/Addiction Counseling; Clinical/Medical Social Work; Mental Health Counseling/Counselor; Mental and Social Health Services and Allied Professions, Other. **Related Knowledge/**

Courses—Therapy and Counseling: Information and techniques needed to rehabilitate physical and mental ailments and to provide career guidance, including alternative treatments, rehabilitation equipment and its proper use, and methods to evaluate treatment effects. **Psychology:** Human behavior and performance, mental processes, psychological research methods, and the assessment and treatment of behavioral and affective disorders. **Sociology and Anthropology:** Group behavior and dynamics; societal trends and influences; and cultures and their history, migrations, ethnicity, and origins. **Philosophy and Theology:** Different philosophical systems and religions, including their basic principles, values, ethics, ways of thinking, customs, and practices and their impact on human culture. **Medicine and Dentistry:** The information and techniques needed to diagnose and treat injuries, diseases, and deformities. This includes symptoms, treatment alternatives, drug properties and interactions, and preventive healthcare measures. **Law and Government:** Laws, legal codes, court procedures, precedents, government regulations, executive orders, agency rules, and the democratic political process.

Work Environment: Indoors; noisy; sitting.

Middle School Teachers, Except Special and Vocational Education

- ❀ Education/Training Required: Bachelor's degree
- ❀ Annual Earnings: $47,900
- ❀ Beginning Wage: $32,630
- ❀ Earnings Growth Potential: Low
- ❀ Growth: 11.2%
- ❀ Annual Job Openings: 75,270
- ❀ Self-Employed: 0.0%
- ❀ Part-Time: 9.5%

Teach students in public or private schools in one or more subjects at the middle, intermediate, or junior high level, which falls between elementary and senior high school as defined by applicable state laws and regulations. Establish and enforce rules for behavior and procedures for maintaining order among the students for whom they are responsible. Adapt teaching methods and instructional materials to meet students' varying needs and interests. Instruct through lectures, discussions, and demonstrations in one or more subjects such as English, mathematics, or social studies. Prepare, administer, and grade tests and assignments to evaluate students' progress. Establish clear objectives for all lessons, units, and projects and communicate these objectives to students. Plan and conduct activities for a balanced program of instruction, demonstration, and work time that provides students with opportunities to observe, question, and investigate. Maintain accurate, complete, and correct student records as required by laws, district policies, and administrative regulations. Observe and evaluate students' performance, behavior, social development, and physical health. Assign lessons and correct homework. Prepare materials and classrooms for class activities. Enforce all administration policies and rules governing students. Confer with parents or guardians, other teachers, counselors, and administrators to resolve students' behavioral and academic problems. Prepare students for later grades by encouraging them to explore learning opportunities and to persevere with challenging tasks. Prepare objectives and outlines for courses of study, following curriculum guidelines or requirements of states and schools. Guide and counsel students with adjustment or academic problems or special academic interests. Meet with parents and guardians to discuss their children's progress and to determine their priorities for their children and their resource needs. Meet with other professionals to discuss individual students' needs and progress. Prepare and implement remedial programs for students requiring extra help. Prepare for assigned classes and show written evidence of preparation upon request of immediate supervisors. Instruct and monitor students in the use and care of equipment and materials to prevent injury and damage.

Personality Type: Social. These occupations frequently involve working with, communicating with, and teaching people and often involve helping or providing service to others.

GOE—Interest Area/Cluster: 05. Education and Training. **Work Group:** 05.02. Preschool, Elementary, and Secondary Teaching and Instructing. **Other Jobs in This Work Group:** Elementary School Teachers, Except Special Education; Kindergarten Teachers, Except Special Education; Secondary School Teachers, Except Special and Vocational Education; Special Education Teachers, Middle School; Special Education Teachers, Preschool, Kindergarten, and Elementary School; Special Education Teachers, Secondary School; Vocational Education Teachers, Middle School; Vocational Education Teachers, Secondary School.

Skills—Learning Strategies: Using multiple approaches when learning or teaching new things. **Instructing:** Teaching others how to do something. **Monitoring:** Assessing how well one is doing when learning or doing something. **Social Perceptiveness:** Being aware of others' reactions and understanding why they react the way they do. **Time Management:** Managing one's own time and the time of others. **Persuasion:** Persuading others to approach things differently. **Negotiation:** Bringing others together and trying to reconcile differences. **Speaking:** Talking to others to effectively convey information.

Education and Training Programs: Junior High/Intermediate/Middle School Education and Teaching; Montessori Teacher Education; Waldorf/Steiner Teacher Education; Art Teacher Education; English/Language Arts Teacher Education; Foreign Language Teacher Education; Health Teacher Education; Family and Consumer Sciences/Home Economics Teacher Education; Technology Teacher Education/Industrial Arts Teacher Education; Mathematics Teacher Education; others. **Related Knowledge/Courses—Sociology and Anthropology:** Group behavior and dynamics; societal trends and influences; and cultures and their history, migrations, ethnicity, and origins. **History and Archeology:** Historical events and their causes, indicators, and impact on particular civilizations and cultures. **Philosophy and Theology:** Different philosophical systems and religions, including their basic principles, values, ethics, ways of thinking, customs, and practices and their impact on human culture. **Education and Training:** Instructional methods and training techniques, including curriculum design principles, learning theory, group and individual teaching techniques, design of individual development plans, and test design principles. **Geography:** Various methods for describing the location and distribution of land, sea, and air masses, including

their physical locations, relationships, and characteristics. **Therapy and Counseling:** Information and techniques needed to rehabilitate physical and mental ailments and to provide career guidance, including alternative treatments, rehabilitation equipment and its proper use, and methods to evaluate treatment effects.

Work Environment: Indoors; noisy; standing.

Multi-Media Artists and Animators

- ❋ Education/Training Required: Bachelor's degree
- ❋ Annual Earnings: $54,550
- ❋ Beginning Wage: $30,620
- ❋ Earnings Growth Potential: High
- ❋ Growth: 25.8%
- ❋ Annual Job Openings: 13,182
- ❋ Self-Employed: 69.7%
- ❋ Part-Time: 22.5%

Create special effects, animation, or other visual images, using film, video, computers, or other electronic tools and media, for use in products or creations such as computer games, movies, music videos, and commercials. Design complex graphics and animation, using independent judgment, creativity, and computer equipment. Create two-dimensional and three-dimensional images depicting objects in motion or illustrating a process, using computer animation or modeling programs. Make objects or characters appear lifelike by manipulating light, color, texture, shadow, and transparency or manipulating static images to give the illusion of motion. Apply story development, directing, cinematography, and editing to animation to create storyboards that show the flow of the animation and map out key scenes and characters. Assemble, typeset, scan, and produce digital camera-ready art or film negatives and printer's proofs. Script, plan, and create animated narrative sequences under tight deadlines, using computer software and hand-drawing techniques. Create basic designs, drawings, and illustrations for product labels, cartons, direct mail, or television. Create pen-and-paper images to be scanned, edited, colored, textured, or animated by computer. Develop briefings, brochures, multimedia presentations, Web pages, promotional products, technical illustrations, and computer artwork for use in products, technical manuals, literature, newsletters, and slide shows. Use models to simulate the behavior of animated objects in the finished sequence. Create and install special effects as required by the script, mixing chemicals and fabricating needed parts from wood, metal, plaster, and clay. Participate in design and production of multimedia campaigns, handling budgeting and scheduling and assisting with such responsibilities as production coordination, background design, and progress tracking. Convert real objects to animated objects through modeling, using techniques such as optical scanning. Implement and maintain configuration control systems.

Personality Type: Artistic. These occupations frequently involve working with forms, designs, and patterns. They often require self-expression, and the work can be done without following a clear set of rules.

GOE—Interest Area/Cluster: 03. Arts and Communication. **Work Group:** 03.09. Media Technology. **Other Jobs in This Work Group:** Broadcast Technicians; Film and Video Editors.

Skills—Operations Analysis: Analyzing needs and product requirements to create a design. **Technology Design:** Generating or adapting equipment and technology to serve user needs. **Time Management:** Managing one's own time and the time of others. **Judgment and Decision Making:** Weighing the relative costs and benefits of a

potential action. **Science:** Using scientific methods to solve problems. **Reading Comprehension:** Understanding written sentences and paragraphs in work-related documents. **Active Listening:** Listening to what other people are saying and asking questions as appropriate. **Programming:** Writing computer programs for various purposes.

Education and Training Programs: Animation, Interactive Technology, Video Graphics and Special Effects; Web Page, Digital/Multimedia and Information Resources Design; Graphic Design; Drawing; Intermedia/Multimedia; Painting; Printmaking. **Related Knowledge/Courses— Fine Arts:** Theory and techniques required to produce, compose, and perform works of music, dance, visual arts, drama, and sculpture. **Design:** Design techniques, principles, tools, and instruments involved in the production and use of precision technical plans, blueprints, drawings, and models. **Computers and Electronics:** Electric circuit boards, processors, chips, and computer hardware and software, including applications and programming. **Communications and Media:** Media production, communication, and dissemination techniques and methods, including alternative ways to inform and entertain via written, oral, and visual media. **English Language:** The structure and content of the English language, including the meaning and spelling of words, rules of composition, and grammar.

Work Environment: Indoors; sitting; using hands on objects, tools, or controls; repetitive motions.

Natural Sciences Managers

* Education/Training Required: Work experience plus degree
* Annual Earnings: $104,040
* Beginning Wage: $62,880
* Earnings Growth Potential: Medium
* Growth: 11.4%
* Annual Job Openings: 3,661
* Self-Employed: 0.6%
* Part-Time: 4.4%

Plan, direct, or coordinate activities in such fields as life sciences, physical sciences, mathematics, and statistics and research and development in these fields. Confer with scientists, engineers, regulators, and others to plan and review projects and to provide technical assistance. Develop client relationships and communicate with clients to explain proposals, present research findings, establish specifications, or discuss project status. Plan and direct research, development, and production activities. Prepare project proposals. Design and coordinate successive phases of problem analysis, solution proposals, and testing. Review project activities and prepare and review research, testing, and operational reports. Hire, supervise, and evaluate engineers, technicians, researchers, and other staff. Determine scientific and technical goals within broad outlines provided by top management and make detailed plans to accomplish these goals. Develop and implement policies, standards, and procedures for the architectural, scientific, and technical work performed to ensure regulatory compliance and operations enhancement. Develop innovative technology and train staff for its implementation. Provide for stewardship of plant and animal resources and habitats, studying land use; monitoring animal populations; and providing shelter, resources, and medical treatment for animals. Conduct own research in field of expertise. Recruit personnel and oversee the development and maintenance of staff competence. Advise and assist in obtaining patents or meeting other legal requirements. Prepare and administer budget, approve and review expenditures, and prepare financial reports. Make presentations at professional meetings to further knowledge in the field.

Personality Type: Enterprising. These occupations frequently involve starting up and carrying out projects and can involve leading people and making many decisions. They sometimes require risk taking and often deal with business.

GOE—Interest Area/Cluster: 15. Scientific Research, Engineering, and Mathematics. **Work Group:** 15.01. Managerial Work in Scientific Research, Engineering, and Mathematics. **Other Jobs in This Work Group:** Engineering Managers.

Skills—Science: Using scientific methods to solve problems. **Mathematics:** Using mathematics to solve problems. **Active Learning:** Working with new material or information to grasp its implications. **Reading Comprehension:** Understanding written sentences and paragraphs in work-related documents. **Writing:** Communicating effectively with others in writing as indicated by the needs of the audience. **Management of Personnel Resources:** Motivating, developing, and directing people as they work; identifying the best people for the job. **Complex Problem Solving:** Identifying complex problems, reviewing the options, and implementing solutions. **Critical Thinking:** Using logic and analysis to identify the strengths and weaknesses of different approaches.

Education and Training Programs: Operations Research; Biology/Biological Sciences, General; Biochemistry; Biophysics; Molecular Biology; Radiation Biology/Radiobiology; Botany/Plant Biology; Plant Pathology/Phytopathology; Plant

Physiology; Botany/Plant Biology, Other; Cell/Cellular Biology and Histology; Anatomy; Cell/Cellular Biology and Anatomical Sciences, Other; Microbiology, General; others. **Related Knowledge/Courses—Biology:** Plant and animal living tissue, cells, organisms, and entities, including their functions, interdependencies, and interactions with each other and the environment. **Chemistry:** The composition, structure, and properties of substances and of the chemical processes and transformations that they undergo. This includes uses of chemicals and their interactions, danger signs, production techniques, and disposal methods. **Engineering and Technology:** Equipment, tools, and mechanical devices and their uses to produce motion, light, power, technology, and other applications. **Law and Government:** Laws, legal codes, court procedures, precedents, government regulations, executive orders, agency rules, and the democratic political process. **Administration and Management:** Principles and processes involved in business and organizational planning, coordination, and execution. This includes strategic planning, resource allocation, manpower modeling, leadership techniques, and production methods. **Physics:** Physical principles, laws, and applications, including air, water, material dynamics, light, atomic principles, heat, electric theory, earth formations, and meteorological and related natural phenomena.

Work Environment: Indoors; noisy; sitting.

Network and Computer Systems Administrators

* Education/Training Required: Bachelor's degree
* Annual Earnings: $64,690
* Beginning Wage: $39,970
* Earnings Growth Potential: Medium
* Growth: 27.0%
* Annual Job Openings: 37,010
* Self-Employed: 0.4%
* Part-Time: 3.1%

The job openings listed here are shared with Computer Security Specialists.

Install, configure, and support organizations' local area networks (LANs), wide area networks (WANs), and Internet systems or segments of network systems. Maintain network hardware and software. Monitor networks to ensure network availability to all system users and perform necessary maintenance to support network availability. May supervise other network support and client server specialists and plan, coordinate, and implement network security measures. Maintain and administer computer networks and related computing environments including computer hardware, systems software, applications software, and all configurations. Perform data backups and disaster recovery operations. Diagnose, troubleshoot, and resolve hardware, software, or other network and system problems, and replace defective components when necessary. Plan, coordinate, and implement network security measures to protect data, software, and hardware. Configure, monitor, and maintain e-mail applications or virus protection software. Operate master consoles to monitor the performance of computer systems and networks, and to coordinate computer network access and use. Load computer tapes and disks, and install software and printer paper or forms. Design, configure, and test computer hardware, networking software, and operating system software. Monitor network performance to determine whether adjustments need to be made and to determine where changes will need to be made in the future. Confer with network users about how to solve existing system problems. Research new technologies by attending seminars, reading trade articles, or taking classes, and implement or recommend the implementation of new technologies. Analyze equipment performance records to determine the need for repair or replacement. Implement and provide technical support for voice services and equipment such as private branch exchanges, voice mail systems, and telecom systems. Maintain inventories of parts for emergency repairs. Recommend changes to improve systems and network configurations, and determine hardware or software requirements related to such changes. Gather data pertaining to customer needs, and use the information to identify, predict, interpret, and evaluate system and network requirements. Train people in computer system use. Coordinate with vendors and with company personnel to facilitate purchases. Perform routine network startup and shutdown procedures, and maintain control records. Maintain logs related to network functions, as well as maintenance and repair records.

Personality Type: Investigative. These occupations frequently involve working with ideas and require an extensive amount of thinking. They can involve searching for facts and figuring out problems mentally.

GOE—Interest Area/Cluster: 11. Information Technology. **Work Group:** 11.01. Managerial Work in Information Technology. **Other Jobs in This Work Group:** Computer and Information Systems Managers.

Skills—Programming: Writing computer programs for various purposes. **Systems Analysis:** Determining how a system should work and how changes will affect outcomes. **Systems Evaluation:** Looking at many indicators of system performance and taking into account their accuracy. **Operation Monitoring:** Watching gauges, dials, or other indicators to make sure a machine is working properly. **Quality Control Analysis:** Evaluating the quality or performance of products, services, or processes. **Troubleshooting:** Determining what is causing an operating error and deciding what to do about it. **Management of Personnel Resources:** Motivating, developing, and directing people as they work; identifying the best people for the job. **Operation and Control:** Controlling operations of equipment or systems.

Education and Training Programs: Computer and Information Sciences and Support Services, Other; Computer and Information Sciences, General; Computer and Information Systems Security; Computer Systems Analysis/Analyst; Computer Systems Networking and Telecommunications; Information Science/Studies; System Administration/Administrator; System, Networking, and LAN/WAN Management/Manager. **Related Knowledge/Courses—Telecommunications:** Transmission, broadcasting, switching, control, and operation of telecommunications systems. **Computers and Electronics:** Electric circuit boards, processors, chips, and computer hardware and software, including applications and programming. **Clerical Practices:** Administrative and clerical procedures and systems such as word-processing systems, filing and records management systems, stenography and transcription, forms, design principles, and other office procedures and terminology. **Administration and Management:** Principles and processes involved in business and organizational planning, coordination, and execution. This includes strategic planning, resource allocation, manpower modeling, leadership techniques, and production methods. **Engineering and Technology:** Equipment, tools, and mechanical devices and their uses to produce motion, light, power, technology, and other applications.

Work Environment: Indoors; noisy; sitting; using hands on objects, tools, or controls; repetitive motions.

Network Designers

- ❋ Education/Training Required: Bachelor's degree
- ❋ Annual Earnings: $71,510
- ❋ Beginning Wage: $37,600
- ❋ Earnings Growth Potential: High
- ❋ Growth: 15.1%
- ❋ Annual Job Openings: 14,374
- ❋ Self-Employed: 6.6%
- ❋ Part-Time: 5.6%

The job openings listed here are shared with Computer Systems Engineers/Architects; Software Quality Assurance Engineers and Testers; Web Administrators; and Web Developers.

Determine user requirements and design specifications for computer networks. Plan and implement network upgrades. Develop network-related documentation. Design, build, or operate equipment configuration prototypes, including network hardware, software, servers, or server operation systems. Coordinate network operations, maintenance, repairs, or upgrades. Adjust network sizes to meet volume or capacity demands. Communicate with vendors to gather information about products, to alert them to future needs, to resolve problems, or to address system maintenance issues. Coordinate installation of new equipment. Coordinate network or design activities with designers of associated networks. Design, organize,

and deliver product awareness, skills transfer, and product education sessions for staff and suppliers. Determine specific network hardware or software requirements, such as platforms, interfaces, bandwidths, or routine schemas. Develop disaster recovery plans. Communicate with customers, sales staff, or marketing staff to determine customer needs. Explain design specifications to integration or test engineers. Develop plans or budgets for network equipment replacement. Prepare design presentations and proposals for staff or customers. Supervise engineers and other staff in the design or implementation of network solutions. Use network computer-aided design (CAD) software packages to optimize network designs. Develop or maintain project reporting systems. Participate in network technology upgrade or expansion projects, including installation of hardware and software and integration testing. Research and test new or modified hardware or software products to determine performance and interoperability. Develop and implement solutions for network problems. Prepare or monitor project schedules, budgets, or cost control systems. Monitor and analyze network performance and data input/output reports to detect problems, identify inefficient use of computer resources, or perform capacity planning. Evaluate network designs to determine whether customer requirements are met efficiently and effectively. Estimate time and materials needed to complete projects. Develop or recommend network security measures, such as firewalls, network security audits, or automated security probes.

Personality Type: Conventional. These occupations frequently involve following set procedures and routines and can include working with data and details more than with ideas. Usually there is a clear line of authority to follow.

GOE—Interest Area/Cluster: 11. Information Technology. **Work Group:** 11.02. Information Technology Specialties. **Other Jobs in This**

Work Group: Computer and Information Scientists, Research; Computer Programmers; Computer Security Specialists; Computer Software Engineers, Applications; Computer Software Engineers, Systems Software; Computer Support Specialists; Computer Systems Analysts; Computer Systems Engineers/Architects; Database Administrators; Network Systems and Data Communications Analysts; Software Quality Assurance Engineers and Testers; Web Administrators; Web Developers.

Skills: No data available.

Education and Training Programs: Computer and Information Sciences, General; Computer Science; Computer Systems Networking and Telecommunications; Computer Engineering, General; Computer Software Engineering. **Related Knowledge/Courses:** No data available.

Work Environment: No data available.

Network Systems and Data Communications Analysts

- ❋ Education/Training Required: Bachelor's degree
- ❋ Annual Earnings: $68,220
- ❋ Beginning Wage: $40,100
- ❋ Earnings Growth Potential: High
- ❋ Growth: 53.4%
- ❋ Annual Job Openings: 35,086
- ❋ Self-Employed: 17.5%
- ❋ Part-Time: 8.6%

Analyze, design, test, and evaluate network systems, such as local area networks (LAN); wide area networks (WAN); and Internet, intranet, and other data communications systems. Perform network modeling, analysis, and planning. Research and recommend network and data communications hardware and software. Includes telecommunications specialists who deal with the interfacing of computer and communications equipment. May supervise computer programmers. Maintain needed files by adding and deleting files on the network server and backing up files to guarantee their safety in the event of problems with the network. Monitor system performance and provide security measures, troubleshooting, and maintenance as needed. Assist users to diagnose and solve data communication problems. Set up user accounts, regulating and monitoring file access to ensure confidentiality and proper use. Design and implement systems, network configurations, and network architecture, including hardware and software technology, site locations, and integration of technologies. Maintain the peripherals, such as printers, that are connected to the network. Identify areas of operation that need upgraded equipment such as modems, fiber-optic cables, and telephone wires. Train users in use of equipment. Develop and write procedures for installation, use, and troubleshooting of communications hardware and software. Adapt and modify existing software to meet specific needs. Work with other engineers, systems analysts, programmers, technicians, scientists, and top-level managers in the design, testing, and evaluation of systems. Test and evaluate hardware and software to determine efficiency, reliability, and compatibility with existing system and make purchase recommendations. Read technical manuals and brochures to determine which equipment meets establishment requirements. Consult customers, visit workplaces, or conduct surveys to determine present and future user needs. Visit vendors, attend conferences or training, and study technical journals to keep up with changes in technology.

Personality Type: Investigative. These occupations frequently involve working with ideas and require an extensive amount of thinking. They can involve searching for facts and figuring out problems mentally.

GOE—Interest Area/Cluster: 11. Information Technology. **Work Group:** 11.02. Information Technology Specialties. **Other Jobs in This Work Group:** Computer and Information Scientists, Research; Computer Programmers; Computer Security Specialists; Computer Software Engineers, Applications; Computer Software Engineers, Systems Software; Computer Support Specialists; Computer Systems Analysts; Computer Systems Engineers/Architects; Database Administrators; Network Designers; Software Quality Assurance Engineers and Testers; Web Administrators; Web Developers.

Skills—Installation: Installing equipment, machines, wiring, or programs to meet specifications. **Technology Design:** Generating or adapting equipment and technology to serve user needs. **Troubleshooting:** Determining what is causing an operating error and deciding what to do about it. **Systems Analysis:** Determining how a system should work and how changes will affect outcomes. **Programming:** Writing computer programs for various purposes. **Systems Evaluation:** Looking at many indicators of system performance and taking into account their accuracy. **Management of Material Resources:** Obtaining and seeing to the appropriate use of equipment, facilities, and materials needed to do certain work. **Operations Analysis:** Analyzing needs and product requirements to create a design.

Education and Training Programs: Computer and Information Sciences, General; Information Technology; Computer Systems Analysis/Analyst; Computer Systems Networking and Telecommunications; System, Networking, and LAN/WAN Management/Manager; Computer and Information Systems Security. **Related Knowledge/Courses—Telecommunications:** Transmission, broadcasting, switching, control, and operation of telecommunications systems. **Computers and Electronics:** Electric circuit boards, processors, chips, and computer hardware and software, including applications and programming. **Customer and Personal Service:** Principles and processes for providing customer and personal services, including needs assessment techniques, quality service standards, alternative delivery systems, and customer satisfaction evaluation techniques. **Engineering and Technology:** Equipment, tools, and mechanical devices and their uses to produce motion, light, power, technology, and other applications. **Education and Training:** Instructional methods and training techniques, including curriculum design principles, learning theory, group and individual teaching techniques, design of individual development plans, and test design principles. **Design:** Design techniques, principles, tools, and instruments involved in the production and use of precision technical plans, blueprints, drawings, and models.

Work Environment: Indoors; sitting.

Nuclear Medicine Technologists

- Education/Training Required: Associate degree
- Annual Earnings: $64,670
- Beginning Wage: $47,370
- Earnings Growth Potential: Low
- Growth: 14.8%
- Annual Job Openings: 1,290
- Self-Employed: 1.0%
- Part-Time: 17.3%

Prepare, administer, and measure radioactive isotopes in therapeutic, diagnostic, and tracer studies, using a variety of radioisotope equipment. Prepare stock solutions of radioactive

materials and calculate doses to be administered by radiologists. Subject patients to radiation. Execute blood volume, red cell survival, and fat absorption studies, following standard laboratory techniques. Detect and map radiopharmaceuticals in patients' bodies, using a camera to produce photographic or computer images. Administer radiopharmaceuticals or radiation intravenously to detect or treat diseases, using radioisotope equipment, under direction of a physician. Produce computer-generated or film images for interpretation by physicians. Calculate, measure, and record radiation dosages or radiopharmaceuticals received, used, and disposed, using computers and following physicians' prescriptions. Perform quality control checks on laboratory equipment and cameras. Maintain and calibrate radioisotope and laboratory equipment. Dispose of radioactive materials and store radiopharmaceuticals, following radiation safety procedures. Process cardiac function studies, using computers. Prepare stock radiopharmaceuticals, adhering to safety standards that minimize radiation exposure to workers and patients. Record and process results of procedures. Explain test procedures and safety precautions to patients and provide them with assistance during test procedures. Gather information on patients' illnesses and medical histories to guide choices of diagnostic procedures for therapies. Measure glandular activity, blood volume, red cell survival, and radioactivity of patient, using scanners, Geiger counters, scintillation counters, and other laboratory equipment. Train and supervise student or subordinate nuclear medicine technologists. Position radiation fields, radiation beams, and patients to allow for most effective treatment of patients' diseases, using computers. Add radioactive substances to biological specimens such as blood, urine, and feces to determine therapeutic drug or hormone levels. Develop treatment procedures for nuclear medicine treatment programs.

Personality Type: Investigative. These occupations frequently involve working with ideas and require an extensive amount of thinking. They can involve searching for facts and figuring out problems mentally.

GOE—Interest Area/Cluster: 08. Health Science. **Work Group:** 08.06. Medical Technology. **Other Jobs in This Work Group:** Biological Technicians; Cardiovascular Technologists and Technicians; Diagnostic Medical Sonographers; Medical and Clinical Laboratory Technicians; Medical and Clinical Laboratory Technologists; Medical Records and Health Information Technicians; Orthotists and Prosthetists; Radiologic Technicians; Radiologic Technologists; Radiologic Technologists and Technicians.

Skills—Operation Monitoring: Watching gauges, dials, or other indicators to make sure a machine is working properly. **Equipment Maintenance:** Performing routine maintenance and determining when and what kind of maintenance is needed. **Quality Control Analysis:** Evaluating the quality or performance of products, services, or processes. **Systems Analysis:** Determining how a system should work and how changes will affect outcomes. **Operation and Control:** Controlling operations of equipment or systems. **Systems Evaluation:** Looking at many indicators of system performance and taking into account their accuracy.

Education and Training Programs: Nuclear Medical Technology/Technologist; Radiation Protection/Health Physics Technician. **Related Knowledge/Courses—Medicine and Dentistry:** The information and techniques needed to diagnose and treat injuries, diseases, and deformities. This includes symptoms, treatment alternatives, drug properties and interactions, and preventive health-care measures. **Biology:** Plant and animal living tissue, cells, organisms, and entities, including their functions, interdependencies, and interactions with each other and the environment.

Chemistry: The composition, structure, and properties of substances and of the chemical processes and transformations that they undergo. This includes uses of chemicals and their interactions, danger signs, production techniques, and disposal methods. **Physics:** Physical principles, laws, and applications, including air, water, material dynamics, light, atomic principles, heat, electric theory, earth formations, and meteorological and related natural phenomena. **Customer and Personal Service:** Principles and processes for providing customer and personal services, including needs assessment techniques, quality service standards, alternative delivery systems, and customer satisfaction evaluation techniques. **Therapy and Counseling:** Information and techniques needed to rehabilitate physical and mental ailments and to provide career guidance, including alternative treatments, rehabilitation equipment and its proper use, and methods to evaluate treatment effects.

Work Environment: Indoors; contaminants; radiation; disease or infections; standing; using hands on objects, tools, or controls.

Nursing Instructors and Teachers, Postsecondary

* Education/Training Required: Doctoral degree
* Annual Earnings: $57,500
* Beginning Wage: $36,020
* Earnings Growth Potential: Medium
* Growth: 22.9%
* Annual Job Openings: 7,337
* Self-Employed: 0.4%
* Part-Time: 27.8%

Demonstrate and teach patient care in classroom and clinical units to nursing students. Includes both teachers primarily engaged in teaching and those who do a combination of both teaching and research. Initiate, facilitate, and moderate classroom discussions. Prepare and deliver lectures to undergraduate or graduate students on topics such as pharmacology, mental health nursing, and community health-care practices. Keep abreast of developments in their field by reading current literature, talking with colleagues, and participating in professional conferences. Prepare course materials such as syllabi, homework assignments, and handouts. Supervise students' laboratory and clinical work. Evaluate and grade students' classwork, laboratory and clinic work, assignments, and papers. Collaborate with colleagues to address teaching and research issues. Plan, evaluate, and revise curricula, course content, and course materials and methods of instruction. Assess clinical education needs and patient and client teaching needs, utilizing a variety of methods. Compile, administer, and grade examinations or assign this work to others. Advise students on academic and vocational curricula and on career issues. Maintain student attendance records, grades, and other required records. Maintain regularly scheduled office hours to advise and assist students. Supervise undergraduate or graduate teaching, internship, and research work. Conduct research in a particular field of knowledge and publish findings in professional journals, books, and/or electronic media. Participate in student recruitment, registration, and placement activities. Serve on academic or administrative committees that deal with institutional policies, departmental matters, and academic issues. Coordinate training programs with area universities, clinics, hospitals, health agencies, and/or vocational schools. Compile bibliographies of specialized materials for outside reading assignments. Select and obtain materials and supplies such as textbooks and laboratory equipment. Participate in campus and community events. Write grant proposals to procure external research funding. Act as advisers to student organizations.

Demonstrate patient care in clinical units of hospitals. Perform administrative duties such as serving as department head.

Personality Type: Social. These occupations frequently involve working with, communicating with, and teaching people and often involve helping or providing service to others.

GOE—Interest Area/Cluster: 05. Education and Training. **Work Group:** 05.03. Postsecondary and Adult Teaching and Instructing. **Other Jobs in This Work Group:** Adult Literacy, Remedial Education, and GED Teachers and Instructors; Agricultural Sciences Teachers, Postsecondary; Anthropology and Archeology Teachers, Postsecondary; Architecture Teachers, Postsecondary; Area, Ethnic, and Cultural Studies Teachers, Postsecondary; Art, Drama, and Music Teachers, Postsecondary; Atmospheric, Earth, Marine, and Space Sciences Teachers, Postsecondary; Biological Science Teachers, Postsecondary; Business Teachers, Postsecondary; Chemistry Teachers, Postsecondary; Communications Teachers, Postsecondary; Computer Science Teachers, Postsecondary; Criminal Justice and Law Enforcement Teachers, Postsecondary; Economics Teachers, Postsecondary; Education Teachers, Postsecondary; Engineering Teachers, Postsecondary; English Language and Literature Teachers, Postsecondary; Environmental Science Teachers, Postsecondary; Farm and Home Management Advisors; Foreign Language and Literature Teachers, Postsecondary; Forestry and Conservation Science Teachers, Postsecondary; Geography Teachers, Postsecondary; Graduate Teaching Assistants; Health Specialties Teachers, Postsecondary; History Teachers, Postsecondary; Home Economics Teachers, Postsecondary; Law Teachers, Postsecondary; Library Science Teachers, Postsecondary; Mathematical Science Teachers, Postsecondary; Philosophy and Religion Teachers, Postsecondary; Physics Teachers, Postsecondary; Political Science Teachers, Postsecondary; Psychology Teachers, Postsecondary; Recreation and Fitness Studies Teachers, Postsecondary; Social Work Teachers, Postsecondary; Sociology Teachers, Postsecondary.

Skills—Science: Using scientific methods to solve problems. **Instructing:** Teaching others how to do something. **Writing:** Communicating effectively with others in writing as indicated by the needs of the audience. **Social Perceptiveness:** Being aware of others' reactions and understanding why they react the way they do. **Reading Comprehension:** Understanding written sentences and paragraphs in work-related documents. **Learning Strategies:** Using multiple approaches when learning or teaching new things. **Service Orientation:** Actively looking for ways to help people. **Critical Thinking:** Using logic and analysis to identify the strengths and weaknesses of different approaches.

Education and Training Programs: Pre-Nursing Studies; Nursing—Registered Nurse Training (RN, ASN, BSN, MSN); Adult Health Nurse/Nursing; Nurse Anesthetist; Family Practice Nurse/Nurse Practitioner; Maternal/Child Health and Neonatal Nurse/Nursing; Nurse Midwife/Nursing Midwifery; Nursing Science (MS, PhD); Pediatric Nurse/Nursing; Psychiatric/Mental Health Nurse/Nursing; Public Health/Community Nurse/Nursing; others. **Related Knowledge/Courses—Therapy and Counseling:** Information and techniques needed to rehabilitate physical and mental ailments and to provide career guidance, including alternative treatments, rehabilitation equipment and its proper use, and methods to evaluate treatment effects. **Biology:** Plant and animal living tissue, cells, organisms, and entities, including their functions, interdependencies, and interactions with each other and the environment. **Sociology and Anthropology:** Group behavior and dynamics; societal trends and influences; and cultures and their history, migrations, ethnicity, and origins. **Medicine and Dentistry:** The information and techniques needed to diagnose and treat injuries, diseases, and deformities. This includes symptoms, treatment alternatives, drug properties and interactions, and preventive health-care measures. **Philosophy and Theology:** Different philosophical systems and religions, including their basic principles, values, ethics, ways of thinking, customs, and practices and their impact on human culture. **Psychology:** Human behavior and performance, mental processes, psychological research methods, and the assessment and treatment of behavioral and affective disorders.

Work Environment: Indoors; disease or infections; sitting.

Obstetricians and Gynecologists

* Education/Training Required: First professional degree
* Annual Earnings: More than $145,600
* Beginning Wage: $100,770
* Earnings Growth Potential: Cannot be calculated
* Growth: 14.2%
* Annual Job Openings: 38,027
* Self-Employed: 14.7%
* Part-Time: 8.1%

The job openings listed here are shared with Anesthesiologists; Family and General Practitioners; Internists, General; Pediatricians, General; Psychiatrists; and Surgeons.

Diagnose, treat, and help prevent diseases of women, especially those affecting the reproductive system and the process of childbirth. Care for and treat women during prenatal, natal, and post-natal periods. Explain procedures and discuss test results or prescribed treatments with patients. Treat diseases of female organs. Monitor patients' condition and progress and re-evaluate treatments as necessary. Perform cesarean sections or other surgical procedures as needed to preserve patients' health and deliver babies safely. Prescribe or administer therapy, medication, and other specialized medical care to treat or prevent illness, disease, or injury. Analyze records, reports, test results, or examination information to diagnose medical condition of patient. Collect, record, and maintain patient information, such as medical histories, reports, and examination results. Advise patients and community members concerning diet, activity, hygiene, and disease prevention. Refer patient to medical specialist or other practitioner when necessary. Consult with, or provide consulting services to, other physicians. Direct and coordinate activities of nurses, students, assistants, specialists, therapists, and other medical staff. Plan, implement, or administer health programs in hospitals, businesses, or communities for prevention and treatment of injuries or illnesses. Prepare government and organizational reports on birth, death, and disease statistics; workforce evaluations; or the medical status of individuals. Conduct research to develop or test medications, treatments, or procedures to prevent or control disease or injury.

Personality Type: Investigative. These occupations frequently involve working with ideas and require an extensive amount of thinking. They can involve searching for facts and figuring out problems mentally.

GOE—Interest Area/Cluster: 08. Health Science. **Work Group:** 08.02. Medicine and Surgery. **Other Jobs in This Work Group:** Anesthesiologists; Family and General Practitioners; Internists, General; Pediatricians, General; Pharmacists; Physician Assistants; Psychiatrists; Registered Nurses; Surgeons.

Skills—Science: Using scientific methods to solve problems. **Judgment and Decision Making:**

Weighing the relative costs and benefits of a potential action. **Reading Comprehension:** Understanding written sentences and paragraphs in work-related documents. **Complex Problem Solving:** Identifying complex problems, reviewing the options, and implementing solutions. **Active Learning:** Working with new material or information to grasp its implications. **Social Perceptiveness:** Being aware of others' reactions and understanding why they react the way they do. **Critical Thinking:** Using logic and analysis to identify the strengths and weaknesses of different approaches. **Instructing:** Teaching others how to do something.

Education and Training Programs: Neonatal-Perinatal Medicine; Obstetrics and Gynecology. **Related Knowledge/Courses—Medicine and Dentistry:** The information and techniques needed to diagnose and treat injuries, diseases, and deformities. This includes symptoms, treatment alternatives, drug properties and interactions, and preventive health-care measures. **Therapy and Counseling:** Information and techniques needed to rehabilitate physical and mental ailments and to provide career guidance, including alternative treatments, rehabilitation equipment and its proper use, and methods to evaluate treatment effects. **Biology:** Plant and animal living tissue, cells, organisms, and entities, including their functions, interdependencies, and interactions with each other and the environment. **Psychology:** Human behavior and performance, mental processes, psychological research methods, and the assessment and treatment of behavioral and affective disorders. **Sociology and Anthropology:** Group behavior and dynamics; societal trends and influences; and cultures and their history, migrations, ethnicity, and origins. **Chemistry:** The composition, structure, and properties of substances and of the chemical processes and transformations that they undergo. This includes uses of chemicals

and their interactions, danger signs, production techniques, and disposal methods.

Work Environment: Indoors; disease or infections; standing; using hands on objects, tools, or controls.

Occupational Therapist Assistants

- ❋ Education/Training Required: Associate degree
- ❋ Annual Earnings: $45,050
- ❋ Beginning Wage: $27,870
- ❋ Earnings Growth Potential: Medium
- ❋ Growth: 25.4%
- ❋ Annual Job Openings: 2,634
- ❋ Self-Employed: 3.5%
- ❋ Part-Time: 17.8%

Assist occupational therapists in providing occupational therapy treatments and procedures. May, in accordance with state laws, assist in development of treatment plans, carry out routine functions, direct activity programs, and document the progress of treatments. Generally requires formal training. Observe and record patients' progress, attitudes, and behavior and maintain this information in client records. Maintain and promote a positive attitude toward clients and their treatment programs. Monitor patients' performance in therapy activities, providing encouragement. Select therapy activities to fit patients' needs and capabilities. Instruct, or assist in instructing, patients and families in home programs, basic living skills, and the care and use of adaptive equipment. Evaluate the daily living skills and capacities of physically, developmentally, or emotionally disabled clients. Aid patients in dressing and grooming themselves. Implement, or assist occupational therapists with implementing, treatment plans designed to help clients function independently. Report to supervisors, verbally or in writing, on patients' progress, attitudes, and behavior. Alter treatment programs to obtain better results if treatment is not having the intended effect. Work under the direction of occupational therapists to plan, implement, and administer educational, vocational, and recreational programs that restore and enhance performance in individuals with functional impairments. Design, fabricate, and repair assistive devices and make adaptive changes to equipment and environments. Assemble, clean, and maintain equipment and materials for patient use. Teach patients how to deal constructively with their emotions. Perform clerical duties such as scheduling appointments, collecting data, and documenting health insurance billings. Transport patients to and from the occupational therapy work area. Demonstrate therapy techniques such as manual and creative arts or games. Order any needed educational or treatment supplies. Assist educational specialists or clinical psychologists in administering situational or diagnostic tests to measure client's abilities or progress.

Personality Type: Social. These occupations frequently involve working with, communicating with, and teaching people and often involve helping or providing service to others.

GOE—Interest Area/Cluster: 08. Health Science. **Work Group:** 08.07. Medical Therapy. **Other Jobs in This Work Group:** Audiologists; Occupational Therapists; Physical Therapist Assistants; Physical Therapists; Radiation Therapists; Recreational Therapists; Respiratory Therapists; Respiratory Therapy Technicians; Speech-Language Pathologists.

Skills—Social Perceptiveness: Being aware of others' reactions and understanding why they react the way they do. **Operations Analysis:** Analyzing needs and product requirements to create a design. **Equipment Selection:** Determining the kind of tools and equipment needed to do a job. **Service Orientation:** Actively looking for ways to help people. **Writing:** Communicating effectively with others in writing as indicated by the needs of the audience. **Persuasion:** Persuading others to approach things differently. **Monitoring:** Assessing how well one is doing when learning or doing something. **Time Management:** Managing one's own time and the time of others.

Education and Training Program: Occupational Therapist Assistant. **Related Knowledge/Courses—Therapy and Counseling:** Information and techniques needed to rehabilitate physical and mental ailments and to provide career guidance, including alternative treatments, rehabilitation equipment and its proper use, and methods to evaluate treatment effects. **Psychology:** Human behavior and performance, mental processes, psychological research methods, and the assessment and treatment of behavioral and affective disorders. **Sociology and Anthropology:** Group behavior and dynamics; societal trends and influences; and cultures and their history, migrations, ethnicity, and origins. **Philosophy and Theology:** Different philosophical systems and religions, including their basic principles, values, ethics, ways of thinking, customs, and practices and their impact on human culture. **Medicine and Dentistry:** The information and techniques needed to diagnose and treat injuries, diseases, and deformities. This includes symptoms, treatment alternatives, drug properties and interactions, and preventive health-care measures. **Biology:** Plant and animal living tissue, cells, organisms, and entities, including their functions, interdependencies, and interactions with each other and the environment.

Work Environment: Indoors; disease or infections; standing; walking and running; using hands on objects, tools, or controls; bending or twisting the body.

Occupational Therapists

* Education/Training Required: Master's degree
* Annual Earnings: $63,790
* Beginning Wage: $42,330
* Earnings Growth Potential: Low
* Growth: 23.1%
* Annual Job Openings: 8,338
* Self-Employed: 8.6%
* Part-Time: 29.8%

Assess, plan, organize, and participate in rehabilitative programs that help restore vocational, homemaking, and daily living skills, as well as general independence, to disabled persons. Plan, organize, and conduct occupational therapy programs in hospital, institutional, or community settings to help rehabilitate those impaired because of illness, injury, or psychological or developmental problems. Test and evaluate patients' physical and mental abilities and analyze medical data to determine realistic rehabilitation goals for patients. Select activities that will help individuals learn work and life-management skills within limits of their mental and physical capabilities. Evaluate patients' progress and prepare reports that detail progress. Complete and maintain necessary records. Train caregivers to provide for the needs of patients during and after therapies. Recommend changes in patients' work or living environments, consistent with their needs and capabilities. Develop and participate in health promotion programs, group activities, or discussions to promote client health, facilitate social adjustment, alleviate stress, and prevent physical or mental disability. Consult with rehabilitation team to select activity programs and coordinate occupational therapy with other therapeutic activities. Plan and implement programs and social activities to help patients learn work and school skills and adjust to handicaps. Design and create, or requisition, special supplies and equipment such as splints, braces and computer-aided adaptive equipment. Conduct research in occupational therapy. Provide training and supervision in therapy techniques and objectives for students and nurses and other medical staff. Help clients improve decision making, abstract reasoning, memory, sequencing, coordination, and perceptual skills, using computer programs. Advise on health risks in the workplace and on health-related transition to retirement. Lay out materials such as puzzles, scissors, and eating utensils for use in therapy, and clean and repair these tools after therapy sessions. Provide patients with assistance in locating and holding jobs.

Personality Type: Social. These occupations frequently involve working with, communicating with, and teaching people and often involve helping or providing service to others.

GOE—Interest Area/Cluster: 08. Health Science. **Work Group:** 08.07. Medical Therapy. **Other Jobs in This Work Group:** Audiologists; Occupational Therapist Assistants; Physical Therapist Assistants; Physical Therapists; Radiation Therapists; Recreational Therapists; Respiratory Therapists; Respiratory Therapy Technicians; Speech-Language Pathologists.

Skills—Systems Evaluation: Looking at many indicators of system performance and taking into account their accuracy. **Systems Analysis:** Determining how a system should work and how changes will affect outcomes. **Social Perceptiveness:** Being aware of others' reactions and understanding why they react the way they do. **Judgment and Decision Making:** Weighing the relative costs and benefits of a potential action. **Service Orientation:** Actively looking for ways to help people. **Persuasion:** Persuading others to approach things differently. **Management of Personnel Resources:** Motivating, developing, and directing people as they work; identifying the best people for the job.

Complex Problem Solving: Identifying complex problems, reviewing the options, and implementing solutions.

Education and Training Program: Occupational Therapy/Therapist. **Related Knowledge/Courses—Therapy and Counseling:** Information and techniques needed to rehabilitate physical and mental ailments and to provide career guidance, including alternative treatments, rehabilitation equipment and its proper use, and methods to evaluate treatment effects. **Psychology:** Human behavior and performance, mental processes, psychological research methods, and the assessment and treatment of behavioral and affective disorders. **Sociology and Anthropology:** Group behavior and dynamics; societal trends and influences; and cultures and their history, migrations, ethnicity, and origins. **Medicine and Dentistry:** The information and techniques needed to diagnose and treat injuries, diseases, and deformities. This includes symptoms, treatment alternatives, drug properties and interactions, and preventive health-care measures. **Biology:** Plant and animal living tissue, cells, organisms, and entities, including their functions, interdependencies, and interactions with each other and the environment. **Education and Training:** Instructional methods and training techniques, including curriculum design principles, learning theory, group and individual teaching techniques, design of individual development plans, and test design principles.

Work Environment: Indoors; disease or infections; standing; using hands on objects, tools, or controls; bending or twisting the body.

Operations Research Analysts

- Education/Training Required: Master's degree
- Annual Earnings: $66,950
- Beginning Wage: $39,760
- Earnings Growth Potential: High
- Growth: 10.6%
- Annual Job Openings: 5,727
- Self-Employed: 0.2%
- Part-Time: 5.6%

Formulate and apply mathematical modeling and other optimizing methods, using a computer to develop and interpret information that assists management with decision making, policy formulation, or other managerial functions. May develop related software, service, or products. Frequently concentrates on collecting and analyzing data and developing decision support software. May develop and supply optimal time, cost, or logistics networks for program evaluation, review, or implementation. Formulate mathematical or simulation models of problems, relating constants and variables, restrictions, alternatives, and conflicting objectives and their numerical parameters. Collaborate with others in the organization to ensure successful implementation of chosen problem solutions. Analyze information obtained from management in order to conceptualize and define operational problems. Perform validation and testing of models to ensure adequacy; reformulate models as necessary. Collaborate with senior managers and decision-makers to identify and solve a variety of problems and to clarify management objectives. Define data requirements; then gather and validate information, applying judgment and statistical tests. Study and analyze information about alternative courses of action in order to determine which plan will offer the best outcomes. Prepare management reports defining and evaluating problems and recommending solutions. Break systems into their component parts, assign numerical values to each component, and examine the mathematical relationships between them. Specify manipulative or computational methods to be applied to models. Observe the current system in operation and gather and analyze information about each of the parts of component problems, using a variety of sources. Design, conduct, and evaluate experimental operational models in cases where models cannot be developed from existing data. Develop and apply time and cost networks in order to plan, control, and review large projects. Develop business methods and procedures, including accounting systems, file systems, office systems, logistics systems, and production schedules.

Personality Type: Investigative. These occupations frequently involve working with ideas and require an extensive amount of thinking. They can involve searching for facts and figuring out problems mentally.

GOE—Interest Area/Cluster: 04. Business and Administration. **Work Group:** 04.05. Accounting, Auditing, and Analytical Support. **Other Jobs in This Work Group:** Accountants; Accountants and Auditors; Auditors; Budget Analysts; Industrial Engineering Technicians; Logisticians; Management Analysts.

Skills—Programming: Writing computer programs for various purposes. **Systems Analysis:** Determining how a system should work and how changes will affect outcomes. **Operations Analysis:** Analyzing needs and product requirements to create a design. **Science:** Using scientific methods to solve problems. **Mathematics:** Using mathematics to solve problems. **Systems Evaluation:** Looking at many indicators of system performance and taking into account their accuracy.

Complex Problem Solving: Identifying complex problems, reviewing the options, and implementing solutions. **Judgment and Decision Making:** Weighing the relative costs and benefits of a potential action.

Education and Training Programs: Educational Evaluation and Research; Educational Statistics and Research Methods; Operations Research; Management Science, General; Management Sciences and Quantitative Methods, Other. **Related Knowledge/Courses—Mathematics:** Numbers and their operations and interrelationships, including arithmetic, algebra, geometry, calculus, and statistics and their applications. **Engineering and Technology:** Equipment, tools, and mechanical devices and their uses to produce motion, light, power, technology, and other applications. **Computers and Electronics:** Electric circuit boards, processors, chips, and computer hardware and software, including applications and programming. **Production and Processing:** Inputs, outputs, raw materials, waste, quality control, costs, and techniques for maximizing the manufacture and distribution of goods. **Economics and Accounting:** Economic and accounting principles and practices, the financial markets, banking, and the analysis and reporting of financial data. **Administration and Management:** Principles and processes involved in business and organizational planning, coordination, and execution. This includes strategic planning, resource allocation, manpower modeling, leadership techniques, and production methods.

Work Environment: Indoors; sitting.

Optometrists

- Education/Training Required: First professional degree
- Annual Earnings: $93,800
- Beginning Wage: $47,980
- Earnings Growth Potential: High
- Growth: 11.3%
- Annual Job Openings: 1,789
- Self-Employed: 25.5%
- Part-Time: 20.8%

Diagnose, manage, and treat conditions and diseases of the human eye and visual system. Examine eyes and visual systems, diagnose problems or impairments, prescribe corrective lenses, and provide treatment. May prescribe therapeutic drugs to treat specific eye conditions. Examine eyes, using observation, instruments, and pharmaceutical agents, to determine visual acuity and perception, focus, and coordination and to diagnose diseases and other abnormalities such as glaucoma or color blindness. Prescribe medications to treat eye diseases if state laws permit. Analyze test results and develop treatment plans. Prescribe, supply, fit, and adjust eyeglasses, contact lenses, and other vision aids. Educate and counsel patients on contact lens care, visual hygiene, lighting arrangements, and safety factors. Remove foreign bodies from eyes. Consult with and refer patients to ophthalmologist or other health care practitioners if additional medical treatment is determined necessary. Provide patients undergoing eye surgeries such as cataract and laser vision correction, with pre- and post-operative care. Prescribe therapeutic procedures to correct or conserve vision. Provide vision therapy and low vision rehabilitation.

Personality Type: Investigative. These occupations frequently involve working with ideas and require an extensive amount of thinking. They can involve searching for facts and figuring out problems mentally.

GOE—Interest Area/Cluster: 08. Health Science. **Work Group:** 08.04. Health Specialties. **Other Jobs in This Work Group:** Chiropractors; Podiatrists.

Skills—Management of Personnel Resources: Motivating, developing, and directing people as they work; identifying the best people for the job. **Systems Evaluation:** Looking at many indicators of system performance and taking into account their accuracy. **Writing:** Communicating effectively with others in writing as indicated by the needs of the audience. **Systems Analysis:** Determining how a system should work and how changes will affect outcomes.

Education and Training Program: Optometry (OD). **Related Knowledge/Courses—Medicine and Dentistry:** The information and techniques needed to diagnose and treat injuries, diseases, and deformities. This includes symptoms, treatment alternatives, drug properties and interactions, and preventive health-care measures. **Biology:** Plant and animal living tissue, cells, organisms, and entities, including their functions, interdependencies, and interactions with each other and the environment. **Therapy and Counseling:** Information and techniques needed to rehabilitate physical and mental ailments and to provide career guidance, including alternative treatments, rehabilitation equipment and its proper use, and methods to evaluate treatment effects. **Physics:** Physical principles, laws, and applications, including air, water, material dynamics, light, atomic principles, heat, electric theory, earth formations, and meteorological and related natural phenomena. **Sales and Marketing:** Principles and methods involved in showing, promoting, and selling products or services. This includes marketing strategies and tactics, product demonstration and sales techniques, and sales control systems. **Economics and**

Optometrists

200 Best Jobs for College Graduates © JIST Works

315

Accounting: Economic and accounting principles and practices, the financial markets, banking, and the analysis and reporting of financial data.

Work Environment: Indoors; disease or infections; sitting; using hands on objects, tools, or controls.

Oral and Maxillofacial Surgeons

* Education/Training Required: First professional degree
* Annual Earnings: More than $145,600
* Beginning Wage: $63,850
* Earnings Growth Potential: Cannot be calculated
* Growth: 9.1%
* Annual Job Openings: 400
* Self-Employed: 30.6%
* Part-Time: 25.9%

Perform surgery on mouth, jaws, and related head and neck structure to execute difficult and multiple extractions of teeth, to remove tumors and other abnormal growths, to correct abnormal jaw relations by mandibular or maxillary revision, to prepare mouth for insertion of dental prosthesis, or to treat fractured jaws. Administer general and local anesthetics. Remove impacted, damaged, and non-restorable teeth. Evaluate the position of the wisdom teeth in order to determine whether problems exist currently or might occur in the future. Collaborate with other professionals such as restorative dentists and orthodontists in order to plan treatment. Perform surgery to prepare the mouth for dental implants and to aid in the regeneration of deficient bone and gum tissues. Remove tumors and other abnormal growths of the oral and facial regions, using surgical instruments. Treat infections of the oral cavity, salivary glands, jaws, and neck. Treat problems affecting the oral mucosa such as mouth ulcers and infections. Provide emergency treatment of facial injuries, including facial lacerations, intra-oral lacerations, and fractured facial bones. Perform surgery on the mouth and jaws in order to treat conditions such as cleft lip and palate and jaw growth problems. Restore form and function by moving skin, bone, nerves, and other tissues from other parts of the body in order to reconstruct the jaws and face. Perform minor cosmetic procedures such as chin and cheekbone enhancements and minor facial rejuvenation procedures including the use of Botox and laser technology. Treat snoring problems, using laser surgery.

Personality Type: Realistic. These occupations frequently involve work activities that include practical, hands-on problems and solutions. They often deal with plants; animals; and real-world materials such as wood, tools, and machinery. Many of the occupations require working outside and don't involve a lot of paperwork or working closely with others.

GOE—Interest Area/Cluster: 08. Health Science. **Work Group:** 08.03. Dentistry. **Other Jobs in This Work Group:** Dental Hygienists; Dentists, General; Orthodontists; Prosthodontists.

Skills—Science: Using scientific methods to solve problems. **Management of Financial Resources:** Determining how money will be spent to get the work done and accounting for these expenditures. **Equipment Selection:** Determining the kind of tools and equipment needed to do a job. **Service Orientation:** Actively looking for ways to help people. **Complex Problem Solving:** Identifying complex problems, reviewing the options, and implementing solutions. **Management of Personnel Resources:** Motivating, developing, and directing people as they work; identifying the best people for the job. **Active Learning:** Working with new material or information to grasp its implications. **Reading Comprehension:** Understanding written sentences and paragraphs in work-related documents.

Education and Training Programs: Oral/Maxillofacial Surgery (Cert, MS, PhD); Dental/Oral Surgery Specialty. **Related Knowledge/Courses— Medicine and Dentistry:** The information and techniques needed to diagnose and treat injuries, diseases, and deformities. This includes symptoms, treatment alternatives, drug properties and interactions, and preventive health-care measures. **Biology:** Plant and animal living tissue, cells, organisms, and entities, including their functions, interdependencies, and interactions with each other and the environment. **Therapy and Counseling:** Information and techniques needed to rehabilitate physical and mental ailments and to provide career guidance, including alternative treatments, rehabilitation equipment and its proper use, and methods to evaluate treatment effects. **Chemistry:** The composition, structure, and properties of substances and of the chemical processes and transformations that they undergo. This includes uses of chemicals and their interactions, danger signs, production techniques, and disposal methods. **Psychology:** Human behavior and performance, mental processes, psychological research methods, and the assessment and treatment of behavioral and affective disorders. **Personnel and Human Resources:** Principles and procedures for personnel recruitment; selection; training; compensation and benefits; labor relations and negotiation; and personnel information systems.

Work Environment: Indoors; disease or infections; standing; using hands on objects, tools, or controls; bending or twisting the body; repetitive motions.

Orthodontists

* Education/Training Required: First professional degree
* Annual Earnings: More than $145,600
* Beginning Wage: $95,740
* Earnings Growth Potential: Cannot be calculated
* Growth: 9.2%
* Annual Job Openings: 479
* Self-Employed: 43.3%
* Part-Time: 25.9%

Examine, diagnose, and treat dental malocclusions and oral cavity anomalies. Design and fabricate appliances to realign teeth and jaws to produce and maintain normal function and to improve appearance. Fit dental appliances in patients' mouths to alter the position and relationship of teeth and jaws and to realign teeth. Study diagnostic records such as medical/dental histories, plaster models of the teeth, photos of a patient's face and teeth, and X rays to develop patient treatment plans. Diagnose teeth and jaw or other dental-facial abnormalities. Examine patients to assess abnormalities of jaw development, tooth position, and other dental-facial structures. Prepare diagnostic and treatment records. Adjust dental appliances periodically to produce and maintain normal function. Provide patients with proposed treatment plans and cost estimates. Instruct dental officers and technical assistants in orthodontic procedures and techniques. Coordinate orthodontic services with other dental and medical services. Design and fabricate appliances, such as space maintainers, retainers, and labial and lingual arch wires.

Personality Type: Investigative. These occupations frequently involve working with ideas and require an extensive amount of thinking. They can involve searching for facts and figuring out problems mentally.

GOE—Interest Area/Cluster: 08. Health Science. **Work Group:** 08.03. Dentistry. **Other Jobs in This Work Group:** Dental Hygienists; Dentists, General; Oral and Maxillofacial Surgeons; Prosthodontists.

Skills—Management of Financial Resources: Determining how money will be spent to get the work done and accounting for these expenditures. **Equipment Selection:** Determining the kind of tools and equipment needed to do a job. **Management of Personnel Resources:** Motivating, developing, and directing people as they work; identifying the best people for the job. **Management of Material Resources:** Obtaining and seeing to the appropriate use of equipment, facilities, and materials needed to do certain work. **Technology Design:** Generating or adapting equipment and technology to serve user needs. **Judgment and Decision Making:** Weighing the relative costs and benefits of a potential action. **Operations Analysis:** Analyzing needs and product requirements to create a design. **Service Orientation:** Actively looking for ways to help people.

Education and Training Programs: Orthodontics/Orthodontology (Cert, MS, PhD); Orthodontics Specialty. **Related Knowledge/Courses—Medicine and Dentistry:** The information and techniques needed to diagnose and treat injuries, diseases, and deformities. This includes symptoms, treatment alternatives, drug properties and interactions, and preventive health-care measures. **Biology:** Plant and animal living tissue, cells, organisms, and entities, including their functions, interdependencies, and interactions with each other and the environment. **Sales and Marketing:** Principles and methods involved in showing, promoting, and selling products or services. This includes marketing strategies and tactics, product demonstration and sales techniques, and sales control

systems. **Economics and Accounting:** Economic and accounting principles and practices, the financial markets, banking, and the analysis and reporting of financial data. **Personnel and Human Resources:** Principles and procedures for personnel recruitment; selection; training; compensation and benefits; labor relations and negotiation; and personnel information systems. **Customer and Personal Service:** Principles and processes for providing customer and personal services, including needs assessment techniques, quality service standards, alternative delivery systems, and customer satisfaction evaluation techniques.

Work Environment: Indoors; disease or infections; sitting; using hands on objects, tools, or controls; bending or twisting the body; repetitive motions.

Paralegals and Legal Assistants

* Education/Training Required: Associate degree
* Annual Earnings: $44,990
* Beginning Wage: $28,360
* Earnings Growth Potential: Medium
* Growth: 22.2%
* Annual Job Openings: 22,756
* Self-Employed: 2.2%
* Part-Time: 11.0%

Assist lawyers by researching legal precedent, investigating facts, or preparing legal documents. Conduct research to support a legal proceeding, to formulate a defense, or to initiate legal action. Prepare legal documents, including briefs, pleadings, appeals, wills, contracts, and real estate closing statements. Prepare affidavits or other documents, maintain document file, and file pleadings with court clerk. Gather and analyze research data, such as statutes; decisions; and legal articles, codes, and documents. Investigate facts and law of cases to determine causes of action and to prepare cases. Call upon witnesses to testify at hearing. Direct and coordinate law office activity, including delivery of subpoenas. Arbitrate disputes between parties and assist in real estate closing process. Keep and monitor legal volumes to ensure that law library is up to date. Appraise and inventory real and personal property for estate planning.

Personality Type: Conventional. These occupations frequently involve following set procedures and routines and can include working with data and details more than with ideas. Usually there is a clear line of authority to follow.

GOE—Interest Area/Cluster: 12. Law and Public Safety. **Work Group:** 12.03. Legal Support. **Other Jobs in This Work Group:** Law Clerks.

Skills—Writing: Communicating effectively with others in writing as indicated by the needs of the audience. **Active Listening:** Listening to what other people are saying and asking questions as appropriate. **Speaking:** Talking to others to effectively convey information. **Time Management:** Managing one's own time and the time of others. **Reading Comprehension:** Understanding written sentences and paragraphs in work-related documents. **Monitoring:** Assessing how well one is doing when learning or doing something.

Education and Training Program: Legal Assistant/Paralegal. **Related Knowledge/Courses— Clerical Practices:** Administrative and clerical procedures and systems such as word-processing systems, filing and records management systems, stenography and transcription, forms, design principles, and other office procedures and terminology. **Law and Government:** Laws, legal codes, court procedures, precedents, government regulations, executive orders, agency rules, and the democratic political process. **Computers and Electronics:** Electric circuit boards, processors, chips, and computer hardware and software, including applications and programming. **Personnel and Human Resources:** Principles and procedures for personnel recruitment; selection; training; compensation and benefits; labor relations and negotiation; and personnel information systems. **English Language:** The structure and content of the English language, including the meaning and spelling of words, rules of composition, and grammar. **Customer and Personal Service:** Principles and processes for providing customer and personal services, including needs assessment techniques, quality service standards, alternative delivery systems, and customer satisfaction evaluation techniques.

Work Environment: Indoors; sitting; repetitive motions.

Pediatricians, General

- ❋ Education/Training Required: First professional degree
- ❋ Annual Earnings: $140,690
- ❋ Beginning Wage: $67,430
- ❋ Earnings Growth Potential: Very high
- ❋ Growth: 14.2%
- ❋ Annual Job Openings: 38,027
- ❋ Self-Employed: 14.7%
- ❋ Part-Time: 8.1%

The job openings listed here are shared with Anesthesiologists; Family and General Practitioners; Internists, General; Obstetricians and Gynecologists; Psychiatrists; and Surgeons.

Diagnose, treat, and help prevent children's diseases and injuries. Examine patients or order, perform, and interpret diagnostic tests to obtain information on medical condition and determine diagnosis. Examine children regularly to assess their growth and development. Prescribe or administer treatment, therapy, medication, vaccination, and other specialized medical care to treat or prevent illness, disease, or injury in infants and children. Collect, record, and maintain patient information, such as medical history, reports, and examination results. Advise patients, parents or guardians, and community members concerning diet, activity, hygiene, and disease prevention. Treat children who have minor illnesses, acute and chronic health problems, and growth and development concerns. Explain procedures and discuss test results or prescribed treatments with patients and parents or guardians. Monitor patients' condition and progress and re-evaluate treatments as necessary. Plan and execute medical care programs to aid in the mental and physical growth and development of children and adolescents. Refer patient to medical specialist or other practitioner when necessary. Direct and coordinate activities of nurses, students, assistants, specialists, therapists, and other medical staff. Provide consulting services to other physicians. Plan, implement, or administer health programs or standards in hospital, business, or community for information, prevention, or treatment of injury or illness. Operate on patients to remove, repair, or improve functioning of diseased or injured body parts and systems. Conduct research to study anatomy and develop or test medications, treatments, or procedures to prevent or control disease or injury. Prepare reports for government or management of birth, death, and disease statistics; workforce evaluations; or medical status of individuals.

Personality Type: Investigative. These occupations frequently involve working with ideas and require an extensive amount of thinking. They can involve searching for facts and figuring out problems mentally.

GOE—Interest Area/Cluster: 08. Health Science. **Work Group:** 08.02. Medicine and Surgery.

Other Jobs in This Work Group: Anesthesiologists; Family and General Practitioners; Internists, General; Obstetricians and Gynecologists; Pharmacists; Physician Assistants; Psychiatrists; Registered Nurses; Surgeons.

Skills—Science: Using scientific methods to solve problems. **Social Perceptiveness:** Being aware of others' reactions and understanding why they react the way they do. **Active Learning:** Working with new material or information to grasp its implications. **Reading Comprehension:** Understanding written sentences and paragraphs in work-related documents. **Persuasion:** Persuading others to approach things differently. **Critical Thinking:** Using logic and analysis to identify the strengths and weaknesses of different approaches. **Management of Financial Resources:** Determining how money will be spent to get the work done and accounting for these expenditures. **Monitoring:** Assessing how well one is doing when learning or doing something.

Education and Training Programs: Child/Pediatric Neurology; Family Medicine; Neonatal-Perinatal Medicine; Pediatric Cardiology; Pediatric Endocrinology; Pediatric Hemato-Oncology; Pediatric Nephrology; Pediatric Orthopedics; Pediatric Surgery; Pediatrics. **Related Knowledge/Courses—Medicine and Dentistry:** The information and techniques needed to diagnose and treat injuries, diseases, and deformities. This includes symptoms, treatment alternatives, drug properties and interactions, and preventive health-care measures. **Therapy and Counseling:** Information and techniques needed to rehabilitate physical and mental ailments and to provide career guidance, including alternative treatments, rehabilitation equipment and its proper use, and methods to evaluate treatment effects. **Biology:** Plant and animal living tissue, cells, organisms, and entities, including their functions, interdependencies, and interactions with each other and the environment.

Psychology: Human behavior and performance, mental processes, psychological research methods, and the assessment and treatment of behavioral and affective disorders. **Chemistry:** The composition, structure, and properties of substances and of the chemical processes and transformations that they undergo. This includes uses of chemicals and their interactions, danger signs, production techniques, and disposal methods. **Sociology and Anthropology:** Group behavior and dynamics; societal trends and influences; and cultures and their history, migrations, ethnicity, and origins.

Work Environment: Indoors; disease or infections; standing; using hands on objects, tools, or controls.

Personal Financial Advisors

- ❋ Education/Training Required: Bachelor's degree
- ❋ Annual Earnings: $67,660
- ❋ Beginning Wage: $33,100
- ❋ Earnings Growth Potential: Very high
- ❋ Growth: 41.0%
- ❋ Annual Job Openings: 17,114
- ❋ Self-Employed: 30.9%
- ❋ Part-Time: 7.7%

Advise clients on financial plans, using knowledge of tax and investment strategies, securities, insurance, pension plans, and real estate. Duties include assessing clients' assets, liabilities, cash flows, insurance coverages, tax statuses, and financial objectives to establish investment strategies. Prepare and interpret for clients information such as investment performance reports, financial document summaries, and income projections. Recommend strategies clients can use to achieve their financial goals and objectives, including specific recommendations in such areas as cash management, insurance coverage, and investment planning. Build and maintain client bases, keeping current client plans up-to-date and recruiting new clients on an ongoing basis. Devise debt liquidation plans that include payoff priorities and timelines. Implement financial planning recommendations, or refer clients to someone who can assist them with plan implementation. Interview clients to determine their current incomes, expenses, insurance coverages, tax statuses, financial objectives, risk tolerances, and other information needed to develop financial plans. Monitor financial market trends to ensure that plans are effective, and to identify any necessary updates. Explain and document for clients the types of services that are to be provided, and the responsibilities to be taken by personal financial advisors. Explain to individuals and groups the details of financial assistance available to college and university students, such as loans, grants, and scholarships. Guide clients in the gathering of information such as bank account records, income tax returns, life and disability insurance records, pension plan information, and wills. Analyze financial information obtained from clients to determine strategies for meeting clients' financial objectives. Meet with clients' other advisors, including attorneys, accountants, trust officers, and investment bankers, to fully understand clients' financial goals and circumstances. Answer clients' questions about the purposes and details of financial plans and strategies. Open accounts for clients, and disburse funds from account to creditors as agents for clients. Authorize release of financial aid funds to students. Participate in the selection of candidates for specific financial aid awards. Research and investigate available investment opportunities to determine whether they fit into financial plans.

Personality Type: Enterprising. These occupations frequently involve starting up and carrying out projects and can involve leading people and making many decisions. They sometimes require risk taking and often deal with business.

GOE—Interest Area/Cluster: 06. Finance and Insurance. **Work Group:** 06.05. Finance/Insurance Sales and Support. **Other Jobs in This Work Group:** Insurance Sales Agents; Sales Agents, Financial Services; Sales Agents, Securities and Commodities; Securities, Commodities, and Financial Services Sales Agents.

Skills—Management of Financial Resources: Determining how money will be spent to get the work done and accounting for these expenditures. **Persuasion:** Persuading others to approach things differently. **Mathematics:** Using mathematics to solve problems. **Speaking:** Talking to others to effectively convey information. **Complex Problem Solving:** Identifying complex problems, reviewing the options, and implementing solutions. **Active Listening:** Listening to what other people are saying and asking questions as appropriate. **Service Orientation:** Actively looking for ways to help people. **Judgment and Decision Making:** Weighing the relative costs and benefits of a potential action.

Education and Training Programs: Finance, General; Financial Planning and Services. **Related Knowledge/Courses—Economics and Accounting:** Economic and accounting principles and practices, the financial markets, banking, and the analysis and reporting of financial data. **Sales and Marketing:** Principles and methods involved in showing, promoting, and selling products or services. This includes marketing strategies and tactics, product demonstration and sales techniques, and sales control systems. **Law and Government:** Laws, legal codes, court procedures, precedents, government regulations, executive orders, agency rules, and the democratic political process. **Customer and Personal Service:** Principles and processes for providing customer and personal services, including needs assessment techniques, quality service standards, alternative delivery systems, and customer satisfaction evaluation techniques. **Mathematics:** Numbers and their operations and interrelationships, including arithmetic, algebra, geometry, calculus, and statistics and their applications. **Computers and Electronics:** Electric circuit boards, processors, chips, and computer hardware and software, including applications and programming.

Work Environment: Indoors; sitting.

Personnel Recruiters

- ❋ Education/Training Required: Bachelor's degree
- ❋ Annual Earnings: $44,380
- ❋ Beginning Wage: $27,340
- ❋ Earnings Growth Potential: Medium
- ❋ Growth: 18.4%
- ❋ Annual Job Openings: 33,588
- ❋ Self-Employed: 2.1%
- ❋ Part-Time: 7.6%

The job openings listed here are shared with Employment Interviewers.

Seek out, interview, and screen applicants to fill existing and future job openings and promote career opportunities within an organization. Establish and maintain relationships with hiring managers to stay abreast of current and future hiring and business needs. Interview applicants to obtain information on work history, training, education, and job skills. Maintain current knowledge of Equal Employment Opportunity (EEO) and affirmative action guidelines and laws, such as the Americans with Disabilities Act (ADA). Perform searches for qualified candidates according to relevant job criteria, using computer databases, networking, Internet recruiting resources, cold calls, media, recruiting firms, and employee referrals. Prepare and maintain employment records. Contact applicants to inform them of employment possibilities, consideration, and selection. Inform potential applicants about facilities, operations, benefits, and job or career opportunities in organizations. Screen and refer applicants to hiring personnel in the organization, making hiring recommendations when appropriate. Arrange for interviews and provide travel arrangements as necessary. Advise managers and employees on staffing policies and procedures. Review and evaluate applicant qualifications or eligibility for specified licensing according to established guidelines and designated licensing codes. Hire applicants and authorize paperwork assigning them to positions. Conduct reference and background checks on applicants. Evaluate recruitment and selection criteria to ensure conformance to professional, statistical, and testing standards, recommending revision as needed. Recruit applicants for open positions, arranging job fairs with college campus representatives. Advise management on organizing, preparing, and implementing recruiting and retention programs. Supervise personnel clerks performing filing, typing, and recordkeeping duties. Project yearly recruitment expenditures for budgetary consideration and control. Serve on selection and examination boards to evaluate applicants according to test scores, contacting promising candidates for interviews. Address civic and social groups and attend conferences to disseminate information concerning possible job openings and career opportunities.

Personality Type: Enterprising. These occupations frequently involve starting up and carrying out projects and can involve leading people and making many decisions. They sometimes require risk taking and often deal with business.

GOE—Interest Area/Cluster: 04. Business and Administration. **Work Group:** 04.03. Human Resources Support. **Other Jobs in This Work Group:** Compensation, Benefits, and Job Analysis Specialists; Employment Interviewers; Employment, Recruitment, and Placement Specialists; Training and Development Specialists.

Skills—Management of Personnel Resources: Motivating, developing, and directing people as they work; identifying the best people for the job. **Negotiation:** Bringing others together and trying to reconcile differences. **Persuasion:** Persuading others to approach things differently. **Management of Financial Resources:** Determining how money will be spent to get the work done and accounting for these expenditures. **Service Orientation:** Actively looking for ways to help people. **Judgment and Decision Making:** Weighing the relative costs and benefits of a potential action. **Monitoring:** Assessing how well one is doing when learning or doing something. **Active Listening:** Listening to what other people are saying and asking questions as appropriate.

Education and Training Programs: Human Resources Management/Personnel Administration, General; Labor and Industrial Relations. **Related Knowledge/Courses—Personnel and Human Resources:** Principles and procedures for personnel recruitment; selection; training; compensation and benefits; labor relations and negotiation; and personnel information systems. **Clerical Practices:** Administrative and clerical procedures and systems such as word-processing systems, filing and records management systems, stenography and transcription, forms, design principles, and other office procedures and terminology. **Sales and Marketing:** Principles and methods involved in showing, promoting, and selling products or services. This includes marketing strategies and tactics, product demonstration and sales techniques, and sales control systems. **Education and Training:** Instructional methods and training techniques, including curriculum design principles, learning theory, group and individual teaching techniques, design of individual development plans, and test design principles. **Administration and Management:** Principles and processes involved in business and organizational planning, coordination, and execution. This includes strategic planning, resource allocation, manpower modeling, leadership techniques, and production methods. **Communications and Media:** Media production, communication, and dissemination techniques and methods, including alternative ways to inform and entertain via written, oral, and visual media.

Work Environment: Indoors; sitting.

Pharmacists

* Education/Training Required: First professional degree
* Annual Earnings: $100,480
* Beginning Wage: $73,010
* Earnings Growth Potential: Low
* Growth: 21.7%
* Annual Job Openings: 16,358
* Self-Employed: 0.5%
* Part-Time: 18.1%

Compound and dispense medications, following prescriptions issued by physicians, dentists, or other authorized medical practitioners. Review prescriptions to assure accuracy, to ascertain the needed ingredients, and to evaluate their suitability. Provide information and advice regarding drug interactions, side effects, dosage, and proper medication storage. Analyze prescribing trends to monitor patient compliance and to prevent excessive usage or harmful interactions. Order and purchase pharmaceutical supplies, medical supplies, and drugs, maintaining stock and storing and handling it properly. Maintain records, such as pharmacy files; patient profiles; charge system files; inventories; control records for radioactive nuclei; and registries of poisons, narcotics, and controlled drugs. Provide specialized services to help patients manage conditions such as diabetes, asthma, smoking cessation, or high blood pressure. Advise customers on the selection of medication brands, medical equipment, and health-care supplies. Collaborate with other health-care professionals to plan, monitor, review, and evaluate the quality and effectiveness of drugs and drug regimens, providing advice on drug applications and characteristics. Compound and dispense medications as prescribed by doctors and dentists by calculating, weighing, measuring, and mixing ingredients or oversee these activities. Offer health promotion and prevention activities—for example, training people to use devices such as blood-pressure or diabetes monitors. Refer patients to other health professionals and agencies when appropriate. Prepare sterile solutions and infusions for use in surgical procedures, emergency rooms, or patients' homes. Plan, implement, and maintain procedures for mixing, packaging, and labeling pharmaceuticals according to policy and legal requirements to ensure quality, security, and proper disposal. Assay radiopharmaceuticals, verify rates of disintegration, and calculate the volume required to produce the desired results to ensure proper dosages. Manage pharmacy operations, hiring and supervising staff, performing administrative duties, and buying and selling nonpharmaceutical merchandise. Work in hospitals, clinics, or for health maintenance organizations (HMOs), dispensing prescriptions, serving as a medical team consultant, or specializing in specific drug therapy areas such as oncology or nuclear pharmacotherapy.

Personality Type: Investigative. These occupations frequently involve working with ideas and require an extensive amount of thinking. They can involve searching for facts and figuring out problems mentally.

GOE—**Interest Area/Cluster:** 08. Health Science. **Work Group:** 08.02. Medicine and Surgery. **Other Jobs in This Work Group:** Anesthesiologists; Family and General Practitioners; Internists, General; Obstetricians and Gynecologists; Pediatricians, General; Physician Assistants; Psychiatrists; Registered Nurses; Surgeons.

Skills—Science: Using scientific methods to solve problems. **Reading Comprehension:** Understanding written sentences and paragraphs in work-related documents. **Social Perceptiveness:** Being aware of others' reactions and understanding why they react the way they do. **Active Listening:** Listening to what other people are saying and asking questions as appropriate. **Instructing:** Teaching others how to do something. **Mathematics:** Using mathematics to solve problems. **Speaking:** Talking to others to effectively convey information. **Critical Thinking:** Using logic and analysis to identify the strengths and weaknesses of different approaches.

Education and Training Programs: Pharmacy (PharmD [USA] PharmD, BS/BPharm [Canada]); Pharmacy Administration and Pharmacy Policy and Regulatory Affairs (MS, PhD); Pharmaceutics and Drug Design (MS, PhD); Medicinal and Pharmaceutical Chemistry (MS, PhD); Natural Products Chemistry and Pharmacognosy (MS, PhD); Clinical and Industrial Drug Development (MS, PhD); Pharmacoeconomics/Pharmaceutical Economics (MS, PhD); Clinical, Hospital, and Managed Care Pharmacy (MS, PhD); others. **Related Knowledge/Courses—Medicine and Dentistry:** The information and techniques needed to diagnose and treat injuries, diseases, and deformities. This includes symptoms, treatment alternatives, drug properties and interactions, and preventive health-care measures. **Chemistry:** The composition, structure, and properties of substances and of the chemical processes and transformations that they undergo. This includes uses of chemicals and their interactions, danger signs, production techniques, and disposal methods. **Therapy and Counseling:** Information and techniques needed to rehabilitate physical and mental ailments and to provide career guidance, including alternative treatments, rehabilitation equipment and its proper use, and methods to evaluate treatment effects. **Biology:** Plant and animal living tissue, cells, organisms, and entities, including their functions, interdependencies, and interactions with each other and the environment. **Psychology:** Human behavior and performance, mental processes, psychological research methods, and the assessment and treatment of behavioral and affective disorders. **Mathematics:** Numbers and their operations and interrelationships, including arithmetic, algebra, geometry, calculus, and statistics and their applications.

Work Environment: Indoors; disease or infections; standing; repetitive motions.

Philosophy and Religion Teachers, Postsecondary

- ❀ Education/Training Required: Doctoral degree
- ❀ Annual Earnings: $56,380
- ❀ Beginning Wage: $32,640
- ❀ Earnings Growth Potential: High
- ❀ Growth: 22.9%
- ❀ Annual Job Openings: 3,120
- ❀ Self-Employed: 0.4%
- ❀ Part-Time: 27.8%

Teach courses in philosophy, religion, and theology. Evaluate and grade students' classwork, assignments, and papers. Initiate, facilitate, and moderate classroom discussions. Prepare and deliver lectures to undergraduate and graduate students on topics such as ethics, logic, and contemporary religious thought. Prepare course materials such as syllabi, homework assignments, and handouts. Compile, administer, and grade examinations or assign this work to others. Keep abreast of developments in their field by reading current literature, talking with colleagues, and participating in professional conferences. Maintain student attendance records, grades, and other required records. Plan, evaluate, and revise curricula, course content, and course materials and methods of instruction. Maintain regularly scheduled office hours to advise and assist students. Select and obtain materials and supplies such as textbooks. Advise students on academic and vocational curricula and on career issues. Conduct research in a particular field of knowledge and publish findings in professional journals, books, or electronic media. Perform administrative duties such as serving as department head. Serve on academic or administrative committees that deal with institutional policies, departmental matters, and academic issues. Collaborate with colleagues to address teaching and research issues. Participate in campus and community events. Participate in student recruitment, registration, and placement activities. Compile bibliographies of specialized materials for outside reading assignments. Supervise undergraduate and graduate teaching, internship, and research work. Act as advisers to student organizations. Write grant proposals to procure external research funding. Provide professional consulting services to government or industry.

Personality Type: Social. These occupations frequently involve working with, communicating with, and teaching people and often involve helping or providing service to others.

GOE—Interest Area/Cluster: 05. Education and Training. **Work Group:** 05.03. Postsecondary and Adult Teaching and Instructing. **Other Jobs in This Work Group:** Adult Literacy, Remedial Education, and GED Teachers and Instructors; Agricultural Sciences Teachers, Postsecondary; Anthropology and Archeology Teachers, Postsecondary; Architecture Teachers, Postsecondary; Area, Ethnic, and Cultural Studies Teachers, Postsecondary; Art, Drama, and Music Teachers, Postsecondary; Atmospheric, Earth, Marine, and Space Sciences Teachers, Postsecondary; Biological Science Teachers, Postsecondary; Business Teachers, Postsecondary; Chemistry Teachers, Postsecondary; Communications Teachers, Postsecondary; Computer Science Teachers, Postsecondary; Criminal Justice and Law Enforcement Teachers, Postsecondary; Economics Teachers, Postsecondary; Education Teachers, Postsecondary; Engineering Teachers, Postsecondary; English Language and Literature Teachers, Postsecondary; Environmental Science Teachers, Postsecondary; Farm and Home Management Advisors; Foreign Language and Literature Teachers, Postsecondary; Forestry and Conservation Science Teachers, Postsecondary; Geography Teachers, Postsecondary; Graduate Teaching Assistants; Health Specialties Teachers, Postsecondary; History Teachers, Postsecondary; Home Economics Teachers, Postsecondary; Law Teachers, Postsecondary; Library Science Teachers, Postsecondary; Mathematical Science Teachers, Postsecondary; Nursing Instructors and Teachers, Postsecondary; Physics Teachers, Postsecondary; Political Science Teachers, Postsecondary; Psychology Teachers, Postsecondary; Recreation and Fitness Studies Teachers, Postsecondary; Social Work Teachers, Postsecondary; Sociology Teachers, Postsecondary.

Skills—Writing: Communicating effectively with others in writing as indicated by the needs of the audience. **Instructing:** Teaching others how to do something. **Reading Comprehension:** Understanding written sentences and paragraphs in work-related documents. **Critical Thinking:** Using logic and analysis to identify the strengths and weaknesses of different approaches. **Speaking:** Talking to others to effectively convey information.

Learning Strategies: Using multiple approaches when learning or teaching new things. **Social Perceptiveness:** Being aware of others' reactions and understanding why they react the way they do. **Persuasion:** Persuading others to approach things differently.

Education and Training Programs: Philosophy; Ethics; Philosophy, Other; Religion/Religious Studies; Buddhist Studies; Christian Studies.; Hindu Studies; Philosophy and Religious Studies, Other; Bible/Biblical Studies; Missions/Missionary Studies and Missiology; Religious Education; Religious/Sacred Music; Theology/Theological Studies; Divinity/Ministry (BD, MDiv.); Pre-Theology/Pre-Ministerial Studies; others. **Related Knowledge/Courses—Philosophy and Theology:** Different philosophical systems and religions, including their basic principles, values, ethics, ways of thinking, customs, and practices and their impact on human culture. **History and Archeology:** Historical events and their causes, indicators, and impact on particular civilizations and cultures. **Sociology and Anthropology:** Group behavior and dynamics; societal trends and influences; and cultures and their history, migrations, ethnicity, and origins. **Foreign Language:** The structure and content of a foreign (non-English) language, including the meaning and spelling of words, rules of composition and grammar, and pronunciation. **English Language:** The structure and content of the English language, including the meaning and spelling of words, rules of composition, and grammar. **Education and Training:** Instructional methods and training techniques, including curriculum design principles, learning theory, group and individual teaching techniques, design of individual development plans, and test design principles.

Work Environment: Indoors; sitting.

Physical Therapist Assistants

- ❋ Education/Training Required: Associate degree
- ❋ Annual Earnings: $44,130
- ❋ Beginning Wage: $27,800
- ❋ Earnings Growth Potential: Medium
- ❋ Growth: 32.4%
- ❋ Annual Job Openings: 5,957
- ❋ Self-Employed: 0.2%
- ❋ Part-Time: 27.1%

Assist physical therapists in providing physical therapy treatments and procedures. May, in accordance with state laws, assist in the development of treatment plans, carry out routine functions, document the progress of treatment, and modify specific treatments in accordance with patient status and within the scope of treatment plans established by physical therapists. Generally requires formal training. Instruct, motivate, safeguard, and assist patients as they practice exercises and functional activities. Observe patients during treatments to compile and evaluate data on their responses and progress, and provide results to physical therapists in person or through progress notes. Confer with physical therapy staffs or others to discuss and evaluate patient information for planning, modifying, and coordinating treatment. Transport patients to and from treatment areas, lifting and transferring them according to positioning requirements. Secure patients into or onto therapy equipment. Administer active and passive manual therapeutic exercises, therapeutic massages, aquatic physical therapy, and heat, light, sound, and electrical modality treatments such as ultrasound. Communicate with or instruct caregivers and family members on patient therapeutic activities and treatment plans. Measure patients' ranges-of-joint motion, body parts, and vital signs to determine effects of treatments or for patient evaluations. Monitor operation of equipment and record use of equipment and administration of treatment. Fit patients for orthopedic braces, prostheses, and supportive devices such as crutches. Train patients in the use of orthopedic braces, prostheses, or supportive devices. Clean work areas and check and store equipment after treatments. Assist patients to dress, undress, or put on and remove supportive devices such as braces, splints, and slings. Attend or conduct continuing education courses, seminars, or in-service activities. Perform clerical duties such as taking inventory, ordering supplies, answering telephones, taking messages, and filling out forms. Prepare treatment areas and electrotherapy equipment for use by physiotherapists. Administer traction to relieve neck and back pain, using intermittent and static traction equipment. Perform postural drainage, percussions and vibrations, and teach deep breathing exercises to treat respiratory conditions.

Personality Type: Social. These occupations frequently involve working with, communicating with, and teaching people and often involve helping or providing service to others.

GOE—Interest Area/Cluster: 08. Health Science. **Work Group:** 08.07. Medical Therapy. **Other Jobs in This Work Group:** Audiologists; Occupational Therapist Assistants; Occupational Therapists; Physical Therapists; Radiation Therapists; Recreational Therapists; Respiratory Therapists; Respiratory Therapy Technicians; Speech-Language Pathologists.

Skills—Service Orientation: Actively looking for ways to help people.

Education and Training Program: Physical Therapist Assistant. **Related Knowledge/Courses—Therapy and Counseling:** Information and techniques needed to rehabilitate physical

and mental ailments and to provide career guidance, including alternative treatments, rehabilitation equipment and its proper use, and methods to evaluate treatment effects. **Medicine and Dentistry:** The information and techniques needed to diagnose and treat injuries, diseases, and deformities. This includes symptoms, treatment alternatives, drug properties and interactions, and preventive health-care measures. **Psychology:** Human behavior and performance, mental processes, psychological research methods, and the assessment and treatment of behavioral and affective disorders. **Biology:** Plant and animal living tissue, cells, organisms, and entities, including their functions, interdependencies, and interactions with each other and the environment. **Customer and Personal Service:** Principles and processes for providing customer and personal services, including needs assessment techniques, quality service standards, alternative delivery systems, and customer satisfaction evaluation techniques. **Education and Training:** Instructional methods and training techniques, including curriculum design principles, learning theory, group and individual teaching techniques, design of individual development plans, and test design principles.

Work Environment: Indoors; disease or infections; standing; walking and running.

Physical Therapists

- ❋ Education/Training Required: Master's degree
- ❋ Annual Earnings: $69,760
- ❋ Beginning Wage: $48,530
- ❋ Earnings Growth Potential: Low
- ❋ Growth: 27.1%
- ❋ Annual Job Openings: 12,072
- ❋ Self-Employed: 8.4%
- ❋ Part-Time: 22.7%

Assess, plan, organize, and participate in rehabilitative programs that improve mobility, relieve pain, increase strength, and decrease or prevent deformity of patients suffering from disease or injury. Perform and document initial exams, evaluating data to identify problems and determine diagnoses prior to interventions. Plan, prepare, and carry out individually designed programs of physical treatment to maintain, improve, or restore physical functioning, alleviate pain, and prevent physical dysfunction in patients. Record prognoses, treatments, responses, and progresses in patients' charts or enter information into computers. Identify and document goals, anticipated progresses, and plans for reevaluation. Evaluate effects of treatments at various stages and adjust treatments to achieve maximum benefits. Administer manual exercises, massages, or traction to help relieve pain, increase patient strength, or decrease or prevent deformity or crippling. Test and measure patients' strength, motor development and function, sensory perception, functional capacity, and respiratory and circulatory efficiency and record data. Instruct patients and families in treatment procedures to be continued at home. Confer with patients, medical practitioners, and appropriate others to plan, implement, and assess intervention programs. Review physicians' referrals and patients' medical records to help determine diagnoses and physical therapy treatments required. Obtain patients' informed consent to proposed interventions. Discharge patients from physical therapy when goals or projected outcomes have been attained, and provide for appropriate follow-up care or referrals. Provide information to patients about proposed interventions, material risks, and expected benefits and any reasonable alternatives. Inform patients when diagnoses reveal findings outside the scope of physical therapy to treat and refer to appropriate practitioners. Direct, supervise, assess, and communicate with supportive personnel. Provide educational information about physical therapy and physical therapists, injury prevention, ergonomics, and ways to promote health. Refer clients to community resources and services. Administer treatment involving application of physical agents, using equipment, moist packs, ultraviolet and infrared lamps, and ultrasound machines.

Personality Type: Social. These occupations frequently involve working with, communicating with, and teaching people and often involve helping or providing service to others.

GOE—Interest Area/Cluster: 08. Health Science. **Work Group:** 08.07. Medical Therapy. **Other Jobs in This Work Group:** Audiologists; Occupational Therapist Assistants; Occupational Therapists; Physical Therapist Assistants; Radiation Therapists; Recreational Therapists; Respiratory Therapists; Respiratory Therapy Technicians; Speech-Language Pathologists.

Skills—Management of Personnel Resources: Motivating, developing, and directing people as they work; identifying the best people for the job. **Systems Analysis:** Determining how a system should work and how changes will affect outcomes. **Social Perceptiveness:** Being aware of others' reactions and understanding why they react the way they do. **Complex Problem Solving:** Identifying complex problems, reviewing the options, and implementing solutions. **Systems Evaluation:** Looking at many indicators of system performance and taking into account their accuracy. **Judgment and Decision Making:** Weighing the relative costs and benefits of a potential action. **Monitoring:** Assessing how well one is doing when learning or doing something. **Speaking:** Talking to others to effectively convey information.

Education and Training Programs: Physical Therapy/Therapist; Kinesiotherapy/Kinesiotherapist. **Related Knowledge/Courses—Therapy and Counseling:** Information and techniques needed to rehabilitate physical and mental ailments and to provide career guidance, including alternative treatments, rehabilitation equipment and its proper use, and methods to evaluate treatment effects. **Medicine and Dentistry:** The information and techniques needed to diagnose and treat injuries, diseases, and deformities. This includes symptoms, treatment alternatives, drug properties and interactions, and preventive health-care measures. **Psychology:** Human behavior and performance, mental processes, psychological research methods, and the assessment and treatment of behavioral and affective disorders. **Education and Training:** Instructional methods and training techniques, including curriculum design principles, learning theory, group and individual teaching techniques, design of individual development plans, and test design principles. **Biology:** Plant and animal living tissue, cells, organisms, and entities, including their functions, interdependencies, and interactions with each other and the environment. **Customer and Personal Service:** Principles and processes for providing customer and personal services, including needs assessment techniques, quality service standards, alternative delivery systems, and customer satisfaction evaluation techniques.

Work Environment: Indoors; disease or infections; standing.

Physician Assistants

* Education/Training Required: Master's degree
* Annual Earnings: $78,450
* Beginning Wage: $46,750
* Earnings Growth Potential: High
* Growth: 27.0%
* Annual Job Openings: 7,147
* Self-Employed: 1.8%
* Part-Time: 15.6%

Under the supervision of physicians, provide health-care services typically performed by a physician. Conduct complete physicals, provide treatment, and counsel patients. May, in some cases, prescribe medication. Must graduate from an accredited educational program for physician assistants. Examine patients to obtain information about their physical conditions. Obtain, compile, and record patient medical data, including health history, progress notes, and results of physical examinations. Interpret diagnostic test results for deviations from normal. Make tentative diagnoses and decisions about management and treatment of patients. Prescribe therapy or medication with physician approval. Administer or order diagnostic tests, such as X-ray, electrocardiogram, and laboratory tests. Instruct and counsel patients about prescribed therapeutic regimens, normal growth and development, family planning, emotional problems of daily living, and health maintenance. Perform therapeutic procedures such as injections, immunizations, suturing and wound care, and infection management. Provide physicians with assistance during surgery or complicated medical procedures. Visit and observe patients on hospital rounds or house calls, updating charts, ordering therapy, and reporting back to physicians. Supervise and coordinate activities of technicians and technical assistants. Order medical and laboratory supplies and equipment.

Personality Type: Social. These occupations frequently involve working with, communicating with, and teaching people and often involve helping or providing service to others.

GOE—Interest Area/Cluster: 08. Health Science. **Work Group:** 08.02. Medicine and Surgery. **Other Jobs in This Work Group:** Anesthesiologists; Family and General Practitioners; Internists, General; Obstetricians and Gynecologists; Pediatricians, General; Pharmacists; Psychiatrists; Registered Nurses; Surgeons.

Skills—Social Perceptiveness: Being aware of others' reactions and understanding why they react the way they do. Systems Analysis: Determining how a system should work and how changes will affect outcomes. Systems Evaluation: Looking at many indicators of system performance and taking into account their accuracy. Persuasion: Persuading others to approach things differently. Complex Problem Solving: Identifying complex problems, reviewing the options, and implementing solutions. Reading Comprehension: Understanding written sentences and paragraphs in work-related documents. Service Orientation: Actively looking for ways to help people. Speaking: Talking to others to effectively convey information.

Education and Training Program: Physician Assistant. Related Knowledge/Courses—Medicine and Dentistry: The information and techniques needed to diagnose and treat injuries, diseases, and deformities. This includes symptoms, treatment alternatives, drug properties and interactions, and preventive health-care measures. Biology: Plant and animal living tissue, cells, organisms, and entities, including their functions, interdependencies, and interactions with each other and the environment. Therapy and Counseling: Information and techniques needed to rehabilitate physical and mental ailments and to provide career guidance, including alternative treatments, rehabilitation equipment and its proper use, and methods to evaluate treatment effects. Psychology: Human behavior and performance, mental processes, psychological research methods, and the assessment and treatment of behavioral and affective disorders. Chemistry: The composition, structure, and properties of substances and of the chemical processes and transformations that they undergo. This includes uses of chemicals and their interactions, danger signs, production techniques, and disposal methods. Sociology and Anthropology: Group behavior and dynamics; societal trends and influences; and cultures and their history, migrations, ethnicity, and origins.

Work Environment: Indoors; disease or infections; standing; using hands on objects, tools, or controls.

Physicists

* Education/Training Required: Doctoral degree
* Annual Earnings: $96,850
* Beginning Wage: $51,870
* Earnings Growth Potential: High
* Growth: 6.8%
* Annual Job Openings: 1,302
* Self-Employed: 0.8%
* Part-Time: 5.2%

Conduct research into phases of physical phenomena, develop theories and laws on basis of observation and experiments, and devise methods to apply laws and theories to industry and other fields. Perform complex calculations as part of the analysis and evaluation of data, using computers. Describe and express observations and conclusions in mathematical terms. Analyze data from research conducted to detect and measure physical phenomena. Report experimental results by writing papers for scientific journals or by presenting information at scientific conferences. Design computer simulations to model physical data so that it can be better understood. Collaborate with other scientists in the design, development, and testing of experimental, industrial, or medical equipment, instrumentation, and procedures. Direct testing and monitoring of contamination of radioactive equipment, and recording of personnel and plant area radiation exposure data. Observe the structure and properties of matter, and the transformation and propagation of energy, using equipment such as masers, lasers, and telescopes, in order to explore and identify the basic principles governing these phenomena. Develop theories and laws on the basis of observation and experiments, and apply these theories and laws to problems in areas such as nuclear energy, optics, and aerospace technology. Teach physics to students. Develop manufacturing, assembly, and fabrication processes of lasers, masers, infrared, and other light-emitting and light-sensitive devices. Conduct application evaluations and analyze results in order to determine commercial, industrial, scientific, medical, military, or other uses for electro-optical devices. Develop standards of permissible concentrations of radioisotopes in liquids and gases. Conduct research pertaining to potential environmental impacts of atomic energy-related industrial development in order to determine licensing qualifications. Advise authorities of procedures to be followed in radiation incidents or hazards, and assist in civil defense planning.

Personality Type: Investigative. These occupations frequently involve working with ideas and require an extensive amount of thinking. They can involve searching for facts and figuring out problems mentally.

GOE—Interest Area/Cluster: 15. Scientific Research, Engineering, and Mathematics. **Work Group:** 15.02. Physical Sciences. **Other Jobs in This Work Group:** Astronomers; Atmospheric and Space Scientists; Chemists; Geographers; Geoscientists, Except Hydrologists and Geographers; Hydrologists; Materials Scientists.

Skills—Programming: Writing computer programs for various purposes. **Science:** Using scientific methods to solve problems. **Mathematics:** Using mathematics to solve problems. **Complex Problem Solving:** Identifying complex problems, reviewing the options, and implementing solutions. **Management of Financial Resources:** Determining how money will be spent to get the work done

and accounting for these expenditures. **Systems Analysis:** Determining how a system should work and how changes will affect outcomes. **Writing:** Communicating effectively with others in writing as indicated by the needs of the audience. **Critical Thinking:** Using logic and analysis to identify the strengths and weaknesses of different approaches.

Education and Training Programs: Astrophysics; Physics, General; Atomic/Molecular Physics; Elementary Particle Physics; Plasma and High-Temperature Physics; Nuclear Physics; Optics/Optical Sciences; Solid State and Low-Temperature Physics; Acoustics; Theoretical and Mathematical Physics; Physics, Other; Health/Medical Physics. **Related Knowledge/Courses—Physics:** Physical principles, laws, and applications, including air, water, material dynamics, light, atomic principles, heat, electric theory, earth formations, and meteorological and related natural phenomena. **Mathematics:** Numbers and their operations and interrelationships, including arithmetic, algebra, geometry, calculus, and statistics and their applications. **Engineering and Technology:** Equipment, tools, and mechanical devices and their uses to produce motion, light, power, technology, and other applications. **Computers and Electronics:** Electric circuit boards, processors, chips, and computer hardware and software, including applications and programming. **English Language:** The structure and content of the English language, including the meaning and spelling of words, rules of composition, and grammar. **Telecommunications:** Transmission, broadcasting, switching, control, and operation of telecommunications systems.

Work Environment: Indoors; sitting.

Physics Teachers, Postsecondary

* Education/Training Required: Doctoral degree
* Annual Earnings: $70,090
* Beginning Wage: $40,580
* Earnings Growth Potential: High
* Growth: 22.9%
* Annual Job Openings: 2,155
* Self-Employed: 0.4%
* Part-Time: 27.8%

Teach courses pertaining to the laws of matter and energy. Includes both teachers primarily engaged in teaching and those who do a combination of both teaching and research. Evaluate and grade students' classwork, laboratory work, assignments, and papers. Prepare and deliver lectures to undergraduate and/or graduate students on topics such as quantum mechanics, particle physics, and optics. Compile, administer, and grade examinations or assign this work to others. Maintain student attendance records, grades, and other required records. Supervise students' laboratory work. Prepare course materials such as syllabi, homework assignments, and handouts. Maintain regularly scheduled office hours to advise and assist students. Supervise undergraduate and/or graduate teaching, internship, and research work. Keep abreast of developments in their field by reading current literature, talking with colleagues, and participating in professional conferences. Plan, evaluate, and revise curricula, course content, and course materials and methods of instruction. Initiate, facilitate, and moderate classroom discussions. Conduct research in a particular field of knowledge and publish findings in professional journals, books, and/or electronic media. Advise students on academic and vocational curricula and on career

issues. Select and obtain materials and supplies such as textbooks and laboratory equipment. Collaborate with colleagues to address teaching and research issues. Participate in student recruitment, registration, and placement activities. Serve on academic or administrative committees that deal with institutional policies, departmental matters, and academic issues. Write grant proposals to procure external research funding. Perform administrative duties such as serving as department head. Act as advisers to student organizations. Provide professional consulting services to government and/ or industry. Compile bibliographies of specialized materials for outside reading assignments. Participate in campus and community events.

Personality Type: Social. These occupations frequently involve working with, communicating with, and teaching people and often involve helping or providing service to others.

GOE—Interest Area/Cluster: 05. Education and Training. **Work Group:** 05.03. Postsecondary and Adult Teaching and Instructing. **Other Jobs in This Work Group:** Adult Literacy, Remedial Education, and GED Teachers and Instructors; Agricultural Sciences Teachers, Postsecondary; Anthropology and Archeology Teachers, Postsecondary; Architecture Teachers, Postsecondary; Area, Ethnic, and Cultural Studies Teachers, Postsecondary; Art, Drama, and Music Teachers, Postsecondary; Atmospheric, Earth, Marine, and Space Sciences Teachers, Postsecondary; Biological Science Teachers, Postsecondary; Business Teachers, Postsecondary; Chemistry Teachers, Postsecondary; Communications Teachers, Postsecondary; Computer Science Teachers, Postsecondary; Criminal Justice and Law Enforcement Teachers, Postsecondary; Economics Teachers, Postsecondary; Education Teachers, Postsecondary; Engineering Teachers, Postsecondary; English Language and Literature Teachers, Postsecondary; Environmental Science Teachers, Postsecondary; Farm and

Home Management Advisors; Foreign Language and Literature Teachers, Postsecondary; Forestry and Conservation Science Teachers, Postsecondary; Geography Teachers, Postsecondary; Graduate Teaching Assistants; Health Specialties Teachers, Postsecondary; History Teachers, Postsecondary; Home Economics Teachers, Postsecondary; Law Teachers, Postsecondary; Library Science Teachers, Postsecondary; Mathematical Science Teachers, Postsecondary; Nursing Instructors and Teachers, Postsecondary; Philosophy and Religion Teachers, Postsecondary; Political Science Teachers, Postsecondary; Psychology Teachers, Postsecondary; Recreation and Fitness Studies Teachers, Postsecondary; Social Work Teachers, Postsecondary; Sociology Teachers, Postsecondary.

Skills—Science: Using scientific methods to solve problems. **Programming:** Writing computer programs for various purposes. **Mathematics:** Using mathematics to solve problems. **Instructing:** Teaching others how to do something. **Writing:** Communicating effectively with others in writing as indicated by the needs of the audience. **Reading Comprehension:** Understanding written sentences and paragraphs in work-related documents. **Learning Strategies:** Using multiple approaches when learning or teaching new things. **Critical Thinking:** Using logic and analysis to identify the strengths and weaknesses of different approaches.

Education and Training Programs: Physics, General; Atomic/Molecular Physics; Elementary Particle Physics; Plasma and High-Temperature Physics; Nuclear Physics; Optics/Optical Sciences; Solid State and Low-Temperature Physics; Acoustics; Theoretical and Mathematical Physics; Physics, Other. **Related Knowledge/Courses— Physics:** Physical principles, laws, and applications, including air, water, material dynamics, light, atomic principles, heat, electric theory, earth formations, and meteorological and related natural phenomena. **Mathematics:** Numbers and their

operations and interrelationships, including arithmetic, algebra, geometry, calculus, and statistics and their applications. **Chemistry:** The composition, structure, and properties of substances and of the chemical processes and transformations that they undergo. This includes uses of chemicals and their interactions, danger signs, production techniques, and disposal methods. **Engineering and Technology:** Equipment, tools, and mechanical devices and their uses to produce motion, light, power, technology, and other applications. **Education and Training:** Instructional methods and training techniques, including curriculum design principles, learning theory, group and individual teaching techniques, design of individual development plans, and test design principles. **Computers and Electronics:** Electric circuit boards, processors, chips, and computer hardware and software, including applications and programming.

Work Environment: Indoors; sitting.

Podiatrists

- ❋ Education/Training Required: First professional degree
- ❋ Annual Earnings: $110,510
- ❋ Beginning Wage: $45,260
- ❋ Earnings Growth Potential: Very high
- ❋ Growth: 9.5%
- ❋ Annual Job Openings: 648
- ❋ Self-Employed: 23.9%
- ❋ Part-Time: 23.6%

Diagnose and treat diseases and deformities of the human foot. Treat bone, muscle, and joint disorders affecting the feet. Diagnose diseases and deformities of the foot, using medical histories, physical examinations, X rays, and laboratory test results. Prescribe medications, corrective devices, physical therapy, or surgery. Treat conditions such as corns, calluses, ingrown nails, tumors, short-ened tendons, bunions, cysts, and abscesses by sur-gical methods. Advise patients about treatments and foot care techniques necessary for prevention of future problems. Refer patients to physicians when symptoms indicative of systemic disorders, such as arthritis or diabetes, are observed in feet and legs. Correct deformities by means of plaster casts and strapping. Make and fit prosthetic appli-ances. Perform administrative duties such as hiring employees, ordering supplies, and keeping records. Educate the public about the benefits of foot care through techniques such as speaking engagements, advertising, and other forums. Treat deformities, using mechanical methods, such as whirlpool or paraffin baths, and electrical methods, such as shortwave and low-voltage currents.

Personality Type: Investigative. These occupa-tions frequently involve working with ideas and require an extensive amount of thinking. They can involve searching for facts and figuring out prob-lems mentally.

GOE—Interest Area/Cluster: 08. Health Sci-ence. **Work Group:** 08.04. Health Specialties. **Other Jobs in This Work Group:** Chiropractors; Optometrists.

Skills—Science: Using scientific methods to solve problems. **Active Listening:** Listening to what other people are saying and asking questions as appropriate. **Complex Problem Solving:** Identi-fying complex problems, reviewing the options, and implementing solutions. **Management of Financial Resources:** Determining how money will be spent to get the work done and account-ing for these expenditures. **Reading Compre-hension:** Understanding written sentences and paragraphs in work-related documents. **Equip-ment Selection:** Determining the kind of tools and equipment needed to do a job. **Active Learn-ing:** Working with new material or information to grasp its implications. **Judgment and Decision**

Making: Weighing the relative costs and benefits of a potential action.

Education and Training Program: Podiat-ric Medicine/Podiatry (DPM). **Related Knowl-edge/Courses—Medicine and Dentistry:** The information and techniques needed to diagnose and treat injuries, diseases, and deformities. This includes symptoms, treatment alternatives, drug properties and interactions, and preventive health-care measures. **Biology:** Plant and animal living tissue, cells, organisms, and entities, including their functions, interdependencies, and interac-tions with each other and the environment. **Ther-apy and Counseling:** Information and techniques needed to rehabilitate physical and mental ail-ments and to provide career guidance, including alternative treatments, rehabilitation equipment and its proper use, and methods to evaluate treat-ment effects. **Sales and Marketing:** Principles and methods involved in showing, promoting, and sell-ing products or services. This includes marketing strategies and tactics, product demonstration and sales techniques, and sales control systems. **Chem-istry:** The composition, structure, and properties of substances and of the chemical processes and transformations that they undergo. This includes uses of chemicals and their interactions, danger signs, production techniques, and disposal meth-ods. **Psychology:** Human behavior and perfor-mance, mental processes, psychological research methods, and the assessment and treatment of behavioral and affective disorders.

Work Environment: Indoors; contaminants; dis-ease or infections; sitting; using hands on objects, tools, or controls; repetitive motions.

Poets, Lyricists, and Creative Writers

* Education/Training Required: Bachelor's degree
* Annual Earnings: $50,660
* Beginning Wage: $26,530
* Earnings Growth Potential: High
* Growth: 12.8%
* Annual Job Openings: 24,023
* Self-Employed: 65.9%
* Part-Time: 21.8%

The job openings listed here are shared with Copy Writers.

Create original written works, such as scripts, essays, prose, poetry, or song lyrics, for publication or performance. Revise written material to meet personal standards and to satisfy needs of clients, publishers, directors, or producers. Choose subject matter and suitable form to express personal feelings and experiences or ideas, or to narrate stories or events. Plan project arrangements or outlines, and organize material accordingly. Prepare works in appropriate format for publication, and send them to publishers or producers. Follow appropriate procedures to get copyrights for completed work. Write fiction or nonfiction prose such as short stories, novels, biographies, articles, descriptive or critical analyses, and essays. Develop factors such as themes, plots, characterizations, psychological analyses, historical environments, action, and dialogue, to create material. Confer with clients, editors, publishers, or producers to discuss changes or revisions to written material. Conduct research to obtain factual information and authentic detail, using sources such as newspaper accounts, diaries, and interviews. Write narrative, dramatic, lyric, or other types of poetry for publication. Attend book launches and publicity events, or conduct public readings. Write words to fit musical compositions, including lyrics for operas, musical plays, and choral works. Adapt text to accommodate musical requirements of composers and singers. Teach writing classes. Write humorous material for publication, or for performances such as comedy routines, gags, and comedy shows. Collaborate with other writers on specific projects.

Personality Type: Artistic. These occupations frequently involve working with forms, designs, and patterns. They often require self-expression, and the work can be done without following a clear set of rules.

GOE—Interest Area/Cluster: 03. Arts and Communication. **Work Group:** 03.02. Writing and Editing. **Other Jobs in This Work Group:** Copy Writers; Editors; Technical Writers; Writers and Authors.

Skills—Writing: Communicating effectively with others in writing as indicated by the needs of the audience. **Social Perceptiveness:** Being aware of others' reactions and understanding why they react the way they do. **Management of Financial Resources:** Determining how money will be spent to get the work done and accounting for these expenditures. **Persuasion:** Persuading others to approach things differently. **Active Listening:** Listening to what other people are saying and asking questions as appropriate. **Reading Comprehension:** Understanding written sentences and paragraphs in work-related documents. **Speaking:** Talking to others to effectively convey information. **Critical Thinking:** Using logic and analysis to identify the strengths and weaknesses of different approaches.

Education and Training Programs: Communication Studies/Speech Communication and Rhetoric; Mass Communication/Media Studies; Family and Consumer Sciences/Human Sciences Communication; English Composition; Creative

Writing; Playwriting and Screenwriting. **Related Knowledge/Courses—Fine Arts:** Theory and techniques required to produce, compose, and perform works of music, dance, visual arts, drama, and sculpture. **Communications and Media:** Media production, communication, and dissemination techniques and methods, including alternative ways to inform and entertain via written, oral, and visual media. **Philosophy and Theology:** Different philosophical systems and religions, including their basic principles, values, ethics, ways of thinking, customs, and practices and their impact on human culture. **Sociology and Anthropology:** Group behavior and dynamics; societal trends and influences; and cultures and their history, migrations, ethnicity, and origins. **Sales and Marketing:** Principles and methods involved in showing, promoting, and selling products or services. This includes marketing strategies and tactics, product demonstration and sales techniques, and sales control systems. **English Language:** The structure and content of the English language, including the meaning and spelling of words, rules of composition, and grammar.

Work Environment: Indoors; sitting; using hands on objects, tools, or controls; repetitive motions.

Political Science Teachers, Postsecondary

- ❋ Education/Training Required: Doctoral degree
- ❋ Annual Earnings: $63,100
- ❋ Beginning Wage: $35,600
- ❋ Earnings Growth Potential: High
- ❋ Growth: 22.9%
- ❋ Annual Job Openings: 2,435
- ❋ Self-Employed: 0.4%
- ❋ Part-Time: 27.8%

Teach courses in political science, international affairs, and international relations. Initiate, facilitate, and moderate classroom discussions. Prepare and deliver lectures to undergraduate or graduate students on topics such as classical political thought, international relations, and democracy and citizenship. Evaluate and grade students' classwork, assignments, and papers. Compile, administer, and grade examinations or assign this work to others. Prepare course materials such as syllabi, homework assignments, and handouts. Keep abreast of developments in their field by reading current literature, talking with colleagues, and participating in professional conferences. Plan, evaluate, and revise curricula, course content, and course materials and methods of instruction. Maintain student attendance records, grades, and other required records. Maintain regularly scheduled office hours in order to advise and assist students. Advise students on academic and vocational curricula and on career issues. Select and obtain materials and supplies such as textbooks. Conduct research in a particular field of knowledge and publish findings in professional journals, books, and electronic media. Supervise undergraduate and graduate teaching, internship, and research work. Collaborate with colleagues to address teaching and research issues. Serve on academic or administrative committees that deal with institutional policies, departmental matters, and academic issues. Participate in student recruitment, registration, and placement activities. Participate in campus and community events. Compile bibliographies of specialized materials for outside reading assignments. Act as advisers to student organizations. Perform administrative duties such as serving as department head. Write grant proposals to procure external research funding. Provide professional consulting services to government and industry.

Personality Type: Social. These occupations frequently involve working with, communicating with, and teaching people and often involve helping or providing service to others.

GOE—Interest Area/Cluster: 05. Education and Training. **Work Group:** 05.03. Postsecondary and Adult Teaching and Instructing. **Other Jobs in This Work Group:** Adult Literacy, Remedial Education, and GED Teachers and Instructors; Agricultural Sciences Teachers, Postsecondary; Anthropology and Archeology Teachers, Postsecondary; Architecture Teachers, Postsecondary; Area, Ethnic, and Cultural Studies Teachers, Postsecondary; Art, Drama, and Music Teachers, Postsecondary; Atmospheric, Earth, Marine, and Space Sciences Teachers, Postsecondary; Biological Science Teachers, Postsecondary; Business Teachers, Postsecondary; Chemistry Teachers, Postsecondary; Communications Teachers, Postsecondary; Computer Science Teachers, Postsecondary; Criminal Justice and Law Enforcement Teachers, Postsecondary; Economics Teachers, Postsecondary; Education Teachers, Postsecondary; Engineering Teachers, Postsecondary; English Language and Literature Teachers, Postsecondary; Environmental Science Teachers, Postsecondary; Farm and Home Management Advisors; Foreign Language and Literature Teachers, Postsecondary; Forestry and Conservation Science Teachers, Postsecondary; Geography Teachers, Postsecondary; Graduate Teaching Assistants; Health Specialties Teachers, Postsecondary; History Teachers, Postsecondary; Home Economics Teachers, Postsecondary; Law Teachers, Postsecondary; Library Science Teachers, Postsecondary; Mathematical Science Teachers, Postsecondary; Nursing Instructors and Teachers, Postsecondary; Philosophy and Religion Teachers, Postsecondary; Physics Teachers, Postsecondary; Psychology Teachers, Postsecondary; Recreation and Fitness Studies Teachers, Postsecondary; Social Work Teachers, Postsecondary; Sociology Teachers, Postsecondary.

Skills—Writing: Communicating effectively with others in writing as indicated by the needs of the audience. **Instructing:** Teaching others how to do something. **Reading Comprehension:** Understanding written sentences and paragraphs in work-related documents. **Learning Strategies:** Using multiple approaches when learning or teaching new things. **Persuasion:** Persuading others to approach things differently. **Critical Thinking:** Using logic and analysis to identify the strengths and weaknesses of different approaches. **Speaking:** Talking to others to effectively convey information. **Active Learning:** Working with new material or information to grasp its implications.

Education and Training Programs: Social Science Teacher Education; Political Science and Government, General; American Government and Politics (United States); Political Science and Government, Other. **Related Knowledge/Courses— History and Archeology:** Historical events and their causes, indicators, and impact on particular civilizations and cultures. **Philosophy and Theology:** Different philosophical systems and religions, including their basic principles, values, ethics, ways of thinking, customs, and practices and their impact on human culture. **Sociology and Anthropology:** Group behavior and dynamics; societal trends and influences; and cultures and their history, migrations, ethnicity, and origins. **Geography:** Various methods for describing the location and distribution of land, sea, and air masses, including their physical locations, relationships, and characteristics. **Law and Government:** Laws, legal codes, court procedures, precedents, government regulations, executive orders, agency rules, and the democratic political process. **English Language:** The structure and content of the English language, including the meaning and spelling of words, rules of composition, and grammar.

Work Environment: Indoors; sitting.

Probation Officers and Correctional Treatment Specialists

* Education/Training Required: Bachelor's degree
* Annual Earnings: $44,510
* Beginning Wage: $28,400
* Earnings Growth Potential: Medium
* Growth: 10.9%
* Annual Job Openings: 18,335
* Self-Employed: 0.1%
* Part-Time: 12.0%

Provide social services to assist in rehabilitation of law offenders in custody or on probation or parole. Make recommendations for actions involving formulation of rehabilitation plan and treatment of offender, including conditional release and education and employment stipulations. Prepare and maintain case folder for each assigned inmate or offender. Write reports describing offenders' progress. Inform offenders or inmates of requirements of conditional release, such as office visits, restitution payments, or educational and employment stipulations. Discuss with offenders how such issues as drug and alcohol abuse and anger management problems might have played roles in their criminal behavior. Gather information about offenders' backgrounds by talking to offenders, their families and friends, and other people who have relevant information. Develop rehabilitation programs for assigned offenders or inmates, establishing rules of conduct, goals, and objectives. Develop liaisons and networks with other parole officers, community agencies, staff in correctional institutions, psychiatric facilities, and after-care agencies to make plans for helping offenders with life adjustments. Arrange for medical, mental health, or substance abuse treatment services according to individual needs and court orders. Provide offenders or inmates with assistance in matters concerning detainers, sentences in other jurisdictions, writs, and applications for social assistance. Arrange for post-release services such as employment, housing, counseling, education, and social activities. Recommend remedial action or initiate court action when terms of probation or parole are not complied with. Interview probationers and parolees regularly to evaluate their progress in accomplishing goals and maintaining the terms specified in their probation contracts and rehabilitation plans. Supervise people on community-based sentences, including people on electronically monitored home detention. Assess the suitability of penitentiary inmates for release under parole and statutory release programs and submit recommendations to parole boards. Investigate alleged parole violations, using interviews, surveillance, and search and seizure. Conduct prehearing and presentencing investigations and testify in court regarding offenders' backgrounds and recommended sentences and sentencing conditions.

Personality Type: Social. These occupations frequently involve working with, communicating with, and teaching people and often involve helping or providing service to others.

GOE—Interest Area/Cluster: 10. Human Service. **Work Group:** 10.01. Counseling and Social Work. **Other Jobs in This Work Group:** Child, Family, and School Social Workers; Clinical Psychologists; Clinical, Counseling, and School Psychologists; Counseling Psychologists; Marriage and Family Therapists; Medical and Public Health Social Workers; Mental Health and Substance Abuse Social Workers; Mental Health Counselors; Rehabilitation Counselors; Substance Abuse and Behavioral Disorder Counselors.

Skills—Social Perceptiveness: Being aware of others' reactions and understanding why they react the way they do. **Persuasion:** Persuading others to approach things differently. **Negotiation:** Bringing others together and trying to reconcile differences. **Management of Personnel Resources:** Motivating, developing, and directing people as they work; identifying the best people for the job. **Time Management:** Managing one's own time and the time of others. **Monitoring:** Assessing how well one is doing when learning or doing something. **Writing:** Communicating effectively with others in writing as indicated by the needs of the audience. **Learning Strategies:** Using multiple approaches when learning or teaching new things.

Education and Training Program: Social Work. **Related Knowledge/Courses—Therapy and Counseling:** Information and techniques needed to rehabilitate physical and mental ailments and to provide career guidance, including alternative treatments, rehabilitation equipment and its proper use, and methods to evaluate treatment effects. **Psychology:** Human behavior and performance, mental processes, psychological research methods, and the assessment and treatment of behavioral and affective disorders. **Sociology and Anthropology:** Group behavior and dynamics; societal trends and influences; and cultures and their history, migrations, ethnicity, and origins. **Philosophy and Theology:** Different philosophical systems and religions, including their basic principles, values, ethics, ways of thinking, customs, and practices and their impact on human culture. **Law and Government:** Laws, legal codes, court procedures, precedents, government regulations, executive orders, agency rules, and the democratic political process. **Public Safety and Security:** Weaponry; public safety; security operations, rules, regulations, precautions, and prevention; and the protection of people, data, and property.

Work Environment: More often indoors than outdoors; very hot or cold; disease or infections; sitting.

Producers

⊛ Education/Training Required: Work experience plus degree
⊛ Annual Earnings: $61,090
⊛ Beginning Wage: $28,980
⊛ Earnings Growth Potential: Very high
⊛ Growth: 11.1%
⊛ Annual Job Openings: 8,992
⊛ Self-Employed: 29.5%
⊛ Part-Time: 9.0%

The job openings listed here are shared with Directors— Stage, Motion Pictures, Television, and Radio; Program Directors; Talent Directors; and Technical Directors/ Managers.

Plan and coordinate various aspects of radio, television, stage, or motion picture production, such as selecting script; coordinating writing, directing, and editing; and arranging financing. Coordinate the activities of writers, directors, managers, and other personnel throughout the production process. Monitor post-production processes to ensure accurate completion of all details. Perform management activities such as budgeting, scheduling, planning, and marketing. Determine production size, content, and budget, establishing details such as production schedules and management policies. Compose and edit scripts or provide screenwriters with story outlines from which scripts can be written. Conduct meetings with staff to discuss production progress and to ensure production objectives are attained. Resolve personnel problems that arise during the production process by acting as liaisons between dissenting parties when necessary. Produce shows for special occasions, such as holidays or testimonials. Edit and write news stories from information collected by reporters. Write and submit proposals to bid on contracts for projects. Hire directors, principal cast members, and key production staff members. Arrange financing for productions. Select plays, scripts, books, or ideas to be produced. Review film, recordings, or rehearsals to ensure conformance to production and broadcast standards. Perform administrative duties such as preparing operational reports, distributing rehearsal call sheets and script copies, and arranging for rehearsal quarters. Obtain and distribute costumes, props, music, and studio equipment needed to complete productions. Negotiate contracts with artistic personnel, often in accordance with collective bargaining agreements. Maintain knowledge of minimum wages and working conditions established by unions or associations of actors and technicians. Plan and coordinate the production of musical recordings, selecting music and directing performers. Negotiate with parties, including independent producers and the distributors and broadcasters who will be handling completed productions. Develop marketing plans for finished products, collaborating with sales associates to supervise product distribution. Determine and direct the content of radio programming.

Personality Type: Enterprising. These occupations frequently involve starting up and carrying out projects and can involve leading people and making many decisions. They sometimes require risk taking and often deal with business.

GOE—Interest Area/Cluster: 03. Arts and Communication. **Work Group:** 03.01. Managerial Work in Arts and Communication. **Other Jobs in This Work Group:** Agents and Business Managers of Artists, Performers, and Athletes; Art Directors; Producers and Directors; Program Directors; Public Relations Managers.

Skills—Monitoring: Assessing how well one is doing when learning or doing something. **Writing:** Communicating effectively with others in writing as indicated by the needs of the audience. **Management of Financial Resources:** Determining how money will be spent to get the work done and accounting for these expenditures. **Management of Personnel Resources:** Motivating, developing, and directing people as they work; identifying the best people for the job. **Negotiation:** Bringing others together and trying to reconcile differences. **Coordination:** Adjusting actions in relation to others' actions. **Equipment Selection:** Determining the kind of tools and equipment needed to do a job. **Speaking:** Talking to others to effectively convey information.

Education and Training Programs: Radio and Television; Drama and Dramatics/Theatre Arts, General; Directing and Theatrical Production; Theatre/Theatre Arts Management; Dramatic/Theatre Arts and Stagecraft, Other; Film/Cinema Studies; Cinematography and Film/Video Production. **Related Knowledge/Courses—Communications and Media:** Media production, communication, and dissemination techniques and methods, including alternative ways to inform and entertain via written, oral, and visual media. **Fine Arts:** Theory and techniques required to produce, compose, and perform works of music, dance, visual arts, drama, and sculpture. **Clerical Practices:** Administrative and clerical procedures and systems such as word-processing systems, filing and records management systems, stenography and transcription, forms, design principles, and other office procedures and terminology. **Sales and Marketing:** Principles and methods involved in showing, promoting, and selling products or services. This includes marketing strategies and tactics, product demonstration and sales techniques, and sales control systems. **Telecommunications:** Transmission, broadcasting, switching, control, and operation of telecommunications systems. **English Language:** The structure and content of the English language, including the meaning and spelling of words, rules of composition, and grammar.

Work Environment: Indoors; sitting.

Program Directors

* Education/Training Required: Work experience plus degree
* Annual Earnings: $61,090
* Beginning Wage: $28,980
* Earnings Growth Potential: Very high
* Growth: 11.1%
* Annual Job Openings: 8,992
* Self-Employed: 29.5%
* Part-Time: 9.0%

The job openings listed here are shared with Directors—Stage, Motion Pictures, Television, and Radio; Producers; Talent Directors; Technical Directors/Managers.

Direct and coordinate activities of personnel engaged in preparation of radio or television station program schedules and programs such as sports or news. Plan and schedule programming and event coverage based on broadcast length; time availability; and other factors such as community needs, ratings data, and viewer demographics. Monitor and review programming to ensure that schedules are met, guidelines are adhered to, and performances are of adequate quality. Direct and coordinate activities of personnel engaged in broadcast news, sports, or programming. Check completed program logs for accuracy and conformance with FCC rules and regulations and resolve program log inaccuracies. Establish work schedules and assign work to staff members. Coordinate activities between departments such as news and programming. Perform personnel duties such as hiring staff and evaluating work performance. Evaluate new and existing programming for suitability and to assess the need for changes, using information such as audience surveys and feedback. Develop budgets for programming and broadcasting activities and monitor expenditures to ensure that they remain within budgetary limits. Confer with directors and production staff to discuss issues such as production and casting problems, budgets, policies, and news coverage. Select, acquire, and maintain programs, music, films, and other needed materials and obtain legal clearances for their use as necessary. Monitor network transmissions for advisories concerning daily program schedules, program content, special feeds, or program changes. Develop promotions for current programs and specials. Prepare copy and edit tape so that material is ready for broadcasting. Develop ideas for programs and features that a station could produce. Participate in the planning and execution of fundraising activities. Review information about programs and schedules to ensure accuracy and provide such information to local media outlets as necessary. Read news, read or record public service and promotional announcements, and otherwise participate as a member of an on-air shift as required. Operate and maintain on-air and production audio equipment. Direct setup of remote facilities and install or cancel programs at remote stations.

Personality Type: Enterprising. These occupations frequently involve starting up and carrying out projects and can involve leading people and making many decisions. They sometimes require risk taking and often deal with business.

GOE—Interest Area/Cluster: 03. Arts and Communication. **Work Group:** 03.01. Managerial Work in Arts and Communication. **Other Jobs in This Work Group:** Agents and Business Managers of Artists, Performers, and Athletes; Art Directors; Producers; Producers and Directors; Public Relations Managers.

Skills—Operations Analysis: Analyzing needs and product requirements to create a design. **Management of Financial Resources:** Determining how money will be spent to get the work done and accounting for these expenditures. **Management of Personnel Resources:** Motivating, developing, and directing people as they work; identifying the best people for the job. **Coordination:** Adjusting actions in relation to others' actions. **Writing:** Communicating effectively with others in writing as indicated by the needs of the audience. **Time Management:** Managing one's own time and the time of others. **Equipment Selection:** Determining the kind of tools and equipment needed to do a job. **Monitoring:** Assessing how well one is doing when learning or doing something.

Education and Training Programs: Radio and Television; Drama and Dramatics/Theatre Arts, General; Directing and Theatrical Production; Theatre/Theatre Arts Management; Dramatic/Theatre Arts and Stagecraft, Other; Film/Cinema Studies; Cinematography and Film/Video Production. **Related Knowledge/Courses—Telecommunications:** Transmission, broadcasting, switching, control, and operation of telecommunications systems. **Communications and Media:** Media production, communication, and dissemination techniques and methods, including alternative ways to inform and entertain via written, oral, and visual media. **Computers and Electronics:** Electric circuit boards, processors, chips, and computer hardware and software, including applications and programming. **Clerical Practices:** Administrative and clerical procedures and systems such as word-processing systems, filing and records management systems, stenography and transcription, forms, design principles, and other office procedures and terminology. **Personnel and Human Resources:** Principles and procedures for personnel recruitment; selection; training; compensation and benefits; labor relations and negotiation; and personnel information systems. **Engineering and Technology:** Equipment, tools, and mechanical devices and their uses to produce motion, light, power, technology, and other applications.

Work Environment: Indoors; noisy; sitting.

Property, Real Estate, and Community Association Managers

- ❋ Education/Training Required: Bachelor's degree
- ❋ Annual Earnings: $43,670
- ❋ Beginning Wage: $20,800
- ❋ Earnings Growth Potential: Very high
- ❋ Growth: 15.1%
- ❋ Annual Job Openings: 49,916
- ❋ Self-Employed: 50.9%
- ❋ Part-Time: 16.1%

Plan, direct, or coordinate selling, buying, leasing, or governance activities of commercial, industrial, or residential real estate properties. Meet with prospective tenants to show properties, explain terms of occupancy, and provide information about local areas. Direct collection of monthly assessments; rental fees; and deposits and payment of insurance premiums, mortgage, taxes, and incurred operating expenses. Inspect grounds, facilities, and equipment routinely to determine necessity of repairs or maintenance. Investigate complaints, disturbances, and violations and resolve problems, following management rules and regulations. Manage and oversee operations, maintenance, administration, and improvement of commercial, industrial, or residential properties. Plan, schedule, and coordinate general maintenance, major repairs, and remodeling or construction projects for commercial or residential properties. Negotiate the sale, lease, or development of property and complete or review appropriate documents and forms. Maintain records of sales, rental or usage activity, special permits issued, maintenance and operating costs, or property availability. Determine and certify the eligibility of prospective tenants, following government regulations.

Prepare detailed budgets and financial reports for properties. Direct and coordinate the activities of staff and contract personnel and evaluate their performance. Maintain contact with insurance carriers, fire and police departments, and other agencies to ensure protection and compliance with codes and regulations. Market vacant space to prospective tenants through leasing agents, advertising, or other methods. Solicit and analyze bids from contractors for repairs, renovations, and maintenance. Review rents to ensure that they are in line with rental markets. Prepare and administer contracts for provision of property services such as cleaning, maintenance, and security services. Purchase building and maintenance supplies, equipment, or furniture. Act as liaisons between on-site managers or tenants and owners. Confer regularly with community association members to ensure their needs are being met. Meet with boards of directors and committees to discuss and resolve legal and environmental issues or disputes between neighbors.

Personality Type: Enterprising. These occupations frequently involve starting up and carrying out projects and can involve leading people and making many decisions. They sometimes require risk taking and often deal with business.

GOE—Interest Area/Cluster: 14. Retail and Wholesale Sales and Service. **Work Group:** 14.01. Managerial Work in Retail/Wholesale Sales and Service. **Other Jobs in This Work Group:** Advertising and Promotions Managers; Funeral Directors; Marketing Managers; Purchasing Managers; Sales Managers.

Skills—Management of Financial Resources: Determining how money will be spent to get the work done and accounting for these expenditures. **Management of Personnel Resources:** Motivating, developing, and directing people as they work; identifying the best people for the job. **Management of Material Resources:** Obtaining and seeing to the appropriate use of equipment, facilities, and materials needed to do certain work. **Time Management:** Managing one's own time and the time of others. **Repairing:** Repairing machines or systems, using the needed tools. **Judgment and Decision Making:** Weighing the relative costs and benefits of a potential action. **Installation:** Installing equipment, machines, wiring, or programs to meet specifications. **Coordination:** Adjusting actions in relation to others' actions.

Education and Training Program: Real Estate. **Related Knowledge/Courses—Sales and Marketing:** Principles and methods involved in showing, promoting, and selling products or services. This includes marketing strategies and tactics, product demonstration and sales techniques, and sales control systems. **Clerical Practices:** Administrative and clerical procedures and systems such as word-processing systems, filing and records management systems, stenography and transcription, forms, design principles, and other office procedures and terminology. **Economics and Accounting:** Economic and accounting principles and practices, the financial markets, banking, and the analysis and reporting of financial data. **Administration and Management:** Principles and processes involved in business and organizational planning, coordination, and execution. This includes strategic planning, resource allocation, manpower modeling, leadership techniques, and production methods. **Customer and Personal Service:** Principles and processes for providing customer and personal services, including needs assessment techniques, quality service standards, alternative delivery systems, and customer satisfaction evaluation techniques. **Building and Construction:** Materials, methods, and the appropriate tools to construct objects, structures, and buildings.

Work Environment: More often indoors than outdoors; sitting.

Prosthodontists

- ✸ Education/Training Required: First professional degree
- ✸ Annual Earnings: More than $145,600
- ✸ Beginning Wage: $75,450
- ✸ Earnings Growth Potential: Cannot be calculated
- ✸ Growth: 10.7%
- ✸ Annual Job Openings: 54
- ✸ Self-Employed: 51.3%
- ✸ Part-Time: 25.9%

Construct oral prostheses to replace missing teeth and other oral structures to correct natural and acquired deformation of mouth and jaws; to restore and maintain oral function, such as chewing and speaking; and to improve appearance. Replace missing teeth and associated oral structures with permanent fixtures, such as crowns and bridges, or removable fixtures, such as dentures. Fit prostheses to patients, making any necessary adjustments and modifications. Design and fabricate dental prostheses or supervise dental technicians and laboratory bench workers who construct the devices. Measure and take impressions of patients' jaws and teeth to determine the shape and size of dental prostheses, using face bows, dental articulators, recording devices, and other materials. Collaborate with general dentists, specialists, and other health professionals to develop solutions to dental and oral health concerns. Repair, reline, and/or rebase dentures. Restore function and aesthetics to traumatic injury victims or to individuals with diseases or birth defects. Use bonding technology on the surface of the teeth to change tooth shape or to close gaps. Treat facial pain and jaw joint problems. Place veneers onto teeth to conceal defects. Bleach discolored teeth to brighten and whiten them.

Personality Type: Investigative. These occupations frequently involve working with ideas and require an extensive amount of thinking. They can involve searching for facts and figuring out problems mentally.

GOE—Interest Area/Cluster: 08. Health Science. **Work Group:** 08.03. Dentistry. **Other Jobs in This Work Group:** Dental Hygienists; Dentists, General; Oral and Maxillofacial Surgeons; Orthodontists.

Skills—Science: Using scientific methods to solve problems. **Management of Financial Resources:** Determining how money will be spent to get the work done and accounting for these expenditures. **Social Perceptiveness:** Being aware of others' reactions and understanding why they react the way they do. **Equipment Selection:** Determining the kind of tools and equipment needed to do a job. **Reading Comprehension:** Understanding written sentences and paragraphs in work-related documents. **Active Learning:** Working with new material or information to grasp its implications. **Complex Problem Solving:** Identifying complex problems, reviewing the options, and implementing solutions. **Technology Design:** Generating or adapting equipment and technology to serve user needs.

Education and Training Programs: Prosthodontics/Prosthodontology (Cert, MS, PhD); Prosthodontics Specialty. **Related Knowledge/Courses—Medicine and Dentistry:** The information and techniques needed to diagnose and treat injuries, diseases, and deformities. This includes symptoms, treatment alternatives, drug properties and interactions, and preventive health-care measures. **Biology:** Plant and animal living tissue, cells, organisms, and entities, including their functions, interdependencies, and interactions with each other and the environment. **Chemistry:** The composition, structure, and properties of substances and of the chemical processes and transformations that they undergo. This includes uses of chemicals and their interactions, danger signs, production techniques, and disposal methods. **Psychology:** Human behavior and performance, mental processes, psychological research methods, and the assessment and treatment of behavioral and affective disorders. **Engineering and Technology:** Equipment, tools, and mechanical devices and their uses to produce motion, light, power, technology, and other applications. **Sales and Marketing:** Principles and methods involved in showing, promoting, and selling products or services. This includes marketing strategies and tactics, product demonstration and sales techniques, and sales control systems.

Work Environment: Indoors; noisy; contaminants; disease or infections; hazardous equipment; using hands on objects, tools, or controls.

Psychiatrists

* Education/Training Required: First professional degree
* Annual Earnings: More than $145,600
* Beginning Wage: $59,090
* Earnings Growth Potential: Cannot be calculated
* Growth: 14.2%
* Annual Job Openings: 38,027
* Self-Employed: 14.7%
* Part-Time: 8.1%

The job openings listed here are shared with Anesthesiologists; Family and General Practitioners; Internists, General; Obstetricians and Gynecologists; Pediatricians, General; and Surgeons.

Diagnose, treat, and help prevent disorders of the mind. Prescribe, direct, and administer psychotherapeutic treatments or medications to treat mental, emotional, or behavioral disorders.

Analyze and evaluate patient data and test findings to diagnose nature and extent of mental disorders. Collaborate with physicians, psychologists, social workers, psychiatric nurses, or other professionals to discuss treatment plans and progress. Gather and maintain patient information and records, including social and medical histories obtained from patients, relatives, and other professionals. Design individualized care plans, using a variety of treatments. Counsel outpatients and other patients during office visits. Examine or conduct laboratory or diagnostic tests on patients to provide information on general physical conditions and mental disorders. Advise and inform guardians, relatives, and significant others of patients' conditions and treatments. Teach, take continuing education classes, attend conferences and seminars, and conduct research and publish findings to increase understanding of mental, emotional, and behavioral states and disorders. Review and evaluate treatment procedures and outcomes of other psychiatrists and medical professionals. Prepare and submit case reports and summaries to government and mental health agencies. Serve on committees to promote and maintain community mental health services and delivery systems.

Personality Type: Investigative. These occupations frequently involve working with ideas and require an extensive amount of thinking. They can involve searching for facts and figuring out problems mentally.

GOE—Interest Area/Cluster: 08. Health Science. **Work Group:** 08.02. Medicine and Surgery. **Other Jobs in This Work Group:** Anesthesiologists; Family and General Practitioners; Internists, General; Obstetricians and Gynecologists; Pediatricians, General; Pharmacists; Physician Assistants; Registered Nurses; Surgeons.

Skills—Social Perceptiveness: Being aware of others' reactions and understanding why they react the way they do. **Systems Evaluation:** Looking at many indicators of system performance and taking into account their accuracy. **Systems Analysis:** Determining how a system should work and how changes will affect outcomes. **Active Listening:** Listening to what other people are saying and asking questions as appropriate. **Writing:** Communicating effectively with others in writing as indicated by the needs of the audience. **Speaking:** Talking to others to effectively convey information. **Reading Comprehension:** Understanding written sentences and paragraphs in work-related documents. **Judgment and Decision Making:** Weighing the relative costs and benefits of a potential action.

Education and Training Programs: Child Psychiatry; Psychiatry; Physical Medical and Rehabilitation/Psychiatry. **Related Knowledge/Courses—Therapy and Counseling:** Information and techniques needed to rehabilitate physical and mental ailments and to provide career guidance, including alternative treatments, rehabilitation equipment and its proper use, and methods to evaluate treatment effects. **Medicine and Dentistry:** The information and techniques needed to diagnose and treat injuries, diseases, and deformities. This includes symptoms, treatment alternatives, drug properties and interactions, and preventive health-care measures. **Psychology:** Human behavior and performance, mental processes, psychological research methods, and the assessment and treatment of behavioral and affective disorders. **Biology:** Plant and animal living tissue, cells, organisms, and entities, including their functions, interdependencies, and interactions with each other and the environment. **Sociology and Anthropology:** Group behavior and dynamics; societal trends and influences; and cultures and their history, migrations, ethnicity, and origins. **Philosophy and Theology:** Different philosophical systems and religions, including their basic principles, values, ethics, ways of thinking, customs, and practices and their impact on human culture.

Work Environment: Indoors; disease or infections; sitting.

Psychology Teachers, Postsecondary

- ❋ Education/Training Required: Doctoral degree
- ❋ Annual Earnings: $60,610
- ❋ Beginning Wage: $34,030
- ❋ Earnings Growth Potential: High
- ❋ Growth: 22.9%
- ❋ Annual Job Openings: 5,261
- ❋ Self-Employed: 0.4%
- ❋ Part-Time: 27.8%

Teach courses in psychology, such as child, clinical, and developmental psychology, and psychological counseling. Prepare and deliver lectures to undergraduate and/or graduate students on topics such as abnormal psychology, cognitive processes, and work motivation. Evaluate and grade students' classwork, laboratory work, assignments, and papers. Initiate, facilitate, and moderate classroom discussions. Compile, administer, and grade examinations or assign this work to others. Keep abreast of developments in their field by reading current literature, talking with colleagues, and participating in professional conferences. Prepare course materials such as syllabi, homework assignments, and handouts. Plan, evaluate, and revise curricula, course content, and course materials and methods of instruction. Maintain student attendance records, grades, and other required records. Supervise undergraduate and/or graduate teaching, internship, and research work. Maintain regularly scheduled office hours to advise and assist students. Conduct research in a particular field of knowledge and publish findings in professional journals, books, and electronic media. Advise students on academic and vocational curricula and on career issues. Select and obtain materials and supplies such as textbooks. Collaborate with colleagues to address teaching and research issues. Serve on academic or administrative committees that deal with institutional policies, departmental matters, and academic issues. Compile bibliographies of specialized materials for outside reading assignments. Participate in student recruitment, registration, and placement activities. Supervise students' laboratory work. Perform administrative duties such as serving as department head. Act as advisers to student organizations. Write grant proposals to procure external research funding. Participate in campus and community events. Provide professional consulting services to government and industry.

Personality Type: Social. These occupations frequently involve working with, communicating with, and teaching people and often involve helping or providing service to others.

GOE—Interest Area/Cluster: 05. Education and Training. **Work Group:** 05.03. Postsecondary and Adult Teaching and Instructing. **Other Jobs in This Work Group:** Adult Literacy, Remedial Education, and GED Teachers and Instructors; Agricultural Sciences Teachers, Postsecondary; Anthropology and Archeology Teachers, Postsecondary; Architecture Teachers, Postsecondary; Area, Ethnic, and Cultural Studies Teachers, Postsecondary; Art, Drama, and Music Teachers, Postsecondary; Atmospheric, Earth, Marine, and Space Sciences Teachers, Postsecondary; Biological Science Teachers, Postsecondary; Business Teachers, Postsecondary; Chemistry Teachers, Postsecondary; Communications Teachers, Postsecondary; Computer Science Teachers, Postsecondary; Criminal Justice and Law Enforcement Teachers, Postsecondary; Economics Teachers, Postsecondary;

Education Teachers, Postsecondary; Engineering Teachers, Postsecondary; English Language and Literature Teachers, Postsecondary; Environmental Science Teachers, Postsecondary; Farm and Home Management Advisors; Foreign Language and Literature Teachers, Postsecondary; Forestry and Conservation Science Teachers, Postsecondary; Geography Teachers, Postsecondary; Graduate Teaching Assistants; Health Specialties Teachers, Postsecondary; History Teachers, Postsecondary; Home Economics Teachers, Postsecondary; Law Teachers, Postsecondary; Library Science Teachers, Postsecondary; Mathematical Science Teachers, Postsecondary; Nursing Instructors and Teachers, Postsecondary; Philosophy and Religion Teachers, Postsecondary; Physics Teachers, Postsecondary; Political Science Teachers, Postsecondary; Recreation and Fitness Studies Teachers, Postsecondary; Social Work Teachers, Postsecondary; Sociology Teachers, Postsecondary.

Skills—Science: Using scientific methods to solve problems. **Learning Strategies:** Using multiple approaches when learning or teaching new things. **Instructing:** Teaching others how to do something. **Social Perceptiveness:** Being aware of others' reactions and understanding why they react the way they do. **Writing:** Communicating effectively with others in writing as indicated by the needs of the audience. **Reading Comprehension:** Understanding written sentences and paragraphs in work-related documents. **Critical Thinking:** Using logic and analysis to identify the strengths and weaknesses of different approaches. **Active Learning:** Working with new material or information to grasp its implications.

Education and Training Programs: Social Science Teacher Education; Psychology Teacher Education; Psychology, General; Clinical Psychology; Cognitive Psychology and Psycholinguistics; Community Psychology; Comparative Psychology; Counseling Psychology; Developmental and Child Psychology; Experimental Psychology; Industrial and Organizational Psychology; Personality Psychology; Physiological Psychology/Psychobiology; others. **Related Knowledge/ Courses—Therapy and Counseling:** Information and techniques needed to rehabilitate physical and mental ailments and to provide career guidance, including alternative treatments, rehabilitation equipment and its proper use, and methods to evaluate treatment effects. **Psychology:** Human behavior and performance, mental processes, psychological research methods, and the assessment and treatment of behavioral and affective disorders. **Sociology and Anthropology:** Group behavior and dynamics; societal trends and influences; and cultures and their history, migrations, ethnicity, and origins. **Philosophy and Theology:** Different philosophical systems and religions, including their basic principles, values, ethics, ways of thinking, customs, and practices and their impact on human culture. **Education and Training:** Instructional methods and training techniques, including curriculum design principles, learning theory, group and individual teaching techniques, design of individual development plans, and test design principles. **English Language:** The structure and content of the English language, including the meaning and spelling of words, rules of composition, and grammar.

Work Environment: Indoors; sitting.

Public Relations Managers

* Education/Training Required: Work experience plus degree
* Annual Earnings: $86,470
* Beginning Wage: $44,870
* Earnings Growth Potential: High
* Growth: 16.9%
* Annual Job Openings: 5,781
* Self-Employed: 1.7%
* Part-Time: 5.4%

Plan and direct public relations programs designed to create and maintain a favorable public image for employer or client or, if engaged in fundraising, plan and direct activities to solicit and maintain funds for special projects and nonprofit organizations. Identify main client groups and audiences and determine the best way to communicate publicity information to them. Write interesting and effective press releases, prepare information for media kits, and develop and maintain company Internet or intranet Web pages. Develop and maintain the company's corporate image and identity, which includes the use of logos and signage. Manage communications budgets. Manage special events such as sponsorship of races, parties introducing new products, or other activities the firm supports to gain public attention through the media without advertising directly. Draft speeches for company executives and arrange interviews and other forms of contact for them. Assign, supervise, and review the activities of public relations staff. Evaluate advertising and promotion programs for compatibility with public relations efforts. Establish and maintain effective working relationships with local and municipal government officials and media representatives. Confer with labor relations managers to develop internal communications that keep employees informed of company activities. Direct activities of external agencies, establishments, and departments that develop and implement communication strategies and information programs. Formulate policies and procedures related to public information programs, working with public relations executives. Respond to requests for information about employers' activities or status. Establish goals for soliciting funds, develop policies for collection and safeguarding of contributions, and coordinate disbursement of funds. Facilitate consumer relations or the relationship between parts of the company such as the managers and employees or different branch offices. Maintain company archives. Manage in-house communication courses. Produce films and other video products, regulate their distribution, and operate film library. Observe and report on social, economic, and political trends that might affect employers.

Personality Type: Enterprising. These occupations frequently involve starting up and carrying out projects and can involve leading people and making many decisions. They sometimes require risk taking and often deal with business.

GOE—Interest Area/Cluster: 03. Arts and Communication. **Work Group:** 03.01. Managerial Work in Arts and Communication. **Other Jobs in This Work Group:** Agents and Business Managers of Artists, Performers, and Athletes; Art Directors; Producers; Producers and Directors; Program Directors.

Skills—Management of Financial Resources: Determining how money will be spent to get the work done and accounting for these expenditures. **Monitoring:** Assessing how well one is doing when learning or doing something. **Social Perceptiveness:** Being aware of others' reactions and understanding why they react the way they do. **Writing:** Communicating effectively with others in writing as indicated by the needs of the audience. **Service Orientation:** Actively looking for ways to help people. **Operations Analysis:** Analyzing

needs and product requirements to create a design. **Speaking:** Talking to others to effectively convey information. **Persuasion:** Persuading others to approach things differently.

Education and Training Program: Public Relations/Image Management. **Related Knowledge/Courses—Sales and Marketing:** Principles and methods involved in showing, promoting, and selling products or services. This includes marketing strategies and tactics, product demonstration and sales techniques, and sales control systems. **Economics and Accounting:** Economic and accounting principles and practices, the financial markets, banking, and the analysis and reporting of financial data. **Foreign Language:** The structure and content of a foreign (non-English) language, including the meaning and spelling of words, rules of composition and grammar, and pronunciation. **Law and Government:** Laws, legal codes, court procedures, precedents, government regulations, executive orders, agency rules, and the democratic political process. **Education and Training:** Instructional methods and training techniques, including curriculum design principles, learning theory, group and individual teaching techniques, design of individual development plans, and test design principles. **English Language:** The structure and content of the English language, including the meaning and spelling of words, rules of composition, and grammar.

Work Environment: Indoors; sitting.

Public Relations Specialists

* Education/Training Required:
  Bachelor's degree
* Annual Earnings: $49,800
* Beginning Wage: $29,580
* Earnings Growth Potential: High
* Growth: 17.6%
* Annual Job Openings: 51,216
* Self-Employed: 4.9%
* Part-Time: 13.9%

Engage in promoting or creating good will for individuals, groups, or organizations by writing or selecting favorable publicity material and releasing it through various communications media. May prepare and arrange displays and make speeches. Prepare or edit organizational publications for internal and external audiences, including employee newsletters and stockholders' reports. Respond to requests for information from the media or designate another appropriate spokesperson or information source. Establish and maintain cooperative relationships with representatives of community, consumer, employee, and public interest groups. Plan and direct development and communication of informational programs to maintain favorable public and stockholder perceptions of an organization's accomplishments and agenda. Confer with production and support personnel to produce or coordinate production of advertisements and promotions. Arrange public appearances, lectures, contests, or exhibits for clients to increase product and service awareness and to promote goodwill. Study the objectives, promotional policies, and needs of organizations to develop public relations strategies that will influence public opinion or promote ideas, products, and services. Consult with advertising agencies or staff to arrange promotional campaigns in all types of media for products, organizations, or

individuals. Confer with other managers to identify trends and key group interests and concerns or to provide advice on business decisions. Coach client representatives in effective communication with the public and with employees. Prepare and deliver speeches to further public relations objectives. Purchase advertising space and time as required to promote client's product or agenda. Plan and conduct market and public opinion research to test products or determine potential for product success, communicating results to client or management.

Personality Type: Enterprising. These occupations frequently involve starting up and carrying out projects and can involve leading people and making many decisions. They sometimes require risk taking and often deal with business.

GOE—Interest Area/Cluster: 03. Arts and Communication. **Work Group:** 03.03. News, Broadcasting, and Public Relations. **Other Jobs in This Work Group:** Reporters and Correspondents.

Skills—Service Orientation: Actively looking for ways to help people. **Management of Financial Resources:** Determining how money will be spent to get the work done and accounting for these expenditures. **Persuasion:** Persuading others to approach things differently. **Writing:** Communicating effectively with others in writing as indicated by the needs of the audience. **Negotiation:** Bringing others together and trying to reconcile differences. **Social Perceptiveness:** Being aware of others' reactions and understanding why they react the way they do. **Judgment and Decision Making:** Weighing the relative costs and benefits of a potential action. **Monitoring:** Assessing how well one is doing when learning or doing something.

Education and Training Programs: Communication Studies/Speech Communication and Rhetoric; Public Relations/Image Management; Political Communication; Health Communication; Family and Consumer Sciences/Human

Sciences Communication. **Related Knowledge/ Courses—Sales and Marketing:** Principles and methods involved in showing, promoting, and selling products or services. This includes marketing strategies and tactics, product demonstration and sales techniques, and sales control systems. **Communications and Media:** Media production, communication, and dissemination techniques and methods, including alternative ways to inform and entertain via written, oral, and visual media. **Customer and Personal Service:** Principles and processes for providing customer and personal services, including needs assessment techniques, quality service standards, alternative delivery systems, and customer satisfaction evaluation techniques. **Sociology and Anthropology:** Group behavior and dynamics; societal trends and influences; and cultures and their history, migrations, ethnicity, and origins. **Clerical Practices:** Administrative and clerical procedures and systems such as word-processing systems, filing and records management systems, stenography and transcription, forms, design principles, and other office procedures and terminology. **Administration and Management:** Principles and processes involved in business and organizational planning, coordination, and execution. This includes strategic planning, resource allocation, manpower modeling, leadership techniques, and production methods.

Work Environment: Indoors; sitting.

Purchasing Managers

- ❈ Education/Training Required: Work experience plus degree
- ❈ Annual Earnings: $85,440
- ❈ Beginning Wage: $48,480
- ❈ Earnings Growth Potential: High
- ❈ Growth: 3.4%
- ❈ Annual Job Openings: 7,243
- ❈ Self-Employed: 2.7%
- ❈ Part-Time: 1.9%

Plan, direct, or coordinate the activities of buyers, purchasing officers, and related workers involved in purchasing materials, products, and services. Maintain records of goods ordered and received. Locate vendors of materials, equipment, or supplies and interview them to determine product availability and terms of sales. Prepare and process requisitions and purchase orders for supplies and equipment. Control purchasing department budgets. Interview and hire staff and oversee staff training. Review purchase order claims and contracts for conformance to company policy. Analyze market and delivery systems to assess present and future material availability. Develop and implement purchasing and contract management instructions, policies, and procedures. Participate in the development of specifications for equipment, products, or substitute materials. Resolve vendor or contractor grievances and claims against suppliers. Represent companies in negotiating contracts and formulating policies with suppliers. Review, evaluate, and approve specifications for issuing and awarding bids. Direct and coordinate activities of personnel engaged in buying, selling, and distributing materials, equipment, machinery, and supplies. Prepare bid awards requiring board approval. Prepare reports regarding market conditions and merchandise costs. Administer online purchasing systems. Arrange for disposal of surplus materials.

Personality Type: Enterprising. These occupations frequently involve starting up and carrying out projects and can involve leading people and making many decisions. They sometimes require risk taking and often deal with business.

GOE—Interest Area/Cluster: 14. Retail and Wholesale Sales and Service. **Work Group:** 14.01. Managerial Work in Retail/Wholesale Sales and Service. **Other Jobs in This Work Group:** Advertising and Promotions Managers; Funeral Directors; Marketing Managers; Property, Real Estate, and Community Association Managers; Sales Managers.

Skills—Management of Material Resources: Obtaining and seeing to the appropriate use of equipment, facilities, and materials needed to do certain work. **Management of Financial Resources:** Determining how money will be spent to get the work done and accounting for these expenditures. **Negotiation:** Bringing others together and trying to reconcile differences. **Operations Analysis:** Analyzing needs and product requirements to create a design. **Mathematics:** Using mathematics to solve problems. **Systems Evaluation:** Looking at many indicators of system performance and taking into account their accuracy. **Operation Monitoring:** Watching gauges, dials, or other indicators to make sure a machine is working properly. **Operation and Control:** Controlling operations of equipment or systems.

Education and Training Program: Purchasing, Procurement/Acquisitions and Contracts Management. **Related Knowledge/Courses—Economics and Accounting:** Economic and accounting principles and practices, the financial markets, banking, and the analysis and reporting of financial data. **Personnel and Human Resources:** Principles and procedures for personnel recruitment; selection; training; compensation and benefits; labor relations and negotiation; and personnel information systems. **Production and**

Processing: Inputs, outputs, raw materials, waste, quality control, costs, and techniques for maximizing the manufacture and distribution of goods. **Administration and Management:** Principles and processes involved in business and organizational planning, coordination, and execution. This includes strategic planning, resource allocation, manpower modeling, leadership techniques, and production methods. **Mathematics:** Numbers and their operations and interrelationships, including arithmetic, algebra, geometry, calculus, and statistics and their applications. **Transportation:** Principles and methods for moving people or goods by air, rail, sea, or road, including their relative costs, advantages, and limitations.

Work Environment: Indoors; noisy; sitting.

Radiation Therapists

- ✱ Education/Training Required: Associate degree
- ✱ Annual Earnings: $70,010
- ✱ Beginning Wage: $46,580
- ✱ Earnings Growth Potential: Low
- ✱ Growth: 24.8%
- ✱ Annual Job Openings: 1,461
- ✱ Self-Employed: 0.0%
- ✱ Part-Time: 10.3%

Provide radiation therapy to patients as prescribed by radiologists according to established practices and standards. Duties may include reviewing prescriptions and diagnoses; acting as liaisons with physicians and supportive care personnel; preparing equipment such as immobilization, treatment, and protection devices; and maintaining records, reports, and files. May assist in dosimetry procedures and tumor localization. Position patients for treatment with accuracy according to prescription. Administer prescribed doses of radiation to specific body parts, using radiation therapy equipment according to established practices and standards. Check radiation therapy equipment to ensure proper operation. Review prescriptions, diagnoses, patient charts, and identification. Follow principles of radiation protection for patients, radiation therapists, and others. Maintain records, reports, and files as required, including such information as radiation dosages, equipment settings, and patients' reactions. Conduct most treatment sessions independently, in accordance with long-term treatment plans and under general direction of patients' physicians. Enter data into computers and set controls to operate and adjust equipment and regulate dosages. Observe and reassure patients during treatments and report unusual reactions to physicians or turn equipment off if unexpected adverse reactions occur. Calculate actual treatment dosages delivered during each session. Check for side effects such as skin irritation, nausea, and hair loss to assess patients' reaction to treatment. Prepare and construct equipment such as immobilization, treatment, and protection devices. Educate, prepare, and reassure patients and their families by answering questions, providing physical assistance, and reinforcing physicians' advice regarding treatment reactions and post-treatment care. Provide assistance to other health care personnel during dosimetry procedures and tumor localization. Help physicians, radiation oncologists, and clinical physicists to prepare physical and technical aspects of radiation treatment plans, using information about patient conditions and anatomies. Photograph treated areas of patients and process film. Act as liaisons with medical physicists and supportive care personnel. Train and supervise student or subordinate radiotherapy technologists. Implement appropriate follow-up care plans. Assist in the preparation of sealed radioactive materials such as cobalt, radium, cesium, and isotopes for use in radiation treatments. Store, sterilize, or prepare the special applicators containing the radioactive substances implanted by physicians.

Personality Type: Social. These occupations frequently involve working with, communicating with, and teaching people and often involve helping or providing service to others.

GOE—Interest Area/Cluster: 08. Health Science. **Work Group:** 08.07. Medical Therapy. **Other Jobs in This Work Group:** Audiologists; Occupational Therapist Assistants; Occupational Therapists; Physical Therapist Assistants; Physical Therapists; Recreational Therapists; Respiratory Therapists; Respiratory Therapy Technicians; Speech-Language Pathologists.

Skills—Operation Monitoring: Watching gauges, dials, or other indicators to make sure a machine is working properly. **Operation and Control:** Controlling operations of equipment or systems. **Quality Control Analysis:** Evaluating the quality or performance of products, services, or processes.

Education and Training Program: Medical Radiologic Technology/Science—Radiation Therapist. **Related Knowledge/Courses—Medicine and Dentistry:** The information and techniques needed to diagnose and treat injuries, diseases, and deformities. This includes symptoms, treatment alternatives, drug properties and interactions, and preventive health-care measures. **Biology:** Plant and animal living tissue, cells, organisms, and entities, including their functions, interdependencies, and interactions with each other and the environment. **Physics:** Physical principles, laws, and applications, including air, water, material dynamics, light, atomic principles, heat, electric theory, earth formations, and meteorological and related natural phenomena. **Psychology:** Human behavior and performance, mental processes, psychological research methods, and the assessment and treatment of behavioral and affective disorders.

Philosophy and Theology: Different philosophical systems and religions, including their basic principles, values, ethics, ways of thinking, customs, and practices and their impact on human culture. **Therapy and Counseling:** Information and techniques needed to rehabilitate physical and mental ailments and to provide career guidance, including alternative treatments, rehabilitation equipment and its proper use, and methods to evaluate treatment effects.

Work Environment: Indoors; radiation; disease or infections; standing; walking and running; using hands on objects, tools, or controls.

Radiologic Technicians

- ✸ Education/Training Required: Associate degree
- ✸ Annual Earnings: $50,260
- ✸ Beginning Wage: $33,910
- ✸ Earnings Growth Potential: Low
- ✸ Growth: 15.1%
- ✸ Annual Job Openings: 12,836
- ✸ Self-Employed: 1.1%
- ✸ Part-Time: 17.3%

The job openings listed here are shared with Radiologic Technologists.

Maintain and use equipment and supplies necessary to demonstrate portions of the human body on X-ray film or fluoroscopic screen for diagnostic purposes. Use beam-restrictive devices and patient-shielding techniques to minimize radiation exposure to patient and staff. Position X-ray equipment and adjust controls to set exposure factors, such as time and distance. Position patient on examining table and set up and adjust equipment to obtain optimum view of specific body area as requested by physician. Determine patients'

X-ray needs by reading requests or instructions from physicians. Make exposures necessary for the requested procedures, rejecting and repeating work that does not meet established standards. Process exposed radiographs, using film processors or computer-generated methods. Explain procedures to patients to reduce anxieties and obtain cooperation. Perform procedures such as linear tomography; mammography; sonograms; joint and cyst aspirations; routine contrast studies; routine fluoroscopy; and examinations of the head, trunk, and extremities under supervision of physician. Prepare and set up X-ray room for patient. Assure that sterile supplies, contrast materials, catheters, and other required equipment are present and in working order, requisitioning materials as necessary. Maintain records of patients examined, examinations performed, views taken, and technical factors used. Provide assistance to physicians or other technologists in the performance of more complex procedures. Monitor equipment operation and report malfunctioning equipment to supervisor. Provide students and other technologists with suggestions of additional views, alternate positioning, or improved techniques to ensure the images produced are of the highest quality. Coordinate work of other technicians or technologists when procedures require more than one person. Assist with on-the-job training of new employees and students and provide input to supervisors regarding training performance. Maintain a current file of examination protocols. Operate mobile X-ray equipment in operating room, in emergency room, or at patient's bedside. Provide assistance in radiopharmaceutical administration, monitoring patients' vital signs and notifying the radiologist of any relevant changes.

Personality Type: Realistic. These occupations frequently involve work activities that include practical, hands-on problems and solutions. They often deal with plants; animals; and real-world materials such as wood, tools, and machinery. Many of the occupations require working outside and don't involve a lot of paperwork or working closely with others.

GOE—Interest Area/Cluster: 08. Health Science. **Work Group:** 08.06. Medical Technology. **Other Jobs in This Work Group:** Biological Technicians; Cardiovascular Technologists and Technicians; Diagnostic Medical Sonographers; Medical and Clinical Laboratory Technicians; Medical and Clinical Laboratory Technologists; Medical Records and Health Information Technicians; Nuclear Medicine Technologists; Orthotists and Prosthetists; Radiologic Technologists; Radiologic Technologists and Technicians.

Skills—Science: Using scientific methods to solve problems. **Operation Monitoring:** Watching gauges, dials, or other indicators to make sure a machine is working properly. **Equipment Selection:** Determining the kind of tools and equipment needed to do a job. **Operation and Control:** Controlling operations of equipment or systems. **Service Orientation:** Actively looking for ways to help people. **Active Listening:** Listening to what other people are saying and asking questions as appropriate. **Negotiation:** Bringing others together and trying to reconcile differences. **Writing:** Communicating effectively with others in writing as indicated by the needs of the audience.

Education and Training Programs: Medical Radiologic Technology/Science—Radiation Therapist; Radiologic Technology/Science—Radiographer; Allied Health Diagnostic, Intervention, and Treatment Professions, Other. **Related Knowledge/Courses—Medicine and Dentistry:** The information and techniques needed to diagnose and treat injuries, diseases, and deformities. This includes symptoms, treatment alternatives, drug properties and interactions, and preventive health-care measures. **Clerical Practices:** Administrative and clerical procedures and systems such as

word-processing systems, filing and records management systems, stenography and transcription, forms, design principles, and other office procedures and terminology. **Psychology:** Human behavior and performance, mental processes, psychological research methods, and the assessment and treatment of behavioral and affective disorders. **Physics:** Physical principles, laws, and applications, including air, water, material dynamics, light, atomic principles, heat, electric theory, earth formations, and meteorological and related natural phenomena. **Biology:** Plant and animal living tissue, cells, organisms, and entities, including their functions, interdependencies, and interactions with each other and the environment. **Chemistry:** The composition, structure, and properties of substances and of the chemical processes and transformations that they undergo. This includes uses of chemicals and their interactions, danger signs, production techniques, and disposal methods.

Work Environment: Indoors; radiation; disease or infections; standing; walking and running; using hands on objects, tools, or controls.

Radiologic Technologists

* Education/Training Required: Associate degree
* Annual Earnings: $50,260
* Beginning Wage: $33,910
* Earnings Growth Potential: Low
* Growth: 15.1%
* Annual Job Openings: 12,836
* Self-Employed: 1.1%
* Part-Time: 17.3%

The job openings listed here are shared with Radiologic Technicians.

Take X rays and Computerized Axial Tomography (CAT or CT) scans or administer

nonradioactive materials into patient's bloodstream for diagnostic purposes. Includes technologists who specialize in other modalities such as computed tomography, ultrasound, and magnetic resonance. Use radiation safety measures and protection devices to comply with government regulations and to ensure safety of patients and staff. Review and evaluate developed X rays, video tape, or computer generated information to determine if images are satisfactory for diagnostic purposes. Position imaging equipment and adjust controls to set exposure times and distances, according to specification of examinations. Explain procedures and observe patients to ensure safety and comfort during scans. Key commands and data into computers to document and specify scan sequences, adjust transmitters and receivers, or photograph certain images. Operate or oversee operation of radiologic and magnetic imaging equipment to produce images of the body for diagnostic purposes. Position and immobilize patients on examining tables. Record, process, and maintain patient data and treatment records, and prepare reports. Take thorough and accurate patient medical histories. Remove and process film. Set up examination rooms, ensuring that all necessary equipment is ready. Monitor patients' conditions and reactions, reporting abnormal signs to physicians. Coordinate work with clerical personnel or other technologists. Provide assistance in dressing or changing seriously ill, injured, or disabled patients. Demonstrate new equipment, procedures, and techniques to staff, and provide technical assistance. Collaborate with other medical team members such as physicians and nurses to conduct angiography or special vascular procedures. Prepare and administer oral or injected contrast media to patients. Monitor video displays of areas being scanned and adjust density or contrast to improve picture quality. Operate fluoroscope to aid physicians to view and guide wires or catheters through blood vessels to areas of interest. Assign duties to radiologic staffs to maintain patient flows and achieve production goals. Perform scheduled maintenance and minor emergency repairs on radiographic equipment. Perform administrative duties such as developing departmental operating budgets, coordinating purchases of supplies and equipment, and preparing work schedules.

Personality Type: Realistic. These occupations frequently involve work activities that include practical, hands-on problems and solutions. They often deal with plants; animals; and real-world materials such as wood, tools, and machinery. Many of the occupations require working outside and don't involve a lot of paperwork or working closely with others.

GOE—Interest Area/Cluster: 08. Health Science. **Work Group:** 08.06. Medical Technology. **Other Jobs in This Work Group:** Biological Technicians; Cardiovascular Technologists and Technicians; Diagnostic Medical Sonographers; Medical and Clinical Laboratory Technicians; Medical and Clinical Laboratory Technologists; Medical Records and Health Information Technicians; Nuclear Medicine Technologists; Orthotists and Prosthetists; Radiologic Technicians; Radiologic Technologists and Technicians.

Skills—Operation Monitoring: Watching gauges, dials, or other indicators to make sure a machine is working properly. **Operation and Control:** Controlling operations of equipment or systems.

Education and Training Programs: Medical Radiologic Technology/Science—Radiation Therapist; Radiologic Technology/Science—Radiographer; Allied Health Diagnostic, Intervention, and Treatment Professions, Other. **Related Knowledge/Courses—Medicine and Dentistry:** The information and techniques needed to diagnose and treat injuries, diseases, and deformities. This includes symptoms, treatment alternatives, drug properties and interactions, and preventive health-care measures. **Physics:** Physical principles, laws, and applications, including air, water, material dynamics, light, atomic principles, heat, electric theory, earth formations, and meteorological and related natural phenomena. **Customer and Personal Service:** Principles and processes for providing customer and personal services, including needs assessment techniques, quality service standards, alternative delivery systems, and customer satisfaction evaluation techniques. **Biology:** Plant and animal living tissue, cells, organisms, and entities, including their functions, interdependencies, and interactions with each other and the environment. **Psychology:** Human behavior and performance, mental processes, psychological research methods, and the assessment and treatment of behavioral and affective disorders. **Chemistry:** The composition, structure, and properties of substances and of the chemical processes and transformations that they undergo. This includes uses of chemicals and their interactions, danger signs, production techniques, and disposal methods.

Work Environment: Indoors; radiation; disease or infections; standing; using hands on objects, tools, or controls; repetitive motions.

Recreation and Fitness Studies Teachers, Postsecondary

- ❋ Education/Training Required: Doctoral degree
- ❋ Annual Earnings: $52,170
- ❋ Beginning Wage: $26,790
- ❋ Earnings Growth Potential: High
- ❋ Growth: 22.9%
- ❋ Annual Job Openings: 3,010
- ❋ Self-Employed: 0.4%
- ❋ Part-Time: 27.8%

Teach courses pertaining to recreation, leisure, and fitness studies, including exercise physiology and facilities management. Evaluate and grade students' classwork, assignments, and papers. Maintain student attendance records, grades, and other required records. Prepare and deliver lectures to undergraduate and graduate students on topics such as anatomy, therapeutic recreation, and conditioning theory. Prepare course materials such as syllabi, homework assignments, and handouts. Maintain regularly scheduled office hours to advise and assist students. Compile, administer, and grade examinations or assign this work to others. Plan, evaluate, and revise curricula, course content, and course materials and methods of instruction. Initiate, facilitate, and moderate classroom discussions. Keep abreast of developments in their field by reading current literature, talking with colleagues, and participating in professional conferences. Advise students on academic and vocational curricula and on career issues. Participate in student recruitment, registration, and placement activities. Collaborate with colleagues to address teaching and research issues. Select and obtain materials and supplies such as textbooks. Participate in campus and community events. Serve on academic or administrative committees that deal with institutional policies, departmental matters, and academic issues. Compile bibliographies of specialized materials for outside reading assignments. Supervise undergraduate or graduate teaching, internship, and research work. Perform administrative duties such as serving as department heads. Prepare students to act as sports coaches. Conduct research in a particular field of knowledge and publish findings in professional journals, books, or electronic media. Act as advisers to student organizations. Write grant proposals to procure external research funding. Provide professional consulting services to government or industry.

Personality Type: Social. These occupations frequently involve working with, communicating with, and teaching people and often involve helping or providing service to others.

GOE—Interest Area/Cluster: 05. Education and Training. **Work Group:** 05.03. Postsecondary and Adult Teaching and Instructing. **Other Jobs in This Work Group:** Adult Literacy, Remedial Education, and GED Teachers and Instructors; Agricultural Sciences Teachers, Postsecondary; Anthropology and Archeology Teachers, Postsecondary; Architecture Teachers, Postsecondary; Area, Ethnic, and Cultural Studies Teachers, Postsecondary; Art, Drama, and Music Teachers, Postsecondary; Atmospheric, Earth, Marine, and Space Sciences Teachers, Postsecondary; Biological Science Teachers, Postsecondary; Business Teachers, Postsecondary; Chemistry Teachers, Postsecondary; Communications Teachers, Postsecondary; Computer Science Teachers, Postsecondary; Criminal Justice and Law Enforcement Teachers, Postsecondary; Economics Teachers, Postsecondary; Education Teachers, Postsecondary; Engineering Teachers, Postsecondary; English Language and Literature Teachers, Postsecondary; Environmental Science Teachers, Postsecondary; Farm and Home Management Advisors; Foreign Language and Literature Teachers, Postsecondary; Forestry and Conservation Science Teachers, Postsecondary; Geography Teachers, Postsecondary; Graduate Teaching Assistants; Health Specialties Teachers, Postsecondary; History Teachers, Postsecondary; Home Economics Teachers, Postsecondary; Law Teachers, Postsecondary; Library Science Teachers, Postsecondary; Mathematical Science Teachers, Postsecondary; Nursing Instructors and Teachers, Postsecondary; Philosophy and Religion Teachers, Postsecondary; Physics Teachers, Postsecondary; Political Science Teachers, Postsecondary; Psychology Teachers, Postsecondary; Social Work Teachers, Postsecondary; Sociology Teachers, Postsecondary.

Skills—Instructing: Teaching others how to do something. **Learning Strategies:** Using multiple approaches when learning or teaching new things. **Science:** Using scientific methods to solve problems. **Social Perceptiveness:** Being aware of others' reactions and understanding why they react the way they do. **Persuasion:** Persuading others to approach things differently. **Time Management:** Managing one's own time and the time of others. **Management of Financial Resources:** Determining how money will be spent to get the work done and accounting for these expenditures. **Writing:** Communicating effectively with others in writing as indicated by the needs of the audience.

Education and Training Programs: Parks, Recreation and Leisure Studies; Health and Physical Education, General; Sport and Fitness Administration/Management. **Related Knowledge/Courses—Education and Training:** Instructional methods and training techniques, including curriculum design principles, learning theory, group and individual teaching techniques, design of individual development plans, and test design principles. **Philosophy and Theology:** Different philosophical systems and religions, including their basic principles, values, ethics, ways of thinking, customs, and practices and their impact on human culture. **Psychology:** Human behavior and performance, mental processes, psychological research methods, and the assessment and treatment of behavioral and affective disorders. **Therapy and Counseling:** Information and techniques needed to rehabilitate physical and mental ailments and to provide career guidance, including alternative treatments, rehabilitation equipment and its proper use, and methods to evaluate treatment effects. **Medicine and Dentistry:** The information and techniques needed to diagnose and treat injuries, diseases, and deformities. This includes symptoms, treatment alternatives, drug properties and interactions, and preventive health-care measures. **Sociology and Anthropology:** Group behavior and dynamics; societal trends and influences; and cultures and their history, migrations, ethnicity, and origins.

Work Environment: More often indoors than outdoors; standing.

Recreation Workers

* Education/Training Required: Bachelor's degree
* Annual Earnings: $21,220
* Beginning Wage: $14,980
* Earnings Growth Potential: Low
* Growth: 12.7%
* Annual Job Openings: 61,454
* Self-Employed: 8.5%
* Part-Time: 38.2%

Conduct recreation activities with groups in public, private, or volunteer agencies or recreation facilities. Organize and promote activities such as arts and crafts, sports, games, music, dramatics, social recreation, camping, and hobbies, taking into account the needs and interests of individual members. Enforce rules and regulations of recreational facilities to maintain discipline and ensure safety. Organize, lead, and promote interest in recreational activities such as arts, crafts, sports, games, camping, and hobbies. Manage the daily operations of recreational facilities. Administer first aid according to prescribed procedures and notify emergency medical personnel when necessary. Ascertain and interpret group interests, evaluate equipment and facilities, and adapt activities to meet participant needs. Greet new arrivals to activities, introducing them to other participants, explaining facility rules, and encouraging participation. Complete and maintain time and attendance forms and inventory lists. Explain principles, techniques, and safety procedures to participants in recreational activities and demonstrate use of materials and equipment. Evaluate recreation areas, facilities, and services to determine if they are producing desired results. Confer with management to discuss and resolve participant complaints. Supervise and coordinate the work activities of personnel, such as training staff members and assigning work duties. Meet and collaborate with agency personnel, community organizations, and other professional personnel to plan balanced recreational programs for participants. Schedule maintenance and use of facilities. Direct special activities or events such as aquatics, gymnastics, or performing arts. Meet with staff to discuss rules, regulations, and work-related problems. Provide for entertainment and set up related decorations and equipment. Encourage participants to develop their own activities and leadership skills through group discussions. Serve as liaison between park or recreation administrators and activity instructors. Evaluate staff performance, recording evaluations on appropriate forms. Oversee the purchase, planning, design, construction, and upkeep of recreation facilities and areas.

Personality Type: Social. These occupations frequently involve working with, communicating with, and teaching people and often involve helping or providing service to others.

GOE—Interest Area/Cluster: 09. Hospitality, Tourism, and Recreation. **Work Group:** 09.02. Recreational Services. **Other Jobs in This Work Group:** No others in group.

Skills—Management of Financial Resources: Determining how money will be spent to get the work done and accounting for these expenditures. **Management of Personnel Resources:** Motivating, developing, and directing people as they work; identifying the best people for the job. **Service Orientation:** Actively looking for ways to help people. **Management of Material Resources:** Obtaining and seeing to the appropriate use of equipment, facilities, and materials needed to do certain work. **Social Perceptiveness:** Being aware of others' reactions and understanding why they react the way they do. **Writing:** Communicating effectively with others in writing as indicated by the needs of the audience. **Equipment Selection:** Determining the kind of tools and equipment needed to do a job. **Systems Evaluation:** Looking at many indicators of system performance and taking into account their accuracy.

Education and Training Programs: Parks, Recreation and Leisure Studies; Parks, Recreation and Leisure Facilities Management; Sport and Fitness Administration/Management; Health and Physical Education/Fitness, Other; Parks, Recreation, Leisure and Fitness Studies, Other. **Related Knowledge/Courses—Psychology:** Human behavior and performance, mental processes, psychological research methods, and the assessment and treatment of behavioral and affective disorders. **Therapy and Counseling:** Information and techniques needed to rehabilitate physical and mental ailments and to provide career guidance, including alternative treatments, rehabilitation equipment and its proper use, and methods to evaluate treatment effects. **Customer and Personal Service:**

Principles and processes for providing customer and personal services, including needs assessment techniques, quality service standards, alternative delivery systems, and customer satisfaction evaluation techniques. **Sociology and Anthropology:** Group behavior and dynamics; societal trends and influences; and cultures and their history, migrations, ethnicity, and origins. **Sales and Marketing:** Principles and methods involved in showing, promoting, and selling products or services. This includes marketing strategies and tactics, product demonstration and sales techniques, and sales control systems. **Clerical Practices:** Administrative and clerical procedures and systems such as word-processing systems, filing and records management systems, stenography and transcription, forms, design principles, and other office procedures and terminology.

Work Environment: Indoors; noisy; more often standing than sitting; using hands on objects, tools, or controls.

Registered Nurses

- ❋ Education/Training Required: Associate degree
- ❋ Annual Earnings: $60,010
- ❋ Beginning Wage: $42,020
- ❋ Earnings Growth Potential: Low
- ❋ Growth: 23.5%
- ❋ Annual Job Openings: 233,499
- ❋ Self-Employed: 0.8%
- ❋ Part-Time: 21.8%

Assess patient health problems and needs, develop and implement nursing care plans, and maintain medical records. Administer nursing care to ill, injured, convalescent, or disabled patients. May advise patients on health maintenance and disease prevention or provide

case management. **Licensing or registration required. Includes advance practice nurses such as nurse practitioners, clinical nurse specialists, certified nurse midwives, and certified registered nurse anesthetists. Advanced practice nursing is practiced by RNs who have specialized formal, post-basic education and who function in highly autonomous and specialized roles.** Monitor, record, and report symptoms and changes in patients' conditions. Maintain accurate, detailed reports and records. Record patients' medical information and vital signs. Order, interpret, and evaluate diagnostic tests to identify and assess patients' conditions. Modify patient treatment plans as indicated by patients' responses and conditions. Direct and supervise less skilled nursing or health care personnel or supervise particular units. Consult and coordinate with health care team members to assess, plan, implement and evaluate patient care plans. Monitor all aspects of patient care, including diet and physical activity. Instruct individuals, families, and other groups on topics such as health education, disease prevention, and childbirth, and develop health improvement programs. Prepare patients for, and assist with, examinations and treatments. Assess the needs of individuals, families, or communities, including assessment of individuals' home or work environments to identify potential health or safety problems. Provide health care, first aid, immunizations, and assistance in convalescence and rehabilitation in locations such as schools, hospitals, and industry. Prepare rooms, sterile instruments, equipment, and supplies, and ensure that stock of supplies is maintained. Inform physicians of patients' conditions during anesthesia. Administer local, inhalation, intravenous, and other anesthetics. Perform physical examinations, make tentative diagnoses, and treat patients en route to hospitals or at disaster site triage centers. Observe nurses and visit patients to ensure proper nursing care. Conduct specified laboratory tests. Direct and coordinate

infection control programs, advising and consulting with specified personnel about necessary precautions. Prescribe or recommend drugs, medical devices, or other forms of treatment such as physical therapy, inhalation therapy, or related therapeutic procedures. Perform administrative and managerial functions such as taking responsibility for a unit's staff, budget, planning, and long-range goals. Hand items to surgeons during operations.

Personality Type: Social. These occupations frequently involve working with, communicating with, and teaching people and often involve helping or providing service to others.

GOE—Interest Area/Cluster: 08. Health Science. **Work Group:** 08.02. Medicine and Surgery. **Other Jobs in This Work Group:** Anesthesiologists; Family and General Practitioners; Internists, General; Obstetricians and Gynecologists; Pediatricians, General; Pharmacists; Physician Assistants; Psychiatrists; Surgeons.

Skills—Negotiation: Bringing others together and trying to reconcile differences. **Systems Analysis:** Determining how a system should work and how changes will affect outcomes. **Operation Monitoring:** Watching gauges, dials, or other indicators to make sure a machine is working properly. **Service Orientation:** Actively looking for ways to help people. **Systems Evaluation:** Looking at many indicators of system performance and taking into account their accuracy.

Education and Training Programs: Nursing—Registered Nurse Training (RN, ASN, BSN, MSN); Adult Health Nurse/Nursing; Nurse Anesthetist; Family Practice Nurse/Nurse Practitioner; Maternal/Child Health and Neonatal Nurse/Nursing; Nurse Midwife/Nursing Midwifery; Nursing Science (MS, PhD); Pediatric Nurse/Nursing; Psychiatric/Mental Health Nurse/Nursing; Public Health/Community Nurse/Nursing; others. **Related Knowledge/Courses—Medicine**

and Dentistry: The information and techniques needed to diagnose and treat injuries, diseases, and deformities. This includes symptoms, treatment alternatives, drug properties and interactions, and preventive health-care measures. **Psychology:** Human behavior and performance, mental processes, psychological research methods, and the assessment and treatment of behavioral and affective disorders. **Therapy and Counseling:** Information and techniques needed to rehabilitate physical and mental ailments and to provide career guidance, including alternative treatments, rehabilitation equipment and its proper use, and methods to evaluate treatment effects. **Biology:** Plant and animal living tissue, cells, organisms, and entities, including their functions, interdependencies, and interactions with each other and the environment. **Philosophy and Theology:** Different philosophical systems and religions, including their basic principles, values, ethics, ways of thinking, customs, and practices and their impact on human culture. **Sociology and Anthropology:** Group behavior and dynamics; societal trends and influences; and cultures and their history, migrations, ethnicity, and origins.

Work Environment: Indoors; disease or infections; standing; walking and running; using hands on objects, tools, or controls.

Rehabilitation Counselors

- ❋ Education/Training Required: Master's degree
- ❋ Annual Earnings: $29,630
- ❋ Beginning Wage: $19,610
- ❋ Earnings Growth Potential: Low
- ❋ Growth: 23.0%
- ❋ Annual Job Openings: 32,081
- ❋ Self-Employed: 5.9%
- ❋ Part-Time: 15.4%

Counsel individuals to maximize the independence and employability of persons coping with personal, social, and vocational difficulties that result from birth defects, illness, disease, accidents, or the stress of daily life. Coordinate activities for residents of care and treatment facilities. Assess client needs and design and implement rehabilitation programs that may include personal and vocational counseling, training, and job placement. Monitor and record clients' progress in order to ensure that goals and objectives are met. Confer with clients to discuss their options and goals so that rehabilitation programs and plans for accessing needed services can be developed. Prepare and maintain records and case files, including documentation such as clients' personal and eligibility information, services provided, narratives of client contacts, and relevant correspondence. Arrange for physical, mental, academic, vocational, and other evaluations to obtain information for assessing clients' needs and developing rehabilitation plans. Analyze information from interviews, educational and medical records, consultation with other professionals, and diagnostic evaluations to assess clients' abilities, needs, and eligibility for services. Develop rehabilitation plans that fit clients' aptitudes, education levels, physical abilities, and career goals. Maintain close contact with clients during job training and placements to resolve problems and evaluate placement adequacy. Locate barriers to client employment, such as inaccessible work sites, inflexible schedules, and transportation problems, and work with clients to develop strategies for overcoming these barriers. Develop and maintain relationships with community referral sources such as schools and community groups. Arrange for on-site job coaching or assistive devices such as specially equipped wheelchairs in order to help clients adapt to work or school environments. Confer with physicians, psychologists, occupational therapists, and other professionals to develop and implement client rehabilitation programs. Develop diagnostic procedures for determining clients' needs. Participate in job development and placement programs, contacting prospective employers, placing clients in jobs, and evaluating the success of placements. Collaborate with clients' families to implement rehabilitation plans that include behavioral, residential, social, and/or employment goals. Collaborate with community agencies to establish facilities and programs to assist persons with disabilities.

Personality Type: Social. These occupations frequently involve working with, communicating with, and teaching people and often involve helping or providing service to others.

GOE—Interest Area/Cluster: 10. Human Service. **Work Group:** 10.01. Counseling and Social Work. **Other Jobs in This Work Group:** Child, Family, and School Social Workers; Clinical Psychologists; Clinical, Counseling, and School Psychologists; Counseling Psychologists; Marriage and Family Therapists; Medical and Public Health Social Workers; Mental Health and Substance Abuse Social Workers; Mental Health Counselors; Probation Officers and Correctional Treatment Specialists; Substance Abuse and Behavioral Disorder Counselors.

Skills—Management of Financial Resources: Determining how money will be spent to get the work done and accounting for these expenditures. **Social Perceptiveness:** Being aware of others' reactions and understanding why they react the way they do. **Writing:** Communicating effectively with others in writing as indicated by the needs of the audience. **Service Orientation:** Actively looking for ways to help people. **Monitoring:** Assessing how well one is doing when learning or doing something. **Coordination:** Adjusting actions in relation to others' actions. **Speaking:** Talking to others to effectively convey information. **Judgment and Decision Making:** Weighing the relative costs and benefits of a potential action.

Education and Training Programs: Vocational Rehabilitation Counseling/Counselor; Assistive/Augmentative Technology and Rehabiliation Engineering. **Related Knowledge/Courses— Therapy and Counseling:** Information and techniques needed to rehabilitate physical and mental ailments and to provide career guidance, including alternative treatments, rehabilitation equipment and its proper use, and methods to evaluate treatment effects. **Psychology:** Human behavior and performance, mental processes, psychological research methods, and the assessment and treatment of behavioral and affective disorders. **Philosophy and Theology:** Different philosophical systems and religions, including their basic principles, values, ethics, ways of thinking, customs, and practices and their impact on human culture. **Education and Training:** Instructional methods and training techniques, including curriculum design principles, learning theory, group and individual teaching techniques, design of individual development plans, and test design principles. **Personnel and Human Resources:** Principles and procedures for personnel recruitment; selection; training; compensation and benefits; labor relations and negotiation; and personnel information systems. **Sociology and Anthropology:** Group behavior and dynamics; societal trends and influences; and cultures and their history, migrations, ethnicity, and origins.

Work Environment: More often indoors than outdoors; sitting; walking and running.

Respiratory Therapists

⚜ Education/Training Required: Associate degree
⚜ Annual Earnings: $50,070
⚜ Beginning Wage: $36,650
⚜ Earnings Growth Potential: Low
⚜ Growth: 22.6%
⚜ Annual Job Openings: 5,563
⚜ Self-Employed: 1.1%
⚜ Part-Time: 15.0%

Assess, treat, and care for patients with breathing disorders. Assume primary responsibility for all respiratory care modalities, including the supervision of respiratory therapy technicians. Initiate and conduct therapeutic procedures; maintain patient records; and select, assemble, check, and operate equipment. Set up and operate devices such as mechanical ventilators, therapeutic gas administration apparatus, environmental control systems, and aerosol generators, following specified parameters of treatment. Provide emergency care, including artificial respiration, external cardiac massage, and assistance with cardiopulmonary resuscitation. Determine requirements for treatment, such as type, method, and duration of therapy; precautions to be taken; and medication and dosages, compatible with physicians' orders. Monitor patient's physiological responses to therapy, such as vital signs, arterial blood gases, and blood chemistry changes, and consult with physician if adverse reactions occur. Read prescription, measure arterial blood gases, and review patient information to assess patient condition. Work as part of a team of physicians, nurses, and other health-care professionals to manage patient care. Enforce safety rules and ensure careful adherence to physicians' orders. Maintain charts that contain patients' pertinent identification and therapy information. Inspect, clean, test, and maintain respiratory therapy equipment to ensure equipment is functioning safely and efficiently, ordering repairs when necessary. Educate patients and their families about their conditions and teach appropriate disease management techniques, such as breathing exercises and the use of medications and respiratory equipment. Explain treatment procedures to patients to gain cooperation and allay fears. Relay blood analysis results to a physician. Perform pulmonary function and adjust equipment to obtain optimum results in therapy. Perform bronchopulmonary drainage and assist or instruct patients in performance of breathing exercises. Demonstrate respiratory care procedures to trainees and other health-care personnel. Teach, train, supervise, and utilize the assistance of students, respiratory therapy technicians, and assistants. Make emergency visits to resolve equipment problems. Use a variety of testing techniques to assist doctors in cardiac and pulmonary research and to diagnose disorders. Conduct tests, such as electrocardiograms (EKGs), stress testing, and lung capacity tests, to evaluate patients' cardiopulmonary functions.

Personality Type: Social. These occupations frequently involve working with, communicating with, and teaching people and often involve helping or providing service to others.

GOE—Interest Area/Cluster: 08. Health Science. **Work Group:** 08.07. Medical Therapy. **Other Jobs in This Work Group:** Audiologists; Occupational Therapist Assistants; Occupational Therapists; Physical Therapist Assistants; Physical Therapists; Radiation Therapists; Recreational Therapists; Respiratory Therapy Technicians; Speech-Language Pathologists.

Skills—Science: Using scientific methods to solve problems. **Mathematics:** Using mathematics to solve problems. **Operation Monitoring:** Watching gauges, dials, or other indicators to make sure a machine is working properly. **Reading**

Comprehension: Understanding written sentences and paragraphs in work-related documents. **Active Learning:** Working with new material or information to grasp its implications. **Troubleshooting:** Determining what is causing an operating error and deciding what to do about it. **Instructing:** Teaching others how to do something. **Service Orientation:** Actively looking for ways to help people.

Education and Training Program: Respiratory Care Therapy/Therapist. **Related Knowledge/Courses—Medicine and Dentistry:** The information and techniques needed to diagnose and treat injuries, diseases, and deformities. This includes symptoms, treatment alternatives, drug properties and interactions, and preventive health-care measures. **Biology:** Plant and animal living tissue, cells, organisms, and entities, including their functions, interdependencies, and interactions with each other and the environment. **Psychology:** Human behavior and performance, mental processes, psychological research methods, and the assessment and treatment of behavioral and affective disorders. **Customer and Personal Service:** Principles and processes for providing customer and personal services, including needs assessment techniques, quality service standards, alternative delivery systems, and customer satisfaction evaluation techniques. **Therapy and Counseling:** Information and techniques needed to rehabilitate physical and mental ailments and to provide career guidance, including alternative treatments, rehabilitation equipment and its proper use, and methods to evaluate treatment effects. **Chemistry:** The composition, structure, and properties of substances and of the chemical processes and transformations that they undergo. This includes uses of chemicals and their interactions, danger signs, production techniques, and disposal methods.

Work Environment: Indoors; disease or infections; standing.

Sales Agents, Financial Services

- ✳ Education/Training Required: Bachelor's degree
- ✳ Annual Earnings: $68,430
- ✳ Beginning Wage: $30,890
- ✳ Earnings Growth Potential: Very high
- ✳ Growth: 24.8%
- ✳ Annual Job Openings: 47,750
- ✳ Self-Employed: 17.7%
- ✳ Part-Time: 6.9%

The job openings listed here are shared with Sales Agents, Securities and Commodities.

Sell financial services such as loan, tax, and securities counseling to customers of financial institutions and business establishments. Determine customers' financial services needs and prepare proposals to sell services that address these needs. Contact prospective customers to present information and explain available services. Sell services and equipment, such as trusts, investments, and check processing services. Prepare forms or agreements to complete sales. Develop prospects from current commercial customers, referral leads, and sales and trade meetings. Review business trends in order to advise customers regarding expected fluctuations. Make presentations on financial services to groups to attract new clients. Evaluate costs and revenue of agreements to determine continued profitability.

Personality Type: Enterprising. These occupations frequently involve starting up and carrying out projects and can involve leading people and making many decisions. They sometimes require risk taking and often deal with business.

GOE—Interest Area/Cluster: 06. Finance and Insurance. **Work Group:** 06.05. Finance/

Insurance Sales and Support. **Other Jobs in This Work Group:** Insurance Sales Agents; Personal Financial Advisors; Sales Agents, Securities and Commodities; Securities, Commodities, and Financial Services Sales Agents.

Skills—Persuasion: Persuading others to approach things differently. **Management of Financial Resources:** Determining how money will be spent to get the work done and accounting for these expenditures. **Service Orientation:** Actively looking for ways to help people. **Negotiation:** Bringing others together and trying to reconcile differences. **Operations Analysis:** Analyzing needs and product requirements to create a design. **Monitoring:** Assessing how well one is doing when learning or doing something. **Speaking:** Talking to others to effectively convey information. **Judgment and Decision Making:** Weighing the relative costs and benefits of a potential action.

Education and Training Programs: Financial Planning and Services; Investments and Securities; Business and Personal/Financial Services Marketing Operations. **Related Knowledge/Courses— Sales and Marketing:** Principles and methods involved in showing, promoting, and selling products or services. This includes marketing strategies and tactics, product demonstration and sales techniques, and sales control systems. **Economics and Accounting:** Economic and accounting principles and practices, the financial markets, banking, and the analysis and reporting of financial data. **Customer and Personal Service:** Principles and processes for providing customer and personal services, including needs assessment techniques, quality service standards, alternative delivery systems, and customer satisfaction evaluation techniques. **Law and Government:** Laws, legal codes, court procedures, precedents, government regulations, executive orders, agency rules, and the democratic political process. **Mathematics:** Numbers and their operations and interrelationships, including arithmetic, algebra, geometry, calculus, and statistics and their applications. **Personnel and Human Resources:** Principles and procedures for personnel recruitment; selection; training; compensation and benefits; labor relations and negotiation; and personnel information systems.

Work Environment: Indoors; sitting.

Sales Agents, Securities and Commodities

- ✵ Education/Training Required: Bachelor's degree
- ✵ Annual Earnings: $68,430
- ✵ Beginning Wage: $30,890
- ✵ Earnings Growth Potential: Very high
- ✵ Growth: 24.8%
- ✵ Annual Job Openings: 47,750
- ✵ Self-Employed: 17.7%
- ✵ Part-Time: 6.9%

The job openings listed here are shared with Sales Agents, Financial Services.

Buy and sell securities in investment and trading firms and develop and implement financial plans for individuals, businesses, and organizations. Complete sales order tickets and submit for processing of client requested transactions. Interview clients to determine clients' assets, liabilities, cash flow, insurance coverage, tax status, and financial objectives. Record transactions accurately and keep clients informed about transactions. Develop financial plans based on analysis of clients' financial status and discuss financial options with clients. Review all securities transactions to ensure accuracy of information and ensure that trades conform to regulations of governing agencies. Offer advice on the purchase or sale of particular securities. Relay buy or sell orders to securities

S

exchanges or to firm trading departments. Identify potential clients, using advertising campaigns, mailing lists, and personal contacts. Review financial periodicals, stock and bond reports, business publications, and other material to identify potential investments for clients and to keep abreast of trends affecting market conditions. Contact prospective customers to determine customer needs, present information, and explain available services. Prepare documents needed to implement plans selected by clients. Analyze market conditions to determine optimum times to execute securities transactions. Explain stock market terms and trading practices to clients. Inform and advise concerned parties regarding fluctuations and securities transactions affecting plans or accounts. Calculate costs for billings and commissions purposes. Supply the latest price quotes on any security, as well as information on the activities and financial positions of the corporations issuing these securities. Prepare financial reports to monitor client or corporate finances. Read corporate reports and calculate ratios to determine best prospects for profit on stock purchases and to monitor client accounts.

Personality Type: Enterprising. These occupations frequently involve starting up and carrying out projects and can involve leading people and making many decisions. They sometimes require risk taking and often deal with business.

GOE—Interest Area/Cluster: 06. Finance and Insurance. **Work Group:** 06.05. Finance/Insurance Sales and Support. **Other Jobs in This Work Group:** Insurance Sales Agents; Personal Financial Advisors; Sales Agents, Financial Services; Securities, Commodities, and Financial Services Sales Agents.

Skills—Management of Financial Resources: Determining how money will be spent to get the work done and accounting for these expenditures. **Persuasion:** Persuading others to approach things differently. **Social Perceptiveness:** Being aware of others' reactions and understanding why they react the way they do. **Negotiation:** Bringing others together and trying to reconcile differences. **Judgment and Decision Making:** Weighing the relative costs and benefits of a potential action. **Service Orientation:** Actively looking for ways to help people. **Speaking:** Talking to others to effectively convey information. **Time Management:** Managing one's own time and the time of others.

Education and Training Programs: Financial Planning and Services; Investments and Securities. **Related Knowledge/Courses—Economics and Accounting:** Economic and accounting principles and practices, the financial markets, banking, and the analysis and reporting of financial data. **Customer and Personal Service:** Principles and processes for providing customer and personal services, including needs assessment techniques, quality service standards, alternative delivery systems, and customer satisfaction evaluation techniques. **Sales and Marketing:** Principles and methods involved in showing, promoting, and selling products or services. This includes marketing strategies and tactics, product demonstration and sales techniques, and sales control systems. **Clerical Practices:** Administrative and clerical procedures and systems such as word-processing systems, filing and records management systems, stenography and transcription, forms, design principles, and other office procedures and terminology. **Law and Government:** Laws, legal codes, court procedures, precedents, government regulations, executive orders, agency rules, and the democratic political process. **Mathematics:** Numbers and their operations and interrelationships, including arithmetic, algebra, geometry, calculus, and statistics and their applications.

Work Environment: Indoors; sitting.

Sales Engineers

- ✸ Education/Training Required:
  Bachelor's degree
- ✸ Annual Earnings: $80,270
- ✸ Beginning Wage: $48,290
- ✸ Earnings Growth Potential: Medium
- ✸ Growth: 8.5%
- ✸ Annual Job Openings: 7,371
- ✸ Self-Employed: 0.0%
- ✸ Part-Time: 2.0%

Sell business goods or services, the selling of which requires a technical background equivalent to a baccalaureate degree in engineering. Plan and modify product configurations to meet customer needs. Confer with customers and engineers to assess equipment needs and to determine system requirements. Collaborate with sales teams to understand customer requirements, to promote the sale of company products, and to provide sales support. Secure and renew orders and arrange delivery. Develop, present, or respond to proposals for specific customer requirements, including request for proposal responses and industry-specific solutions. Sell products requiring extensive technical expertise and support for installation and use, such as material handling equipment, numerical-control machinery, and computer systems. Diagnose problems with installed equipment. Prepare and deliver technical presentations that explain products or services to customers and prospective customers. Recommend improved materials or machinery to customers, documenting how such changes will lower costs or increase production. Provide technical and non-technical support and services to clients or other staff members regarding the use, operation, and maintenance of equipment. Research and identify potential customers for products or services. Visit prospective buyers at commercial, industrial, or other establishments to show samples or catalogs and to inform them about product pricing, availability, and advantages. Create sales or service contracts for products or services. Arrange for demonstrations or trial installations of equipment. Keep informed on industry news and trends; products; services; competitors; relevant information about legacy, existing, and emerging technologies; and the latest product-line developments. Attend company training seminars to become familiar with product lines. Provide information needed for the development of custom-made machinery. Develop sales plans to introduce products in new markets. Write technical documentation for products. Identify resale opportunities and support them to achieve sales plans. Document account activities, generate reports, and keep records of business transactions with customers and suppliers.

Personality Type: Enterprising. These occupations frequently involve starting up and carrying out projects and can involve leading people and making many decisions. They sometimes require risk taking and often deal with business.

GOE—Interest Area/Cluster: 14. Retail and Wholesale Sales and Service. **Work Group:** 14.02. Technical Sales. **Other Jobs in This Work Group:** No others in group.

Skills—Operations Analysis: Analyzing needs and product requirements to create a design. **Science:** Using scientific methods to solve problems. **Systems Evaluation:** Looking at many indicators of system performance and taking into account their accuracy. **Technology Design:** Generating or adapting equipment and technology to serve user needs. **Programming:** Writing computer programs for various purposes. **Installation:** Installing equipment, machines, wiring, or programs to meet specifications. **Equipment Selection:** Determining the kind of tools and equipment needed to do a job. **Mathematics:** Using mathematics to solve problems.

Education and Training Programs: Aerospace Engineering; Agricultural Engineering; Chemical Engineering; Computer Engineering; Construction Engineering; Electrical, Electronics and Communications Engineering; Environmental Engineering; Forest Engineering; Industrial Engineering; Manufacturing Engineering; Materials Engineering; Mechanical Engineering; Metallurgical Engineering; Mining and Mineral Engineering; Nuclear Engineering; Petroleum Engineering; Transportation and Highway Engineering; Water Resources Engineering; others. **Related Knowledge/Courses—Sales and Marketing:** Principles and methods involved in showing, promoting, and selling products or services. This includes marketing strategies and tactics, product demonstration and sales techniques, and sales control systems. **Engineering and Technology:** Equipment, tools, and mechanical devices and their uses to produce motion, light, power, technology, and other applications. **Design:** Design techniques, principles, tools, and instruments involved in the production and use of precision technical plans, blueprints, drawings, and models. **Physics:** Physical principles, laws, and applications, including air, water, material dynamics, light, atomic principles, heat, electric theory, earth formations, and meteorological and related natural phenomena. **Computers and Electronics:** Electric circuit boards, processors, chips, and computer hardware and software, including applications and programming. **Customer and Personal Service:** Principles and processes for providing customer and personal services, including needs assessment techniques, quality service standards, alternative delivery systems, and customer satisfaction evaluation techniques.

Work Environment: Indoors; sitting; repetitive motions.

Sales Managers

- ❋ Education/Training Required: Work experience plus degree
- ❋ Annual Earnings: $94,910
- ❋ Beginning Wage: $45,860
- ❋ Earnings Growth Potential: Very high
- ❋ Growth: 10.2%
- ❋ Annual Job Openings: 36,392
- ❋ Self-Employed: 2.2%
- ❋ Part-Time: 4.1%

Direct the actual distribution or movement of products or services to customers. Coordinate sales distribution by establishing sales territories, quotas, and goals, and establish training programs for sales representatives. Analyze sales statistics gathered by staff to determine sales potential and inventory requirements and monitor the preferences of customers. Resolve customer complaints regarding sales and service. Oversee regional and local sales managers and their staffs. Plan and direct staffing, training, and performance evaluations to develop and control sales and service programs. Determine price schedules and discount rates. Review operational records and reports to project sales and determine profitability. Monitor customer preferences to determine focus of sales efforts. Prepare budgets and approve budget expenditures. Confer or consult with department heads to plan advertising services and to secure information on equipment and customer specifications. Direct and coordinate activities involving sales of manufactured products, services, commodities, real estate, or other subjects of sale. Confer with potential customers regarding equipment needs and advise customers on types of equipment to purchase. Direct foreign sales and service outlets of an organization. Advise dealers and distributors on policies and operating procedures to ensure functional effectiveness of businesses. Visit franchised dealers to stimulate interest in establishment or expansion of leasing programs. Direct clerical staff to keep records of export correspondence, bid requests, and credit collections, and to maintain current information on tariffs, licenses, and restrictions. Direct, coordinate, and review activities in sales and service accounting and recordkeeping, and in receiving and shipping operations. Assess marketing potential of new and existing store locations, considering statistics and expenditures. Represent company at trade association meetings to promote products.

Personality Type: Enterprising. These occupations frequently involve starting up and carrying out projects and can involve leading people and making many decisions. They sometimes require risk taking and often deal with business.

GOE—Interest Area/Cluster: 14. Retail and Wholesale Sales and Service. **Work Group:** 14.01. Managerial Work in Retail/Wholesale Sales and Service. **Other Jobs in This Work Group:** Advertising and Promotions Managers; Funeral Directors; Marketing Managers; Property, Real Estate, and Community Association Managers; Purchasing Managers.

Skills—Management of Personnel Resources: Motivating, developing, and directing people as they work; identifying the best people for the job. **Systems Analysis:** Determining how a system should work and how changes will affect outcomes. **Management of Financial Resources:** Determining how money will be spent to get the work done and accounting for these expenditures. **Persuasion:** Persuading others to approach things differently. **Negotiation:** Bringing others together and trying to reconcile differences. **Systems Evaluation:** Looking at many indicators of system performance and taking into account their accuracy. **Social Perceptiveness:** Being aware of others'

reactions and understanding why they react the way they do. **Speaking:** Talking to others to effectively convey information.

Education and Training Programs: Consumer Merchandising/Retailing Management; Business/Commerce, General; Business Administration and Management, General; Marketing/Marketing Management, General; Marketing, Other. **Related Knowledge/Courses—Sales and Marketing:** Principles and methods involved in showing, promoting, and selling products or services. This includes marketing strategies and tactics, product demonstration and sales techniques, and sales control systems. **Personnel and Human Resources:** Principles and procedures for personnel recruitment; selection; training; compensation and benefits; labor relations and negotiation; and personnel information systems. **Economics and Accounting:** Economic and accounting principles and practices, the financial markets, banking, and the analysis and reporting of financial data. **Administration and Management:** Principles and processes involved in business and organizational planning, coordination, and execution. This includes strategic planning, resource allocation, manpower modeling, leadership techniques, and production methods. **Customer and Personal Service:** Principles and processes for providing customer and personal services, including needs assessment techniques, quality service standards, alternative delivery systems, and customer satisfaction evaluation techniques. **Psychology:** Human behavior and performance, mental processes, psychological research methods, and the assessment and treatment of behavioral and affective disorders.

Work Environment: Indoors; sitting.

School Psychologists

- ❋ Education/Training Required: Doctoral degree
- ❋ Annual Earnings: $62,210
- ❋ Beginning Wage: $37,300
- ❋ Earnings Growth Potential: High
- ❋ Growth: 15.8%
- ❋ Annual Job Openings: 8,309
- ❋ Self-Employed: 34.2%
- ❋ Part-Time: 24.0%

The job openings listed here are shared with Clinical Psychologists and with Counseling Psychologists.

Investigate processes of learning and teaching and develop psychological principles and techniques applicable to educational problems. Compile and interpret students' test results, along with information from teachers and parents, to diagnose conditions and to help assess eligibility for special services. Report any pertinent information to the proper authorities in cases of child endangerment, neglect, or abuse. Assess an individual child's needs, limitations, and potential, using observation, review of school records, and consultation with parents and school personnel. Select, administer, and score psychological tests. Provide consultation to parents, teachers, administrators, and others on topics such as learning styles and behavior modification techniques. Promote an understanding of child development and its relationship to learning and behavior. Collaborate with other educational professionals to develop teaching strategies and school programs. Counsel children and families to help solve conflicts and problems in learning and adjustment. Develop individualized educational plans in collaboration with teachers and other staff members. Maintain student records, including special education reports, confidential records, records of services provided, and behavioral data. Serve as a resource to help families and schools deal with crises, such as separation and loss. Attend workshops, seminars, or professional meetings to remain informed of new developments in school psychology. Design classes and programs to meet the needs of special students. Refer students and their families to appropriate community agencies for medical, vocational, or social services. Initiate and direct efforts to foster tolerance, understanding, and appreciation of diversity in school communities. Collect and analyze data to evaluate the effectiveness of academic programs and other services, such as behavioral management systems. Provide educational programs on topics such as classroom management, teaching strategies, or parenting skills. Conduct research to generate new knowledge that can be used to address learning and behavior issues.

Personality Type: Investigative. These occupations frequently involve working with ideas and require an extensive amount of thinking. They can involve searching for facts and figuring out problems mentally.

GOE—Interest Area/Cluster: 15. Scientific Research, Engineering, and Mathematics. **Work Group:** 15.04. Social Sciences. **Other Jobs in This Work Group:** Anthropologists; Anthropologists and Archeologists; Archeologists; Economists; Historians; Industrial-Organizational Psychologists; Political Scientists; Sociologists.

Skills—Social Perceptiveness: Being aware of others' reactions and understanding why they react the way they do. **Negotiation:** Bringing others together and trying to reconcile differences. **Learning Strategies:** Using multiple approaches when learning or teaching new things. **Persuasion:** Persuading others to approach things differently. **Writing:** Communicating effectively with others in writing as indicated by the needs of the audience. **Active Listening:** Listening to what other people are saying and asking questions as appropriate. **Service Orientation:** Actively looking for ways to help people. **Active Learning:** Working with new material or information to grasp its implications.

Education and Training Programs: Educational Assessment, Testing, and Measurement; Psychology, General; Clinical Psychology; Counseling Psychology; Developmental and Child Psychology; School Psychology; Psychoanalysis and Psychotherapy. **Related Knowledge/Courses—Therapy and Counseling:** Information and techniques needed to rehabilitate physical and mental ailments and to provide career guidance, including alternative treatments, rehabilitation equipment and its proper use, and methods to evaluate treatment effects. **Psychology:** Human behavior and performance, mental processes, psychological research methods, and the assessment and treatment of behavioral and affective disorders. **Sociology and Anthropology:** Group behavior and dynamics; societal trends and influences; and cultures and their history, migrations, ethnicity, and origins. **Philosophy and Theology:** Different philosophical systems and religions, including their basic principles, values, ethics, ways of thinking, customs, and practices and their impact on human culture. **Education and Training:** Instructional methods and training techniques, including curriculum design principles, learning theory, group and individual teaching techniques, design of individual development plans, and test design principles. **Medicine and Dentistry:** The information and techniques needed to diagnose and treat injuries, diseases, and deformities. This includes symptoms, treatment alternatives, drug properties and interactions, and preventive health-care measures.

Work Environment: Indoors; sitting.

Secondary School Teachers, Except Special and Vocational Education

- ❋ Education/Training Required: Bachelor's degree
- ❋ Annual Earnings: $49,420
- ❋ Beginning Wage: $32,920
- ❋ Earnings Growth Potential: Low
- ❋ Growth: 5.6%
- ❋ Annual Job Openings: 93,166
- ❋ Self-Employed: 0.0%
- ❋ Part-Time: 7.8%

Instruct students in secondary public or private schools in one or more subjects at the secondary level, such as English, mathematics, or social studies. May be designated according to subject matter specialty, such as typing instructors, commercial teachers, or English teachers. Establish and enforce rules for behavior and procedures for maintaining order among the students for whom they are responsible. Instruct through lectures, discussions, and demonstrations in one or more subjects such as English, mathematics, or social studies. Establish clear objectives for all lessons, units, and projects and communicate those objectives to students. Prepare, administer, and grade tests and assignments to evaluate students' progress. Prepare materials and classrooms for class activities. Adapt teaching methods and instructional materials to meet students' varying needs and interests. Assign and grade classwork and homework. Maintain accurate and complete student records as required by laws, district policies, and administrative regulations. Enforce all administration policies and rules governing students. Observe and evaluate students' performance, behavior, social development, and physical health. Plan and conduct activities for a

S

balanced program of instruction, demonstration, and work time that provides students with opportunities to observe, question, and investigate. Prepare students for later grades by encouraging them to explore learning opportunities and to persevere with challenging tasks. Guide and counsel students with adjustment and/or academic problems or special academic interests. Instruct and monitor students in the use and care of equipment and materials to prevent injuries and damage. Prepare for assigned classes and show written evidence of preparation upon request of immediate supervisors. Meet with parents and guardians to discuss their children's progress and to determine their priorities for their children and their resource needs. Confer with parents or guardians, other teachers, counselors, and administrators in order to resolve students' behavioral and academic problems. Use computers, audiovisual aids, and other equipment and materials to supplement presentations. Prepare objectives and outlines for courses of study, following curriculum guidelines or requirements of states and schools. Meet with other professionals to discuss individual students' needs and progress.

Personality Type: Social. These occupations frequently involve working with, communicating with, and teaching people and often involve helping or providing service to others.

GOE—Interest Area/Cluster: 05. Education and Training. **Work Group:** 05.02. Preschool, Elementary, and Secondary Teaching and Instructing. **Other Jobs in This Work Group:** Elementary School Teachers, Except Special Education; Kindergarten Teachers, Except Special Education; Middle School Teachers, Except Special and Vocational Education; Special Education Teachers, Middle School; Special Education Teachers, Preschool, Kindergarten, and Elementary School; Special Education Teachers, Secondary School; Vocational Education Teachers, Middle School; Vocational Education Teachers, Secondary School.

Skills—Learning Strategies: Using multiple approaches when learning or teaching new things. **Social Perceptiveness:** Being aware of others' reactions and understanding why they react the way they do. **Persuasion:** Persuading others to approach things differently. **Monitoring:** Assessing how well one is doing when learning or doing something. **Instructing:** Teaching others how to do something. **Time Management:** Managing one's own time and the time of others. **Negotiation:** Bringing others together and trying to reconcile differences. **Service Orientation:** Actively looking for ways to help people.

Education and Training Programs: Junior High/Intermediate/Middle School Education and Teaching; Secondary Education and Teaching; Teacher Education, Multiple Levels; Waldorf/Steiner Teacher Education; Agricultural Teacher Education; Art Teacher Education; Business Teacher Education; Driver and Safety Teacher Education; English/Language Arts Teacher Education; Foreign Language Teacher Education; Health Teacher Education; others. **Related Knowledge/Courses—History and Archeology:** Historical events and their causes, indicators, and impact on particular civilizations and cultures. **Philosophy and Theology:** Different philosophical systems and religions, including their basic principles, values, ethics, ways of thinking, customs, and practices and their impact on human culture. **Sociology and Anthropology:** Group behavior and dynamics; societal trends and influences; and cultures and their history, migrations, ethnicity, and origins. **Education and Training:** Instructional methods and training techniques, including curriculum design principles, learning theory, group and individual teaching techniques, design of individual development plans, and test design principles. **Geography:** Various methods for describing the location and distribution of land, sea, and air masses, including their physical locations, relationships, and characteristics.

Therapy and Counseling: Information and techniques needed to rehabilitate physical and mental ailments and to provide career guidance, including alternative treatments, rehabilitation equipment and its proper use, and methods to evaluate treatment effects.

Work Environment: Indoors; noisy; standing.

Social and Community Service Managers

- ❀ Education/Training Required: Bachelor's degree
- ❀ Annual Earnings: $54,530
- ❀ Beginning Wage: $32,480
- ❀ Earnings Growth Potential: High
- ❀ Growth: 24.7%
- ❀ Annual Job Openings: 23,788
- ❀ Self-Employed: 5.9%
- ❀ Part-Time: 11.6%

Plan, organize, or coordinate the activities of a social service program or community outreach organization. Oversee the program or organization's budget and policies regarding participant involvement, program requirements, and benefits. Work may involve directing social workers, counselors, or probation officers. Establish and maintain relationships with other agencies and organizations in community to meet community needs and to ensure that services are not duplicated. Prepare and maintain records and reports, such as budgets, personnel records, or training manuals. Direct activities of professional and technical staff members and volunteers. Evaluate the work of staff and volunteers to ensure that programs are of appropriate quality and that resources are used effectively. Establish and oversee administrative procedures to meet objectives set by boards of directors or senior management. Participate in the determination of organizational policies regarding such issues as participant eligibility, program requirements, and program benefits. Research and analyze member or community needs to determine program directions and goals. Speak to community groups to explain and interpret agency purposes, programs, and policies. Recruit, interview, and hire or sign up volunteers and staff. Represent organizations in relations with governmental and media institutions. Plan and administer budgets for programs, equipment, and support services. Analyze proposed legislation, regulations, or rule changes to determine how agency services could be impacted. Act as consultants to agency staff and other community programs regarding the interpretation of program-related federal, state, and county regulations and policies. Implement and evaluate staff training programs. Direct fundraising activities and the preparation of public relations materials.

Personality Type: Enterprising. These occupations frequently involve starting up and carrying out projects and can involve leading people and making many decisions. They sometimes require risk taking and often deal with business.

GOE—Interest Area/Cluster: 07. Government and Public Administration. **Work Group:** 07.01. Managerial Work in Government and Public Administration. **Other Jobs in This Work Group:** No others in group.

Skills—Social Perceptiveness: Being aware of others' reactions and understanding why they react the way they do. **Management of Personnel Resources:** Motivating, developing, and directing people as they work; identifying the best people for the job. **Service Orientation:** Actively looking for ways to help people. **Systems Evaluation:** Looking at many indicators of system performance and taking into account their accuracy. **Negotiation:** Bringing others together and trying to reconcile differences. **Persuasion:** Persuading others to approach things differently. **Monitoring:** Assessing how well one is doing when learning or doing something. **Writing:** Communicating effectively with others in writing as indicated by the needs of the audience.

Education and Training Programs: Human Services, General; Community Organization and Advocacy; Public Administration; Business/Commerce, General; Business Administration and Management, General; Non-Profit/Public/Organizational Management; Entrepreneurship/Entrepreneurial Studies; Business, Management, Marketing, and Related Support Services, Other. **Related Knowledge/Courses—Sociology and Anthropology:** Group behavior and dynamics; societal trends and influences; and cultures and their history, migrations, ethnicity, and origins. **Therapy and Counseling:** Information and techniques needed to rehabilitate physical and mental ailments and to provide career guidance, including alternative treatments, rehabilitation equipment and its proper use, and methods to evaluate treatment effects. **Psychology:** Human behavior and performance, mental processes, psychological research methods, and the assessment and treatment of behavioral and affective disorders. **Philosophy and Theology:** Different philosophical systems and religions, including their basic principles, values, ethics, ways of thinking, customs, and practices and their impact on human culture. **Clerical Practices:** Administrative and clerical procedures and systems such as word-processing systems, filing and records management systems, stenography and transcription, forms, design principles, and other office procedures and terminology. **Education and Training:** Instructional methods and training techniques, including curriculum design principles, learning theory, group and individual teaching techniques, design of individual development plans, and test design principles.

Work Environment: Indoors; noisy; sitting.

Social Work Teachers, Postsecondary

* Education/Training Required: Doctoral degree
* Annual Earnings: $56,240
* Beginning Wage: $33,840
* Earnings Growth Potential: Medium
* Growth: 22.9%
* Annual Job Openings: 1,292
* Self-Employed: 0.4%
* Part-Time: 27.8%

Teach courses in social work. Initiate, facilitate, and moderate classroom discussions. Evaluate and grade students' classwork, assignments, and papers. Prepare and deliver lectures to undergraduate or graduate students on topics such as family behavior, child and adolescent mental health, and social intervention evaluation. Keep abreast of developments in their field by reading current literature, talking with colleagues, and participating in professional conferences. Supervise students' laboratory work and fieldwork. Conduct research in a particular field of knowledge and publish findings in professional journals, books, or electronic media. Prepare course materials such as syllabi, homework assignments, and handouts. Maintain regularly scheduled office hours to advise and assist students. Supervise undergraduate or graduate teaching, internship, and research work. Plan, evaluate, and revise curricula, course content, and course materials and methods of instruction. Collaborate with colleagues and with community agencies to address teaching and research issues. Compile, administer, and grade examinations or assign this work to others. Advise students on academic and vocational curricula and on career issues. Maintain student attendance records, grades, and other required records. Write grant proposals to procure external research funding. Serve on academic or administrative committees that deal with institutional policies, departmental matters, and academic issues. Perform administrative duties such as serving as department head. Compile bibliographies of specialized materials for outside reading assignments. Select and obtain materials and supplies such as textbooks and laboratory equipment. Participate in student recruitment, registration, and placement activities. Participate in campus and community events. Provide professional consulting services to government and industry. Act as advisers to student organizations.

Personality Type: Social. These occupations frequently involve working with, communicating with, and teaching people and often involve helping or providing service to others.

GOE—Interest Area/Cluster: 05. Education and Training. **Work Group:** 05.03. Postsecondary and Adult Teaching and Instructing. **Other Jobs in This Work Group:** Adult Literacy, Remedial Education, and GED Teachers and Instructors; Agricultural Sciences Teachers, Postsecondary; Anthropology and Archeology Teachers, Postsecondary; Architecture Teachers, Postsecondary; Area, Ethnic, and Cultural Studies Teachers, Postsecondary; Art, Drama, and Music Teachers, Postsecondary; Atmospheric, Earth, Marine, and Space Sciences Teachers, Postsecondary; Biological Science Teachers, Postsecondary; Business Teachers, Postsecondary; Chemistry Teachers, Postsecondary; Communications Teachers, Postsecondary; Computer Science Teachers, Postsecondary; Criminal Justice and Law Enforcement Teachers, Postsecondary; Economics Teachers, Postsecondary; Education Teachers, Postsecondary; Engineering Teachers, Postsecondary; English Language and Literature Teachers, Postsecondary; Environmental Science Teachers, Postsecondary; Farm and Home Management Advisors; Foreign Language and Literature Teachers, Postsecondary; Forestry and Conservation Science Teachers, Postsecondary; Geography Teachers, Postsecondary; Graduate Teaching Assistants; Health Specialties Teachers, Postsecondary; History Teachers, Postsecondary; Home Economics Teachers, Postsecondary; Law Teachers, Postsecondary; Library Science Teachers, Postsecondary; Mathematical Science Teachers, Postsecondary; Nursing Instructors and Teachers, Postsecondary; Philosophy and Religion Teachers, Postsecondary; Physics Teachers, Postsecondary; Political Science Teachers, Postsecondary; Psychology Teachers, Postsecondary; Recreation and Fitness Studies Teachers, Postsecondary; Sociology Teachers, Postsecondary.

Skills—Social Perceptiveness: Being aware of others' reactions and understanding why they react the way they do. **Service Orientation:** Actively looking for ways to help people. **Instructing:** Teaching others how to do something. **Learning Strategies:** Using multiple approaches when learning or teaching new things. **Writing:** Communicating effectively with others in writing as indicated by the needs of the audience. **Complex Problem Solving:** Identifying complex problems, reviewing the options, and implementing solutions. **Critical Thinking:** Using logic and analysis to identify the strengths and weaknesses of different approaches. **Negotiation:** Bringing others together and trying to reconcile differences.

Education and Training Programs: Teacher Education and Professional Development, Specific Subject Areas, Other; Social Work; Clinical/Medical Social Work. **Related Knowledge/Courses—Therapy and Counseling:** Information and techniques needed to rehabilitate physical and mental ailments and to provide career guidance, including alternative treatments, rehabilitation equipment and its proper use, and methods to evaluate treatment effects. **Sociology and Anthropology:** Group behavior and dynamics; societal trends and influences; and cultures and their history, migrations, ethnicity, and origins. **Psychology:** Human behavior and performance, mental processes, psychological research methods, and the assessment and treatment of behavioral and affective disorders. **Philosophy and Theology:** Different philosophical systems and religions, including their basic principles, values, ethics, ways of thinking, customs, and practices and their impact on human culture. **Education and Training:** Instructional methods and training techniques, including curriculum design principles, learning theory, group and individual teaching techniques, design of individual development plans, and test design principles. **English Language:** The structure and content of the English language, including the meaning and spelling of words, rules of composition, and grammar.

Work Environment: Indoors; sitting.

Sociology Teachers, Postsecondary

- ❈ Education/Training Required: Doctoral degree
- ❈ Annual Earnings: $58,160
- ❈ Beginning Wage: $31,310
- ❈ Earnings Growth Potential: High
- ❈ Growth: 22.9%
- ❈ Annual Job Openings: 2,774
- ❈ Self-Employed: 0.4%
- ❈ Part-Time: 27.8%

Teach courses in sociology. Evaluate and grade students' classwork, assignments, and papers. Prepare and deliver lectures to undergraduate and graduate students on topics such as race and ethnic relations, measurement and data collection, and workplace social relations. Initiate, facilitate, and moderate classroom discussions. Prepare course materials such as syllabi, homework assignments, and handouts. Compile, administer, and grade examinations or assign this work to others. Keep abreast of developments in their field by reading current literature, talking with colleagues, and participating in professional conferences. Maintain student attendance records, grades, and other required records. Maintain regularly scheduled office hours in order to advise and assist students. Plan, evaluate, and revise curricula, course content, and course materials and methods of instruction. Advise students on academic and vocational curricula and on career issues. Collaborate with colleagues to address teaching and research issues. Conduct research in a particular field of knowledge and publish findings in professional journals, books, or electronic media. Select and obtain materials and supplies such as textbooks and laboratory equipment. Supervise undergraduate and graduate teaching, internship, and research work. Serve on academic or administrative committees that deal with institutional policies, departmental matters, and academic issues. Participate in student recruitment, registration, and placement activities. Perform administrative duties such as serving as department head. Supervise students' laboratory work and fieldwork. Write grant proposals to procure external research funding. Act as advisers to student organizations. Compile bibliographies of specialized materials for outside reading assignments. Participate in campus and community events. Provide professional consulting services to government and industry.

Personality Type: Social. These occupations frequently involve working with, communicating with, and teaching people and often involve helping or providing service to others.

GOE—Interest Area/Cluster: 05. Education and Training. **Work Group:** 05.03. Postsecondary and Adult Teaching and Instructing. **Other Jobs in This Work Group:** Adult Literacy, Remedial Education, and GED Teachers and Instructors;

Agricultural Sciences Teachers, Postsecondary; Anthropology and Archeology Teachers, Postsecondary; Architecture Teachers, Postsecondary; Area, Ethnic, and Cultural Studies Teachers, Postsecondary; Art, Drama, and Music Teachers, Postsecondary; Atmospheric, Earth, Marine, and Space Sciences Teachers, Postsecondary; Biological Science Teachers, Postsecondary; Business Teachers, Postsecondary; Chemistry Teachers, Postsecondary; Communications Teachers, Postsecondary; Computer Science Teachers, Postsecondary; Criminal Justice and Law Enforcement Teachers, Postsecondary; Economics Teachers, Postsecondary; Education Teachers, Postsecondary; Engineering Teachers, Postsecondary; English Language and Literature Teachers, Postsecondary; Environmental Science Teachers, Postsecondary; Farm and Home Management Advisors; Foreign Language and Literature Teachers, Postsecondary; Forestry and Conservation Science Teachers, Postsecondary; Geography Teachers, Postsecondary; Graduate Teaching Assistants; Health Specialties Teachers, Postsecondary; History Teachers, Postsecondary; Home Economics Teachers, Postsecondary; Law Teachers, Postsecondary; Library Science Teachers, Postsecondary; Mathematical Science Teachers, Postsecondary; Nursing Instructors and Teachers, Postsecondary; Philosophy and Religion Teachers, Postsecondary; Physics Teachers, Postsecondary; Political Science Teachers, Postsecondary; Psychology Teachers, Postsecondary; Recreation and Fitness Studies Teachers, Postsecondary; Social Work Teachers, Postsecondary.

Skills—Science: Using scientific methods to solve problems. **Instructing:** Teaching others how to do something. **Writing:** Communicating effectively with others in writing as indicated by the needs of the audience. **Learning Strategies:** Using multiple approaches when learning or teaching new things. **Social Perceptiveness:** Being aware of others' reactions and understanding why they react the

way they do. **Critical Thinking:** Using logic and analysis to identify the strengths and weaknesses of different approaches. **Reading Comprehension:** Understanding written sentences and paragraphs in work-related documents. **Speaking:** Talking to others to effectively convey information.

Education and Training Programs: Social Science Teacher Education; Sociology. **Related Knowledge/Courses—Sociology and Anthropology:** Group behavior and dynamics; societal trends and influences; and cultures and their history, migrations, ethnicity, and origins. **Philosophy and Theology:** Different philosophical systems and religions, including their basic principles, values, ethics, ways of thinking, customs, and practices and their impact on human culture. **History and Archeology:** Historical events and their causes, indicators, and impact on particular civilizations and cultures. **Education and Training:** Instructional methods and training techniques, including curriculum design principles, learning theory, group and individual teaching techniques, design of individual development plans, and test design principles. **English Language:** The structure and content of the English language, including the meaning and spelling of words, rules of composition, and grammar. **Geography:** Various methods for describing the location and distribution of land, sea, and air masses, including their physical locations, relationships, and characteristics.

Work Environment: Indoors; sitting.

Software Quality Assurance Engineers and Testers

- ❋ Education/Training Required: Associate degree
- ❋ Annual Earnings: $71,510
- ❋ Beginning Wage: $37,600
- ❋ Earnings Growth Potential: High
- ❋ Growth: 15.1%
- ❋ Annual Job Openings: 14,374
- ❋ Self-Employed: 6.6%
- ❋ Part-Time: 5.6%

The job openings listed here are shared with Computer Systems Engineers/Architects, Network Designers, Web Administrators, and Web Developers.

Develop and execute software test plans in order to identify software problems and their causes. Design test plans, scenarios, scripts, or procedures. Test system modifications to prepare for implementation. Document software defects, using a bug tracking system, and report defects to software developers. Develop testing programs that address areas such as database impacts, software scenarios, regression testing, negative testing, error or bug retests, or usability. Identify, analyze, and document problems with program function, output, online screens, or content. Monitor bug resolution efforts and track successes. Create or maintain databases of known test defects. Plan test schedules or strategies in accordance with project scope or delivery dates. Participate in product design reviews to provide input on functional requirements, product designs, schedules, or potential problems. Review software documentation to ensure technical accuracy, compliance, or completeness, or to mitigate risks. Document test procedures to ensure replicability and compliance with standards. Develop or specify standards, methods, or procedures to determine product quality or release readiness. Update automated test scripts to ensure currency. Investigate customer problems referred by technical support. Install, maintain, or use software testing programs. Provide feedback and recommendations to developers on software usability and functionality. Monitor program performance to ensure efficient and problem-free operations. Install and configure recreations of software production environments to allow testing of software performance. Collaborate with field staff or customers to evaluate or diagnose problems and recommend possible solutions. Conduct software compatibility tests with programs, hardware, operating systems, or network environments. Identify program deviance from standards, and suggest modifications to ensure compliance. Design or develop automated testing tools. Coordinate user or third party testing. Perform initial debugging procedures by reviewing configuration files, logs, or code pieces to determine breakdown sources. Visit beta testing sites to evaluate software performance. Evaluate or recommend software for testing or bug tracking.

Personality Type: Investigative. These occupations frequently involve working with ideas and require an extensive amount of thinking. They can involve searching for facts and figuring out problems mentally.

GOE—Interest Area/Cluster: 11. Information Technology. **Work Group:** 11.02. Information Technology Specialties. **Other Jobs in This Work Group:** Computer and Information Scientists, Research; Computer Programmers; Computer Security Specialists; Computer Software Engineers, Applications; Computer Software Engineers, Systems Software; Computer Support Specialists; Computer Systems Analysts; Computer Systems Engineers/Architects; Database Administrators; Network Designers; Network Systems and Data

Communications Analysts; Web Administrators; Web Developers.

Skills—Quality Control Analysis: Evaluating the quality or performance of products, services, or processes. **Programming:** Writing computer programs for various purposes. **Systems Analysis:** Determining how a system should work and how changes will affect outcomes. **Systems Evaluation:** Looking at many indicators of system performance and taking into account their accuracy. **Troubleshooting:** Determining what is causing an operating error and deciding what to do about it. **Technology Design:** Generating or adapting equipment and technology to serve user needs. **Operations Analysis:** Analyzing needs and product requirements to create a design. **Writing:** Communicating effectively with others in writing as indicated by the needs of the audience.

Education and Training Programs: Computer and Information Sciences, General; Information Technology; Information Science/Studies; Computer Science; Computer and Information Sciences and Support Services, Other; Computer Engineering, General; Computer Software Engineering; Computer Engineering Technologies/Technicians, Other. **Related Knowledge/Courses—Computers and Electronics:** Electric circuit boards, processors, chips, and computer hardware and software, including applications and programming. **Engineering and Technology:** Equipment, tools, and mechanical devices and their uses to produce motion, light, power, technology, and other applications. **Design:** Design techniques, principles, tools, and instruments involved in the production and use of precision technical plans, blueprints, drawings, and models. **English Language:** The structure and content of the English language, including the meaning and spelling of words, rules of composition, and grammar. **Mathematics:** Numbers and their operations and interrelationships, including arithmetic, algebra, geometry, calculus, and statistics and their applications. **Clerical Practices:** Administrative and clerical procedures and systems such as word-processing systems, filing and records management systems, stenography and transcription, forms, design principles, and other office procedures and terminology.

Work Environment: Indoors; sitting; using hands on objects, tools, or controls; repetitive motions.

Special Education Teachers, Middle School

- ✳ Education/Training Required: Bachelor's degree
- ✳ Annual Earnings: $48,940
- ✳ Beginning Wage: $33,690
- ✳ Earnings Growth Potential: Low
- ✳ Growth: 15.8%
- ✳ Annual Job Openings: 8,846
- ✳ Self-Employed: 0.3%
- ✳ Part-Time: 9.6%

Teach middle school subjects to educationally and physically handicapped students. Includes teachers who specialize and work with audibly and visually handicapped students and those who teach basic academic and life processes skills to the mentally impaired. Establish and enforce rules for behavior and policies and procedures to maintain order among students. Maintain accurate and complete student records and prepare reports on children and activities as required by laws, district policies, and administrative regulations. Prepare materials and classrooms for class activities. Confer with parents, administrators, testing specialists, social workers, and professionals to develop individual educational plans designed to promote students' educational, physical, and social development. Develop and implement strategies to meet the needs of students with a variety of handicapping conditions. Teach socially acceptable behavior, employing techniques such as behavior modification and positive reinforcement. Modify the general education curriculum for special-needs students based upon a variety of instructional techniques and instructional technology. Employ special educational strategies and techniques during instruction to improve the development of sensory- and perceptual-motor skills, language, cognition, and memory. Confer with parents or guardians, other teachers, counselors, and administrators to resolve students' behavioral and academic problems. Instruct through lectures, discussions, and demonstrations in one or more subjects such as English, mathematics, or social studies. Coordinate placement of students with special needs into mainstream classes. Meet with parents and guardians to discuss their children's progress and to determine their priorities for their children and their resource needs. Guide and counsel students with adjustment or academic problems or special academic interests. Prepare, administer, and grade tests and assignments to evaluate students' progress. Observe and evaluate students' performance, behavior, social development, and physical health. Establish clear objectives for all lessons, units, and projects and communicate those objectives to students. Teach students personal development skills such as goal setting, independence, and self-advocacy. Plan and conduct activities for a balanced program of instruction, demonstration, and work time that provides students with opportunities to observe, question, and investigate.

Personality Type: Social. These occupations frequently involve working with, communicating with, and teaching people and often involve helping or providing service to others.

GOE—Interest Area/Cluster: 05. Education and Training. **Work Group:** 05.02. Preschool, Elementary, and Secondary Teaching and Instructing.

Other Jobs in This Work Group: Elementary School Teachers, Except Special Education; Kindergarten Teachers, Except Special Education; Middle School Teachers, Except Special and Vocational Education; Secondary School Teachers, Except Special and Vocational Education; Special Education Teachers, Preschool, Kindergarten, and Elementary School; Special Education Teachers, Secondary School; Vocational Education Teachers, Middle School; Vocational Education Teachers, Secondary School.

Skills—Learning Strategies: Using multiple approaches when learning or teaching new things. **Social Perceptiveness:** Being aware of others' reactions and understanding why they react the way they do. **Instructing:** Teaching others how to do something. **Monitoring:** Assessing how well one is doing when learning or doing something. **Persuasion:** Persuading others to approach things differently. **Writing:** Communicating effectively with others in writing as indicated by the needs of the audience. **Negotiation:** Bringing others together and trying to reconcile differences. **Time Management:** Managing one's own time and the time of others.

Education and Training Programs: Special Education and Teaching, General; Education/Teaching of the Gifted and Talented; Education/Teaching of Individuals Who are Developmentally Delayed; Education/Teaching of Individuals in Early Childhood Special Education Programs. **Related Knowledge/Courses—Geography:** Various methods for describing the location and distribution of land, sea, and air masses, including their physical locations, relationships, and characteristics. **History and Archeology:** Historical events and their causes, indicators, and impact on particular civilizations and cultures. **Psychology:** Human behavior and performance, mental processes, psychological research methods, and the assessment and treatment of behavioral and affective disorders. **Therapy and Counseling:** Information and techniques needed to rehabilitate physical and mental ailments and to provide career guidance, including alternative treatments, rehabilitation equipment and its proper use, and methods to evaluate treatment effects. **Sociology and Anthropology:** Group behavior and dynamics; societal trends and influences; and cultures and their history, migrations, ethnicity, and origins. **Education and Training:** Instructional methods and training techniques, including curriculum design principles, learning theory, group and individual teaching techniques, design of individual development plans, and test design principles.

Work Environment: Indoors; noisy; standing.

Special Education Teachers, Preschool, Kindergarten, and Elementary School

- ❋ Education/Training Required: Bachelor's degree
- ❋ Annual Earnings: $48,350
- ❋ Beginning Wage: $32,700
- ❋ Earnings Growth Potential: Low
- ❋ Growth: 19.6%
- ❋ Annual Job Openings: 20,049
- ❋ Self-Employed: 0.3%
- ❋ Part-Time: 9.6%

Teach elementary and preschool school subjects to educationally and physically handicapped students. Includes teachers who specialize and work with audibly and visually handicapped students and those who teach basic academic and life processes skills to the mentally impaired. Instruct students in academic subjects, using a variety of techniques such as phonetics, multisensory learning, and repetition to reinforce learning and to meet students' varying needs and interests. Employ special educational strategies and techniques during instruction to improve the development of sensory- and perceptual-motor skills, language, cognition, and memory. Teach socially acceptable behavior, employing techniques such as behavior modification and positive reinforcement. Modify the general education curriculum for special-needs students based upon a variety of instructional techniques and technologies. Meet with parents and guardians to discuss their children's progress and to determine their priorities for their children and their resource needs. Plan and conduct activities for a balanced program of instruction, demonstration, and work time that provides students with opportunities to observe, question, and investigate. Establish and enforce rules for behavior and policies and procedures to maintain order among the students for whom they are responsible. Confer with parents, administrators, testing specialists, social workers, and professionals to develop individual educational plans designed to promote students' educational, physical, and social development. Maintain accurate and complete student records and prepare reports on children and activities as required by laws, district policies, and administrative regulations. Establish clear objectives for all lessons, units, and projects and communicate those objectives to students. Develop and implement strategies to meet the needs of students with a variety of handicapping conditions. Prepare classrooms for class activities and provide a variety of materials and resources for children to explore, manipulate, and use, both in learning activities and imaginative play. Confer with parents or guardians, teachers, counselors, and administrators to resolve students' behavioral and academic problems. Observe and evaluate students' performance, behavior, social development, and physical health. Teach students personal development skills such as goal setting, independence, and self-advocacy.

Personality Type: Social. These occupations frequently involve working with, communicating with, and teaching people and often involve helping or providing service to others.

GOE—Interest Area/Cluster: 05. Education and Training. **Work Group:** 05.02. Preschool, Elementary, and Secondary Teaching and Instructing. **Other Jobs in This Work Group:** Elementary School Teachers, Except Special Education; Kindergarten Teachers, Except Special Education; Middle School Teachers, Except Special and Vocational Education; Secondary School Teachers, Except Special and Vocational Education; Special Education Teachers, Middle School; Special Education Teachers, Secondary School; Vocational Education Teachers, Middle School; Vocational Education Teachers, Secondary School.

Skills—Learning Strategies: Using multiple approaches when learning or teaching new things. **Instructing:** Teaching others how to do something. **Social Perceptiveness:** Being aware of others' reactions and understanding why they react the way they do. **Monitoring:** Assessing how well one is doing when learning or doing something. **Negotiation:** Bringing others together and trying to reconcile differences. **Time Management:** Managing one's own time and the time of others. **Coordination:** Adjusting actions in relation to others' actions. **Writing:** Communicating effectively with others in writing as indicated by the needs of the audience.

Education and Training Programs: Special Education and Teaching, General; Education/Teaching of Individuals with Hearing Impairments, Including Deafness; Education/Teaching of the Gifted and Talented; Education/Teaching of Individuals with Emotional Disturbances; Education/Teaching of Individuals with Mental Retardation; Education/Teaching of Individuals with Multiple Disabilities; Education/Teaching of Individuals with Orthopedic and Other Physical Health Impairments; others. **Related Knowledge/Courses—Psychology:** Human behavior and performance, mental processes, psychological research methods, and the assessment and treatment of behavioral and affective disorders. **History and Archeology:** Historical events and their causes, indicators, and impact on particular civilizations and cultures. **Therapy and Counseling:** Information and techniques needed to rehabilitate physical and mental ailments and to provide career guidance, including alternative treatments, rehabilitation equipment and its proper use, and methods to evaluate treatment effects. **Geography:** Various methods for describing the location and distribution of land, sea, and air masses, including their physical locations, relationships, and characteristics. **Philosophy and Theology:** Different philosophical systems and religions, including their basic principles, values, ethics, ways of thinking, customs, and practices and their impact on human culture. **Sociology and Anthropology:** Group behavior and dynamics; societal trends and influences; and cultures and their history, migrations, ethnicity, and origins.

Work Environment: Indoors; noisy; standing.

Speech-Language Pathologists

- ❁ Education/Training Required: Master's degree
- ❁ Annual Earnings: $60,690
- ❁ Beginning Wage: $40,200
- ❁ Earnings Growth Potential: Low
- ❁ Growth: 10.6%
- ❁ Annual Job Openings: 11,160
- ❁ Self-Employed: 8.8%
- ❁ Part-Time: 24.6%

Assess and treat persons with speech, language, voice, and fluency disorders. May select alternative communication systems and teach their use. May perform research related to speech and language problems. Monitor patients' progress and adjust treatments accordingly. Evaluate hearing and speech/language test results and medical or background information to diagnose and plan treatment for speech, language, fluency, voice, and swallowing disorders. Administer hearing or speech and language evaluations, tests, or examinations to patients to collect information on type and degree of impairments, using written and oral tests and special instruments. Record information on the initial evaluation, treatment, progress, and discharge of clients. Develop and implement treatment plans for problems such as stuttering, delayed language, swallowing disorders, and inappropriate pitch or harsh voice problems, based on own assessments and recommendations of physicians, psychologists, or social workers. Develop individual or group programs in schools to deal with speech or language problems. Instruct clients in techniques for more effective communication, including sign language, lip reading, and voice improvement. Teach clients to control or strengthen tongue, jaw, face muscles, and breathing mechanisms. Develop speech exercise programs to reduce disabilities. Consult with and advise educators or medical staff on speech or hearing topics, such as communication strategies or speech and language stimulation. Instruct patients and family members in strategies to cope with or avoid communication-related misunderstandings. Design, develop, and employ alternative diagnostic or communication devices and strategies. Conduct lessons and direct educational or therapeutic games to assist teachers dealing with speech problems. Refer clients to additional medical or educational services if needed. Participate in conferences or training, or publish research results, to share knowledge of new hearing or speech disorder treatment methods or technologies. Communicate with non-speaking students, using sign language or computer technology. Provide communication instruction to dialect speakers or students with limited English proficiency. Use computer applications to identify and assist with communication disabilities.

Personality Type: Social. These occupations frequently involve working with, communicating with, and teaching people and often involve helping or providing service to others.

GOE—Interest Area/Cluster: 08. Health Science. **Work Group:** 08.07. Medical Therapy. **Other Jobs in This Work Group:** Audiologists; Occupational Therapist Assistants; Occupational Therapists; Physical Therapist Assistants; Physical Therapists; Radiation Therapists; Recreational Therapists; Respiratory Therapists; Respiratory Therapy Technicians.

Skills—Learning Strategies: Using multiple approaches when learning or teaching new things. **Instructing:** Teaching others how to do something. **Social Perceptiveness:** Being aware of others' reactions and understanding why they react the way they do. **Speaking:** Talking to others to effectively convey information. **Monitoring:** Assessing how well one is doing when learning or

S

doing something. **Service Orientation:** Actively looking for ways to help people. **Reading Comprehension:** Understanding written sentences and paragraphs in work-related documents. **Active Learning:** Working with new material or information to grasp its implications.

Education and Training Programs: Communication Disorders, General; Speech-Language Pathology/Pathologist; Audiology/Audiologist and Speech-Language Pathology/Pathologist; Communication Disorders Sciences and Services, Other. **Related Knowledge/Courses—Therapy and Counseling:** Information and techniques needed to rehabilitate physical and mental ailments and to provide career guidance, including alternative treatments, rehabilitation equipment and its proper use, and methods to evaluate treatment effects. **Psychology:** Human behavior and performance, mental processes, psychological research methods, and the assessment and treatment of behavioral and affective disorders. **Sociology and Anthropology:** Group behavior and dynamics; societal trends and influences; and cultures and their history, migrations, ethnicity, and origins. **Medicine and Dentistry:** The information and techniques needed to diagnose and treat injuries, diseases, and deformities. This includes symptoms, treatment alternatives, drug properties and interactions, and preventive health-care measures. **Education and Training:** Instructional methods and training techniques, including curriculum design principles, learning theory, group and individual teaching techniques, design of individual development plans, and test design principles. **English Language:** The structure and content of the English language, including the meaning and spelling of words, rules of composition, and grammar.

Work Environment: Indoors; disease or infections; sitting.

Statisticians

* Education/Training Required: Master's degree
* Annual Earnings: $69,900
* Beginning Wage: $38,140
* Earnings Growth Potential: High
* Growth: 8.5%
* Annual Job Openings: 3,433
* Self-Employed: 6.0%
* Part-Time: 13.1%

Engage in the development of mathematical theory or apply statistical theory and methods to collect, organize, interpret, and summarize numerical data to provide usable information. May specialize in fields such as bio-statistics, agricultural statistics, business statistics, economic statistics, or other fields. Report results of statistical analyses, including information in the form of graphs, charts, and tables. Process large amounts of data for statistical modeling and graphic analysis, using computers. Identify relationships and trends in data, as well as any factors that could affect the results of research. Analyze and interpret statistical data in order to identify significant differences in relationships among sources of information. Prepare data for processing by organizing information, checking for any inaccuracies, and adjusting and weighting the raw data. Evaluate the statistical methods and procedures used to obtain data in order to ensure validity, applicability, efficiency, and accuracy. Evaluate sources of information in order to determine any limitations in terms of reliability or usability. Plan data collection methods for specific projects and determine the types and sizes of sample groups to be used. Design research projects that apply valid scientific techniques and utilize information obtained from baselines or historical data in order to structure uncompromised and efficient analyses. Develop an understanding of fields to which statistical methods are to be applied in order to determine whether methods and results are appropriate. Supervise and provide instructions for workers collecting and tabulating data. Apply sampling techniques or utilize complete enumeration bases in order to determine and define groups to be surveyed. Adapt statistical methods in order to solve specific problems in many fields, such as economics, biology, and engineering. Develop and test experimental designs, sampling techniques, and analytical methods. Examine theories, such as those of probability and inference, in order to discover mathematical bases for new or improved methods of obtaining and evaluating numerical data.

Personality Type: Conventional. These occupations frequently involve following set procedures and routines and can include working with data and details more than with ideas. Usually there is a clear line of authority to follow.

GOE—Interest Area/Cluster: 15. Scientific Research, Engineering, and Mathematics. **Work Group:** 15.06. Mathematics and Data Analysis. **Other Jobs in This Work Group:** Actuaries; Mathematical Technicians; Mathematicians; Social Science Research Assistants.

Skills—Programming: Writing computer programs for various purposes. **Science:** Using scientific methods to solve problems. **Mathematics:** Using mathematics to solve problems. **Writing:** Communicating effectively with others in writing as indicated by the needs of the audience. **Active Learning:** Working with new material or information to grasp its implications. **Negotiation:** Bringing others together and trying to reconcile differences. **Complex Problem Solving:** Identifying complex problems, reviewing the options, and implementing solutions. **Operations Analysis:** Analyzing needs and product requirements to create a design.

Education and Training Programs: Biostatistics; Mathematics, General; Applied Mathematics; Statistics, General; Mathematical Statistics and Probability; Statistics, Other; Business Statistics. **Related Knowledge/Courses—Mathematics:** Numbers and their operations and interrelationships, including arithmetic, algebra, geometry, calculus, and statistics and their applications. **Computers and Electronics:** Electric circuit boards, processors, chips, and computer hardware and software, including applications and programming. **English Language:** The structure and content of the English language, including the meaning and spelling of words, rules of composition, and grammar. **Law and Government:** Laws, legal codes, court procedures, precedents, government regulations, executive orders, agency rules, and the democratic political process. **Education and Training:** Instructional methods and training techniques, including curriculum design principles, learning theory, group and individual teaching techniques, design of individual development plans, and test design principles.

Work Environment: Indoors; sitting; using hands on objects, tools, or controls; repetitive motions.

Substance Abuse and Behavioral Disorder Counselors

- ❋ Education/Training Required: Bachelor's degree
- ❋ Annual Earnings: $35,580
- ❋ Beginning Wage: $23,780
- ❋ Earnings Growth Potential: Low
- ❋ Growth: 34.3%
- ❋ Annual Job Openings: 20,821
- ❋ Self-Employed: 5.8%
- ❋ Part-Time: 15.4%

Counsel and advise individuals with alcohol; tobacco; drug; or other problems, such as gambling and eating disorders. May counsel individuals, families, or groups or engage in prevention programs. Counsel clients and patients individually and in group sessions to assist in overcoming dependencies, adjusting to life, and making changes. Complete and maintain accurate records and reports regarding the patients' histories and progress, services provided, and other required information. Develop client treatment plans based on research, clinical experience, and client histories. Review and evaluate clients' progress in relation to measurable goals described in treatment and care plans. Interview clients, review records, and confer with other professionals to evaluate individuals' mental and physical condition and to determine their suitability for participation in a specific program. Intervene as advocate for clients or patients to resolve emergency problems in crisis situations. Provide clients or family members with information about addiction issues and about available services and programs, making appropriate referrals when necessary. Modify treatment plans to comply with changes in client status. Coordinate counseling efforts with mental health professionals and other health professionals such as doctors, nurses, and social workers. Attend training sessions to increase knowledge and skills. Plan and implement follow-up and aftercare programs for clients to be discharged from treatment programs. Conduct chemical dependency program orientation sessions. Counsel family members to assist them in understanding, dealing with, and supporting clients or patients. Participate in case conferences and staff meetings. Act as liaisons between clients and medical staff. Coordinate activities with courts, probation officers, community services, and other post-treatment agencies. Confer with family members or others close to clients to keep them informed of treatment planning and progress. Instruct others in program methods, procedures, and functions. Follow progress of discharged patients to determine effectiveness of treatments. Develop, implement, and evaluate public education, prevention, and health promotion programs, working in collaboration with organizations, institutions, and communities.

Personality Type: Social. These occupations frequently involve working with, communicating with, and teaching people and often involve helping or providing service to others.

GOE—Interest Area/Cluster: 10. Human Service. **Work Group:** 10.01. Counseling and Social Work. **Other Jobs in This Work Group:** Child, Family, and School Social Workers; Clinical Psychologists; Clinical, Counseling, and School Psychologists; Counseling Psychologists; Marriage and Family Therapists; Medical and Public Health Social Workers; Mental Health and Substance Abuse Social Workers; Mental Health Counselors; Probation Officers and Correctional Treatment Specialists; Rehabilitation Counselors.

Skills—Social Perceptiveness: Being aware of others' reactions and understanding why they react the way they do. **Persuasion:** Persuading others to approach things differently. **Service Orientation:** Actively looking for ways to help people. **Negotiation:** Bringing others together and trying to reconcile differences. **Active Listening:** Listening to what other people are saying and asking questions as appropriate. **Learning Strategies:** Using multiple approaches when learning or teaching new things. **Writing:** Communicating effectively with others in writing as indicated by the needs of the audience. **Complex Problem Solving:** Identifying complex problems, reviewing the options, and implementing solutions.

Education and Training Programs: Substance Abuse/Addiction Counseling; Clinical/Medical Social Work; Mental and Social Health Services and Allied Professions, Other. **Related**

Knowledge/Courses—Therapy and Counseling: Information and techniques needed to rehabilitate physical and mental ailments and to provide career guidance, including alternative treatments, rehabilitation equipment and its proper use, and methods to evaluate treatment effects. **Psychology:** Human behavior and performance, mental processes, psychological research methods, and the assessment and treatment of behavioral and affective disorders. **Sociology and Anthropology:** Group behavior and dynamics; societal trends and influences; and cultures and their history, migrations, ethnicity, and origins. **Philosophy and Theology:** Different philosophical systems and religions, including their basic principles, values, ethics, ways of thinking, customs, and practices and their impact on human culture. **Customer and Personal Service:** Principles and processes for providing customer and personal services, including needs assessment techniques, quality service standards, alternative delivery systems, and customer satisfaction evaluation techniques. **Education and Training:** Instructional methods and training techniques, including curriculum design principles, learning theory, group and individual teaching techniques, design of individual development plans, and test design principles.

Work Environment: Indoors; disease or infections; sitting.

Surgeons

- ✺ Education/Training Required: First professional degree
- ✺ Annual Earnings: More than $145,600
- ✺ Beginning Wage: $104,410
- ✺ Earnings Growth Potential: Cannot be calculated
- ✺ Growth: 14.2%
- ✺ Annual Job Openings: 38,027
- ✺ Self-Employed: 14.7%
- ✺ Part-Time: 8.1%

The job openings listed here are shared with Anesthesiologists; Family and General Practitioners; Internists, General; Obstetricians and Gynecologists; Pediatricians, General; and Psychiatrists.

Treat diseases, injuries, and deformities by invasive methods, such as manual manipulation, or by using instruments and appliances. Analyze patient's medical history, medication allergies, physical condition, and examination results to verify operation's necessity and to determine best procedure. Operate on patients to correct deformities, repair injuries, prevent and treat diseases, or improve or restore patients' functions. Follow established surgical techniques during the operation. Prescribe preoperative and postoperative treatments and procedures, such as sedatives, diets, antibiotics, and preparation and treatment of the patient's operative area. Examine patient to provide information on medical condition and surgical risk. Diagnose bodily disorders and orthopedic conditions and provide treatments, such as medicines and surgeries, in clinics, hospital wards, and operating rooms. Direct and coordinate activities of nurses, assistants, specialists, residents, and other medical staff. Provide consultation and surgical assistance to other physicians and surgeons. Refer patient to medical specialist or other practitioners when necessary. Examine instruments, equipment, and operating room to ensure sterility. Prepare case histories. Manage surgery services, including planning, scheduling and coordination, determination of procedures, and procurement of supplies and equipment. Conduct research to develop and test surgical techniques that can improve operating procedures and outcomes.

Personality Type: Investigative. These occupations frequently involve working with ideas and require an extensive amount of thinking. They can involve searching for facts and figuring out problems mentally.

GOE—Interest Area/Cluster: 08. Health Science. **Work Group:** 08.02. Medicine and Surgery. **Other Jobs in This Work Group:** Anesthesiologists; Family and General Practitioners; Internists, General; Obstetricians and Gynecologists; Pediatricians, General; Pharmacists; Physician Assistants; Psychiatrists; Registered Nurses.

Skills—Science: Using scientific methods to solve problems. **Reading Comprehension:** Understanding written sentences and paragraphs in work-related documents. **Judgment and Decision Making:** Weighing the relative costs and benefits of a potential action. **Complex Problem Solving:** Identifying complex problems, reviewing the options, and implementing solutions. **Management of Financial Resources:** Determining how money will be spent to get the work done and accounting for these expenditures. **Critical Thinking:** Using logic and analysis to identify the strengths and weaknesses of different approaches. **Equipment Selection:** Determining the kind of tools and equipment needed to do a job. **Technology Design:** Generating or adapting equipment and technology to serve user needs.

Education and Training Programs: Colon and Rectal Surgery; Critical Care Surgery; General Surgery; Hand Surgery; Neurological Surgery/

Neurosurgery; Orthopedics/Orthopedic Surgery; Otolaryngology; Pediatric Orthopedics; Pediatric Surgery; Plastic Surgery; Sports Medicine; Thoracic Surgery; Urology; Vascular Surgery; Adult Reconstructive Orthopedics (Orthopedic Surgery); Orthopedic Surgery of the Spine. **Related Knowledge/Courses—Medicine and Dentistry:** The information and techniques needed to diagnose and treat injuries, diseases, and deformities. This includes symptoms, treatment alternatives, drug properties and interactions, and preventive health-care measures. **Biology:** Plant and animal living tissue, cells, organisms, and entities, including their functions, interdependencies, and interactions with each other and the environment. **Therapy and Counseling:** Information and techniques needed to rehabilitate physical and mental ailments and to provide career guidance, including alternative treatments, rehabilitation equipment and its proper use, and methods to evaluate treatment effects. **Psychology:** Human behavior and performance, mental processes, psychological research methods, and the assessment and treatment of behavioral and affective disorders. **Chemistry:** The composition, structure, and properties of substances and of the chemical processes and transformations that they undergo. This includes uses of chemicals and their interactions, danger signs, production techniques, and disposal methods. **Customer and Personal Service:** Principles and processes for providing customer and personal services, including needs assessment techniques, quality service standards, alternative delivery systems, and customer satisfaction evaluation techniques.

Work Environment: Indoors; contaminants; radiation; disease or infections; standing; using hands on objects, tools, or controls.

Surveyors

* Education/Training Required: Bachelor's degree
* Annual Earnings: $51,630
* Beginning Wage: $28,590
* Earnings Growth Potential: High
* Growth: 23.7%
* Annual Job Openings: 14,305
* Self-Employed: 3.7%
* Part-Time: 4.6%

Make exact measurements and determine property boundaries. Provide data relevant to the shape, contour, gravitation, location, elevation, or dimension of land or land features on or near Earth's surface for engineering, mapmaking, mining, land evaluation, construction, and other purposes. Verify the accuracy of survey data including measurements and calculations conducted at survey sites. Calculate heights, depths, relative positions, property lines, and other characteristics of terrain. Search legal records, survey records, and land titles to obtain information about property boundaries in areas to be surveyed. Prepare and maintain sketches, maps, reports, and legal descriptions of surveys to describe, certify, and assume liability for work performed. Direct or conduct surveys to establish legal boundaries for properties, based on legal deeds and titles. Prepare or supervise preparation of all data, charts, plots, maps, records, and documents related to surveys. Write descriptions of property boundary surveys for use in deeds, leases, or other legal documents. Compute geodetic measurements and interpret survey data to determine positions, shapes, and elevations of geomorphic and topographic features. Determine longitudes and latitudes of important features and boundaries in survey areas using theodolites, transits, levels, and satellite-based global positioning systems (GPS). Record the results of surveys including the shape, contour, location, elevation, and dimensions of land or land features. Coordinate findings with the work of engineering and architectural personnel, clients, and others concerned with projects. Establish fixed points for use in making maps, using geodetic and engineering instruments. Train assistants and helpers, and direct their work in such activities as performing surveys or drafting maps. Plan and conduct ground surveys designed to establish baselines, elevations, and other geodetic measurements. Adjust surveying instruments to maintain their accuracy. Analyze survey objectives and specifications to prepare survey proposals or to direct others in survey proposal preparation. Develop criteria for survey methods and procedures. Survey bodies of water to determine navigable channels and to secure data for construction of breakwaters, piers, and other marine structures. Conduct research in surveying and mapping methods using knowledge of techniques of photogrammetric map compilation and electronic data processing.

Personality Type: Realistic. These occupations frequently involve work activities that include practical, hands-on problems and solutions. They often deal with plants; animals; and real-world materials such as wood, tools, and machinery. Many of the occupations require working outside and don't involve a lot of paperwork or working closely with others.

GOE—Interest Area/Cluster: 02. Architecture and Construction. **Work Group:** 02.03. Architecture/Construction Engineering Technologies. **Other Jobs in This Work Group:** No others in group.

Skills—Operation Monitoring: Watching gauges, dials, or other indicators to make sure a machine is working properly. **Management of Personnel Resources:** Motivating, developing, and directing people as they work; identifying the best people for the job. **Operation and Control:**

Controlling operations of equipment or systems. **Repairing:** Repairing machines or systems, using the needed tools.

Education and Training Program: Surveying Technology/Surveying. **Related Knowledge/ Courses—Geography:** Various methods for describing the location and distribution of land, sea, and air masses, including their physical locations, relationships, and characteristics. **Design:** Design techniques, principles, tools, and instruments involved in the production and use of precision technical plans, blueprints, drawings, and models. **Building and Construction:** Materials, methods, and the appropriate tools to construct objects, structures, and buildings. **History and Archeology:** Historical events and their causes, indicators, and impact on particular civilizations and cultures. **Engineering and Technology:** Equipment, tools, and mechanical devices and their uses to produce motion, light, power, technology, and other applications. **Mathematics:** Numbers and their operations and interrelationships, including arithmetic, algebra, geometry, calculus, and statistics and their applications.

Work Environment: Outdoors; very hot or cold; hazardous equipment; minor burns, cuts, bites, or stings; standing; using hands on objects, tools, or controls.

Technical Writers

- ❋ Education/Training Required: Bachelor's degree
- ❋ Annual Earnings: $60,390
- ❋ Beginning Wage: $36,490
- ❋ Earnings Growth Potential: Medium
- ❋ Growth: 19.5%
- ❋ Annual Job Openings: 7,498
- ❋ Self-Employed: 6.0%
- ❋ Part-Time: 6.5%

Write technical materials, such as equipment manuals, appendices, or operating and maintenance instructions. May assist in layout work. Organize material and complete writing assignment according to set standards regarding order, clarity, conciseness, style, and terminology. Maintain records and files of work and revisions. Edit, standardize, or make changes to material prepared by other writers or establishment personnel. Confer with customer representatives, vendors, plant executives, or publisher to establish technical specifications and to determine subject material to be developed for publication. Review published materials and recommend revisions or changes in scope, format, content, and methods of reproduction and binding. Select photographs, drawings, sketches, diagrams, and charts to illustrate material. Study drawings, specifications, mockups, and product samples to integrate and delineate technology, operating procedure, and production sequence and detail. Interview production and engineering personnel and read journals and other material to become familiar with product technologies and production methods. Observe production, developmental, and experimental activities to determine operating procedure and detail. Arrange for typing, duplication, and distribution of material. Assist in laying out material for publication. Analyze developments in specific field to determine need for revisions in previously published materials and development of new material. Review manufacturer's and trade catalogs, drawings, and other data relative to operation, maintenance, and service of equipment. Draw sketches to illustrate specified materials or assembly sequence.

Personality Type: Artistic. These occupations frequently involve working with forms, designs, and patterns. They often require self-expression, and the work can be done without following a clear set of rules.

GOE—Interest Area/Cluster: 03. Arts and Communication. Work Group: 03.02. Writing and Editing. Other Jobs in This Work Group: Copy Writers; Editors; Poets, Lyricists and Creative Writers; Writers and Authors.

Skills—Writing: Communicating effectively with others in writing as indicated by the needs of the audience. Technology Design: Generating or adapting equipment and technology to serve user needs. Quality Control Analysis: Evaluating the quality or performance of products, services, or processes. Active Listening: Listening to what other people are saying and asking questions as appropriate. Operations Analysis: Analyzing needs and product requirements to create a design. Reading Comprehension: Understanding written sentences and paragraphs in work-related documents. Coordination: Adjusting actions in relation to others' actions. Active Learning: Working with new material or information to grasp its implications.

Education and Training Programs: Communication Studies/Speech Communication and Rhetoric; Technical and Business Writing; Business/Corporate Communications. Related Knowledge/Courses—Communications and Media: Media production, communication, and dissemination techniques and methods, including alternative ways to inform and entertain via written, oral, and visual media. Clerical Practices: Administrative and clerical procedures and systems such as word-processing systems, filing and records management systems, stenography and transcription, forms, design principles, and other office procedures and terminology. English Language: The structure and content of the English language, including the meaning and spelling of words, rules of composition, and grammar. Computers and Electronics: Electric circuit boards, processors, chips, and computer hardware and software, including applications and programming. Education and

Training: Instructional methods and training techniques, including curriculum design principles, learning theory, group and individual teaching techniques, design of individual development plans, and test design principles. Engineering and Technology: Equipment, tools, and mechanical devices and their uses to produce motion, light, power, technology, and other applications.

Work Environment: Indoors; sitting; using hands on objects, tools, or controls; repetitive motions.

Training and Development Managers

- ❊ Education/Training Required: Work experience plus degree
- ❊ Annual Earnings: $84,340
- ❊ Beginning Wage: $46,450
- ❊ Earnings Growth Potential: High
- ❊ Growth: 15.6%
- ❊ Annual Job Openings: 3,759
- ❊ Self-Employed: 1.6%
- ❊ Part-Time: 2.7%

Plan, direct, or coordinate the training and development activities and staff of organizations. Prepare training budgets for departments or organizations. Evaluate instructor performances and the effectiveness of training programs, providing recommendations for improvements. Analyze training needs to develop new training programs or modify and improve existing programs. Conduct or arrange for ongoing technical training and personal development classes for staff members. Plan, develop, and provide training and staff development programs, using knowledge of the effectiveness of methods such as classroom training, demonstrations, on-the-job training, meetings, conferences, and workshops. Conduct orientation sessions and arrange on-the-job training for new hires. Confer with management and conduct surveys to identify training needs based on projected production processes, changes, and other factors. Train instructors and supervisors in techniques and skills for training and dealing with employees. Develop and organize training manuals, multimedia visual aids, and other educational materials. Develop testing and evaluation procedures. Review and evaluate training and apprenticeship programs for compliance with government standards. Coordinate established courses with technical and professional courses provided by community schools and designate training procedures.

Personality Type: Enterprising. These occupations frequently involve starting up and carrying out projects and can involve leading people and making many decisions. They sometimes require risk taking and often deal with business.

GOE—Interest Area/Cluster: 04. Business and Administration. **Work Group:** 04.01. Managerial Work in General Business. **Other Jobs in This Work Group:** Chief Executives; Compensation and Benefits Managers; General and Operations Managers; Human Resources Managers.

Skills—Systems Evaluation: Looking at many indicators of system performance and taking into account their accuracy. **Management of Financial Resources:** Determining how money will be spent to get the work done and accounting for these expenditures. **Systems Analysis:** Determining how a system should work and how changes will affect outcomes. **Management of Personnel Resources:** Motivating, developing, and directing people as they work; identifying the best people for the job. **Negotiation:** Bringing others together and trying to reconcile differences. **Persuasion:** Persuading others to approach things differently. **Learning Strategies:** Using multiple approaches when learning or teaching new things. **Service Orientation:** Actively looking for ways to help people.

Education and Training Programs: Human Resources Management/Personnel Administration, General; Human Resources Development. **Related Knowledge/Courses—Education and Training:** Instructional methods and training techniques, including curriculum design principles, learning theory, group and individual teaching techniques, design of individual development plans, and test design principles. **Personnel and Human Resources:** Principles and procedures for personnel recruitment; selection; training; compensation and benefits; labor relations and negotiation; and personnel information systems. **Sociology and Anthropology:** Group behavior and dynamics; societal trends and influences; and cultures and their history, migrations, ethnicity, and origins. **Sales and Marketing:** Principles and methods involved in showing, promoting, and selling products or services. This includes marketing strategies and tactics, product demonstration and sales techniques, and sales control systems. **Therapy and Counseling:** Information and techniques needed to rehabilitate physical and mental ailments and to provide career guidance, including alternative treatments, rehabilitation equipment and its proper use, and methods to evaluate treatment effects. **English Language:** The structure and content of the English language, including the meaning and spelling of words, rules of composition, and grammar.

Work Environment: Indoors; sitting.

Training and Development Specialists

- Education/Training Required: Work experience plus degree
- Annual Earnings: $49,630
- Beginning Wage: $28,600
- Earnings Growth Potential: High
- Growth: 18.3%
- Annual Job Openings: 35,862
- Self-Employed: 2.3%
- Part-Time: 7.6%

Conduct training and development programs for employees. Monitor, evaluate and record training activities and program effectiveness. Offer specific training programs to help workers maintain or improve job skills. Assess training needs through surveys, interviews with employees, focus groups, or consultation with managers, instructors, or customer representatives. Develop alternative training methods if expected improvements are not seen. Organize and develop, or obtain, training procedure manuals and guides and course materials such as handouts and visual materials. Present information, using a variety of instructional techniques and formats such as role playing, simulations, team exercises, group discussions, videos, and lectures. Evaluate training materials prepared by instructors, such as outlines, text, and handouts. Design, plan, organize, and direct orientation and training for employees or customers of industrial or commercial establishments. Monitor training costs to ensure budget is not exceeded, and prepare budget reports to justify expenditures. Select and assign instructors to conduct training. Schedule classes based on availability of classrooms, equipment, and instructors. Keep up with developments in their individual areas of expertise by reading current journals, books, and magazine articles. Supervise instructors, evaluate instructor performances, and refer instructors to classes for skill development. Coordinate recruitment and placement of training program participants. Attend meetings and seminars to obtain information for use in training programs, or to inform management of training program statuses. Negotiate contracts with clients, including desired training outcomes, fees, and expenses. Devise programs to develop executive potential among employees in lower-level positions. Screen, hire, and assign workers to positions based on qualifications. Refer trainees to employer relations representatives, to locations offering job placement assistance, or to appropriate social services agencies if warranted.

Personality Type: Social. These occupations frequently involve working with, communicating with, and teaching people and often involve helping or providing service to others.

GOE—Interest Area/Cluster: 04. Business and Administration. **Work Group:** 04.03. Human Resources Support. **Other Jobs in This Work Group:** Compensation, Benefits, and Job Analysis Specialists; Employment Interviewers; Employment, Recruitment, and Placement Specialists; Personnel Recruiters.

Skills—Systems Evaluation: Looking at many indicators of system performance and taking into account their accuracy. **Systems Analysis:** Determining how a system should work and how changes will affect outcomes. **Learning Strategies:** Using multiple approaches when learning or teaching new things. **Management of Personnel Resources:** Motivating, developing, and directing people as they work; identifying the best people for the job. **Management of Financial Resources:** Determining how money will be spent to get the work done and accounting for these expenditures. **Instructing:** Teaching others how to do something. **Negotiation:** Bringing others together and trying to reconcile differences. **Writing:** Communicating

200 Best Jobs for College Graduates © JIST Works

395

effectively with others in writing as indicated by the needs of the audience.

Education and Training Programs: Human Resources Management/Personnel Administration, General; Organizational Behavior Studies. **Related Knowledge/Courses—Education and Training:** Instructional methods and training techniques, including curriculum design principles, learning theory, group and individual teaching techniques, design of individual development plans, and test design principles. **Sociology and Anthropology:** Group behavior and dynamics; societal trends and influences; and cultures and their history, migrations, ethnicity, and origins. **Sales and Marketing:** Principles and methods involved in showing, promoting, and selling products or services. This includes marketing strategies and tactics, product demonstration and sales techniques, and sales control systems. **Clerical Practices:** Administrative and clerical procedures and systems such as word-processing systems, filing and records management systems, stenography and transcription, forms, design principles, and other office procedures and terminology. **Personnel and Human Resources:** Principles and procedures for personnel recruitment; selection; training; compensation and benefits; labor relations and negotiation; and personnel information systems. **Psychology:** Human behavior and performance, mental processes, psychological research methods, and the assessment and treatment of behavioral and affective disorders.

Work Environment: Indoors; sitting.

Treasurers and Controllers

- ✸ Education/Training Required: Work experience plus degree
- ✸ Annual Earnings: $95,310
- ✸ Beginning Wage: $51,910
- ✸ Earnings Growth Potential: High
- ✸ Growth: 12.6%
- ✸ Annual Job Openings: 57,589
- ✸ Self-Employed: 4.6%
- ✸ Part-Time: 4.2%

The job openings listed here are shared with Financial Managers, Branch or Department.

Direct financial activities, such as planning, procurement, and investments, for all or part of an organization. Prepare and file annual tax returns or prepare financial information so that outside accountants can complete tax returns. Prepare or direct preparation of financial statements, business activity reports, financial position forecasts, annual budgets, and/or reports required by regulatory agencies. Supervise employees performing financial reporting, accounting, billing, collections, payroll, and budgeting duties. Delegate authority for the receipt, disbursement, banking, protection, and custody of funds, securities, and financial instruments. Maintain current knowledge of organizational policies and procedures, federal and state policies and directives, and current accounting standards. Conduct or coordinate audits of company accounts and financial transactions to ensure compliance with state and federal requirements and statutes. Receive and record requests for disbursements; authorize disbursements in accordance with policies and procedures. Monitor financial activities and details such as reserve levels to ensure that all legal and regulatory requirements are met. Monitor and evaluate the performance of accounting and other financial staff; recommend and implement personnel actions such as promotions and dismissals. Develop and maintain relationships with banking, insurance, and non-organizational accounting personnel in order to facilitate financial activities. Coordinate and direct the financial planning, budgeting, procurement, or investment activities of all or part of an organization. Develop internal control policies, guidelines, and procedures for activities such as budget administration, cash and credit management, and accounting. Analyze the financial details of past, present, and expected operations in order to identify development opportunities and areas where improvement is needed. Advise management on short-term and long-term financial objectives, policies, and actions. Provide direction and assistance to other organizational units regarding accounting and budgeting policies and procedures and efficient control and utilization of financial resources. Evaluate needs for procurement of funds and investment of surpluses and make appropriate recommendations.

Personality Type: Conventional. These occupations frequently involve following set procedures and routines and can include working with data and details more than with ideas. Usually there is a clear line of authority to follow.

GOE—Interest Area/Cluster: 06. Finance and Insurance. **Work Group:** 06.01. Managerial Work in Finance and Insurance. **Other Jobs in This Work Group:** Financial Managers; Financial Managers, Branch or Department.

Skills—Management of Financial Resources: Determining how money will be spent to get the work done and accounting for these expenditures. **Management of Material Resources:** Obtaining and seeing to the appropriate use of equipment, facilities, and materials needed to do certain work. **Judgment and Decision Making:** Weighing the relative costs and benefits of a potential action. **Management of Personnel Resources:**

Motivating, developing, and directing people as they work; identifying the best people for the job. **Mathematics:** Using mathematics to solve problems. **Negotiation:** Bringing others together and trying to reconcile differences. **Time Management:** Managing one's own time and the time of others. **Persuasion:** Persuading others to approach things differently.

Education and Training Programs: Accounting and Finance; Accounting and Business/Management; Finance, General; International Finance; Public Finance; Credit Management; Finance and Financial Management Services, Other. **Related Knowledge/Courses—Economics and Accounting:** Economic and accounting principles and practices, the financial markets, banking, and the analysis and reporting of financial data. **Administration and Management:** Principles and processes involved in business and organizational planning, coordination, and execution. This includes strategic planning, resource allocation, manpower modeling, leadership techniques, and production methods. **Personnel and Human Resources:** Principles and procedures for personnel recruitment; selection; training; compensation and benefits; labor relations and negotiation; and personnel information systems. **Law and Government:** Laws, legal codes, court procedures, precedents, government regulations, executive orders, agency rules, and the democratic political process. **Mathematics:** Numbers and their operations and interrelationships, including arithmetic, algebra, geometry, calculus, and statistics and their applications. **English Language:** The structure and content of the English language, including the meaning and spelling of words, rules of composition, and grammar.

Work Environment: Indoors; sitting.

Veterinarians

❋ Education/Training Required: First professional degree
❋ Annual Earnings: $75,230
❋ Beginning Wage: $44,150
❋ Earnings Growth Potential: High
❋ Growth: 35.0%
❋ Annual Job Openings: 5,301
❋ Self-Employed: 17.1%
❋ Part-Time: 13.4%

Diagnose and treat diseases and dysfunctions of animals. May engage in a particular function, such as research and development, consultation, administration, technical writing, sale or production of commercial products, or rendering of technical services to commercial firms or other organizations. Includes veterinarians who inspect livestock. Examine animals to detect and determine the nature of diseases or injuries. Treat sick or injured animals by prescribing medication, setting bones, dressing wounds, or performing surgery. Inoculate animals against various diseases such as rabies and distemper. Collect body tissue, feces, blood, urine, or other body fluids for examination and analysis. Operate diagnostic equipment such as radiographic and ultrasound equipment and interpret the resulting images. Advise animal owners regarding sanitary measures, feeding, and general care necessary to promote health of animals. Educate the public about diseases that can be spread from animals to humans. Train and supervise workers who handle and care for animals. Provide care to a wide range of animals or specialize in a particular species, such as horses or exotic birds. Euthanize animals. Establish and conduct quarantine and testing procedures that prevent the spread of diseases to other animals or to humans and that comply with applicable government regulations. Conduct postmortem studies and analyses to determine the causes of animals' deaths. Perform administrative duties such as scheduling appointments, accepting payments from clients, and maintaining business records. Drive mobile clinic vans to farms so that health problems can be treated or prevented. Direct the overall operations of animal hospitals, clinics, or mobile services to farms. Specialize in a particular type of treatment such as dentistry, pathology, nutrition, surgery, microbiology, or internal medicine. Inspect and test horses, sheep, poultry, and other animals to detect the presence of communicable diseases. Research diseases to which animals could be susceptible. Plan and execute animal nutrition and reproduction programs. Inspect animal housing facilities to determine their cleanliness and adequacy. Determine the effects of drug therapies, antibiotics, or new surgical techniques by testing them on animals.

Personality Type: Investigative. These occupations frequently involve working with ideas and require an extensive amount of thinking. They can involve searching for facts and figuring out problems mentally.

GOE—Interest Area/Cluster: 08. Health Science. **Work Group:** 08.05. Animal Care. **Other Jobs in This Work Group:** Veterinary Technologists and Technicians.

Skills—Science: Using scientific methods to solve problems. **Management of Financial Resources:** Determining how money will be spent to get the work done and accounting for these expenditures. **Reading Comprehension:** Understanding written sentences and paragraphs in work-related documents. **Judgment and Decision Making:** Weighing the relative costs and benefits of a potential action. **Complex Problem Solving:** Identifying complex problems, reviewing the options, and implementing solutions. **Management of Personnel Resources:** Motivating, developing, and directing people as they work; identifying the best people for the job. **Equipment Selection:** Determining the kind of tools and equipment needed to do a job. **Management of Material Resources:** Obtaining and seeing to the appropriate use of equipment, facilities, and materials needed to do certain work.

Education and Training Programs: Veterinary Medicine (DVM); Veterinary Sciences/Veterinary Clinical Sciences, General (Cert, MS, PhD); Veterinary Anatomy (Cert, MS, PhD); Veterinary Physiology (Cert, MS, PhD); Veterinary Microbiology and Immunobiology (Cert, MS, PhD); Veterinary Pathology and Pathobiology (Cert, MS, PhD); Veterinary Toxicology and Pharmacology (Cert, MS, PhD); Large Animal/Food Animal and Equine Surgery and Medicine (Cert, MS, PhD); others. **Related Knowledge/Courses—Biology:** Plant and animal living tissue, cells, organisms, and entities, including their functions, interdependencies, and interactions with each other and the environment. **Medicine and Dentistry:** The information and techniques needed to diagnose and treat injuries, diseases, and deformities. This includes symptoms, treatment alternatives, drug properties and interactions, and preventive healthcare measures. **Chemistry:** The composition, structure, and properties of substances and of the chemical processes and transformations that they undergo. This includes uses of chemicals and their interactions, danger signs, production techniques, and disposal methods. **Therapy and Counseling:** Information and techniques needed to rehabilitate physical and mental ailments and to provide career guidance, including alternative treatments, rehabilitation equipment and its proper use, and methods to evaluate treatment effects. **Sales and Marketing:** Principles and methods involved in showing, promoting, and selling products or services. This includes marketing strategies and tactics, product demonstration and sales techniques, and sales control systems. **Customer and Personal Service:** Principles and processes for providing customer and personal services, including needs assessment techniques, quality service standards, alternative delivery systems, and customer satisfaction evaluation techniques.

Work Environment: Indoors; noisy; contaminants; disease or infections; standing; using hands on objects, tools, or controls.

Veterinary Technologists and Technicians

* Education/Training Required: Associate degree
* Annual Earnings: $27,970
* Beginning Wage: $18,840
* Earnings Growth Potential: Low
* Growth: 41.0%
* Annual Job Openings: 14,674
* Self-Employed: 0.2%
* Part-Time: 20.8%

Perform medical tests in a laboratory environment for use in the treatment and diagnosis of diseases in animals. Prepare vaccines and serums for prevention of diseases. Prepare tissue samples; take blood samples; and execute laboratory tests, such as urinalysis and blood counts. Clean and sterilize instruments and materials and maintain equipment and machines. Administer anesthesia to animals, under the direction of a veterinarian, and monitor animals' responses to anesthetics so that dosages can be adjusted. Care for and monitor the condition of animals recovering from surgery. Prepare and administer medications, vaccines, serums, and treatments as prescribed by veterinarians. Perform laboratory tests on blood, urine, and feces, such as urinalyses and blood counts, to assist in the diagnosis and treatment of animal health problems.

Administer emergency first aid, such as performing emergency resuscitation or other life-saving procedures. Collect, prepare, and label samples for laboratory testing, culture, or microscopic examination. Clean and sterilize instruments, equipment, and materials. Provide veterinarians with the correct equipment and instruments as needed. Fill prescriptions, measuring medications and labeling containers. Prepare animals for surgery, performing such tasks as shaving surgical areas. Take animals into treatment areas and assist with physical examinations by performing such duties as obtaining temperature, pulse, and respiration data. Observe the behavior and condition of animals and monitor their clinical symptoms. Take and develop diagnostic radiographs, using X-ray equipment. Maintain laboratory, research, and treatment records, as well as inventories of pharmaceuticals, equipment, and supplies. Give enemas and perform catheterizations, ear flushes, intravenous feedings, and gavages. Prepare treatment rooms for surgery. Maintain instruments, equipment, and machinery to ensure proper working condition. Perform dental work such as cleaning, polishing, and extracting teeth. Clean kennels, animal holding areas, surgery suites, examination rooms, and animal loading/unloading facilities to control the spread of disease. Provide information and counseling regarding issues such as animal health care, behavior problems, and nutrition. Provide assistance with animal euthanasia and the disposal of remains. Dress and suture wounds and apply splints and other protective devices. Perform a variety of office, clerical, and accounting duties, such as reception, billing, bookkeeping, or selling products.

Personality Type: Realistic. These occupations frequently involve work activities that include practical, hands-on problems and solutions. They often deal with plants; animals; and real-world materials such as wood, tools, and machinery. Many of the occupations require working outside and don't involve a lot of paperwork or working closely with others.

GOE—Interest Area/Cluster: 08. Health Science. **Work Group:** 08.05. Animal Care. **Other Jobs in This Work Group:** Veterinarians.

Skills—Science: Using scientific methods to solve problems. **Operation Monitoring:** Watching gauges, dials, or other indicators to make sure a machine is working properly. **Instructing:** Teaching others how to do something. **Equipment Maintenance:** Performing routine maintenance and determining when and what kind of maintenance is needed. **Social Perceptiveness:** Being aware of others' reactions and understanding why they react the way they do. **Operation and Control:** Controlling operations of equipment or systems. **Mathematics:** Using mathematics to solve problems. **Reading Comprehension:** Understanding written sentences and paragraphs in work-related documents.

Education and Training Program: Veterinary/Animal Health Technology/Technician and Veterinary Assistant. **Related Knowledge/Courses—Biology:** Plant and animal living tissue, cells, organisms, and entities, including their functions, interdependencies, and interactions with each other and the environment. **Medicine and Dentistry:** The information and techniques needed to diagnose and treat injuries, diseases, and deformities. This includes symptoms, treatment alternatives, drug properties and interactions, and preventive health-care measures. **Chemistry:** The composition, structure, and properties of substances and of the chemical processes and transformations that they undergo. This includes uses of chemicals and their interactions, danger signs, production techniques, and disposal methods. **Sales and Marketing:** Principles and methods involved in showing, promoting, and selling products or services. This includes marketing strategies and tactics, product demonstration and sales techniques, and sales control systems. **Customer and Personal Service:** Principles and processes for providing customer and personal services, including needs assessment techniques, quality service standards, alternative delivery systems, and customer satisfaction evaluation techniques. **Mathematics:** Numbers and their operations and interrelationships, including arithmetic, algebra, geometry, calculus, and statistics and their applications.

Work Environment: Indoors; contaminants; radiation; disease or infections; minor burns, cuts, bites, or stings; standing.

Web Administrators

- ❋ Education/Training Required: Bachelor's degree
- ❋ Annual Earnings: $71,510
- ❋ Beginning Wage: $37,600
- ❋ Earnings Growth Potential: High
- ❋ Growth: 15.1%
- ❋ Annual Job Openings: 14,374
- ❋ Self-Employed: 6.6%
- ❋ Part-Time: 5.6%

The job openings listed here are shared with Computer Systems Engineers/Architects; Network Designers; Software Quality Assurance Engineers and Testers; and Web Developers.

Manage Web environment design, deployment, development, and maintenance activities. Perform testing and quality assurance of Web sites and Web applications. Back up or modify applications and related data to provide for disaster recovery. Determine sources of Web page or server problems, and take action to correct such problems. Review or update Web page content or links in a timely manner, using appropriate tools. Monitor systems for intrusions or denial of service attacks, and report security breaches to appropriate personnel. Implement Web site security measures, such as firewalls or message encryption. Administer Internet/intranet infrastructure, including components such as Web, file transfer protocol (FTP), news, and mail servers. Collaborate with development teams to discuss, analyze, or resolve usability issues. Test backup or recovery plans regularly and resolve any problems. Monitor Web developments through continuing education, reading, or participation in professional conferences, workshops, or groups. Implement updates, upgrades, and patches in a timely manner to limit loss of service. Identify or document backup or recovery plans. Collaborate with Web developers to create and operate internal and external Web sites, or to manage projects, such as e-marketing campaigns. Install or configure Web server software or hardware to ensure that directory structure is well-defined, logical, secure, and that files are named properly. Gather, analyze, or document user feedback to locate or resolve sources of problems. Develop Web site performance metrics. Identify or address interoperability requirements. Document installation or configuration procedures to allow maintenance and repetition. Identify, standardize, and communicate levels of access and security. Track, compile, and analyze Web site usage data. Test issues such as system integration, performance, and system security on a regular schedule or after any major program modifications. Recommend Web site improvements, and develop budgets to support recommendations. Inform Web site users of problems, problem resolutions, or application changes and updates. Document application and Web site changes or change procedures. Develop or implement procedures for ongoing Web site revision.

Personality Type: Conventional. These occupations frequently involve following set procedures and routines and can include working with data and details more than with ideas. Usually there is a clear line of authority to follow.

GOE—Interest Area/Cluster: 11. Information Technology. **Work Group:** 11.02. Information Technology Specialties. **Other Jobs in This Work Group:** Computer and Information Scientists, Research; Computer Programmers; Computer Security Specialists; Computer Software Engineers, Applications; Computer Software Engineers, Systems Software; Computer Support Specialists; Computer Systems Analysts; Computer Systems Engineers/Architects; Database Administrators; Network Designers; Network Systems and Data Communications Analysts; Software Quality Assurance Engineers and Testers; Web Developers.

Skills—Programming: Writing computer programs for various purposes. **Systems Evaluation:** Looking at many indicators of system performance and taking into account their accuracy. **Systems Analysis:** Determining how a system should work and how changes will affect outcomes. **Troubleshooting:** Determining what is causing an operating error and deciding what to do about it. **Operations Analysis:** Analyzing needs and product requirements to create a design. **Technology Design:** Generating or adapting equipment and technology to serve user needs. **Installation:** Installing equipment, machines, wiring, or programs to meet specifications. **Equipment Selection:** Determining the kind of tools and equipment needed to do a job.

Education and Training Programs: Computer and Information Sciences, General; Information Technology; Information Science/Studies; Computer Science; Web Page, Digital/Multimedia and Information Resources Design; Computer Systems Networking and Telecommunications; System, Networking, and LAN/WAN Management/Manager; Web/Multimedia Management and Webmaster; Computer and Information Sciences and Support Services, Other; E-Commerce/Electronic Commerce. **Related Knowledge/**

Courses—Computers and Electronics: Electric circuit boards, processors, chips, and computer hardware and software, including applications and programming. **Telecommunications:** Transmission, broadcasting, switching, control, and operation of telecommunications systems. **Design:** Design techniques, principles, tools, and instruments involved in the production and use of precision technical plans, blueprints, drawings, and models. **Communications and Media:** Media production, communication, and dissemination techniques and methods, including alternative ways to inform and entertain via written, oral, and visual media. **Sales and Marketing:** Principles and methods involved in showing, promoting, and selling products or services. This includes marketing strategies and tactics, product demonstration and sales techniques, and sales control systems. **Engineering and Technology:** Equipment, tools, and mechanical devices and their uses to produce motion, light, power, technology, and other applications.

Work Environment: Indoors; sitting; using hands on objects, tools, or controls; repetitive motions.

Web Developers

- ❋ Education/Training Required: Bachelor's degree
- ❋ Annual Earnings: $71,510
- ❋ Beginning Wage: $37,600
- ❋ Earnings Growth Potential: High
- ❋ Growth: 15.1%
- ❋ Annual Job Openings: 14,374
- ❋ Self-Employed: 6.6%
- ❋ Part-Time: 5.6%

The job openings listed here are shared with Computer Systems Engineers/Architects; Network Designers; Software Quality Assurance Engineers and Testers; and Web Administrators.

Develop and design Web applications and Web sites. Create and specify architectural and technical parameters. Direct Web site content creation, enhancement, and maintenance. Design, build, or maintain Web sites, using authoring or scripting languages, content creation tools, management tools, and digital media. Perform or direct Web site updates. Write, design, or edit Web page content, or direct others producing content. Confer with management or development teams to prioritize needs, resolve conflicts, develop content criteria, or choose solutions. Back up files from Web sites to local directories for instant recovery in case of problems. Identify problems uncovered by testing or customer feedback, and correct problems or refer problems to appropriate personnel for correction. Evaluate code to ensure that it is valid, is properly structured, meets industry standards and is compatible with browsers, devices, or operating systems. Maintain understanding of current Web technologies or programming practices through continuing education, reading, or participation in professional conferences, workshops, or groups. Analyze user needs to determine technical requirements. Develop or validate test routines and schedules to ensure that test cases mimic external interfaces and address all browser and device types. Develop databases that support Web applications and Web sites. Renew domain name registrations. Collaborate with management or users to develop e-commerce strategies and to integrate these strategies with Web sites. Write supporting code for Web applications or Web sites. Communicate with network personnel or Web site hosting agencies to address hardware or software issues affecting Web sites. Design and implement Web site security measures such as firewalls or message encryption. Perform Web site tests according to planned schedules, or after any Web site or product revisions. Select programming languages, design tools, or applications. Incorporate technical considerations into Web site design plans, such as budgets, equipment, performance requirements, or legal issues including accessibility and privacy. Respond to user e-mail inquiries, or set up automated systems to send responses. Develop or implement procedures for ongoing Web site revision.

Personality Type: Conventional. These occupations frequently involve following set procedures and routines and can include working with data and details more than with ideas. Usually there is a clear line of authority to follow.

GOE—Interest Area/Cluster: 11. Information Technology. **Work Group:** 11.02. Information Technology Specialties. **Other Jobs in This Work Group:** Computer and Information Scientists, Research; Computer Programmers; Computer Security Specialists; Computer Software Engineers, Applications; Computer Software Engineers, Systems Software; Computer Support Specialists; Computer Systems Analysts; Computer Systems Engineers/Architects; Database Administrators; Network Designers; Network Systems and Data Communications Analysts; Software Quality Assurance Engineers and Testers; Web Administrators.

Skills—Programming: Writing computer programs for various purposes. **Troubleshooting:** Determining what is causing an operating error and deciding what to do about it. **Operations Analysis:** Analyzing needs and product requirements to create a design. **Technology Design:** Generating or adapting equipment and technology to serve user needs. **Systems Evaluation:** Looking at many indicators of system performance and taking into account their accuracy. **Quality Control Analysis:** Evaluating the quality or performance of products, services, or processes. **Systems Analysis:** Determining how a system should work and how changes will affect outcomes. **Complex Problem Solving:** Identifying complex problems, reviewing the options, and implementing solutions.

Education and Training Programs: Computer and Information Sciences, General; Information Technology; Information Science/Studies; Computer Science; Web Page, Digital/Multimedia and Information Resources Design; Computer Systems Networking and Telecommunications; System, Networking, and LAN/WAN Management/Manager; Web/Multimedia Management and Webmaster; Computer and Information Sciences and Support Services, Other; E-Commerce/Electronic Commerce. **Related Knowledge/Courses— Computers and Electronics:** Electric circuit boards, processors, chips, and computer hardware and software, including applications and programming. **Design:** Design techniques, principles, tools, and instruments involved in the production and use of precision technical plans, blueprints, drawings, and models. **Sales and Marketing:** Principles and methods involved in showing, promoting, and selling products or services. This includes marketing strategies and tactics, product demonstration and sales techniques, and sales control systems. **Communications and Media:** Media production, communication, and dissemination techniques and methods, including alternative ways to inform and entertain via written, oral, and visual media. **Telecommunications:** Transmission, broadcasting, switching, control, and operation of telecommunications systems. **Clerical Practices:** Administrative and clerical procedures and systems such as word-processing systems, filing and records management systems, stenography and transcription, forms, design principles, and other office procedures and terminology.

Work Environment: Indoors; sitting; using hands on objects, tools, or controls; repetitive motions.

Index

C

E

M

U–V

W–Z